Attorney for the Damned

EDITED AND WITH NOTES BY
ARTHUR WEINBERG

FOREWORD BY
JUSTICE WILLIAM O. DOUGLAS

SIMON AND SCHUSTER · NEW YORK · 1957

To
LILA
who helped, encouraged,
and kept the twins
from sabotaging

FOREWORD

WHILE THERE HAS been much written about Clarence Darrow, nothing gives quite the full flavor of the man as do these addresses. Here is Darrow in the raw—as fresh as the day he spoke.

These pages contain for the most part addresses which Darrow delivered to juries in criminal cases. There are in addition speeches on controversial people and subjects. Throughout each of them runs a common thread—his antagonism toward bigotry, prejudice, ignorance, and hate.

Some say that Darrow in his later years became bitter and conservative. But in his prime he certainly was a fearless liberal, representing many lost causes. Darrow represented both the poor and the rich. There was no class line among his clientele. But he never, I think, represented the strong against the weak, the mighty against the masses. When those lines were drawn, he was always on the side of the underdog fighting for equal protection, due process, and a fair trial.

The institution through which Darrow achieved his great distinction was the jury. Darrow knew that juries are more to be trusted than judges when it comes to the protection of the *life* and *liberty* of the citizen.

There were prosecutors who tried to unleash in the courtroom the passions of the mob and stampede the jury with fear and fright. Darrow always stood between the mob and the jury, pleading for sanity, reason, and objectivity.

Darrow knew the terrors of race riots and calmed juries with talk of tolerance and equal rights that still rings true to the democratic ideal.

Most criminal lawyers do not leave their own bailiwick to risk the unknown elements in distant communities. Darrow was the exception; and the price he paid is dramatically revealed in the McNamara case in California.

Darrow met religious bigotry head-on. He exposed it with a relentless fury. What his religion may have been, I do not know. But he obviously believed in an infinite God who was the Maker of all humanity.

Darrow, following in the tradition of Beccaria, the eighteenth-century Italian legal philosopher, was opposed to capital punishment. Darrow saw in murders and other crimes the working of forces far too imponderable to measure. He thought that the "right-wrong" test of insanity, pronounced in 1843 by the House of Lords in *M'Naghten's Case*,[1] was archaic. He would, I am sure, have been delighted with the rule announced in 1954 by the Court of Appeals for the District of Columbia in *Durham* v. *United States*[2] that "an accused is not criminally responsible if his unlawful act was the product of mental disease or mental defect." That test was reflected in his recurring appeals to judges and juries on the issue of insanity. Darrow may not have been steeped in psychoanalytic theories; but his instinct was true to modern psychiatry, and his eloquence made a powerful impact on judges and on juries.

Darrow was champion of labor at a time when a union was considered more a group bent on conspiracy than a lawful association that could use the strike and the boycott to raise wages and improve working conditions. This was the time when government by injunction was in its heyday, when the awful power of contempt was used to punish strikers.[3] This was the time when courts were saying, "We cannot say by law that the laborer shall have just such a price for his services."[4] Darrow pleaded for the men and women—the flesh and blood—that made the wheels of industry move. He placed them as high in the social scales as the capital invested in industry.

Darrow was widely read and well versed in the humanities. His addresses sparkle with analogies, with historic examples, with figures of speech taken from the masters.

[1] M'Naghten's Case, 8 Eng. Rep. 200.
[2] Durham v. United States, 214 F(2d) 862, 874-875.
[3] In re Debs, 158 U.S. 564.
[4] King v. Ohio & M Ry., 14 Fed. Cas. 539, 541.

But his intellectual achievements were not the secret of his success. Darrow knew people. He ran the gamut of emotions in his jury speeches. His arguments are a full orchestration, carrying great power even in cold print. They must have been overwhelming as they came from his tongue. Yet he was not the flamboyant type. His words were the simple discourse of ordinary conversation. They had the power of deep conviction, the strength of any plea for fair play, the pull of every protest against grinding down the faces of the poor, the appeal of humanity against forces of greed and exploitation.

Darrow used the law to promote social justice as he saw it. Yet the law and the lawyers were to him reactionary forces. Their faces were usually turned backward. Great reforms came not from within the law but from without. It was not the judges and barristers who made the significant advances toward social justice. They were made in conventions of the people and in legislative halls. Yet Darrow, working through the law, brought prestige and honor to it during a long era of intolerance.

—WILLIAM O. DOUGLAS

CONTENTS

"conspiracy to advocate the overthrow of the government by force."

PART THREE

AGAINST PRIVILEGE

PART FOUR

FOR JUSTICE

a juror in the McNamara case. He accuses his enemies as
conspirators against his freedom.

INTRODUCTION

"THE POWERFUL ORATOR *hulking his way slowly, thoughtfully, extemporizing . . . hands in pocket, head down and eyes up, wondering what it is all about, to the inevitable conclusion which he throws off with a toss of his shrugging shoulders: 'I don't know . . . We don't know . . . Not enough to kill or even to judge one another.'" The words are Lincoln Steffens' writing the review of Darrow's* The Story of My Life *in which Steffens called him* "the attorney for the damned."

But behind the words is a more public image, a vivid impression of Darrow in a typical pose: an expanse of crumpled white shirt over that relaxed chest and stomach, one thumb hooked in his galluses, the other hand extended to make a point, striding forward in baggy gray pants and a loose, hopelessly stretched jacket pushed back on his shoulders—striding forward and then stopping, staring straight into the jurors' eyes, turning, head hung in thought as the retreating voice comes over the shoulder slowly, carefully, then all at once booming again. Sometimes witty, smiling; sometimes angry, scathing, merciless. Sometimes with tears streaming down his cheeks, as in this unpublished poetic portrait by the poet Edgar Lee Masters, a former law partner, written in 1922:

> This is a man with an old face, always old . . .
> There was pathos, in his face, and in his eyes,
> And early weariness; and sometimes tears in his eyes,
> Which he let slip unconsciously on his cheek,
> Or brushed away with an unconcerned hand.
> There were tears for human suffering, or for a glance
> Into the vast futility of life,
> Which he had seen from the first, being old
> When he was born.

There are many who claim that Darrow was chiefly an orator who played on the emotions of his listeners. He would be the last to deny it. He always insisted that man acted mainly through emotion anyway. His pleas, however, always had a powerful rational basis, and it could hardly be said that he avoided the philosophical and social issues involved. Though reason was his constant appeal and futile hope for man, his real weapons were emotional because he was himself deeply involved in his cases. He visited Leopold and Loeb regularly in Joliet until his health prevented it, and in a letter to his friend Allen Crandall * he admitted: "I put up $1,000 of the money that released Haywood from jail during the war. I got another $1,500 from a friend. We were both glad when he made his get-a-away." † He insisted "there is no such crime as a crime of thought; there are only crimes of action." He told juries: "I am not bound to believe them right in order to take their case, and you are not bound to believe them right in order to find them not guilty."

But the passion was for something deeper and more difficult to define than the individual defendants whom he saved. It is not the conventional approach for a lawyer to tell a jury that his client is his least concern. Yet he did it in the trial of this same Haywood in 1907. Said Darrow to the Boise, Idaho jury: "Mr. Haywood is not my greatest concern. Other men have died before him. Wherever men have looked upward and onward, worked for the poor and the weak, they have been sacrificed."

In the Communist Labor party case in Chicago in 1920, Darrow told the jury: "If you want to convict these twenty men, then do it. I ask no consideration on behalf of any of them. They are no better than any other twenty men, they are no better than the millions who have been prosecuted—yes, and convicted in cases like this."

In the case of Leopold and Loeb he told Judge Caverly in his plea for their lives: "I am not pleading so much for these boys as I am for the infinite number of others to follow, those who perhaps cannot be as well defended as these boys have been, those who

---

* From *The Man from Kinsman.*

† Haywood and more than 100 IWWs were tried and convicted in 1918 for hindering the war effort. Released on bond, Haywood made his "get-a-way" by fleeing to Soviet Russia, there to die a disillusioned man as far as the Bolsheviks were concerned.

may go down in the tempest without aid. It is of them I am thinking and for them I am begging of this court not to turn backward
to the barbarous and cruel past."

In many of his courtroom pleas he directed his ire against an
individual: it might be the prosecutor, a witness for the opposing
side, or the complainant. The reader will come across this tactic in
plea after plea, for it is one of Darrow's favorite means of making
the jury sympathize, not only with the defendant, but with any
man who is under brutal scrutiny for his motives and frailties.

He was bitter in his denunciation of the state's attorney in the
Kidd case; in the Chicago Communist case he set his sights against
a state's witness, Ole Hanson, the former mayor of Seattle; in the
Haywood case, his sarcasm was directed against Harry Orchard,
the state's main witness who had admitted committing 26 murders but had now "got religion"; in his own defense, Darrow decried the prosecutor and the forces of the employers who he
claimed were out to get him.

In the case of Leopold and Loeb, his anger was directed against
Dr. William O. Krohn, an alienist who was a state's witness. He
charged him with "going up and down the land peddling perjury."
And then he turned his attention to one of the assistant prosecutors—Joseph Savage. Said Darrow: "Now, Your Honor, I shall discuss that more in detail a little later and I only say it now because
my friend Mr. Savage—did you pick him for his name or his ability
or his learning?—because my friend Mr. Savage, in as cruel a
speech as he knew how to make, said to this Court that we pleaded
guilty because we were afraid to do anything else. Your Honor,
that is true."

Darrow's views never fell in line with orthodox thinking. Many
of the causes he defended in his day were unpopular. To stand on
principle in their defense meant incurring the wrath and overt
disapproval of the majority. Yet he never feared the consequences.

Many of the men he defended on murder charges were innocent
men. Others offered the plea of self-defense; still others had miti-
gating circumstances. "For some of them there was not much to
say," he wrote, "except that killing by law is the wrong way to
deal with the killer."

He liked "to defend men and women charged with crime." To

him, it was never just another case. He was always interested in the psychology of human conduct—why some act one way and some another.

"I was dealing with life, with its fears, its aspirations and despairs. With me it was going to the foundation of motive and conduct and adjustments for human beings, instead of blindly talking hatred and vengeance and that subtle, indefinable quality that men call 'justice' and of which nothing really is known," he wrote in his autobiography.

This theme—the cause and effect of men's actions—is repeated throughout his life: in his summations to juries, in his debates and lectures and writings.

Shortly before he died on March 13, 1938, Darrow repeated an oft-made observation on crime and criminals: If doctors were to treat the causes of physical illness as lawyers and judges handle crime, "treatment of disease would again be like 'black magic.'"

From the time he first came to Chicago as a young lawyer in 1888, to his final public service on the NRA Review Board, Darrow followed his own convictions, as he understood them, wherever they led.

Arriving in Chicago a year after the Haymarket Anarchists had been executed, he found a city in debate with itself, inflamed with agitation and reaction to the hanging of the men. One of the main regrets of Darrow's life was that he had not been able to help defend the eight charged with throwing a bomb into the police ranks, killing seven and wounding 67, during the mass meeting protesting police brutality in the McCormick Works strike.

To this day, no one knows who actually perpetrated the act, but the Anarchists were convicted and four of them hanged. One was given a fifteen-year prison term, another committed suicide the night before he was to be executed, and the remaining two had their death sentences commuted to life imprisonment.

Darrow took part in the amnesty movement for the imprisoned men. He also made the friendship of John Peter Altgeld who, shortly after becoming governor of Illinois, reviewed the case of the Haymarket labor men, found the trial a travesty on justice, and in 1894 pardoned the men in jail and exonerated those who had been executed. With this act the governor signed his own political death warrant, but he and Darrow remained close friends, and for the last years of the governor's life he was Darrow's law partner.

Soon after his arrival in Chicago, Darrow joined the Single Tax Club. He began to participate in the debates at the club which led to his speaking at other public meetings.

It was at a Free Trade convention in 1888 at which Henry George was the main speaker that Darrow made his initial impact as a public speaker. DeWitt C. Creiger who was to be elected Chicago's mayor in a few weeks was among those who heard him.

It was Altgeld at the height of his popularity as a politician who urged Mayor Creiger to appoint Darrow assistant corporation counsel of Chicago, from which post he stepped into the position of acting corporation counsel a short time later.

After several years as the city's legal adviser, Darrow resigned to become general attorney for the Chicago and Northwestern Railway Company. In 1894, while he was attorney for the railroad, the American Railway Union "struck" the line. "Neither before nor since has any such railroad strike happened in America," Darrow later wrote. "The strike grew out of a demand for better wages and conditions. The railroads refused to grant the demands."

Darrow sympathized with the strikers. He found it increasingly difficult to reconcile his own feelings with those of the corporation he represented. The railroads went into the Federal court and obtained an injunction against the strikers. Eugene Victor Debs, president of the union, and all the members of the union's board were indicted by the Federal grand jury for "conspiracy."

It was then that Clarence Darrow—well on the way to becoming a successful and recognized corporation attorney—resigned his position as attorney for the railroad to represent Debs and the executive board of the ARU.

Referring to Darrow in his autobiography only as the head of the law firm, Masters wrote in 1936: "He posed as an altruist and a friend of the oppressed, but I doubted him." Darrow himself seems to have admitted the partial truth of this remark when he answered those who praised his quitting the railway to defend Debs by saying: "Like the man who buys 10¢ worth of relief from the beggar on the street, I am buying relief too."

In 1934, at the age of 77, Darrow went to Washington at the

invitation of President Franklin D. Roosevelt, General Hugh Johnson, head of the National Recovery Administration, and Donald Richberg, its chief counsel. The veteran liberal and labor attorney was asked to become chairman of a Board of Review to investigate charges that the NRA was favoring Big Business "although claiming their sympathies were being directed toward the small dealers and concerns."

The Darrow Review Board held 47 public hearings, examined 34 codes under the NRA, and also examined about 3,000 complaints during a four-month period. After the first of three reports submitted to the President, Newsweek *magazine commented: "Clarence Darrow is on one of his peculiarly cool and deadly rampages again. As a foreman of a kind of governmental grand jury to tell the administration how the NRA is working, he has brought in a report saying it's doing perfectly terrible."*

In his conclusions to the third report, Darrow acknowledged the good NRA was attempting in such instances as abolishing child labor and shortening the work week, but he charged: "It may safely be said that not in many years have monopolistic tendencies in industry been so forwarded and strengthened as they have been through the perversion of an act excellently intended to restore prosperity and promote general welfare."

The New York Times *headlined:*

DARROW BOARD FINDS NRA
TENDS TOWARD MONOPOLIES

Both Johnson and Richberg felt that the liberal Darrow had betrayed them, and the General stormed: "A more superficial, intemperate and inaccurate document than the report, I have never seen."

But again Darrow was speaking for what he believed right. His report on NRA was the prelude to the United States Supreme Court decision which declared that board unconstitutional.

Some said that he was not a very good lawyer. He knew little law, he was too lazy to do much research. But Joseph Welch, the Boston attorney of Army-McCarthy fame, said: "He was never careless as to facts. . . . The single greatest trait of Darrow's char-

acter was that he was so brave and fearless. He was so brave and so fearless, that he did not realize that he was either."

In his autobiography, Lincoln Steffens describes the [enigmatic] character of this impassioned man: "At three o'clock he is a hero for courage, nerve, and calm judgment, but at a quarter past three he may be a coward for fear, collapse, and panicky mentality. He is more of a poet than a fighting attorney. He is a great fighter, as he is a good lawyer. His power and his weakness is in the highly sensitive, emotional nature which sets his seething mind in motion in that loafing body."

During the anthracite coal arbitration in 1903, Darrow pointed out to the commission appointed by President Theodore Roosevelt that all of the advantages in the hearings were in favor of the operators: "Their social advantages are better, their religious privileges are better, they speak the English language better. They are not children. They can hire . . . expert accountants, and they have got the advantage of us in almost every particular, and we will admit all that." The chairman could not refrain from interrupting: "All except the lawyers."

Nathan Leopold, co-defendant with Richard Loeb in the famous murder-kidnaping case, whom Darrow saved from the gallows, remembered more than legal acumen when he said, from the prison cell in which he is serving a life sentence for the crime, that Darrow was "the kindest man I have ever known. To me, at least, Mr. Darrow's fundamental characteristic was his deep-seated all-embracing kindness. . . . He hated superficiality and refused to conform for conformity's sake."

The New York Times said of him: "He resorted to no quillets of the law. He was defending justice in his conception of it, a justice tempered with sympathy and humanity."

The Chicago Daily News commenting on his death wrote that "in the pure sense of the word, Darrow was not a criminal lawyer. He was rather a practicing philosopher, a student of society, of crime, its causes and cures."

Whatever kind of lawyer he was, he certainly was more than a lawyer. As Federal Judge William H. Holly, friend and former partner said: "Few lawyers have the wide and varied intellectual *interests that Clarence Darrow enjoys. Perhaps no other lawyer in the land has his aptitude for history, science, philosophy and other branches of study that especially attract him." Judge Holly delivered the eulogy at Darrow's funeral, and provided an epitaph which fits the man exactly.*

"He loved mercy. We may not know what justice is. No judge who sentences a prisoner to the electric chair is more certain of the righteousness of his judgment than the mob that hangs or burns its victim. Whether the offender is legally executed by the sheriff, or illegally hanged by the mob, we cannot be sure whether it is justice or vengeance that has been satisfied.

"But mercy is a quality that we can all recognize, and in his heart was infinite pity and mercy for the poor, the oppressed, the weak and erring—all races, all colors, all creeds and all human kind. Clarence Darrow made the way easier for man. He preached not doctrine but love and pity, the only virtues that can make this world any better."

* * * *

This selection of the spoken words of Clarence Darrow will, I hope, give this generation an understanding and appreciation of how much of an era, and yet how far in advance of his time, was this man. In editing the material, I have attempted to keep the flavor, the color, the feeling of each selection, deleting only the irrelevant legal digressions and the minutiae of stenographic reporting. Each plea is preceded by a foreword giving the setting, the legal background, and the human factors involved. The verdict and subsequent effects of the trial are contained in an afterword to each selection.

Among the sources referred to by the editor for this book, in addition to those listed in the Bibliography, were Darrow's own writings, back issues of newspapers and magazines, pamphlets, court records, personal reminiscings to the editor by Paul Darrow, the attorney's only child, and Darrow's associates. Also, Irving Stone's biography, Clarence Darrow for the Defense, *Charles Yale Harrison's biography,* Clarence Darrow, *and Arthur Garfield Hays's* Let Freedom Ring.

I am deeply grateful to Supreme Court Justice William O. Douglas, one of the leading jurists of our time and one who exem-

plifies the courage so necessary when freedom is attacked, for consenting to write the Foreword to this book.

I want to thank the numerous libraries at which I did my research, including Newberry Library in Chicago, the Chicago Public Library, University of Chicago Harper Library, the Free Library of Philadelphia, and the New York Public Library.

I want to express my appreciation to Richard L. Grossman of Simon and Schuster, and to my friend, novelist Louis Zara, for encouragement. To my Chicago associates at Fairchild Publications who lived through the book with me. To Ewing C. Baskette for the loan of a rare copy of the Haywood plea. To my in-laws Sam and Blanche Shaffer, and my father, A. M. Weinberg, who co-operated in much-needed baby-sitting as my wife worked with me on the project. And to my wife, without whom this project would never have been started or completed.

Chicago, Illinois   —Arthur Weinberg
May 1957

PART ONE

AGAINST
VENGEANCE

Crime and Criminals

ADDRESS TO THE PRISONERS IN THE COOK COUNTY JAIL
1902

THE WARDEN of the Cook County Jail in Chicago, who knew Clarence Darrow as a criminologist, lawyer and writer, invited him to speak before the inmates of the jail. Darrow accepted the invitation. This was in 1902.

The prisoners marched into the auditorium where they heard what is today still considered one of the most extraordinary and unique speeches ever delivered to such an audience.

IF I LOOKED at jails and crimes and prisoners in the way the ordinary person does, I should not speak on this subject to you. The reason I talk to you on the question of crime, its cause and cure, is that I really do not in the least believe in crime. There is no such thing as a crime as the word is generally understood. I do not believe there is any sort of distinction between the real moral conditions of the people in and out of jail. One is just as good as the other. The people here can no more help being here than the people outside can avoid being outside. I do not believe that people are in jail because they deserve to be. They are in jail simply because they cannot avoid it on account of circumstances which are entirely beyond their control and for which they are in no way responsible.

I suppose a great many people on the outside would say I was doing you harm if they should hear what I say to you this afternoon, but you cannot be hurt a great deal anyway, so it will not matter. Good people outside would say that I was really teaching you things that were calculated to injure society, but it's worth while now and then to hear something different from what you ordinarily get from preachers and the like. These will tell you that you should be good and then you will get rich and be happy. Of course we know that people do not get rich by being good, and that is the reason why so many of you people try to get rich some other way, only you do not understand how to do it quite as well as the fellow outside.

There are people who think that everything in this world is an accident. But really there is no such thing as an accident. A great many folks admit that many of the people in jail ought to be there, and many who are outside ought to be in. I think none of them ought to be here. There ought to be no jails; and if it were not for the fact that the people on the outside are so grasping and heartless in their dealings with the people on the inside, there would be no such institution as jails.

I do not want you to believe that I think all you people here are angels. I do not think that. You are people of all kinds, all of you doing the best you can—and that is evidently not very well. You are people of all kinds and conditions and under all circumstances. In one sense everybody is equally good and equally bad. We all do the best we can under the circumstances. But as to the exact things for which you are sent here, some of you are guilty and did the particular act because you needed the money. Some of you did it because you are in the habit of doing it, and some of you because you are born to it, and it comes to be as natural as it does, for instance, for me to be good.

Most of you probably have nothing against me, and most of you would treat me the same as any other person would, probably better than some of the people on the outside would treat me, because you think I believe in you and they know I do not believe in them. While you would not have the least thing against me in the world, you might pick my pockets. I do not think all of you would, but I think some of you would. You would not have anything against me, but that's your profession, a few of you. Some of the rest of you, if my doors were unlocked, might come in if you saw anything you wanted—not out of any malice to me, but because that is your trade. There is no doubt there are quite a number of people in this jail who would pick my pockets. And still I know this—that when I get outside pretty nearly everybody picks my pocket. There may be some of you who would hold up a man on the street, if you did not happen to have something else to do, and needed the money; but when I want to light my house or my office the gas company holds me up. They charge me one dollar for something that is worth twenty-five cents. Still all these people are good people; they are pillars of society and support the churches, and they are respectable.

When I ride on the streetcars I am held up—I pay five cents for a ride that is worth two and a half cents, simply because a body of men have bribed the city council and the legislature, so that all the rest of us have to pay tribute to them.

If I do not want to fall into the clutches of the gas trust and choose to burn oil instead of gas, then good Mr. Rockefeller holds me up, and he uses a certain portion of his money to build universities and support churches which are engaged in telling us how to be good.

Some of you are here for obtaining property under false pretenses—yet I pick up a great Sunday paper and read the advertisements of a merchant prince—"Shirtwaists for 39 cents, marked down from $3.00."

When I read the advertisements in the paper I see they are all lies. When I want to get out and find a place to stand anywhere on the face of the earth, I find that it has all been taken up long ago before I came here, and before you came here, and somebody says, "Get off, swim into the lake, fly into the air; go anywhere, but get off." That is because these people have the police and they have the jails and the judges and the lawyers and the soldiers and all the rest of them to take care of the earth and drive everybody off that comes in their way.

A great many people will tell you that all this is true, but that it does not excuse you. These facts do not excuse some fellow who reaches into my pocket and takes out a five-dollar bill. The fact that the gas company bribes the members of the legislature from year to year, and fixes the law, so that all you people are compelled to be "fleeced" whenever you deal with them; the fact that the streetcar companies and the gas companies have control of the streets; and the fact that the landlords own all the earth—this, they say, has nothing to do with you.

Let us see whether there is any connection between the crimes of the respectable classes and your presence in the jail. Many of you people are in jail because you have really committed burglary; many of you, because you have stolen something. In the meaning of the law, you have taken some other person's property. Some of you have entered a store and carried off a pair of shoes because you did not have the price. Possibly some of you have committed murder. I cannot tell what all of you did. There are a great many people here who have done some of these things who really do not know themselves why they did them. I think I know why you did them—every one of you; you did these things because you were bound to do them. It looked to you at the time as if you had a chance to do them or not, as you saw fit; but still, after all, you had no choice. There may be people here who had some money in their pockets and who still went out and got some more money in a way society forbids. Now, you may not yourselves see exactly why it was you did this thing, but if you look at the question deeply enough and carefully enough you will see that there were circumstances that drove you to do exactly the thing which you did. You could not help it any more than we outside can help taking the positions that we take. The reformers who tell you to be good and you will be happy, and the people on the outside who have property to protect—they think that the only way to do it is by building jails and locking you up in cells on weekdays and praying for you Sundays.

I think that all of this has nothing whatever to do with right conduct. I think it is very easily seen what has to do with right conduct. Some so-called criminals—and I will use this word because it is handy, it means nothing to me—I speak of the criminals who get caught as distinguished from the criminals who catch them—some of these so-called criminals are in jail for their first offenses, but nine tenths of you are in jail because you did not have a good lawyer and, of course, you did not have a good lawyer because you did not have enough money to pay a good lawyer. There is no very great danger of a rich man going to jail.

Some of you may be here for the first time. If we would open the doors and let you out, and leave the laws as they are today, some of you would be back tomorrow. This is about as good a place as you can get anyway. There are many people here who are so in the habit of coming that they would not know where else to go. There are people who are born with the tendency to break into jail every chance they get, and they cannot avoid it. You cannot figure out your life and see why it was, but still there is a reason for it; and if we were all wise and knew all the facts, we could figure it out.

In the first place, there are a good many more people who go to jail in the wintertime than in summer. Why is this? Is it because people are more wicked in winter? No, it is because the coal trust begins to get in its grip in the winter. A few gentlemen take possession of the coal, and unless the people will pay seven or eight dollars a ton for something that is worth three dollars, they will have to freeze. Then there is nothing to do but to break into jail, and so there are many more in jail in the winter than in summer. It costs more for gas in the winter because the nights are longer, and people go to jail to save gas bills. The jails are electric-lighted. You may not know it, but these economic laws are working all the time, whether we know it or do not know it.

There are more people who go to jail in hard times than in good times—few people, comparatively, go to jail except when they are hard up. They go to jail because they have no other place to go. They may not know why, but it is true all the same. People are not more wicked in hard times. That is not the reason. The fact is true all over the world that in hard times more people go to jail than in good times, and in winter more people go to jail than in summer. Of course it is pretty hard times for people who go to jail at any time. The people who go to jail are almost always poor people—people who have no other place to live, first and last. When times are hard, then you find large numbers of people who go to jail who would not otherwise be in jail.

Long ago, Mr. Buckle, who was a great philosopher and historian, collected facts, and he showed that the number of people who are arrested increased just as the price of food increased. When they put up the price of gas ten cents a thousand, I do not know who will go to jail, but I do know that a certain number of people will go. When the meat combine raises the price of beef, I do not know who is going to jail, but I know that a large number of people are bound to go. Whenever the Standard Oil Company raises the price of oil, I know that a certain number of girls who are seamstresses, and who work night after night long hours for somebody else, will be compelled to go out on the streets and ply another trade, and I know that Mr. Rockefeller and his associates are responsible and not the poor girls in the jails.

First and last, people are sent to jail because they are poor. Sometimes, as I say, you may not need money at the particular time, but you wish to have thrifty forehanded habits, and do not always wait until you are in absolute want. Some of you people are perhaps plying the trade, the profession, which is called burglary. No man in his right senses will go into a strange house in the dead of night and prowl around with a dark lantern through unfamiliar rooms and take chances of his life, if he has plenty of the good things of the world in his own home. You would not take any such chances as that. If a man had clothes in his clothes-press and beefsteak in his pantry and money in the bank, he would not navigate around nights in houses where he knows nothing about the premises whatever. It always requires experience and education for this profession, and people who fit themselves for it are no more to blame than I am for being a lawyer. A man would not hold up another man on the street if he had plenty of money in his own pocket. He might do it if he had one dollar or two dollars, but he wouldn't if he had as much money as Mr. Rockefeller has. Mr. Rockefeller has a great deal better hold-up game than that.

The more that is taken from the poor by the rich, who have the chance to take it, the more poor people there are who are compelled to resort to these means for a livelihood. They may not understand it, they may not think so at once, but after all they are driven into that line of employment.

There is a bill before the legislature of this state to punish kidnaping children with death. We have wise members of the legislature. They know the gas trust when they see it and they always see it—they can furnish light enough to be seen; and this legislature thinks it is going to stop kidnaping children by making a law punishing kidnapers of children with death. I don't believe in kidnaping children, but the legislature is all wrong. Kidnaping children is not a crime, it is a profession. It has been developed with the times. It has been developed with our modern industrial conditions. There are many ways of making money— many new ways that our ancestors knew nothing about. Our ancestors knew nothing about a billion-dollar trust; and here comes some poor fellow who has no other trade and he discovers the profession of kidnaping children.

This crime is born, not because people are bad; people don't kidnap other people's children because they want the children or because they are devilish, but because they see a chance to get some money out of it. You cannot cure this crime by passing a law punishing by death kidnapers of children. There is one way to cure it. There is one way to cure all these offenses, and that is to give the people a chance to live. There is no other way, and there never was any other way since the world began; and the world is so blind and stupid that it will not see. If every man and woman and child in the world had a chance to make a decent, fair, honest living, there would be no jails and no lawyers and no courts. There might be some persons here or there with some peculiar formation of their brain, like Rockefeller, who would do these things simply to be doing them; but they would be very, very few, and those should be sent to a hospital and treated, and not sent to jail; and they would entirely disappear in the second generation, or at least in the third generation.

I am not talking pure theory. I will just give you two or three illustrations.

The English people once punished criminals by sending them away. They would load them on a ship and export them to Australia. England was owned by lords and nobles and rich people. They owned the whole earth over there, and the other people had to stay in the streets. They could not get a decent living. They used to take their criminals and send them to Australia—I mean the class of criminals who got caught. When these criminals got over there, and nobody else had come, they had the whole continent to run over, and so they could raise sheep and furnish their own meat, which is easier than stealing it. These criminals then became decent, respectable people because they had a chance to live. They did not commit any crimes. They were just like the English people who sent them there, only better. And in the second generation the descendants of those criminals were as good and respectable a class of people as there were on the face of the earth, and then they began building churches and jails themselves.

A portion of this country was settled in the same way, landing prisoners down on the southern coast; but when they got here and had a whole continent to run over and plenty of chances to make a living, they became respectable citizens, making their own living just like any other citizen in the world. But finally the descendants of the English aristocracy who sent the people over to Australia found out they were getting rich, and so they went over to get possession of the earth as they always do, and they organized land syndicates and got control of the land and ores, and then they had just as many criminals in Australia as they did in England. It was not because the world had grown bad; it was because the earth had been taken away from the people.

Some of you people have lived in the country. It's prettier than it is here. And if you have ever lived on a farm you understand that if you put a lot of cattle in a field, when the pasture is short they will jump over the fence; but put them in a good field where there is plenty of pasture, and they will be law-abiding cattle to the end of time. The human animal is just like the rest of the animals, only a little more so. The same thing that governs in the one governs in the other.

Everybody makes his living along the lines of least resistance. A wise man who comes into a country early sees a great undeveloped land. For instance, our rich men twenty-five years ago saw that Chicago was small and knew a lot of people would come here and settle, and they readily saw that if they had all the land around here it would be worth a good deal, so they grabbed the land. You cannot be a landlord because somebody has got it all. You must find some other calling. In England and Ireland and Scotland less than five per cent own all the land there is, and the people are bound to stay there on any kind of terms the landlords give. They must live the best they can, so they develop all these various professions—burglary, picking pockets and the like.

Again, people find all sorts of ways of getting rich. These are diseases like everything else. You look at people getting rich, organizing trusts and making a million dollars, and somebody gets the disease and he starts out. He catches it just as a man catches the mumps or the measles; he is not to blame, it is in the air. You will find men speculating beyond their means, because the mania of money-getting is taking possession of them. It is simply a disease—nothing more, nothing less. You cannot avoid catching it; but the fellows who have control of the earth have the advantage of you. See what the law is: when these men get control of things, they make the laws. They do not make the laws to protect anybody; courts are not instruments of justice. When your case gets into court it will make little difference whether you are guilty or innocent, but it's better if you have a smart lawyer. And you cannot have a smart lawyer unless you have money. First and last it's a question of money. Those men who own the earth make the laws to protect what they have. They fix up a sort of fence or pen around what they have, and they fix the law so the fellow on the outside cannot get in. The laws are really organized for the protection of the men who rule the world. They were never organized or enforced to do justice. We have no system for doing justice, not the slightest in the world.

Let me illustrate: Take the poorest person in this room. If the community had provided a system of doing justice, the poorest person in this room would have as good a lawyer as the richest, would he not? When you went into court you would have just as long a trial and just as fair a trial as the richest person in Chicago. Your case would not be tried in fifteen or twenty minutes, whereas it would take fifteen days to get through with a rich man's case.

Then if you were rich and were beaten, your case would be taken to the Appellate Court. A poor man cannot take his case to the Appellate Court; he has not the price. And then to the Supreme Court. And if he were beaten there he might perhaps go to the United States Supreme Court. And he might die of old age before he got into jail. If you are poor, it's a quick job. You are almost known to be guilty, else you would not be there. Why should anyone be in the criminal court if he were not guilty? He would not be there if he could be anywhere else. The officials have no time to look after all these cases. The people who are on the outside, who are running banks and building churches and making jails, they have no time to examine 600 or 700 prisoners each year to see whether they are guilty or innocent. If the courts were organized to promote justice the people would elect somebody to defend all these criminals, somebody as smart as the prosecutor—and give him as many detectives and as many assistants to help, and pay as much money to defend you as to prosecute you. We have a very able man for state's attorney, and he has many assistants, detectives and policemen without end, and judges to hear the cases—everything handy.

Most all of our criminal code consists in offenses against property. People are sent to jail because they have committed a crime against property. It is of very little consequence whether one hundred people more or less go to jail who ought not to go—you must protect property, because in this world property is of more importance than anything else.

How is it done? These people who have property fix it so
they can protect what they have. When somebody commits a
crime it does not follow that he has done something that is
morally wrong. The man on the outside who has committed no
crime may have done something. For instance: to take all
the coal in the United States and raise the price two dollars
or three dollars when there is no need of it, and thus kill thousands of babies and send thousands of people to the poorhouse
and tens of thousands to jail, as is done every year in the United
States—this is a greater crime than all the people in our jails
ever committed; but the law does not punish it. Why? Because
the fellows who control the earth make the laws. If you and I
had the making of the laws, the first thing we would do would
be to punish the fellow who gets control of the earth. Nature
put this coal in the ground for me as well as for them and
nature made the prairies up here to raise wheat for me as well
as for them, and then the great railroad companies came along
and fenced it up.

Most all of the crimes for which we are punished are property
crimes. There are a few personal crimes, like murder—but they
are very few. The crimes committed are mostly those against
property. If this punishment is right the criminals must have
a lot of property. How much money is there in this crowd?
And yet you are all here for crimes against property. The people
up and down the Lake Shore have not committed crime; still
they have so much property they don't know what to do with it.
It is perfectly plain why these people have not committed crimes
against property; they make the laws and therefore do not need
to break them. And in order for you to get some property you
are obliged to break the rules of the game. I don't know but
what some of you may have had a very nice chance to get rich
by carrying a hod for one dollar a day, twelve hours. Instead of
taking that nice, easy profession, you are a burglar. If you had
been given a chance to be a banker you would rather follow that.
Some of you may have had a chance to work as a switchman on
a railroad where you know, according to statistics, that you cannot live and keep all your limbs more than seven years, and you
can get fifty dollars or seventy-five dollars a month for taking

your lives in your hands; and instead of taking that lucrative position you chose to be a sneak thief, or something like that. Some of you made that sort of choice. I don't know which I would take if I was reduced to this choice. I have an easier choice.

I will guarantee to take from this jail, or any jail in the world, five hundred men who have been the worst criminals and law-breakers who ever got into jail, and I will go down to our lowest streets and take five hundred of the most abandoned prostitutes, and go out somewhere where there is plenty of land, and will give them a chance to make a living, and they will be as good people as the average in the community.

There is a remedy for the sort of condition we see here. The world never finds it out, or when it does find it out it does not enforce it. You may pass a law punishing every person with death for burglary, and it will make no difference. Men will commit it just the same. In England there was a time when one hundred different offenses were punishable with death, and it made no difference. The English people strangely found out that so fast as they repealed the severe penalties and so fast as they did away with punishing men by death, crime decreased instead of increased; that the smaller the penalty the fewer the crimes.

Hanging men in our county jails does not prevent murder. It makes murderers.

And this has been the history of the world. It's easy to see how to do away with what we call crime. It is not so easy to do it. I will tell you how to do it. It can be done by giving the people a chance to live—by destroying special privileges. So long as big criminals can get the coal fields, so long as the big criminals have control of the city council and get the public streets for streetcars and gas rights—this is bound to send thousands of poor people to jail. So long as men are allowed to monopolize all the earth, and compel others to live on such terms as these men see fit to make, then you are bound to get into jail.

The only way in the world to abolish crime and criminals is to abolish the big ones and the little ones together. Make fair conditions of life. Give men a chance to live. Abolish the right of private ownership of land, abolish monopoly, make the world partners in production, partners in the good things of life. Nobody would steal if he could get something of his own some easier way. Nobody will commit burglary when he has a house full. No girl will go out on the streets when she has a comfortable place at home. The man who owns a sweatshop or a department store may not be to blame himself for the condition of his girls, but when he pays them five dollars, three dollars, and two dollars a week, I wonder where he thinks they will get the rest of their money to live. The only way to cure these conditions is by equality. There should be no jails. They do not accomplish what they pretend to accomplish. If you would wipe them out there would be no more criminals than now. They terrorize nobody. They are a blot upon any civilization, and a jail is an evidence of the lack of charity of the people on the outside who make the jails and fill them with the victims of their greed.

"TOO RADICAL," was the comment of one prisoner when a guard later asked him what he thought of the speech.

Darrow's friends, too, were distressed when they heard about the talk. "Your theories might be true, Clarence," they insisted, "but you should never have told them to criminals in a jail."

Darrow's reaction to his friends' thinking is best expressed in the introduction to the lecture which he had printed in pamphlet form.

Wrote Darrow: "Realizing the force of the suggestion that the truth should not be spoken to all people, I have caused these remarks to be printed on rather good paper and in a somewhat expensive form. In this way the truth does not become cheap and vulgar, and is only placed before those whose intelligence and affluence will prevent their being influenced by it."

The pamphlet sold for five cents.

The Crime of Compulsion

LEOPOLD AND LOEB
Chicago, 1924

ROPE WILL NOT CURE
CRIME, DARROW SAYS
IN PLEA FOR SLAYERS

[Headline, Chicago Daily News, August 25, 1924]

"Your boy has been kidnaped. He is in safe custody. You will hear from us in the morning," said a cultivated voice over the telephone to Jacob Franks, a prominent and respected Chicago businessman.

The next morning the father received a letter reading: "This is a strictly commercial proposition." The letter asked for $10,000 ransom to be paid in old twenty- and fifty-dollar bills for the safe return of fourteen-year-old Bobby Franks.

Mr. Franks was making arrangements to meet the kidnapers when the police notified him that the body of a young boy had been found. The father refused even to go to the morgue to see the body, insisting that the kidnapers had promised they would not harm his son. An uncle of the boy finally went.

The telephone rang at the Franks' home. This time the kidnapers told Mr. Franks that a taxi would pick him up shortly, that he should go to a drugstore at 1463 East 63 Street.

Just as the cab arrived, the telephone rang again. It was the boy's uncle. The boy in the morgue was Bobby Franks.

*   *   *

A pair of glasses found near the body was the turning point in the investigation of the case. These horn-rimmed glasses linked Nathan Leopold, Jr., son of a Chicago millionaire, to the crime.

Questioned by the state's attorney as to his whereabouts on the day of the crime, he said he had been out driving with a friend, Richard Loeb, son of a vice-president of Sears, Roebuck & Company. Young Loeb was brought in for questioning.

Finally, both boys confessed to the kidnaping and murder of Bobby Franks.

The state's attorney immediately issued a formal statement: "I have a hanging case."

Richard Loeb, seventeen, had long wanted to commit the "perfect crime": kidnaping, murder, ransom. He told his close friend, Nathan Leopold, Jr., eighteen, of his scheme and asked for his help. Leopold had no particular desire to participate in such an act, but nevertheless agreed to co-operate because he had an "exalted" opinion of Loeb. The crime was committed, the boys later admitted, "for the sake of a thrill."

Both teen-agers were brilliant students. Leopold was the youngest graduate of the University of Chicago, and Loeb the youngest to be graduated from the University of Michigan.

The 67-year-old Darrow was asked to defend the boys after they had confessed. Even as he was making his decision, newspaper headlines were already proclaiming: "Millions to defend killers."

The state's attorney's office summarized the case: "If your father had $10,000,000, he'd spend at least $5,000,000 to prevent your being hanged. The fathers of these boys have an estimated combined fortune of $15,000,-000, and we suppose it will be these millions versus the death penalty."

When Darrow accepted the case, foes and many friends alike felt the veteran attorney had "sold out" for the fee he was to get.[1] To Darrow,

---

[1] After the trial Darrow sent several notes asking representatives of the Loeb and Leopold families to come to his office to discuss the fee. When they finally came, he mentioned $200,000 as a "reasonable" fee. They appeared shocked.

In his biography of Darrow, published while the attorney was alive, Charles Yale Harrison reported that Darrow "reminded them of their agreement to the Bar Association to arbitrate the matter, but one member of the youths' families reminded Darrow that they would be at a disadvantage because of the fact that Darrow was a lawyer. After a few days, representatives of the families thought that an arbitrator would have awarded one hundred thousand dollars to Darrow, because the next day they came around and offered seventy-five thousand dollars. Disgusted with the negotiations, Dar-

however, this was a case in which he could effectively present his views on capital punishment.

Realizing the necessity of stopping the talk of a "million-dollar defense," the families of the boys, through Darrow, issued a statement: "There will be no large sums of money spent, either for legal or medical talent. . . . Lawyers' fees shall be determined by a committee composed of officers of the Chicago Bar Association. . . . In no way will the families of the accused boys use money in any attempt to defeat justice."

A few days before the trial opened, the Chicago Tribune offered to broadcast the proceedings over its radio station and asked for the opinion of the public through a poll. The Chicago Evening American, in biting satire, suggested in answer to the Tribune's offer that the local White Sox baseball park be used as an open-air courtroom. The public, fearing that its children would be exposed to unsavory testimony, voted 6,569 to 4,169 against such a broadcast, and the Tribune dropped the idea.

The trial of the State of Illinois versus Nathan Leopold, Jr., and Richard Loeb opened July 21, 1924 in the courtroom of John R. Caverly, Chief Justice of the Criminal Court of Cook County.

State's Attorney Robert E. Crowe, a former Cook County circuit court judge, was chief prosecutor. His assistants were Thomas Marshall, Joseph P. Savage, John Sbarbaro and Milton D. Smith.

For the defense: Clarence Darrow, and the Bachrach brothers, Benjamin and Walter, who were relatives of the Loebs.

The public and the newspapers followed the cry of the prosecutor calling for hanging of the boys. The defense was only interested in saving the lives of the two teen-agers.

On the opening day of the trial, July 21, 1924, the defense startled the court, the newspapers and the country when it pleaded the youths guilty. "We dislike to throw this burden upon this Court or any court but we feel that we must," said Darrow. "We ask the Court to permit us to offer evidence as to the mental condition of these young men to show the degree of responsibility that they had. We wish to offer this evidence in mitigation of the punishment."

Darrow explained later: "We are not going to introduce evidence of insanity, but we do intend to show that our clients are mentally diseased."

State's Attorney Crowe insisted: "We shall go ahead with our evidence and shall demand the death penalty for both Loeb and Leopold."

Darrow answered, speaking at times to the prosecutor and at other times

---

row accepted, and told them to send their check along. The next day it arrived. It was for seventy thousand dollars.

"As Darrow had an arrangement with his firm by which they were to supply him with assistants, clerical help, et cetera, and he was to divide all his fees equally with the firm, his net fee was thirty-five thousand dollars. Of this amount the federal and state governments took five thousand dollars in taxes, leaving a net of thirty thousand dollars."

to the judge: "I never saw so much enthusiasm for the death penalty as I have seen here. It's been discussed as a holiday, like a day at the races."

Both the State and the defense brought alienists into the case to substantiate their contentions.

Darrow began his summation August 22, 1924. The afternoon newspaper carried a banner head:

DARROW PLEADS FOR MERCY: MOBS RIOT

It then went on in a sub-headline:

BAILIFF'S ARM BROKEN AND WOMAN FAINTS AS FRENZIED
MOB STORMS PAST GUARDS; JUDGE CALLS FOR 20
POLICE; FEARS SOME WILL BE KILLED

More people than all the courtrooms in the old Cook County Court building could accommodate mobbed Judge Caverly's court when it was learned Darrow was to speak.

The crowd "fought like animals to . . . hear Darrow speak," a newspaper reported.

Judge Caverly himself found it hard to get into the courtroom. So did Nathan Leopold, Sr., and his son Foreman. Assistant State's Attorney Savage had to fight his way in.

Judge Caverly ordered the courtroom doors closed. The bailiff protested: "Judge, there are four of your friends outside."

"Let them stay outside," snapped Judge Caverly.

As the veteran attorney pleaded for the boys' lives, Loeb dug his fist in his eyes and Leopold unsuccessfully tried to hold back tears.

Judge Caverly sat on the bench, chin cupped in his right hand. Attentive. Watching.

"You may stand them up on the trap door of the scaffold, and choke them to death, but that act will be infinitely more cold-blooded, whether justified or not, than any act that these boys have committed or can commit."

Your Honor, it has been almost three months since the great responsibility of this case was assumed by my associates and myself. I am willing to confess that it has been three months of great anxiety—a burden which I gladly would have been spared excepting for my feelings of affection toward some of the members of one of these unfortunate families. This responsibility is almost too great for anyone to assume, but we lawyers can no more choose than the court can choose.

Our anxiety over this case has not been due to the facts that are connected with this most unfortunate affair, but to the almost un-heard-of publicity it has received; to the fact that newspapers all over this country have been giving it space such as they have al-most never before given to any case. The fact that day after day the people of Chicago have been regaled with stories of all sorts about it, until almost every person has formed an opinion.

And when the public is interested and demands a punishment, no matter what the offense, great or small, it thinks of only one punishment, and that is death.

It may not be a question that involves the taking of human life; it may be a question of pure prejudice alone; but when the public speaks as one man it thinks only of killing.

We have been in this stress and strain for three months. We did what we could and all we could to gain the confidence of the public, who in the end really control, whether wisely or unwisely.

It was announced that there were millions of dollars to be spent on this case. Wild and extravagant stories were freely published as though they were facts. Here was to be an effort to save the lives of two boys by the use of money in fabulous amounts, amounts such as these families never even had.

We announced to the public that no excessive use of money would be made in this case, neither for lawyers nor for psychia-trists, nor in any other way. We have faithfully kept that prom-ise.

The psychiatrists, it has been shown by the evidence in this case, are receiving a per diem, and only a per diem, which is the same as is paid by the State.

The attorneys, at their own request, have agreed to take such amount as the officers of the Chicago Bar Association may think is proper in this case.

If we fail in this defense it will not be for lack of money. It will be on account of money. Money has been the most serious handicap that we have met. There are times when poverty is fortunate.

I insist, Your Honor, that had this been the case of two boys of these defendants' ages, unconnected with families supposed to have great wealth, there is not a state's attorney in Illinois who would not have consented at once to a plea of guilty and a punishment in the penitentiary for life. Not one.

No lawyer could have justified any other attitude. No prosecution could have justified it.

We could have come into this court without evidence, without argument, and this court would have given to us what every judge in the city of Chicago has given to everybody in the city of Chicago since the first capital case was tried. We would have had no contest.

We are here with the lives of two boys imperiled, with the public aroused.

For what?

Because, unfortunately, the parents have money. Nothing else.

I told Your Honor in the beginning that never had there been a case in Chicago, where on a plea of guilty a boy under twenty-one had been sentenced to death. I will raise that age and say, never has there been a case where a human being under the age of twenty-three has been sentenced to death. And, I think I am safe in saying, although I have not examined all the records and could not—but I think I am safe in saying—that never has there been such a case in the state of Illinois.

And yet this court is urged, aye, threatened, that he must hang two boys contrary to precedents, contrary to the acts of every judge who ever held court in this state.

Why?

Tell me what public necessity there is for this.

Why need the state's attorney ask for something that never before has been demanded?

Why need a judge be urged by every argument, moderate and immoderate, to hang two boys in the face of every precedent in Illinois, and in the face of the progress of the last fifty years?

Lawyers stand here by the day and read cases from the Dark

Ages, where judges have said that if a man had a grain of sense left and a child if he was barely out of his cradle, could be hanged because he knew the difference between right and wrong. Death sentences for eighteen, seventeen, sixteen and fourteen years have been cited. Brother Marshall [1] has not half done his job. He should read his beloved Blackstone again.

I have heard in the last six weeks nothing but the cry for blood. I have heard from the office of the state's attorney only ugly hate.

I have heard precedents quoted which would be a disgrace to a savage race.

I have seen a court urged almost to the point of threats to hang two boys, in the face of science, in the face of philosophy, in the face of humanity, in the face of experience, in the face of all the better and more humane thought of the age.

Why did not my friend, Mr. Marshall, who dug up from the relics of the buried past these precedents that would bring a blush of shame to the face of a savage, read this from Blackstone:

"Under fourteen, though an infant shall be judged to be incapable of guile prima facie, yet if it appeared to the court and the jury that he was capable of guile, and could discern between good and evil, he may be convicted and suffer death."

Thus a girl thirteen has been burned for killing her mistress.

How this case would delight Dr. Krohn! [2]

He would lick his chops over that more gleefully than over his dastardly homicidal attempt to kill these boys.

One boy of ten and another of nine years of age who had killed their companion were sentenced to death; and he of ten actually hanged.

Why?

He knew the difference between right and wrong. He had learned that in Sunday school.

Age does not count.

Why, Mr. Savage [3] says age makes no difference, and that if this court should do what every other court in Illinois has done

---

[1] Thomas Marshall, Assistant State's Attorney.
[2] Dr. William Krohn, alienist who testified for the State.
[3] Joseph P. Savage, Assistant State's Attorney.

since its foundation, and refuse to sentence these boys to death, no one else would ever be hanged in Illinois.

Well, I can imagine some results worse than that. So long as this terrible tool is to be used for a plaything, without thought or consideration, we ought to get rid of it for the protection of human life.

My friend Marshall has read Blackstone by the page, as if it had something to do with a fairly enlightened age, as if it had something to do with the year 1924, as if it had something to do with Chicago, with its boys' courts and its fairly tender protection of the young.

Now, Your Honor, I shall discuss that more in detail a little later, and I only say it now because my friend Mr. Savage—did you pick him for his name or his ability or his learning?—because my friend Mr. Savage, in as cruel a speech as he knew how to make, said to this court that we pleaded guilty because we were afraid to do anything else.

Your Honor, that is true.

We have said to the public and to this court that neither the parents, nor the friends, nor the attorneys would want these boys released. That they are as they are. Unfortunate though it be, it is true, and those closest to them know perfectly well that they should not be released, and that they should be permanently isolated from society. We have said that, and we mean it. We are asking this court to save their lives, which is the least and the most that a judge can do.

We did plead guilty before Your Honor because we were afraid to submit our case to a jury. I would not for a moment deny to this court or to this community a realization of the serious danger we were in and how perplexed we were before we took this more unusual step.

I can tell Your Honor why.

I have found that years and experience with life tempers one's emotions and makes him more understanding of his fellow-man.

Why, when my friend Savage is my age, or even yours, he will read his address to this court with horror.

I am aware that as one grows older he is less critical. He is not so sure. He is inclined to make some allowance for his fellow-man. I am aware that a court has more experience, more judgment and more kindliness than a jury.

Your Honor, it may be hardly fair to the court; I am aware that I have helped to place a serious burden upon your shoulders. And at that, I have always meant to be your friend. But this was not an act of friendship.

I know perfectly well that where responsibility is divided by twelve, it is easy to say: "Away with him."

But, Your Honor, if these boys hang, you must do it. There can be no division of responsibility here. You can never explain that the rest overpowered you. It must be by your deliberate, cool, premeditated act, without a chance to shift responsibility.

It was not a kindness to you. We placed this responsibility on your shoulders because we were mindful of the rights of our clients, and we were mindful of the unhappy families who have done no wrong.

Now, let us see, Your Honor, what we had to sustain us. Of course, I have known Your Honor for a good many years. Not intimately. I could not say that I could even guess from my experience what Your Honor might do, but I did know something. I knew, Your Honor, that ninety unfortunate human beings had been hanged by the neck until dead in the city of Chicago in our history. We would not have civilization except for those ninety that were hanged, and if we cannot make it ninety-two we will have to shut up shop. Some ninety human beings have been hanged in the history of Chicago, and of those only four have been hanged on the plea of guilty—one out of twenty-two.

I know that in the last ten years four hundred and fifty people have been indicted for murder in the city of Chicago and have pleaded guilty. Four hundred and fifty have pleaded guilty in the city of Chicago, and only one has been hanged! And my friend who is prosecuting this case[1] deserves the honor of that hanging while he was on the bench. But his victim was forty years old.

Your Honor will never thank me for unloading this responsibility upon you, but you know that I would have been untrue to

---

[1] Robert E. Crowe, State's Attorney.

my clients if I had not concluded to take this chance before a court, instead of submitting it to a poisoned jury in the city of Chicago. I did it knowing that it would be an unheard-of thing for any court, no matter who, to sentence these boys to death.

And, so far as that goes, Mr. Savage is right. I hope, Your Honor, that I have made no mistake.

I could have wished that the state's attorney's office had met this case with the same fairness that we have met it.

It has seemed to me as I have listened to this case, five or six times repeating the story of this tragedy, spending days to urge Your Honor that a condition of mind could not mitigate, or that tender years could not mitigate, it has seemed to me that it ought to be beneath the representative of a proud state like this to invoke the dark and cruel and bloody past to affect this court and compass these boys' death.

Your Honor, I must for a moment criticize the arguments that have preceded me. I can read to you in a minute my friend Marshall's argument, barring Blackstone. But the rest of his arguments and the rest of Brother Savage's argument, I can sum up in a minute: Cruel; dastardly; premeditated; fiendish; abandoned and malignant heart—sounds like a cancer—cowardly; cold-blooded!

Now that is what I have listened to for three days against two minors, two children, who have no right to sign a note or make a deed.

Cowardly?

Well, I don't know. Let me tell you something that I think is cowardly, whether their acts were or not. Here is Dickie Loeb, and Nathan Leopold, and the State objects to anybody calling one "Dickie" and the other "Babe" although everybody does, but they think they can hang them easier if their names are Richard and Nathan, so we will call them Richard and Nathan.

Eighteen and nineteen years old at the time of the homicide.

Here are three officers watching them. They are led out and in this jail and across the bridge waiting to be hanged. Not a chance to get away. Handcuffed when they get out of this room. Not a chance. Penned in like rats in a trap. And for a lawyer with psychological eloquence to wave his fist in front of their faces and shout "Cowardly!" does not appeal to me as a brave act. It does not commend itself to me as a proper thing for a state's attorney or his assistant; for even defendants not yet hanged have some rights with an official.

Cold-blooded? Why? Because they planned, and schemed, and arranged and fixed?

Yes. But here are the officers of justice, so-called, with all the power of the state, with all the influence of the press, to fan this community into a frenzy of hate; with all of that, who for months have been planning and scheming, and contriving and working to take these two boys' lives.

You may stand them up on the trap door of the scaffold, and choke them to death, but that act will be infinitely more cold-blooded, whether justified or not, than any act that these boys have committed or can commit.

Cold-blooded!

Let the State, who is so anxious to take these boys' lives, set an example in consideration, kindheartedness and tenderness before they call my clients cold-blooded.

I have heard this crime described—this most distressing and unfortunate homicide, as I would call it; this cold-blooded murder, as the State would call it.

I call it a homicide particularly distressing because I am defending.

They call it a cold-blooded murder because they want to take human lives.

Call it what you will.

I have heard this case talked of, and I have heard these lawyers say that this is the coldest-blooded murder that the civilized world ever has known. I don't know what they include in the civilized world. I suppose Illinois. Although they talk as if they did not. But we will assume Illinois. This is the most cold-blooded murder, says the State, that ever occurred.

Now, Your Honor, I have been practicing law a good deal longer than I should have, anyhow for forty-five or forty-six years, and during a part of that time I have tried a good many criminal cases, always defending. It does not mean that I am better. It probably means that I am more squeamish than the other fellows. It means neither that I am better nor worse. It means the way I am made. I cannot help it.

I have never yet tried a case where the state's attorney did not say that it was the most cold-blooded, inexcusable, premeditated case that ever occurred. If it was murder, there never was such a murder. If it was robbery, there never was such a robbery. If it was a conspiracy, it was the most terrible conspiracy that ever happened since the Star Chamber passed into oblivion. If it was larceny, there never was such a larceny.

Now, I am speaking moderately. All of them are the worst. Why? Well, it adds to the credit of the state's attorney to be connected with a big case. That is one thing. They can say:

"Well, I tried the most cold-blooded murder case that ever was tried, and I convicted them, and they are dead," or:

"I tried the worst forgery case that ever was tried, and I won that. I never did anything that was not big."

Lawyers are apt to say that.

And then there is another thing, Your Honor: Of course, I generally try cases to juries, and these adjectives always go well with juries; bloody, cold-blooded, despicable, cowardly, dastardly, cruel, heartless—the whole litany of the state's attorney's office generally goes well with a jury. The twelve jurors, being good themselves, think it is a tribute to their virtue if they follow the litany of the state's attorney.

I suppose it may have some effect with the court; I do not know. Anyway, those are the chances we take when we do our best to save life and reputation.

"Here, your clients have pleaded guilty to the most cold-blooded murder that ever took place in the history of the world. And how does a judge dare to refuse to hang by the neck until dead two cowardly ruffians who committed the coldest-blooded murder in the history of the world?"

That is a good talking point.

I want to give some attention to this cold-blooded murder, Your Honor.

Was it a cold-blooded murder?

Was it the most terrible murder that ever happened in the state of Illinois?

Was it the most dastardly act in the annals of crime?

No.

I insist, Your Honor, that under all fair rules and measurements, this was one of the least dastardly and cruel of any that I have known anything about.

Now, let us see how we should measure it.

They say that this was a cruel murder, the worst that ever happened. I say that very few murders ever occurred that were as free from cruelty as this.

There ought to be some rule to determine whether a murder is exceedingly cruel or not.

Of course, Your Honor, I admit that I hate killing, and I hate it no matter how it is done—whether you shoot a man through the heart, or cut his head off with an ax, or kill him with a chisel or tie a rope around his neck. I hate it. I always did. I always shall.

But there are degrees, and if I might be permitted to make my own rules I would say that if I were estimating what was the most cruel murder, I might first consider the sufferings of the victim.

Now, probably the State would not take that rule. They would say the one that had the most attention in the newspapers. In that way they have got me beaten at the start.

But I would say the first thing to consider is the degree of pain to the victim.

Poor little Bobby Franks suffered very little. There is no excuse for his killing. If to hang these two boys would bring him back to life, I would say let them hang, and I believe their parents would say so, too. But:

> *The moving finger writes, and having writ,*
> *Moves on; nor all your piety nor wit*
> *Shall lure it back to cancel half a line,*
> *Nor all your tears wash out a word of it.*

Robert Franks is dead, and we cannot call him back to life. It was all over in fifteen minutes after he got into the car, and he probably never knew it or thought of it. That does not justify it. It is the last thing I would do. I am sorry for the poor boy. I am sorry for his parents. But it is done.

Of course I cannot say with the certainty of Mr. Savage that he would have been a great man if he had grown up. At fourteen years of age I don't know whether he would or not. Savage, I suppose, is a mind reader, and he says that he would. He has a fantasy, which is hanging. So far as the cruelty to the victim is concerned, you can scarce imagine one less cruel.

Now, what else would stamp a murder as being a most atrocious crime?

First, I put the victim, who ought not to suffer; and next, I would put the attitude of those who kill.

What was the attitude of these two boys?

It may be that the state's attorney would think that it was particularly cruel to the victim because he was a boy.

Well, my clients are boys, too, and if it would make more serious the offense to kill a boy, it should make less serious the offense of the boys who do the killing.

What was there in the conduct of these two boys which showed a wicked, malignant and abandoned heart beyond that of anybody else who ever lived? Your Honor, it is simply foolish.

Everybody who thinks knows the purpose of this. Counsel knows that under all the rules of the courts they have not the slightest right to ask this court to take life. Yet they urge it upon this court by falsely characterizing this as being the cruelest act that ever occurred. What about these two boys—the second thing that would settle whether it was cruel or not?

Mr. Marshall read case after case of murders and he said: "Why, those cases don't compare with yours. Yours is worse." Worse, why? What were those cases? Most of his cases were robbery cases—where a man went out with a gun to take a person's money, and shot him down. Some of them were cases where a man killed from spite and hatred and malice. Some of them were cases of special atrocities, most connected with money. A man kills someone to get money, he kills someone through hatred. What is this case?

This is a senseless, useless, purposeless, motiveless act of two boys. Now, let me see if I can prove it. There was not a particle of hate, there was not a grain of malice, there was no opportunity to be cruel except as death is cruel—and death is cruel.

There was absolutely no purpose in it all, no reason in it all, and no motive for it all.

Now, let me see whether I am right or not.

I mean to argue this thoroughly, and it seems to me that there is no chance for a court to hesitate upon the facts in this case.

I want to try to do it honestly and plainly, and without any attempt at frills or oratory; to state the facts of this case just as the facts exist, and nothing else.

What does the State say about it?

*　　*　　*

In order to make this the most cruel thing that ever happened, of course they must have a motive. And what, do they say, was the motive?

Your Honor, if there was ever anything so foolish, so utterly futile as the motive claimed in this case, then I have never listened to it.

What did Tom Marshall say?

What did Joe Savage say?

"The motive was to get ten thousand dollars," say they.

These two boys, neither one of whom needed a cent, scions of wealthy people, killed this little inoffensive boy to get ten thousand dollars?

First let us call your attention to the opening statement of Judge Crowe, where we heard for the first time the full details of this homicide after a plea of Guilty.

All right. He said these two young men were heavy gamblers, and they needed the money to pay gambling debts—or on account of gambling.

Now, Your Honor, he said this was atrocious, most atrocious; and they did it to get the money because they were gamblers and needed it to pay gambling debts.

What did he prove?

He put on one witness, and one only, who had played bridge with both of them in college, and he said they played for five cents a point.

Now, I trust Your Honor knows better than I do how much of a game that would be. At poker I might guess, but I know little about bridge.

But what else?

He said that in a game one of them lost ninety dollars to the other one.

They were playing against each other, and one of them lost ninety dollars?

Ninety dollars!

Their joint money was just the same; and there is not another word of evidence in this case to sustain the statement of Mr. Crowe, who pleads to hang these boys. Your Honor, is it not trifling?

It would be trifling, excepting, Your Honor, that we are dealing in human life. And we are dealing in more than that; we are dealing in the future fate of two families. We are talking of placing a blot upon the escutcheon of two houses that do not deserve it. And all that they can get out of their imagination is that there was a game of bridge and one lost ninety dollars to the other, and therefore they went out and committed murder.

* * *

But let us go further than that. Who were these two boys? And how did it happen?

On a certain day they killed poor little Robert Franks. I will not go over the paraphernalia, the letter demanding money, the ransom, because I will discuss that later in another connection. But they killed him. These two boys. They were not to get ten thousand dollars; they were to get five thousand dollars if it worked, that is, five thousand dollars each. Neither one could get more than five, and either one was risking his neck in the job. So each one of my clients was risking his neck for five thousand dollars, if that had anything to do with it, which it did not.

Did they need the money?

Why, at this very time, and a few months before, Dickie Loeb had three thousand dollars in a checking account in the bank. Your Honor, I would be ashamed to talk about this except that in all apparent seriousness they are asking to kill these two boys on the strength of this flimsy foolishness.

At that time Richard Loeb had a three-thousand-dollar checking account in the bank. He had three Liberty Bonds, one of which was past due, and the interest on each of them had not been collected for three years. I said, had not been collected; not a penny's interest had been collected—and the coupons were there for three years. And yet they would ask to hang him on the theory that he committed this murder because he needed money.

In addition to that we brought his father's private secretary here, who swears that whenever he asked for it, he got a check, without ever consulting the father. She had an open order to give him a check whenever he wanted it, and she had sent him a check in February, and he had lost it and had not cashed it. So he got another in March.

Your Honor, how far would this kind of an excuse go on the part of the defense? Anything is good enough to dump into a pot where the public are clamoring, and where the stage is set and where loud-voiced young attorneys are talking about the sanctity of the law, which means killing people; anything is enough to justify a demand for hanging.

How about Leopold?

Leopold was in regular receipt of one hundred and twenty-five dollars a month; he had an automobile; paid nothing for board and clothes and expenses; he got money whenever he wanted it, and he had arranged to go to Europe and had bought his ticket and was going to leave about the time he was arrested in this case.

He passed his examination for the Harvard Law School, and was going to take a short trip to Europe before it was time for him to attend the fall term. His ticket had been bought, and his father was to give him three thousand dollars to make the trip.

Your Honor, jurors sometimes make mistakes, and courts do, too. If on this evidence the court is to construe a motive out of this case, then I insist that human liberty is not safe and human life is not safe. A motive could be construed out of any set of circumstances and facts that might be imagined.

In addition to that, these boys' families were extremely

wealthy. The boys had been reared in luxury, they had never been denied anything; no want or desire left unsatisfied; no debts; no need of money; nothing.

And yet they murdered a little boy against whom they had nothing in the world, without malice, without reason, to get five thousand dollars each. All right. All right, Your Honor, if the court believes it, if anyone believes it—I can't help it.

That is what this case rests on. It could not stand up a minute without motive. Without it, it was the senseless act of immature and diseased children, as it was; a senseless act of children, wandering around in the dark and moved by some emotion that we still perhaps have not the knowledge or the insight into life to understand thoroughly.

Now, let me go on with it. What else do they claim?

I want to say to Your Honor that you may cut out every expert in this case, you may cut out every lay witness in this case, you may decide this case upon the facts as they appear here alone; and there is no sort of question that these boys were mentally diseased.

I do not know, but I do not believe that there is any man who knows this case, who does not know that it can be accounted for only on the theory of the mental disease of these two lads.

*   *   *

The State says, in order to make out the wonderful mental processes of these two boys, that they fixed up a plan to go to Ann Arbor to get a typewriter, and yet when they got ready to do this act, they went down the street a few doors from their house and bought a rope; they went around the corner and bought acid; then went somewhere else nearby and bought tape; they went down to the hotel and rented a room, and then gave it up, and went to another hotel, and rented one there. And then Dick Loeb went to the hotel room, took a valise containing his library card and some books from the library, left it two days in the room, until the hotel took the valise and took the books. Then he went to another hotel and rented another room. He might just as well have sent his card with the ransom letter.

They went to the Rent-a-Car place and hired a car. All this clumsy machinery was gone through without intelligence or method or rational thought. I submit, Your Honor, that no one, unless he had an afflicted mind, together with youth, could possibly have done it.

But let's get to something stronger than that. Were these boys in their right minds? Here were two boys with good intellect, one eighteen and one nineteen. They had all the prospects that life could hold out for any of the young—one a graduate of Chicago and another of Ann Arbor; one who had passed his examination for the Harvard Law School and was about to take a trip in Europe, another who had passed at Ann Arbor, the youngest in his class, with three thousand dollars in the bank. Boys who never knew what it was to want a dollar; boys who could reach any position that was given to boys of that kind to reach; boys of distinguished and honorable families, families of wealth and position, with all the world before them. And they gave it all up for nothing, nothing! They took a little companion of one of them, on a crowded street, and killed him, for nothing, and sacrificed everything that could be of value in human life upon the crazy scheme of a couple of immature lads.

Now, Your Honor, you have been a boy; I have been a boy. And we have known other boys. The best way to understand somebody else is to put yourself in his place.

Is it within the realm of your imagination that a boy who was right, with all the prospects of life before him, who could choose what he wanted, without the slightest reason in the world would lure a young companion to his death, and take his place in the shadow of the gallows?

I do not care what Dr. Krohn may say; he is liable to say anything, except to tell the truth, and he is not liable to do that. No one who has the process of reasoning could doubt that a boy who would do that is not right.

How insane they are I care not, whether medically or legally. They did not reason; they could not reason; they committed the most foolish, most unprovoked, most purposeless, most causeless act that any two boys ever committed, and they put themselves where the rope is dangling above their heads.

There are not physicians enough in the world to convince any thoughtful, fair-minded man that these boys are right. Was their act one of deliberation, of intellect, or were they driven by some force such as Dr. White[1] and Dr. Glueck[2] and Dr. Healy[3] have told this court?

There are only two theories: one is that their diseased brains drove them to it; the other is the old theory of possession by devils, and my friend Marshall could have read you books on that, too, but it has been pretty well given up in Illinois.

That they were intelligent and sane and sound and reasoning is unthinkable. Let me call Your Honor's attention to another thing.

Why did they kill little Bobby Franks?

Not for money, not for spite, not for hate. They killed him as they might kill a spider or a fly, for the experience. They killed him because they were made that way. Because somewhere in the infinite processes that go to the making up of the boy or the man something slipped, and those unfortunate lads sit here hated, despised, outcasts, with the community shouting for their blood.

Are they to blame for it? There is no man on earth who can mention any purpose for it all or any reason for it all. It is one of those things that happened; that happened, and it calls not for hate but for kindness, for charity, for consideration.

I heard the state's attorney talk of mothers.

Mr. Savage is talking for the mothers, and Mr. Crowe is thinking of the mothers, and I am thinking of the mothers. Mr. Savage, with the immaturity of youth and inexperience, says that if we hang them there will be no more killing. This world has been one long slaughterhouse from the beginning until today, and killing goes on and on and on, and will forever. Why

[1] Dr. W. A. White, alienist, defense witness.
[2] Dr. Benjamin Glueck, alienist, defense witness.
[3] Dr. William J. Healy, alienist, defense witness.

not read something, why not study something, why not think instead of blindly shouting for death?

Kill them. Will that prevent other senseless boys or other vicious men or vicious women from killing? No!

It will simply call upon every weak-minded person to do as they have done. I know how easy it is to talk about mothers when you want to do something cruel. But I am thinking of the mothers too. I know that any mother might be the mother of a little Bobby Franks, who left his home and went to his school, and who never came back. I know that any mother might be the mother of Richard Loeb and Nathan Leopold, just the same. The trouble is this, that if she is the mother of a Nathan Leopold or of a Richard Loeb, she has to ask herself the question:

"How came my children to be what they are? From what ancestry did they get this strain? How far removed was the poison that destroyed their lives? Was I the bearer of the seed that brings them to death?"

Any mother might be the mother of any of them. But these two are the victims. I remember a little poem that gives the soliloquy of a boy about to be hanged, a soliloquy such as these boys might make:

> The night my father got me
> His mind was not on me;
> He did not plague his fancy
> To muse if I should be
> The son you see.
>
> The day my mother bore me
> She was a fool and glad,
> For all the pain I cost her,
> That she had borne the lad
> That borne she had.
>
> My father and my mother
> Out of the light they lie;
> The warrant would not find them,
> And here, 'tis only I
> Shall hang so high.

O let not man remember
The soul that God forgot,
But fetch the county sheriff
And noose me in a knot,
And I will rot.

And so the game is ended,
That should not have begun.
My father and my mother
They had a likely son,
And I have none.

No one knows what will be the fate of the child he gets or the child she bears; the fate of the child is the last thing they consider. This weary old world goes on, begetting, with birth and with living and with death; and all of it is blind from the beginning to the end. I do not know what it was that made these boys do this mad act, but I do know there is a reason for it. I know they did not beget themselves. I know that any one of an infinite number of causes reaching back to the beginning might be working out in these boys' minds, whom you are asked to hang in malice and in hatred and injustice, because someone in the past has sinned against them.

I am sorry for the fathers as well as the mothers, for the fathers who give their strength and their lives for educating and protecting and creating a fortune for the boys that they love; for the mothers who go down into the shadow of death for their children, who nourish them and care for them, and risk their lives, that they may live, who watch them with tenderness and fondness and longing, and who go down into dishonor and disgrace for the children that they love.

All of these are helpless. We are all helpless. But when you are pitying the father and the mother of poor Bobby Franks, what about the fathers and mothers of these two unfortunate boys, and what about the unfortunate boys themselves, and what about all the fathers and all the mothers and all the boys and all the girls who tread a dangerous maze in darkness from birth to death?

Do you think you can cure it by hanging these two? Do you think you can cure the hatreds and the maladjustments of the world by hanging them? You simply show your ignorance and your hate when you say it. You may here and there cure hatred with love and understanding, but you can only add fuel to the flames by cruelty and hate.

What is my friend's idea of justice? He says to this court, whom he says he respects—and I believe he does—Your Honor, who sits here patiently, holding the lives of these two boys in your hands:

"Give them the same mercy that they gave to Bobby Franks."

Is that the law? Is that justice? Is this what a court should do? Is this what a state's attorney should do? If the state in which I live is not kinder, more humane, more considerate, more intelligent than the mad act of these two boys, I am sorry that I have lived so long.

I am sorry for all fathers and all mothers. The mother who looks into the blue eyes of her little babe cannot help musing over the end of the child, whether it will be crowned with the greatest promises which her mind can image or whether he may meet death upon the scaffold. All she can do is to rear him with love and care, to watch over him tenderly, to meet life with hope and trust and confidence, and to leave the rest with fate.

*   *   *

Your Honor, last night I was speaking about what is perfectly obvious in this case, that no human being could have done what these boys did, excepting through the operation of a diseased brain. I do not propose to go through each step of this terrible deed—it would take too long. But I do want to call the attention of this court to some of the other acts of these two boys, in this distressing and weird homicide; acts which show conclusively that there could be no reason for their conduct.

Without any excuse, without the slightest motive, not moved by money, not moved by passion or hatred, by nothing except the vague wanderings of children, they rented a car, and about four o'clock in the afternoon started to find somebody to kill. For nothing.

They went over to the Harvard School. Dick's little brother was there, on the playground. Dick went there himself in open daylight, known by all of them. He had been a pupil there himself. The school was near his home, and he looked over the little boys.

Your Honor has been in these courts for a long time; you have listened to murder cases before. Has any such case ever appeared here or in any of the books? Has it ever come to the human experience of any judge, or any lawyer, or any person of affairs? Never once!

Ordinarily there would be no sort of question of the condition of these boys' minds. The question is raised only because their parents have money.

They first picked out a little boy named Levinson, and Dick trailed him around.

As I think of that story of Dick trailing this little boy around, there comes to my mind a picture of Dr. Krohn—for sixteen years going in and out of the courtrooms in this building and other buildings, trailing victims without regard to the name or sex or age or surroundings. But he had a motive, and his motive was cash, as I will show further. One was the mad act of a child; the other the cold, deliberate act of a man getting his living by dealing in blood.

Dick abandons that lead; Dick and Nathan are in the car, and they see Bobby Franks on the street, and they call to him to get into the car. It is about five o'clock in the afternoon, in the long summer days, on a thickly settled street, built up with homes, the houses of their friends and their companions, known to everybody, automobiles appearing and disappearing, and they take him in the car—for nothing.

If there had been a question of revenge, yes; if there had been a question of hate, where no one cares for his own fate, intent only on accomplishing his end, yes. But without any motive or any reason they pick up this little boy right in sight of their own homes, and surrounded by their neighbors. They drive a little way, on a populous street, where everybody can see, where eyes may be at every window as they pass by. They hit him over the head with a chisel and kill him, and go on about their business, driving this car within half a block of Loeb's home, within the same distance of Franks's home, drive it past the neighbors that they know, in the open highway, in broad daylight. And still men will say that they have a bright intellect, and, as Dr. Krohn puts it, can orient themselves and reason as well as he can, possibly, and that it is the sane act of sane men.

I say again, whatever madness and hate and frenzy may do to the human mind, there is not a single person who reasons who can believe that one of these acts was the act of men—of brains—that were not diseased. There is no other explanation for it. And had it not been for the wealth and the weirdness and the notoriety, they would have been sent to the psychopathic hospital for examination, and been taken care of, instead of the State demanding that this court take the last pound of flesh and the last drop of blood from two irresponsible lads.

They pull the dead boy into the back seat, and wrap him in a blanket, and this funeral car starts on its route.

If ever any death car went over the same route or the same kind of a route driven by sane people, I have never heard of it, and I fancy no one else has ever heard of it.

This car is driven for twenty miles. First down through thickly populated streets, where everyone knows the boys and their families, and has known them for years, till they come to the Midway Boulevard, and then take the main line of a street which is traveled more than any other street on the South Side except in the Loop, among automobiles that can scarcely go along on account of the number, straight down the Midway through the regular route of Jackson Park, Nathan Leopold driving this car, and Dick Loeb on the back seat, and the dead boy with him.

The slightest accident, the slightest misfortune, a bit of curiosity, an arrest for speeding—anything would bring destruction. For what? For nothing! The mad acting of the fool in *King Lear* is the only thing I know of that compares with it. And yet doctors will swear that it is a sane act. They know better.

They go down a thickly populated street through South Chicago, and then for three miles take the longest street to go through this city—built solid with business buildings, filled with automobiles backed upon the street, with streetcars on the track, with thousands of peering eyes; one boy driving and the other on the back seat, with the corpse of little Bobby Franks, the blood streaming from him, wetting everything in the car.

And yet they tell me that this is sanity; they tell me that the brains of these boys are not diseased. You need no experts; you need no X rays; you need no study of the endocrines. Their conduct shows exactly what it was, and shows that this Court has before him two young men who should be examined in a psychopathic hospital and treated kindly and with care.

They get through South Chicago, and they take the regular automobile road down toward Hammond. There is the same situation—hundreds of machines; any accident might encompass their ruin. They stop at the forks of the road, and leave little Bobby Franks, soaked with blood, in the machine, and get their dinner, and eat it without an emotion or a qualm.

Your Honor, we do not need to believe in miracles; we need not resort to that in order to get blood. If it were any other case, there could not be a moment's hesitancy as to what to do.

I repeat, you may search the annals of crime, and you can find no parallel. It is utterly at variance with every motive and every act and every part of conduct that influences normal people in the commission of crime. There is not a sane thing in all of this from the beginning to the end. There was not a normal act in any of it, from its inception in a diseased brain, until today, when they sit here awaiting their doom.

But we are told that they planned. Well, what does that mean? A maniac plans, an idiot plans, an animal plans, any brain that functions may plan; but their plans were the diseased plans of the diseased mind. Do I need to argue it? Does anybody need more than to glance at it? Is there any man with a fair intellect and a decent regard for human life and the slightest bit of heart that does not understand this situation?

And still, Your Honor, on account of its weirdness and its strangeness and its advertising, we are forced to fight. For what? Forced to plead to this court that two boys, one eighteen and the other nineteen, may be permitted to live in silence and solitude and disgrace and spend all their days in the penitentiary, asking this court and the state's attorney to be merciful enough to let these two boys be locked up in a prison until they die.

What do they want? Tell me, is a lifetime for the young boys spent behind prison bars—is that not enough for this mad act? And is there any reason why this great public should be regaled by a hanging?

I cannot understand it, Your Honor. It would be past belief, excepting that to the four corners of the earth the news of this weird act has been carried and men have been stirred, and the primitive has come back, and the intellect has been stifled, and men have been controlled by feelings and passions and hatred which should have died centuries ago.

My friend Savage pictured to you the putting of this dead boy in this culvert. Well, no one can minutely describe any killing and not make it shocking. It is shocking. It is shocking because we love life and because we instinctively draw back from death. It is shocking wherever it is and however it is, and perhaps all death is almost equally shocking.

But here is the picture of a dead boy, past pain, when no harm can come to him, put in a culvert, after taking off his clothes so that the evidence would be destroyed; and that is pictured to this court as a reason for hanging. Well, Your Honor, that does not appeal to me as strongly as the hitting over the head of little Robert Franks with a chisel. The boy was dead.

I could say something about the death penalty that, for some mysterious reason, the State wants in this case. Why do they want it? To vindicate the law? Oh, no. The law can be vindicated without killing anyone else. It might shock the fine sensibilities of the state's counsel that this boy was put into a culvert and left after he was dead, but, Your Honor, I can think of a scene that makes this pale into insignificance. I can think, and only think, Your Honor, of taking two boys, one eighteen and the other nineteen, irresponsible, weak, diseased, penning them in a cell, checking off the days and the hours and the minutes until they will be taken out and hanged. Wouldn't it be a glorious day for Chicago? Wouldn't it be a glorious triumph for the state's attorney? Wouldn't it be a glorious triumph of justice in this land? Wouldn't it be a glorious illustration of Christianity and kindness and charity? I can picture them, wakened in the gray light of morning, furnished a suit of clothes by the State, led to the scaffold, their feet tied, black caps drawn over their heads, stood on a trap door, the hangman pressing a spring so that it gives way under them; I can see them fall through space—and—stopped by the rope around their necks.

This would surely expiate placing Bobby Franks in the culvert after he was dead. This would doubtless bring immense satisfaction to some people. It would bring a greater satisfaction because it would be done in the name of justice. I am always suspicious of righteous indignation. Nothing is more cruel than righteous indignation. To hear young men talk glibly of justice. Well, it would make me smile if it did not make me sad. Who knows what it is? Does Mr. Savage know? Does Mr. Crowe know? Do I know? Does Your Honor know? Is there any human machinery for finding it out? Is there any man who can weigh me and say what I deserve? Can Your Honor? Let us be honest. Can Your Honor appraise yourself, and say what you deserve? Can Your Honor appraise these two young men and say what they deserve? Justice must take account of infinite circumstances which a human being cannot understand.

If there is such a thing as justice it could only be administered by one who knew the inmost thoughts of the man to whom he was meting it out. Aye, who knew the father and mother and the grandparents and the infinite number of people back of him. Who knew the origin of every cell that went into the body, who could understand the structure and how it acted. Who could tell how the emotions that sway the human being affected that particular frail piece of clay. It means more than that. It means that you must appraise every influence that moves men, the civilization where they live, and all society which enters into the making of the child or the man! If Your Honor can do it—if you can do it you are wise, and with wisdom goes mercy.

No one with wisdom and with understanding, no one who is honest with himself and with his own life, whoever he may be, no one who has seen himself the prey and the sport and the plaything of the infinite forces that move man, no one who has tried and who has failed—and we have all tried and we have all failed—no one can tell what justice is for someone else or for himself; and the more he tries and the more responsibility he takes, the more he clings to mercy as being the one thing which he is sure should control his judgment of men.

It is not so much mercy either, Your Honor. I can hardly understand myself pleading to a court to visit mercy on two boys by shutting them into a prison for life.

For life! Where is the human heart that would not be satisfied with that?

Where is the man or woman who understands his own life and who has a particle of feeling that could ask for more? Any cry for more roots back to the hyena; it roots back to the hissing serpent; it roots back to the beast and the jungle. It is not a part of man. It is not a part of that feeling which, let us hope, is growing, though scenes like this sometimes make me doubt that it is growing. It is not a part of that feeling of mercy and pity and understanding of each other which we believe has been slowly raising man from his low estate. It is not a part of the finer instincts which are slow to develop; of the wider knowledge which is slow to come, and slow to move us when it comes. It is not a part of all that makes the best there is in man. It is not a part of all that promises any hope for the future and any justice for the present. And must I ask that these boys get mercy by spending the rest of their lives in prison, year following year, month following month, and day following day, with nothing to look forward to but hostile guards and stone walls? It ought not to be hard to get that much mercy in any court in the year 1924.

These boys left this body down in the culvert, and they came back and telephoned home that they would be too late for supper. Here, surely, was an act of consideration on the part of Leopold, telephoning home that he would be late for supper. Dr. Krohn says he must be able to think and act because he could do this. But the boy who, through habit, would telephone his home that he would be late for supper had not a tremor or a thought or a shudder at taking the life of little Bobby Franks for nothing, and he has not had one yet. He was in the habit of doing what he did when he telephoned—that was all; but in the presence of life and death, and a cruel death, he had no tremor and no thought.

They came back. They got their dinners. They parked the bloody automobile in front of Leopold's house. They cleaned it to some extent that night and left it standing in the street in front of their home.

"Oriented," of course. "Oriented." They left it there for the night, so that anybody might see and might know. They took it into the garage the next day and washed it, and then poor little Dickie Loeb—I shouldn't call him Dickie, and I shouldn't call him poor, because that might be playing for sympathy, and you have no right to ask for sympathy in this world; you should ask for justice, whatever that may be; and only state's attorneys know.

And then in a day or so we find Dick Loeb with his pockets stuffed with newspapers telling of the Franks tragedy. We find him consulting with his friends in the club, with the newspaper reporters; and my experience is that the last person that a conscious criminal associates with is a reporter. He shuns them even more than he does a detective, because they are smarter and less merciful. But he picks up a reporter, and he tells him he has read a great many detective stories, and he knows just how this would happen and that the fellow who telephoned must have been down on Sixty-third Street, and the way to find him is to go down Sixty-third Street and visit the drugstores, and he would go with him.

And Dick Loeb pilots reporters around the drugstores where the telephoning was done, and he talks about it, and he takes the newspapers, and takes them with him, and he is having a glorious time. And yet he is "perfectly oriented," in the language of Dr. Krohn. "Perfectly oriented." Is there any question about the condition of his mind? Why was he doing it? He liked to hear about it. He had done something that he could not boast of directly, but he did want to hear other people talk about it, and he looked around there and helped them find the place where the telephone message was sent out.

Your Honor has had experience with criminals and you know how they act. Was any such thing as this ever heard of before on land or sea? Does not the man who knows what he is doing, who for some reason has been overpowered and commits what is called a crime, keep as far away from it as he can? Does he go to the reporters and help them hunt it out? There is not a single act in this case that is not the act of a diseased mind, not one.

Talk about scheming. Yes, it is the scheme of disease; it is the scheme of infancy; it is the scheme of fools; it is the scheme of irresponsibility from the time it was conceived until the last act of the tragedy. And yet we have to talk about it, and argue about it, when it is obvious to anyone who cares to know the truth.

But they must be hanged, because everybody is talking about the case, and their people have money.

Am I asking for much in this case?

Let me see for a moment now. Is it customary to get anything on a plea of Guilty? How about the state's attorney? Do they not give you something on a plea of Guilty? How many times has Your Honor listened to the state's attorney come into this court, with a man charged with robbery with a gun, which means from ten years to life, and on condition of a plea of Guilty, ask to have the gun charge stricken out, and get a sentence of three to twenty years, with a chance to see daylight inside of three years? How many times? How many times has the state's attorney himself asked consideration for everything including murder, not only for the young, but even the old? How many times have they come into this court, and into every court, not only here but everywhere, and asked for it? Your Honor knows. I will guarantee that three times out of four in criminal cases, and much more than that in murder, ninety-nine times out of one hundred, and much more than that; I would say not twice in a thousand times has the State failed to give consideration to the defendant on a plea.

How many times has Your Honor been asked to change a sentence, and not hold a man guilty of robbery with a gun, and give him a chance on a plea of Guilty—not a boy but a man?

How many times have others done it, and over and over and over again? And it will be done so long as justice is fairly administered; and in a case of a charge of robbery with a gun, coupled with larceny, how many times have both the robbery and the gun been waived, and a plea of larceny made, so that the defendant might be released in a year?

✻   ✻   ✻

How many times has mercy come even from the state's attorney's office? I am not criticizing. It should come and I am telling this court what this court knows. And yet forsooth, for some reason, here is a case of two immature boys of diseased mind, as plain as the light of day, and they say you can get justice only by shedding their last drop of blood!

Why? I can ask the question easier than I can answer it. Why? It is unheard of, unprecedented in this court, unknown among civilized men. And yet this court is to make an example or civilization will fail. I suppose civilization will survive if Your Honor hangs them. But it will be a terrible blow that you shall deal. Your Honor will be turning back over the long, long road we have traveled. You will be turning back from the protection of youth and infancy. Your Honor would be turning back from the treatment of children. Your Honor would be turning back to the barbarous days which Brother Marshall seems to love, when they burned people thirteen years of age. You would be dealing a staggering blow to all that has been done in the city of Chicago in the last twenty years for the protection of infancy and childhood and youth.

And for what? Because the people are talking about it. Nothing else. It would not mean, Your Honor, that your reason was convinced. It would mean in this land of ours, where talk is cheap, where newspapers are plenty, where the most immature expresses his opinion, and the more immature the stronger, that a court couldn't help feeling the great pressure of the public opinion which they say exists in this case.

Coming alone in this courtroom with obscure defendants, doing what has been done in this case, coming with the outside world shut off, as in most cases, and saying to this court and counsel:

"I believe that these boys ought not to be at large; I believe they are immature and irresponsible, and I am willing to enter a plea of Guilty and let you sentence them to life imprisonment," how long do you suppose Your Honor would hesitate? Do you suppose the state's attorneys would raise their voices in protest?

You know it has been done too many times. And here for the first time, under these circumstances, this court is told that you must make an example.

*   *   *

Can you administer law without consideration? Can you administer what approaches justice without it? Can this court or any court administer justice by consciously turning his heart to stone and being deaf to all the finer instincts which move men? Without those instincts I wonder what would happen to the human race?

If a man could judge a fellow in coldness without taking account of his own life, without taking account of what he knows of human life, without some understanding—how long would we be a race of real human beings? It has taken the world a long time for man to get to even where he is today. If the law was administered without any feeling of sympathy or humanity or kindliness, we would begin our long, slow journey back to the jungle that was formerly our home.

How many times has assault with intent to rob or kill been changed in these courts to assault and battery? How many times has felony been waived in assault with a deadly weapon and a man or boy given a chance? And we are asking a chance to be shut up in stone walls for life. For life. It is hard for me to think of it, but that is the mercy we are asking from this court, which we ought not to be required to ask, and which we should have as a matter of right in this court and which I have faith to believe we will have as a matter of right.

Is this new? Why, I undertake to say that even the state's attorney's office—and if he denies it I would like to see him bring in the records—I will undertake to say that in three cases out of four of all kinds and all degrees, clemency has been shown.

Three hundred and forty murder cases in ten years with a plea of Guilty in this county. All the young who pleaded guilty, every one of them—three hundred and forty in ten years with one hanging on a plea of Guilty, and that a man forty years of age. And yet they say we come here with a preposterous plea for mercy. When did any plea for mercy become preposterous in any tribunal in all the universe?

We are satisfied with justice, if the court knows what justice is, or if any human being can tell what justice is. If anybody can look into the minds and hearts and the lives and the origin of these two youths and tell what justice is, we would be content. But nobody can do it without imagination, without sympathy, without kindliness, without understanding, and I have faith that this Court will take this case, with his conscience, and his judgment and his courage and save these boys' lives.

Now, Your Honor, let me go a little further with this. I have gone over some of the high spots in this tragedy. This tragedy has not claimed all the attention it has had on account of its atrocity. There is nothing to that.

What is it?

There are two reasons, and only two that I can see. First is the reputed extreme wealth of these families; not only the Loeb and Leopold families, but the Franks family, and of course it is unusual. And next is the fact it is weird and uncanny and motiveless. That is what attracted the attention of the world.

Many may say now that they want to hang these boys; but I know that giving the people blood is something like giving them their dinner. When they get it they go to sleep. They may for the time being have an emotion, but they will bitterly regret it. And I undertake to say that if these two boys are sentenced to death and are hanged, on that day a pall will settle over the people of this land that will be dark and deep, and at least cover every humane and intelligent person with its gloom. I wonder if it will do good. I wonder if it will help the children—and there is an infinite number like these. I marveled when I heard Mr. Savage talk. I do not criticize him. He is young and enthusiastic. But has he ever read anything? Has he ever thought? Was there ever any man who had studied science, who has read anything of criminology or philosophy— was there ever any man who knew himself who could speak with the assurance with which he speaks?

What about this matter of crime and punishment, anyhow? I may know less than the rest, but I have at least tried to find out, and I am fairly familiar with the best literature that has been written on that subject in the last hundred years. The more men study, the more they doubt the effect of severe punishment on crime. And yet Mr. Savage tells this court that if these boys are hanged, there will be no more murder.

Mr. Savage is an optimist. He says that if the defendants are hanged there will be no more boys like these.

I could give him a sketch of punishment—punishment beginning with the brute which killed something because something hurt it; the punishment of the savage. If a person is injured in the tribe, they must injure somebody in the other tribe; it makes no difference who it is, but somebody. If one is killed his friends or family must kill in return.

You can trace it all down through the history of man. You can trace the burnings, the boilings, the drawings and quarterings, the hanging of people in England at the crossroads, carving them up and hanging them as examples for all to see.

We can come down to the last century when nearly two hundred crimes were punishable by death, and by death in every form; not only hanging—that was too humane—but burning, boiling, cutting into pieces, torturing in all conceivable forms.

You can read the stories of the hangings on a high hill, and the populace for miles around coming out to the scene, that everybody might be awed into goodness. Hanging for picking pockets—and more pockets were picked in the crowd that went to the hanging than had been known before. Hangings for murder—and men were murdered on the way there and on the way home. Hangings for poaching, hangings for everything, and hangings in public, not shut up cruelly and brutally in a jail, out of the light of day, wakened in the nighttime and led forth and killed, but taken to the shire town on a high hill, in the presence of a multitude, so that all might see that the wages of sin were death.

❋   ❋   ❋

I know that every step in the progress of humanity has been met and opposed by prosecutors, and many times by courts. I know that when poaching and petty larceny were punishable by death in England, juries refused to convict. They were too humane to obey the law; and judges refused to sentence. I know that when the delusion of witchcraft was spreading over Europe, claiming its victims by the millions, many a judge so shaped his cases that no crime of witchcraft could be punished in his court. I know that these trials were stopped in America because juries would no longer convict. I know that every step in the progress of the world in reference to crime has come from the human feelings of man. It has come from that deep well of sympathy which, in spite of all our training and all our conventions and all our teaching, still lives in the human breast. Without it there could be no human life on this weary old world.

Gradually the laws have been changed and modified, and men look back with horror at the hangings and the killings of the past. What did they find in England? That as they got rid of these barbarous statutes, crimes decreased instead of increased; as the criminal law was modified and humanized, there was less crime instead of more. I will undertake to say, Your Honor, that you can scarcely find a single book written by a student—and I will include all the works on criminology of the past—that has not made the statement over and over again that as the penal code was made less terrible, crimes grew less frequent.

* * *

Now let us see a little about the psychology of man.

If these two boys die on the scaffold—which I can never bring myself to imagine—if they do die on the scaffold, the details of this will be spread over the world. Every newspaper in the United States will carry a full account. Every newspaper of Chicago will be filled with the gruesome details. It will enter every home and every family.

Will it make men better or make men worse? I would like to put that to the intelligence of man, at least such intelligence as they have. I would like to appeal to the feelings of human beings so far as they have feelings—would it make the human heart softer or would it make hearts harder? How many men would be colder and crueler for it? How many men would enjoy the details? And you cannot enjoy human suffering without being affected for better or for worse; those who enjoyed it would be affected for the worse.

What influence would it have upon the millions of men who will read it? What influence would it have upon the millions of women who will read it, more sensitive, more impressionable, more imaginative than men? Would it help them if Your Honor should do what the State begs you to do? What influence would it have upon the infinite number of children who will devour its details as Dickie Loeb has enjoyed reading detective stories? Would it make them better or would it make them worse? The question needs no answer. You can answer it from the human heart. What influence, let me ask you, will it have for the unborn babes still sleeping in their mother's womb? And what influence will it have on the psychology of the fathers and mothers yet to come? Do I need to argue to Your Honor that cruelty only breeds cruelty?—that hatred only causes hatred? —that if there is any way to soften this human heart, which is hard enough at its best, if there is any way to kill evil and hatred and all that goes with it, it is not through evil and hatred and cruelty; it is through charity, and love and understanding?

How often do people need to be told this? Look back at the world. There is not a man who is pointed to as an example to the world who has not taught it. There is not a philosopher, there is not a religious leader, there is not a creed that has not taught it. This is a Christian community, so-called, at least it boasts of it, and yet they would hang these boys in a Christian community. Let me ask this court, is there any doubt about whether these boys would be safe in the hands of the founder of the Christian religion? It would be blasphemy to say they would not. Nobody could imagine, nobody could even think of it. And yet there are men who want to hang them for a childish, purposeless act, conceived without the slightest malice in the world.

Your Honor, I feel like apologizing for urging it so long. It is not because I doubt this court. It is not because I do not know something of the human emotions and the human heart. It is not that I do not know that every result of logic, every page of history, every line of philosophy and religion, every precedent in this court, urges this court to save life. It is not that. I have become obsessed with this deep feeling of hate and anger that has swept across this city and this land. I have been fighting it, battling with it, until it has fairly driven me mad, until I sometimes wonder whether every religious human emotion has not gone down in the raging storm.

I am not pleading so much for these boys as I am for the infinite number of others to follow, those who perhaps cannot be as well defended as these have been, those who may go down in the storm and the tempest without aid. It is of them I am thinking, and for them I am begging of this court not to turn backward toward the barbarous and cruel past.

Now, Your Honor, who are these two boys?

Leopold, with a wonderfully brilliant mind; Loeb, with an unusual intelligence; both from their very youth crowded like hothouse plants to learn more and more and more. Dr. Krohn says that they are intelligent. In spite of that, it is true: they are unusually intelligent. But it takes something besides brains to make a human being who can adjust himself to life.

Brains are not the chief essential in human conduct. The emotions are the urge that makes us live; the urge that makes us work or play, or move along the pathways of life. They are the instinctive things. In fact, intellect is a late development of life. Long before it was evolved, the emotional life kept the organism in existence until death. Whatever our action is, it comes from the emotions, and nobody is balanced without them.

* * *

The question of intellect means the smallest part of life. Back of this are man's nerves, muscles, heart, blood, lungs—in fact, the whole organism; the brain is the least part in human development. Without the emotion-life man is nothing. How is it with these two boys? Is there any question about them?

I insist there is not the slightest question about it. All teaching and all training appeals, not only to the intellectual, but to emotional life. A child is born with no ideas of right and wrong, just with plastic brain, ready for such impressions as come to him, ready to be developed. Lying, stealing, killing are not wrong to the child. These mean nothing.

Gradually his parents and his teachers tell him things, teach him habits, show him that he may do this and he may not do that, teach him the difference between his and mine. No child knows this when he is born. He knows nothing about property or property rights. They are given to him as he goes along. He is like the animal that wants something and goes out and gets it, kills it, operating purely from instinct, without training.

The child is gradually taught, and habits are built up. These habits are supposed to be strong enough so that they will form inhibitions against conduct when the emotions come in conflict with the duties of life. Dr. Singer[1] and Dr. Church,[2] both of them, admitted exactly what I am saying now. The child of himself knows nothing about right and wrong, and the teaching built up gives him habits, so he will be able to control certain instincts that surge upon him, and which surge upon everyone who lives. If the instinct is strong enough and the habit weak enough, the habit goes down before it. Both of these eminent men admit it. There can be no question about it. His conduct depends upon the relative strength of the instinct and the habit that has been built up.

Education means fixing these habits so deeply in the life of man that they stand in stead when he needs them to keep him in the path—and that is all it does mean. Suppose one sees a thousand-dollar bill and nobody present. He may have the impulse to take it. If he does not take it, it will be because his emotional nature revolts at it, through habit and through training. If the emotional nature does not revolt at it he will do it. That is why people do not commit what we call crime; that, and caution. All education means is the building of habits so that certain conduct revolts you and stops you, saves you; but without an emotional

[1] Dr. Harold D. Singer, alienist, State witness.
[2] Dr. Church, alienist, State witness.

[54]

nature you cannot do that. Some are born practically without it. How about this case?

The State put on three alienists and Dr. Krohn. Two of them, Dr. Patrick[1] and Dr. Church, are undoubtedly able men. One of them, Dr. Church, is a man whom I have known for thirty years, and for whom I have the highest regard.

On Sunday, June first, before any of the friends of these boys or their counsel could see them, while they were in the care of the state's attorney's office, they brought them in to be examined by these alienists. I am not going to discuss that in detail as I may later on. Dr. Patrick said that the only thing unnatural he noted about it was that they had no emotional reactions. Dr. Church said the same. These are their alienists, not ours. These boys could tell this gruesome story without a change of countenance, without the slightest feelings. There were no emotional reactions to it. What was the reason? I do not know. How can I tell why? I know what causes the emotional life. I know it comes from the nerves, the muscles, the endocrine glands, the vegetative system. I know it is the most important part of life. I know it is practically left out of some. I know that without it men cannot live. I know that without it they cannot act with the rest. I know they cannot feel what you feel and what I feel; that they cannot feel the moral shocks which come to men who are educated and who have not been deprived of an emotional system or emotional feelings. I know it, and every person who has honestly studied this subject knows it as well. Is Dickie Loeb to blame because out of the infinite forces that conspired to form him, the infinite forces that were at work producing him ages before he was born, that because out of these infinite combinations he was born without it? If he is, then there should be a new definition for justice. Is he to blame for what he did not have and never had? Is he to blame that his machine is imperfect? Who is to blame? I do not know. I have never in my life been interested so much in fixing blame as I have in relieving people from blame. I am not wise enough to fix it. I know that somewhere in the past that entered into him something missed. It may be defective

[1] Dr. Hugh T. Patrick, alienist, State witness.

nerves. It may be a defective heart or liver. It may be defective endocrine glands. I know it is something. I know that nothing happens in this world without a cause.

I know, Your Honor, that if you, sitting here in this court, and in this case, had infinite knowledge, you could lay your fingers on it, and I know you would not visit it on Dickie Loeb. I asked Dr. Church and I asked Dr. Singer whether, if they were wise enough to know, they could not find the cause, and both of them said yes. I know that they and Loeb are just as they are, and that they did not make themselves. There are at least two theories of man's responsibility. There may be more. There is the old theory that if a man does something it is because he willfully, purposely, maliciously, and with a malignant heart sees fit to do it. And that goes back to the possession of man by devils. The old indictments used to read that a man being possessed of a devil did so and so. But why was he possessed with the devil? Did he invite him in? Could he help it?

Very few half-civilized people believe that doctrine any more. Science has been at work, humanity has been at work, scholarship has been at work, and intelligent people now know that every human being is the product of the endless heredity back of him and the infinite environment around him. He is made as he is and he is the sport of all that goes before him and is applied to him, and under the same stress and storm you would act one way and I act another, and poor Dickie Loeb another.

Dr. Church said so and Dr. Singer said so, and it is the truth. Take a normal boy, Your Honor. Do you suppose he could have taken a boy into an automobile without any reason and hit him over the head and killed him? I might just as well ask you whether you thought the sun could shine at midnight in this latitude. It is not a part of normality. Something was wrong.

I am asking Your Honor not to visit the grave and dire and terrible misfortunes of Dickie Loeb and Nathan Leopold upon these two boys. I do not know where to place it. I know it is somewhere in the infinite economy of nature, and if I were wise enough I could find it. I know it is there, and to say that because they are as they are you should hang them, is brutality and cruelty, and savors of the fang and claw.

There can be no question on the evidence in this case. Dr. Church and Dr. Patrick both testified that these boys have no emotional reactions in reference to this crime. Every one of the alienists on both sides has told this court what no doubt this court already knew, that the emotions furnish the urge and the drive to life. A man can get along without his intellect, and most people do, but he cannot get along without his emotions. When they did make a brain for man, they did not make it good enough to hurt, because emotions can still hold sway. He eats and he drinks, he works and plays and sleeps, in obedience to his emotional system. The intellectual part of man acts only as a judge over his emotions, and then he generally gets it wrong, and has to rely on his instincts to save him.

These boys—I do not care what their mentality; that simply makes it worse—are emotionally defective. Every single alienist who has testified in this case has said so. The only person who did not was Dr. Krohn. While I am on that subject, lest I forget the eminent doctor, I want to refer to one or two things. In the first place, all these alienists that the State called came into the state's attorney's office and heard these boys tell their story of this crime, and that is all they heard.

Now, Your Honor is familiar with Chicago the same as I am, and I am willing to admit right here and now that the two ablest alienists in Chicago are Dr. Church and Dr. Patrick. There may be abler ones, but we lawyers do not know them.

And I will go further: If my friend Crowe had not got to them first, I would have tried to get them. There is no question about it at all. I said I would have tried to; I didn't say I would, and yet I suspect I would. And I say that, Your Honor, without casting the slightest reflection on either of them, for I really have a high regard for them, and aside from that a deep friendship for Dr. Church. And I have considerable regard for Dr. Singer. I will go no further now.

We could not get them, and Mr. Crowe was very wise, and he deserves a great deal of credit for the industry, the research and the thoroughness that he and his staff have used in detecting this terrible crime.

He worked with intelligence and rapidity. If here and there

he trampled on the edges of the Constitution I am not going to talk about it here. If he did it, he is not the first one in that office and probably will not be the last who will do it, so let that go. A great many people in this world believe the end justifies the means. I don't know but that I do myself. And that is the reason I never want to take the side of the prosecution, because I might harm an individual. I am sure the State will live anyhow.

Before the defense had a chance, the State got in two alienists, Church and Patrick, and also called Dr. Krohn, and they sat around hearing these boys tell their stories, and that is all.

Your Honor, they were not holding an examination. They were holding an inquest, and nothing else. It has not the slightest reference to, or earmarks of, an examination for sanity. It was just an inquest; a little premature, but still an inquest.

What is the truth about it? What did Patrick say? He said that it was not a good opportunity for examination. What did Church say? He said that it was not a good opportunity for an examination. What did Krohn say? "Fine—a fine opportunity for an examination," the best he had ever heard of, or that ever anybody had, because their souls were stripped naked. Krohn is not an alienist. He is an orator. He said, because their souls were naked to them. Well, if Krohn's was naked, there would not be much to show.

But Patrick and Church said the conditions were unfavorable for an examination, that they never would choose it, that their opportunities were poor. And yet Krohn states the contrary— Krohn, who by his own admissions, for sixteen years has not been a physician, but has used a license for the sake of haunting these courts, civil and criminal, and going up and down the land peddling perjury.

*   *   *

Your Honor, the mind, of course, is an illusive thing. Whether it exists or not no one can tell. It cannot be found as you find the brain. Its relation to the brain and the nervous system is uncertain. It simply means the activity of the body, which is coordinated with the brain. But when we do find from human conduct that we believe there is a diseased mind, we naturally speculate on how it came about. And we wish to find always, if possible, the reason why it is so. We may find it; we may not find it; because the unknown is infinitely wider and larger than the known, both as to the human mind and as to almost everything else in the universe.

*　　*　　*

I have tried to study the lives of these two most unfortunate boys. Three months ago, if their friends and the friends of the family had been asked to pick out the most promising lads of their acquaintance, they probably would have picked these two boys. With every opportunity, with plenty of wealth, they would have said that those two would succeed.

In a day, by an act of madness, all this is destroyed, until the best they can hope for now is a life of silence and pain, continuing to the end of their years.

How did it happen?

Let us take Dickie Loeb first.

*　　*　　*

I do not claim to know how it happened; I have sought to find out. I know that something, or some combination of things, is responsible for this mad act. I know that there are no accidents in nature. I know that effect follows cause. I know that, if I were wise enough, and knew enough about this case, I could lay my finger on the cause. I will do the best I can, but it is largely speculation.

The child, of course, is born without knowledge.

Impressions are made upon its mind as it goes along. Dickie Loeb was a child of wealth and opportunity. Over and over in this court Your Honor has been asked, and other courts have been asked, to consider boys who have no chance; they have been asked to consider the poor, whose home had been the street, with no education and no opportunity in life, and they have done it, and done it rightfully.

But, Your Honor, it is just as often a great misfortune to be the child of the rich as it is to be the child of the poor. Wealth has its misfortunes. Too much, too great opportunity and advantage, given to a child has its misfortunes, and I am asking Your Honor to consider the rich as well as the poor (and nothing else). Can I find what was wrong? I think I can. Here was a boy at a tender age, placed in the hands of a governess, intellectual, vigorous, devoted, with a strong ambition for the welfare of this boy. He was pushed in his studies, as plants are forced in hothouses. He had no pleasures, such as a boy should have, except as they were gained by lying and cheating.

Now, I am not criticizing the nurse. I suggest that some day Your Honor look at her picture. It explains her fully. Forceful, brooking no interference, she loved the boy, and her ambition was that he should reach the highest perfection. No time to pause, no time to stop from one book to another, no time to have those pleasures which a boy ought to have to create a normal life. And what happened? Your Honor, what would happen? Nothing strange or unusual. This nurse was with him all the time, except when he stole out at night, from two to fourteen years of age. He, scheming and planning as healthy boys would do, to get out from under her restraint; she, putting before him the best books, which children generally do not want; and he, when she was not looking, reading detective stories, which he devoured, story after story, in his young life. Of all of this there can be no question.

What is the result? Every story he read was a story of crime. We have a statute in this state, passed only last year, if I recall it, which forbids minors reading stories of crime. Why? There is only one reason. Because the legislature in its wisdom felt that it would produce criminal tendencies in the boys who read them. The legislature of this state has given its opinion, and forbidden boys to read these books. He read them day after day. He never stopped. While he was passing through college at Ann Arbor he was still reading them. When he was a senior he read them, and almost nothing else.

Now, these facts are beyond dispute. He early developed the tendency to mix with crime, to be a detective; as a little boy shadowing people on the street; as a little child going out with his fantasy of being the head of a band of criminals and directing them on the street. How did this grow and develop in him? Let us see. It seems to be as natural as the day following the night. Every detective story is a story of a sleuth getting the best of it: trailing some unfortunate individual through devious ways until his victim is finally landed in jail or stands on the gallows. They all show how smart the detective is, and where the criminal himself falls down.

This boy early in his life conceived the idea that there could be a perfect crime, one that nobody could ever detect; that there could be one where the detective did not land his game—a perfect crime. He had been interested in the story of Charley Ross, who was kidnaped. He was interested in these things all his life. He believed in his childish way that a crime could be so carefully planned that there would be no detection, and his idea was to plan and accomplish a perfect crime. It would involve kidnaping and involve murder.

*　　*　　*

There had been growing in Dickie's brain, dwarfed and twisted—as every act in this case shows it to have been dwarfed and twisted—there had been growing this scheme, not due to any wickedness of Dickie Loeb, for he is a child. It grew as he grew; it grew from those around him; it grew from the lack of the proper training until it possessed him. He believed he could beat the police. He believed he could plan the perfect crime. He had thought of it and talked of it for years—had talked of it as a child, had worked at it as a child—this sorry act of his, utterly irrational and motiveless, a plan to commit a perfect crime which must contain kidnaping, and there must be ransom, or else it could not be perfect, and they must get the money.

The State itself in opening this case said that it was largely for experience and for a thrill, which it was. In the end the State switched it onto the foolish reason of getting cash.

Every fact in this case shows that cash had almost nothing to do with it, except as a factor in the perfect crime; and to commit the perfect crime there must be a kidnaping, and a kidnaping where they could get money, and that was all there was of it. Now, these are the two theories of this case, and I submit, Your

Honor, under the facts in this case, that there can be no question but that we are right. This fantasy grew in the mind of Dickie Loeb almost before he began to read. It developed as a child just as kleptomania has developed in many a person and is clearly recognized by the courts. He went from one thing to another—in the main insignificant, childish things. Then, the utterly foolish and stupid and unnecessary thing of going to Ann Arbor to steal from a fraternity house, a fraternity of which he was a member. And, finally, the planning for this crime. Murder was the least part of it; to kidnap and get the money, and kill in connection with it—that was the childish scheme growing up in these childish minds. And they had it in mind for five or six months—planning what? Planning where every step was foolish and childish; acts that could have been planned in an hour or a day; planning this, and then planning that, changing this and changing that; the weird actions of two mad brains.

Counsel have laughed at us for talking about fantasies and hallucinations. They had laughed at us in one breath, but admitted in another. Let us look at that for a moment, Your Honor. Your Honor has been a child. I well remember that I have been a child. And while youth has its advantages, it has its grievous troubles. There is an old prayer, "Though I grow old in years, let me keep the heart of a child." The heart of a child—with its abundant life, its disregard for consequences, its living in the moment, and for the moment alone, its lack of responsibility, and its freedom from care.

The law knows and has recognized childhood for many and many a long year. What do we know about childhood? The brain of the child is the home of dreams, of castles, of visions, of illusions and of delusions. In fact, there could be no childhood without delusions, for delusions are always more alluring than facts. Delusions, dreams and hallucinations are a part of the warp and woof of childhood. You know it and I know it. I remember, when I was a child, the men seemed as tall as the trees, the trees as tall as the mountains. I can remember very well when, as a little boy, I swam the deepest spot in the river for the first time. I swam breathlessly and landed with as much sense of glory and triumph as Julius Caesar felt when he led his army across the

Rubicon. I have been back since, and I can almost step across the same place, but it seemed an ocean then. And those men whom I thought so wonderful were dead and left nothing behind. I had lived in a dream. I had never known the real world which I met, to my discomfort and despair, and that dispelled the illusions of my youth.

The whole life of childhood is a dream and an illusion, and whether they take one shape or another shape depends not upon the dreamy boy but on what surrounds him. As well might I have dreamed of burglars and wished to be one as to dream of policemen and wished to be one. Perhaps I was lucky, too, that I had no money. We have grown to think that the misfortune is in not having it. The great misfortune in this terrible case is the money. That has destroyed their lives. That has fostered these illusions. That has promoted this mad act. And, if Your Honor shall doom them to die, it will be because they are the sons of the rich.

Do you suppose that if they lived up here on the Northwest Side and had no money, with the evidence as clear in this case as it is, that any human being would want to hang them? Excessive wealth is a grievous misfortune in every step in life. When I hear foolish people, when I read malicious newspapers talking of excessive fees in this case, it makes me ill. That there is nothing bigger in life, that it is presumed that no man lives to whom money is not the first concern, that human instincts, sympathy and kindness and charity and logic can only be used for cash. It shows how deeply money has corrupted the hearts of most men.

Now, to get back to Dickie Loeb. He was a child. The books he read by day were not the books he read by night. We are all of us molded somewhat by the influences around us, and of those, to people who read, perhaps books are the greatest and the strongest influences.

I know where my life has been molded by books, amongst other things. We all know where our lives have been influenced by books. The nurse, strict and jealous and watchful, gave him one kind of book; by night he would steal off and read the other.

Which, think you, shaped the life of Dickie Loeb? Is there any kind of question about it? A child. Was it pure maliciousness? Was a boy of five or six or seven to blame for it? Where did he get it? He got it where we all get our ideas, and these books became a part of his dreams and a part of his life, and as he grew up his visions grew to hallucinations.

He went out on the street and fantastically directed his companions, who were not there, in their various moves to complete the perfect crime. Can there be any sort of question about it?

Suppose, Your Honor, that instead of this boy being here in this court, under the plea of the State that Your Honor shall pronounce a sentence to hang him by the neck until dead, he had been taken to a pathological hospital to be analyzed, and the physicians had inquired into his case. What would they have said? There is only one thing that they could possibly have said. They would have traced everything back to the gradual growth of the child.

That is not all there is about it. Youth is hard enough. The only good thing about youth is that it has no thought and no care; and how blindly we can do things when we are young!

Where is the man who has not been guilty of delinquencies in youth? Let us be honest with ourselves. Let us look into our own hearts. How many men are there today—lawyers and congressmen and judges, and even state's attorneys—who have not been guilty of some mad act in youth? And if they did not get caught, or the consequences were trivial, it was their good fortune.

We might as well be honest with ourselves, Your Honor. Before I would tie a noose around the neck of a boy I would try to call back into my mind the emotions of youth. I would try to remember what the world looked like to me when I was a child. I would try to remember how strong were these instinctive, persistent emotions that moved my life. I would try to remember how weak and inefficient was youth in the presence of the surging, controlling feelings of the child. One that honestly remembers and asks himself the question and tries to unlock the door that he thinks is closed, and calls back the boy, can understand the boy.

But, Your Honor, that is not all there is to boyhood. Nature is strong and she is pitiless. She works in her own mysterious

way, and we are her victims. We have not much to do with it
ourselves. Nature takes this job in hand, and we play our parts.
In the words of old Omar Khayyam, we are only:

> *But helpless pieces in the game He plays*
> *Upon this checkerboard of nights and days;*
> *Hither and thither moves, and checks, and slays,*
> *And one by one back in the closet lays.*

What had this boy to do with it? He was not his own father;
he was not his own mother; he was not his own grandparents.
All of this was handed to him. He did not surround himself with
governesses and wealth. He did not make himself. And yet he is
to be compelled to pay.

There was a time in England, running down as late as the
beginning of the last century, when judges used to convene court
and call juries to try a horse, a dog, a pig, for crime. I have in my
library a story of a judge and jury and lawyers trying and convicting an old sow for lying down on her ten pigs and killing
them.

What does it mean? Animals were tried. Do you mean to tell
me that Dickie Loeb had any more to do with his making than
any other product of heredity that is born upon the earth?

At this period of life it is not enough to take a boy—Your
Honor, I wish I knew when to stop talking about this question
that always has interested me so much—it is not enough to take
a boy filled with his dreams and his fantasies and living in an
unreal world, but the age of adolescence comes on him with all
the rest.

What does he know? Both these boys are in the adolescent age.
Both these boys, as every alienist in this case on both sides tells
you, are in the most trying period of the life of a child—both
these boys, when the call of sex is new and strange; both these
boys, at a time of seeking to adjust their young lives to the
world, moved by the strongest feelings and passions that have
ever moved men; both these boys, at the time boys grow insane,
at the time crimes are committed. All of this is added to all the
rest of the vagaries of their lives. Shall we charge them with

full responsibility that we may have a hanging? That we may deck Chicago in a holiday garb and let the people have their fill of blood; that you may put stains upon the heart of every man, woman and child on that day, and that the dead walls of Chicago will tell the story of the shedding of their blood?

For God's sake, are we crazy? In the face of history, of every line of philosophy, against the teaching of every religionist and seer and prophet the world has ever given us, we are still doing what our barbaric ancestors did when they came out of the caves and the woods.

From the age of fifteen to the age of twenty or twenty-one, the child has the burden of adolescence, of puberty and sex thrust upon him. Girls are kept at home and carefully watched. Boys without instruction are left to work the period out for themselves. It may lead to excess. It may lead to disgrace. It may lead to perversion. Who is to blame? Who did it? Did Dickie Loeb do it?

Your Honor, I am almost ashamed to talk about it. I can hardly imagine that we are in the twentieth century. And yet there are men who seriously say that for what nature has done, for what life has done, for what training has done, you should hang these boys.

Now, there is no mystery about this case, Your Honor. I seem to be criticizing their parents. They had parents who were kind and good and wise in their way. But I say to you seriously that the parents are more responsible than these boys. And yet few boys had better parents.

Your Honor, it is the easiest thing in the world to be a parent. We talk of motherhood, and yet every woman can be a mother. We talk of fatherhood, and yet every man can be a father. Nature takes care of that. It is easy to be a parent. But to be wise and farseeing enough to understand the boy is another thing; only a very few are so wise and so farseeing as that. When I think of the light way nature has of picking our parents and populating the earth, having them born and die, I cannot hold human beings to the same degree of responsibility that young lawyers hold them when they are enthusiastic in a prosecution. I know what it means.

I know there are no better citizens in Chicago than the fathers of these poor boys. I know there were no better women than their mothers. But I am going to be honest with this court, if it is at the expense of both. I know that one of two things happened to Richard Loeb: that this terrible crime was inherent in his organism, and came from some ancestor; or that it came through his education and his training after he was born. Do I need to prove it? Judge Crowe said at one point in this case, when some witness spoke about their wealth, that "probably that was responsible."

To believe that any boy is responsible for himself or his early training is an absurdity that no lawyer or judge should be guilty of today. Somewhere this came to the boy. If his failing came from his heredity, I do not know where or how. None of us are bred perfect and pure; and the color of our hair, the color of our eyes, our stature, the weight and fineness of our brain, and everything about us could, with full knowledge, be traced with absolute certainty to somewhere. If we had the pedigree it could be traced just the same in a boy as it could in a dog, a horse or a cow.

I do not know what remote ancestors may have sent down the seed that corrupted him, and I do not know through how many ancestors it may have passed until it reached Dickie Loeb.

All I know is that it is true, and there is not a biologist in the world who will not say that I am right.

If it did not come that way, then I know that if he was normal, if he had been understood, if he had been trained as he should have been it would not have happened. Not that anybody may not slip, but I know it and Your Honor knows it, and every schoolhouse and every church in the land is an evidence of it. Else why build them?

Every effort to protect society is an effort toward training the youth to keep the path. Every bit of training in the world proves it, and it likewise proves that it sometimes fails. I know that if this boy had been understood and properly trained—properly for him—and the training that he got might have been the very best for someone; but if it had been the proper training for him he would not be in this courtroom today with the noose above his head. If there is responsibility anywhere, it is back of him; somewhere in the infinite number of his ancestors, or in his surroundings, or in both. And I submit, Your Honor, that under every principle of natural justice, under every principle of conscience, of right, and of law, he should not be made responsible for the acts of someone else.

I say this again, without finding fault with his parents, for whom I have the highest regard, and who doubtless did the best they could. They might have done better if they had not had so much money. I do not know. Great wealth often curses all who touch it.

This boy was sent to school. His mind worked; his emotions were dead. He could learn books, but he read detective stories. There never was a time since he was old enough to move back and forth, according to what seemed to be his volition, when he was not haunted with these fantasies.

The State made fun of Dr. White, the ablest and, I believe, the best psychiatrist in America today, for speaking about this boy's mind running back to the Teddy bears he used to play with, and in addressing somebody he was wont to say, "You know, Teddy—"

Well, Your Honor, is it nothing but the commonplace action of the commonplace child or the ordinary man? A set of emotions, thoughts, feelings take possession of the mind and we find them recurring and recurring over and over again.

I catch myself many and many a time repeating phrases of my childhood, and I have not quite got into my second childhood yet. I have caught myself doing this while I still could catch myself. It means nothing. We may have all the dreams and visions and build all the castles we wish, but the castles of youth should be discarded with youth, and when they linger to the time when boys should think wiser things, then it indicates a diseased mind.

"When I was young, I thought as a child, I spoke as a child, I understood as a child; but now I have put off childish things," said the Psalmist twenty centuries ago.

It is when these dreams of boyhood, these fantasies of youth still linger, and the growing boy is still a child—a child in emotion, a child in feeling, a child in hallucinations—that you can say that it is the dreams and the hallucinations of childhood that are responsible for his conduct. There is not an act in all this horrible tragedy that was not the act of a child, the act of a child wandering around in the morning of life, moved by the new feelings of a boy, moved by the uncontrolled impulses which his teaching was not strong enough to take care of, moved by the dreams and the hallucinations which haunt the brain of a child. I say, Your Honor, that it would be the height of cruelty, of injustice, of wrong and barbarism to visit the penalty upon this poor boy.

Your Honor, again I want to say that all parents can be criticized; likewise grandparents and teachers. Science is not so much interested in criticism as in finding causes. Sometime education will be more scientific. Sometime we will try to know the boy before we educate and as we educate him. Sometime we will try to know what will fit the individual boy, instead of putting all boys through the same course, regardless of what they are.

This boy needed more of home, more love, more directing. He needed to have his emotions awakened. He needed guiding hands along the serious road that youth must travel. Had these been given him, he would not be here today.

Now, Your Honor, I want to speak of the other lad, Babe.

Babe is somewhat older than Dick, and is a boy of remarkable mind—away beyond his years. He is a sort of freak in this direction, as in others; a boy without emotions, a boy obsessed of philosophy, a boy obsessed of learning, busy every minute of his life.

He went through school quickly; he went to college young; he could learn faster than almost everybody else. His emotional life was lacking, as every alienist and witness in this case excepting Dr. Krohn has told you. He was just a half-boy, an intellect, an intellectual machine going without balance and without a governor, seeking to find out everything there was in life intellectually; seeking to solve every philosophy but using his intellect only.

Of course his family did not understand him; few men would. His mother died when he was young; he had plenty of money;

everything was given to him that he wanted. Both these boys with unlimited money; both these boys with automobiles; both these boys with every luxury around them and in front of them. They grew up in this environment.

Babe took up philosophy. I call him Babe, not because I want it to affect Your Honor, but because everybody else does. He is the youngest of the family and I suppose that is why he got his nickname. We will call him a man. Mr. Crowe thinks it is easier to hang a man than a boy, and so I will call him a man if I can think of it.

He grew up in this way. He became enamored of the philosophy of Nietzsche.

Your Honor, I have read almost everything that Nietzsche ever wrote. He was a man of a wonderful intellect; the most original philosopher of the last century. A man who probably has made a deeper imprint on philosophy than any other man within a hundred years, whether right or wrong. More books have been written about him than probably all the rest of the philosophers in a hundred years. More college professors have talked about him. In a way he has reached more people, and still he has been a philosopher of what we might call the intellectual cult. Nietzsche believed that some time the superman would be born, that evolution was working toward the superman.

He wrote one book, *Beyond Good and Evil,* which was a criticism of all moral codes as the world understands them; a treatise holding that the intelligent man is beyond good and evil; that the laws for good and the laws for evil do not apply to those who approach the superman. He wrote on the will to power. He wrote some ten or fifteen volumes on his various philosophical ideas. Nathan Leopold is not the only boy who has read Nietzsche. He may be the only one who was influenced in the way that he was influenced.

It is not how he would affect you. It is not how he would affect me. The question is how he did affect the impressionable, visionary, dreamy mind of a boy.

At seventeen, at sixteen, at eighteen, while healthy boys were playing baseball or working on the farm or doing odd jobs, he was reading Nietzsche, a boy who never should have seen it at that early age. Babe was obsessed of it, and here are some of the things which Nietzsche taught:

"Why so soft, oh, my brethren? Why so soft, so unresisting and yielding? Why is there so much disavowal and abnegation in your heart? Why is there so little fate in your looks? For all creators are hard, and it must seem blessedness unto you to press your hand upon millenniums and upon wax. This new table, oh, my brethren, I put over you: Become hard. To be obsessed by moral consideration presupposes a very low grade of intellect. We should substitute for morality the will to our own end, and consequently to the means to accomplish that.

"A great man, a man that nature has built up and invented in a grand style, is colder, harder, less cautious and more free from the fear of public opinion. He does not possess the virtues which are compatible with respectability, with being respected, nor any of those things which are counted among the virtues of the herd."

Nietzsche held a contemptuous, scornful attitude to all those things which the young are taught as important in life; a fixing of new values which are not the values by which any normal child has ever yet been reared—a philosophical dream, containing more or less truth, that was not meant by anyone to be applied to life.

Again he says:

"The morality of the master class is irritating to the taste of the present day because of its fundamental principle that a man has obligation only to his equals; that he may act to all of lower rank and to all that are foreign, as he pleases."

In other words, man has no obligations; he may do with all other men and all other boys, and all society, as he pleases—the superman was a creation of Nietzsche, but it has permeated every college and university in the civilized world.

Quoting from a professor of a university:

"Although no perfect superman has yet appeared in history, Nietzsche's types are to be found in the world's great figures—Alexander, Napoleon—in the wicked heroes such as the Borgias, Wagner's Siegfried and Ibsen's Brand—and the great cosmopolitan intellects such as Goethe and Stendhal. These were the gods of Nietzsche's idolatry.

"The superman-like qualities lie not in their genius, but in their freedom from scruple. They rightly felt themselves to be above the law. What they thought was right, not because sanctioned by any law, beyond themselves, but because they did it. So the superman will be a law unto himself. What he does will come from the will and superabundant power within him."

Your Honor, I could read for a week from Nietzsche, all to the same purpose, and the same end.

Counsel have said that because a man believes in murder that does not excuse him.

Quite right. But this is not a case like the anarchists' case where a number of men, perhaps honestly believing in revolution and knowing the consequences of their act and knowing its illegal character, were held responsible for murder.

Of course the books are full of statements that the fact that a man believes in committing a crime does not excuse him.

That is not this case, and counsel must know that it is not this case. Here is a boy at sixteen or seventeen becoming obsessed with these doctrines. There isn't any question about the facts. Their own witnesses tell it and every one of our witnesses tell it. It was not a casual bit of philosophy with him; it was his life. He believed in a superman. He and Dickie Loeb were the supermen. There might have been others, but they were two, and two chums. The ordinary commands of society were not for him.

Many of us read this philosophy but know that it has no actual application to life; but not he. It became a part of his being. It was his philosophy. He lived it and practiced it; he thought it applied to him, and he could not have believed it excepting that it either caused a diseased mind or was the result of a diseased mind.

Now let me call your attention hastily to just a few facts in connection with it. One of the cases is a New York case, where a man named Freeman became obsessed in a very strange way of religious ideas. He read the story of Isaac and Abraham and he felt a call that he must sacrifice his son. He arranged an altar in his parlor. He converted his wife to the idea. He took his little babe and put it on the altar and cut its throat. Why? Because he was obsessed of that idea. Was he sane? Was he normal? Was his mind diseased? Was this poor fellow responsible? Not in the least. And he was acquitted because he was the victim of a delusion. Men are largely what their ideas make them. Boys largely what their ideas make them.

Here is a boy who by day and by night, in season and out, was talking of the superman, owing no obligations to anyone; whatever gave him pleasure he should do, believing it just as another man might believe a religion or any philosophical theory.

You remember that I asked Dr. Church about these religious cases and he said, "Yes, many people go to the insane asylum on account of them," that "They place a literal meaning on parables and believe them thoroughly." I asked Dr. Church, whom I again say I believe to be an honest man, and an intelligent man —I asked him whether the same thing might be done or might come from a philosophical belief, and he said, "If one believed it strongly enough."

And I asked him about Nietzsche. He said he knew something of Nietzsche, something of his responsibility for the war, for which he perhaps was not responsible. He said he knew something about his doctrines. I asked him what became of him, and he said he was insane for fifteen years just before the time of his death. His very doctrine is a species of insanity.

Here is a man, a wise man—perhaps not wise, but brilliant— a thoughtful man who has made his impress upon the world. Every student of philosophy knows him. His own doctrines made him a maniac. And here is a young boy, in the adolescent age, harassed by everything that harasses children, who takes this philosophy and believes it literally. It is a part of his life. It is his life. Do you suppose this mad act could have been done by him in any other way? What could he have to win from this homicide?

A boy with a beautiful home, with automobiles, a graduate of college, going to Europe, and then to study law at Harvard; as brilliant in intellect as any boy that you could find; a boy with every prospect that life might hold out to him; and yet he goes out and commits this weird, strange, wild, mad act, that he may die on the gallows or live in a prison cell until he dies of old age or disease.

He did it, obsessed of an idea, perhaps to some extent influenced by what has not been developed publicly in this case—perversions that were present in the boy. Both signs of insanity; both, together with this act, proving a diseased mind.

Is there any question about what was responsible for him?

What else could be? A boy in his youth, with every promise that the world could hold out before him—wealth and position and intellect, yes, genius, scholarship, nothing that he could not obtain, and he throws it away, and mounts the gallows or goes into a cell for life. It is too foolish to talk about. Can Your Honor imagine a sane brain doing it? Can you imagine it coming from anything but a diseased mind? Can you imagine it is any part of normality? And yet, Your Honor, you are asked to hang a boy of his age, abnormal, obsessed of dreams and visions, a philosophy that destroyed his life, when there is no sort of question in the world as to what caused his downfall.

Now, I have said that, as to Loeb, if there is anybody to blame, it is back of him. Your Honor, lots of things happen in this world that nobody is to blame for. In fact, I am not very much for settling blame myself. If I could settle the blame on somebody else for this special act, I would wonder why that somebody else did it, and I know if I could find that out, I would move it back still another peg.

I know, Your Honor, that every atom of life in all this universe is bound up together. I know that a pebble cannot be thrown into the ocean without disturbing every drop of water in the sea. I know that every life is inextricably mixed and woven with every other life. I know that every influence, conscious and unconscious, acts and reacts on every living organism, and that no one can fix the blame. I know that all life is a series of infinite chances, which sometimes result one way and sometimes another. I have not the infinite wisdom that can fathom it; neither has any other human brain. But I do know that if back of it is a power that made it, that power alone can tell, and if there is no power, then it is an infinite chance, which man cannot solve.

Why should this boy's life be bound up with Friedrich Nietzsche who died thirty years ago, insane, in Germany? I don't know.

I only know it is. I know that no man who ever wrote a line that I read failed to influence me to some extent. I know that every life I ever touched influenced me, and I influenced it; and that it is not given to me to unravel the infinite causes and say, "This is I, and this is you. I am responsible for so much; and you are responsible for so much." I know—I know that in the infinite universe everything has its place and that the smallest particle is a part of all. Tell me that you can visit the wrath of fate and chance and life and eternity upon a nineteen-year-old boy! If you could, justice would be a travesty and mercy a fraud.

I might say further about Nathan Leopold—where did he get this philosophy?—at college? He did not make it, Your Honor. He did not write these books, and I will venture to say there are at least ten thousand books on Nietzsche and his philosophy. I never counted them, but I will venture to say that there are that many in the libraries of the world.

No other philosopher ever caused the discussion that Nietzsche has caused. There is no university in the world where the professors are not familiar with Nietzsche; not one. There is not an intellectual man in the world whose life and feelings run to philosophy who is not more or less familiar with the Nietzschean philosophy. Some believe it, and some do not believe it. Some read it as I do, and take it as a theory, a dream, a vision, mixed with good and bad, but not in any way related to human life. Some take it seriously. The universities perhaps do not all teach it, for perhaps some teach nothing in philosophy; but they give the boys the books of the masters, and tell them what they taught, and discuss the doctrines.

There is not a university in the world of any high standing where the professors do not tell you about Nietzsche, and discuss it, or where the books cannot be found.

I will guarantee that you can go down to the University of

Chicago today—into its big library—and find over a thousand volumes on Nietzsche, and I am sure I speak moderately. If this boy is to blame for this, where did he get it? Is there any blame attached because somebody took Nietzsche's philosophy seriously and fashioned his life on it? And there is no question in this case that it is true. Then who is to blame? The university would be more to blame than he is. The scholars of the world would be more to blame than he is. The publishers of the world—and Nietzsche's books are published by one of the biggest publishers in the world—are more to blame than he. Your Honor, it is hardly fair to hang a nineteen-year-old boy for the philosophy that was taught him at the university.

Now, I do not want to be misunderstood about this. Even for the sake of saving the lives of my clients, I do not want to be dishonest and tell the court something that I do not honestly think in this case. I do not believe that the universities are to blame. I do not think they should be held responsible. I do think, however, that they are too large, and that they should keep a closer watch, if possible, upon the individual. But, you cannot destroy thought because, forsooth, some brain may be deranged by thought. It is the duty of the university, as I conceive it, to get the great storehouse of the wisdom of the ages, and to let students go there, and learn, and choose. I have no doubt but that it has meant the death of many; that we cannot help. Every changed idea in the world has had its consequences. Every new religious doctrine has created its victims. Every new philosophy has caused suffering and death. Every new machine has carved up men while it served the world. No railroad can be built without the destruction of human life. No great building can be erected but that unfortunate workmen fall to the earth and die. No great movement that does not bear its toll of life and death; no great ideal but does good and harm, and we cannot stop because it may do harm.

I have no idea in this case that this act would ever have been committed or participated in by him excepting for the philosophy which he had taken literally, which belonged to older boys and older men, and which no one can take literally and practice literally and live. So, Your Honor, I do not mean to unload this act on that man or this man, or this organization or that organization. I am trying to trace causes. I am trying to trace them honestly. I am trying to trace them with the light I have. I am trying to say to this court that these boys are not responsible for this; and that their act was due to this and this, and this and this; and asking this court not to visit the judgment of its wrath upon them for things for which they are not to blame.

✻   ✻   ✻

These boys, neither one of them, could possibly have committed this act excepting by coming together. It was not the act of one; it was the act of two. It was the act of their planning, their conniving, their believing in each other; their thinking themselves supermen. Without it they could not have done it. It would not have happened. Their parents happened to meet, these boys happened to meet; some sort of chemical alchemy operated so that they cared for each other, and poor Bobby Franks's dead body was found in the culvert as a result. Neither of them could have done it alone.

I want to call your attention, Your Honor, to the two letters in this case which settle this matter to my mind conclusively; not only the condition of these boys' minds, but the terrible fate that overtook them.

Your Honor, I am sorry for poor Bobby Franks, and I think anybody who knows me knows that I am not saying it simply to talk. I am sorry for the bereaved father and the bereaved mother, and I would like to know what they would do with these poor unfortunate lads who are here in this court today. I know something of them, of their lives, of their charity, of their ideas, and nobody here sympathizes with them more than I.

On the twenty-first day of May poor Bobby Franks, stripped and naked, was left in a culvert down near the Indiana line. I know it came through the act of mad boys. Mr. Savage told us that Franks, if he lived, would have been a great man and have accomplished much. I want to leave this thought with Your Honor now. I do not know what Bobby Franks would have been had he grown to be a man. I do not know the laws that control one's growth. Sometimes, Your Honor, a boy of great promise is cut off in his early youth. Sometimes he dies and is placed in a culvert. Sometimes a boy of great promise stands on a trap door and is hanged by the neck until dead. Sometimes he dies of diphtheria. Death somehow pays no attention to age, sex, prospects, wealth or intellect.

It comes, and perhaps—I can only say perhaps, for I never professed to unravel the mysteries of fate, and I cannot tell; but I can say perhaps—the boy who died at fourteen did as much as if he had died at seventy, and perhaps the boy who died as a babe did as much as if he had lived longer. Perhaps, somewhere in fate and chance, it might be that he lived as long as he should.

And I want to say this, that the death of poor little Bobby Franks should not be in vain. Would it mean anything if on account of that death, these two boys were taken out and a rope tied around their necks and they died felons? Would that show that Bobby Franks had a purpose in his life and a purpose in his death? No, Your Honor, the unfortunate and tragic death of this young lad should mean something. It should mean an appeal to the fathers and the mothers, an appeal to the teachers, to the religious guides, to society at large. It should mean an appeal to all of them to appraise children, to understand the emotions that control them, to understand the ideas that possess them, to teach them to avoid the pitfalls of life.

Society, too, should assume its share of the burdens of this case, and not make two more tragedies, but use this calamity as best it can to make life safer, to make childhood easier and more secure, to do something to cure the cruelty, the hatred, the chance, and the willfulness of life.

I have discussed somewhat in detail these two boys separately. Their coming together was the means of their undoing. Your Honor is familiar with the facts in reference to their association. They had a weird, almost impossible relationship. Leopold, with his obsession of the superman, had repeatedly said that Loeb was his idea of the superman. He had the attitude toward him that one has to his most devoted friend, or that a man has to a lover. Without the combination of these two, nothing of this sort probably could have happened.

* * *

Now, Your Honor, I shall pass that subject. I think all of the facts of this extraordinary case, all of the testimony of the alienists, all that Your Honor has seen and heard, all their friends and acquaintances who have come here to enlighten this court—I think all of it shows that this terrible act was the act of immature and diseased brains, the act of children.

Nobody can explain it in any other way.

No one can imagine it in any other way.

It is not possible that it could have happened in any other way.

And, I submit, Your Honor, that by every law of humanity, by every law of justice, by every feeling of righteousness, by every instinct of pity, mercy and charity, Your Honor should say that because of the condition of these boys' minds, it would be monstrous to visit upon them the vengeance that is asked by the State.

* * *

I want to discuss now another thing which this court must consider and which to my mind is absolutely conclusive in this case. That is, the age of these boys.

I shall discuss it more in detail than I have discussed it before, and I submit, Your Honor, that it is not possible for any court to hang these two boys if he pays any attention whatever to the modern attitude toward the young, if he pays any attention whatever to the precedents in this county, if he pays any attention to the humane instincts which move ordinary man.

I have a list of executions in Cook County beginning in 1840, which I presume covers the first one, because I asked to have it go to the beginning. Ninety poor unfortunate men have given up their lives to stop murder in Chicago. Ninety men have been hanged by the neck until dead, because of the ancient superstition that in some way hanging one man keeps another from committing a crime. The ancient superstition, I say, because I defy the State to point to a criminologist, a scientist, a student, who has ever said it. Still we go on, as if human conduct was not influenced and controlled by natural laws the same as all the rest of the universe is the subject of law. We treat crime as if it had no cause. We go on saying, "Hang the unfortunates, and it will end." Was there ever a murder without a cause? Was there ever a crime without a cause? And yet all punishment proceeds upon the theory that there is no cause; and the only way to treat crime is to intimidate everyone into goodness and obedience to law. We lawyers are a long way behind.

Crime has its cause. Perhaps all crimes do not have the same cause, but they all have some cause. And people today are seeking to find out the cause. We lawyers never try to find out. Scientists are studying it; criminologists are investigating it; but we lawyers go on and on, punishing and hanging, and thinking that by general terror we can stamp out crime.

It never occurs to the lawyer that crime has a cause as certainly as disease, and that the way to treat any abnormal condition rationally is to remove the cause.

If a doctor were called on to treat typhoid fever he would probably try to find out what kind of milk or water the patient drank, and perhaps clean out the well so that no one else could get typhoid from the same source. But if a lawyer was called on to treat a typhoid patient, he would give him thirty days in jail, and then he would think that nobody else would ever dare to take it. If the patient got well in fifteen days, he would be kept until his time was up; if the disease was worse at the end of thirty days, the patient would be released because his time was out.

As a rule, lawyers are not scientists. They have learned the doctrine of hate and fear, and they think that there is only one way to make men good, and that is to put them in such terror that they do not dare to be bad. They act unmindful of history, and science, and all the experience of the past.

Still, we are making some progress. Courts give attention to some things that they did not give attention to before.

Once in England they hanged children seven years of age; not necessarily hanged them, because hanging was never meant for punishment; it was meant for an exhibition. If somebody committed crime, he would be hanged by the head or the heels, it didn't matter much which, at the four crossroads, so that every-body could look at him until his bones were bare, and so that people would be good because they had seen the gruesome result of crime and hate.

Hanging was not necessarily meant for punishment. The cul-prit might be killed in any other way, and then hanged—yes. Hanging was an exhibition. They were hanged on the highest hill, and hanged at the crossroads, and hanged in public places, so that all men could see. If there is any virtue in hanging, that was the logical way, because you cannot awe men into goodness unless they know about the hanging. We have not grown bet-ter than the ancients. We have grown more squeamish; we do not like to look at it, that is all. They hanged them at seven years; they hanged them again at eleven and fourteen.

We have raised the age of hanging. We have raised it by the humanity of courts, by the understanding of courts, by the prog-ress in science which at last is reaching the law; and of ninety men hanged in Illinois from its beginning, not one single person under twenty-three was ever hanged upon a plea of Guilty—not one. If Your Honor should do this, you would violate every precedent that has been set in Illinois for almost a century. There can be no excuse for it, and no justification for it, because this is the policy of the law which is rooted in the feelings of humanity, which are deep in every human being that thinks and feels. There have been two or three cases where juries have con-victed boys younger than this, and where courts on convictions have refused to set aside the sentence. But this was because a jury had decided it.

* * *

Your Honor, if in this court a boy of eighteen and a boy of nineteen should be hanged on a plea of Guilty, in violation of every precedent of the past, in violation of the policy of the law to take care of the young, in violation of all the progress that has been made and of the humanity that has been shown in the care of the young, in violation of the law that places boys in reformatories instead of prisons—if Your Honor, in violation of all that and in the face of all the past, should stand here in

Chicago alone to hang a boy on a plea of Guilty, then we are turning our faces backward toward the barbarism which once possessed the world. If Your Honor can hang a boy of eighteen, some other judge can hang him at seventeen, or sixteen, or fourteen. Some day, if there is any such thing as progress in the world, if there is any spirit of humanity that is working in the hearts of men, someday men would look back upon this as a barbarous age which deliberately set itself in the way of progress, humanity and sympathy, and committed an unforgivable act.

* * *

Now, Your Honor, I have spoken about the war. I believed in it. I don't know whether I was crazy or not. Sometimes I think perhaps I was. I approved of it; I joined in the general cry of madness and despair. I urged men to fight. I was safe because I was too old to go. I was like the rest. What did they do? Right or wrong, justifiable or unjustifiable—which I need not discuss today—it changed the world. For four long years the civilized world was engaged in killing men. Christian against Christian; barbarians uniting with Christians to kill Christians; anything to kill. It was taught in every school, aye in the Sunday schools. The little children played at war. The toddling children on the street. Do you suppose this world has ever been the same since then? How long, Your Honor, will it take for the world to get back the humane emotions that were slowly growing before the war? How long will it take the calloused hearts of men before the scars of hatred and cruelty shall be removed?

We read of killing one hundred thousand men in a day. We read about it and we rejoiced in it—if it was the other fellows who were killed. We were fed on flesh and drank blood. Even down to the prattling babe. I need not tell Your Honor this, because you know; I need not tell you how many upright, honorable young boys have come into this court charged with murder, some saved and some sent to their death, boys who fought in this war and learned to place a cheap value on human life. You know it and I know it. These boys were brought up in it. The tales of death were in their homes, their playgrounds, their schools; they were in the newspapers that they read; it was a part of the common frenzy. What was a life? It was nothing. It was the least sacred thing in existence and these boys were trained to this cruelty.

It will take fifty years to wipe it out of the human heart, if ever. I know this, that after the Civil War in 1865, crimes of this sort increased marvelously. No one needs to tell me that crime has no cause. It has as definite a cause as any other disease, and I know that out of the hatred and bitterness of the Civil War crime increased as America had never known it before. I know that growing out of the Napoleonic wars there was an era of crime such as Europe had never seen before. I know that Europe is going through the same experience today; I know it has followed every war; and I know it has influenced these boys so that life was not the same to them as it would have been if the world had not been made red with blood. I protest against the crimes and mistakes of society being visited upon them. All of us have our share of it. I have mine. I cannot tell and I shall never know how many words of mine might have given birth to cruelty in place of love and kindness and charity.

Your Honor knows that in this very court crimes of violence have increased, growing out of the war. Not necessarily by those who fought but by those that learned that blood was cheap, and human life was cheap, and if the State could take it lightly why not the boy? There are causes for this terrible crime. There are causes, as I have said, for everything that happens in the world. War is a part of it; education is a part of it; birth is a part of it; money is a part of it—all these conspired to compass the destruction of these two poor boys.

Has the court any right to consider anything but these two boys? The State says that Your Honor has a right to consider the welfare of the community, as you have. If the welfare of the community would be benefited by taking these lives, well and good. I think it would work evil that no one could measure. Has Your Honor a right to consider the families of these two defendants? I have been sorry, and I am sorry for the bereavement of Mr. and Mrs. Franks, for those broken ties that cannot be healed. All I can hope and wish is that some good may come from it all. But as compared with the families of Leopold and Loeb, the Franks are to be envied—and everyone knows it.

I do not know how much salvage there is in these two boys. I hate to say it in their presence, but what is there to look forward to? I do not know but that Your Honor would be merciful if you tied a rope around their necks and let them die; merciful to them, but not merciful to civilization, and not merciful to those who would be left behind. To spend the balance of their lives in prison is mighty little to look forward to, if anything. Is it anything? They may have the hope that as the years roll around they might be released. I do not know. I do not know. I will be honest with this court as I have tried to be from the beginning. I know that these boys are not fit to be at large. I believe they will not be until they pass through the next stage of life, at forty-five or fifty. Whether they will be then, I cannot tell. I am sure of this; that I will not be here to help them. So far as I am concerned, it is over.

I would not tell this court that I do not hope that some time, when life and age have changed their bodies, as it does, and has changed their emotions, as it does—that they may once more return to life. I would be the last person on earth to close the door to any human being that lives, and least of all to my clients. But what have they to look forward to? Nothing. And I think here of the stanza of Housman:

> Now hollow fires burn out to black,
>   And lights are fluttering low:
> Square your shoulders, lift your pack
>   And leave your friends and go.
> O never fear, lads, naught's to dread,
>   Look not left nor right:
> In all the endless road you tread
>   There's nothing but the night.

I care not, Your Honor, whether the march begins at the gallows or when the gates of Joliet close upon them, there is nothing but the night, and that is little for any human being to expect.

But there are others to consider. Here are these two families, who have led honest lives, who will bear the name that they bear, and future generations must carry it on.

Here is Leopold's father—and this boy was the pride of his life. He watched him, he cared for him, he worked for him; the boy was brilliant and accomplished, he educated him, and he thought that fame and position awaited him, as it should have awaited. It is a hard thing for a father to see his life's hopes crumble into dust.

Should he be considered? Should his brothers be considered? Will it do society any good or make your life safer, or any human being's life safer, if it should be handed down from generation to generation, that this boy, their kin, died upon the scaffold?

And Loeb's, the same. Here are the faithful uncle and brother, who have watched here day by day, while Dickie's father and his mother are too ill to stand this terrific strain, and shall be waiting for a message which means more to them than it can mean to you or me. Shall these be taken into account in this general bereavement?

Have they any rights? Is there any reason, Your Honor, why their proud names and all the future generations that bear them shall have this bar sinister written across them? How many boys and girls, how many unborn children, will feel it? It is bad enough, however it is. But it's not yet death on the scaffold. It's not that. And I ask Your Honor, in addition to all that I have said, to save two honorable families from a disgrace that never ends, and which could be of no avail to help any human being that lives.

* * *

Now, I must say a word more and then I will leave this with you where I should have left it long ago. None of us are unmindful of the public; courts are not, and juries are not. We placed our fate in the hands of a trained court, thinking that he would be more mindful and considerate than a jury. I cannot say how people feel. I have stood here for three months as one might stand at the ocean trying to sweep back the tide. I hope the seas are subsiding and the wind is falling, and I believe they are, but I wish to make no false pretense to this court. The easy thing and the popular thing to do is to hang my clients. I know it. Men and women who do not think will applaud. The cruel and thoughtless will approve. It will be easy today; but in Chicago, and reaching out over the length and breadth of the land, more and more fathers and mothers, the humane, the kind and the hopeful, who are gaining an understanding and asking questions not only about these poor boys, but about their own— these will join in no acclaim at the death of my clients. They would ask that the shedding of blood be stopped, and that the normal feelings of man resume their sway. And as the days and the months and the years go on, they will ask it more and more. But, Your Honor, what they shall ask may not count. I know the easy way. I know Your Honor stands between the future and the past. I know the future is with me, and what I stand for here; not merely for the lives of these two unfortunate lads, but for all boys and all girls; for all of the young, and, as far as possible, for all of the old. I am pleading for life, understanding, charity, kindness, and the infinite mercy that considers all. I am pleading that we overcome cruelty with kindness, and hatred with love. I know the future is on my side.

Your Honor stands between the past and the future. You may hang these boys; you may hang them by the neck until they are dead. But in doing it you will turn your face toward the past. In doing it you are making it harder for every other boy who, in ignorance and darkness, must grope his way through the mazes which only childhood knows. In doing it you will make it harder for unborn children. You may save them and make it easier for every child that sometime may stand where these boys stand. You will make it easier for every human being with an aspiration and a vision and a hope and a fate.

I am pleading for the future; I am pleading for a time when hatred and cruelty will not control the hearts of men, when we can learn by reason and judgment and understanding and faith that all life is worth saving, and that mercy is the highest attribute of man.

I feel that I should apologize for the length of time I have taken. This case may not be as important as I think it is, and I am sure I do not need to tell this court, or to tell my friends that I would fight just as hard for the poor as for the rich. If I should succeed in saving these boys' lives and do nothing for the progress of the law, I should feel sad, indeed. If I can succeed, my greatest reward and my greatest hope will be that I have done something for the tens of thousands of other boys, for the countless unfortunates who must tread the same road in blind childhood that these poor boys have trod; that I have done something to help human understanding, to temper justice with mercy, to overcome hate with love.

I was reading last night of the aspiration of the old Persian poet, Omar Khayyam. It appealed to me as the highest that I can vision. I wish it was in my heart, and I wish it was in the hearts of all.

> So I be written in the Book of Love,
> I do not care about that Book above;
> Erase my name or write it as you will,
> So I be written in the Book of Love.

TEARS WERE STREAMING DOWN the judge's face as Darrow finished his plea. A newspaper reported, "The stuffed courtroom was like a black hole. Hardly a breath of air moved in it. Yet the crowd that was massed around Darrow sat motionless in attention as the weary old man gathered up all the threads of his argument for the final restatement."

Another newspaper said the lines in Darrow's face were "deeper, the eyes haggard. But there was no sign of physical weariness in the speech, only a spiritual weariness with the cruelties of the world."

Chicago newspapers and many others throughout the country printed Darrow's more-than-twelve-hour plea in full or in part.

A newspaper reporter said, "There was scarcely any telling where his voice had finished and where silence had begun. His own eyes were not the only ones that held tears."

State's Attorney Crowe summed up the case for the State. He talked for two days. Court adjourned.

On September 10, 1924, the Chief Justice of the Criminal Court of Cook County sentenced the defendants to imprisonment for life on the murder indictment and 99 years on the kidnaping charge.

Editorialized the New York Morning Telegram the following day: "Law, the bastard daughter of justice, handed her mother a frightful beating in Chicago yesterday."

The New York Times said: "Had the youthful murderers been poor and friendless, they would have escaped capital punishment precisely as Leopold and Loeb have escaped it."

The boys were taken to Joliet penitentiary.

There, twelve years later, Loeb was killed in a prison fight. Leopold, who is still in the penitentiary, has made several unsuccessful pleas for his freedom.

Is Capital Punishment a Wise Policy?

DEBATE WITH JUDGE TALLEY
New York, 1924

THIRTEEN DAYS after a Chicago judge's decision saved Leopold and Loeb from hanging, a New York judge attacked Clarence Darrow's view on criminology and capital punishment.

The challenge was hurled by Judge Alfred J. Talley, Court of General Sessions, New York City.

Said the judge in a statement to the press: "It is not the criminals, actual or potential, that need a neuropathic hospital. It is the people who slobber over them in an effort to find excuses for their crime.

"The demand of the hour in America, above all other countries," continued Judge Talley, "is for jurors with conscience, judges with courage, and prisons which are neither country clubs nor health resorts. . . . There are lots of sick people who concern themselves with crime, but the criminals are not among them."

About a month later, on September 23, 1924, Judge Talley debated Clarence Darrow on the subject: "Is Capital Punishment a Wise Policy?"

The debate was held in the Manhattan Opera House under the auspices of the League for Public Discussion. Tickets sold from $1.65 to $4.40 and every seat in the Opera House was filled.

Warden Lewis E. Lawes of Sing Sing prison was temporary chairman, and the Honorable Louis Marshall was chairman.

Darrow was interrupted by either applause or laughter about 45 times during his first presentation, and about 20 times during his rebuttal.

YES: *Judge Alfred J. Talley*
NO: *Clarence Darrow*

Affirmative (JUDGE TALLEY):[1]

T HE PENALTY of death is the only thing the criminal fears, Judge Talley asserted in his opening remarks.

He questioned whether this is the time to abolish capital punishment, with the large number of murders being committed.

Judge Talley divided his initial presentation into two parts: (1) the right of the State to impose capital punishment; and (2) the expediency and necessity of enforcing that kind of punishment.

He pointed out that were his life in imminent danger "neither God nor man would question my right to defend my life." If the individual has that right to kill in self-defense, the Judge asked, why has not the State, "which is nothing more than an aggregation of individuals, the same right to defend itself against unjust aggression and unjust attack?"

Judge Talley asserted that those who want to take away from the State the power to impose the death sentence seek to "despoil the symbol of justice."

"The object of punishment of crime must be deterrent, and it must be vindicative—not vindicative in the sense of revengeful, but it must be imposed so that the law and its majesty and sanctity may be vindicated," the Judge explained.

[1] Arguments by Judge Talley have been condensed by the editor.

Negative (MR. DARROW):

I HAD THIS STAND moved up so I could get next to the audience. I hope I will not be obliged to spend too much time on my friend's address. I don't think I shall need to.

First, I deny his statement that every man's heart tells him it is wrong to kill. I think every man's heart desires killing. Personally, I never killed anybody that I know of. But I have had a great deal of satisfaction now and then reading obituary notices, and I used to delight, with the rest of my hundred-per-cent patriotic friends, when I saw ten or fifteen thousand Germans being killed in a day.

Everybody loves killing. Some of them think it is too messy for them. Every human being that believes in capital punishment loves killing, and the only reason they believe in capital punishment is because they get a kick out of it. Nobody kills anyone for love, unless they get over it temporarily or otherwise. But they kill the one they hate. And before you can get a trial to hang somebody or electrocute him, you must first hate him and then get a satisfaction over his death.

There is no emotion in any human being that is not in every single human being. The degree is different, that is all. And the degree is not always different in different people. It depends likewise on circumstances, on time and on place.

I shall not follow my friend into the labyrinth of statistics. Statistics are a pleasant indoor sport—not so good as crossword puzzles—and they prove nothing to any sensible person who is familiar with statistics.

I might just observe, in passing, that in all of these states where the mortality by homicide is great, they have capital punishment and always have had it. A logical man, when he found out that the death rate increased under capital punishment, would suggest some other way of dealing with it.

I undertake to say—and you can look them up yourselves, for I haven't time to bother with it (and there is nothing that lies like statistics)—I will guarantee to take any set of statistics and take a little time to it and prove they mean directly the opposite of what is claimed. But I will undertake to say that you can show by statistics that the states in which there was no capital punishment have a very much smaller percentage of homicides.

I know it is true. That doesn't prove anything, because, as a rule, they are states with a less diverse population, without as many large cities, without as much mixture of all sorts of elements which go to add to the general gaiety—and homicide is a product of that. There is no sort of question but what those states in the United States where there is no capital punishment have a lower percentage than the others. But that doesn't prove the question. It is a question that cannot be proven one way or the other by statistics. It rests upon things, upon feelings and emotions and arguments, much deeper than statistics.

The death rate from homicide in Memphis and in some other Southern cities is high. Why? Well, it is an afternoon's pleasure to kill a Negro—that is about all. Everybody knows it.

The death rate recently in the United States and all over the world has increased. Why? The same thing has happened that has happened in every country in the world since time began. A great war always increases death rates.

We teach people to kill, and the State is the one that teaches them. If the State wishes that its citizens respect human life, then the State should stop killing. It can be done in no other way, and it will perhaps not be fully done that way. There are infinite reasons for killing. There are infinite circumstances under which there are more or less deaths. It never did depend and never can depend upon the severity of the punishment.

* * *

But let's see what there is in this argument. He says, "Everybody who kills, dreads hanging." Well, he has had experience as a lawyer on both sides. I have had experience on one side. I know that everybody who is taken into court on a murder charge desires to live, and they do not want to be hanged or electrocuted. Even a thing as alluring as being cooked with electricity doesn't appeal to them.

But that hasn't anything to do with it. What was the state of mind when the homicide was committed? The state of mind is one thing when a homicide is committed and another thing weeks or months afterward, when every reason for committing it is gone. There is no comparison between them. There never can be any comparison between them.

We might ask why people kill. I don't want to dispute with him about the right of the State to kill people. Of course, they have got a right to kill them. That is about all we do. The great industry of the world for four long years was killing. They have got a right to kill, of course, that is, they have got the power. And you have got a right to do what you get away with. The words power and right, so far as this is concerned, mean exactly the same thing. So nobody who has any knowledge of philosophy would pretend to say that the State had not the right to kill.

But why not do a good job of it? If you want to get rid of killings by hanging people or electrocuting them because these are so terrible, why not make a punishment that is terrible? This isn't so much. It lasts but a short time. There is no physical torture in it. Why not boil them in oil, as they used to do? Why not burn them at the stake? Why not sew them into a bag with serpents and throw them out to sea? Why not take them out on the sand and let them be eaten by ants? Why not break every bone in their body on the rack, as has been done for such serious offenses as heresy and witchcraft?

Those were the good old days in which the Judge should have held court. Glorious days, when you could kill them by the millions because they worshiped God in a different way from that which the State provided, or when you could kill old women for witchcraft! There might be some sense in it if you could kill young ones, but not old ones. Those were the glorious days of capital punishment. And there wasn't a judge or a preacher who didn't think that the life of the State depended upon their right to hang old women for witchcraft and to persecute others for worshiping God in the wrong way.

Why, our capital punishment isn't worth talking about, so far as its being a preventive is concerned. It isn't worth discussing. Why not call back from the dead and barbarous past the hundred and sixty- or seventy-odd crimes that were punishable by death in England? Why not once more re-enact the Blue Laws of our own country and kill people right? Why not resort to all the tortures that the world has always resorted to to keep men in the straight and narrow path? Why reduce it to a paltry question of murder?

Everybody in this world has some pet aversion to something, and on account of that pet aversion they would like to hang somebody. If the prohibitionists made the law, they would be in favor of hanging you for taking a drink, or certainly for bootlegging, because to them that is the most heinous crime there is.

Some men slay or murder. Why? As a matter of fact, murder as murder is very rare; and the people who commit it, as a rule, are of a much higher type than others. You may go to any penitentiary and, as a rule, those who have been convicted of murder become the trusties; whereas, if you are punishing somebody as a sneak thief or a counterfeiter or a confidence man, they never get over it—never.

Now, I don't know how injustice is administered in New York. I just know about Chicago. But I am glad to learn from the gentleman that if a man is so poor in New York that he can't hire a lawyer, that he has a first-class lawyer appointed to defend him—a first-class lawyer appointed to defend him. Don't take a chance and go out and kill anybody on the statement made by my friend.

I suppose anybody can go out and kill somebody and ask to have my friend, Sam Untermeyer, appointed. There never was such a thing. Here and there, a good lawyer may have defended people for nothing. But no court ever interferes with a good lawyer's business by calling him in and compelling him to give his time. They have been lawyers too recently themselves to ever work a trick like that on a lawyer. As a rule, it is the poor and the weak and the friendless who furnish the victims of the law.

Let me take another statement of my friend. He said, "Oh, we don't hang anybody if they kill when they are angry; it is only when they act premeditatedly." Yes, I have been in courts and heard judges instruct people on this premeditated act. It is only when they act under their judgment and with due consideration. He would also say that if a man is moved by anger, but if he doesn't strike the deadly blow until such time as reason and judgment have a chance to possess him, even if it is a second— how many times have I heard judges say, "Even if it is a second?" What does any judge know about premeditation? What does anybody know about it? How many people are there in this world that can premeditate on anything? I will strike out the "pre" and say how many people are there that can meditate?

How long does it take the angry man for his passions to cool when he is in the presence of the thing that angers him? There never was a premeditated murder in any sense of psychology or science. There are planned murders—planned, yes—but back of every murder and back of every human act are sufficient causes that move the human machine beyond their control.

The other view is an outworn, outlawed, unscientific theory of the metaphysicians. Does anybody ever act in this world without a motive? Did they ever act without a sufficient motive? And who am I to say that John Smith premeditated? I might premeditate a good deal quicker than John Smith did. My judgment might have a chance to act quicker than John Smith's judgment had a chance to act.

We have heard talk of justice. Is there anybody who knows what justice is? No one on earth can measure out justice. Can you look at any man and say what he deserves—whether he deserves hanging by the neck until dead or life in prison or thirty days in prison or a medal? The human mind is blind to all who seek to look in at it and to most of us that look out from it. Justice is something that man knows little about. He may know something about charity and understanding and mercy, and he should cling to these as far as he can.

❂   ❂   ❂

There is just one thing in all this question. It is a question of how you feel, that is all. It is all inside of you. If you love the thought of somebody being killed, why, you are for it. If you hate the thought of somebody being killed, you are against it.

Let me just take a little brief review of what has happened in this world. They used to hang people on the crossways and on a high hill, so that everybody would be awed into goodness by the sight. They have tortured them in every way that the brain of man could conceive. They have provided every torture known or that could be imagined for one who believed differently from his fellow-man—and still the belief persisted. They have maimed and scarred and starved and killed human beings since man began penning his fellow-man. Why? Because we hate him. And what has added to it is that they have done it under the false ideal of self-righteousness.

I have heard parents punish their children and tell their children it hurt the parents more than it did the child. I don't believe it. I have tried it both ways, and I don't believe it. I know better.

Gradually, the world has been lopping off these punishments. Why? Because we have grown a little more sensitive, a little more imaginative, a little kindlier, that is all.

Why not re-enact the code of Blackstone's day? Why, the judges were all for it—every one of them—and the only way we got rid of these laws was because juries were too humane to obey the courts.

That is the only way we got rid of punishing old women, of hanging old women in New England—because, in spite of all the courts, the juries would no longer convict them for a crime that never existed. And in that way they have cut down the crimes in England for punishment by death from one hundred and seventy to two. What is going to happen if we get rid of them? Is the world coming to an end? The earth has been here ages and ages before man came. It will be here ages and ages after he disappears, and the amount of people you hang won't make the slightest difference with it.

Now, why am I opposed to capital punishment? It is too horrible a thing for a State to undertake. We are told by my friend "Oh, the killer does it; why shouldn't the State?" I would hate to live in a State that I didn't think was better than a murderer.

But I told you the real reason. The people of the State kill a man because he killed someone else—that is all—without the slightest logic, without the slightest application to life, simply from anger, nothing else!

I am against it because I believe it is inhuman, because I believe that as the hearts of men have softened they have gradually gotten rid of brutal punishment, because I believe that it will only be a few years until it will be banished forever from every civilized country—even New York; because I believe that it has no effect whatever to stop murder.

Now let's make that simple and see. Where do the murders come from? I would say the second largest class of what we call murders grow out of domestic relations. They follow those deep and profound feelings that are at the basis of life—and the feelings which give the greatest joy are susceptible of the greatest pain when they go a-riot.

Can you imagine a woman following a man around with a pistol to kill him that would stop if you said, "Oh, you will be hanged!" Nothing doing—not if the world was coming to an end! Can you imagine a man doing it? Not at all. They think of it afterward, but not before.

They come from acts like burglary and robbery. A man goes out to rob or to burglarize. Somebody catches him or stops him or recognizes him, and he kills to save himself. Do you suppose there was ever a burglar or robber since the world began who would not kill to save himself? Is there anybody who wouldn't? It doesn't make any difference who. Wouldn't he take a chance shooting? Anyone would do it. Why, my friend himself said he would kill in self-defense. That is what they do. If you are going to stop them, you ought to hang them for robbery—which would be a good plan—and then, of course, if one started out to rob, he would kill the victim before he robbed him.

There isn't, I submit, a single admissible argument in favor of capital punishment. Nature loves life. We believe that life should be protected and preserved. The thing that keeps one from killing is the emotion they have against it; and the greater the sanctity that the State pays to life, the greater the feeling of sanctity the individual has for life.

There is nothing in the history of the world that ever cheapened human life like our great war; next to that, the indiscriminate killing of men by the States.

My friend says a man must be proven guilty first. Does anybody know whether anybody is guilty? There is a great deal implied in that. For me to do something or for you to do something is one thing; for some other man to do something quite another. To know what one deserves requires infinite study, which no one can give to it. No one can determine the condition of the brain that did the act. It is out of the question.

All people are products of two things, and two things only—their heredity and their environment. And they act in exact accord with the heredity which they took from all the past, and for which they are in no wise responsible, and the environment, which reaches out to the farthest limit of all life that can influence them. We all act from the same way. And it ought to teach us to be charitable and kindly and understanding of our fellowman.

BEFORE introducing Judge Talley for his affirmative refutation, the chairman answered Mr. Darrow's assertion that a "first-class lawyer" is not assigned by the courts to defend a man charged with murder. "I can give testimony to the fact that that is very frequently done here (New York City)," he said.

The chairman also took issue with Mr. Darrow's assertion that the judges never did anything in England to stop the conviction of people for 160 different offenses—the conviction being followed by execution. "I merely wish to remind Mr. Darrow," said the chairman, "that the great reform in the subject of criminal law wrought in England was through the judges, against Parliament—the people."

Affirmative Rebuttal (JUDGE TALLEY):

THE ASSERTION that everybody loves a killing is a "shocking statement to make upon a public platform," Judge Talley answered Clarence Darrow.

"It is because we abhor the man who kills an innocent victim that we demand that his life shall pay the forfeit for his act. It is not because we love the killing—it is because we hate the killing—that we stand for adequate and sensible punishment that will vindicate justice in our life," said the judge.

He charged that there never was a greater fallacy projected upon the people of this or any other country than that "the criminality that we have had since the war (World War I) is the result of it."

There isn't a judge on the bench, continued the New York jurist, that would assign an "incompetent, helpless lawyer to defend a man charged with murder."

He then pointed out that the State does not kill in anger. "The State kills in order that the majesty of justice may be vindicated and that people who would violate its laws must, by the example of that killing, be deterred from taking life."

The judge also noted that Darrow who asked for charity for the murderer made no suggestion about "charity for the woman that is left alone or with helpless children to support whose husband has been stricken down by the revolver or knife of an assassin."

Neither poverty, nor heredity or environment are the cause of a crime, said the judge.

Negative Rebuttal (MR. DARROW):

FIFTEEN MINUTES in which to answer my friend and the chairman is, perhaps, a little short; but still I can do it.

I want to say, in spite of the chairman having the added dignity of a chairman, that every single statement that I made is true as to the judges and the people. The long list of one hundred and seventy crimes was abolished in England because juries would not convict, until here and there, as Mr. Marshall says, some decent judges circumvented the law. For God's sake, Mr. Marshall, a great lawyer like you talking about judges circumventing the law!

Now, there is no use of mincing matters over this. There isn't any human being who ever investigated this subject that doesn't know it. Every step in humanity, in the administraton of the law, has been against courts and by the people—every step. It is all right for judges to write essays about it after it has happened. But over and over again, as in New England, they instructed juries to hang old women for witchcraft, and they refused. And every clergyman stood there, urging it. But they refused, and the old women were not hanged—and that was abolished in New England.

Neither am I making a misstatement when I say that good lawyers are not appointed to defend poor clients. Now, look that up. There may be, here and there, some conspicuous case, but the run of poor clients in a court is without the help of lawyers who are fit to do it. And I will guarantee that every man waiting for death in Sing Sing is there without the aid of a good lawyer.

Now, look that up. I know about these good lawyers. They don't do it. Do you suppose you can get a member of the Bar Association to give his time for nothing? No, he leaves it to us criminal lawyers. Nothing doing—they are taking care of the wealth of corporations. That is what they are doing.

A VOICE: How about you?

MR. DARROW: You want to know about me? I have defended more than half of my clients for nothing. Ever since I began the practice of law, I have given more than a third of the time of every man in my office for nothing. If you want to know about me, that is the truth.

A VOICE: Was it by appointment?

MR. DARROW: No, I never was appointed in my life—never. No judge would take my time by appointing me, any more than they do any lawyer when he wants to get paid for his services.

Now, I am going to finish this debate.

My friend doesn't believe in heredity. I didn't suppose there was more than one man in the United States who didn't believe in heredity. I knew that Mr. Bryan didn't. Am I to enter into a discussion about the ABCs of science? There isn't a scientist on earth who doesn't believe and say that man is the product of heredity and environment alone. Of course, it takes one from the Dark Ages to believe in killing human beings.

He talks of logic. He says I don't believe in free will (I do not) and that, therefore, I would say that no man should be confined. Does that follow? No.

Why do we send people to prison? Because we want to hurt them? No. We send them in self-defense, because for some reason they can't adjust themselves to life. And no other reason than that is admissible, and no humane person believes any other reason is admissible.

Why? You want to know about it? If you do, read, study. There have been a great number of scientific men whose work has been for the benefit of the human race. A great many of these have been students of criminology. Yet, we heard them sneered at this afternoon by men who know nothing, men who dare say that heredity is all "bunk."

Well, of course, it seems kind of hopeless to teach people anything. I wonder if the gentleman believes in heredity in the breeding of cattle. I wonder if he believes in heredity in the breeding of pigs. I wonder if he believes in heredity—well, didn't he ever see any heredity in a human being? Didn't you see your mother, your father, your grandmother, your grandfather? Why discuss it? Everybody knows it. And those who don't know it, don't want to know it—that's all.

I did not say that every case in prison was that of a poor person. I said that almost all of them were. My friend said that, probably, to make the utterly absurd statement about a terrible crime—the most terrible, he said—because he read it in the newspapers. He doesn't know anything about it—but it is common for a judge to pass judgment upon things he is not acquainted with.

I said that the great mass of people in prison are the poor. Am I right or am I wrong?

Where do you live that you don't know it? I want to get you to look into this question. And you can't do it in a minute. You can sing hosannas when some poor devil is sent to Kingdom Come, but you can't understand without thought and study. And, contrary to my friend, everybody doesn't think. He says everybody born has free will. Have they? Everybody born has free will—what do you think of that?

Now, am I right in my statement that it is the poor who fill prisons and who go to the scaffold and who are prosecuted and persecuted? Nobody who knows anything about it believes that the rich are the ones, or any considerable fraction of the rich.

He hasn't given me time to shed tears over the victims of the murderers. I am as sorry for them as he is, because I hate cruelty; no matter who suffers, I hate it. I don't love it and get pleasure out of it when it is done by hanging somebody by the neck until dead—no.

But, now, let me tell you. You can find out. I will guarantee that you can go through the Tombs and you won't find one out of a thousand that isn't poor. You may go to Sing Sing and you will not find one out of a thousand who isn't poor. Since the world began, a procession of the weak and the poor and the helpless has been going to our jails and our prisons and to their deaths. They have been judged as if they were strong and rich and intelligent. They have been victims, whether punishable by death for one crime or one hundred and seventy crimes.

And, we say, this is no time to soften the human heart. Isn't it? Whenever it is the hardest, that is the best time to get at it. When is the time? If he is right, why not re-enact the penal codes of the past? What do you suppose the American Bar Association knows about this subject?

A VOICE: More than you.

MR. DARROW: Do you think so? Then you don't know what you are talking about. Their members are too busy defending corporations. There isn't a criminologist in the world that hasn't said what I have said. And you may read any history or any philosophy and they each and every one point out that after every great war in the world, wherever it was, crimes of violence increased. Do I need to prove it?

Let me ask you this: Do you think man, in any sense, is a creature of environment? Do you think you people could, day by day, wish and hope and pray for the slaughter of thousands of Germans because they were your enemies, and not become callous to suffering? Do you think that children of our schools and our Sunday schools could be taught killing and be as kindly and as tender after it as before? Do you think man does not feel every emotion that comes to him, no matter from what source it comes? Do you think this war did not brutalize the hearts of millions of people in this world? And are you going to cure it by brutalizing it still more by capital punishment?

If capital punishment would cure these dire evils that he tells us about, why in the world should there be any more killing? We have had it always. We have had it long enough. It should have been abolished long ago.

In the end, this question is simply one of the humane feelings against the brutal feelings. One who likes to see suffering, out of what he thinks is a righteous indignation, or any other, will hold fast to capital punishment. One who has sympathy, imagination, kindness and understanding, will hate it and detest it as he hates and detests death.

The "Unwritten Law"

THE MASSIE CASE
Honolulu, 1932

DARROW PLEA
IS BASED ON
HUMAN BEINGS

[Headline, Honolulu Advertiser, April 28, 1932]

CLARENCE DARROW, who had retired four years earlier, spent his seventy-fifth birthday in Honolulu pleading the case of four defendants in what is known as the Massie case.

"Many times I have been asked why I went to Honolulu. I was not sure then, and am not sure now," the defense attorney wrote five years before he died.

But there were several reasons which might explain his undertaking the case. To Darrow, it was a study of psychology, and he was always interested in man's puzzling behavior. In addition, the 1929 depression had practically wiped out his savings and he admitted he needed the fee, which reportedly was $25,000.

Thalia Massie, wife of a United States Navy officer stationed on the Island, was raped by five men. The Massies had been to a party. Mrs. Massie left at midnight after a quarrel with her husband. She was walking toward her home when she was accosted. Four of the men—none of whom was white—were arrested and identified by Mrs. Massie as her assailants. They were brought to trial. The jury disagreed and they were released on bail.

While awaiting the retrial of the accused, the victim's husband, Lieutenant Thomas H. Massie, forced one of the Japanese assailants, who was out on bond, to confess. The Japanese, however, had photographs taken of the welts on his back from Massie's beating. When Massie told his lawyer of the confession, the lawyer advised that a confession obtained in this manner would never hold up in court.

Determined to get a confession, the lieutenant, with a false subpoena, kidnaped the leader of the assailants, Joseph Kahahawai. Lieutenant Massie was aided by his mother-in-law Mrs. Fortescue and two sailors.

Kahahawai was brought to Mrs. Fortescue's home. There he confessed to raping Mrs. Massie. Lieutenant Massie fatally shot him.

The Island was seething with race dissension—first, because of the assault on Mrs. Massie; then, the disagreement of the jury in the original trial of the assailants; and, finally, the murder of Kahahawai.

Darrow, however, had made it clear before he left the States that his defense would not be a question of race, but rather of "causes and motives."

The trial against Lieutenant Massie, Mrs. Fortescue and the two sailors opened early in April 1932, in the small courtroom of Circuit Judge Charles S. Davis.

The chief prosecutor was J. C. Kelley.

For the defense: Clarence Darrow and George Leisure, a Wall Street lawyer.

In the selection of the jury, each side had used three of its twenty-four challenges by the end of the first day. The prosecution challenged two whites and a Chinese; the defense used its challenges against two Hawaiians and one Japanese. By the end of the second day, eight challenges had been used by both sides.

Jury selection was completed four days after the trial opened. The jury was composed of one Hawaiian, three Chinese, one Portuguese, the rest native-born Americans.

During the trial, newspapermen commented that the mind of the veteran of the courts had lost none of its cunning. There may have been some doubts of this when, at one point, the attorney of many legal battles forgot the name of one of the defendants. He turned to the prosecutor and asked the name:

PROSECUTOR: Don't you know?

DARROW: Yes, but it popped my mind.

PROSECUTOR: It's Lord.

DARROW: Yes, Lord—that's right.

And he turned back to the jury.

Many persons stood in line through the night to hear Darrow's plea the following morning. Places in line sold for five dollars, and in some instances for as much as twenty-five dollars.

"I have put this case without appeal to the nationality or race of any juror, asking them to pass on it as a human case."

GENTLEMEN: We are getting close to the end of this case. It has been a long, serious, tedious trial, and you of the jury probably have had the worst of it.

This case illustrates the working of human destiny more than any other case I have handled. It illustrates the effect of sorrow and mishap on human minds and lives, and shows us how weak and powerless human beings are in the hands of relentless powers.

Eight months ago Mrs. Fortescue was in Washington, respected and known like any other woman.

Eight months ago Lieutenant Massie worked himself up to the rank of lieutenant in the navy, respected, courageous and intelligent.

His young wife, handsome and attractive, was known and respected and admired by the community.

In that short space of time they are in a criminal court and the jury asked to send them to prison for life.

What has happened is a long series of events, beginning at a certain time, ending we don't know where.

A whole family—their life, future, name—bound up in a criminal act committed by someone else in which they had no part.

About eight months ago Massie and his wife went to a dance. They were young, happy. He was following the profession he had chosen, and she was the wife of a navy officer—brave, courageous and fearless.

Today they are in this court, in the hands of you twelve men, to settle their fate. I ask you gentlemen to consider carefully, seriously. The power is given to you to do justice in this case.

We contend that for months Massie's mind had been affected by all that was borne upon him: grief, sorrow, trouble, day after day, week after week, and month after month. What do you think would have happened to any one of you under the same condition? We measure other people by ourselves. We place ourselves in their place and say, "How would we have acted?" We have no further way of telling, except perhaps from the conditions of the life in which we live.

As to the early history of this case—they went to a dance with their friends. About half-past eleven in the evening, Mrs. Massie, who didn't especially care for these festivities, went out for a walk intending to go down the street and come back and join her husband again at the dance. It was only a few steps from safety to destruction.

What did Massie learn from her a few hours later? An unbelievable story—almost—at least an unthinkable one about which even my friend who opened this argument for the State said: "It was a terrible story"—so terrible that he pitied them. Still, he asked you to send these people to prison.

She had gone but a short way when four or five men drove up behind her in an automobile, dragged her into it, beat her, and broke her jaw in two places. They were ruffians, unknown to her. And after that they dragged her into the bushes, and she was raped by four or five men.

Can you imagine anything worse that could have happened or any greater calamity that could have fallen upon that family? They had nothing to do with it—not the slightest.

She was going on her way as she had a right to go, and in the twinkling of an eye her whole life, the life of the family, was changed and they are now here in this court for you to say whether they will go to prison—for life!

Is there a more terrible story anywhere in literature? I don't know whether there is—or who it was—or where I can find that sad tale but right here. You and all the other people in the city have been chosen to take care of their fate. I hope you will in kindness and humanity and understanding—no one else but you can do this.

She was left on that lonely road in pain and agony and suffering. In this Mrs. Massie suffered the greatest humiliation that a woman can suffer at the hands of man. She had done nothing! Massie had done nothing! So far, suffering has been inflicted on them. Suffering that few people encounter in their lives.

Massie dances until the dance is nearly over. He is ready to go home. He looks for his wife. She is not there. He goes to a friend's house. She is not there. He calls home, and she isn't there. He looks wherever he can and he calls home again and she sobs out a part of the story over the telephone, part of the story as terrible, as cruel, as any story I ever heard: "Hurry home, something terrible has happened to me!"

Tommy (Lieutenant Massie) rushes home! She meets him at the door and sobs and tells him this terrible story—isn't that enough to unsettle any man's mind? Suppose you'd heard it!— then and there—what effect would it have had on your mind— what effect would it have had on anybody's mind!

Shock, grief, and sorrow, at times protracted, sometimes at once, causes a human mind to break down in the end. This was only the beginning—here was his wife: she told him that they had broken her jaw, that she thought they had knocked out her teeth, that they had hit her on the jaw, that they had beaten her, taken her into the machine, dragged her into the bushes, ravished her and left her by the road to find her way home.

Do you remember the subsequent story? The police were called to pick up the trail. No one raised even a doubt about this story, except the originators of a few vile slanders which were carried from tongue to tongue. Has anybody placed their finger upon a single fact to contradict the saddest tale that was ever brought to a husband?

What did Mrs. Massie do? All of this she told her husband. They had reason to believe and fear infection and that she might be placed in a family way from these men who dragged her into the bushes and ravished her. She took the best precautions she could. She gave her information to the police and they jested and hinted and quarreled and haggled about what should be done.

There have been people who spread around in this community stories I don't believe true. They concocted these terrible stories and what effect did they have on Massie? May I ask what effect they would have had on you, and how you would have stood them? Massie attended to his days' duties as best he could. He went back and forth, nursing his wife, working all day and attending her at night for weeks. It was all that any husband could do, or any man could do. He lost sleep. He lost courage. He lost hope. He was distraught! And all this load was on his shoulders!

Any cause for it? Our insane institutions are filled with men and women who had less cause for insanity than he had. Everyone knows it. The mind isn't too easy to understand at the best. But what happens to the human mind? It does one thing with one person and another thing with another. You know what it did to Massie's. Do you think he is responsible, or has been, from that terrible night?

What did he do? Days he worked. At night he nursed his wife. Could anybody do more? The slow, long, terrible times. The doctor attending her helped Massie too. Gentlemen, just think how much is involved here now. Here was the assault, the rape, the pain, the days and the nights, and what else? Dr. Withington told them that they must take the greatest pain to guard against disease and pregnancy. So he watched her day by day. Day by day Tommy tended to his duties. He nursed his wife at night. Well, how would it affect you? Finally the doctor said, "You must have an operation to prevent pregnancy."

Here is a man—his wife—she is bearing inside of her the germs of—who? Does anybody know? Not he, but someone of the four ruffians who assaulted her and left a wreck of her. The doctor was not only a physician, but a friend. He asked no question. He didn't even read the statutes. He wasn't afraid the district attorney would indict him for abortion. You know what a friend would do, what an intelligent physician did do. So he took away what was there. He did it out of kindness and consideration— and prescribed for Massie, too.

Now, gentlemen, don't you suppose all this trouble might have been what ailed him? Would you take a chance on your own mind or any other person's, strong or weak?

It is almost inconceivable that so much could happen to one

family. In time, four men were indicted for the crime. Tommy was away on duty some of the time. Part of the time he was in the courtroom during the trial of the assailants. A strange circumstance, indeed, that the jury disagreed in that case. I don't know, I don't see why. But anyway, after all their work, and all their worry, the jury disagreed. What effect did that have?

Many have no doubt raised the question that has been raised over and over since man organized courts—"Can't I get justice?" Is there a chance to get any? Months passed and this case still was not retried.

Then began a campaign such as has been waged against few men and women. Out of the clear air, with nothing on which to rest, strange, slanderous stories were spread over these Islands about Lieutenant Massie and his ravished wife. Stories that she had never been raped, or else that she ravished herself. Stories that her husband, whose faithfulness the doctor has related to you, and it has been plainly evident to every person who sat in this courtroom during these long trying days, broke his wife's jaw. Then they spread the rumor that it was some Navy person who had ravished her. This spread all over the Islands. Everybody heard it. It came to Tommy, it came to Mrs. Massie. And it came to her mother.

Gentlemen, I wonder what Fate has against this family anyhow? And I wonder when it will get through taking its toll and leave them to go in peace, to try and make their own life in comfort for the rest of their days.

Here is the mother. What about her? They wired to her and she came. Poems and rhymes have been written about mothers. I don't want to bring forth further eulogies which are more or less worth while, but I want to call your attention to something more primitive than that. Nature. It is not a case of the greatness of a mother. It is the case of what nature has done. I don't care whether it is a human mother, a mother of beasts or birds of the air, they are all alike.

To them there is one all-important thing and that is a child that they carried in their womb. Without that feeling which is so strong in all life, there would be no life preserved upon this earth. She acted as every mother acts. She felt as your mothers have felt, because the family is the preservation of life. What did she do? Immediately she started on a long trip to her daughter. The daughter was married and a long way off, but she was still her daughter. I don't care if a mother is seventy-five and her daughter fifty, it is still the mother and the child.

Everything else is forgotten in the emotion that carries her back to the time when this was a little baby in her arms which she bore and loved. Your mother was that way and my mother, and there can be no other way, because life can be preserved in no other way. The mother started on a trip of 5,000 miles, over land and sea, to her child. And here she is now in this courtroom waiting to go to the penitentiary.

Gentlemen, let me say this: If this husband and this mother and these faithful boys go to the penitentiary, it won't be the first time that a penitentiary has been sanctified by its inmates.

When people come to your beautiful Islands, one of the first places that they will wish to see is the prison where the mother and the husband are confined because they moved under emotion. If that does happen, that prison will be the most conspicuous building on this Island, and men will wonder how it happened and will marvel at the injustice and cruelty of men and will pity the inmates and blame Fate for the cruelty, persecution and sorrow that has followed this family.

Gentlemen, you are asked to send these people to the penitentiary. Do you suppose that if you had been caught in the hands of Fate—would you have done differently? No, we are not made that way. Life doesn't come that way. It comes from a devotion of mothers, of husbands, loves of men and women, that's where life comes from. Without this love, this devotion, the world will be desolate and cold and will take its lonely course around the sun alone! Without a human heartbeat, there will be nothing except thin air. Every instinct that moves human beings, every feeling that is with you or any of your kin, every feeling that moves in the mother of the animal is with us in this case. You can't fight against it. If you do you are fighting against nature and life.

Gentlemen of the jury, this campaign against Massie and Mrs. Massie began very, very early. It was very strong when the jury disagreed. Stories have been peddled all over this town that Massie and his wife were about to get a divorce. They said that another Navy officer was out that night with Mrs. Massie.

Stories have been peddled up and down in the streets and broadcast against this woman who had been raped, and the husband was doing all he could to help her as any husband would. What effect could it have on the mind of this defendant?

Gentlemen of the jury, it was bad enough that the wife was raped. These vile stories were circulated and caused great anxiety and agony. All this is bad enough. But now you are asked that they must spend the rest of their lives in prison. All right, gentlemen, you have the power, but let me say to you—that if on top of all else that has been heaped upon the devoted heads of this family, if they should be sent to prison, it would place a blot upon the fair name of these Islands that all the Pacific seas would never wash away.

There is, somewhere deep in the feelings and instincts of a man, a yearning for justice, an idea of what is right and wrong, of what is fair between man and man, that came before the first law was written and will abide after the last one is dead. Picture Tommy's and his wife's minds, when he went up and down investigating these stories. He doubted his friends and he thought he heard people's footsteps on the lawn outside in the dead of the night, and he went out to see and he was harassed and worried from the time this happened until now.

How much could you, how much could any human mind stand? Some men have gone insane by a word, by fear, by fright, others by slow degree, by long trouble, by mishap.

Poor Massie, strong and vigorous, when all of these things were heaped on him. What did he do? He began to rid his mind somewhat of his own troubles and of the persecution of the men who performed this deed. He began to think of vindicating his wife from this slander. She had been lied about, she had been abused with talk.

Massie was discouraged. Months of slander since his wife had been dragged into the bushes and raped; months of abuse. He had ideas and fears and delusions. The doctor tried to quiet his fears, but they could not be quieted. He couldn't work—and work has been the first and last aid of many other unfortunates.

He wanted to get a confession. For what? To get somebody imprisoned? No—that did not concern him—he was concerned with the girl, whom he had taken in marriage when she was sixteen—sweet sixteen.

Mrs. Fortescue was worrying about the delay of what she thought was justice, and what other people thought was justice. I fairly well know what law is, but I don't often know what justice is—it is a pattern according to our own personal conceptions.

Mrs. Fortescue, too, believed it necessary to get a confession. The last thing they wanted to do was to shoot or kill.

What did they do? They formed a plan to take Kahahawai to their house and get a confession. They never conceived it to be illegal—it was the ends they thought of—not the means. Are Jones and Lord, two common seamen, bad? There are some human virtues that are not common—loyalty, devotion.

Jones had been out there to see that the slanderers didn't kill—but slanderers don't kill that way. He was faithful as a dog, he was loyal when a shipmate asked for help. Was he bad? There are so many ways to measure goodness and badness.

There isn't a single thing that either of these two boys did that should bring censure.

I know the state's attorney would rather convict four people instead of two, but I think he would compromise on two—that ought to be enough for one day.

If you needed a friend, would you take one of these gobs, or would you wait outside prayer meetings on Wednesday night—I guess that's the right night? I say to you I would take one of these, rather than the others.

Tommy had prepared this warrant or subpoena, woven, like Joseph's coat, of many colors. Jones handed it to the Hawaiian boy and said Major Ress wanted to see him.

They did not want to kill—they made no plan to kill—they didn't know what to do when it happened. And the house was not a good place to kill—one family thirty feet away, another house twenty-five feet away. A lovely place to kill someone, isn't it?

Tommy, I say Tommy because he will never be anything else

to me. I have not known him long, but I have learned to love him and respect him. Tommy was driving the car when it came to the courthouse—this man got in. Tommy for months had been subject to delusions and fears that bring insanity.

There is nothing in this evidence to indicate that they ever meant to kill—there was never any talk about killing, as far as this evidence is concerned.

I would not want to do anything to add to the sorrow of the mother of the boy (Kahahawai), or the father of the boy, or the cousin, who sit here. They have human feelings. I have too. I want you to have human feelings too. Any man without human feeling is without life.

The party entered the house. Tommy had a .45, which *is* much surer death than a .32, and this unfortunate boy was killed with a .32.

It's of no consequence who fired that shot—I am arguing the facts, and the only facts as you get them. Is there any reason in the world why Massie, on top of all these other troubles, should assume the added burden of assuming the responsibility of this killing?

I haven't always had the highest opinion of the average human being; man is none too great at best. He is moved by everything that reaches him, but I have no reason to think there is anybody on this jury who will disregard the truth for some fantastic, imaginary theory. Tommy has told you the fact that there was no intention of killing.

When Kahahawai said, "Yes, I done it," everything was blotted out—here was the man who had ruined his wife.

No man can judge another unless he places himself in the position of the other before he pronounces the verdict.

If you can put yourself in his place, if you can think of his raped wife, of his months of suffering and mental anguish; if you can confront the unjust, cruel fate that unrolled before him, then you can judge—but you cannot judge any man otherwise.

If you put yourself in Tommy Massie's place, what would you have done? I don't know about you, or you, or you, or you—but at least ten out of twelve men would have done just what poor

Tommy Massie did. The thing for which you are asked to send him to prison for the rest of his life.

I shan't detain you much longer. Again I say I cannot understand why the prosecution raises a doubt as to who fired the shot and how.

Massie was there! He rose! The picture came before him! He doubtless shot! One bullet was shot and only one.

Massie saw the picture of his wife pleading, injured, raped—and he shot. There could have been nobody else. And then what? Had any preparations been made to get out this body? What could they do? What would you have done with a dead man on your hands? You would want to protect yourselves. It might be the wrong thing to do—but it's only human.

What is the first instinct? Flight. To the mountains, to the sea, anywhere but where they were. Here was the dead body—they couldn't leave it—perhaps they could get rid of it. There isn't one in ten thousand who wouldn't get away, no matter how.

That isn't the plan of conduct of someone who had thought out a definite plan; it is the hasty, half-co-ordinated instinct of one surprised in a situation. And finally they were caught. The first few officers found that these people wouldn't speak. This is an hour after the shooting.

Gradually, Lieutenant Massie was coming back to consciousness and realizing where he was. Where is the mystery in a man cracking after six or eight months of worry?

We are now realizing that many acts have been punished as crimes that are acts of insanity. Why? Because lawyers have been too cruel to look for insanity; because an act is considered as a crime, not as a consequence of causes.

He asked for a cigarette, a simple reaction, something you're used to, something to do. Does a man think every time he takes a cigarette? No. It doesn't mean a thing. I have been a cigarette smoker, and I could ask for a cigarette in my sleep.

Any man in any situation may do it. Neither does turning away from a camera indicate anything; it may be just instinct, and means nothing.

As time went on, he, of course, began to recover. Two hours later at the city attorney's office he had recovered enough to refuse to answer questions.

He had had delusions, had lost flesh, had been ill. It's a wonder he didn't go crazy the first night. Many men have gone insane for less, many have gone insane without others realizing it until later.

I believe I've covered this case as far as I care to go. There are little things here and there, but the broad facts are before you.

It was a hard, cruel, fateful episode in the lives of these poor people. Is it possible that anyone should think of heaping more sorrows on their devoted heads, to increase their burden and add to their wrongs?

If so, I cannot understand it. There are many things in this world that I cannot understand.

Can anyone say that they are of the type on whom prison gates should close to increase their sufferings? Have they ever stolen, assaulted, forged?

They are here because of what has happened to them. Take these poor pursued, suffering people, take them into your care as you would have them take you if you were in their place.

Take them not with anger, but with pity and understanding.

I'd hate to leave here thinking that I had made anyone's life harder, had not sympathized with suffering, had created, not relieved, suffering.

I have looked at this Island, which is a new country to me. I've never had any prejudice against any race on earth. I didn't learn it, and I defy anyone to find any word of mine to contradict what I say. To me these questions of race must be solved by understanding—not by force.

*　　*　　*

I have put this case without appeal to the nationality or race of any juror, asking them to pass on it as a human case.

We're all human beings. Take this case with its dire disasters, written all over by the hand of fate, as a case of your own, and I'll be content with your verdict.

What we do is affected by things around us; we're made more than we make.

I want you to help this family, to understand them. If you understand them, that's all that's necessary.

I'd like to think I had done my small part to bring peace and justice to an Island wracked and worn by strife.

You have not only the fate but the life of these four people. What is there for them if you pronounce a sentence of doom on them? What have they done?

You are a people to heal, not to destroy. I place this in your hands asking you to be kind and considerate both to the living and the dead.

DURING HIS PLEA, which was broadcast to the mainland, Darrow brought tears to his listeners as he recounted how Mrs. Massie was bruised and beaten.

When Darrow had finished his plea, he appeared exhausted. He had talked for four hours and twenty minutes, and although he had held up well throughout, his age showed as he walked back to his chair.

The Honolulu Advertiser reported: "With words that unfolded like the immortal pages of a Greek tragedy, Clarence Darrow laid before the Massie-Fortescue jury the reasons upon which he is asking their freedom."

The jury was out two days. Their verdict: guilty of manslaughter. But they recommended leniency. The verdict was unexpected. Reactions were strong both in the States and in Hawaii. Senator J. Hamilton Lewis of Illinois urged President Hoover to investigate the case; Representative Thatcher of Kentucky, the home state of Lieutenant Massie, circulated a petition in the house asking the governor of the Island to pardon Massie and the others.

Darrow later wrote of this case: "Of course, all the attorneys for the prosecution and those for the defense, as well as the judge, knew that legally my clients were guilty of murder. Everyone, however, was talking about the 'unwritten law.' "

Judge Davis had stressed in his instructions to the jury that no one has a right to take the law into his own hands. It was these instructions which left the jury no choice but to render the verdict they did.

However, before the defendants had served more than an hour, their sentence was commuted by the governor of the Island.

Then, for the first time in his life, Darrow was asked to be on the prosecutor's side. The attorney general of the Island asked his help in prosecuting Mrs. Massie's assailants in the retrial. The attorney for the defense declined, pointing out that never in his more than half-century of practice had he ever prosecuted anyone, and it was too late to start now.

What Darrow did do before he left was to convince the State and Mrs. Massie to drop further prosecution, to let the whole affair be forgotten as soon as possible.

PART TWO

❦

AGAINST
PREJUDICE

Freedom Knows No Limits

THE COMMUNIST TRIAL
Chicago, 1920

DARROW DARES
JURY TO CONVICT
REDS ON TRIAL

[Headline, Chicago *Daily Tribune*, July 31, 1920]

AFTER the First World War, about one-half of the states passed espionage acts which Clarence Darrow described as "forbidding free discussion either orally or in the press." Illinois passed such a statute in 1919.

This was the background for the Communist Labor case in Chicago in 1920 when twenty Communists were arrested and charged with advocating the overthrow of the government by force. The indictment rested upon the fact that the defendants were members of the newly formed Communist Labor party.

All were arrested in one of the many "red raids" which United States Attorney General A. Mitchell Palmer was then conducting. In this era radicals of all descriptions were rounded up. Some were indicted and convicted, others deported.

The dramatic trial of the twenty members of the Communist Labor party was held in the Criminal Court of Chicago. Judge Oscar Hebel presided. Prosecuting attorneys were Frank Comerford, Lloyd Heth and Marvin

Barnhart. At the defense table, in addition to Darrow, was William S. Forrest.

The defendants were intellectuals; many of them were native-born Americans, including Winnetka, Illinois millionaire William Bross Lloyd, who was one of the organizers of the Communist Labor party in America. William Bross Lloyd was the son of Henry Demarest Lloyd, author of *Wealth Against Commonwealth.*

Other defendants included: Samuel Ash, Max Bedacht, Oscar Jesse Brown, Jack Carney, N. J. Christensen, L. K. England, Edwin Firth, Samuel Hankin, L. E. Katterfeld, Niels Kjar, Charles Krumbein, Ludwig Lore, James E. Meisinger, Edgar Owen, Arthur Procter, Karl F. Sandberg, Perry Shipman, Morris S. Stolar and John Vogel.

The chief witness for the prosecution was Ole Hanson, former mayor of Seattle, Washington, the city which a year earlier had been plagued with a general strike.

Hanson testified that prior to the strike, the unions in Seattle had tried to make him promise to turn over to them the city's lighting plant. He also asserted that James Duncan, a defense witness, gave him a copy of Lenin's *The Soviets at Work* and explained that this book contained the idea behind the Seattle strike.

While Duncan was on the witness stand, the prosecuting attorney appeared unusually eager to cross-examine him. The prosecutor's actions attracted the attention of the jury and caused Darrow to complain to the judge. The judge instructed the jury to "oblige the Court by paying strict attention to the testimony and not to the actions of the opposing attorneys while it is being given."

As Duncan was leaving the stand, the prosecuting attorney claimed he heard him say, "He (Hanson) is the biggest liar I ever heard."

The judge did not hear this and asked for a clarification of the incident. During the explanation, Hanson tried to speak to the judge. Darrow objected. A heated exchange occurred. The Chicago Daily News reported that "Hanson was led from the courtroom when the passage between him and Clarence Darrow threatened to develop into physical conflict."

The State's case showed that Lloyd had driven down Chicago's State Street with both an American and a red flag flying from his car. A few weeks later Lloyd told a Socialist meeting in Milwaukee: "What we want is preparedness. We want to organize so if you want every Socialist in Milwaukee at a certain place at a certain time, with a rifle or a bad egg in his hand, he will be there."

In his closing remarks, Prosecuting Attorney Comerford said, "For days attorneys Forrest and Darrow have made eloquence a defense. But the truth as it appeared in evidence has not been touched."

Said Attorney Barnhart for the State: "He (Lloyd) had the red flag tied over the American flag to show his contempt for Old Glory. Think of it, gentlemen—this defendant indicating his contempt for the government by displaying the red flag of the revolution."

Darrow followed with his summation to the jury:

"You can only protect your liberties in this world by protecting the other man's freedom. You can only be free if I am free."

GENTLEMEN OF THE JURY: I have for a good many years been arguing cases in court and, in my own way as a lawyer, asking jurors to forget their prejudices and their feelings and deliver a verdict according to the evidence, uninfluenced by fear or passion or heat.

I must say that in all my experience, which now covers forty-two years, it seems to me I never saw a case where every cheap feeling has been appealed to; where every inference has been drawn; where the world has been traveled over; where false and misleading ideas of law and of fact have been stated; where everything has been urged to swing a jury from their duty that they might join the mob, as has been done in this case.

Gentlemen, from the beginning to the end there has been no attempt at fairness; there has been no effort to see that these defendants had a trial that was such a trial as should be had in an American court, or in an Indian court, or in a cannibal court. There is no mean and sordid motive, there is not one influence that could be used on this jury, that has not been urged in this case against the liberty of my clients.

Now, gentlemen, let me be plain about it. If you want to convict these twenty men, then do it. I ask no consideration on behalf of any one of them. If you have any idea in your heads that I want you to protect them or save them, forget it. They are no better than any other twenty men; they are no better than the millions and tens of millions down through the ages who have been prosecuted—yes, and convicted, in cases like this; and if it is necessary for my clients, gentlemen, to show that America is like all the rest, if it is necessary that my clients shall go to prison to show it, then let them go. They can afford it if you gentlemen can; make no mistake about that.

If under this hue and cry of today—which I say is moved and instigated by a gang of profiteers who would strangle freedom that they might get rich; who would traffic in the blood of men; who have determined that in this country no voice of criticism shall be raised against them—gentlemen, if it can be done, all right. Perhaps it can; but there is no more reason why my clients should be saved than anybody else; although they have been called cowards for doing what not a single lawyer in this case would dare to do, to stand up against a mob. They are not cowards enough to beg, and if you want to convict them for this, then convict them. But I want to have my say first, and I shall attempt to say it honestly; and I fancy not one of this jury, after I am done, can say that I have dodged or sidestepped or appealed to any cheap sentiment or passion to get my clients free. I am not interested in them. I will submit this case squarely to this jury to see what you are going to do in the cause of freedom of speech, and the principles for which men have shed their blood in every age and every land. Still less am I interested in winning a case. I might have been once but the best wish I could have for myself would be that I never had to enter a courthouse again. I have served my time, and I am only interested in one thing in this case. I am interested in the policy of this country. I am interested in the verdict of this jury as to whether this country shall be ruled by the conscienceless men who would stifle freedom of speech when it interferes with their gold; or whether this jury will stand by the principles of the fathers and, whether so far as you can, you will stop this mad wave that threatens to engulf the liberty of the American citizens.

*　　*　　*

My good friend Barnhart says, "How is it that Mr. Darrow can defend this case? Mr. Darrow did all he could toward bringing the American people to believe it was their duty to enter this World War, and how can he defend twenty men on a charge like this?"

I am surprised and just a little disappointed that my brother should ask that question. I am defending this case for two reasons, and I will put the more unimportant one first. When I entered the practice of my profession years ago I determined that there never should be a case, however unpopular, or whatever the feeling, where I would refuse to do my duty to defend that case; and I can honestly say to this jury that I have kept the faith; that I have never turned my back upon any defendant no matter what the charge. When the cry is the loudest the defendant needs the lawyer most; when every other man has turned against him the law provides that he should have a lawyer—one who cannot only be his lawyer, but his friend. And I have done that.

But the most important reason I am defending this case is that I have seldom known a case where I believed so heartily that I am right as this.

I believe in this case and my duty in this case. Mr. Barnhart wonders, because I was in favor of the war. I was in favor of it. From the time Belgium was invaded, long before we got into it, I believed it to be our duty, and I believed it without any feeling against Germany of any sort. But if I had believed that this war would not have left the world freer, I would not have believed in it. If I had believed that after one autocracy had been overthrown, that here in America, where we cherish individual liberty, here in America, twenty states would pass a statute like this, which we had got along without one hundred and fifty years, so that great interests might silence every human voice while they were robbing the American people; if I had believed that this would result, perhaps I would not have believed we should have entered this war.

I believed in the war; I believed in it to make the world freer and fairer and better for all mankind; I believed that Europe would be freer; I believed that America would be freer, and I did the best I could. But there is something that I believe in more than I do in my country, and that is human freedom.

I have loved America first of all because she stood for this. Make us a nation of slaves, and I shall love it no more.

It was not an excess of patriotism 100 per cent or 200 per cent, or a million per cent, that made me believe in this war. I believed in it two years before we ever got into it; and I would have believed in it just the same whether we had been in it or not; and if our Congress should have delivered us to the support of Germany, I could not have stood with the United States.

Gentlemen, I am always watchful of anybody when he over-does patriotism. If I did not like the United States better than any other country, I would not stay here because I could go away; in that regard I have an advantage over some others who must stay. But I do like America. I was born here. I know its people. In the main, I like its institutions. I do not like every-thing it does and I never shall like everything it does.

There is no legislature that can pass a law that will make me think black is white; I know better; and there is no court that can decide a case that will make me think black is white. I might stand it, but it would not change my opinion; and I know enough of other countries to know that we have no monopoly on the virtue of the world. I know that other countries feel as our country does—that their country is best; and it is all right that they should. But I know enough about the world to know that no country has all the good; and the wise man picks his ideas and his views and his facts wherever he can get them. They are the common heritage of men. They belong to no land and to no country, and there are things that are higher than patriotism— love of justice, the devotion to truth, the love of freedom. These were born before national lines were made, and they will live until the last heartbeat dies in man. When they are dead no man will have a country worth protecting or a life worth saving. These are some of the things that never change, but boundaries change according to the needs and customs and habits of men.

Gentlemen of the jury, I do not mean to tell you twelve men that you are the greatest men who ever lived or the wisest men who ever lived; I don't know what is lurking back of your skulls. I know that mixed with every man is an infinite heritage, and I do not know what is there. But I do know this, that a jury of twelve men is the one protection between a human being and those who attack him; and I know, gentlemen of the jury, that when that safeguard is lost, then man's freedom is gone.

You twelve men have been told that if you acquit these defendants, you will leave the box despised; that you will endorse everything that these defendants believe.

If you gentlemen should find in favor of these defendants, then the Communists might go out and take your home, your furniture, and all that you possess.

Now, gentlemen, let us see about it. I don't know how those things may affect this jury, yet I have talked to juries for many, many years.

If you are the right kind of jurors, and I fancy that most men are that, you would sacrifice your home or your furniture or even your reputations with the mob, to do your duty in this case; and you would not have been jurors if we had not thought you would; because we know how easy it is to appeal to the mob. I have nothing to promise you. The Communist state is so far away that I cannot promise you a home on the Lake Shore Drive if you find these defendants not guilty. You would all be dead long before you ever saw it. I cannot even promise you a reward in heaven, for that I know nothing about. I have no promise to offset what you will lose if our wicked clients invade your homes and take your towels and napkins and linen; it is left for the State to do that.

Gentlemen, I can only ask you to decide this case upon the facts as you have heard them, in the light of the law as you understand it, in the light of the history of the country, whose institutions you and I are bound to protect.

I shall not argue to you whether the defendants' ideas are right or wrong. I am not bound to believe them right in order to take their case, and you are not bound to believe them right in order to find them not guilty. I don't know whether they are right or wrong and you don't know whether they are right or wrong. But I do know this—I know that the humblest and the meanest man who lives, I know that the idlest and the silliest man who lives, should have his say. I know he ought to speak his mind. And I know that the Constitution is a delusion and a snare if the weakest and the humblest man in the land cannot be defended in his right to speak and his right to think as much as the greatest and the strongest in the land. I am not here to defend their opinions. I am here to defend their right to express their opinions.

I don't know whether your ideas are right or wrong. No one knows except these attorneys for the State, and the fewer ideas that men have the surer they are that they are right.

How do you settle whether your opinions are right or wrong? There is nothing to measure them by; I have done the best I could through many years to search for truth. Sometimes I have thought I had a gleam of truth; sometimes I felt that I had in my hands the truth, a truth that could not be disputed, but that would be true forever. Sometimes I thought I had found it; and then again I thought I had lost it; and the truth I so fondly held in my hands was only an empty dream, and not the truth at all; and I have searched again and again, and here I find it and there I lose it; and I expect it will be this way until the end. It is not given to man to be sure of the truth. There are no standards, there are no measures; everything is dumped in on his imperfect brain. He weighs it the best he can and finds out the best way he can whether it is true or false; and he never knows. Therefore, gentlemen, above everything else on earth, men should cling fast to their right to examine every question; to listen to everyone, no matter who he is; to hear the spoken words and read the written words; because if you shut men's mouths and paralyze their minds, then the greatest truth that is necessary for the welfare of the human race may die.

Gentlemen, nature works in a mysterious way. When a new truth comes upon the earth, or a great idea necessary for mankind is born, where does it come from? Not from the police force or the prosecuting attorneys or the judges or the lawyers or the doctors; not there. It comes from the despised, and the outcast; it comes perhaps from jails and prisons; it comes from men who have dared to be rebels and think their thoughts; and their fate has been the fate of rebels. This generation gives them graves while another builds them monuments; and there is no exception to it. It has been true since the world began, and it will be true no doubt forever.

It has been true in America; it has been true in every other country in the world. It may be true again. What I say is what every man on this jury knows—you worship dead heroes who died for truth. They were despised and called cowards by prosecutors who were earning a salary, and they were put to death; but future generations have uncovered their graves from the slime that prosecutors have thrown over them, and they have shown to the world the great thoughts and ideas of these martyrs who died that you and I might be saved. It is true the world over. It may be that the human race can never do better; I cannot tell; perhaps there is not much to expect from it. But all the same we are obliged to do the best we can, and appeal over and over and over again to the consideration and enlightenment and the feeling of men against the things that have gone before; and that is what I am asking here.

It has been many a day since any body of men has been dogged and hounded, with every right violated, to get them into prison, as these twenty men have been.

Gentlemen, Mr. Barnhart says, "They do not believe in the Constitution" and "They have dared to criticize the Constitution." They are not on trial for that, gentlemen. If Mr. Barnhart was more familiar with history, and probably if he was not prosecuting this case he would be more familiar with history without knowing anything more about it than he knows now, he would know that from the beginning of the government down to the present time, many of the ablest men, from Thomas Jefferson and Patrick Henry down, have never believed in our Federal Constitution. They have believed that it was the work of men who had personal interests to serve.

When you get through with this case and my clients are safely housed away in Joliet, and the State is satisfied—and the world is saved—you might pick up Professor Beard, professor of the University of Pennsylvania, and read his book on the Constitution. He is a professor and still he has not been convicted.

Are they trying this case like any other? Here is my client,

Owen. Has he right to the protection of the law? And yet the cheap policeman who, Mr. Barnhart says, is a clean-cut, fine, right-living man—how does he know it? And if he knows it, how do you know it? And if it is true, what of it?

I repeat it, put it down again—a cheap policeman twice violated the Constitution, the Federal Constitution and the State Constitution, outraged every right the defendant had while a prosecuting attorney was standing by his side down in Moline.

They entered his home; they had no search warrant. They overhauled his papers. They found a flag, a red one, which he had the same right to have in his house that you have to keep a green one, or a yellow one, or any other color, and he impudently rolled it up and put another flag on the wall, nailed it there. What right did he have to do that, gentlemen?

What about this kind of patriotism that violates your right and mine, that violates the Constitution to get you and to get me? They overhauled his papers, they went through his desk, they rifled everything he had, they went through his room, and they brag of it, in a court of justice.

Gentlemen, this officer should be impeached and would be impeached if the Constitution was in force in Illinois.

What right had a state's attorney, who ought to support the Constitution of the United States and the state of Illinois, what right had he to violate the law in this way?

Has it come to that pass in this country, that because you want to get a man, officers of the law can trample on human rights and Constitutional rights and red-handed violate every principle of justice and then excuse it in a court of justice?

From the beginning to the end, this case has been marked by the most flagrant violation of law, by every effort to magnify, to create passion and prejudice, that you gentlemen might forget those things that are dear to the heart of every real American, that are more essential than any other; that you gentlemen might forget what America once stood for; that you might do your ignoble part toward bridling the tongue of man, toward paralyzing his mind, toward stifling his thought, toward uprooting and destroying forever that freedom of speech which has been the cornerstone of American institutions. You are really asked to make America the home of the tyrant, the informer and the usurer, who is willing to trample laws and constitutions and human rights beneath his feet, that he may plunder undisturbed.

Most of what has been used to this jury to stir up feeling in your souls has been the separate acts of individuals; mostly before this law was passed. Not one of these has the slightest bearing to prove conspiracy in this case. We can only ask you that no frenzy of the mob, whether from the mouth of the district attorney, or any other source, shall drive you from the plain law and the facts that have been proven in this case.

Lloyd's speech in Milwaukee has nothing to do with a conspiracy. Whether that speech was a joke or was serious, I will not attempt to discuss; Mr. Forrest has done that. But I will say this in passing, that if it was serious it was as mild as a summer's shower compared with many of the statements of these guardians of the law who are responsible for the conditions that exist in the United States. We have heard the statement of men in high places, that certain people who dared to express their opinion should be stood up against the wall and shot. Such a furor was created by the press of the country against Senator La Follette that it was suggested that he be stood up against the wall and shot. We have heard men of position and standing in America declare that people who have dared to criticize the actions of those who are getting rich should be put in a cement ship with leaden sails and sent out to sea. Every violent appeal that could be conceived by the brain of man has been used by the powerful and the strong. If there is anything that would provoke individuals who do not see questions as the property interests have seen fit to put them, it is the wild fanatical statements of these men who are responsible for these acts. Mr. Lloyd's letter and Mr. Lloyd's speech are nothing but reaction against the tyranny and oppression, the cruel statements of those people who would seal the lips of every man who disagrees with all they say and do.

What about this letter of Owen's? Owen says, "My son is a musician, and my highest ambition for him is that he will be a rebel, and that he will be the musician of the revolution." That is what Owen says, and although it is a personal letter which had no connection with any human being in this case, although it could throw no light on this case, it is paraded to this jury that you might say that Owen should be sent to prison because he wrote that letter.

Now, gentlemen, I am not going to apologize for that letter. I understand Mr. Owen; he has a high ambition for his boy. None of the cringing, cowardly time-servers will ever reach that height. If the son succeeds in his father's ambition, he may fill a felon's grave, and the time-serving cowards who always stand for the things that pay because they pay, may help send him there; but it is the rebels to whom monuments have been built. All through the ages, from Moses down, the men who have never followed the opinions and ideas of the people around them, are the men who have been building for the future. They have hewn steps out of the solid rock; they have worked in thorns and brambles and hard places that a stairway might be built for you and for me. They are like Moses, who, defying custom and habit and giving up ease and security, and having that faith which great mortals have, could see far off something better than the world had known. They have led their people through long years of sacrifice to the Promised Land. But these poor rebels have never seen that land, for when they reached that spot their eyes were too dim to see, or they were laid in a felon's grave while the time-servers walked over their bodies to the goal.

What do you suppose would happen to the world except for these rebels? I wish there were more of them. What do you suppose would have happened to the workingmen except for the rebels all the way down through history? Think of the complaisant, cowardly people who never raise their voices against the powers that be. If there had been only these, you gentlemen would be hewers of wood and drawers of water. You gentlemen would have been slaves. You gentlemen owe whatever you have and whatever you hope for to those brave rebels who dared to think and dared to speak and dared to act; and if this jury should make it harder for any man to be a rebel, you would be doing the most you could for the damnation of the human race. It is easier to believe something because somebody tells you it is true. It is easy to run with the hounds and bay to death those who may be better than yourself; it was easy for the people of New England to join in the mad rush and hang old women for witchcraft; it was easy for the people who lived in the days of the Inquisition to light the fires around men who dared to think; but it is those same rebels whose burning bodies have been the flame that has lighted the human race to something better than the world has ever known.

I sympathize with Mr. Owen in his high ambition that his boy shall be a rebel, and that he may furnish the music for the revolution. Whether the revolution ever comes or not, his voice will be joined with the voices of almost every man whose name is immortal, and his music will be the strain that stirred the hearts of men. If he should meet this high ambition, I am glad for man, but sorry for him. It means a stony road, a rocky path; it means want, contumely, abuse and sacrifice, sorrow and a neglected grave.

No matter how brave we are, no matter how determined we may be, no matter how these fantastic lights dazzle and beckon us with the promise of some far-off dream, no matter what we see, what we hope, or what we feel—to all of us who have been more or less rebels in this world, the thought often comes, after all, is it worth the while? After all, should not I have closed my eyes on the dreams and the visions and the hopes; should not I have left the world where the world seems proud to be, and lived in luxury and ease with the good people of the earth? If you find him guilty for this letter you will not condemn him, you will condemn yourselves.

Much has been said about the red flag. I say, gentlemen, that I have as much right to have a red flag as you have to own a green one, or a yellow one, or one of any other color. I have a right to one flag or a dozen flags, and the jury has never yet been found who could deny it.

Let me tell you something about this red flag. I will tell you why every tyrant on earth has hated it; I will tell you why every man with stolen money in his pocket has hated it; I will tell you why the men back of this law hated it; although they have no wit and no imagination. Their wit and their imagination, if they ever had any, has been traded for dollars.

What is this red flag? Gentlemen, the Communist Labor party did not invent the red flag. The Socialists did not invent the red flag. The Democrats did not invent the red flag. It is older than that. It is older than any of those parties. Christopher Columbus did not. It is older than that. It was not invented at Bunker Hill, although it was present. It was invented long before that. No man can tell you when it was first used. We can come pretty near it, though.

Since the workingman has grown enough to have the wit to think, and since he has found a voice for himself, although that voice is weak and feeble, the red flag has been the flag of the common man. It was the flag of the workingman long before Greece, and in Greece it was the flag of the workingman; in the Roman Empire it was the flag of the workingman; in ancient France, in Germany, in Russia, in Switzerland, in England, in Spain and in the United States. And yet these fool legislators think they can stamp out the institutions and the customs and the habits of a people.

Let us see where it came from. As near as we can find out, the rulers and kings and aristocrats who get their power from the Almighty—nobody ever saw the Almighty hand it down or even read the credentials of the aristocrats or kings—they had a white flag, or a blue flag; a blue flag, representing their blue blood which was pure and unsoiled, and the white flag, representing no color whatever and could not be soiled; only working people could be soiled, because you could only soil your hands with work.

The common people had a red flag. It came from the god of the sun, the red rays of the sun, as far back as you can read in history; when it took a more definite meaning, it meant the common red blood which courses through the veins of all men alike. It represents the brotherhood of man. That is where it came from.

In the early days of the Romans the workingman did not fight. It would not do for the workingman to learn to fight; he might fight the ruler. He had no arms, and you remember the noise that is raised here by the counsel in this case because the Russians propose to arm the proletariat? No, they should not. The other fellow should have the guns. They always did have them. Not the proletariat—these should have hoes and pick-axes and spades and scythes. That is their job. The other fellows should carry the guns because they do not use pick-axes. While the poor man is working, they will do their part by shooting him, especially if he does not work.

Finally the Romans did take the poor man into their armies and legions to fight. Of course, they found out long ago that the workingman's red blood would do just as well to fight with as any other kind, and when they took him he carried the red banner. He carried the red banner alongside of the blue banner of the blue bloods; and the rulers, with the well-known tricks on the psychology of the mind, threw these red banners far out into the line of the enemy, and the workingmen, who loved their red flag, would rush madly into the opposing ranks for their beloved flag that it should not be polluted by their enemy. It represented their dreams, their hopes and their ambitions, and they defended it with their lives. It was present in the battles of the Romans.

When the skilled workmen in the Middle Ages began to establish their trade unions, in France and in Germany, their trade-union flag was a flag of red, because it is the flag of the common man, who understood that the blood which courses through his veins was the same color as the blood that courses through the veins of every human being that ever lived. It was the flag used in Germany and in England, and is the flag today of a large part of the trade unions of the world, and it will be their flag when you get through with this infamous prosecution. It will be their flag whether this jury shall say innocent or guilty.

This flag was the flag of the first colonists in the United States. It flew proudly at the battle of Bunker Hill with other flags of all kinds. This flag flew where Washington had command. It flew at the Battle of Brandywine. The nuns of Bethlehem embroidered one with the greatest care and sent it to the

Commander that he might rally his men under that banner to fight for America against Great Britain.

*   *   *

Every idea has its flag. There is something about a flag which catches the eye, and through the eye the imagination. There are flags which represent temperance. There are flags which represent each nation of the world, and all the ideas of the world; some ideas perhaps bad, and some ideas good. There are flags that represent people. There are flags that represent a class. This red flag, as far back as you can go in the history of the world, has been labor's flag. It will be labor's flag, gentlemen, whatever you may do.

The man who thinks that you can change the customs and habits of a country by passing a law is a shallow man, who knows nothing of history and still less of philosophy. The red flag has been the emblem of the workers as far back as history can go, gentlemen, and I want to say further that this emblem has stood after long tribulation through the ages.

It has waved when the workingman was enslaved; when he was bought and sold; and later when he formed his unions and met in caves and waste places, under the ban of the law; when he was sent to prison be re he dared to haggle over his wages. When he was enslav France and his life was in the hands of the king; when capitalists, even in America, would make him a slave. It has represented the sufferings of workingmen throughout all these years. It is his banner, and you cannot take it from him by a verdict in this case. It will be his banner so long as red is the color of the blood that runs through the veins of men, and so long as the breaking clouds of dawn are crimsoned by the glorious rays of the rising sun.

I do not know why the common man should not rule if he can. Maybe he cannot. All this may be a dream. It may be that fixed in the constituency of life is the status of their power; that there must always be rich and always be poor. I do not know. I used to think that perhaps there need not always be poor and need not always be rich. I may have been wrong.

[136]

* * *

There have been great souls ever since men began to think who have believed in public ownership of land; and there are very few people who believe in unqualified private ownership today. Counsel know very well, if they have common observation, that this doctrine has been preached openly for more than forty years in the United States, and fairly well for more than one hundred and fifty years in the world.

Mr. Forrest read here yesterday from the New Testament to show that Christ was a Communist and that his disciples were Communists; and Mr. Comerford shouted, "Do you compare your people with Him, are they lineal descendants of Him?" Let me answer: Yes. They are lineal descendants, and you would have sent Christ to jail just the same as you would these defendants, just the same as the prosecutor in his day did it; just the same as there have always been prosecutors to send to jail every man who had a dream beyond the narrow vision of his fellow-man.

The doctrines of these defendants are just the same; and they are lineal descendants of the Communists of the early Christian days; Communists have been in the world since man was born. It was not new when Christ came upon the earth. Men have not only professed it, but they have lived it. Now, it may be replied that these were primitive people and that civilized man got over it. I do not know whether that is true or not, and neither do I care. That communism has been a well-known doctrine for ages, every intelligent man knows, although the Wall Street gentlemen have just found it out. These I do not count intelligent. Every intelligent man knows it. The prophets and the teachers and the seers all down through the ages have taught it. When it came to the early Christian times, all the disciples and apostles were Communists who owned all their property together and who taught that private property was wrong. Their doctrine came from Christ, and Christ got it from somewhere else. It has always been in the world. It was the principle all through the Middle Ages. It is the doctrine of Karl

Marx, who has left a greater impress upon this world than any other political economist who ever lived. It was the doctrine of Robert Dale Owen, who sacrificed his whole life for his fellow-man. It has been the doctrine of most of the great idealists and dreamers of the world. I do not know whether it will come or not.

I will tell you where it comes from, gentlemen. It is in you. It is in every juror in this box to a limited degree. It is in every state's attorney who is prosecuting in this case, in a very limited degree. It is in every man who has sympathy for his fellows. It is in every man whose sympathy goes out to his fellow-man. It is in every man who hates poverty, not because he is poor, but because other men are poor. It is born of sympathy; it is born of love; it is born of the feeling of common brotherhood in man; it will live so long as mothers love their children; so long as idealists love the human race; so long as men hope and strive and dream. Whether we shall ever accomplish it, I do not know. No man can tell.

I do not know whether communism would work. I do not know whether we can ever get a state of society where men are good enough, ideal enough, kindly enough and human enough to say, "Here is mine, I will throw it in with yours, and we will work together for the common good." Perhaps that cannot be. I shudder to think that we cannot; I have cherished that dream and that hope and that illusion even when I knew that it could not come. I do not know whether it is scientific. Of course, some of these scientific gentlemen can tell; but there is something higher than science. I do not know whether you can work it out in cold mathematics or not. Man is one-fourth unselfish and three-fourths selfish. Scientists would probably say, tell me some way to get the one-quarter to overcome the three-quarters. I don't know in mathematics, but just in proportion as a man is an idealist, just in proportion as he cares for his fellow-man, just in that proportion he will cling to these dreams, whether he believes that they can ever come true or not. I have had my dreams. I do not know whether socialism or communism will work or not. I do know that capitalism does not work. I do know that our present system of industry is a crazy quilt that allows no man to be really honest, that allows no man to be unselfish, that allows no man to live without sacrificing his fellow-man.

I know that the present system does not work. I know that it makes men greedy and selfish and mean. I know it stifles every good motive in man. I know that under the present system no one on earth can be as good as he would be. I know that capitalism does not work and never can work. None of these devout lovers of the capitalistic state, all of whom are sure they are going to heaven—not one of them would want to go to heaven if it was run on the same scheme as the earth. Not one of them believes that this system could live anywhere except upon the earth. My clients believe that a system fit for heaven is fit for earth. They are dreamers. Their principles were formed by all the ages. They did not make them. These have come down to them in a direct line from most of the idealists of the world. Karl Marx voiced it better than anyone else. They are dreamers. It is true counsel has slurred them. But why, gentlemen? Why? One of the commonest and cheapest things that the representatives of the State can do in criminal cases is to slur the defendants. It is easy because they are helpless, and the attorneys have ample chance. They are under indictment. They cannot rise to reply and neither can they hit them over the head with an ax. They have to stand it. The men who hold these opinions hold them because they are idealists. That is the reason. Gentlemen, I cannot tell whether this scheme will work, but it is what they believe. They have the same right to their belief under the laws of this country as you have to yours; and all of you told me over and over again that you would protect the right of another man the same as you would protect your own rights.

Gentlemen, somebody is interested in this case. We have a statute with the word *unlawful* in it, which we insist means nothing. They insist it may mean strikes, and so it may if they can get the judges to so interpret it. Today they are after these men. Tomorrow they will be after Gompers[1] and the trade unions and everybody who dares defy their power. They know

[1] Samuel Gompers, president, American Federation of Labor.

perfectly well that these men are reformers; but the men who are responsible for this law would be glad to get the three or four million trade unionists who are banded together for the protection of each other's rights, and not only for the protection of each other's rights but for the protection of the right of every other man to express his opinion. They know that in the next year or two mills will close, railway employees will be discharged. Then will be a good time to send trade unionists to prison. Do you suppose they care for these men on trial? Oh, no. They have got too much brains for that, although I would not accuse the backers of this law of being overly intelligent. They are out to rule the world. They are out to make money. They are out to destroy whatever is between them and their prey. Today it is these twenty men. Tomorrow it will be somebody else. You can only protect your liberties in this world by protecting the other man's freedom. You can only be free if I am free. The same thing that would get me may be used to get you, and the government that is not strong enough to protect all its citizens ought not to live upon the face of this earth.

These men are dreamers. They are idealists. They believe that somewhere in the future there can come a condition of society where property will be owned in common, and they do not believe in paying for it, either. They have a perfectly good legal right to take it without paying for it, provided an amendment is made to the Constitution of the United States, which I venture we can do before we can get that far.

Taking property without compensation is only a technical point to send people to jail. They believe in praying, "Thy Kingdom come, Thy will be done on earth as it is done in Heaven." Still, nobody wants it done on earth. That is, nobody who has much, and who wants something more. But, gentlemen, we ought to be careful of our dreamers and our idealists. If a man can have a dream and an ideal in this sordid world, he ought to have it; for the world is hard enough, it is cruel enough, it is selfish enough.

There is enough greed, there is enough envy and there is enough hate in this world; and if now and then men can have a vision that there will be a system where all men will be brothers, where there will be no more haggling and bickering, where there will be no poverty, no rich and poor, where man will live in love and brotherhood—if they have that dream, that ideal ought to be saved to the human race, whether it shall ever come true or not.

Gentlemen of the jury, I have been trying to point out some of the things that have been emphasized in this case. They told you about the proletariat and bourgeois. Mr. Barnhart says you are all bourgeois. Well, now, I don't know what difference it makes to you whether you are or not, but I don't think there are more than two bourgeois on this jury, and I am not going to mention their names.

Mr. Barnhart gave you the definition of a proletariat, and he says it is a man who works for wages, who has no property and so forth. He says there are definitions which show a good deal worse than that, that it is the meanest workingman.

That is right, Mr. Barnhart, that was the definition of the proletariat for long ages.

For long years to be a workingman was to be mean, was to be bought and sold, was to be flogged and killed, was to be the property of the master, body and soul. In France before the Revolution the workingman meant men without property, and they were. It does not mean that today, and the proletariat does not mean that today. It means simply this: those who do not make their money by employing other people. That is all it means. It means a man who works for wages, either with his hand or his brain, as against a bourgeois who employs men to work.

Almost all the people belong to the proletariat class—almost all is a little too strong, but much more than half; and it would be out of the question to have the bourgeois without the proletariat, because as long as there are big industries owned by somebody there must be a number of men to work in those industries.

My clients believe in a time when the owners of the industries should be workers, that is all. They believe in a time to be

reached by a different organization of society, when these industries shall all be owned by the men who work in them—that is
what they mean.

Is there anything wrong about that, gentlemen of the jury?

It may never come, but I fancy that no man who has sympathy
for the human race does not wish that sometime those who
labor should have the whole product of their toil. Probably it
will never come, but I wish that the time might come when
the men who work in the industries would own the industries.
I would take a chance, although I know that under that system
I would have to go to work myself.

Most all of you men on this jury work for others. Is there
any reason why the proletariat should not control the State?
Through all the long, cruel years the men who have worked
have had no voice in the State. Gentlemen, how much have
they got now? How much has the workingman to say about the
laws of his country? You were not born yesterday. How much
have you to say as to who will be president or mayor or senator
or anything else? Every man knows that the common man has
practically nothing to say about it.

I might go to the polls in November and vote for Cox or for
Harding. But what had I to say about the forces that came together and put me in a position where I must vote for one or
the other? And I would not vote for either if I could help it;
and almost no one else would.

Who of you, gentlemen of the jury, had anything to say about
who was to be mayor last spring? You might have had a chance
to vote for one of two men, neither of whom you wanted, and
that is the most, it amounts to nothing.

I would like to see the proletariat rule for a while, but I
have few delusions left; they might not do any better than the
others. I have seen workingmen that were not saints, lots of
them. I am not trying to uphold the workingman or his opinion
on the ground that he is a saint; he is not; he is human. But I
know that through all the past this world has been ruled by
property, and if there can ever come a time when the workingman can rule it, I will say he ought to have that chance to see

what he can do; and yet to tell you that is to believe in the "dictatorship of the proletariat"—well, why not?

I would like to see the proletariat have a chance to rule; the others have had it long enough, and these never have. The proletariat may lose their idealism as they get a better chance in the world; that often happens, too. But if it was nothing excepting for a change, I would like to see it tried. I would like to see those who have been a burden on the world for all these ages give some of the others a chance, to see what they could do.

We have been told by the gentlemen here, "Why, your men do not even believe in the labor unions."

Well, suppose they do not, gentlemen? I presume that statement is made for some of the jurors here who belong to labor unions.

Suppose my clients do not believe in them? I have always believed in them; they may be wrong, and they may be right. The labor unions have no guarantee that they are right. These men believe there should be a change in the labor unions, that is what they think. They think long use of power has made them conservative. So it has. Perhaps they are better for being conservative, or maybe they would be better if they were more radical.

My clients have a right to their opinion. No man can tell whether their opinion is best or not until you try it out. We are told that they do not believe in socialism. Whence comes all this sympathy of my friends, the prosecutors, for unionism and socialism? Wonders will never cease.

These gentlemen are standing here and condemning my clients because they are not for labor unions and they are not for socialism.

They will tell a different story when they have socialism on the rack.

You will hear a different story when this law catches you, and they are really after the labor organizations of the United States.

And I will tell you why they say it—because, forsooth, somebody on this jury might say, "Well, if they do not believe in socialism they must be bad; if they do not believe in trade unionism they must be bad; if they do not believe in this thing or that thing or the other things they must be bad."

These men have a right to their own opinions, just the same right that you have and the same right that I have and the same right that every man should have, and that opinion may be good or bad. And they tell us another thing, gentlemen. They say the Communist Labor party has endorsed Lenin and Trotzky, and that they believe in them. They say that my clients are sympathetic with Lenin and Trotzky; and they are, gentlemen; they are. And what are you going to do about it? I will tell you what I think about it, not because it is my thought, but because it is my position in this case. I am willing to stand with them upon that question, without the slightest fear as to any intelligent jury in the United States.

I don't know whether Lenin's government and Trotzky's government are the best or not. I have no chance to know. I have read the ordinary lies of the ordinary papers. I have read about Lenin and Trotzky being defeated one day and the next day carrying their banner through the lines of the opposing army. I have been fed on all these stories and I know not what to think of them, and I confess I do not care. I have no chance to know, neither has any other man a chance to know. Every man's idea of Russia is clouded, more or less, by his own feelings. I can say for myself that whatever the government of Russia is I wish it well.

I know this, that every American with the least drop of red blood in his veins hates the past of Russia. I know that you cannot find a human American—a human American who does not hate the Czar and all his works. I know that any man who loves liberty, any man who loves humanity, would not be willing to get rid of the new and replace it with the old; and I know you cannot overthrow the new unless you replace it with the old.

I know something of Russia; I have been a student of her literature for years; I have read much of her history. I know that she has been the last word of tyranny in Europe for more than a thousand years. I know that she has had a government of arbitrary power; a government of despotism, tempered by assassination; a government where all the good and all the brave and all the liberty-loving people of Russia have been killed or sent to Siberia and left to rot their life away because they loved their fellow-man. I know that you cannot get an American citizen who values his reputation who dares say a word for the past, not one.

And yet, gentlemen, that government which has been the government of Russia for ages, that government could not be overcome unless something was put in its place, and the despotism of all the years could not be washed away except in tears and blood.

*　　*　　*

I do not know whether the government of Lenin and Trotzky can stand or not; I do not know, neither do I care. I know it is there today and I know what was there before; I know it was time for the old to die and time for the new to be ushered in; and if it takes another revolution and another and a hundred others, I am glad at least that the government of the Czar no longer soaks the earth with blood.

I cannot tell what is in store for Russia. I hope good for her, as well as I do for all the other weary sons of man. I hope for her as I do for Austria, borne down by disaster and by want. I hope for her as I hope for all the people of the earth.

Sometime when the clouds are lifted and the night is over we may know. It is given to no man to see the future. Back of the heavy curtain which hides the present Russia from the future, back of that curtain no human eye can see. Still we know that the fates are weaving, that they are throwing the shuttle back and forth to fashion the future pattern of the human race. What the pattern shall be neither you nor I can tell. We can only meet the future of Russia and the world as we meet the future in our lives. We can meet it with fortitude, hope and trust.

I know that no decent man wants the past to come to Russia again. I know that no man would ask for it except for cash. To attempt to predict the future of a government born in the throes of a great world war, born in the anguish and poverty of a great people, to do that, gentlemen, is to attempt to do something that is beyond the ken of man. Sometime we will know. I hope at least that the present will last until the old is dead, beyond recall.

When I hear about a Russian princess waiting on a table in a restaurant in Constantinople it does not bother me; the only question that bothers me is whether she will make a good waitress, that is all. I don't know what right she had to be a princess. The newspapers can print these stories, but they will draw no tears from me. As long as somebody waits on the table I would just as soon it would be a princess as anyone else, provided she knows how to do the job. There were many, many weary ages when royalty was served by serfs, but their turn has come; their turn has come.

Gentlemen, I believe I speak for my clients, I know I speak for myself, and I believe I speak for every man who loves freedom and fairness and justice, when I say that I wish Russia well; that I hope the past has gone forever; when I say that I believe that no American soldiers should be in Russia today; when I say that I believe that it is an unspeakable crime that they should be there; when I say that I believe that no other land on earth should stand against their right of self-government, and their right to work out their own destiny as the fates shall will. And yet, gentlemen of the jury, everything has been said that the wit of man could devise, to get you in such a frame of mind that you will have no sense of justice and fairness, that you will throw aside your judgment and yield to your passion in this case because my clients welcome the dawn of revolution in Russia.

Why, in this they believe what Wilson did; what Wilson did when he learned that the old regime was overthrown and that a new power had taken its place; when he issued his message to the Russian people, congratulating them on the fact that Russia had awakened, and that the people, after the long, long night of the past, were claiming the right to liberty, the right to self-government, the right to freedom; and that Russia had taken her place among the other nations of the world standing for the liberty of man.

I don't suppose the end has come for Russia. The truth is, the end never comes for anything. There is no way to fix this weary world so it will stay and still be right. As long as the world shall last there will be wrongs, and if no man objected and no man rebelled, those wrongs would last forever. The objector and the rebel who raises his voice against what he believes to be the injustice of the present and the wrongs of the past is the one who hunches the world along.

Now, let me tell you another little incident here to show the prejudice of these gentlemen.

When they burglarized my client's house in the daytime, in violation of the State Constitution and in violation of the provisions of the Federal Constitution, they took from him a circular. Gentlemen, you remember it; Mr. Barnhart read it, with tears in his voice, and said, "My God, can it be?"

What was it? Now, let me show you what they are trying to do to you. That circular said that on the fourteenth day of November—my client Kjar, I had almost forgotten his name—now, it was Kjar who had a circular announcing that on the fourteenth day of November there was to be a picnic. It was on the same date as the one that the Bolsheviks came into power in Russia; the anniversary of the overthrow of the Russian government; they were celebrating it; there were to be pictures of street scenes of Russia on the day when the old regime had fallen, and the people with high hopes and fine dreams, dreams that perhaps will never be realized, were ushering in the new.

All right, gentlemen, the world is full of those pictures. "The king is dead; long live the king."

There never was a king who died but what the deluded people thanked God that the king was dead and looked forward with joy and hope because a new king was to rule. The old was dead, and in their imagination they dreamed of plenty of prosperity, of food for the people, of not too much work, but plenty of wages, of good things to come because there was a new king; and when his turn came to die they thanked God that he was dead and another king had come.

Gentlemen, the poor old human race has been doing that forever, thanking God for the things they have got rid of, dreaming their dreams and smoking their pipes, and living and dying in the delusion that some time the kingdom of heaven was to come to earth.

All right, gentlemen; I am glad after all the long and weary ages, that Russia had hers; I am glad and I hope that they were happy for a time. I hope they rejoiced over the death of the old; I hope they rejoiced at the passing of that night which had hung over Russia for long, weary years. On the seventh day of November, 1917, the old was overthrown and the new was born, and on the seventh day of November, 1919, two years later, my clients—

COMERFORD: You are mistaken, Mr. Darrow.

DARROW: What is that?

COMERFORD: You are mistaken, if you will pardon me. That was the overthrow of the Kerensky government, not the overthrow of the Czar.

DARROW: Oh, pshaw.

COMERFORD: I simply interrupt, thinking you want to be accurate.

DARROW: Of all the little, foolish, insignificant things that men pick out, it is that the overthrow of the Kerensky government was not the real overthrow of the Czar.

Every man who knows anything about Kerensky never had the slightest faith in him and counsel knows it. He has been driven out of most of the important countries of Europe. He left Russia and his country. He was the first that followed the Czar, and he left without stopping to take the government with him or doing anything except make speeches, a typical oratorical word peddler, in no way fitted for the job. If his place had not been taken by Lenin, then the old tyrants whom you love and whom you would bring back to power to complete the destruction of that unhappy people, would have come back. There was nothing between the Russian people and the monarchy but

Lenin, good or bad, and he has held that country for three years, and I am glad he has.

As I say, gentlemen, I am glad of it, and when something better shall come I will be infinitely glad of that; but the man who wishes Lenin's power destroyed, that man is working for the whip and the lash and the dungeon, which made slaves of Russians for a thousand years.

Now, don't make any mistake about that, gentlemen; there can be no mistake about it.

Now, my deluded clients, if they had come to me and asked whether they should celebrate the overthrow of the Czar, I would have said, "No, you are crazy; the people don't want it; let them alone; you may not belong in the penitentiary because you think you can help the world, but you belong in the insane asylum, for the world doesn't want to be helped." That is what I would have said; then I would probably have gone and tried to help. That is the difference between reason and impulse.

My clients held a celebration on November 7, 1919, two years after Lenin assumed the government in Russia, to keep the old regime out of power; and Jack Carney I suppose made a speech. Well, I hope he enjoyed making it and had a good time. They showed pictures of the celebration in Moscow, where the people came together in mad acclaim, because the old was dead and the new was born.

How I do like to look at those pictures of those enthusiasts who had a dream of what was coming true. I do not like to look at the picture after it has come true. They are like the pictures of the troops in Berlin marching proudly to the front, and the troops in Vienna marching proudly to the front, and the troops in France marching proudly to the front, and the troops everywhere marching proudly to the front; and now the glory is over for the war is done.

They had this celebration on the seventh of November, two years after Lenin came into power.

Well, now, gentlemen, let me tell you a little story. It won't take me very long to tell it and it is applicable to this case.

I got a card on the fourteenth day of June, I think it was,

just a little while ago. Some aristocratic gentlemen, who believe in jails for Chicago, were holding a celebration over the fall of the Bastille in Paris a hundred and fifty-odd years ago.

Of course they believed in jails here; but the French people, in 1789 or thereabouts, destroyed the Bastille in Paris by a mob, and we could celebrate that unconstitutional event in Chicago.

Isn't it marvelous how a Chicago man does like liberty in some other country?

I can get together all the bankers in Chicago for a feast in commemoration of the French revolution, and after they get quieted down a little about their money and over their fear of Bolshevism we could get them all together in commemoration of the Russian revolution and the triumph of Lenin.

You can get men to be patriotic over freedom for any country on earth except their own; and that is a misfortune, that is all. That is what my clients here did not know. They thought that men could be just as patriotic over liberty at home as they could over liberty abroad.

No, it cannot be done. It just cannot be done. But I got that invitation. I had accepted it a few years before. This time I did not because I was busy trying to find twelve good men and true in this case, like Diogenes going out with his lantern to hunt an honest man; I don't suppose he knew whether he had found him, and I don't know whether I did, but still we all keep on trying.

Well, our people got together to celebrate the fall of the Bastille in France. I approved, although I did not celebrate; I approve of any bastille falling now and then. It was high time that tumbled; in my mind's eye I saw this picture.

I saw a land that had been fair and great; a land where the rulers, through their worthless lives, their reckless waste and their disregard of human rights, had destroyed freedom and made brutes of men; where they had driven the people to beggary that they might be rich and profligate; where they had taken all for the king and left nothing for the poor; where if the poor disobeyed their masters they were killed; where the serf was a slave; I saw that land suffering under centuries of cruelty, injustice and wrong. Almost in a night I saw her slaves arise against the French laws and constitution; I saw them rise against the institutions that the strong had made—against the church and the state, and in one mad frenzy sweep these from the earth. I saw that long line from Versailles marching on Paris, a line led by an old woman in the front, with a butcher knife in her hand and a great apron filled with human heads; I heard them singing the "Marseillaise," the song of freedom, as they went out to wreak vengeance and death upon the rulers for the long night of cruelty and injustice that had drenched the fair land of France with blood and tears. I saw them moving like the mad waves, a nation aroused to action against the tyranny of the ages. I saw this mob led by the inspiring martial strains of the "Marseillaise." I saw them surround the Bastille and pound it into dust; I saw coming from its grimy dungeons men who had been so long confined that there were no records of the time they were shut in, or the charge on which they came; men whose eyes were dazzled by the light of day when they left their gloomy cells; I saw the pent-up feeling born of the oppression of all the ages turned loose in Paris. I saw the mad holiday of an oppressed and outraged people drunk with power.

For a time at least these despised ones were rulers, for the old was dead and the new was born. I saw their banners and read thereon liberty, equality, fraternity. And on the fourteenth day of July we celebrated the madness of that righteous mob; we rejoiced over the destruction of the old and the birth of the new. All this was in Chicago, where live the comfortable people who are prosecuting this case, the comfortable people who love justice when it is far away, the comfortable people who take a rebel to their hearts if he is a long way off. These smug men celebrated it; and the respectables of America have been celebrating it for fifty years because the event was in France, and long ago.

And yet we are condemned because our dreamers went mad with joy over the same kind of a revolution in Russia two years ago.

Wait fifty years and you will find another prosecutor—you will find another prosecutor trying to send men to jail in Chicago while his employers are having a dinner to celebrate the revolution in Russia that overthrew the Czar.

Are any of you sorry for the French revolution? I wonder if these prosecutors are sorry for it.

Liberty was enthroned, the old was destroyed and a new France was born. Today we are celebrating it. The new rulers of France kept their place by the guillotine and the sword; they killed the king and they killed the queen, but the people lived.

I remember a striking passage in Carlyle, the great Scotch philosopher. He told of the cruelties of France in this mad debauch of liberty. Carlyle said, "Yes, the guillotine was busy; yes, blood flowed and men were killed, the nobles raved and cursed and cried aloud, but this was the difference: through all the long ages it had been the poor who were killed; it had been the poor who died in a thousand ways; now the rich were killed, the guillotine was busy with the thousands who made the most noise. The heads of those who were chopped off were the heads of those who cried the loudest and who could make their complaints heard by the world, while the poor, the common man, who, for years had died in a thousand different ways, had met his end in the dumb silence of despair. He was silent with no one to listen to his wrongs until one day he arose in his wrath and swept the powerful from the earth."

The people had their way in Paris until the man on horseback came, and all the civilized world has been wishing that Napoleon were still alive that he might have commanded in this last great war. Still Napoleon was hated more than any man the world had known; England feared him, Germany hated him, all the world despised him; they feared and hated the revolution then, that revolution which Victor Hugo called the greatest event in history, that revolution which we all approve today.

Gentlemen, we forget. If the people of Chicago can celebrate the fall of the Bastille, why should not my clients celebrate the fall of Nicholas, old Nick?

I wish they could have got along without killing him or shedding any royal blood, but with all the crimes of all the

Czars on his head, nothing else could have been written in the book of fate.

Long ago it was written down that "without the shedding of blood there can be no remission of sins." It would be strange, indeed, if the blood that had been shed in France, if the sufferings that Russia has undergone, could be paid for in any other coin but blood.

* * *

Gentlemen, the prosecutors are trying to send to the penitentiary twenty men, and incidentally, gentlemen of the jury, seeking to violate the Constitution of the United States and of the state of Illinois; seeking to place freedom of thought and freedom of speech under such a ban that no man will ever dare to think or ever dare to speak again in a land which once was free.

Inferences have been thrown out here that a sympathetic strike is an illegal strike.

I do not know what these gentlemen will say and I do not care. If they want to argue to this jury that a sympathetic strike is an illegal strike, all right, gentlemen; it will not be the only absurd thing that you have heard argued to this jury. I have respect for a man who strikes because he himself needs, or thinks he needs, more to take care of his family or himself, or for any other purpose of the kind. I have respect for the men who lay down their tools and take a chance to better conditions for themselves.

But, gentlemen, when a man who has a job and is making no claim for himself, when a man who has a job will lay down his tools and quit his job out of sympathy for his fellow-man, who he believes is not treated right, I have infinitely more respect for him; it shows a higher idealism, it shows a greater sense of justice when a man does this for for someone else, than when he does it for himself.

Long ago it was written that "greater love hath no man than this, that he would give his life for his friend." Greater love has no organization than that it will lay down its tools in sympathy with its fellow-man.

I may do something for myself and I am entitled to no credit for it; but when I will risk privation and want and financial loss and ostracism from my fellow-men, for the sake of bettering the conditions of the rest, who I feel are suffering injustice, then I am entitled to credit; and I care not how many lawyers argue that a sympathetic strike is illegal, and I care not how many legislatures declare it, or how often judges say it. So long as men have human hearts and human feelings and human sympathies and kindly emotions, men will know that it is not. They will know that the man who fights for his fellow-man is a better man than the one who fights for himself.

There are some things higher than the laws. There is an innate sense of justice; there is a human sympathy on which the race lives, which is its preservation. And these have persisted, while laws have come and gone; and woe be to the law that gets in front of it, for no prosecutor is strong enough to defend it.

You cannot do it, gentlemen; it will not be tried in this case. I wish it would, I wish counsel would insist on what they started out to do, instead of coming into this court at the eleventh hour, after all this array before this jury, and after every effort that has been made to fasten the Seattle strike on these defendants.

Let us see about the Seattle strike which it is claimed the defendants endorsed. This began with the shipyards strike in January 1919.

The shipyards, as we gather from this testimony, were financed and owned by the people in the East. Of course they were; everything is financed and owned by people in the East. These sedition statutes were financed and passed in more than twenty states after the war had closed, by people in the East.

It is perfectly plain that twenty states passing these same laws immediately after the close of the war were moved by a common purpose, and were influenced by a common organization, and that those statutes are there because someone wanted them. And that, too, after we had lived for a hundred and fifty years without them.

That is what I say about it. You can think of it, do as you will, but sometime, when reason has regained its throne, if it ever does, or what is more probable, when the human race has taken some new frenzy and forgotten the old, America will repent in sackcloth and ashes for the injustice that has been done to men under these panic laws.

Now, they called the Seattle strike, and they called it in sympathy with the shipbuilders.

*　　*　　*

What did they do when they commenced this strike? They did what no strikers ever did in Chicago in my experience; they did what I don't recall any other committee ever doing, although they may have done it.

Before they ever called this strike, they made arrangements so that everyone could be fed, whether he was a striker or not.

Of course, there were some people who ate at home. I suppose they did not all eat in restaurants, they never do in any community that I know anything about.

The unions were not bound to furnish food for Seattle. Men who are engaged in an industrial struggle have the right to carry on their struggle, and if the other side cannot live, let them make terms, that is all.

But these men in Seattle went further than men generally go. The first thing they did was to provide places to eat and places to buy milk, and provided that the lights should not be turned off.

Gas was left flowing, electricity was left running, telephones were running and everybody was fed; the only man who was creating any disturbance was Mayor Ole Hanson.

Now let me say a little about Ole Hanson, gentlemen.

He was the mayor of Seattle, a man who, like everybody else, is just the kind of a fellow that the Lord makes him. You cannot add to him or take away from him. At least it would be dangerous to take much away from him, and I am afraid you cannot add to him.

He was mayor. This strike came on the town; very likely he could not help it. His town is not the first one where a strike has occurred; we have had them here in Chicago; we have had them in New York; we have had them in practically every big city in the country; and we will probably have them for years to come. There is nothing strange or remarkable about it; the only strange and remarkable thing about this is that it was such a general strike. There was peace and order, and the citizens were well protected, which shows exactly what the strikers tried to do and what they did do.

Ole Hanson, evidently figuring with the Chamber of Commerce, or with some of the other people of wealth and influence in the community, allowed himself to be influenced by them. That is almost always the case. He was the mayor of this city. He has not shown, in a single instance, that there was any trouble, any riot, any assault or any fear of trouble. No one in this case has shown where, in a single instance, there was any effort to take hold of the business of the city or any interference in any way with any of the municipal departments; and yet they started here with a flourish to prove to you that Seattle was an illustration of what was meant in this Manifesto, of taking possession of political power.

Where did anybody try it; where was it done? Where was it suggested; where did this thing come from, anyhow?

Ole Hanson had no such thought, at least not before he left Seattle; he had no such thought while he was acting as mayor; he had no such thought while he was dealing with the organization.

Every proclamation issued by the workers, every statement issued in connection with this strike, showed that they were engaged simply in a sympathetic strike, to help the shipworkers. They called on the businessmen by proclamation saying, "That your interests lie with us as against these nonresident ship-owners; if wages are raised there will be more money to spend with you."

This certainly does not indicate any intention of taking over the city, taking over the industries, or doing anything except using their power to get more wages for their fellows, who no doubt deserved them. But whether they deserved them or not they thought they did and that was enough.

Hanson had several interviews, most of them flatly contradicted by Duncan, many of them utterly inconsistent with his own statements made at other times and shown in this case.

Where does he show that anybody ever undertook to take his job or any other job or perform any of the functions that he or the city administrations were performing or take anybody's industry or anybody's business?

And yet, gentlemen, they come here and carry that inference to this jury.

Now let me show you something which proves that no one ever dreamed of such a thing until counsel thought it was necessary to make a case.

Notice of this strike was given, as I recall, on Sunday, the second of February, that the strike was to take place on Thursday, the sixth. It did take place on Thursday the sixth. On Wednesday, the fifth, Ole Hanson had a conference with the labor men in charge of this strike. He had a right to take every precaution necessary for the city during the time of the strike.

He had another conference the sixth and another one the seventh, and on the seventh, as he says, a committee of workingmen came in headed by Duncan; came to his office, and he boastfully says he kept them waiting from ten o'clock in the morning until three o'clock in the afternoon. They came there at his request, to see what could be done to call off this strike, which was just a day old; a strike which was never meant for anything except to gain the point by the workers of the shipyards; he kept them waiting there, he says, all the afternoon.

Duncan denies this. He says Hanson called in his friends from the Chamber of Commerce and they had a conference, but Ole Hanson says that while he was keeping these men waiting in his outside office, he got busy and gave to the evening papers what he called his proclamation; and here it is, gentlemen, Ole Hanson's proclamation. I fancy this is the first proclamation that he ever issued, and it probably will be the last.

I want to call your attention, gentlemen, to what is in it, and to what is not in it, as showing the falsity of these witnesses; to show you that nobody ever had the remotest thought of taking possession of the city of Seattle or doing anything except winning this strike. As shown to you, the strike was conducted for perfectly lawful purposes by a body of patriotic workingmen, and the only bad thing about it was that Hanson thought it was bad.

Now what did Ole think on the seventh day of February, 1919, when he issued his proclamation?

Here it is:

"To the people of Seattle: By virtue of the authority vested in me as Mayor I hereby guarantee to all the people of Seattle absolute and complete protection."

And yet, from the beginning to the end, not a man was interfered with in any way.

"They should go about their daily work and business in perfect security."

Why not?

"We have fifteen hundred policemen, fifteen hundred regular soldiers from Camp Lewis, and can and will secure, if necessary, every soldier in the Northwest to protect life, business and property."

All of which were safer in that four or five days of strike than before or since, in the history of Seattle.

"The time has come for every person in Seattle to show their Americanism."

To show their Americanism?

"Go about your daily duties without fear. We will see to it—" We will see to it?

"—that you have food, transportation, water, light, gas and all necessities. The anarchists in this community shall not rule its affairs."

The anarchists in this community shall not rule its affairs?

"All persons violating the law will be dealt with summarily."

It is signed "Ole Hanson, Mayor."

Now, gentlemen, up to that time and after that time not a single voice had been raised against business and good order, not a single thing had happened in Seattle, as peaceable as on a Sunday morning, and everybody says so including their witnesses.

Property and life were properly secured, and yet they have carried the inference here, and Hanson has said that he heard a wild speech at the corner of Fourth Avenue and some other street, that the strikers were going to assume the control of the city.

Now, gentlemen, pray tell me why, on the seventh day of February, after this strike had been brewing for a week; after repeated conferences by the mayor with the strike committee; after this sleuth had been going in and out and making his reports; after every effort had been made to stir up violence by these agents; after all this time, pray tell me why Ole Hanson issued his proclamation and never in any way referred to any effort of these strikers to take control of the city; to interfere with property; to usurp the functions of the State; or to do a single unlawful thing?

Think you, gentlemen, that if there had been any effort to do any of these things, Ole would not have spoken of it?

Think you the proclamations would not have come so thick and fast that he would never need another line of advertising as long as he lived?

Think you that this cheap, advertising, money-mad man would have overlooked an opportunity to bring to the world what they were doing? Do you think that he would have overlooked an opportunity to be advertised on all the fences and all the signboards all over the United States, so that he might make money for the heroism he showed in this battle?

Why didn't he say something about it? Why didn't he call the attention of the city of Seattle to it? Why didn't he call the attention of the government of the United States to this fact, if it had been a fact? Why did he never raise his voice or raise his hand to protect the administration of the city, if the city was in any danger?

Never once did he refer to this until he began to coin his

notoriety into money; then this great patriot talked about something that never happened.

*   *   *

Is Ole Hanson hard to understand? Is he? Doesn't he show, all over him, the marks of a cheap poser? Doesn't he show all over him evidence of a lightheaded notoriety hunter? Think of it, gentlemen. Imagine one of you. Suppose you had been the hero of this bloody strike. Suppose you have preserved civilization and Americanism, because you were such a great and such a brave and such a noble mayor. Suppose that you had bared your breast to this mob that opens up milk stations and eating houses and carefully guards the peace of the city. Suppose that you had earned the plaudits of your fellow-men and the encomiums of the press. Suppose that you had done that and suppose that you had been heralded by state's attorneys as the great savior of the world; what would you have done?

Well, I fancy you would have stuck to your job. I fancy you would have stayed right there and run the job. But not Ole, oh no, not Ole. When he was advertised from one end of America to another for his fool proclamation because he was the jumping-jack mayor of Seattle, when his advertising was worth thousands in lecture courses, he forthwith lays down his job and leaves Seattle to go to the dogs, or to the workingmen, as the case might be.

The captain deserts the army, and the pilot gets off the ship and lets Seattle go to the devil while he rakes in the shekels.

Now, that is Ole; that is Ole Hanson, the cheap vaudeville performer.

If there was a museum down here on Clark Street, that is where you would find him this afternoon, with the stuffed white horse that figured in the Cronin case.

He left the mayoralty of Seattle to make seventy thousand dollars a year lecturing. We asked him why he did it. What did he say?

Why, he said he needed the money.

That is a fine excuse for a patriot, and pretty near all of the professional patriots need the money; that is the reason they are professional patriots—they need the money.

And that shocked even Frank Comerford. This great patriot left the city in the hands of a mob, because he needed the money; so Frank tried to help him out by asking him how many children he had, and he said he had nine children and three grandchildren.

Well, of course, if a man has nine children and three grandchildren, he might do anything to get a living, even come down here and lie, and I suppose that is the theory of his examination.

Nine children and three grandchildren, and yet he probably had almost all of them when he got the people to elect him mayor, and as quick as he got some fame and some notoriety that he could work into cash he left his job and took the cash.

Now, gentlemen, you can take his story if you want to, but I will undertake to say that in any ordinary case, where the feelings and passions of men are not involved, a story like this would not be looked at for a single minute.

And what did we show about that strike?

Why, we even converted the counsel on the other side, which was some job, gentlemen.

I don't think we converted their reason; we just put them in a position where they thought it would be foolish to tell you anything else, that is all.

*　　*　　*

Well now, gentlemen, I fancy you people know something about strikes. You do if you have lived long in Chicago or in any civilized community. There will be strikes until the industrial system is changed, if it ever is changed, which it probably never will be.

Counsel insists that the Communist Labor party is seeking control of industry. Is there any reason on earth why the poor should not control industry if they can? I submit there is none. If I thought they could do with it what many of these dreamers think they can do, I would say, speed the day. But whether they can or not, they have a right to try.

But my clients despise the ballot. Gentlemen, you would be slaves today if you had depended on voting. Men might never vote and they might get their rights, and they might vote forever, and be slaves. Men may take their choice of methods; so long as we have the semblance of freedom in the world, they may do either, they may do both, and they may do neither. If you gentlemen only got what you voted for, you would get mighty little. Voting is a habit, sometimes wise, and sometimes unwise. I generally vote when there is something important. I sometimes vote, but for the life of me, I do not know where my vote ever brought results. Of course you cannot be a professional patriot unless you are terribly strong for voting. Voting came directly from God Almighty. The man who gets something he does not vote for, is a sinner. Of course, it is all right to vote for something you do not get; but you must never get anything you do not vote for.

I say again, that a strike, a general strike or a special strike, is perfectly lawful. If a general strike results in violence, you may punish the violence, and that is all. It may be violence will result from a strike. Violence often comes where the feelings of men are deeply roused on questions that affect large masses of men. We are made that way; but you cannot stop the progress of the world because something is liable to happen, any more than you can stop the building of a skyscraper because somebody is sure to get killed while it is building. That is incidental to it; and if there has to be bloodshed because of changes, that is no reason why the changes should not come. If you take out of the history of the world all the progress that has come through violence, you would not have enough state's attorneys left to send men to jail for striking. Men would still be using clubs and living in caves. The world moves in wonderfully mysterious ways and the logic of lawyers never was the logic of the universe. A lawyer might want to make the Mississippi Valley fertile and rich and productive, and he would pass a law; but nature sixty, seventy, one hundred thousand years ago sent a glacier down through the valley which ground and pulverized the soil to make it ready for the homes of men. Nature works one way and lawyers work another. Lawyers sometimes think they are the bosses, but nature is the boss; and if lawyers had sense enough to conform their endeavors to natural lines, they would not make such fools of themselves. They would not be everlastingly flying in the face of what must be.

Now, what about a general strike and what about changing the conditions of industry and forms of institutions in any way except by pushing a ballot into a box? Now, gentlemen, I insist that you have a perfect right to change any law or custom or institution by a strike the same as by a ballot. Let us see. It seems to be the theory of counsel that strikes must be confined to raising the pay or shortening the hours or changing the conditions of workingmen. That is not the law and never was the law. I have the right to go out and urge the people of the United States never to do another day's work until the Eighteenth Amendment is repealed, and I would do it if I thought I could get them to stop. I have the right to urge men not to work until any law is changed. It has been done over and over and over in the history of the world, and it will be done more and more.

Does man live by the ballot alone? How many of you men are members of unions? Most of you have the eight-hour law. Did you wait to vote to get it? Did you get it by any vote you ever cast? I say no. How did they get the eight-hour day in this country? I have read the history of it. I was present with some of it. I know how it came about. I know it came by workingmen laying down their tools and saying, we will no longer work until we get an eight-hour day. Not only did they get an eight-hour day in this manner, but that is the way they got the fifteen-hour day; that is the way they got the twelve-hour day; that is the way they got the ten-hour day and then the eight-hour day; not by voting, but by laying down their tools; and then let me tell you what happened. After that was over and after the victory was won, then these time-servers, these politicians who make up the legislatures of most of the states in the Union, in order to get the union vote, passed laws making an eight-hour workday. No law was passed until after the victory was won.

We have now pretty generally an eight-hour working day in America; sometime we will have a shorter one. I don't know when. Personally I do not care when, but we will have a shorter one, but none of those eight-hour working days ever came by legislation. Men used to toil ten, twelve and fifteen hours for the smallest amount that would keep body and soul together. Gentlemen, we had an illustration of it on this jury. Half of the men excused from jury service were men who had been only to the fourth grade in school; in this great city, in this great land, where you can vote four or five times a year if you want —half of them, almost half of them, had not passed the fourth grade, and not one out of ten had ever had a chance to read or study since they had left the common school. I want to know whether any of you people who work for wages, which is most of you, and who have a better chance than your ancestors had, whether you are thanking God for the politicians who gave it to you. If you do you are silly. I want to know whether you ever voted these wages to yourself, or did you go out and get them. Did you get your friends to stand together and say, we will not go down in the mine and dig coal for men unless we have enough for ourselves and our families, and unless we have reasonable hours to work and reasonable conditions of life. We will not risk our lives on engines unless we have reasonable appliances; unless we have reasonable wages; unless we have reasonable hours. And you got it by fighting for it. You could not get it by voting. There are too many law-makers. There is Congress, the Senate and the President and the Supreme Court and the state legislature and another supreme court and lawyers and everybody else to be satisfied before you get it, and you would die before you could vote it to yourself.

That is the way you have got it in the past, and that is the way you will get it in the future; and you gentlemen can make the most of it. Now, I don't need to tell you gentlemen that it has been gained that way; you all know it. I don't object to voting; I seldom miss a chance; but there are many things in this world besides voting; many, many things, and voting is a very small part of a man's life, and very, very few are the things he gets from it; but the way these gentlemen talk one would think that all you had to do was to go out and vote. You do not even need to be educated, or to study. You do not even need to understand political questions. The education of voters is much more important than the voting. The actions of men are much more important than voting.

Now, gentlemen, strikes have often been called in industrial matters, and everybody knows it. They have been called to affect political matters just the same. Belgium had two recent strikes. I cannot tell you the second time, but as I recall, it was about five or six years ago they had the last one and the other one a few years before. Only a very small fraction of the Belgian people could vote. Of course, those were the blue-bloods who were extremely patriotic; workingmen did not vote. They worked. They did not even vote for a change of law because they could not vote. It might have made a difference or might not, if they had. What did they do? They struck. They said, we will work no longer until we get a chance to vote. We will strike. Just as our ancestors struck at Boston Harbor. We said we would send no more taxes to England until we were represented in England, and we struck by force and violence and "unlawful" means.

The Belgians went out as a man and parliament was called together and gave them limited suffrage, just as limited as they dared, but of course, limited; two years passed and they struck again. About two years before the war, they struck for complete suffrage and refused to work until they got it; and parliament was called together and they got it because they struck. A political strike, and not a drop of blood was shed, not a drop. If men had died, none the less the strike would have been legal; none the less it would have been just; none the less it would have worked.

*　　*　　*

In many of the civilized countries of the world, often in the United States, purely political strikes have been called. One had just been threatened with the railroad workers until a commission was appointed to settle their grievances again; and they called off their strike until the commission was appointed. They waited faithfully until they had the time to settle it, and it was settled by a political commission appointed to prevent it. Why, gentlemen, the idea that human progress rests on the ballot is so absurd that no thinking man ever conceived it. Men lived in this world long before they voted. Men tilled the soil and dug in the mines and felled the trees, raised families and built up a civilization without the ballot; and they can build up a civilization and keep what they have and hold it even in spite of it. Nothing takes the place of work, of energy, of devotion, of standing for your rights, of individual action. When this country or any people sees fit to give up all the things which have brought America the wealth and power she has, and which has brought our individual workmen what power they have; when they see fit to give it up and trust only to the ballot, they are lost, and every intelligent man knows that they are lost. It is good in its place, but its place is secondary to the efforts of men; its place comes after education; its place comes after organization; it comes after all the forces that have made us great and that have made us free. These are the things that count. Gentlemen, my clients are condemned here because they said in their platform that while they voted, they believed the ballot was secondary to education and organization. All right, gentlemen, you have your views about it, but my clients are right, and you jurors, through your daily life, and daily conduct, and in your relations to society, know it well. Education, organization with your fellow-man, for your industries and your institutions, these are the things that you rely upon for your life and your progress and the progress of the society in which you live, and everybody knows it who has tried to think of it or who cares to think.

A question was asked by the prosecutors of you jurors as to whether you believed in "legal freedom." For God's sake, tell me what is "legal freedom." It is a tricky catch-phrase that has ever been used to enslave men. What is "legal freedom"? Everybody always had "legal freedom." The men who were roasted to death by the Spanish Inquisition had "legal freedom." That is, they had all the freedom that the law gave them. The old men and the old women of America who were hung for witchcraft, enjoyed "legal freedom." No man who ever knew the meaning of that word "freedom" ever attached to it the word "legal." "Freedom" is "freedom," and nothing is done by a government that is not legal. If it is not legal, they make it legal; and men in the past who had their tongues pulled out, who were pierced with red-hot irons, who were boiled in oil, who were tied to stakes, who were bent on the rack and tortured until they died, who had every limb torn from them, who had their nails pulled out and splinters run into their flesh, all were enjoying "legal freedom" while they were tortured and killed. That is what you will enjoy if in this country of ours the evil forces back of this prosecution can have their way and provide their kind of "freedom." The time will come very soon when America will be ashamed of her cowardly attempt to send men to jail under laws of this kind; ashamed of the suppression of freedom of thought and freedom of speech which is making a madhouse of a once free land.

My clients are abused because the Communist Labor party expressed sympathy for the I.W.W. I have read more or less about the Industrial Workers of the World. I know where the newspapers have placed them. They have been so often prosecuted and condemned that most men in America hesitate to sympathize with them; and yet, gentlemen, they have done a work for a class of workers that no other labor organizations could do or ever did do; and if you have read the stories in the *Atlantic Monthly,* or even in our daily papers, you have seen that these men have organized the transient laborers, the men who were taking a temporary job at this, that and the other kind of work, and could not be members of the old organizations because they did not stay long enough in a place, men with no support who were imposed on in a thousand different ways. They have brought this transient labor together. Only recently an investigation has been made by the American Loyal Legion, and it reported that they had done a much-needed work in providing decent places where men could live and decent conditions for people who had no chance.

Now, about shop committees and mass action in the shops: What is a labor union for except to connect up for the mass action of its members? Why, gentlemen, you must have lived in the Dark Ages. Do you not know about shop committees? Do you not know that in most lines of industry that have shown the greatest progress, every organization has its shop committee? And almost every question is put up to that shop committee, and unless that shop committee can agree with the employer it is submitted to arbitration. These men are dealing openly with their employers in this way, and many, many of them have their shop committees all over the United States. Mass action by shop committees—when did this become wicked? When did it transpire that because somebody advocated mass action by shop committees that we will send him to jail? All right, gentlemen, there they are. If you think it would help matters, why, it is all in your hands.

And, gentlemen, the conquest of the State, what of it? Why should not the workingman make a conquest of the power of the State? That is what they have been talking about trying to do; it is what everybody has tried to do. I fancy in this general mix-up the workingman has never had a chance at the power of the State; no organization could believe in the conquest of the power of the State unless it believed in the State. Unless it wanted to use that organization and believed in it. Is there any more reason why the workingman should not make the conquest of the State than any other part of society? Why should these men be sent to jail because they wanted to make the conquest of the power of the State? Every political party in America is trying to do it, and is doing it. The Republican party is now very busy making the conquest of the power of the State, and doing everything it can think of that they may make the conquest of power. The Socialist party has always done it; the Democrats have done it when they were out and tried to keep it when they were in. My clients' policy is just like the policy of everyone else, excepting this—they think they would use it for the benefit of the workingman. Perhaps even if these men did make the conquest of the power of the State, their dreams would not come true; I cannot tell, but they have a right to try; they have a right to think, they have a right to proselyte, they have the right to their opinion and to make their opinion heard. This is what I plead for, and I am not interested in whether their opinions are right or wrong. If they are wrong, the American people under free discussion can find the wrong; and if by any chance these opinions shall convert the United States, then the United States needs converting. The prosecution has taken these phrases, which are innocent, which are in common use, which are used by every political party, which are used in all campaigns, which are absolutely harmless —and have twisted them into damning phrases that this jury might send these men to jail.

I might prophesy that the world will change one way or another. I might prophesy that good will shall sometime abide with man to such an extent that we shall all dwell together in unity and peace. I might prophesy that sometime on healing wings the dove would descend upon the earth and there would be no more wars nor rumors of wars; that every man would love his fellow-man and the whole world seek the highest good of all; where want shall be forever banished; where there shall be no more ignorance and no more greed; where there shall be no children working in industries that great institutions may get rich; where there shall be no poverty; where disease will be conquered; where there will be that peace and good will on earth that the religious have always said prevailed in heaven. I might prophesy. I don't know whether it is coming or not. I rather suspect it is not; if it does come, I fancy, gentlemen, I will be too dead to know anything about it. At least I will be so blind I cannot see it, but I might prophesy it.

I can make another prophecy. It has been made by sociologists, by captains of industry, by bankers, by preachers, by politicians, by labor leaders—I can make a prophecy that even this country which I love more than any other in spite of the faults which I believe she has, that even this country, through the greed of wealth, ever seeking and reaching and grabbing more and more, taking from you and from me, from the hungry children that toil in mills; taking from the consumers of the world until nothing is left; taking as they would be taking now except for the rebels who oppose them: I can prophesy that they will do here what they did in Russia; will crush the workingman in darkness and night, until some day America will see the greatest and bloodiest revolution that the world has ever known. I can prophesy that, and it has been prophesied again and again in America, and I would be well within my rights if I announce this dream. It may come and it may not. Any dream or every dream may be true or false. I would be simply saying that I see the danger that this may come. This is not urging you gentlemen to go and get your gun and get it quick and go out tonight and take the City Hall. It is not urging anyone to force and violence. It is giving my opinion, and I still have the right of an American citizen to express my opinion, at least if no spy or prosecutor is looking—I still have that right.

I do not know what the future holds in store for us. Life is not all a summer's dream, whether it is the individual or national life. We are born. We are tossed on the sea of fate. We are driven here and we are driven there. We have our joys and our pains. We have our pleasure and our distress. We die and no man knows where he is bound, or whether there is a port. We live on faith and we live on hope and we nerve ourselves to stand the hard rebuffs of life; we take it as it is, and nations are only aggregations of men.

I have always loved this country. I love its broad prairies, its great mountains, its noble rivers, its dense forests, its wealth of mines, hidden in the earth; I love the freedom that has come from new ideas, from a Constitution made by rebels and protected by rebels, from a Constitution born in strife and tempest and rebellion. I love it for what it has been, materially and spiritually; I love it because over its vast areas one can find a free breath of pure air, because of its intellectual freedom; here one may live; he may speak the thought that is in him; he may develop and grow; if he will he may be free; and without freedom nothing is of value. I love it for these and for these I will fight. I know the danger of security and ease and power. I know that freedom produces wealth and then wealth destroys freedom. I know that the nation that is not watchful of its liberty will lose it. I know that the individual that will not stand for his rights will have no rights, and I believe the first duty of every

American citizen is to protect himself and his country in all the liberties we have and all that we can get.

I want to say to you that all through the ages the blood of the martyrs stains the pathway of the human race. Every step in progress has been marked by blood and tears. Nothing ever came to the old world that was worth the while that did not cost life and blood and anguish of body and of soul. Martyrs have filled the world with graves. They have died for what they thought and spoke, but the monuments of the world have been built to them. Little detectives and prosecutors and courts and juries have condemned them to death. Still, the human race has moved forward over their mangled forms, and its path has been lighted by the burning bodies of these devoted ones.

I do not know what will befall freedom now, but I know that the future is ours. I know that history makes clear the injustice of the past. I know that the dead have risen triumphant over the judgment of juries and courts.

Now, gentlemen, no man can speak freely what is in him if he fears the jail. You cannot write freely with manacles on your hands. You cannot speak or write or think freely with detectives on your track. You can only be yourself in the open, clear light of day; giving what the infinite says through you; giving it freely as it comes. There can be no free thought without free speech. Of what avail to think if I may not write or speak?

Gentlemen, I do not pretend to know the future that is in store for America. I know that nations, like individuals, are born and live their time and die. We are young. Our life should be long. While we live we should preserve all the freedom that we have and strive for more.

We should protect our Constitution as our fathers gave it. Protect it not in the letter but in the soul. I do not know what the future holds in store for America or the human race. I am willing to take my chance, and I want to take my chances by leaving every man free to bring his contribution to the world; by leaving every man free to express his thought; by leaving every man free to throw his opinions into the great crucible that we may work it out. This is freedom. It is the freedom we have believed in. It is the freedom we have worked for, and, gentlemen, it is the freedom I urge you to protect and save. I do not urge it for myself or for my clients—they are the smallest concern to me; but I urge you for the sake of your common country, for the sake of what is even nearer and dearer than that, the liberty of men, the freedom of the human soul, which alone makes life worth the living; I ask you to say that men shall be free, and if in the open discussions between free men my clients triumph, well and good; they ought to triumph; and if they are wrong their theories must go down. I urge you to stand for the right of men to think; for the right to speak boldly and unafraid; the right to be master of their souls; the right to live free and to die free. There is no other cause that is so much worth while. There is no other sentiment or emotion that ever moved the human soul as priceless as this.

Gentlemen, I submit this case, assuring you that my clients are my last concern; I ask you to do your part in the great cause of human freedom, for which men have ever fought and died.

THE TRIAL had lasted ten weeks. The jury was out only a few hours. They returned a verdict of Guilty, sentencing the defendants to terms ranging from one to five years in addition to fines. Lloyd was given a one-to-five-year sentence and a fine of $2,000.

Frank S. Reid, jury foreman, told newspapermen after the trial: "This is our country. It is the best country in the world. It is good enough for us. If others do not think it is good enough for them, let them get out and stay out.

"Although no evidence of overt acts was presented," he continued, "we were certain that had the defendants carried their revolutionary program to its logical conclusion, or had it run its course, a state of anarchy would have been brought about."

The case was appealed to the Illinois Supreme Court. The lower court was affirmed. But Chief Justice Orrin Carter of the State Supreme Court wrote a "vigorous" dissenting opinion.

Said the Justice: "Under the Illinois Act of 1919, it would seem that provisions were designed not so much perhaps to punish those who commit violent acts to overthrow the government, but rather it was drafted for the purpose of forbidding any person who held opinions distasteful to the majority of our citizens to express these opinions.

"Is there anything that can take the place of open and free discussion in a country like ours, that is controlled by public opinion? Is it better to drive such people into the woods, the corners, and the dark places of the world, to conspire in silence and secretly? Is it not best to allow free discussion in this country of all public questions as to the necessity of changing laws and the form of government?"

Quoting from this opinion, Illinois Governor Len Small on November 29, 1922 pardoned sixteen of the defendants before they had served a day of their sentence.

Though twenty men were originally arrested and convicted, L. E. Katterfeld who fled to Russia and Max Bedacht forfeited bond for nonappearance in court; Edwin Firth died during the trial; and Oscar Jesse Brown died before the pardon was announced.

You Can't Teach That!

THE SCOPES EVOLUTION CASE

Dayton, Tennessee, 1925

3,000 AT
APE TRIAL
GET THRILL

[Headline, Louisville (Ky.) Courier-Journal, July 21, 1925]

"ISN'T IT DIFFICULT to realize that a trial of this kind is possible in the twentieth century in the United States of America?" Clarence Darrow commented at one point during the "evolution trial" to Arthur Garfield Hays, who was one of several lawyers who had joined Darrow in the defense of Scopes.

But there it was! Dayton, Tennessee, in the summer of 1925, on the front pages of newspapers throughout the country! And even the newest media of communication—radio—broadcast from this little town.

It was in Robinson's drugstore on the main street of Dayton that the whole thing actually started. George Rappelyea, 31, a mining engineer, Thomas Scopes, 24-year-old high-school teacher, and several others were discussing the new "anti-evolution" law when Rappelyea suggested that Dayton act as a test case and Scopes teach the theory of evolution in his class.

The new law read: "Be it enacted by the General Assembly of the State of Tennessee, that it shall be unlawful for any teacher in any of the universities, normals and all other public schools of the State, which are supported in whole or in part by the public school funds of the State, to teach any theory that denies the story of the divine creation of man as taught in the Bible, and to teach instead that man has descended from a lower order of animals."

Mr. Hays reported in his book Let Freedom Ring: "The sensational character of the undertaking which would make Dayton world-famous was not an unwelcome feature. No time was to be lost. Other communities, once they caught the idea, would compete for the attraction of a trial involving science, the Bible and Tennessee."

Scopes agreed to test this law; he discussed evolution in his class. His friends—as agreed—called the local authorities. The high-school teacher was indicted, and the prelude to the "monkey trial" was completed.

However, so hurriedly was the charge against Scopes drawn up that on the opening day of the trial a new grand jury had to be called to correct a technicality in the indictment.

Events moved fast. William Jennings Bryan, who was now living in Florida, volunteered to help the prosecution. It was the Great Commoner, more than any other man, who, perhaps, was largely responsible for the anti-evolution law. Bryan headed the fundamentalist movement. He stumped the South urging legislatures to pass such laws.

In addition to Bryan for the State were Attorney General E. T. Stewart, Ben and J. Gordon McKenzie, Sue and Herbert Hicks, and W. J. Bryan, Jr.

The American Civil Liberties Union which had offered its services to anyone testing the anti-evolution law, sent Mr. Hays, Dudley Field Malone and Darrow to Dayton. In his more than fifty years of legal practice, the Scopes trial was the only time Darrow ever volunteered his services in a case. In fact, the trial cost Darrow about $2,000 of his own money for expenses.

Bryan felt he was fighting atheism and agnosticism. To Darrow—son of Amirus, furniture maker, town undertaker and "village infidel"—"Education was in danger from the source that always hampered it—religious fanaticism."

*   *   *

The quiet little town became a combined Coney Island, revival meeting and circus. Hot dog and lemonade vendors, fundamentalists, IWWs, anarchists, native Tennesseans, revivalists, Holy Rollers, free-thinkers, artists, and more than 100 newspapermen came to Dayton. Western Union installed twenty-two telegraph wires in the city for the use of the newspapermen.

Dayton was ready! Signs greeted visitors: "Read your Bible," "Where will you spend eternity?" "God is love," "Sweethearts come to Jesus."

The Eighteenth Tennessee Circuit Court, Judge John T. Raulston presiding, opened with prayer in a mobbed courtroom, on an unbearably hot Friday, July 10, 1925. "Not just an ordinary prayer, but an argumentative one, directed straight at the defense," wrote Mr. Hays.

Eleven of the twelve men finally selected on the jury went to church regularly; six of them were Baptists, four Methodists, and one a member of Disciples of Christ.

The townsmen all wanted to get on the jury, to have a part in the "Big Story" datelined Dayton. But the prospective jurors were to miss the highlights of the event, because most of the dramatic moments were arguments of law from which they were excluded, rather than the hearing of evidence. They were not to be in the courtroom when Darrow examined Bryan in the closing days of the trial.

Nor were they to hear Darrow's arraignment of the law.

"I think this case will be remembered because it is the first case of this sort since we stopped trying people in America for witchcraft, because here we have done our best to turn back the tide that has sought to force itself upon this modern world, of testing every fact in science by a religious dictum."

I F THE COURT PLEASE. I shall always remember that this Court is the first one that ever gave me the great title of "Colonel" and I hope it will stick to me when I get back North.

THE COURT: I want you to take it back to your home with you, Colonel.

MR. DARROW: That is what I am trying to do.

But, so far as coming from other cities is concerned, why, Your Honor, it is easy here. I came from Chicago, and my friend Malone, and friend Hays, came from New York, and on the other side we have a distinguished and very pleasant gentleman who came from California and another who is prosecuting this case, and who is responsible for this foolish, mischievous and wicked act, who comes from Florida.

This case we have to argue is a case at law, and hard as it is for me to bring my mind to conceive it, almost impossible as it is to put my mind back into the sixteenth century, I am going to argue it as if it was serious, and as if it was a death struggle between two civilizations.

We have been informed that the legislature has the right to prescribe the course of study in the public schools. Within reason, they no doubt have. They could not prescribe a course of study, I am inclined to think, under your constitution, which omitted arithmetic and geography and writing. Neither, under the rest of the constitution, if it shall remain in force in the state, could they prescribe it if the course of study was only to teach religion; because several hundred years ago, when our people believed in freedom, and when no men felt so sure of their own sophistry that they were willing to send a man to jail who did not believe them, the people of Tennessee adopted a constitution, and they made it broad and plain, and said that the people of Tennessee should always enjoy religious freedom in its broadest terms. So I assume that no legislature could fix a course of study which violated that. For instance, suppose the legislature should say, "We think the religious privileges and duties of the citizens of Tennessee are much more important than education; we agree with the distinguished governor of the state, if religion must go, or learning must go, why, let learning go." I do not know how much it would have to go, but let it go. "And therefore, we will establish a course in the public schools of teaching that the Christian religion as unfolded in the Bible, is true, and that every other religion, or mode or system of ethics, is false; and to carry that out, no person in the public schools shall be permitted to read or hear anything except Genesis, *Pilgrim's Progress*, Baxter's *Saint Rest*, and *In His Image*." Would that be constitutional? If it is, the Constitution is a lie and a snare and the people have forgotten what liberty means.

I remember, long ago, Mr. Bancroft wrote this sentence, which is true: "That it is all right to preserve freedom in constitutions, but when the spirit of freedom has fled from the hearts of the people, then its matter is easily sacrificed under law." And so it is, unless there is left enough of the spirit of freedom in the state of Tennessee, and in the United States, there is not a single line of any constitution that can withstand bigotry and ignorance when it seeks to destroy the rights of the individual; and bigotry and ignorance are ever active. Here, we find today, as brazen and as bold an attempt to destroy learning as was ever made in the Middle Ages, and the only difference is we have not provided that they shall be burned at the stake, but there is time for that, Your Honor. We have to approach these things gradually.

Now, let us see what we claim with reference to this law. If this proceeding both in form and substance, can prevail in this court, then, Your Honor, no law—no matter how foolish, wicked, ambiguous, or ancient—but can come back to Tennessee. All the guarantees go for nothing. All of the past has gone, will be forgotten—if this can succeed.

I am going to begin with some of the simpler reasons why it is absolutely absurd to think that this statute, indictment, or any part of the proceedings in this case are legal; and I think the sooner we get rid of it in Tennessee the better for the peace of Tennessee, and the better for the pursuit of knowledge in the world.

* * *

The statute should be comprehensible. It should not be written in Chinese anyway. It should be in passing English, so that common human beings would understand what it meant, and so a man would know whether he is liable to go to jail when he is teaching; not so ambiguous as to be a snare or a trap to get someone who does not agree with you. It should be plain, simple and easy. Does this statute state what you shall teach and what you shall not? Oh, no! Oh, no! Not at all. Does it say you cannot teach the earth is round because Genesis says it is flat? No. Does it say you cannot teach that the earth is millions of ages old, because the account in Genesis makes it less than six thousand years old? Oh, no. It doesn't state that. If it did you could understand it. It says you shan't teach any theory of the origin of man that is contrary to the divine theory contained in the Bible.

Now let us pass up the word "divine"! No legislature is strong enough in any state in the Union to characterize and pick any book as being divine. Let us take it as it is. What is the Bible? Your Honor, I have read it myself. I might read it more or more wisely. Others may understand it better. Others may think they understand it better when they do not. But in a general way I know what it is. I know there are millions of people in the world who look on it as being a divine book, and I have not the slightest objection to it. I know there are millions of people in the world who derive consolation in their times of trouble and solace in times of distress from the Bible. I would be pretty near the last one in the world to do anything or take any action to take it away. I feel just exactly the same toward the religious creed of every human being who lives. If anybody finds anything in this life that brings them consolation and health and happiness I think they ought to have it, whatever they get. I haven't any fault to find with them at all. But what is it?

The Bible is not one book. The Bible is made up of 66 books written over a period of about 1,000 years, some of them very early and some of them comparatively late. It is a book primarily of religion and morals. It is not a book of science. Never was and was never meant to be. Under it there is nothing prescribed that would tell you how to build a railroad or a steamboat or to make anything that would advance civilization. It is not a textbook or a text on chemistry. It is not big enough to be. It is not a book on geology; they knew nothing about geology. It is not a book on biology; they knew nothing about it. It is not a work on evolution; that is a mystery. It is not a work on astronomy. The man who looked out at the universe and studied the heavens had no thought but that the earth was the center of the universe. But we know better than that. We know that the sun is the center of the solar system. And that there are an infinity of other systems around about us. They thought the sun went around the earth and gave us light and gave us night. We know better. We know the earth turns on its axis to produce days and nights. They thought the earth was created 4,004 years before the Christian Era. We know better. I doubt if there is a person in Tennessee who does not know better. They told it the best they knew. And while suns may change all you may learn of chemistry, geometry and mathematics, there are no doubt certain primitive, elemental instincts in the organs of man that remain the same. He finds out what he can and yearns to know more and supplements his knowledge with hope and faith.

That is the province of religion and I haven't the slightest fault to find with it. Not the slightest in the world. One has one thought and one another, and instead of fighting each other as in the past, they should support and help each other. Let's see, now. Can Your Honor tell what is given as the origin of man as shown in the Bible? Is there any human being who can tell us? There are two conflicting accounts in the first two chapters. There are scattered all through it various acts and ideas. But to pass that up for the sake of argument, no teacher in any school in the state of Tennessee can know that he is violating a law, but must test every one of its doctrines by the Bible, must he not? You cannot say two times two equals four, or a man is an educated animal if evolution is forbidden. It does not specify what you cannot teach, but says you cannot teach anything that conflicts with the Bible. Then just imagine making it a criminal code that is so uncertain and impossible that every man must be sure that he has read everything in the Bible and not only read it but understands it, or he might violate the criminal code. Who is the chief mogul that can tell us what the Bible means? He or they should write a book and make it plain and distinct, so we would know. Let us look at it. There are in America at least 500 different sects or churches, all of which quarrel with each other on the importance and nonimportance of certain things or the construction of certain passages. All along the line they do not agree among themselves and cannot agree among themselves. They never have and probably never will. There is a great division between the Catholics and the Protestants. There is such a disagreement that my client, who is a schoolteacher, not only must know the subject he is teaching, but he must know everything about the Bible in reference to evolution. And he must be sure that he expresses this right or else some fellow will come along here, more ignorant perhaps than he, and say, "You made a bad guess and I think you have committed a crime." No criminal statute can rest that way. There is not a chance for it, for this criminal statute and every criminal statute must be plain and simple. If Mr. Scopes is to be indicted and prosecuted because he taught a wrong theory of the origin of life, why not tell him what he must teach? Why not say that you must teach that man was made of the dust; and still stranger, not directly from the dust, without taking any chances on it, whatever, that Eve was made out of Adam's rib? You will know what I am talking about.

Now my client must be familiar with the whole book, and must know all about all of these warring sects of Christians and know which of them is right and which wrong, in order that he will not commit crime. Nothing was heard of all that until the fundamentalists got into Tennessee. I trust that when they prosecute their wildly made charge upon the intelligence of some other sect they may modify this mistake and state in simple language what was the account contained in the Bible that could not be taught. So, unless other sects have something to do with it, we must know just what we are charged with doing. This statute, I say, Your Honor, is indefinite and uncertain. No man could obey it, no court could enforce it and it is bad for indefiniteness and uncertainty. Look at that indictment up there. If that is a good indictment I never saw a bad one. Now, I do not expect, Your Honor, my opinion to go because it is my opinion; because I am like all lawyers who practice Law—I have made mistakes in my judgment of law. I will probably make more of them. I insist that you might just as well hand my client a piece of blank paper and then send the sheriff after him to jail him.

The State by constitution is committed to the doctrine of education, committed to schools. It is committed to teaching and I assume when it is committed to teaching it is committed to teaching the truth—ought to be anyhow—plenty of people to do the other. It is committed to teaching literature and science. My friend has suggested that literature and science might conflict. I cannot quite see how, but that is another question. But that indicates the policy of the state of Tennessee and wherever it is used in construing the unconstitutionality of this act it can only be used as an indication of what the State meant and you could not pronounce a statute void on it.

*　❁　❁

Now, let's see, Your Honor, there isn't any court in the world that can uphold the spirit of the law by simply upholding its letters. I read somewhere—I don't know where—that the letter killeth, but the spirit giveth life. I think I read it out of *The Prince of Peace*. I don't know where I did, but I read it. If this section of the constitution which guarantees religious liberty in Tennessee cannot be sustained in the spirit it cannot be sustained in the letter. What does it mean? What does it mean? I know two intelligent people can agree only for a little distance, like a company walking along a road. They may go together a few blocks and then one branches off. The remainder go together a few more blocks and another branches off, and still further someone else branches off; and the human minds are just that way, provided they are free, of course. The fundamentalists may be put in a trap so they cannot think differently if at all, probably not at all, but leave two free minds and they may go together a certain distance, but not all the way together. There are no two human machines alike and no two human beings have the same experiences, and their ideas of life and philosophy grow out of their construction of the experiences that we meet on our journey through life. It is impossible, if you leave freedom in the world, to mold the opinions of one man upon the opinions of another—only tyranny can do it—and your constitutional provision, providing a freedom of religion, was meant to meet that emergency. I will go further—there is nothing else—since man—I don't know whether I dare say *evolved*—still, this isn't a school—since man was created out of the dust of the earth—out of hand—there is nothing else, Your Honor, that has caused the difference of opinion, of bitterness, of hatred, of war, of cruelty, that religion has caused. With that, of course, it has given consolation to millions.

But it is one of those particular things that should be left solely between the individual and his Maker, or his God, or whatever takes expression with him, and it is no one else's concern.

How many creeds and cults are there this whole world over? No man could enumerate them. At least about five hundred different Christian creeds, all made up of differences, Your Honor, every one of them, and these subdivided into small differences, until they reach every member of every congregation. Because to think is to differ. And then there are any number of creeds older and any number of creeds younger, than the Christian creed, any number of them; the world has had them forever. They have come and they have gone, they have abided their time and have passed away; some of them are here still, some may be here forever, but there has been a multitude, due to the multitude and manifold differences in human beings. And it was meant by the constitutional convention of Tennessee to leave these questions of religion between man and whatever he worshiped, to leave him free. Has the Mohammedan any right to stay here and cherish his creed? Has the Buddhist a right to live here and cherish his creed? Can the Chinaman who comes here to wash our clothes, can he bring his joss and worship it? Is there any man that holds a religious creed, no matter where he came from, or how old it is or how false it is, is there any man that can be prohibited by any act of the legislature of Tennessee? Impossible? The constitution of Tennessee, as I understand, was copied from the one that Jefferson wrote, so clear, simple, direct, to encourage the freedom of religious opinion, and said in substance, that no act shall ever be passed to interfere with complete religious liberty. Now is this it or is not this it? What do you say? What does it do? We will say I am a scientist, no, I will take that back; I am a pseudo-scientist, because I believe in evolution; pseudo-scientist named by somebody who neither knows or cares what science is, except to grab it by the throat and throttle it to death. I am a pseudo-scientist, and I believe in evolution. Can a legislative body say, "You cannot read a book or take a lesson, or make a talk on science until you first find out whether you are saying against Genesis"? It can unless that constitutional provision protects me. It can.

Can it say to the astronomer, "You cannot turn your tele-scope upon the infinite planets and suns and stars that fill space, lest you find that the earth is not the center of the universe and there is not any firmament between us and the heaven"? Can it? It could—except for the work of Thomas Jefferson, which has been woven into every state constitution of the Union, and has stayed there like the flaming sword to protect the rights of man against ignorance and bigotry; and when it is permitted to over-whelm them, then we are taken in such a sea of blood and ruin that all the miseries and tortures and carrion of the Middle Ages would be as nothing. They would need to call back these men once more. But are the provisions of the constitutions that they left, are they enough to protect you and me, and every-one else in a land which we thought was free? Now, let us see what it says: "All men have a natural and indefeasible right to worship Almighty God according to the dictates of their own conscience."

That takes care even of the despised modernist, who dares to be intelligent. "That no man can of right be compelled to at-tend, erect or support any place of worship, or to maintain any minister against his consent; that no human authority can in any case whatever control or interfere with the rights of conscience in any case whatever"—that does not mean "whatever," that means, "barring fundamentalist propaganda." It does not mean "whatever" at all times, sometimes maybe—and that "no prefer-ence shall be given by law to any religious establishment or mode of worship." Does it? Could you get any more preference, Your Honor, by law? Let us see. Here is the state of Tennessee, living peacefully, surrounded by its beautiful mountains, each one of which contains evidence that the earth is millions of years old, people quiet, not all agreeing upon any one subject, and not necessary. If I could not live in peace with people I did not agree with, why, what? I could not live. Here is the state of Tennessee going along in its own business, teaching evolution for years, state boards handing out books on evolution, professors in colleges, teachers in schools, lawyers at the bar, physicians, ministers, a great percentage of the intelligent citi-zens of the state of Tennessee evolutionists, have not even thought it was necessary to leave their church. They believed that they could appreciate and understand and make their own simple and human doctrine of the Nazarene, to love their neighbor, be kindly with them, not to place a fine on and not try to send to jail some man who did not believe as they believed, and got along all right with it, too, until something happened. They have not thought it necessary to give up their church, because they believed that all that was here was not made on the first six days of creation, but that it had come by a slow process of developments extending over the ages, that one thing grew out of another. There are people who believed that organic life and the plants and the animals and man and the mind of man, and the religion of man are the subjects of evolution, and they have not got through, and that the God in which they believed did not finish creation on the first day, but that He is still working to make something better and higher still out of human beings, who are next to God, and that evolution has been working forever and will work forever—they believe it.

And along comes somebody who says "we have got to believe it as I believe it. It is a crime to know more than I know." And they publish a law to inhibit learning. Now, what is in the way of it? First, what does the law say? This law says that it shall be a criminal offense to teach in the public schools any account of the origin of man that is in conflict with the divine account in the Bible. It makes the Bible the yardstick to measure every man's intellect, to measure every man's intelligence and to measure every man's learning. Are your mathematics good? Turn to Elijah 1:2 [sic]. Is your philosophy good? See II Samuel 3. Is your astronomy good? See Genesis 2:7. Is your chemistry good? See—well, chemistry, see Deuteronomy 3:6, or anything that tells about brimstone. Every bit of knowledge that the mind has must be submitted to a religious test. Now, let us see, it is a travesty upon language, it is a travesty upon justice, it is a travesty upon the constitution to say that any citizen of Tennessee can be deprived of his rights by a legislative body in the face of the constitution. Tell me, Your Honor, if this is not good, then what? Then, where are we coming out? I want to argue that in connection with another question here which is equally plain.

Of course, I used to hear when I was a boy you could lead a horse to water, but you could not make him drink water. I could lead a man to water, but I could not make him drink, either. And you can close your eyes and you won't see, cannot see, refuse to open your eyes—stick your fingers in your ears and you cannot hear—if you want to. But your life and my life and the life of every American citizen depends after all upon the tolerance and forbearance of his fellow-man. If men are not tolerant, if men cannot respect each other's opinions, if men cannot live and let live, then no man's life is safe, no man's life is safe.

Here is a country made up of Englishmen, Irishmen, Scotch, German, Europeans, Asiatics, Africans, men of every sort and men of every creed and men of every scientific belief. Who is going to begin this sorting out and say, "I shall measure you; I know you are a fool, or worse; I know and I have read a creed telling what I know and I will make people go to Heaven even if they don't want to go with me. I will make them do it." Where is the man that is wise enough to do it?

Let us look at this act, Your Honor. Here is a law which makes it a crime to teach any theory of the origin of man excepting that contained in the divine account, which we find in the Bible. All right. Now that act applies to what? Teachers in the public schools. Now I have seen somewhere a statement of Mr. Bryan's that the fellow that made the pay check had a right to regulate the teachers. All right, let us see. I do not question the right of the legislature to fix the courses of study, but the state of Tennessee has no right under the police power of the State to carve out a law which applies to schoolteachers, a law which is a criminal statute and nothing else; which makes no effort to prescribe the school law or course of study. It says that John Smith who teaches evolution is a criminal if he teaches it in the public schools. There is no question about this act; there is no question where it belongs; there is no question of its origin. Nobody would claim that the act could be passed for a minute excepting that teaching evolution was in the nature of a criminal act; that it smacked of policemen and criminals and jails and grand juries; that it was in the nature of something that was criminal and, therefore, the State should forbid it.

It cannot stand a minute in this court on any theory than that it is a criminal act, simply because they say it contravenes the teaching of Moses without telling us what those teachings are. Now, if this is the subject of a criminal act, then it cannot make a criminal out of a teacher in the public schools and leave a man free to teach it in a private school. It cannot make it criminal for a teacher in the public schools to teach evolution, and for the same man to stand among the hustings and teach it. It cannot make it a criminal act for this teacher to teach evolution and permit books upon evolution to be sold in every store in the state of Tennessee and to permit the newspapers from foreign cities to bring into your peaceful community the horrible utterances of evolution. Oh, no, nothing like that. If the state of Tennessee has any force in this day of fundamentalism, in this day when religious bigotry and hatred is being kindled all over our land, see what can be done?

Now, Your Honor, there is an old saying that nits make lice. I don't know whether you know what it makes possible down here in Tennessee. I know, I was raised in Ohio. It is a good idea to clear the nits, safer and easier.

To strangle puppies is good when they grow up into mad dogs, maybe. I will tell you what is going to happen, and I do not pretend to be a prophet, but I do not need to be a prophet to know. Your Honor knows the fires that have been lighted in America to kindle religious bigotry and hate. You can take judicial notice of them if you cannot of anything else. You know that there is no suspicion which possesses the minds of men like bigotry and ignorance and hatred.

If today you can take a thing like evolution and make it a crime to teach it in the public school, tomorrow you can make it a crime to teach it in the private school, and the next year you can make it a crime to teach it from the hustings or in the church. At the next session you may ban books and the newspapers. Soon you may set Catholic against Protestant and Protestant against Protestant, and try to foist your own religion upon the minds of men. If you can do one you can do the other. Ignorance and fanaticism is ever busy and needs feeding. Always it is feeding and gloating for more. Today it is the public-school teachers, tomorrow the private. The next day the preachers and the lecturers, the magazines, the books, the newspapers. After a while, Your Honor, it is the setting of man against man and creed against creed until, with flying banners and beating drums, we are marching backward to the glorious ages of the sixteenth century when bigots lighted fagots to burn the men who dared to bring any intelligence and enlightenment and culture to the human mind.

ON THE THIRD MORNING of the trial, Darrow objected to court sessions being opened by prayer. He said, "I do not object to the jury or anyone else praying in secret or in private, but I do object to the turning of this courtroom into a meetinghouse in the trial of this case."

Replied the judge in overruling the objection: "I do not want to be unreasonable about anything, but I believe I have a right, I am responsible for the conduct of the court. It has been my custom since I have been a judge to have prayers in the courtroom when it was convenient, and I know of no reason why I should not follow up this custom, so I will overrule the objection."

❧   ❧   ❧

When the jurors finally took their seats for the first time on the fourth day of the trial, the foreman, J. R. Thompson, asked the Court: "If it ain't out of order, I would like to make the request, the unanimous request of the jury, to take up the matter of some electric fans here. The heat is fearful."

MCKENZIE: Nothing would give me greater pleasure than to have them installed, but on account of the depleted state of the treasury, I do not believe the county can do it.

MALONE: I will buy some fans.

COURT: Colonel Thompson, I will divide my fan. Perhaps we can borrow some small fans and place them on the table, Mr. County Judge. Maybe we can place some small fans on the table.

❧   ❧   ❧

The examination of witnesses started. Howard Morgan, a fourteen-year-old student in Scopes's class, testified that Scopes had taught: "The earth was once a hot molten mass, too hot for plant or animal life to exist upon it; in the sea the earth cooled off; there was a little germ of one-cell organism formed and this organism kept on evolving and from this was man." Scopes, said the youth, classified man as a "mammal."

DARROW: Now, what do you mean by classify?

MORGAN: Well, it means classify these animals we mentioned, that men were just the same as them.

DARROW: He did not say a cat was the same as a man?

MORGAN: No, sir: he said that man had reasoning power, that these animals did not.

DARROW: There is some doubt about that.

The defense wanted to present expert testimony. This testimony, Darrow said, would show "first, what evolution is, and second, that any interpretation of the Bible that intelligent men could possibly make is not in conflict with any story of creation, while the Bible, in many ways, is in conflict with every known science, and there isn't a human being on earth who believes it literally. We expect to show that it isn't in conflict with the theory of evolution. We expect to show what evolution is, and the interpretation of the Bible that prevails with men of intelligence who have studied it."

The court ruled against the introduction of the expert testimony. However, the court said, it would permit such testimony to be admitted as affidavits. Whereupon Bryan asked if the State would be able to cross-examine these witnesses who would testify for the "information of the judge."

When Judge Raulston asked Bryan for the purpose of this cross-examination, Darrow interjected: "To show prejudice. Nothing else."

Darrow asked the court to have the remainder of the day off so the defense could draft statements on what they intended to prove. The judge objected, to which Darrow said: "We want to make a statement here of what we expect to prove. I do not understand why every request of the State and every suggestion of the prosecution should meet with an endless loss of time; and a bare suggestion of anything that is perfectly competent on our part should be immediately overruled."

JUDGE RAULSTON: I hope you do not mean to reflect upon the court?

DARROW: Well, Your Honor has the right to hope.

JUDGE RAULSTON: I have a right to do something else perhaps.

DARROW: All right, all right.

This exchange took place on a Friday just before court adjourned.

Monday morning, when court convened, Darrow was cited for contempt.

Later in the day Darrow apologized to the court saying, "I have been practicing law for forty-seven years and I have been pretty busy, and most of the time in court. I have had many a case where I have had to do what I have been doing here—fighting the public opinion of the people, in the community where I was trying the case—even in my own town—and I never yet have in all my time had any criticism by the court for anything I have done in court.

"That is, I have tried to treat the court fairly and a little more than fairly, because when I recognize the odds against me, I try to lean the other way the best I can; and I don't think any such occasion ever arose before in my practice. I am not saying this, Your Honor, to influence you, but to put myself right.

"I do think, however, Your Honor, that I went further than I should have gone. So far as its having been premeditated or made for the purpose of insult to the court, I had not the slightest thought of that. One thing snapped out after another, as other lawyers have done in this case—not, however, where the judge was involved—and apologized for it afterward. So far as the people of Tennessee are concerned, Your Honor suggested that in your opinion—I don't know as I was ever in a community in my life where my religious ideas differed as widely from the great mass as I have found them since I have been in Tennessee. Yet, I came here a perfect stranger and I can say what I have said before: that I have not found upon anybody's part—any citizen here in this town or outside—the slightest discourtesy. I have been treated better, kindlier and more hospitably than I fancy would have been the case in the North, and that is due largely to the ideas that Southern people have, and they are, perhaps, more hospitable than we are up North.

"Now, I certainly meant nothing against the state of Tennessee, which I don't think is in any way involved. Your Honor knows that these things come up in court time and time again, and that it is not unusual perhaps in a case where there is a feeling that grows out of proceedings like this, that some lawyers will overstep the bounds. I am quite certain that I did that. I do not see how Your Honor could have helped taking notice of it, and I have regretted it ever since, on my own account and on account of the profession that I am in, where I have tried to conform to all rules and think I have done it remarkably well. I don't want this court, or any of my brethren down here in Tennessee, to think that I am not mindful of the rules of court, which I am, and mean to be, and I haven't the slightest fault to find with the court. Personally, I don't think it constitutes a contempt, but I am quite certain that the remark should not have been made and the court could not help taking notice of it. I am sorry that I made it ever since I got time to read it, and I want to apologize to the court for it."

His apology was accepted, but not until the judge first delivered a fundamentalist sermon. Said the judge: "My friends, and Colonel Darrow, the Man that I believe came into the world to save man from sin, the Man that died on the cross that man might be redeemed, taught that it was godly to forgive; and were it not for the forgiving nature of Himself I would fear for man. The Savior died on the cross pleading with God for the men who crucified Him. I believe in that Christ. I believe in these principles.

"I accept Colonel Darrow's apology. I am sure his remarks were not premeditated. I am sure that if he had had time to have thought and deliberated he would not have spoken those words. He spoke those words, perhaps, just at a moment when he felt that he had suffered perhaps one of the greatest disappointments of his life when the court had held against him. Taking that view of it, I feel that I am justified in speaking for the people of the great state that I represent when I speak as I do to say to him that we forgive him and we forget it and we commend him to go back home and learn in his heart the words of the Man who said: 'If you thirst come unto Me and I will give thee life.' "

Darrow again created excitement when he asked the judge that a sign reading "Read your Bible," which faced the jury, be removed.

DARROW: Your Honor, I think it my duty to make this motion. Off to the left of where the jury sits a little bit, and about ten feet in front of them, is a large sign about ten feet long reading "Read your Bible," and a hand pointing to it. The word Bible is in large letters, perhaps a foot and a half long, and the printing—

COURT: Hardly that long, I think.

DARROW: Why, we will call it a foot.

COURT: Compromise on a foot.

DARROW: I move that it be removed.

GEN. McKENZIE: If Your Honor please, why should it be removed? It is their defense and stated before the court that they do not deny the Bible, that they expected to introduce proof to make it harmonize. Why should we remove the sign cautioning the people to read the Word of God just to satisfy the others in the case?

COURT: Of course, you know I stand for the Bible, but your son has suggested that we agree to take it down.

GEN. McKENZIE: I do not agree with my son.

MALONE: The house is divided against itself.

J. G. McKENZIE: If Your Honor please, I believe in the Bible as strong as anybody else here, but if that sign is objectionable to the attorneys for the defense, and they do not want to be repeatedly reminded of the fact that they should read their Bible, I think this court ought to remove it.

DARROW: We might agree to get up a sign of equal size on the other side and in the same position reading "Hunter's Biology," or "Read your evolution." This sign can have no effect but to influence this case. I read the Bible myself—more or less—and it is pretty good reading in places.

COURT: If the presence of the sign irritates anyone, or if anyone thinks it might influence the jury in any way, I have no purpose except to give both sides a fair trial in this case. Feeling that way about it, I will let the sign come down.

The defense had lined up nationally known scientists to testify as experts in the case. But the judge's ruling left these men sitting in the courtroom as spectators.

Among the scientists were Dr. Maynard M. Metcalf, zoologist at Johns Hopkins University; Charles Hubbard Judd, director of the School of Education, University of Chicago; Jacob G. Lipman, dean of the College of Agriculture and director of the New Jersey agricultural experiment station, State University of New Jersey, New Brunswick, New Jersey; Dr. Fay-Cooper Cole, anthropologist, University of Chicago; Wilbur A. Nelson, state geologist of Tennessee; Kirtley F. Mather, chairman, Department of Geology, Harvard University; Dr. Winterton C. Curtis, zoologist, University of Missouri; and Prof. Horatio Hackett Newman, zoologist, University of Chicago.

When the court refused the defense permission to put these men on the witness stand, many of the newspapermen left Dayton because they felt the judge's ruling ended the case.

But the climax to the trial was yet to come. Hays asked the court's permission to put Bryan on the stand as an expert on the Bible. The judge agreed, as did Bryan.

Whether this request by Hays was a bigger surprise to Bryan or Darrow was never discovered. Both Malone and Hays insisted that Darrow examine the Great Commoner.

The July heat continued torrid. The crowd in the courtroom made the building a hazard, so the judge moved court into the yard, and there Bryan and Darrow met in a duel of words and tempers.

Bryan sat coatless, shirt collar tucked under, sleeves rolled up, fanning himself with a palm leaf fan. Darrow stood facing him, also in shirtsleeves. At one point, Darrow ripped his sleeve while pounding the table to emphasize his position.

Darrow's examination of Bryan lasted a whole day.

MR. HAYS: The defense desires to call Mr. Bryan as a witness. We should want to take Mr. Bryan's testimony for the purposes of our record, even if Your Honor thinks it is not admissible in general, so we wish to call him now.

THE COURT: If you ask him about any confidential matter, I will protect him, of course.

MR. DARROW: I do not intend to do that.

THE COURT: On scientific matters, Colonel Bryan can speak for himself.

MR. BRYAN: If Your Honor please, I insist that Mr. Darrow can be put on the stand, and Mr. Malone and Mr. Hays.

THE COURT: Call anybody you desire. Ask them any questions you wish.

BRYAN: Then, we will call all three of them.

DARROW: Not at once?

BRYAN: Where do you want me to sit?

THE COURT: Mr. Bryan, you are not objecting to going on the stand?

BRYAN: Not at all.

THE COURT: Do you want Mr. Bryan sworn?

DARROW: No.

BRYAN: I can make affirmation; I can say "So help me God, I will tell the truth."

DARROW: No, I take it you will tell the truth, Mr. Bryan. You have given considerable study to the Bible, haven't you, Mr. Bryan?

BRYAN: Yes, sir, I have.

D: Well, we all know you have; we are not going to dispute that at all. But you have written and published articles almost weekly, and sometimes have made interpretations of various things?

B: I would not say interpretations, Mr. Darrow, but comments on the lesson.

D: If you comment to any extent, these comments have been interpretations.

B. I presume that my discussion might be to some extent interpretations, but they have not been primarily intended as interpretations.

❋　　❋　　❋

D: Do you claim that everything in the Bible should be literally interpreted?

B: I believe everything in the Bible should be accepted as it is given there; some of the Bible is given illustratively. For instance: "Ye are the salt of the earth." I would not insist that man was actually salt, or that he had flesh of salt, but it is used in the sense of salt as saving God's people.

D: But when you read that Jonah swallowed the whale—or that the whale swallowed Jonah—excuse me, please—how do you literally interpret that?

B: When I read that a big fish swallowed Jonah—it does not say whale.

D: Doesn't it? Are you sure?

B: That is my recollection of it. A big fish, and I believe it, and I believe in a God who can make a whale and can make a man and make both do what He pleases.

D: Mr. Bryan, doesn't the New Testament say a whale?

B: I am not sure. My impression is that it says fish; but it does not make so much difference; I merely called your attention to where it says fish—it does not say whale.

D: But in the New Testament it says whale, doesn't it?

B: That may be true; I cannot remember in my own mind what I read about it.

D: Now, you say, the big fish swallowed Jonah, and he there remained how long—three days—and then he spewed him upon the land. You believe that the big fish was made to swallow Jonah?

B: I am not prepared to say that; the Bible merely says it was done.

D: You don't know whether it was the ordinary run of fish, or made for that purpose?

B: You may guess; you evolutionists guess.

D: But when we do guess, we have a sense to guess right.

B: But do not do it often.

D: You are not prepared to say whether that fish was made especially to swallow a man or not?

B: The Bible doesn't say, so I am not prepared to say.

D: You don't know whether that was fixed up specially for the purpose?

B: No, the Bible doesn't say.

D: But do you believe He made them—that He made such a fish and that it was big enough to swallow Jonah?

B: Yes, sir. Let me add: one miracle is just as easy to believe as another.

D: It is for you.

B: It is for me.

D: Just as hard?

B: It is hard to believe for you, but easy for me. A miracle is a thing performed beyond what man can perform. When you get beyond what man can do, you get within the realm of miracles; and it is just as easy to believe in the miracle of Jonah as any other miracle in the Bible.

D: Perfectly easy to believe that Jonah swallowed the whale?

B: If the Bible said so; the Bible doesn't make as extreme statements as evolutionists do.

D: That may be a question, Mr. Bryan, about some of those you have known?

B: The only thing is, you have a definition of fact that includes imagination.

D: And you have a definition that excludes everything but imagination?

STEWART: I object to that as argumentative.

BRYAN: You—

DARROW: The witness must not argue with me, either. Do you consider the story of Jonah and the whale a miracle?

B: I think it is.

D: Do you believe Joshua made the sun stand still?

B: I believe what the Bible says. I suppose you mean that the earth stood still?

D: I don't know. I am talking about the Bible now.

B: I accept the Bible absolutely.

D: The Bible says Joshua commanded the sun to stand still for the purpose of lengthening the day, doesn't it; and you believe it?

B: I do.

D: Do you believe at that time the sun went around the earth?

B: No, I believe that the earth goes around the sun.

D: Do you believe that the men who wrote it thought that

the day could be lengthened or that the sun could be stopped?

B: I don't know what they thought.

D: You don't know?

B: I think they wrote the fact without expressing their own thoughts.

D: Have you an opinion as to whether or not the men who wrote that thought—

STEWART: I want to object, Your Honor; it has gone beyond the pale of any issue that could possibly be injected into this lawsuit, except by imagination. I do not think the defendant has a right to conduct the examination any further and I ask Your Honor to exclude it.

THE COURT: I will hear Mr. Bryan.

BRYAN: It seems to me it would be too exacting to confine the defense to the facts; if they are not allowed to get away from the facts, what have they to deal with?

THE COURT: Mr. Bryan is willing to be examined. Go ahead.

DARROW: Have you an opinion as to whether—whoever wrote the book, I believe Joshua, the Book of Joshua, thought the sun went around the earth or not?

BRYAN: I believe that he was inspired.

D: Can you answer my question?

B: When you let me finish the statement.

D: It is a simple question, but finish it.

B: You cannot measure the length of my answer by the length of your question. (*Laughter*)

D: No, except that the answer be longer. (*Laughter*)

B: I believe that the Bible is inspired, with an inspired author. Whether one who wrote as he was directed to write understood the things he was writing about, I don't know.

D: Whoever inspired it? Do you think whoever inspired it believed that the sun went around the earth?

B: I believe it was inspired by the Almighty, and He may have used language that could be understood at that time.

D: Was—

B: Instead of using language that could not be understood until Darrow was born. (*Laughter and applause*)

D: So, it might have been subject to construction, might it not?

B: It might have been phrased in language that could be understood then.

D: That means it is subject to construction?

B: That is your construction. I am answering your question.

D: Is that correct?

B: That is my answer to it.

D: Can you answer?

B: I might say, Isaiah spoke of God sitting upon the circle of the earth.

D: I am not talking about Isaiah.

THE COURT: Let him illustrate, if he wants to.

DARROW: Is it your opinion that passage was subject to construction?

BRYAN: Well, I think anybody can put his own construction upon it, but I do not mean that necessarily that is a correct construction. I have answered the question.

D: Don't you believe that in order to lengthen the day it would have been construed that the earth stood still?

B: I would not attempt to say what would have been necessary, but I know this, that I can take a glass of water that would fall to the ground without the strength of my hand and to the extent of the glass of water I can overcome the law of gravitation and lift it up. Whereas without my hand it would fall to the ground. If my puny hand can overcome the law of gravitation, the most universally understood, to that extent, I would not set power to the hand of Almighty God that made the universe.

D: I read that years ago. Can you answer my question directly? If the day was lengthened by stopping either the earth or the sun, it must have been the earth?

B: Well, I should say so.

D: Yes? But it was language that was understood at that time, and we now know that the sun stood still as it was with the earth.

B: Well, no—

D: We know also the sun does not stand still?

B: Well, it is relatively so, as Mr. Einstein would say.

D: I ask you if it does stand still?

B: You know as well as I know.

D: Better. You have no doubt about it.

B: No. And the earth moves around.

D: Yes?

B: But I think there is nothing improper if you will protect the Lord against your criticism.

D: I suppose He needs it?

B: He was using language at that time the people understood.

D: And that you call "interpretation"?

B: No, sir; I would not call it interpretation.

D: I say, you would call it interpretation at this time, to say it meant something then?

B: You may use your own language to describe what I have to say, and I will use mine in answering.

D: Now, Mr. Bryan, have you ever pondered what would have happened to the earth if it had stood still?

B: No.

D: You have not?

B: No; the God I believe in could have taken care of that, Mr. Darrow.

D: I see. Have you ever pondered what would naturally happen to the earth if it stood still suddenly?

B: No.

D: Don't you know it would have been converted into a molten mass of matter?

B: You testify to that when you get on the stand. I will give you a chance.

D: Don't you believe it?

B: I would want to hear expert testimony on that.

D: You have never investigated that subject?

B: I don't think I have ever had the question asked.

D: Or ever thought of it?

B: I have been too busy on things that I thought were of more importance than that.

D: You believe the story of the flood to be a literal interpretation?

B: Yes, sir.

D: When was that flood?

B: I would not attempt to fix the date. The date is fixed, as suggested this morning.

D: About 4004 B.C.?

B: That has been the estimate of a man that is accepted today. I would not say it is accurate.

D: That estimate is printed in the Bible?

B: Everybody knows, at least, I think most of the people know, that was the estimate given.

D: But what do you think the Bible itself says? Don't you know how it was arrived at?

B: I never made a calculation.

D: A calculation from what?

B: I could not say.

D: From the generations of man?

B: I would not want to say that.

D: What do you think?

B: I do not think about things I don't think about.

D: Do you think about things you do think about?

B: Well, sometimes. (*Laughter*)

POLICEMAN: Let us have order.

DARROW: Mr. Bryan, you have read these dates over and over again?

BRYAN: Not very accurately; I turn back sometimes to see what the time was.

D: You want to say now you have no idea how these dates were computed?

B: No, I don't say, but I have told you what my idea was. I said I don't know how accurate it was.

D: You say from the generations of man—

STEWART: I am objecting to his cross-examining his own witness.

DARROW: He is a hostile witness.

THE COURT: I am going to let Mr. Bryan control—

BRYAN: I want him to have all the latitude he wants. For I am going to have some latitude when he gets through.

DARROW: You can have latitude and longitude. (*Laughter*)

THE COURT: Order.

STEWART: The witness is entitled to be examined as to the legal evidence of it. We were supposed to go into the origin of the case, and we have nearly lost the day, Your Honor.

MR. MCKENZIE: I object to it.

STEWART: Your Honor, he is perfectly able to take care of this, but we are attaining no evidence. This is not competent evidence.

BRYAN: These gentlemen have not had much chance—they did not come here to try this case. They came here to try revealed religion. I am here to defend it, and they can ask me any question they please.

THE COURT: All right. (*Applause*)

DARROW: Great applause from the bleachers.

BRYAN: From those whom you call "yokels."

D: I have never called them yokels.

B: That is the ignorance of Tennessee, the bigotry.

D: You mean who are applauding you? (*Applause*)

B: Those are the people whom you insult.

D: You insult every man of science and learning in the world because he does not believe in your fool religion.

THE COURT: I will not stand for that.

DARROW: For what he is doing?

THE COURT: I am talking to both of you.

STEWART: This has gone beyond the pale of a lawsuit, Your Honor. I have a public duty to perform, under my oath, and I ask the Court to stop it. Mr. Darrow is making an effort to insult the gentleman on the witness stand, and I ask that it be stopped, for it has gone beyond the pale of a lawsuit.

THE COURT: To stop it now would not be just to Mr. Bryan. He wants to ask the other gentleman questions along the same line.

STEWART: It will all be incompetent.

BRYAN: The jury is not here.

THE COURT: I do not want to be strictly technical.

DARROW: Then Your Honor rules, and I accept.

STEWART: The jury is not here.

DARROW: How long ago was the flood, Mr. Bryan?

BRYAN: Let me see Usher's calculation about it?

D. Surely. (*Hands a Bible to the witness*)

BRYAN: It is given here as 2348 years B.C.

D: Well, 2348 years B.C. You believe that all the living things that were not contained in the ark were destroyed?

B: I think the fish may have lived.

D: Outside of the fish?

B: I cannot say.

D: You cannot say?

B: No, except that just as it is, I have no proof to the contrary.

D: I am asking you whether you believe?

B: I do.

D: That all living things outside of the fish were destroyed?

B: What I say about the fish is merely a matter of humor.

D: I understand.

B: Due to the fact a man wrote up here the other day to ask whether all the fish were destroyed, and the gentleman who received the letter told him the fish may have lived.

D: I am referring to the fish, too.

B: I accept that, as the Bible gives it, and I have never found any reason for denying, disputing, or rejecting it.

D: Let us make it definite, 2348 years?

B: I didn't say that. That is the time given there (*Indicating a Bible*), but I don't pretend to say that is exact.

D: You never figured it out, these generations, yourself?

B: No, sir; not myself.

D: But the Bible you have offered in evidence says 2340-something, so that 4200 years ago there was not a living thing on the earth, excepting the people on the ark and the animals in the ark and the fishes?

B: There have been living things before that.

D: I mean at that time?

B: After that.

D: Don't you know there are any number of civilizations that are traced back to more than 5000 years?

B: I know we have people who trace things back according to the number of ciphers they have. But I am not satisfied they are accurate.

D: You are not satisfied there is any civilization that can be traced back 5000 years?

B: I would not want to say there is because I have no evidence of it that is satisfactory.

D: Would you say there is not?

B: Well, so far as I know, but when the scientists differ, from 24,000,000 to 306,000,000 in their opinion, as to how long ago life came here, I want them nearer, to come nearer together before they demand of me to give up my belief in the Bible.

D: Do you say that you do not believe that there were any civilizations on this earth that reach back beyond 5000 years?

B: I am not satisfied by any evidence that I have seen.

D: I didn't ask you what you are satisfied with. I asked you if you believe it?

B: Will you let me answer it?

THE COURT: Go right on.

BRYAN: I am satisfied by no evidence that I have found, that would justify me in accepting the opinions of these men against what I believe to be the inspired Word of God.

DARROW: And you believe every nation, every organization of men, every animal in the world outside of the fishes—

B: The fish, I want you to understand, is merely a matter of humor.

D: I believe the Bible says so. Take the fishes in?

B: Let us get together and look over this.

D: Probably we would better; we will after we get through. You believe that all the various human races on the earth have come into being in the last 4000 years or 4200 years, whatever it is?

B: No, it would be more than that.

D: 1927?

B: Some time after creation, before the flood.

D: 1927 added to it?

B: The flood is 2300 and something, and creation, according to the estimate there, is further back than that.

D: Then you don't understand me. If we don't get together on it, look at the book. This is the year of grace 1925, isn't it?

Let us put down 1925. Have you a pencil? (*One of the defense attorneys hands Mr. Darrow a pencil*)

B: Add to that 4004?

D: Yes.

B: That is the date (*Referring to the Bible*) given here on the first page, according to Bishop Usher, which I say I only accept because I have no reason to doubt it. On that page he gives it.

D: 1925 plus 4004 is 5929 years, if a fallible person is right in his addition. Now, then, what do you subtract from that?

B: That is the beginning.

D: I was talking about the flood.

B: 2348 on that, we said.

D: Less than that?

B: No; subtract that from 4000; it would be about 1700 years.

D: That is the same thing?

B: No; subtracted it is 2300 and something before the beginning of the Christian era, about 1700 years after the creation.

DARROW: If I add 2300 years, that is the beginning of the Christian era?

BRYAN: Yes, sir.

D: If I add 1925 to that I will get it, won't I?

B: Yes, sir.

D: That makes 4262 years. If it is not correct, we can correct it.

B: According to the Bible, there was a civilization before that, destroyed by the flood.

D: Let me make this definite. You believe that every civilization on the earth and every living thing, except possibly fishes, that came out of the ark were wiped out by the flood?

B: At that time.

D: At that time. And then, whatever human beings, including all the tribes, that inhabited the world, and have inhabited the world, and who run their pedigree straight back, and all the animals, have come onto the earth since the flood?

B: Yes.

D: Within 4200 years. Do you know a scientific man on the face of the earth that believes any such thing?

B: I cannot say, but I know some scientific men who dispute entirely the antiquity of man as testified to by other scientific men.

D: Oh, that does not answer the question. Do you know of a single scientific man on the face of the earth that believes any such thing as you stated, about the antiquity of man?

B: I don't think I have ever asked one the direct question.

D: Quite important, isn't it?

B: Well, I don't know as it is.

D: It might not be?

B: If I had nothing else to do except speculate on what our remote ancestors were and what our remote descendants may be—but I have been more interested in Christians living right now, to make it much more important than speculation on either the past or the future.

D: You have never had any interest in the age of the various races and people and civilization and animals that exist upon the earth today? Is that right?

B: I have never felt a great deal of interest in the effort that has been made to dispute the Bible by the speculations of men, or the investigations of men.

D: Are you the only human being on earth who knows what the Bible means?

STEWART: I object.

THE COURT: Sustained.

DARROW: You do know that there are thousands of people who profess to be Christians who believe the earth is much more ancient and that the human race is much more ancient?

BRYAN: I think there may be.

D: And you never have investigated to find out how long man has been on the earth?

B: I have never found it necessary.

D: For any reason, whatever it is?

B: To examine every speculation; but if I had done it I never would have done anything else.

D: I ask for a direct answer.

B: I do not expect to find out all those things, and I do not expect to find out about races.

D: I didn't ask you that. Now, I ask you if you know if it was interesting enough, or important enough for you to try to find out about how old these ancient civilizations were?

B: No; I have not made a study of it.

D: Don't you know that the ancient civilizations of China are 6000 or 7000 years old, at the very least?

B: No; they would not run back beyond the creation, according to the Bible, 6000 years.

D: You don't know how old they are, is that right?

B: I don't know how old they are, but probably you do. I think you would give the preference to anybody who opposed the Bible, and I give the preference to the Bible.

D: I see. Well, you are welcome to your opinion. Have you any idea how old the Egyptian civilization is?

B: No.

D: Do you know of any record in the world, outside of the story of the Bible, which conforms to any statement that it is 4200 years ago or thereabouts that all life was wiped off the face of the earth?

B: I think they have found records.

D: Do you know of any?

B: Records reciting the flood, but I am not an authority on the subject.

D: Now, Mr. Bryan, will you say if you know of any record, or have ever heard of any records, that describe that a flood existed 4200 years ago, or about that time, which wiped all life off the earth?

B: The recollection of what I have read on that subject is not distinct enough to say whether the records attempted to fix a time, but I have seen in the discoveries of archeologists where they have found records that described the flood.

D: Mr. Bryan, don't you know that there are many old religions that describe the flood?

B: No, I don't know.

D: You know there are others besides the Jewish?

B: I don't know whether there are records of any other religion which refer to this flood.

D: Don't you ever examine religion so far as to know that?

B: Outside of the Bible?

D: Yes.

B: No; I have not examined to know that, generally.

D: You have never examined any other religions?

B: Yes, sir.

D: Have you ever read anything about the origins of religions?

B: Not a great deal.

D: You have never examined any other religion?

B: Yes, sir.

D: And you don't know whether any other religion ever gave a similar account of the destruction of the earth by the flood?

B: The Christian religion has satisfied me, and I have never felt it necessary to look up some competing religions.

D: Do you consider that every religion on earth competes with the Christian religion?

B: I think everybody who does not believe in the Christian religion believes so—

D: I am asking what you think.

B: I do not regard them as competitive because I do not think they have the same source as we have.

D: You are wrong in saying "competitive."

B: I would not say competitive, but the religious unbelievers.

D: Unbelievers of what?

B: In the Christian religion.

D: What about the religion of Buddha?

B: I can tell you something about that, if you want to know.

D: What about the religion of Confucius or Buddha?

B: Well, I can tell you something about that, if you would like to know.

D: Did you ever investigate them?

B: Somewhat.

D: Did you regard them as competitive?

B: No, I think they are very inferior. Would you like for me to tell you what I know about it?

D: No.

B: Well, I shall insist on giving it to you.

D: You won't talk about free silver, will you?

B: Not at all.

STEWART: I object to him—counsel—going any further with this examination and cross-examining his own witness. He is your own witness.

DARROW: Well, now, General, you understand we are making up a record, and I assume that every lawyer knows perfectly well that we have a right to cross-examine a hostile witness. Is there any doubt about that?

STEWART: Under the law in Tennessee if you put a witness on and he proves to be hostile to you, the law provides the method by which you may cross-examine him. You will have to make an affidavit that you are surprised at his statement, and you may do that.

BRYAN: Is there any way by which a witness can make an affidavit that the attorney is also hostile?

DARROW: I am not hostile to you. I am hostile to your views, and I suppose that runs with me, too.

B: But I think when the gentlemen asked me about Confucius I ought to be allowed to answer his question.

D: Oh, tell it, Mr. Bryan, I won't object to it.

B: I had occasion to study Confucianism when I went to China. I got all I could find about what Confucius said, and then I bought a book that told us what Menches said about what Confucius said, and I found that there were several direct and strong contrasts between the teachings of Jesus and the teachings of Confucius. In the first place, one of his followers asked if there was any word that would express all that was necessary to know in the relations of life, and he said, "Isn't reciprocity such a word?" I know of no better illustration of the difference between Christianity and Confucianism than the contrast that is brought out there. Reciprocity is a calculating selfishness. If a person does something for you, you do something for him and keep it even. That is the basis of the philosophy of Confucius. Christ's doctrine was not reciprocity. We were told to help people not in proportion as they had helped us—not in proportion as they might have helped us, but in proportion to their needs, and there is all the difference in the world between a religion that teaches you just to keep even with other people and the religion that teaches you to spend yourself for other people and to help them as they need help.

D: There is no doubt about that; I haven't asked you that.

B: That is one of the differences between the two.

D: Do you know how old the Confucian religion is?

B: I can't give you the exact date of it.

D: Did you ever investigate to find out?

B: Not to be able to speak definitely as to date, but I can tell you something I read, and will tell you.

D: Wouldn't you just as soon answer my questions? And get along?

B: Yes, sir.

D: Of course, if I take any advantage of misquoting you, I don't object to being stopped. Do you know how old the religion of Zoroaster is?

B: No, sir.

D: Do you know they are both more ancient than the Christian religion?

B: I am not willing to take the opinion of people who are trying to find excuses for rejecting the Christian religion when they attempt to give dates and hours and minutes, and they will have to get together and be more exact than they have yet been able, to compel me to accept just what they say as if it were absolutely true.

D: Are you familiar with James Clark's book on the ten great religions?

B: No.

D: He was a Unitarian minister, wasn't he? You don't think he was trying to find fault, do you?

B: I am not speaking of the motives of men.

D: You don't know how old they are, all these other religions?

B: I wouldn't attempt to speak correctly, but I think it is much more important to know the differences between them than to know the age.

D: Not for the purpose of this inquiry, Mr. Bryan. Do you know about how many people there were on this earth at the beginning of the Christian era?

B: No, I don't think I ever saw a census on that subject.

D: Do you know about how many people there were on this earth 3,000 years ago?

B: No.

D: Did you ever try to find out?

B: When you display my ignorance, could you not give me the facts so I would not be ignorant any longer? Can you tell me how many people there were when Christ was born?

D: You know, some of us might get the facts and still be ignorant.

B: Will you please give me that? You ought not to ask me a question when you don't know the answer to it.

D: I can make an estimate.

B: What is your estimate?

D: Wait until you get to me. Do you know anything about how many people there were in Egypt 3500 years ago, or how many people there were in China 5000 years ago?

B: No.

D: Have you ever tried to find out?

B: No, sir. You are the first man I ever heard of who has been interested in it. (*Laughter*)

D: Mr. Bryan, am I the first man you ever heard of who has been interested in the age of human societies and primitive man?

B: You are the first man I ever heard speak of the number of people at those different periods.

D: Where have you lived all your life?

B: Not near you. (*Laughter and applause*)

D: Nor near anybody of learning?

B: Oh, don't assume you know it all.

D: Do you know there are thousands of books in our libraries on all those subjects I have been asking you about?

B: I couldn't say, but I will take your word for it.

D: Did you ever read a book on primitive man? Like Tyler's *Primitive Culture,* or Boas, or any of the great authorities?

B: I don't think I ever read the ones you have mentioned.

D: Have you read any?

B: Well, I have read a little from time to time. But I didn't pursue it, because I didn't know I was to be called as a witness.

D: You have never in all your life made any attempt to find out about the other peoples of the earth—how old their civilizations are—how long they had existed on the earth, have you?

B: No, sir; I have been so well satisfied with the Christian religion that I have spent no time trying to find arguments against it.

D: Were you afraid you might find some?

B: No, sir; I am not afraid now that you will show me any.

D: You remember that man who said—I am not quoting literally—that one could not be content though he rose from the dead—you suppose you could be content?

B: Well, will you give the rest of it, Mr. Darrow?

D: No.

B: Why not?

D: I am not interested.

B: Why scrap the Bible—"they have Moses and the prophets"?

D: Who has?

B: That is the rest of the quotation you didn't finish.

D: And so you think if they have Moses and the prophets they don't need to find out anything else?

B: That was the answer that was made there.

D: And you follow the same rule?

B: I have all the information I want to live by and to die by.

D: And that's all you are interested in?

B: I am not looking for any more on religion.

D: You don't care how old the earth is, how old man is and how long the animals have been here?

B: I am not so much interested in that.

D: You have never made any investigation to find out?

B: No, sir, I have never.

D: All right.

B: Now, will you let me finish the question.

D: What question was that? If there is anything more you want to say about Confucius I don't object.

B: Oh, yes, I have got two more things.

D: If Your Honor please I don't object, but his speeches are not germane to my question.

MR. HICKS: Your Honor, he put him on.

.THE COURT: You went into it and I will let him explain.

DARROW: I asked him certain specific questions about Confucius.

HICKS: The questions he is asking are not germane, either.

DARROW: I think they are.

BRYAN: I mentioned the word reciprocity to show the difference between Christ's teachings in that respect and the teachings of Confucius. I call your attention to another difference. One of the followers of Confucius asked him, "What do you think of the doctrine that you should reward evil with good?" and the answer of Confucius was, "Reward evil with justice and reward good with good. Love your enemies. Overcome evil with good," and there is a difference between the two teachings —a difference incalculable in its effect and in— The third difference—people who scoff at religion and try to make it appear that Jesus brought nothing into the world, talk about the Golden Rule of Confucius. Confucius said, "Do not unto others what you would not have others do unto you." It was purely negative. Jesus taught, "Do unto others as you would have others do unto you." There is all the difference in the world between a negative harmlessness and a positive helpfulness and the Christian religion is a religion of helpfulness, of service, embodied in the language of Jesus when he said, "Let him who would be chiefest among you be the servant of all." Those are the three differences between the teachings of Jesus and the teachings of Confucius, and they are very strong differences on very important questions. Now, Mr. Darrow, you asked me if I knew anything about Buddha.

D: You want to make a speech on Buddha, too?

B: No, sir; I want to answer your question on Buddha.

D: I asked you if you knew anything about him.

B: I do.

D: Well, that's answered, then.

B: Buddha—

D: Well, wait a minute, you answered the questions—

THE COURT: I will let him tell what he knows.

DARROW: All he knows?

THE COURT: Well, I don't know about that.

BRYAN: I won't insist on telling all I know. I will tell more than Mr. Darrow wants told.

DARROW: Well, all right, tell it, I don't care.

B: Buddhism is an agnostic religion.

D: To what—what do you mean by agnostic?

B: I don't know.

D: You don't know what you mean?

B: That is, what "agnosticism" is—I don't know. When I was in Rangoon, Burma, one of the Buddhists told me that they were going to send a delegation to an agnostic congress that was to be held soon at Rome and I read in an official document—

D: Do you remember his name?

B: No, sir, I don't.

D: What did he look like; how tall was he?

B: I think he was about as tall as you, but not so crooked.

D: Do you know about how old a man he was—do you know whether he was old enough to know what he was talking about?

B: He seemed to be old enough to know what he was talking about. (*Laughter*)

D: If Your Honor please, instead of answering plain specific questions we are permitting the witness to regale the crowd with what some black man said to him when he was traveling in Rang—who, India?

B: He was dark-colored, but not black.

THE COURT: I will let him go ahead and answer.

BRYAN: I wanted to say that I then read a paper that he gave me, an official paper of the Buddhist church, and it advocated the sending of delegates to that agnostic congress at Rome, arguing that it was an agnostic religion, and I will give you other evidence of it. I went to call on a Buddhist teacher.

DARROW: I object to Mr. Bryan making a speech every time I ask him a question.

THE COURT: Let him finish this answer and then you can go ahead.

BRYAN: I went to call on a Buddhist priest and found him at

his noon meal, and there was an Englishman there who was also a Buddhist. He went over as ship's carpenter and became a Buddhist and had been for about six years and while I waited for the Buddhist priest I talked to the Englishman and I asked him what was the most important thing in Buddhism and he said the most important thing was you didn't have to believe to be a Buddhist.

DARROW: You know the name of the Englishman?

B: No, sir; I don't know his name.

D: What did he look like?

B: He was what I would call an average-looking man.

D: How could you tell he was an Englishman?

B: He told me so.

D: Do you know whether he was truthful or not?

B: No, sir, but I took his word for it.

THE COURT: Well, get along, Mr. Darrow, with your examination.

D: Mr. Bryan, could you tell me how old the earth is?

B: No, sir, I couldn't.

D: Could you come anywhere near it?

B: I wouldn't attempt to. I could possibly come as near as the scientists do, but I had rather be more accurate before I give a guess.

D: You don't think much of scientists, do you?

B: Yes, sir, I do, sir.

D: Is there any scientist in the world you think much of?

B: I do.

D: Who?

B: Well, I think the bulk of the scientists—

D: I don't want that kind of an answer, Mr. Bryan. Who are they?

B: I will give you George M. Price, for instance.

D: Who is he?

B: Professor of geology in a college.

D: Where?

B: He was out near Lincoln, Nebraska.

D: How close to Lincoln, Nebraska?

B: About three or four miles. He is now in a college out in California.

D: Where is the college?

B: At Lodi.

D: That is a small college?

B: I didn't know you had to judge a man by the size of the college—I thought you judged him by the size of the man.

D: I thought the size of the college made some difference?

B: It might raise a presumption in the minds of some, but I think I would rather find out what he believed.

D: You would rather find out whether his belief corresponds with your views or prejudices or whatever they are before you said how good he was?

B: Well, you know the word "prejudice" is—

D: Well, belief, then.

B: I don't think I am any more prejudiced for the Bible than you are against it.

D: Well, I don't know.

B: Well, I don't know either. It is my guess.

D: You mentioned Price because he is the only human being in the world so far as you know that signs his name as geologist that believes like you do?

B: No, there is a man named Wright, who taught at Oberlin.

D: I will get to Mr. Wright in a moment. Who publishes his book?

B: I can't tell you. I can get you the book.

D: Don't you know? Don't you know it is Revell & Co., Chicago?

B: I couldn't say.

D: He publishes yours, doesn't he?

B: Yes, sir.

STEWART: Will you let me make an exception? I don't think it is pertinent about who publishes a book.

DARROW: He has quoted a man that every scientist in this country knows is a mountebank and a pretender and not a geologist at all.

THE COURT: You can ask him about the man, but don't ask him about who publishes the book.

DARROW: Do you know anything about the college he is in?

BRYAN: No, I can't tell you.

D: Do you know how old his book is?

B: No, sir; it is a recent book.

D: Do you know anything about his training?

B: No, I can't say on that.

D: Do you know of any geologist on the face of the earth who ever recognized him?

B: I couldn't say.

*　*　*

D: How old does Mr. Price say the earth is?

B: I haven't examined the book in order to answer questions on it.

D: Then you don't know anything about how old he says it is?

B: He speaks of the layers that are supposed to measure age and points out that they are not uniform and not always the same and that attempts to measure age by those layers where they are not in the order in which they are usually found makes it difficult to fix the exact age.

D: Does he say anything whatever about the age of the earth?

B: I wouldn't be able to testify.

D: You didn't get anything about the age from him?

B: Well, I know he disputes what you say and has very good evidence to dispute it—what some others say about the age.

D: Where did you get your information about the age of the earth?

B: I am not attempting to give you information about the age of the earth.

D: Then you say there was Mr. Wright, of Oberlin?

B: That was rather I think on the age of man than upon the age of the earth.

[215]

D: There are two Mr. Wrights, of Oberlin?

B: I couldn't say.

D: Both of them geologists. Do you know how long Mr. Wright says man has been on the earth?

B: Well, he gives the estimates of different people.

D: Does he give any opinion of his own?

B: I think he does.

D: What is it?

B: I am not sure.

D: What is it?

B: It was based upon the last glacial age—that man has appeared since the last glacial age.

D: Did he say there was no man on earth before the last glacial age?

B: I think he disputes the finding of any proof—where the proof is authentic—but I had rather read him than quote him. I don't like to run the risk of quoting from memory.

D: You couldn't say then how long Mr. Wright places it?

B: I don't attempt to tell you.

D: When was the last glacial age?

B: I wouldn't attempt to tell you that.

D: Have you any idea?

B: I wouldn't want to fix it without looking at some of the figures.

D: That was since the tower of Babel, wasn't it?

B: Well, I wouldn't want to fix it. I think it was before the time given in here, and that was only given as the possible appearance of man and not the actual.

D: Have you any idea how far back the last glacial age was?

B: No, sir.

D: Do you know whether it was more than 6000 years ago?

B: I think it was more than 6000 years.

D: Have you any idea how old the earth is?

B: No.

D: The book you have introduced in evidence tells you, doesn't it?

B: I don't think it does, Mr. Darrow.

D: Let's see whether it does; is this the one?

B: That is the one, I think.

D: It says B.C. 4004.

B: That is Bishop Usher's calculation.

D: That is printed in the Bible you introduced?

B: Yes, sir.

D: And numerous other Bibles?

B: Yes, sir.

D: Printed in the Bible in general use in Tennessee?

B: I couldn't say.

D: And Scofield's Bible?

B: I couldn't say about that.

D: You have seen it somewhere else?

B: I think that is the chronology usually used.

D: Does the Bible you have introduced for the jury's consideration say that?

B: Well, you will have to ask those who introduced that.

D: You haven't practiced law for a long time, so I will ask you if that is the King James version that was introduced? That is your marking, and I assume it is?

B: I think that is the same one.

D: There is no doubt about it, is there, gentlemen?

STEWART: That is the same one.

DARROW: Would you say that the earth was only 4000 years old?

BRYAN: Oh, no; I think it is much older than that.

D: How much?

B: I couldn't say.

D: Do you say whether the Bible itself says it is older than that?

B: I don't think the Bible says itself whether it is older or not.

D: Do you think the earth was made in six days?

B: Not six days of twenty-four hours.

D: Doesn't it say so?

B: No, sir.

STEWART: I want to interpose another objection. What is the purpose of this examination?

BRYAN: The purpose is to cast ridicule on everybody who believes in the Bible, and I am perfectly willing that the world shall know that these gentlemen have no other purpose than ridiculing every Christian who believes in the Bible.

DARROW: We have the purpose of preventing bigots and ignoramuses from controlling the education of the United States and you know it, and that is all.

B: I am glad to bring out that statement. I want the world to know that this evidence is not for the view Mr. Darrow and his associates have filed affidavits here stating, the purpose of which, I understand, is to show that the Bible story is not true.

MALONE: Mr. Bryan seems anxious to get some evidence in the record that would tend to show that those affidavits are not true.

BRYAN: I am not trying to get anything into the record. I am simply trying to protect the Word of God against the greatest atheist or agnostic in the United States. (*Prolonged applause*) I want the papers to know I am not afraid to get on the stand in front of him and let him do his worst. I want the world to know. (*Prolonged applause*)

DARROW: I wish I could get a picture of these clackers.

STEWART: I am not afraid of Mr. Bryan being perfectly able to take care of himself, but this examination cannot be a legal examination and it cannot be worth a thing in the world, and, Your Honor, I respectfully except to it, and call on Your Honor, in the name of all that is legal, to stop this examination and stop it here.

HAYS: I rather sympathize with the general, but Mr. Bryan is produced as a witness because he is a student of the Bible and he presumably understands what the Bible means. He is one of the foremost students in the United States, and we hope to show Mr. Bryan, who is a student of the Bible, what the Bible really means in connection with evolution. Mr. Bryan has already stated that the world is not merely 6000 years old and that is very helpful to us, and where your evidence is coming from, this Bible, which goes to the jury, is that the world started in 4004 B.C.

BRYAN: You think the Bible says that?

HAYS: The one you have taken in evidence says that.

BRYAN: I don't concede that it does.

HAYS: You know that that chronology is made up by adding together all of the ages of the people in the Bible, counting their ages; and now then, let us show the next stage from a Bible student, that these things are not to be taken literally, but that each man is entitled to his own interpretation.

STEWART: The court makes the interpretation.

HAYS: But the court is entitled to information on what is the interpretation of an expert Bible student.

STEWART: This is resulting in a harangue and nothing else.

DARROW: I didn't do any of the haranguing; Mr. Bryan has been doing that.

STEWART: You know absolutely you have done it.

DARROW: Oh, all right.

MALONE: Mr. Bryan doesn't need any support.

STEWART: Certainly he doesn't need any support, but I am doing what I conceive my duty to be, and I don't need any advice, if you please, sir. (*Applause*)

THE COURT: That would be irrelevant testimony if it was going to the jury. Of course, it is excluded from the jury on the point it is not competent testimony, on the same ground as the affidaviting.

HICKS: Your Honor, let me say a word right there. It is in the discretion of the Court how long you will allow them to question witnesses for the purpose of taking testimony to the Supreme Court. Now, we, as taxpayers of this county, feel that this has gone beyond reason.

THE COURT: Well, now, that taxpayers' complaint doesn't appeal to me so much, when it is only fifteen or twenty minutes' time.

DARROW: I would have been through in half an hour if Mr. Bryan had answered my questions.

STEWART: They want to put in affidavits as to what other witnesses would swear, why not let them put in affidavits as to what Mr. Bryan would swear?

BRYAN: God forbid.

MALONE: I will just make this suggestion.

STEWART: It is not worth anything to them, if Your Honor please, even for the record in the Supreme Court.

HAYS: Is not it worth anything to us if Mr. Bryan will accept the story of creation in detail, and if Mr. Bryan, as a Bible student, states you cannot take the Bible necessarily as literally true?

STEWART: The Bible speaks for itself.

HAYS: You mean to say the Bible itself tells whether these are parables? Does it?

STEWART: We have left all annals of procedure behind. This is a harangue between Colonel Darrow and his witness. He makes so many statements that he is forced to defend himself.

DARROW: I do not do that.

STEWART: I except to that as not pertinent to this lawsuit.

THE COURT: Of course, it is not pertinent, or it would be before the jury.

STEWART: It is not worth anything before a jury.

THE COURT: Are you about through, Mr. Darrow?

DARROW: I want to ask a few more questions about the creation.

THE COURT: I know. We are going to adjourn when Mr. Bryan comes off the stand for the day. Be very brief, Mr. Darrow. Of course—I believe I will make myself clearer—of course, it is incompetent testimony before the jury. The only reason I am allowing this to go in at all is that they may have it in the Appellate Courts, as showing what the affidavit would be.

BRYAN: The reason I am answering is not for the benefit of the Superior court. It is to keep these gentlemen from saying I was afraid to meet them and let them question me, and I want the Christian world to know that any atheist, agnostic, or unbeliever, can question me any time as to my belief in God, and I will answer him.

DARROW: I want to take an exception to this conduct of this witness. He may be very popular down here in the hills. I do not need to have his explanation for his answer.

THE COURT: Yes.

BRYAN: If I had not, I would not have answered the question.

HAYS: May I be heard? I do not want Your Honor to think we are asking questions of Mr. Bryan with the expectation that the higher court will not say that those questions are proper testimony. The reason I state this is this: your law speaks for the Bible. Your law does not say the literal interpretation of the Bible. If Mr. Bryan, who is a student of the Bible, will state that everything in the Bible need not be interpreted literally, that each man must judge for himself; if he will state that, of course, then Your Honor would charge the jury. We are not bound by a literal interpretation of the Bible. If I have made my argument clear enough for the attorney-general to understand, I will retire.

STEWART: I will admit you have frequently been difficult of comprehension, and I think you are as much to blame as I am.

HAYS: I know I am.

STEWART: I think this is not legal evidence for the record in the Appellate Courts. The King James version of the Bible, as Your Honor says—

THE COURT: I cannot say that.

STEWART: Your Honor has held the court takes judicial knowledge of the King James version of the Bible.

THE COURT: No, sir; I did not do that.

STEWART: Your Honor charged the grand jury and read from that.

THE COURT: I happened to have the Bible in my hand, it happened to be a King James edition, but I will charge the jury, gentlemen, the Bible generally used in Tennessee, as the book ordinarily understood in Tennessee, as the Bible, I do not think it is proper for us to say to the jury what Bible.

STEWART: Of course, that is all we could ask of Your Honor. This investigation or interrogation, of Mr. Bryan as a witness —Mr. Bryan is called to testify, was of the counsel for the prosecution in this case, and has been asked something, perhaps less than a thousand questions, of course, not personal to this case, and it has resulted in an argument, an argument about every other question cannot be avoided. I submit, Your Honor, it is not worth anything in the record at all, if it is not legal testimony. Mr. Bryan is willing to testify and is able to defend himself. I except it, if the Court please, and ask Your Honor to stop it.

HAYS: May I ask a question? If your contention is correct that this law does not necessarily mean that the Bible is to be taken literally, word for word, is not this competent evidence?

STEWART: Why could you not prove it by your scientists?

DARROW: We are calling one of the foremost Bible students. You vouch for him.

MALONE: We are offering the best evidence.

McKENZIE: Do you think this evidence is competent before a jury?

DARROW: I think so.

THE COURT: It is not competent evidence for the jury.

McKENZIE: Nor is it competent in the Appellate Courts, and these gentlemen would no more file the testimony of Colonel Bryan as a part of the record in this case than they would file a rattlesnake and handle it themselves.

DARROW, HAYS AND MALONE: (In unison) We will file it. We will file it. File every word of it.

BRYAN: Your Honor, they have not asked a question legally, and the only reason they have asked any question is for the purpose, as the question about Jonah was asked, for a chance to give this agnostic an opportunity to criticize a believer in the Word of God; and I answered the question in order to shut his mouth so that he cannot go out and tell his atheistic friends that I would not answer his question. That is the only reason, no more reason in the world.

MALONE: Your Honor, on this very subject, I would like to say that I would have asked Mr. Bryan—and I consider myself as good a Christian as he is—every question that Mr. Darrow has asked him for the purpose of bringing out whether or not there is to be taken in this court only a literal interpretation of the Bible, or whether, obviously, as these questions indicate, if a general and liberal construction cannot be put upon the parts of the Bible which have been covered by Mr. Darrow's questions. I hope for the last time no further attempt will be made by counsel on the other side of the case, or Mr. Bryan, to say the defense is concerned at all with Mr. Darrow's particular religious views or lack of religious views. We are here as lawyers with the same right to our views. I have the same right to mine as a Christian as Mr. Bryan has to his, and we do not intend to have this case charged by Mr. Darrow's agnosticism or Mr. Bryan's brand of Christianity. (*A great applause*)

THE COURT: I will pass on each question as asked, if it is objected to.

DARROW: Mr. Bryan, do you believe that the first woman was Eve?

BRYAN: Yes.

D: Do you believe she was literally made out of Adam's rib?

B: I do.

D: Did you ever discover where Cain got his wife?

B: No, sir; I leave the agnostics to hunt for her.

D: You have never found out?

B: I have never tried to find out.

D: You have never tried to find out?

B: No.

D: The Bible says he got one, doesn't it? Were there other people on the earth at that time?

B: I cannot say.

D: You cannot say. Did that ever enter your consideration?

B: Never bothered me.

D: There were no others recorded, but Cain got a wife.

B: That is what the Bible says.

D: Where she came from you do not know. All right. Does the statement, "The morning and the evening were the first day," and "The morning and the evening were the second day," mean anything to you?

B: I do not think it necessarily means a twenty-four-hour day.

D: You do not?

B: No.

D: What do you consider it to be?

B: I have not attempted to explain it. If you will take the second chapter—let me have the book. (*Examines the Bible*)

The fourth verse of the second chapter says: "These are the generations of the heavens and of the earth, when they were created in the day that the Lord God made the earth and the heavens." The word "day" there in the very next chapter is used to describe a period. I do not see that there is any necessity for construing the words, "the evening and the morning," as meaning necessarily a twenty-four-hour day, "in the day when the Lord made the heaven and the earth."

D: Then, when the Bible said, for instance, "and God called the firmament heaven. And the evening and the morning were the second day," that does not necessarily mean twenty-four hours?

B: I do not think it necessarily does.

D: Do you think it does or does not?

B: I know a great many think so.

D: What do you think?

B: I do not think it does.

D: You think those were not literal days?

B: I do not think they were twenty-four-hour days.

D: What do you think about it?

B: That is my opinion—I do not know that my opinion is better on that subject than those who think it does.

D: You do not think that?

B: No. But I think it would be just as easy for the kind of God we believe in to make the earth in six days as in six years or in 6,000,000 years or in 600,000,000 years. I do not think it important whether we believe one or the other.

D: Do you think those were literal days?

B: My impression is they were periods, but I would not attempt to argue as against anybody who wanted to believe in literal days.

D: Have you any idea of the length of the periods?

B: No; I don't.

D: Do you think the sun was made on the fourth day?

B: Yes.

D: And they had evening and morning without the sun?

B: I am simply saying it is a period.

D: They had evening and morning for four periods without the sun, do you think?

B: I believe in creation as there told, and if I am not able to explain it I will accept it. Then you can explain it to suit yourself.

D: Mr. Bryan, what I want to know is, do you believe the sun was made on the fourth day?

B: I believe just as it says there.

D: Do you believe the sun was made on the fourth day?
B: Read it.

D: I am very sorry; you have read it so many times you would know, but I will read it again:

"And God said, let there be lights in the firmament of the heaven, to divide the day from the night; and let them be for signs, and for seasons, and for days, and years. And let them be for lights in the firmament of the heaven, to give light upon the earth; and it was so. And God made two great lights; the greater light to rule the day, and the lesser light to rule the night; He made the stars also. And God set them in the firmament of the heaven, to give light upon the earth, and to rule over the day and over the night, and to divide the light from the darkness; and God saw that it was good. And the evening and the morning were the fourth day."

Do you believe, whether it was a literal day or a period, the sun and the moon were not made until the fourth day?

B: I believe they were made in the order in which they were given there, and I think in the dispute with Gladstone and Huxley on that point—

D: Cannot you answer my question?

B: I prefer to agree with Gladstone.

D: I do not care about Gladstone.

B: Then prefer to agree with whomever you please.

D: Cannot you answer my question?

B: I have answered it. I believe that it was made on the fourth day, in the fourth day.

D: And they had the evening and the morning before that time for three days or three periods. All right, that settles it.

Now, if you call those periods, they may have been a very long time.

B: They might have been.

D: The creation might have been going on for a very long time.

B: It might have continued for millions of years.

D: Yes. All right. Do you believe the story of the temptation of Eve by the serpent?

B: I do.

D: Do you believe that after Eve ate the apple, or gave it to Adam, whichever way it was, that God cursed Eve, and at that time decreed that all womankind thenceforth and forever should suffer the pains of childbirth in the reproduction of the earth?

B: I believe what it says, and I believe the fact as fully—

D: That is what it says, doesn't it?

B: Yes.

D: And for that reason, every woman born of woman, who has to carry on the race, has childbirth pains because Eve tempted Adam in the Garden of Eden?

B: I will believe just what the Bible says. I ask to put that in the language of the Bible, for I prefer that to your language. Read the Bible and I will answer.

D: All right, I will do that: "And I will put enmity between thee and the woman"—that is referring to the serpent?

B: The serpent.

D: (*Reading*) ". . . and between thy seed and her seed; it shall bruise thy head, and thou shalt bruise his heel. Unto the woman he said, I will greatly multiply thy sorrow and thy conception; in sorrow thou shalt bring forth children; and thy desire shall be to thy husband, and he shall rule over thee." That is right, is it?

B: I accept it as it is.

D: And you believe that came about because Eve tempted Adam to eat the fruit?

B: Just as it says.

D: And you believe that is the reason that God made the serpent to go on his belly after he tempted Eve?

B: I believe the Bible as it is, and I do not permit you to

put your language in the place of the language of the Almighty. You read that Bible and ask me questions, and I will answer them. I will not answer your questions in your language.

D: I will read it to you from the Bible—in your language. "And the Lord God said unto the serpent, because thou hast done this, thou art cursed above all cattle, and above every beast of the field; upon thy belly shalt thou go and dust shalt thou eat all the days of thy life."

Do you think that is why the serpent is compelled to crawl upon his belly?

B: I believe that.

D: Have you any idea how the snake went before that time.

B: No, sir.

D: Do you know whether he walked on his tail or not?

B: No, sir. I have no way to know. (*Laughter*)

D: Now, you refer to the cloud that was put in the heaven after the flood as the rainbow. Do you believe in that?

B: Read it.

D: All right, Mr. Bryan, I will read it for you.

B: Your Honor, I think I can shorten this testimony. The only purpose Mr. Darrow has is to slur at the Bible, but I will answer his question. I will answer it all at once, and I have no objection in the world, I want the world to know that this man, who does not believe in a God, is trying to use a court in Tennessee—

D: I object to that.

B: (*Continuing*) —to slur at it, and while it will require time, I am willing to take it.

D: I object to your statement. I am examining you on your fool ideas that no intelligent Christian on earth believes.

THE COURT: Court is adjourned until tomorrow morning.

THE DAY AFTER Darrow's examination of Bryan, Judge Raulston refused further questioning and ordered Bryan's testimony stricken from the record.

With this decision of the judge, Darrow asked the jury be brought in and instructed to return a verdict of Guilty. This, he said, would permit the defense to appeal to a higher court and get a decision on the constitutionality of the State's anti-evolution law. The jury was called in. The judge told the jury that if they found the defendant guilty without naming the fine, the Court would impose a $100 minimum.

The jury followed Judge Raulston's instructions.

The Court then called Scopes to the bench. "The jury has found you guilty," said the judge. He imposed a $100 fine.

In his hurry to pass sentence the judge forgot to ask Scopes if he had anything to say. Realizing this, he backtracked.

COURT: Oh—have you anything to say, Mr. Scopes, as to why this court should not impose punishment upon you?

SCOPES: Your Honor, I feel that I have been convicted of violating an unjust statute. I will continue in the future, as I have in the past, to oppose this law in any way I can. Any other action would be in violation of my ideal of academic freedom—that is, to teach the truth as guaranteed in our Constitution, of personal and religious freedom. I think the fine is unjust.

COURT: The Court now imposes on you a fine of $100 and costs.

Bail was set at $500. The Baltimore Sun acted as bondsman.

A few days after the trial ended, William Jennings Bryan died. Said Darrow: "A man who for years had fought excessive drinking, now lies dead from indigestion caused by overeating."

On appeal of the case by the defense, the Tennessee Supreme Court reversed the lower court's decision on a technicality: the Court had set the fine instead of the jury. The highest court in Tennessee also ordered the case dismissed.

You Can't Live There!

THE SWEET CASE

Detroit, 1926

"YOU'RE ALL PREJUDICED"
DARROW TELLS JURY

[Headline, Detroit *Free Press*, May 12, 1926]

HOUSING SEGREGATION by the mob was the issue in the Sweet trial in Detroit in 1926.

The Negro population of the city had jumped from about 6,000 in 1910 to about 70,000 at the time of the Sweet case sixteen years later. Most of the increase came during the war when Detroit was in the midst of an unprecedented boom in the automobile industry.

The manufacturers brought Negro laborers from the South into the city. However, neither the manufacturers nor the city made any provisions for housing, and the newcomers were jammed into an already overcrowded area.

"The Negro workmen could stay in the automobile factories in the daytime, but they had no place to stay at night, so they expanded the Negro section and some of them moved out to what was called the white district," Darrow said.

This set the stage for the Sweet case.

Dr. Ossian H. Sweet was a successful gynecologist. He had received his M.D. degree from Howard University. He had worked under Madame Curie and was interested in the effects of radium, particularly on cancer. Later he was to study in Vienna.

Returning from Europe, the Sweets first stayed with the parents of Dr. Sweet's wife until they purchased a home. This new home was located at Garland and Charlevoix, a lower-middle-class white neighborhood. In September of 1925, Dr. Sweet, his wife and their two-year-old baby girl moved into this home.

But Dr. Sweet anticipated trouble. Other Negroes moving into homes in white neighborhoods had been intimidated by so-called Improvement Associations and were forced to move out. So with the Sweets' belongings went ten guns and a supply of ammunition.

A white crowd gathered around the house the first night, September 8, but it was relatively quiet. The second night a larger crowd—estimated at several hundred—gathered in the neighborhood of the Sweet home. About eight policemen were on duty to prevent disorder. But now cries of "Niggers!" rumbled through the street.

Dr. Sweet's two brothers, Otis, a dentist, and Henry, a student, together with seven friends, were in the house on the second night with Dr. and Mrs. Sweet. The baby was at her grandmother's home.

The police testified at the trial that all was quiet on the street when suddenly shots were fired from the windows of the Sweet house. A white man, Leon Breiner, sitting nearby smoking his pipe, was killed, and another white man wounded.

The eleven Negroes in the house were immediately arrested and charged with first-degree murder. Arthur Garfield Hays, one of the attorneys for the defense, later commented in court that if the baby had been home she, too, probably would have been arrested.

The National Association for the Advancement of Colored People wired Darrow in Chicago: Would he become chief counsel? They were told Darrow was in New York. Charles H. Studin and Arthur Spingarn, attorneys for the Association, James Weldon Johnson, Negro poet, and Walter White, who was later to become the Association's secretary, met with Darrow in Hays's home.

Spingarn related the Sweet story to Darrow. Darrow was sympathetic; he said he understood the problem of Spingarn's race. Spingarn told the Chicago attorney that though he was a member of the NAACP, he was not a Negro.

Darrow turned to Studin and said, "You know what I mean," to which Studin replied that neither was he a Negro.

"I won't make that mistake with you," Darrow said to blond-haired, blue-eyed Walter White. White answered, "But I am Negro."

This settled it for Darrow. He became chief counsel for the Sweet case, and with him to Detroit went Hays. Also associated with him in this trial were Walter M. Nelson, Julian W. Perry, Cecil O. Rowlette and Charles H. Mahoney of Detroit.

The trial of the eleven Negroes began October 30, 1925, before Judge Frank Murphy of Recorder's Court. Judge Murphy later became a justice of the United States Supreme Court.

Robert M. Toms was prosecuting attorney and Lester S. Moll was his assistant. Darrow throughout the trial referred to Toms as "a nice fellow."

In her pamphlet, "Clarence Darrow's Two Great Trials," Marcet Haldeman-Julius reported that in Detroit Darrow was in a more formal mood than in Dayton, Tennessee, at the Scopes trial. "The famous galluses were safely hidden under well-pressed vest and coat. Almost invariably his gray hair was neatly brushed."

Selection of the jury was long and difficult. When the panel was called, only one colored person was on it and he was peremptorily dismissed.

The defense contended during the trial that the eleven Negroes had used their constitutional rights of self-defense. It was important for the defense to prove that there had been anti-Negro agitation.

The prosecution, on the other hand, contended that there had been no such agitation and that there was no mob around the Sweet home at the time of the killing.

While State witnesses testified they were in the neighborhood of the Sweet home merely because of curiosity, Darrow sat slouched in his chair working a crossword puzzle.

The defense charged that when the neighborhood heard a colored family had bought a home in the area, a "Water Works Improvement Association" had been formed.

Darrow in his cross-examination tried to prove that the purpose of the Association was to keep Negroes out of the neighborhood. Typical was his questioning of State witness Eben E. Draper. Darrow asked Draper whether his joining the Association was prompted by the Sweets' purchasing a home in the area. Draper answered, "Possibly."

DARROW: Did it?

DRAPER: Yes.

DARROW: You joined that club to aid in keeping that a white district?

DRAPER: Yes.

DARROW: At the meeting in the school, was any reference made to keeping the district free from colored people?

DRAPER: Yes.

A youngster of fifteen, a witness for the State, gave the defense the break it was looking for.

Darrow asked him how many people were in the neighborhood.

WITNESS: There was a great crowd—no, I won't say a great crowd, a large crowd—well, there were a few people and the officers were keeping them moving.

DARROW: Have you talked with anyone about the case?

WITNESS: Lieutenant Johnson [the police detective].

DARROW: And when you started to answer the question you forgot to say "a few people," didn't you?

WITNESS: Yes, sir.

Darrow in his plea asked for a verdict of Not Guilty. He pointed out: "The Sweets spent their first night in their first home afraid to go to bed. The next night they spent in jail. Now the State wants them to spend the rest of their lives in the penitentiary. The State claims there was no mob there that night. Gentlemen, the State has put on enough witnesses who said they were there, to make a mob.

"There are persons in the North and the South who say a black man is inferior to a white and should be controlled by the whites. There are those who recognize his rights and say he should try and enjoy them. To me this case is a cross-section of human history. It involves the future, and the hope of some of us that the future shall be better than the past."

The jury was out forty-six hours. No decision could be reached. Judge Murphy declared a mistrial. The jury was dismissed. That was November 27, 1925.

The defense asked that if there were to be any more trials, each defendant be tried separately.

About five months later, in April 1926, the trial of Henry Sweet, younger brother of Dr. Sweet, opened, again in Judge Murphy's court. This time with Darrow appeared Mr. Perry and Thomas W. Chawke.

It took a week to impanel the jury; 165 prospective jurors were questioned. Most were dismissed for cause; peremptory challenges were used against twenty.

When the jury was finally impaneled, it was made up of a retired steamship steward, locomotive engineer, pharmacist, machinist, electrician, electroplater, grocery store manager, a former army man who was at the time of the trial a Water Board employee, a steamship line executive, a retired lumberman, an electrical engineer and contractor, and a watchman. They ranged in age from 24 to 82 years.

The trial was practically identical to the first except for Darrow's plea.

The ex-army man on the jury many times dozed off during the examination and the remark was often heard in the courtroom that "Number eight is asleep again." But he was wide awake during Darrow's final arguments which lasted for seven hours.

"The life of the Negro race has been a life of tragedy, of injustice, of oppression. The law has made him equal, but man has not. And, after all, the last analysis is, what has man done?—and not what has the law done?"

I F THE COURT PLEASE, gentlemen of the jury: You have listened so long and patiently that I do not know whether you are able to stand much more. I want to say, however, that while I have tried a good many cases in the forty-seven or forty-eight years that I have lived in courthouses, that in one way this has been one of the pleasantest trials I have ever been in. The kindness and the consideration of the Court is such as to make it easy for everybody, and I have seldom found as courteous, gentlemanly and kindly opponents as I have had in this case. I appreciate their friendship. Lawyers are apt to look at cases from different standpoints, and I sometimes find it difficult to understand how a lawyer on the other side can think as he thinks and say what he says; I, being an extremely reasonable man and entirely free from all kinds of prejudices myself, find this hard to comprehend.

My friend Mr. Moll says, gentlemen, that this isn't a race question. This is a murder case. We don't want any prejudice; we don't want the other side to have any. Race and color have nothing to do with this case. This is a case of murder.

I insist that there is nothing but prejudice in this case; that if it was reversed and eleven white men had shot and killed a black while protecting their home and their lives against a mob of blacks, nobody would have dreamed of having them indicted. I know what I am talking about, and so do you. They would have been given medals instead. Ten colored men and one woman are in this indictment, tried by twelve jurors, gentlemen. Every one of you are white, aren't you? At least you all think so. We haven't one colored man on this jury. We couldn't get one. One was called and he was disqualified. You twelve white men are trying a colored man on race prejudice.

Now, let me ask you whether you are not prejudiced. I want to put this square to you, gentlemen. I haven't any doubt but that every one of you is prejudiced against colored people. I want you to guard against it. I want you to do all you can to be fair in this case, and I believe you will. A number of you have answered the question that you are acquainted with colored people. One juror I have in mind, who is sitting here, said there were two or three families living on the street in the block where he lives, and he had lived there for a year or more, but he didn't know their names and had never met them. Some of the rest of you said that you had employed colored people to work for you, are even employing them now. All right. You have seen some colored people in this case. They have been so far above the white people that live at the corner of Garland and Charlevoix that they can't be compared, intellectually, morally and physically, and you know it. How many of you jurors, gentlemen, have ever had a colored person visit you in your home? How many of you have ever visited in their homes? How many of you have invited them to dinner at your house? Probably not one of you. Now, why, gentlemen? There isn't one of you men but what knows just from the witnesses you have seen in this case that there are colored people who are intellectually the equal of all of you. Am I right? Colored people living right here in the city of Detroit are intellectually the equals and some of them superior to most of us. Is that true? Some of them are people of more character and learning than most of us.

* * *

Now, why don't you individually, and why don't I, and why doesn't every white person whose chances have been greater and whose wealth is larger, associate with them? There is only one reason, and that is prejudice. Can you give any other reason for it? They would be intellectual companions. They have good manners. They are clean. They are all of them clean enough to wait on us, but not clean enough to associate with. Is there any reason in the world why we don't associate with them excepting prejudice? I think not one man of this jury wants to be prejudiced. It is forced into us almost from our youth, until somehow or other we feel we are superior to these people who have black faces.

Now, gentlemen, I say you are prejudiced. I fancy everyone of you is, otherwise you would have some companions amongst these colored people. You will overcome it, I believe, in the trial of this case. But they tell me there is no race prejudice, and it is plain nonsense, and nothing else.

Who are we, anyway? A child is born into this world without any knowledge of any sort. He has a brain which is a piece of putty; he inherits nothing in the way of knowledge or of ideas. If he is white, he knows nothing about color. He has no antipathy to the black. The black and the white both will live together and play together, but as soon as the baby is born we begin giving him ideas. We begin planting seeds in his mind. We begin telling him he must do this and he must not do that. We tell him about race and social equality and the thousands of things that men talk about until he grows up. It has been trained into us, and you, gentlemen, bring that feeling into this jury box.

You need not tell me you are not prejudiced. I know better. We are not very much but a bundle of prejudices anyhow. We are prejudiced against other people's color. Prejudiced against other men's religions; prejudiced against other people's politics. Prejudiced against people's looks. Prejudiced about the way they dress. We are full of prejudices. You can teach a man anything beginning with the child; you can make anything out of him, and we are not responsible for it. Here and there some of us haven't any prejudices on some questions, but if you look deep enough you will find them; and we all know it.

All I hope for, gentlemen of the jury, is this: that you are strong enough, and honest enough, and decent enough to lay it aside in this case and decide it as you ought to. And I say, there is no man in Detroit that doesn't know that these defendants, every one of them, did right. There isn't a man in Detroit who doesn't know that the defendant did his duty, and that this case is an attempt to send him and his companions to prison because they defended their constitutional rights. It is a wicked attempt, and you are asked to be a party to it. You know it. I don't need to talk to this jury about the facts in this case. There is no man who can read or can understand that does not know the facts. Is there prejudice in it?

Now, let's see. I don't want to lean very much on your intelligence. I don't need much. I just need a little. Would this case be in this court if these defendants were not black? Would we be standing in front of you if these defendants were not black? Would anybody be asking you to send a boy to prison for life for defending his brother's home and protecting his own life, if his face wasn't black? What were the people in the neighborhood of Charlevoix and Garland Streets doing on that fatal night? There isn't a child that doesn't know. Have you any doubt as to why they were there? Was Mr. Moll right when he said that color has nothing to do with the case? There is nothing else in this case but the feeling of prejudice which has been carefully nourished by the white man until he doesn't know that he has it himself. While I admire and like my friend Moll very much, I can't help criticizing his argument. I suppose I may say what old men are apt to say, in a sort of patronizing way, that his zeal is due to youth and inexperience. That is about all we have to brag about as we get older, so we ought to be permitted to do that. Let us look at this case.

Mr. Moll took particular pains to say to you, gentlemen, that these eleven people here are guilty of murder; he calls this a cold-blooded, deliberate and premeditated murder; that is, they were there to kill. That was their purpose. Eleven, he said. I am not going to discuss the case of all of them just now, but I am starting where he started. He doesn't want any misunderstanding. Amongst that eleven is Mrs. Sweet, the wife of Dr. Sweet. She is a murderer, gentlemen? The state's attorney said so, and the assistant state's attorney said so. The state's attorney would have to endorse it because he himself stands by what his assistant says. Pray, tell me what has Mrs. Sweet done to make her a murderer? She is the wife of Dr. Sweet. She is the mother of his little baby. She left the child at her mother's home while she moved into this highly cultured community near Goethe Street. Anyway, the baby was to be safe; but she took her own chance, and she didn't have a gun; none was provided for her. Brother Toms drew from the witnesses that there were ten guns, and ten men. He didn't leave any for her. Maybe she had a penknife, but there is no evidence on that question. What did she do, gentlemen? She is put down here as a murderer. She wasn't even upstairs. She didn't even look out of a window. She was down in the back kitchen cooking a ham to feed her family and friends, and a white mob came to drive them out of their home before the ham was served for dinner. She is a murderer, and all of these defendants who were driven out of their home must go to the penitentiary for life if you can find twelve jurors somewhere who have enough prejudice in their hearts, and hatred in their minds.

Now, that is this case, gentlemen, and that is all there is to this case. Take the hatred away, and you have nothing left. Mr. Moll says that this is a case between Breiner and Henry Sweet.

MOLL: No, I did not say any such thing.

DARROW: Well, let me correct it. He says that he holds a brief for Breiner. That is right; isn't it?

MOLL: That is right.

DARROW: Well, I will put it just as it is, he holds a brief for Breiner, this prosecuting attorney. He is wrong. If he holds a brief for Breiner, he should throw it in the stove. It has no place in a court of justice. The question here is whether these defendants or this defendant is guilty of murder. It has nothing to do with Breiner. He says that I wiggled and squirmed every time they mentioned Breiner. Well, now, I don't know. Did I? Maybe I did. I didn't know it. I have been around courtrooms so long that I fancy I could listen to anything without moving a hair. Maybe I couldn't.

I rather think my friend is pretty wise. He said that I don't like to hear them talk about Breiner. I don't, gentlemen, and I might have shown it. This isn't the first case I was ever in. I don't like to hear the state's attorney talk about the blood of a victim. It has such a mussy sound. I wish they would leave it out. I will be frank with you about it. I don't think it has any place in a case. I think it tends to create prejudice and feeling and it has no place, and it is always dangerous. And perhaps— whether I showed it or not, my friend read my mind. I don't like it.

Now, gentlemen, as he talked about Breiner, I am going to talk about him, and it isn't easy, either. It isn't easy to talk about the dead, unless you "slobber" over them and I am not going to "slobber" over Breiner. I am going to tell you the truth about it. Why did he say that he held a brief for Breiner, and ask you to judge between Breiner and Henry Sweet? You know why he said it. To get a verdict, gentlemen. That is why he said it. Had it any place in this case? Henry Sweet never knew that such a man lived as Breiner. Did he? He didn't shoot at him. Somebody shot out into that crowd and Breiner got it. Nobody had any feeling against him. But who was Breiner, any-way? I will tell you who he was. I am going to measure my words when I state it, and I am going to make good before I am through in what I say.

*　*　*

Who was he? He was a conspirator in as foul a conspiracy as was ever hatched in a community; in a conspiracy to drive from their homes a little family of black people. Not only that, but to destroy these blacks and their home. Now, let me see whether I am right. What do we know of Breiner? He lived two blocks from the Sweet home. On the fourteenth day of July, seven hundred people met at the schoolhouse and the schoolhouse was too small, and they went out into the yard. This schoolhouse was right across the street from the Sweet house.

Every man in that community knew all about it. Every man in that community understood it. And in that schoolhouse a man rose and told what they had done in his community; that by main force they had driven Negro families from their homes, and that when a Negro moved to Garland Street, their people would be present to help. That is why Mr. Breiner came early to the circus on September 9, 1925. He went past that house, back and forth, two or three times that night. What was he doing? "Smoking his pipe." What were the rest of them doing? They were a part of a mob and they had no rights, and the Court will tell you so, I think. And, if he does, gentlemen, it is your duty to accept it.

* * *

Gentlemen, it is a reflection upon anybody's intelligence to say that everyone did not know why this mob was there. You know! Every one of you know why. They came early to take their seats at the ringside. Didn't they? And Breiner sat at one point where the stones were thrown, didn't he? Was he a member of that mob? Gentlemen, that mob was bent not only on making an assault upon the rights of the owners of that house, not only making an assault upon their persons and their property, but they were making an assault on the constitution and the laws of the nation and the state under which they live.

* * *

Gentlemen, my friend said that he wasn't going to mince matters. I think I will, because I know the prejudice is the other way. You can pick twelve men in these black faces that are watching your deliberations and have throughout all these weary days, and with them I would not need to mince matters; but I must be very careful not to shock your sensibilities. I must state just as much or as near the facts as I dare to state without shocking you and be fair to my client.

It was bad enough for a mob, by force and violation of law, to attempt to drive these people from their house but, gentlemen, it is worse to send them to prison for life for defending their home. Think of it. That is this case. Are we human? Hardly.

Did the witnesses for the State appearing here tell the truth? You know they did not. I am not going to analyze the testimony of every one of them. But they did not tell the truth and they did not mean to tell the truth. Let me ask you this question, gentlemen: Mr. Moll says that these colored people had a perfect right to live in that house. He did not say it was an outrage to molest them. Oh, no, he said they had a perfect right to live in that house. But the mob met there to drive them out. That is exactly what they did, and they have lied and lied and lied to send these defendants to the penitentiary for life, so that they will not go back to their home.

Now, you know that the mob met there for that purpose. They violated the Constitution and the law; they violated every human feeling, and threw justice and mercy and humanity to the winds, and they made a murderous attack upon their neighbor because his face was black. Which is the worse, to do that or lie about it? In describing this mob, I heard the word "few" from the State's witnesses so many times that I could hear it in my sleep, and I presume that when I am dying I will hear that "few," "few," "few" stuff that I heard in Detroit from people who lied and lied and lied. What was this "few?" And who were they, and how did they come there?

I can't tell you about every one of these witnesses, but I can tell you about some of them. Too many. I can't even carry all of their names in my mind and I don't want to. There are other things more interesting—bugs, for instance. Anything is more interesting to carry in your mind than the names of that bunch, and yet I am going to say something for them, too, because I know something about human nature and life; and I want to be fair, and if I did not want to, I think perhaps it would pay me to be.

Are the people who live around the corner of Charlevoix and Garland worse than other people? There isn't one of you who doesn't know that they lied. There isn't one of you who does not know that they tried to drive those people out and now are trying to send them to the penitentiary so that they can't move back; all in violation of the law, and are trying to get you to do the job. Are they worse than other people? I don't know as they are. How much do you know about prejudice? Race prejudice. Religious prejudice. These feelings that have divided men and caused them to do the most terrible things. Prejudices have burned men at the stake, broken them on the rack, torn every joint apart, destroyed people by the million. Men have done this on account of some terrible prejudice which even now is reaching out to undermine this republic of ours and to destroy the freedom that has been the most cherished part of our institutions. These witnesses honestly believe that they are better than blacks. I do not. They honestly believe that it is their duty to keep colored people out. They honestly believe that blacks are an inferior race and yet if they look at themselves, I don't know how they can.

*   *   *

Gentlemen, lawyers are very intemperate in their statements. My friend, Moll, said that my client here was a coward. A coward, gentlemen. Here, he says, were a gang of gunmen, and cowards—shot Breiner through the back. Nobody saw Breiner, of course. If he had his face turned toward the house, while he was smoking there, waiting for the shooting to begin, it wasn't our fault. It wouldn't make any difference which way he turned. I suppose the bullet would have killed him just the same, if he had been in the way of it. If he had been at home, it would not have happened. Who are the cowards in this case? Cowards, gentlemen! Eleven people with black skins, eleven people, gentlemen, whose ancestors did not come to America because they wanted to, but were brought here in slave ships, to toil for nothing, for the whites—whose lives have been taken in nearly every state in the Union—they have been victims of riots all over this land of the free. They have had to take what is left after everybody else had grabbed what he wanted. The only place where he has been put in front is on the battlefield. When we are fighting we give him a chance to die, and the best chance. But, everywhere else, he has been food for the flames, and the ropes, and the knives, and the guns and hate of the white, regardless of law and liberty, and the common sentiments of justice that should move men. Were they cowards?

No, gentlemen, they may have been gunmen. They may have tried to murder. But they were not cowards. Eleven people, knowing what it meant, with the history of the race behind them, with the knowledge of shootings and killings and insult and injury without end, eleven of them go into a house, gentlemen, with no police protection, in the face of a mob, and the hatred of a community, and take guns and ammunition and fight for their rights, and for your rights and for mine, and for the rights of every being that lives. They went in and faced a mob seeking to tear them to bits. Call them something besides cowards. The cowardly curs were in the mob gathered there with the backing of the law. A lot of children went in front and threw the stones. They stayed for two days and two nights in front of this home, and by their threats and assault were trying to drive the Negroes out. Those were the cowardly curs, and you know it. I suppose there isn't any ten of them that would come out in the open daylight against those ten. Oh no, gentlemen, their blood is too pure for that. They can only act like a band of coyotes baying some victim who has no chance. And then my clients are called cowards.

All right, gentlemen, call them something else. These blacks have been called many names along down through the ages, but there have been those through the sad years who believed in justice and mercy and charity and love and kindliness, and there have been those who believed that a black man should have some rights, even in a country where he was brought in chains. There are those even crazy enough to hope and to dream that sometime he will come from under this cloud and take his place amongst the people of the world. If he does, it will be through his courage and his culture. It will be by his intelligence and his scholarship and his effort, and I say, gentlemen of the jury, no honest, right-feeling man, whether on a jury or anywhere else, would place anything in his way in this great struggle behind him and before him.

*   *   *

What are you, gentlemen? And what am I? I don't know. I can only go a little way toward the source of my own being. I know my father and I know my mother. I know my grandmothers and my grandfathers on both sides, but I didn't know my great-grandfathers and great-grandmothers on either side, and I don't know who they were. All that a man can do in this direction is but little. He can only slightly raise the veil that hangs over all the past. He can peer into the darkness just a little way and that is all. I know that somewhere around 1600, as the record goes, some of my ancestors came from England. Some of them. I don't know where all of them came from, and I don't think any human being knows where all his ancestors came from. But back of that, I can say nothing. What do you know of yours? I will tell you what I know, or what I think I know, gentlemen. I will try to speak as modestly as I can, knowing the uncertainty of human knowledge, because it is uncertain. The best I can do is to go a little way back. I know that back of us all and each of us is the blood of all the world. I know that it courses in your veins and mine. It has all come out of the infinite past, and I can't pick out mine and you can't pick out yours, and it is only the ignorant who know, and I believe that back of that—back of that—is what we call the lower order of life; back of that there lurks the instinct of the distant serpent, of the carnivorous tiger. All the elements have been gathered together to make the mixture that is you and I and all the race, and nobody knows anything about his own. Gentlemen, I wonder who we are anyhow, to be so proud about our ancestry? We had better try to do something to be proud of ourselves; we had better try to do something kindly, something humane, to some human being, than to brag about our ancestry, of which none of us know anything.

Now, let us go back to the street again. I don't know. Perhaps I weary you. Perhaps these things that seem important to me are unimportant, but they are all a part of the great human tragedy that stands before us. And if I could do something, which I can't, to make the world better, I would try to have it more tolerant, more kindly, more understanding; could I do that and nothing else, I would be glad.

* * *

The police department went up there on the morning of the eighth, in the city of Detroit, in the state of Michigan, U.S.A., to see that a family were permitted to move into a home that they owned without getting their throats cut by the noble Nordics who inhabit that jungle. Fine, isn't it? No race question in this? Oh, no, this is a murder case, and yet, in the forenoon of the eighth, they sent four policemen there, to protect a man and his wife, with two little truckloads of household furniture, who were moving into that place. Pretty tough, isn't it? Aren't you glad you are not black? You deserve a lot of credit for it, don't you, because you didn't choose black ancestry? People ought to be killed who chose black ancestry. The policemen went there to protect the lives and the small belongings of these humble folks who moved into their home. What are these black people to do?

I seem to wander from one thing to another without much sequence. I must get back again to the colored man. You don't want him. Perhaps you don't want him next to you. Suppose you were colored. Did any of you ever dream that you were colored? Did you ever wake up out of a nightmare when you dreamed that you were colored? Would you be willing to have my client's skin? Why? Just because somebody is prejudiced! Imagine yourselves colored, gentlemen. Imagine yourselves back in the Sweet house on that fatal night. That is the only right way to treat this case, and the Court will tell you so. Would you move there? Where would you move? Dancy says there were six or seven thousand colored people here sixteen years ago. And seventy-one thousand five years ago. Gentlemen, why are they here? They came here as you came here, under the laws of trade and business, under the instincts to live; both the white and the colored, just the same; the instincts of all animals to propagate their kind, the feelings back of life and on which life depends. They came here to live. Your factories were open for them. Mr. Ford hired them. The automobile companies hired them. Everybody hired them. They were all willing to give them work, weren't they? Every one of them. You and I are willing to give them work, too. We are willing to have them in our houses to take care of the children and do the rough work that we shun ourselves. They are not offensive, either. We invited them; pretty nearly all the colored population has come to Detroit in the last fifteen years; most of them, anyhow. They have always had a corner on the meanest jobs. The city must grow, or you couldn't brag about it. The colored people must live somewhere. Everybody is willing to have them live somewhere else. The people at the corner of Garland and Charlevoix would be willing to have them go to some other section. Everybody would be willing to have them go somewhere else.

Somewhere they must live. Are you going to kill them? Are you going to say that they can work, but they can't get a place to sleep? They can toil in the mill, but can't eat their dinner at home. We want them to build automobiles for us, don't we? We even let them become our chauffeurs. Oh, gentlemen, what is the use! You know it is wrong. Every one of you knows it is wrong. You know that no man in conscience could blame a Negro for almost anything. Can you think of these people without shouldering your own responsibility? Don't make it harder for them, I beg you.

They sent four policemen in the morning to help this little family move in. They had a bedstead, a stove and some bedding, ten guns and some ammunition, and they had food to last them through a siege. I feel that they should have taken less furniture and more food and guns.

Gentlemen, nature works in a queer way. I don't know how this question of color will ever be solved, or whether it will be solved. Nature has a way of doing things. There is one thing about nature, she has plenty of time. She would make broad prairies so that we can raise wheat and corn to feed men. How does she do it? She sends a glacier plowing across a continent, and takes fifty thousand years to harrow it and make it fit to till and support human life. She makes a man. She tries endless experiments before the man is done. She wants to make a race and it takes an infinite mixture to make it. She wants to give us some conception of human rights, and some kindness and charity, and she makes pain and suffering and sorrow and death. It all counts. That is a rough way, but it is the only way. It all counts in the great, long, broad scheme of things. I look on a trial like this with a feeling of disgust and shame. I can't help it now. It will be after we have learned in the terrible and expensive school of human experience that we will be willing to find each other and understand each other.

*　　*　　*

Now, let us get to the bare facts of this case. The city of Detroit had the police force there to help these people move into their home. When they unloaded their goods, men and women on the street began going from house to house. They went from house to house to sound the alarm, "the Negroes are coming," as if a foreign army was invading their homes; as if a wild beast had come down out of the mountains in the olden times. Can you imagine those colored people? They didn't dare move without thinking of their color. Where we go into a hotel unconsciously, or a church, if we choose, they do not. Of course, colored people belong to a church, and they have a YMCA. That is, a Jim Crow YMCA. The black Christians cannot mix with the white Christians. They will probably have a Jim Crow Heaven where the white angels will not be obliged to meet the black angels, except as servants.

       ✿   ✿   ✿

Gentlemen, they say there is nothing to justify this shooting; it was an orderly, neighborly crowd; an orderly, neighborly crowd. They came there for a purpose and intended to carry it out. How long, pray, would these men wait penned up in that house? How long would you wait? The very presence of the crowd was a mob, as I believe the Court will tell you. Suppose a crowd gathers around your house; a crowd which doesn't want you there; a hostile crowd, for a part of two days and two nights, until the police force of this city is called in to protect you. How long, tell me, are you going to live in that condition with a mob surrounding your house and the police force standing in front of it? How long should these men have waited? You wouldn't have waited. Counsel say they had just as good reason to shoot on the eighth as on the ninth. Concede it. They did not shoot. They waited and hoped and prayed that in some way this crowd would pass them by and grant them the right to live. The mob came back the next night and the colored people waited while they were gathering; they waited while they were coming from every street and every corner, and while the officers were supine and helpless and doing nothing. And they waited until dozens of stones were thrown against the house on the roof, probably—I don't know how many. Nobody knows how many. They waited until the windows were broken before they shot. Why did they wait so long? I think I know. How much chance had these people for their lives after they shot, surrounded by a crowd as they were? They would never take a chance unless they thought it was necessary to take the chance. Eleven black people penned up in the face of a mob. What chance did they have?

Suppose they shot before they should. What is the theory of counsel in this case? Nobody pretends there is anything in this case to prove that our client Henry fired the fatal shot. There isn't the slightest. It wasn't a shot that would fit the gun he had. The theory of this case is that he was part of a combination to do something. Now, what was that combination, gentlemen? Your own sense will tell you what it was. Did they combine to go there and kill somebody? Were they looking for somebody to murder? Dr. Sweet scraped together his small earnings by his industry and put himself through college, and he scraped together his small earnings of three thousand dollars to buy that home because he wanted to kill somebody?

It is silly to talk about it. He bought that home just as you buy yours, because he wanted a home to live in, to take his wife and to raise his family. There is no difference between the love of a black man for his offspring and the love of a white. He and his wife had the same feeling of fatherly and motherly affection for their child that you gentlemen have for yours, and that your father and mother had for you. They bought that home for that purpose; not to kill somebody. They might have feared trouble, as they probably did, and as the evidence shows that every man with a black face fears it, when he moves into a home that is fit for a dog to live in. It is part of the curse that, for some inscrutable reason, has followed the race—if you call it a race—and which curse, let us hope, sometime the world will be wise enough and decent enough and human enough to wipe out.

They went there to live. They knew the dangers. Why do you suppose they took these guns and this ammunition and these men there? Because they wanted to kill somebody? It is utterly absurd and crazy. They took them there because they thought it might be necessary to defend their home with their lives and they were determined to do it. They took guns there that in case of need they might fight, fight even to death for their home, and for each other, for their people, for their race, for their rights under the Constitution and the laws under which all of us live; and unless men and women will do that, we will soon be a race of slaves, whether we are black or white. "Eternal vigilance is the price of liberty," and it has always been so and always will be. Do you suppose they were in there for any other purpose?

Gentlemen, there isn't a chance that they took arms there for anything else. They did go there knowing their rights, feeling their responsibility, and determined to maintain those rights if it meant death to the last man and the last woman, and no one could do more. No man lived a better life or died a better death than fighting for his home and his children, for himself, and for the eternal principles upon which life depends. Instead of being here under indictment, for murder, they should be honored for the brave stand they made for their rights and ours. Some day, both white and black, irrespective of color, will honor the memory of these men, whether they are inside prison walls or outside, and will recognize that they fought not only for themselves, but for every man who wishes to be free.

Did they shoot too quick? Tell me just how long a man needs wait for a mob? The Court, I know, will instruct you on that. How long do you need to wait for a mob? We have been told that because a person trespasses on your home or on your ground you have no right to shoot him. Is that true? If I go up to your home in a peaceable way, and go on your ground, or on your porch, you have no right to shoot me. You have a right to use force to put me off if I refuse to go, even to the extent of killing me. That isn't this case, gentlemen. That isn't the case of a neighbor who went up to the yard of a neighbor without permission and was shot to death. Oh, no. The Court will tell you the difference, unless I am mistaken, and I am sure I am not; unless I mistake the law, and I am sure I do not. This isn't a case of a man who trespasses upon the ground of some other man and is killed. It is the case of an un-lawful mob, which in itself is a crime; a mob bent on mischief; a mob that has no rights. They are too dangerous. It is like a fire. One man may do something. Two will do much more; three will do more than three times as much; a crowd will do something that no man ever dreamed of doing. The law recognizes it. It is the duty of every man—I don't care who he is—to disperse a mob. It is the duty of the officers to disperse them. It was the duty of the inmates of the house, even though they had to kill somebody to do it.

Now, gentlemen, I wouldn't ask you to take the law on my statement. The Court will tell you the law. A mob is a criminal combination of itself. Their presence is enough. You need not wait until it spreads. It is there, and that is enough. There is no other law; there hasn't been for years, and it is the law which will govern this case.

Now, gentlemen, how long did they need to wait? Why, it is silly. How long would you wait? How long do you suppose ten white men would be waiting? Would they have waited as long? I will tell you how long they needed to wait. I will tell you what the law is, and the Court will confirm me, I am sure. Every man may act upon appearances as they seem to him. Every man may protect his own life. Every man has the right to protect his own property. Every man is bound under the law to disperse a mob even to the extent of taking life. It is his duty to do it, but back of that he has the human right to go to the extent of killing to defend his life. He has a right to defend the life of his kinsman, servant, his friends, or those about him, and he has a right to defend, gentlemen, not from real danger, but from what seems to him real danger at the time.

Here is Henry Sweet, the defendant in this case, a boy. How many of you know why you are trying him? What had he to do with it? Why is he in this case? A boy, twenty-one years old, working his way through college, and he is just as good a boy as the boy of any juror in this box; just as good a boy as you people were when you were boys, and I submit to you, he did nothing whatever that was wrong. Of course, we lawyers talk and talk and talk, as if we feared results. I don't mean to trifle with you. I always fear results. When life or liberty is in the hands of a lawyer, he realizes the terrible responsibility that is on him, and he fears that some word will be left unspoken, or some thought will be forgotten. I would not be telling you the truth if I told you that I did not fear the result of this important case; and when my judgment and my reason come to my aid and take counsel with my fears, I know, and I feel perfectly well that no twelve American jurors, especially in any Northern land, could be brought together who would dream of taking a boy's life or liberty under circumstances like this. That is what my judgment tells me, but my fears perhaps cause me to go further and to say more when I should not have said as much.

Now, let me tell you when a man has the right to shoot in self-defense, and in defense of his home; not when these vital things in life are in danger, but when he thinks they are. These despised blacks did not need to wait until the house was beaten down above their heads. They didn't need to wait until every window was broken. They didn't need to wait longer for that mob to grow more inflamed. There is nothing so dangerous as ignorance and bigotry when it is unleashed as it was here. The Court will tell you that these inmates of this house had the right to decide upon appearances, and if they did, even though they were mistaken, they are not guilty. I don't know but they could safely have stayed a little longer. I don't know but it would have been well enough to let this mob break a few more windowpanes. I don't know but it would have been better and been safe to let them batter down the house before they shot. I don't know. How am I to tell, and how are you to tell?

You are twelve white men, gentlemen. You are twelve men sitting here eight months after all this occurred, listening to the evidence, perjured and otherwise, in this court, to tell whether they acted too quickly or too slowly. A man may be running an engine on the railroad. He may stop too quickly or too slowly. In an emergency he is bound to do one or the other, and the jury a year after, sitting in cold blood, may listen to the evidence and say that he acted too quickly. What do they know about it? You must sit out there upon a moving engine with your hand on the throttle and facing danger and must decide and act quickly. Then you can tell.

Cases often occur in the courts, which doesn't speak very well for the decency of courts, but they have happened, where men have been shipwrecked at sea, a number of the men having left the ship and gone into a small boat to save their lives; they have floated around for hours and tossed on the wild waves of an angry sea; their food disappearing, the boat heavy and likely to sink and no friendly sail in sight . . . What are they to do? Will they throw some of their companions off the boat and save the rest? Will they eat some to save the others? If they kill anybody, it is because they want to live. Every living thing wants to live. The strongest instinct in life is to keep going. You have seen a tree upon a rock send a shoot down for ten or fifteen or twenty feet, to search for water, to draw it up, that it may still survive; it is a strong instinct with animals and with plants, with all sentient things, to keep alive. Men are out in a boat, in an angry sea, with little food, and less water. No hope in sight. What will they do? They throw a companion overboard to save themselves, or they kill somebody to save themselves. Juries have come into court and passed on the question of whether they should have waited longer, or not. Later, the survivors were picked up by a ship and perhaps, if they had waited longer, all would have been saved. Yet a jury, months after it was over, sitting safely in their jury box, pass upon the question of whether they acted too quickly or not. Can they tell? No. To decide that case, you must be in a small boat, with little food and water; in a wild sea, with no sail in sight, and drifting around for hours or days in the face of the deep, beset by hunger and darkness and fear and hope. Then you can tell; but, no man can tell without it. It can't be done, gentlemen, and the law says so, and this Court will tell you so.

Let me tell you what you must do, gentlemen. It is fine for lawyers to say, naïvely, that nothing happened. No foot was set upon that ground; as if you had to put your foot on the premises. You might put your hand on. The foot isn't sacred. No foot was set upon their home. No shot was fired, nothing except that the house was stoned and windows broken, and an angry crowd was outside seeking their destruction. That is all. That is all, gentlemen. I say that no American citizen, unless he is black, need wait until an angry mob sets foot upon his premises before he kills. I say that no free man need wait to see just how far an aggressor will go before he takes life. The first instinct a man has is to save his life. He doesn't need to experiment. He hasn't time to experiment. When he thinks it is time to save his life, he has the right to act. There isn't any question about it. It has been the law of every English-speaking country so long as we have had law. Every man's home is his castle, which even the king may not enter. Every man has a right to kill, to defend himself or his family, or others, either in the defense of the home or in the defense of themselves. So far as that branch of the case is concerned, there is only one thing that this jury has a right to consider, and that is whether the defendants acted in honest fear of danger. That is all. Perhaps they could have safely waited longer. I know a little about psychology. If I could talk to a man long enough, and not too long, and he talk to me a little, I could guess fairly well what is going on in his head, but I can't understand the psychology of a mob, and neither can anybody else. We know it is unreasoning. We know it is filled with hatred. We know it is cruel. We know it has no heart, no soul, and no pity. We know it is as cruel as the grave. No man has a right to stop and dicker while waiting for a mob.

❖   ❖   ❖

Now, let us look at these fellows. Here were eleven colored men, penned up in the house. Put yourselves in their place. Make yourselves colored for a little while. It won't hurt, you can wash it off. They can't, but you can; just make yourself black for a little while; long enough, gentlemen, to judge them, and before any of you would want to be judged, you would want your juror to put himself in your place. That is all I ask in this case, gentlemen. They were black, and they knew the history of the black. Our friend makes fun of Dr. Sweet and Henry

YOU CAN'T LIVE THERE!

Sweet talking these things all over in the short space of two months. Well, gentlemen, let me tell you something, that isn't evidence. This is just theory. This is just theory, and nothing else. I should imagine that the only thing that two or three colored people talk of when they get together is race. I imagine that they can't rub color off their faces or rub it out of their minds. I imagine that it is with them always. I imagine that the stories of lynchings, the stories of murders, the stories of oppression is a topic of constant conversation. I imagine that everything that appears in the newspapers on this subject is carried from one to another until every man knows what others know, upon the topic which is the most important of all to their lives.

What do you think about it? Suppose you were black. Do you think you would forget it even in your dreams? Or would you have black dreams? Suppose you had to watch every point of contact with your neighbor and remember your color, and you knew your children were growing up under this handicap. Do you suppose you would think of anything else? Do you suppose this boy coming in here didn't know all about the conditions, and did not learn all about them? Did he not know about Detroit? Do you suppose he hadn't read the story of his race? He is intelligent. He goes to school. He would have been a graduate now, except for this long hesitation, when he is waiting to see whether he goes back to college or goes to jail. Do you suppose that black students and teachers are discussing it? Anyhow, gentlemen, what is the use? The jury isn't supposed to be entirely ignorant. They are supposed to know something. These black people were in the house with the black man's psychology, and with the black man's fear, based on what they had heard and what they had read and what they knew. I don't need to go far. I don't need to travel to Florida. I don't even need to talk about the Chicago riots. The testimony showed that in Chicago a colored boy on a raft had been washed to a white bathing beach, and men and boys of my race stoned him to death. A riot began, and some hundred and twenty were killed. I don't need to go to Washington or to St. Louis. Let us take Detroit. I don't need to go far either in space or time. Let us take this city. Now, gentlemen, I am not saying that the white people of Detroit are different from the white people of any other city. I know what has been done in Chicago. I know what prejudice growing out of race and religion has done the world over, and all through time. I am not blaming Detroit. I am stating what has happened, that is all. And I appeal to you, gentlemen, to do your part to save the honor of this city, to save its reputation, to save yours, to save its name, and to save the poor colored people who cannot save themselves.

I was told there had not been a lynching of a colored man in thirty years or more in Michigan. All right. Why, I can remember when the early statesmen of Michigan cared for the colored man and when they embodied the rights of the colored men in the constitution and statutes. I can remember when they laid the foundation that made it possible for a man of any color or any religion, or any creed, to own his home wherever he could find a man to sell it. I remember when civil rights laws were passed that gave the Negro the right to go where the white man went and as he went. There are some men who seem to think those laws were wrong. I do not. Wrong or not, it is the law, and if you were black you would protest with every fiber of your body your right to live. Michigan used to protect the rights of colored people. There were not many of them here, but they have come in the last few years, and with them has come prejudice. Then, too, the Southern white man has followed his black slave. But that isn't all. Black labor has come in competition with white. Prejudices have been created where there was no prejudice before. We have listened to the siren song that we are a superior race and have superior rights, and that the black man has none. It is a new idea in Detroit that a colored man's home can be torn down about his head because he is black. There are some eighty thousand blacks here now, and they are bound to reach out. They have reached out in the past, and they will reach out in the future. Do not make any mistake, gentlemen. I am making no promises. I know the instinct for life. I know it reaches black and white alike. I know that you cannot confine any body of people to any particular place; and, as the population grows, the colored people will go farther.

I know it, and you must change the law or you must take it as it is, or you must invoke the primal law of nature and get back to clubs and fists, and if you are ready for that, gentlemen, all right, but do it with your eyes open. That is all I care for. You must have a government of law or blind force, and if you are ready to let blind force take the place of law, the responsibility is on you, not on me.

Now, let us see what has happened here. So far as I know, there had been nothing of the sort happened when Dr. Sweet bought his home. He took an option on it in May, and got his deed in June; and in July, in that one month, while he was deliberating on moving, there were three cases of driving Negro families out of their homes in Detroit. This was accomplished by stones, clubs, guns and mobs. Suppose one of you were colored and had bought a house on Garland Avenue. Take this just exactly as it is. You bought it in June, intending to move in July, and you read and heard about what happened in another part of the city. Would you have waited? Would you have waited a month, as Sweet did?

Remember, these men didn't have any too much money. Dr. Sweet paid three thousand dollars on his home, leaving a loan on it of sixteen thousand dollars more. He had to scrape together some money to buy his furniture, and he bought fourteen hundred dollars' worth the day after he moved in and paid two hundred dollars down. Gentlemen, it is only right to consider Dr. Sweet and his family. He has a little child. He has a wife. They must live somewhere. If they could not, it would be better to take them out and kill them, and kill them decently and quickly. Had he any right to be free? They determined to move in and to take nine men with them. What would you have done, gentlemen? If you had courage, you would have done as Dr. Sweet did. You would have been crazy or a coward if you hadn't. Would you have moved in alone? No, you would not have gone alone. You would have taken your wife. If you had a brother or two, you would have taken them because you would know that you could rely on them, and you would have taken those nearest to you. And you would have moved in just as Dr. Sweet did. Wouldn't you? He didn't shoot the first night.

He didn't look for trouble. He kept his house dark so that the neighbors wouldn't see him. He didn't dare have a light in his house, gentlemen, for fear of the neighbors. Noble neighbors, who were to have a colored family in their neighborhood. He had the light put out in the front part of the house, so as not to tempt any of the mob to violence.

Now, let us go back a little. What happened before this? I don't need to go over the history of the case. Everybody who wants to understand knows it, and many who don't want to understand it. As soon as Dr. Sweet bought this house, the neighbors organized the "Water Works Park Improvement Association." They were going to aid the police. They didn't get a chance to try to aid them until that night. They were going to regulate automobile traffic. They didn't get any chance to regulate automobile traffic until that night. They were going to protect the homes and make them safe for children. The purpose was clear, and every single member reluctantly said that they joined it to keep colored people out of the district. They might have said it first as well as last. People, even in a wealthy and aristocratic neighborhood like Garland and Charlevoix, don't give up a dollar without expecting some profit; not a whole dollar. Sometimes two in one family, the husband and wife, joined. They got in quick. The woods were on fire. Something had to be done, as quick as they heard that Dr. Sweet was coming; Dr. Sweet, who had been a bellhop on a boat, and a bellhop in hotels, and fired furnaces and sold popcorn and worked his way with his great handicap through school and through college, and graduated as a doctor, and gone to Europe and taken another degree; Dr. Sweet, who knew more than any man in the neighborhood ever would know or ever want to know. He deserved more for all he had done. When they heard he was coming, then it was time to act, and act together, for the sake of their homes, their families and their firesides, and so they got together.

❊   ❊   ❊

I shall not talk to you much longer. I am sorry I talked so long. But this case is close to my heart.

Gentlemen, who are these people who were in this house? Were they people of character? Were they people of standing? Were they people of intelligence?

First, there was Dr. Sweet. Gentlemen, a white man does pretty well when he does what Dr. Sweet did. A white boy who can start in with nothing, and put himself through college, study medicine, taking post-graduate work in Europe, earning every penny of it as he goes along, shoveling snow and coal, and working as a bellhop on boats, working at every kind of employment that he can get to make his way, is some fellow. But Dr. Sweet has the handicap of the color of his face. And there is no handicap more terrible than that. Supposing you had your choice, right here this minute, would you rather lose your eyesight or become colored? Would you rather lose your hearing or be a Negro? Would you rather go out there on the street and have your leg cut off by a streetcar, or have a black skin?

I don't like to speak of it; I do not like to speak of it in the presence of these colored people, whom I have always urged to be as happy as they can. But it is true. Life is a hard game anyhow. But, when the cards are stacked against you, it is terribly hard. And they are stacked against a race for no reason but that they are black.

Who are these men who were in this house? There was Dr. Sweet. There was his brother, who was a dentist. There was this young boy who worked his way for three years through college, with a little aid from his brother, and who was on his way to graduate. Henry's future is now in your hands. There was his companion, who was working his way through college— all gathered in that house. Were they hoodlums? Were they criminals? Were they anything except men who asked for a chance to live; who asked for a chance to breathe the free air and make their own way, earn their own living, and get their bread by the sweat of their brow?

❋　　❋　　❋

Gentlemen, these black men shot. Whether any bullets from their guns hit Breiner, I do not care. I will not discuss it. It is passing strange that the bullet that went through him, went directly through, not as if it were shot from some higher place. It was not the bullet that came from Henry Sweet's rifle; that is plain. It might have come from the house; I do not know, gentlemen, and I do not care. There are bigger issues in this case than that. The right to defend your home, the right to defend your person, is as sacred a right as any human being could fight for, and as sacred a cause as any jury could sustain.

That issue not only involves the defendants in this case, but it involves every man who wants to live, every man who wants freedom to work and to breathe; it is an issue worth fighting for, and worth dying for, it is an issue worth the attention of this jury, who have a chance that is given to few juries to pass upon a real case that will mean something in the history of a race.

These men were taken to the police station. Gentlemen, there was never a time that these black men's rights were protected in the least; never once. They had no rights—they are black. They were to be driven out of their home under the law's protection. When they defended their home, they were arrested and charged with murder. They were taken to a police station, manacled. And they asked for a lawyer. And, every man, if he has any brains at all, asks for a lawyer when he is in the hands of the police. If he does not want to have a web woven around him, to entangle or ensnare him, he will ask for a lawyer. And, the lawyer's first aid to the injured always is, "Keep your mouth shut." It is not a case of whether you are guilty or not guilty. That makes no difference. "Keep your mouth shut." The police grabbed them, as is their habit. They got the county attorney to ask questions. What did they do? They did what everybody does, helpless, alone, and unadvised. They did not know, even, that anybody was killed. At least there is no evidence that they knew. But, they knew that they had been arrested for defending their own rights to live; and they were there in the hands of their enemies; and they told the best story they could think of at the time—just as ninety-nine men out of a hundred always do. Whether they are guilty or not guilty makes no difference. But lawyers and even policemen should have protected their rights.

Some things that these defendants said were not true, as is always the case. The prosecutor read a statement from this boy, which is conflicting. In two places he says that he shot "over them." In another he said that he shot "at them." He probably said it in each place but the reporter probably got one of them wrong. But Henry makes it perfectly explicit, and when you go to your jury room and read it all, you will find that he does. In another place he said he shot to defend his brother's home and family. He says that in two or three places. You can also find he said that he shot so that they would run away and leave them to eat their dinner. They are both there. These conflicting statements you will find in all cases of this sort. You always find them, where men have been sweated, without help, without a lawyer, groping around blindly, in the hands of the enemy, without the aid of anybody to protect their rights. Gentlemen, from the first to the last, there has not been a substantial right of these defendants that was not violated.

We come now to lay this man's case in the hands of a jury of our peers—the first defense and the last defense is the protection of home and life as provided by our law. We are willing to leave it here. I feel, as I look at you, that we will be treated fairly and decently, even understandingly and kindly. You know what this case is. You know why it is. You know that if white men had been fighting their way against colored men, nobody would ever have dreamed of a prosecution. And you know that, from the beginning of this case to the end, up to the time you write your verdict, the prosecution is based on race prejudice and nothing else.

Gentlemen, I feel deeply on this subject; I cannot help it. Let us take a little glance at the history of the Negro race. It only needs a minute. It seems to me that the story would melt hearts of stone. I was born in America. I could have left it if I had wanted to go away. Some other men, reading about this land of freedom that we brag about on the Fourth of July, came voluntarily to America. These men, the defendants, are here because they could not help it. Their ancestors were captured in the jungles and on the plains of Africa, captured as you capture wild beasts, torn from their homes and their kindred; loaded into slave ships, packed like sardines in a box, half of them dying on the ocean passage; some jumping into the sea in their frenzy, when they had a chance to choose death in place of slavery. They were captured and brought here. They could not help it. They were bought and sold as slaves, to work without pay, because they were black. They were subjected to all of this for generations, until finally they were given their liberty, so far as the law goes—and that is only a little way, because, after all, every human being's life in this world is inevitably mixed with every other life and, no matter what laws we pass, no matter what precautions we take, unless the people we meet are kindly and decent and human and liberty-loving, then there is no liberty. Freedom comes from human beings, rather than from laws and institutions.

Now, that is their history. These people are the children of slavery. If the race that we belong to owes anything to any human being, or to any power in this universe, it owes it to these black men. Above all other men, they owe an obligation and a duty to these black men which can never be repaid. I never see one of them, that I do not feel I ought to pay part of the debt of my race—and if you gentlemen feel as you should feel in this case, your emotions will be like mine.

Gentlemen, you were called into this case by chance. It took us a week to find you, a week of culling out prejudice and hatred. Probably we did not cull it all out at that; but we took the best and the fairest that we could find. It is up to you.

Your verdict means something in this case. It means something more than the fate of this boy. It is not often that a case is submitted to twelve men where the decision may mean a milestone in the progress of the human race. But this case does. And I hope and I trust that you have a feeling of responsibility that will make you take it and do your duty as citizens of a great nation, and, as members of the human family, which is better still.

Let me say just a parting word for Henry Sweet, who has well nigh been forgotten. I am serious, but it seems almost like a reflection upon this jury to talk as if I doubted your verdict. What has this boy done? This one boy now that I am culling out from all of the rest, and whose fate is in your hands—can you tell me what he has done? Can I believe myself? Am I standing in a court of justice, where twelve men on their oaths are asked to take away the liberty of a boy twenty-one years of age, who has done nothing more than what Henry Sweet has done?

Gentlemen, you may think he shot too quick; you may think he erred in judgment; you may think that Dr. Sweet should not have gone there, prepared to defend his home. But, what of this case of Henry Sweet? What has he done? I want to put it up to you, each of you, individually. Dr. Sweet was his elder brother. He had helped Henry through school. He loved him. He had taken him into his home. Henry had lived with him and his wife; he had fondled his baby. The doctor had promised Henry money to go through school. Henry was getting his education, to take his place in the world, gentlemen—and this is a hard job. With his brother's help, he had worked himself through college up to the last year. The doctor had bought a home. He feared danger. He moved in with his wife and he asked this boy to go with him. And this boy went to help defend his brother and his brother's wife and his child and his home.

Do you think more of him or less of him for that? I never saw twelve men in my life—and I have looked at a good many faces of a good many juries—I never saw twelve men in my life, that, if you could get them to understand a human case, were not true and right.

Should this boy have gone along and helped his brother? Or should he have stayed away? What would you have done? And yet, gentlemen, here is a boy, and the president of his college came all the way here from Ohio to tell you what he thinks of him. His teachers have come here, from Ohio, to tell you what they think of him. The Methodist bishop has come here to tell you what he thinks of him.

So, gentlemen, I am justified in saying that this boy is as kindly, as well disposed, as decent a man as any one of you twelve. Do you think he ought to be taken out of his school and sent to the penitentiary? All right, gentlemen, if you think so, do it. It is your job, not mine. If you think so, do it. But if you do, gentlemen, if you should ever look into the face of your own boy, or your own brother, or look into your own heart, you will regret it in sackcloth and ashes. You know, if he committed any offense, it was being loyal and true to his brother whom he loved. I know where you will send him, and it will not be to the penitentiary.

Now, gentlemen, just one more word, and I am through with this case. I do not live in Detroit. But I have no feeling against this city. In fact, I shall always have the kindest remembrance of it, especially if this case results as I think and feel that it will. I am the last one to come here to stir up race hatred, or any other hatred. I do not believe in the law of hate. I may not be true to my ideals always, but I believe in the law of love, and I believe you can do nothing with hatred. I would like to see a time when man loves his fellow-man, and forgets his color or his creed. We will never be civilized until that time comes. I know the Negro race has a long road to go. I believe the life of the Negro race has been a life of tragedy, of injustice, of oppression. The law has made him equal, but man has not. And, after all, the last analysis is, what has man done?—and not what has the law done? I know there is a long road ahead of him, before he can take the place which I believe he should take. I know that before him there is suffering, sorrow, tribulation and death among the blacks, and perhaps the whites. I am sorry. I would do what I could to avert it. I would advise patience; I would advise toleration; I would advise understanding; I would advise all of those things which are necessary for men who live together.

Gentlemen, what do you think is your duty in this case? I have watched day after day, these black, tense faces that have crowded this court. These black faces that now are looking to you twelve whites, feeling that the hopes and fears of a race are in your keeping.

This case is about to end, gentlemen. To them, it is life. Not one of their color sits on this jury. Their fate is in the hands of twelve whites. Their eyes are fixed on you, their hearts go out to you, and their hopes hang on your verdict.

This is all. I ask you, on behalf of this defendant, on behalf of these helpless ones who turn to you, and more than that—on behalf of this great state, and this great city which must face this problem, and face it fairly—I ask you, in the name of progress and of the human race, to return a verdict of Not Guilty in this case!

THE JURY returned its verdict the following day, May 19, 1926: Not Guilty. None of the other cases was tried.

The Sweets never moved back into the house. For a long time their house at Garland and Charlevoix streets remained vacant. Today, thirty-one years later, both white and colored live in the neighborhood.

PART THREE

AGAINST
PRIVILEGE

Somewhere There Is a Conspiracy

THE KIDD CASE
Oshkosh, Wisconsin, 1898

DARROW SPEAKS FOR KIDD
CHICAGO ATTORNEY SAYS PRESENT
CASE IS AN INCIDENT OF GREAT
SOCIAL PROBLEM AGITATING THE WORLD

[Headline, Milwaukee *Sentinel*, November 1, 1898]

"As INTERESTING as a novel," said William Dean Howells, Atlantic Monthly editor, of Clarence Darrow's final summation in the woodworkers' conspiracy case of 1898.

The Milwaukee Journal reported that when Darrow delivered his plea the courtroom was packed, and "Mr. Darrow held the audience spellbound."

A strike in the sash, door and blind industry in Oshkosh, Wisconsin was the spark that led to the filing of charges against Thomas I. Kidd, general secretary, Amalgamated Woodworkers' International Union, and George Zentner and Michael Troiber, both of Oshkosh, who acted as picket captains during the fourteen-week strike. The three defendants were accused of "criminal conspiracy" to injure the business of the Paine Lumber Company.

Under Wisconsin law, indictments were not necessary; the district attorney filed a complaint.

The trial was held in the Municipal Court of Oshkosh.

The Woodworkers' Union asked Darrow, the son of a woodworker and already famous in his defense of Eugene Victor Debs, to defend the three union men.

To Darrow, this case was but a continuation of the criminal conspiracy conviction of Debs.

At the defense table with Darrow were two local lawyers, Harry I. Weed and Earl P. Finch.

Representing the State were H. Quartermass, district attorney, and F. W. Houghton, a special counsel appointed to assist the district attorney at $15 a day.

In his defense of the union men, Darrow was determined to show that the state of Wisconsin was actually not the complainant in the case; but that it was George M. Paine, head of the lumber company, who was responsible for the district attorney's filing the complaint.

The prosecuting staff inadvertently helped pinpoint this when Mr. Houghton, on the first day Paine appeared to testify, rushed to the industrialist's side, led him to the lawyers' table and shook his hand warmly before putting him on the witness stand.

Darrow commented about this in his summation: "Houghton," he said, "would have been glad to lick the dust from Paine's boots had he been given the opportunity to perform the service."

The State called Darrow an outsider, a trouble-maker, and decried his radical ideas.

The Milwaukee Journal, on the other hand, said of Darrow that "by his indomitable energy, his marked ability and his honest, frank, fearless advocacy of his sincere belief in what he champions, he has commanded the confidence of all who believe with him, and the respect of the great majority who do not."

Darrow himself maintained that the fundamental question posed by the Kidd case was "whether when a body of men desiring to benefit their conditions, and the condition of their fellow-men, shall strike . . . these men can be put to jail."

*"There is a conspiracy, dark and damnable
. . . somebody is guilty of one of the foulest
conspiracies that ever disgraced a free nation.
. . . There are criminals in this case . . .
who . . . have not been guilty of the paltry
crime of conspiring to save their fellow-men,
but criminals who have conspired against
the framework of those institutions that
have made these same criminals great and
strong . . ."*

GENTLEMEN OF THE JURY: The defendants in this case, Thomas I. Kidd, George Zentner and Michael Troiber, are on trial charged with a conspiracy to injure the business of the Paine Lumber Company, by means of a strike, and the incidents arising therefrom. While you have been occupied for the last two weeks in listening to the evidence in this case, and while the Court will instruct you as to the technical rules of law under which this evidence is to be applied, still it is impossible to present the case to you without a broad survey of the great questions that are agitating the world today. For whatever its form, this is really not a criminal case. It is but an episode in the great battle for human liberty, a battle which was commenced when the tyranny and oppression of man first caused him to impose upon his fellows and which will not end so long as the children of one father shall be compelled to toil to support the children of another in luxury and ease.

The Paine Company may hire its lawyers and import its leprous detectives into your peaceful community; it may send these defendants to jail; but so long as injustice and inhumanity exist, so long as employers grow fat and rich and powerful through their robbery and greed, so long as they build their palaces from the unpaid labor of their serfs, so long as they rob childhood of its life and sunshine and joy, you will find other conspirators, thank God, that will take the place of these as fast as the doors of the jail shall close upon them. If other conspirators should be wanting to fill up the gaps made vacant by the prosecutions of the courts and the verdicts of juries, then I should be ashamed of the country in which I live. This is not a criminal case, and every actor concerned in this drama understands it well. Counsel may argue here and there concerning the crossing of a *t* or the dotting of an *i;* they may argue that certain letters were written in haste and that others should have been answered sooner; they may argue that certain heated words should have remained unspoken, and that other language was wrongly used. They may argue as they please about the minor details of this case, but deep in your hearts and in mine, deep in the mind of every man who thinks, is the certain knowledge that this drama in which you play such an important part is but a phase of the great social question that moves the world. You have been told of disorder, and tumult, and riot. Gentlemen, I love order and quiet and peace, but it is idle for you and me to seek to nicely weigh and calmly deliberate upon the responsibility for these tumultuous acts of men. Counsel on the other side cannot fix the responsibility; no more can I, nor you. I look back at that mad riot around McMillen's mill. I understand full well the elements of terror and lawlessness and crime that were present in that wild, tumultuous crowd. I look back at the men and women and the little children gathered there, the Americans, Bohemians, Germans, Austrians—each with their native tongues, whose combined voice was like the babbling of the waves upon the sea, and I know that no man was responsible for the turbulent, surging, rising flood; I know it was but an incident in a great struggle which commenced so many centuries ago and which will and must continue until human liberty is secured and equality has come to dwell on earth. It was an incident alone, and if one man had been absent, or 100 men had been absent, that threatening, tumultuous mob would have been present just the same.

You may send these men to jail tomorrow if you will, and you may destroy even George M. Paine and Nathan Paine, whose malice have made them pursue these defendants into the very temple of justice. Aye, if all the chief actors should be numbered with the dead, and the conditions still remained, the same babbling, overflowing, threatening sea of men and women would gather once again.

Let me repeat, this is not a criminal case, and malicious as these Paines are, I have no idea that they would prosecute this case simply to put Kidd in jail. These employers are using this court of justice because in their misguided cupidity, they believe that they may be able to destroy what little is left of that spirit of independence and manhood which they have been slowly crushing from the breasts of those who toil for them.

Ordinarily men are brought into a criminal court for the reason that they are bad. Thomas I. Kidd is brought into this court because he is good, and they understand it well. If Thomas I. Kidd had been mean and selfish and designing, if he had held out his hand to take the paltry bribes that these men pass out wherever they find one so poor and weak as to take their dirty gold, this case would not be here today. Kidd is a defendant in these criminal proceedings because he loves his fellow-men. This is not the first case of its kind in the history of the world, and I am afraid it will not be the last. It is not the first time that evil men, men who are themselves criminals, have used the law for the purpose of bringing righteous ones to death or to jail, and so long as this great battle is waged, these incidents will continue to mark the history of the strife.

Let us understand exactly who are the parties to this case. Counsel for the prosecution will stand before this jury with hypocritical voice and false words, and say it is the great state of Wisconsin on the one hand and these three defendants upon the other. I say that this is not true, and every person in the hearing of my voice knows that it is not true.

Who is the state of Wisconsin, and how does the state of Wisconsin act? It moves only through its officers, ordinary men, strong in some ways, weak in others, subject to all those influences that move you and me and every other man that lives. Mr. Quartermass, the District Attorney, represents the state of Wisconsin. He comes into court, moved and influenced by the people of the community where he lives, by some more, by some less. He is persuaded to file an information charging a crime or offense against his fellow-citizens, and he haltingly complies with the request. He is simply the tool that is used, nothing more and nothing less; and the seal of the state of Wisconsin is not broad enough and heavy enough to cover up the infamy which caused this information to be filed branding these three men as criminals before the law. I do not intend to find special fault with Quartermass. He is like the rest of us—the way the Lord made him, and no one can tell how much influence was brought to bear upon him.

I am not a resident of Oshkosh, but I know from the inadvertent truths that George M. Paine gave us on the witness stand, and from the way he has sent his son into this courtroom to act as a bloodhound and a spy, for which I am thankful, for the more Paines there are the better it suits me; I know from George M. Paine's testimony that in the days of the strike he went up and down these streets and consulted lawyers to see if he could not send Kidd to jail. I know from the testimony of Frank Blood that Nathan Paine declared that they did not care for George Zentner and Michael Troiber, but they wanted to get Kidd in jail. I know from the manipulations of Mr. Houghton, the Assistant District Attorney, who is the power behind the throne, and so do you. I know that Quartermass filed this information because George Paine told him to do so.

It is not the first time in the history of the world that people in place and power and position have bowed down to the demands of gold. We had an illustration of it here the other day. You saw Brother Houghton. He sat here driving his witnesses to the stand in front of Nathan Paine; he called these poor men, who were in the employ of Nathan Paine and live off the poor morsels that he sees fit to throw them from the rich man's table, and he called them up one after another, with their slave-driver before them, to have them testify against their friends. From his manner I thought Brother Houghton was really playing for a job as a slave-driver in the factory after his law practice is done. But I noticed this: when George M. Paine lent his august presence to this room, which place, although the temple of justice, was scarce good enough to hold him—when in all his majesty and splendor he sat down beside Mr. Houghton, instead of out in the vulgar crowd where his workmen were herded; before he was placed on the stand Brother Houghton turned to him and shook him warmly by the hand. It was the only witness that he shook by the hand or whom he seemed to know. I thought he would have been glad to have licked the dust from Paine's boots, had he been given the opportunity to perform this service.

These are the influences, gentlemen of the jury, these are the influences that falsely make the great state of Wisconsin appear here as prosecutor. Gentlemen, thank God Brother Houghton is not the guardian of the honor of the state of Wisconsin. He may think he is a great man, but he need not deceive himself by believing he is the state of Wisconsin. Gentlemen, before any citizens of Wisconsin can be deprived of their life, or their liberty, or before any citizens of Illinois can be deprived of their life or their liberty, under the laws of this state a jury of Wisconsin men must take this liberty away. Quartermass may indict at the instance of Paine, but it takes a jury to convict, gentlemen; it takes a jury to convict.

Now, I do not propose to be hard on Brother Quartermass. It would not be good policy; and really, I do not feel that way. He is a very nice fellow, but he does not appear to have a great deal of influence with himself. He has made an assignment of the state of Wisconsin—not for the benefit of creditors, but for the benefit of Paine's lumber company. Paine has used almost everything else in Oshkosh, men, women, little children, and now Brother Quartermass has made an assignment of the state to him. After he gets through with it, I hope he will pass it back to you people, who really ought to have something to say about it. Is there any doubt about who are the parties to this case? I do not care how long Brother Houghton talks about it. He can talk about it two days if he can afford it and the jury can. But you know, and I know, and George M. Paine knows, that this is an effort of George M. Paine and his son to send these men to jail, because they are interfering with his business. They cannot make so much money if Thomas I. Kidd is allowed to live. They started out by consulting lawyers to see how they could get him out of town, and they have wound up by consulting the district attorney to see how they can keep him here; and that is all there is of it.

*   *   *

Brother Houghton felt one heartbeat of human kindness and he joined this conspiracy. You remember his visit to Kidd during the strike; nobody sent for him. That is the trouble with him. They did not send for him, but he felt within him one touch of that human kindness that makes all the world kin, and he put his law book under his arm and went down to call on Kidd in the midst of the strike. Now, Brother Houghton, perhaps you, like all the rest of us, when it comes to the great day of judgment, if there ever shall be such a day—and perhaps you ought to hope that there will not be—but when your time comes, and you are called upon to answer for the deeds done in the body, you will be very glad of this little bit of a credit growing out of your sympathetic visit to Thomas I. Kidd. It may be about the only thing that will be thrown into the scales on the other side to make up for the evil you have done. But this conspiracy did touch Brother Houghton, and in the midst of the strike he went down to the boys who were engaged in this conflict and told them that the Paine Lumber Company were criminals, for the law provided that they must pay their workmen weekly instead of once a month. And Brother Houghton is about the only one that ever charged these people with violating the law.

But he told Mr. Kidd in those days when the strike was on, and when he did not know but his services might possibly be needed—no, I will take that back. I will give him the benefit of the doubt and say that there welled up in his breast a little bit of the feeling of pity and tenderness and kindness which, let us hope, is in the hearts of all, even George M. Paine and his worthy son—and moved by that, he went down to see Mr. Kidd, to offer his sympathy, and he told him that these employers were violating the law, and the men had a right to demand a weekly pay-day. And then, gentlemen, after going to this man with kind words and a sympathetic handshake, after seeking him out himself, and seeming to befriend him, after getting his confidence and his trust, he turns around for fifteen dollars a day to try to send him to jail. Shame on you! There should be things that a man would not do, even for twenty dollars a day, and this ought to have been one. If you had been standing beside that meek and lowly Jesus, whom you once sought to follow, as one of his disciples, and had received his love and benedictions, and had counseled with him in his supreme efforts to help the world, and the masters and rulers of that day had offered you twenty dollars a day, you would have turned around and procured his indictment and then read the Sermon on the Mount to the jury to convict him.

Gentlemen, there are occasions when the instinct of humanity and a man's love for justice and his devotion to the right ought to be so strong that no paltry piece of gold could change them. But it depends upon the man. Mr. Houghton was in this conspiracy. I will guarantee he has asked the Court to instruct you that it does not matter whether a man went into the conspiracy at first or not. If he got in he is guilty, and this is the law. Gentlemen, if the unexpected should happen—and I will speak seriously, if I can, about such an improbable event, because I do not think Oshkosh is entirely in the dark—if the unexpected should happen, and you gentlemen, for the good of the community, should keep Mr. Kidd here and find a verdict of Guilty, for God's sake, gentlemen, don't forget to include in your verdict Mr. Houghton, too. Then I hope for Kidd's sake that the jailer will give them separate cells while they are serving out their time.

Gentlemen, you and I may have different views of the way things should be done. Probably no two of you looking at the injustice and oppression of the earth and desiring to better it, would go at it in exactly the same way. But I undertake to say that there was not a well-meaning citizen in the town of Oshkosh, not a man who had in him one drop of the milk of human kindness, that did not wish these poor boys could win. And yet, after the strike is over and all is done and peace has come again, these malignant employers, not satisfied with the past, are bound still to pursue these defendants in the false name of the state of Wisconsin, for the sake of teaching these men that if they ever dare again to assert their rights, the door of the jail will be open to receive them. The malice of George M. Paine is exceeded only by his avarice and his cupidity. It was not enough that he should take the toil and the sweat and the life of these poor men for starvation wages; it was not enough that he should import his spies into this town to dog and destroy and incite them; it was not enough that they should go back to work as best they could; but when all is past and gone, he dares to take the law into his polluted hands, the law which should be holy and above suspicion, and which was made to protect him, and to protect you and me, to take this law and use it as a dagger to stab these men to death.

Paine had to find three conspirators, and he took Michael Troiber. And I will speak of him later, and tell you why he took him; but for fear I might forget it, I want to say a word for him now. I do not know what sort of a man he is. I never saw him before. I probably shall never see him again, unless Paine pursues him further, and then I hope to be present, because I want to be where Paine is until he dies, and then I want to be where he is not. But, gentlemen, whoever Troiber is, he is not a great man—a common man, a plain man, probably an ignorant man in the reckoning of this world; a poor Austrian, born beyond the seas, hearing there, no doubt, as others have heard, of the wonderful opportunities that were offered beneath the Stars and Stripes, and coming here with high hopes and grand aspirations to make a home for himself and his children, where he should be free and happy and contented and prosperous; and he came here, and fell into the clutches of George M. Paine at ninety cents a day.

If the emigration companies, instead of sending information to the poor of other lands in reference to the beauties and the glorious opportunities of America, would send a picture of George M. Paine and his prison pen, we would not have so many aliens in this land today. Troiber came here, as thousands of others have come from all nations of the earth, to lend his brawn and muscle and life to the building up of this great land—and he worked for ninety cents a day until he grew old and stunted and haggard and worn, and thought he had a right to demand something more; and then George M. Paine conspired to lock him up in jail; and he hired these lawyers as bloodhounds to bay him inside the doors.

Michael Troiber is an Austrian by birth. He came here as others have come. However much George M. Paine may have robbed and abused him, he is entitled to the same protection from a jury of his adopted countrymen as every other man; and, gentlemen, I know he will get it. And it is not because I fear that he will not that I take the time today to talk to you. I do not fear it, and to tell you the honest truth, in one way I do not care. I say to you honestly, as man to man, that this jury cannot convict Thomas I. Kidd. You can convict yourselves, but you cannot convict him. You may return a verdict of Guilty against these men, but in the face of the civilized world, and in the view of every man who has a mind to think and a heart to feel, you will write your own infamy in the verdict you return. Let me say to you, gentlemen of the jury, the battle in which these defendants are engaged is your fight the same as theirs. There is not a man upon this jury but what has the same interest in these burning questions of the day as the defendant Kidd. Not one. I do not want you to mistake our position in this case. I am not appealing to you for Thomas I. Kidd. I am appealing to you for the stunted men and suffering women and dependent children who cannot speak. I appeal for them, and not for him; and I say, gentlemen, their lives—their future and their happiness—is in your keeping as much as they were in his.

*　　*　　*

You remember the extract from the principles of the International Woodworkers' Association read by Quartermass to convict these defendants. I will undertake to say this: that Brother Quartermass never read anything in his life before that had as much sense in it as the principles contained in this little book, and in Thomas I. Kidd's speech, which he also read to you. There is more sense in these than in a hundred volumes of musty law books; and also more truth, justice, humanity, brotherhood and fellowship. And I want to say, and I should like to have Mr. Houghton write it down as a text for the sermon he will deliver when I am done, that until these sentiments—contained in this little book and in the speech of Thomas I. Kidd, and I can include those utterances of the greatest conspirator that the world has ever seen, Jesus Christ—are written into the Constitution of America, we will never have the liberty and equality of which our politicians boast. And when they are written there, as they will be one day, gentlemen, whether you send Thomas I. Kidd to jail or not—you might hang him if you could, and one day they will be written there, whether you and I shall be living or dead —and when they are, then George M. Paine's son will have no better opportunity in the world than these poor, stunted children, whose life he has wasted away by the luxury and extravagance of his own. These principles will be some time adopted; and Brother Quartermass can keep on reading Thomas I. Kidd's speech, and he may pick out the most incendiary part if he wants to—the worst of it is better than anything he has been in the habit of reading—and if he understood it better he would read it better; but I will refer to that again.

Now, who is Zentner? I have spoken of Troiber, but I think you gentlemen need to be introduced to Zentner. You probably will not know him when you convict him. The evidence is ten times stronger against Brother Houghton than it is against Zentner. Why, it is a good deal stronger against Brother Houghton's pastor than it is against Zentner, for the preacher admits that he made a speech and we haven't heard of any of Zentner's. You can get the ex-mayor and the businessmen and the preachers and the lawyers, and all of them easier than Zentner. Who is he? His name has been mentioned two or three times as a man who called off the names of pickets, and that is all. He was not present at any fight. He made no speeches, and therefore he could not be a very good labor agitator, for you know the first thing necessary for a labor agitator is to make a speech; and if that is all that is necessary, I have an idea Brother Houghton might be a labor agitator. But you must have a heart back of it, and that might bar him. But who is Zentner? He has been referred to as captain of the pickets, and that is all. Now, gentlemen, it is not much, of course. George M. Paine wants you to convict this man, and you had better do it, for it is not every day that he asks a

favor of his fellow-citizens. Of course anything the old gentleman wants we should be glad to give if we have it around anywhere; and if he wants to send a man or two to jail, what right
have we to object? Who are we to stand in the way of his majesty,
as he takes off his gloves in this courtroom and enlightens us regarding the things that are not true, as I will show you when I
come to refer to George M. Paine? I have not really got to him
yet. He wants you to bundle up Zentner and send him to jail.
There is only one thing I fail to understand about this. Of course
Zentner has not done anything; his name has hardly been mentioned. But still, as a matter of form, we might find out what
Zentner did. He is referred to in this testimony as having been
a captain of pickets. Now, do you want to send him to jail for a
year because he was a captain of pickets? If so, all right. Let him
go. He will undoubtedly have better food there than he could
get off the wages that George M. Paine would pay him, and he
can keep warm through the winter better than he could off the
money that Paine would see fit to dole out to him. I think, gentlemen, it would be a mighty good scheme for the woodworkers
of Oshkosh if they could go to jail for the winter. By the way,
where are those rules of Paine's prison? I can recite them. I
have been learning them. I want to refer a minute to them.
Still I scarcely need them, because I once had occasion to examine the regulations of a prison, and am familiar with all these
rules. Why, George M. Paine, the ancient patriarch, undoubtedly
thinks he is supporting all these people, and they would starve if
it was not for him; if he did not throw a crust to them the same
as he does to his dog.

Gentlemen, George M. Paine is not supporting these men.
These men and women and little children are supporting him.
It is through their labor and their toil that he has grown rich
and prosperous and great. Here are some of the things that are
expected of a man who goes to work for Paine:

"The following rules are made in the interest of good order
and strict attention to business:

"All employees are to be in their places when the bell rings
and whistle blows for starting, and must not absent themselves
except in case of necessity.

"Employees who quit their places or the employ of this company without our consent or a reasonable notice of such intention, are subject to damages therefor; and such persons will not be paid until the next regular pay day following."

This man is not only an employer, but he is a judge up there. He can impose fines and penalties, and I am really surprised that this great man did not try Kidd and Zentner and Troiber himself, instead of coming down here into this little court of justice to ask your aid. Talk about the power of Kidd, and the ruler of Persia, how about George M. Paine?

"Loud talking or shouting in or around the mill and factory cannot be allowed except in case of accident or fire."

I suppose the old gentleman is nervous; and if he is, they ought not to talk loud. It is very kind of him to let them shout when there is a fire. Some men would not do it; but George M. Paine is good, and so if there is a fire they can shout, or if anyone gets hurt, they can talk loud. It's a beautiful institution.

"No unnecessary talking will be allowed during working hours."

Well, there is a great deal of nonsense said in talking, as you will find out when Brother Houghton closes this case; and George M. Paine doesn't believe in nonsense, and so he says, "No unnecessary talking will be allowed during working hours." Under certain conditions and circumstances it is the privilege of American citizens to talk more or less, and we have several constitutional guarantees that are in force, more or less, in different parts of the United States in relation to liberty of speech, but they evidently don't work around Paine's factory to any great extent. I take it that this rule has been copied verbatim from the rules governing penitentiaries in this state and others. If there is anything that George M. Paine prides himself on it is being up to date. There is not a modern improvement that he has not got. I guarantee that he has visited every penal institution of the United States in some capacity or other—and if he has not he should. And that is not all. He has not only copied their rules, that the poor devil who works there for six or seven dollars a week cannot speak loud except in case of fire, and he cannot go out excepting he raise his hand like a little boy in school, and he cannot speak to his neighbor because it hinders him in his work; but in the last addition they made to their factory they got another improvement, and when the poor slaves go in there at a quarter to seven in the morning they lock the door to keep them there; and when the whistle sounds at twelve they send their guards around to unlock the doors. And when one o'clock comes again, this high priest of jailers sends his turnkey back to lock up his American citizens once more so that they cannot leave the mill until nighttime comes.

What kind of an institution have you got that you are trying to send to jail honest men because they seek to better their condition?

Why, gentlemen, the only difference that I can see between the state's prison and George M. Paine's factory is that Paine's men are not allowed to sleep on the premises. American citizens do not exactly relish the idea of being locked up even in a factory; they have inherited certain foolish traditions of liberty that make them object, but they doubtless get over these prejudices in time. Don't be in such a hurry, gentlemen—give them a little time, a little time.

And because these men dared to go to Paine and ask for higher wages, because they had the effrontery to ask for a few more pennies of that wealth that they are grinding out at his machines, because they asked a little more of that money which comes from the sashes and the doors and the blinds which he sends to fourteen states of this great union, he wants to send them to jail. How is it that under our free institutions a man like this could be born? He is not content with robbing and despoiling all whom he has touched with his polluted grasp, but if his employees dare to raise their hand for justice, they are to be answered by a prison pen.

Gentlemen, I say again it is not for fear of this verdict that I speak to you. If you could pick out twelve American citizens anywhere in this broad land who would be so lost to pity and justice and the common human sentiments that stir the hearts of men as to send these defendants to jail, then I should weep in sorrow for the land in which I live.

Gentlemen of the jury, it is the theory of the State in this case, so far as they have a theory, that Mr. Kidd was responsible for this strike. Now, there is one beauty about a conspiracy case; there is one thing that made it valuable to ancient tyrants, and that makes it equally valuable to modern tyrants, and that is that you do not need much of any theory to carry it on, and this makes it possible for Brother Houghton to try the case. If there is somebody you want to get, as there always is, because most of us have enemies, excepting Paine—but if there happens to be someone you are after, then you make a charge of conspiracy, and you are allowed to prove what the defendant said and did, and what everybody else said and did over any length of time that you see fit to carry it, and there you get your conspiracy. Conspiracy is the child of the Star Chamber Court of England, and it has come down to us, like most bad things and many good ones, from the remote past, without much modification. Whenever a king wanted to get rid of somebody, whenever a political disturber was in someone's way, then they brought a charge of conspiracy, and they not only proved everything he said, but everything everyone else said and everyone else did.

George M. Paine should have lived in those good old days. He should have been one of those barons with a castle on the Rhine, whose edict went up and down the river, and who, whenever he wanted a head, would send for it without the formality of a jury.

George M. Paine is a sort of a misfit in republican institutions and in democratic days, where the people, theoretically at least, are supposed to have rights that are equal to those of barons and of kings. It was in those old days, even after courts commenced to protect the rights of individuals, they invented the crime of conspiracy. It was not only a conspiracy to try to kill the king, but it was a conspiracy to talk about killing him, and it was a conspiracy even for several to imagine the death of the king. And it was in these good old days that this wise jury convicted this man of writing the poetry that Brother Quartermass read and referred to. Brother Quartermass read it and then remarked, "And they convicted him." Why, if the names of that jury were blazoned upon the wall in this court of justice today, even Brother Houghton would turn and view them with contempt. And yet, to satisfy their boss, George M. Paine, who, when he wants a thing wants it, and wants it badly, they would have you go back to those trials of a hundred years ago, when they convicted a man for writing poetry dedicated to liberty and common sense. They convicted him, gentlemen, because he wrote a poem lauding Thomas Paine and his *Rights of Man*. They convicted him because he said a word in favor of a man who perhaps did as much for American liberty and for universal liberty as any man who ever lived.

My God, how Brother Houghton's mouth would have watered if he had been given a chance to convict Thomas Paine for daring to proclaim the rights of man!

I have not sized up the religion of this jury, and perhaps I have made a mistake. I see Brother Houghton has made a note of what I say, and as near as I can read it from here it is something about Thomas Paine. Now, gentlemen, whether you are Protestants or agnostics, or Catholics, or pagans, or Paine men, I take it that in this day and generation any singer of songs who would write verses in laudation of the rights of man should rather be canonized as a saint than convicted by a jury of his peers. We can write verses now, but in Oshkosh, under the benign rule of Brother Quartermass, we dare not make speeches even at the funeral of a dead comrade without having them construed into treason and conspiracy and riot. Shame on you, Brother Quartermass. You are a better man than that. You should never have allowed George Paine to invade your office and use the state of Wisconsin for this unholy purpose. Because I want to say again that you are not a bad fellow at all. It is George Paine that I am after.

When these manufacturers set out to get rid of Kidd they started for injunctions. Now, an injunction is a sort of an invention of the devil. But they evidently could not find a judge in Oshkosh that could be used for that purpose. Not one. George M. Paine, when he was on the stand, admitted, although his memory is very faulty—excepting in matters that he wishes to tell —but he admitted that he did try to get these men enjoined, but he could not do it. The judges would not do it; and then he sought to have them arrested, and he went to Quartermass, and he hired lawyers, and he paid for them, I hope, because no man is so mean that he won't pay a lawyer. They may rob the men that work for them, but they would not rob Brother Houghton. They would pay the lawyers even if they had to make a cut of ten or fifteen per cent on the wages of the poor slaves that work in their factories. And they did all this, and of course there was but one thing they could not do. They could not prosecute Kidd for vagrancy, because he is getting twenty dollars a week. Twenty dollars a week. Being a labor agitator is the best business on earth, gentlemen of the jury, the best business on earth. They could not prosecute him for vagrancy, and so they unearthed this old Star Chamber proceeding, the same proceedings that in every age of the world have been used to condemn patriots and heretics and the great and the humane of the earth because miserable tyrants desired their blood; and they sought the aid of the law of conspiracy; and they did not need in this state, gentlemen, to go before a grand jury with their evidence, but they got Quartermass, the District Attorney, with a scratch of his pen, to bring these men into court charged as criminals, because—because they loved their fellow-men, and for no other reason than that.

There is a conspiracy, dark and damnable, and I want to say boldly, and you may make a note of it, Brother Houghton, if you wish, that somebody is guilty of one of the foulest conspiracies that ever disgraced a free nation. If my clients here are innocent, and you know they are, and these persecutors know they are—if my clients are innocent, then George M. Paine and George M. Paine's son, and "other men to us unknown," in the language of your wonderful information, other men, gentlemen, are guilty of entering the temple of justice and using the law, which was made to guard and protect and shelter you and me and these defendants, for the purpose of hounding innocent men to their death or to a prison pen.

In the light of this evidence, in the light of what has transpired here from the day when the first question was asked until now, I say to you that someone is guilty, and that before a just judge, and in the presence of all honest men, and before the consciences of all who have honor and soul, George M. Paine and Nathan Paine will stand forever accused as two men who conspired to send their fellow-men to jail without cause, without shadow of law, simply because these defendants were in their way.

It was an ancient law that a man who conspired to use the courts to destroy his fellow-men was guilty of treason to the State. He had laid his hand upon the State itself; he had touched the bulwark of human liberty. When he assaulted the freedom of one man he assaulted the liberty of every other subject of the State. And when George M. Paine raised his hand to strike a blow against the liberty of Thomas I. Kidd, he raised a hand to strike a blow at your freedom and mine, and he conspired to destroy the institutions under which we live. There are criminals in this case, gentlemen, criminals who in the eye of heaven and in the light of justice have not been guilty of the paltry crime of conspiring to save their fellow-men, but criminals who have conspired against the framework of those institutions that have made these same criminals great and strong; and you know their names; and I know their names; and whether written here or not, if there is a book where the deeds of men are recorded by a Judge who can look beneath the hollow pretenses of hollow hearts, upon that record George M. Paine's name and Nathan Paine's name are written down as men who conspired against the liberty of their fellows and against the country in which they live.

Now, gentlemen, I want to say a few words in relation to the labor question, which is really the controversy involved in this case, because that is all there is of it. Back of all this prosecution is the effort on the part of George M. Paine to wipe these labor organizations out of existence, and you know it. That's all there is of it.

In many well-ordered penitentiaries outside of Oshkosh they have a rule that people cannot converse at all, and the reason is that they may not conspire. And down in the dark coal mines in the anthracite regions of Pennsylvania where those human moles burrow in the earth for the benefit of the great, monstrous, greedy corporations that are corrupting the life-blood of the nation, there they work men in chain gangs, and put an Italian, an Austrian, a German, an American and a Bohemian together so they cannot understand each other when they speak, so that they may not combine and conspire, because in combination, and in combination alone, is strength. They do this, gentlemen of the jury, so that each one of those tiny atoms, each poor laborer, with his little family, perhaps, around him, working for a dollar a day, or eighty cents a day, is bound to compete with the combination of men, with all the wealth that all their lives can create. On the one hand these powerful interests are organized thoroughly, completely, and they act together; and they turn to those poor slaves, whose liberty they take, and say to them, "We will consult with you, but come alone to our office, and then we will talk." They say this because they wish to meet the weak and puny and helpless single individual with the great and powerful wealth and strength of their mighty corporations. And that is what Paine said. "I would not answer the letter because it came from a labor organization; and I did not know who it was. I will meet my men alone and talk with them. There are only two parties to a contract, the employer and the employed." Yes, gentlemen, they would meet their men alone. Fie on you for hypocrites and cowards, who would combine every manufacturer in the city of Oshkosh, not into a "union," but into an "association." A body of employers living from the unpaid labor of the poor is an "association." A body of their slaves is a "labor union." George M. Paine says, "I will not meet your union; I will not meet your committee. If one of you has anything to say, come to me alone and talk." And they did go alone, and what did they get? Gentlemen, what did they get?

This was the beginning of the strike. It was not the speech of Thomas I. Kidd. All the orators on earth could never bring dissatisfaction and riot where justice rules; and all the hired lawyers on earth can never keep down the seething, boiling sea of discontent that is based on sin, and crime, and wrong. Herman Daus went to his employer, and who is Herman Daus? A union man. You saw him before you; intelligent and honest-looking;

and yet these men say he is a criminal. Herman Daus is a respectable citizen of Oshkosh; one who has toiled and labored and helped to rear your beautiful town. He has worked for eight or ten years in these mills; he is a skilled workman; has given that much of his life to his employer and worked at a machine where any day the wheels or knives might clip his fingers instead of the wood. Eight or ten years' experience, and getting a dollar and a quarter a day; seven dollars and a half a week; only about a dollar a day for the number of days that a man must live, for he must live Sundays as well as other days, unless perhaps he is so religious that he can go to Brother Houghton's Sunday school and needs no food except his teachings. Seven dollars and a half a week for a man who had worked at dangerous machinery for ten years, and they had promised him a raise; and he went singly, singly, the way this great corporation desired to have a man meet them; singly—the cowards. I do not know whether he carried his cap in his hand; I suppose so. If he did not he should have. I do not know whether he said "Your lordship." If he did not, he should have been better trained. I do not know whether he knelt down before them like a vassal of the ancient days, and in the way that an Oshkosh lord wishes his vassals to kneel. If he did not, it was his mistake. But he did decently ask for a raise. And what did they say? They said, "Go to hell, God damn you. I can get a damn sight better man than you are for a dollar and a quarter a day." These gentlemen, these high-toned gentlemen, who come into this court of justice with kid gloves and well-brushed clothes, who can study manners at foreign courts, and send their children to foreign lands to be educated; and yet, when a poor laborer asks them for something more than seven dollars and a half a week, they tell him to go to hell. Well, he would not have far to go, Mr. Paine.

There was another man who worked in Paine's mill and he said, "I want a raise"; and the boss answered, "Well, you get out of here or I'll give you a raise in the pants." What beautiful gentlemen these are! Won't it be a pleasure, gentlemen of the jury, just to accommodate them by passing out a verdict of Guilty! This is the way they want to be met, singly and alone. After these men have toiled all these years and are growing old in their business and their service, they are kicked aside like dogs. Mark this, gentlemen, no one has disputed these statements, or any others; and they could not dispute them; they are absolutely true. This is the way the laboring men of Oshkosh were treated by the employers who had waxed great and rich at their expense. And you are asked to cure their discontent by sending Kidd to jail. Gentlemen, let me ask you, do you suppose that while George M. Paine pays a dollar and a quarter a day for skilled labor, that there are jails enough on earth to hold the criminals who will rise in rebellion against such conditions? Aye, gentlemen, if the jails could have put down insurrection and rebellion, then you and I would not be living in America today. If the jails and the penitentiaries and the scaffolds could have strangled and wiped out rebellion and riot and insurrection, there would have been no American republic for us to protect and uphold. You gentlemen who wish to bring back the good old days of the past, you gentlemen with all your power and your wealth, cannot crush discontent and unrest from the hearts of men.

You have heard a great deal of evidence as to whether Thomas I. Kidd provoked this strike. I do not care whether he did or did not. Gentlemen, if it was in my power tomorrow to provoke another strike in this city that would succeed, I would do it, even though the jail opened to receive me. I would do it for the duty I owe to my fellow-men. I do not care whether Kidd provoked this strike or not. I know, gentlemen, that he did what he could in his poor way, with his poor strength, to fight those great monopolies in the interest of the men and women and little children that he loves; and for that you are asked to send him to jail.

What was the condition of labor in this city when he came? Let me call your attention to the fact that of all the witnesses that testified in relation to wages, there was only one man who received more than a dollar and a quarter a day. Just one; and that man was the foreman, having seven under him, besides doing his own work, and he received sixteen and a half cents an hour. Aside from that, amongst the fifteen or twenty who testified, none received more than a dollar and a quarter a day, and each told instances of others who had received ninety cents, eighty cents, and even less; and this has not been disputed for one moment by these men. Not only that, gentlemen, but according to Mr. Paine's report, which he submitted to that ornamental body, the state board of arbitration (not ornamental, but useless enough to be ornamental), according to that report one quarter of all the people that he employs in his mill are little children and girls.

*　　*　　*

Now, gentlemen, just a word more and I will leave this report to you, and Mr. Houghton may say what he pleases about it. Seven eighths of the men, seven eighths of the men, gentlemen, not boys, not girls, but seven eighths of all the men working for Mr. Paine, according to his own statement, receive less than a dollar and a half a day. This strike and this movement were gotten up for that seven eighths, and they know it, and you know it. We are not in this crusade for the benefit of the men who get three and four dollars a day to do the slave-driving for their masters. We are in it, gentlemen, and will stay in it so long as breath is spared us, for the benefit of the seven eighths of our fellow-citizens who labor that their master may grow rich and great. We appear for the seven eighths whose wages they sought to raise; and you take that seven eighths, and take the lowest estimate as Mr. Quartermass took it, and it averages a dollar and ten cents a day—in this land of the free and of great opportunities. It was to better this condition that these men, your citizens, are branded as conspirators and felons, and are hounded by this company and its men. You may figure it yourselves. Seven eighths of those men, according to their own report, taking the lowest figures they give, receive an average of a dollar and ten cents a day—in this nation, in this city where Paine can have a plant worth a million, and warehouses scattered from the Atlantic to the Pacific coast. And the poor devil who is bound to work for what amounts to less than a dollar a day, for him there is nothing but indictments, and prosecutions, and jail, if this conspiracy succeeds.

And that is not all the tale these figures tell. Here is another part of it. One quarter of all the people who work for Paine are children and women. And these are not included in the wages quoted. You have seen some of the children; some of them came up on the witness stand. One quarter are little children and women. Now, I personally agree with Mr. Kidd. I believe a woman should have every opportunity in this world that she wants and needs; every advantage given to a man; but it is only necessity that drives these girls into Paine's sweatshop for ten hours a day. Let me tell you why women and children work for Paine. In this day of civilization, when the ingenuity of man is constantly inventing machinery to take the place of human toil, it is found that girls or little children can do the work that men did before. Paine has been able to get machines to do the labor that once required the work of a skilled mechanic —the head of the family. By the aid of these wonderful machines Paine can take the wife from her home, and the children from the school and cradle, and place them at the machines, and send the father out in the streets to tramp. This is the problem that confronts the laborer of the United States. This is the problem that confronts every one of these labor unions and every one of these labor leaders, and every sociologist who cares anything for his fellow-men.

Let me tell you one place where Mr. Paine made a statement on this stand that was false. Not that he forgot; not that he quibbled; not that he evaded; he did that in every word he uttered, every word he spoke. But I asked Mr. Paine the question if he employed girls, and he said yes. And I asked, "What do those girls do?" "Ah," he says, "those girls take little bits of sticks and saw them up on little saws." That is what Mr. Paine said to this jury, under the sanction of this oath and with the fear of perjury staring him in the face. And what is the evidence? Now I do not know whether Paine is familiar with his factory or not. Possibly he has no more interest in his factory than Quartermass has in the prosecution of criminal cases in this court; but he did not tell the truth. We proved, by witness after witness, that these sixteen-year-old girls take heavy doors, hardwood doors and oak doors, and mold and saw them on the machines; and they have not denied it, excepting that Mr. Paine told you that these girls sawed little sticks on little saws. I suppose these saws scarcely moved; harmless saws that were simply toys. What these girls do has been proven over and over by the witnesses in this case. They do what the men do. They take these heavy doors and lift them and saw them and mold them, and take the places of their fathers and their brothers, that Paine may send his goods into more states, and more territories, and his children to foreign lands.

And what about the children? Let us add to what the seven eighths receive the wages paid to children and the girls, and they work at saws and machines where their fathers worked before, and where some of them work today; and it proves, gentlemen of the jury, according to Paine's figures, as given in this report, that the average pay of all is ninety-six cents per day. That is what a man receives in the city of Oshkosh if he falls into the clutches of George M. Paine. And now let me call your attention to this: not one single witness has been called by them who has testified to the rate of wages—not one. Every man we put upon the witness stand was asked about wages—each person—and they told us; and the wages ranged from ninety cents to a dollar and a quarter for the men, and they told us of others that got much less. We placed little boys upon the stand, and they told their story too, and all of this is undisputed and beyond any possibility of contradiction. And yet they say that these underfed and under-paid toilers were contented and prosperous and happy till Thomas I. Kidd came to Oshkosh. Happy, and prosperous, and contented! Gentlemen, it was a sweeping indictment that the state's attorney made when he told you that sixteen hundred of his fellow-citizens were guilty of conspiracy; but when he tells you that sixteen hundred of your fellow-citizens were happy and contented under these starvation wages, the indictment is more sweeping still. An American, or a citizen of any other nation on earth, who would be contented with wages like that has no right to enjoy the benefits of free government; and they cannot enjoy such benefits very long; they soon become slaves, and that is what this taskmaster wants. He would wish them to make doors without food—aye, without lumber, too, as the men who toiled in Egypt were asked to make bricks without straw, until the agitators, Moses and the rest, led them out. I do not know whether Moses was prosecuted for it or not. He would have been if Houghton had been alive and been paid fifteen dollars a day for his services.

* * *

That was the condition which confronted the Oshkosh woodworkers when they dared—when they dared—what? Why, to ask Mr. Paine for more wages. When they dared to write him a letter. A body of workers, a body of employees actually daring to write a letter to George M. Paine! Why, you ought to send them to jail for it; and it's too bad that they can't be hanged. We had these little children—and let me call your attention to some few facts in relation to these little children. Mr. Houghton said he would have been glad to get as much as they did when he was their age. I do not know whether he meant it or not. I do not know whether Mr. Houghton worked when he was their age or not. I hope not. But he saw fit to say as these little children marched past him, not producing much effect on him, for a man can carry out a large bluff on fifteen dollars a day, "I wish I could have been able to get as much when I was a child of their age."

Now, gentlemen, let us think of it a minute. The child is the father to the man. He is the one on whom must rest in the future the burdens and responsibilities and duties of citizenship and government. After you and I have played our parts and gone our way, they must carry on the battles which we commenced, and do the best they can. Responsibility comes soon enough, and trouble and sorrow come soon enough, and age comes soon enough at best; and there is none too much of joy and sunshine and happiness in the world. It ought to be that these little children should be spared for a time at least before they learn that the world is cruel and hard and unkind and false. And yet, our modern civilization, with its wondrous contrivances, has reached into the cradle and taken these little children in the morning of their youth and set them to work to grind out dollars for George M. Paine. You remember the story of the Arab chief who was lured from his desert home and taken to a factory town, and shown the glory and the magnificence and the great triumphs of civilization. He was taken to a mill where little children were busy feeding wheels and tending machines, and this was pointed out as one of the triumphs and glories of the civilization of this Western world. The chief asked if these were young criminals who were placed at work, and he was told that they were simply factory hands; then he replied, "Take me back to my desert home. I had rather wander a wild Arab on the plain where at least childhood is free than be in your civilization, where you set your children to work in prison shops."

Gentlemen, if all that Oshkosh can show for the civilization of this day—if all that Oshkosh can show is these stunted, starved children, that have made it great, then I say it would be better if not one brick was left standing upon another in your town, and that you give back the soil to the original savage who once roamed the shores of your lovely lake. You are not going forward. You are going backward when you take these little children from their homes and work them up into gold for Paine.

*　*　*

Gentlemen, I want to know if you think that while George M. Paine can set one of these little children at work in his mill at that tender age, you can settle the labor question by sending an agitator to jail? If so, do it. Do it, and crush out the last spark of manhood that remains in the employees of George M. Paine. Do it, and obliterate the last ray of hope from the lives of these little children of Oshkosh who are forced into their premature graves. I want to say to George M. Paine and to those who thrive from the toil of these little ones, that you are paying too great a price for the gold you make. When it comes to grinding your fellow-men to the dust, when it comes to taking the mothers and sisters from their homes, and robbing childhood of its sunshine and its joy, you are paying too much for what you get. I want to say that the luxury and the profligacy and the advantages that have come to these employers' families have come through the unpaid toil of the men who serve them. And I want to say to you, George M. Paine and Nathan Paine, that your wives and your daughters, when they cover themselves with their gowns of silk, have not been clothed by the worm alone, but that their raiment has been spun from the bowels of these little babes.

❖   ❖   ❖

George M. Paine says that his plant is worth a million dollars. It is built from the toil of these children and from the labor of these unpaid men.

It is perhaps something of a habit of mine, as it ought to be of every man's, to think of these little children. I remember that poor agitator of Judea—and the jury found Him guilty, too, Brother Quartermass, and you weren't there—I think of Him as He went out, not to the great and powerful and the mill owners, they did not worship Him then—they worship Him now, it's so long ago it's safe. If Paine had been living then he would have helped to crucify Him instead of building a church in His name. I think of Him as He looked at the little innocent children, the only ones in this sad old world of ours who have learned nothing of suffering and sin—as He looked at the uncorrupted children and said, "Suffer the little children to come unto me and forbid them not, for of such is the Kingdom of Heaven." And then I think of George M. Paine, as he drags his hypocritical robes about him and kneels down in a temple mockingly reared to that meek and lowly Jesus, and repeats in his prayers, "Suffer the little children to come unto me and forbid them not, for of such is the prison pen of George M. Paine." Gentlemen, if the spectacle that you have witnessed in the trial of this case would not justify any strike—any strike to save manhood and woman-hood and liberate these little slaves, then I have made a poor estimate of human nature, and of you who pass upon this case.

I have talked to you about the conditions that existed in Oshkosh, conditions which are not denied. In all these days of prodding and searching and bringing witnesses upon this stand, most of whom knew nothing about this case, they have not denied these horrible conditions that exist at your very doors. But they say we entered into a conspiracy. A conspiracy for what? If you are to find my clients guilty of conspiracy in this case I want you to settle first of all in your own minds what was the purpose of this felonious conspiracy which these gentlemen tell us of.

We are told that there were sixteen hundred and three conspirators who live in Oshkosh, and three who came here from other towns. And what does that mean? They have had the effrontery to stand before this jury, composed, I assume, of intelligent men, composed, I presume, of men who wish to do what is right under their conscience, and in the sight of their God, and to tell them that these sixteen hundred and three men are guilty of conspiracy. I do not know your town very well. I am learning about it. I am getting acquainted with George M. Paine better than his neighbors ever did before, and I wish I could get him acquainted with himself, which I can't. But I do say that if I were the prosecuting attorney of this county I should hesitate before I told a jury that sixteen hundred and three of my fellow-citizens were felons and conspirators. Sixteen hundred men and boys of Oshkosh, the brawn and sinew of your city, the men who take their dinner pails in the morning and go to work in these prisons for a small pittance, and go home at night tired and weary and worn for the life that has gone out of them for the benefit of George M. Paine. Sixteen hundred criminals, all of whom are your citizens and your neighbors, and yet this district attorney assures you that they are criminals, whom you should send to jail. It is an outrageous slander upon your city. It is an outrageous insult to every man in Oshkosh that is obliged to live by his toil. Sixteen hundred men, ground to death by these employers, dared—actually dared—to organize the Oshkosh Woodworkers' Union. Where did you gentlemen come from? I should think, gentlemen, that you lived not later than the end of the seventeenth century, and that in some mysterious way you had fallen asleep and taken a long Rip Van Winkle nap, and wakened here in the closing days of the nineteenth century, with the musty cobwebs of the past obscuring all the light of day. I will undertake to say that you gentlemen cannot find any intelligent political economist, or intelligent law books, if there are any such books, you cannot find in the utterances of men of standing and character for the last hundred years, such statements as you have made to this jury about the criminality of men.

Let me tell you something of labor organizations. I have studied this question because I believe in it, because I love it as I do my very life; because it has been the strongest passion of my years; because in this great battle between the powerful and the weak I have ever been and will ever be with the weak so long as the breath is left in my body to speak. I have read it—not, gentlemen, for this case, not for the dirty gold of Paine—but I have read it because I loved it, and because in my own way I wished to do what I could for the thousands—aye, the millions of people who are yet poorer than myself. I know the history of the labor movement; I know what it has come through. I know the difficulties it is in today. I know the past is a dark, dark chapter of infamy and wrong; and yet, gentlemen, these lawyers have been groping amongst the dead ashes of the past, with a dark lantern, to find the blackest pages of human history, to ask you gentlemen to adopt them in the closing years of this nineteenth century.

There was a time in England, which is the mother of all this agitation, there was a time when the poor serf that lived on his lord's estate was sold with the land; when a man bought his farm he bought the serf with it. There was a time a little later when the poor laboring man did not dare leave his own county without getting permission of his employer, as Paine's slaves are bound to do when they leave his mill for a moment's time. There was a day later when the first glimmerings of a new morning for the world commenced to dawn upon the labor agitators and the conspirators and the humanitarians of that old world. There was a time when they came together and organized to protect and help themselves. And what did they meet? They met their Houghtons—men hired to send them to jail. They met the prison pen. Aye, gentlemen, they met the scaffold and the flames. They were hunted to death because they dared to associate and combine with their fellows to make themselves better men and give a little more freedom to the human race. The early history of trade unionism shows that the first associations came together in the forests, in the rocks, in the waste places, where no human eye could see. Pinkerton detectives had not been invented then, but there were bloodhounds in those days, as there are lawyers now, and those hunted, outlawed men held their meetings in the forest, in the rocks and the caves, and they buried their archives in the earth where the Houghtons could not get them to drag them forth to the light. And in those days, if you were a man who labored for a living, and went to your neighbor and said to him, "My friend, you ought to ask for higher pay," you were a villain and an outcast, and the prison pen opened to receive you. To say to your neighbor out of the depths of your heart and out of a generous instinct, "You are not getting enough, and you ought to ask for more," was enough to consign you to jail by the Houghtons of a hundred years ago. To belong to these labor organizations was a crime—a crime to simply join them; and these prosecutors have ransacked the ancient cobwebs of the past and brought out these law books containing the opinions of imbecile judges in the employ of powerful knaves and quoted their utterances to be adopted in this year 1898, and in the United States. It was a crime in those days, as these men would make it in Oshkosh for a workingman to do anything but work, work patiently and unquestioningly for the man he served.

But that is not the law of today. The law is generally behind, because lawyers look to the past for their precedents, and are ever governed by the dead. The reformers of the world have always led the lawyers of the world. These despised reformers saw the morning and the sunlight rising far away, so far that the poor, weak, practical mortals of the earth could see only darkness as they looked out upon the night. And these reformers have gone forth crying in the wilderness, and have been sent to jail and to the scaffold because they loved their fellow-men. But today I take it that every intelligent person who has investigated this question, outside of the counsel for the State, understand that workingmen have the right to organize; understand that if laborers are not satisfied with their conditions, they may stop work; they may stop work singly or collectively, exactly as they please, and no court will say them nay. That is the law today, and if it is not the law, it ought to be. This hideous conspiracy in Oshkosh, where sixteen hundred of your fellow-citizens were plotting in the dark, was a labor union; that is all.

What have these nameless men who make up these sixteen hundred members done? What have they done that they should be branded before this jury and this community as criminals and felons? Why, gentlemen, these sixteen hundred men, and I suppose sixteen hundred more, and sixteen hundred more, and still sixteen hundred more of your fellow-citizens had the temerity to associate themselves into unions for their mutual good. And for that you are told that they are conspirators, and that you should send them to jail to satisfy Paine. Has anything been proven against them, excepting that they joined the labor union, and that they dared to strike? Disguise it as you may, cover it as you will, there is but one thing in this case, and that is the right of these men to organize for their own defense and to strike if they see fit. This is not a criminal case. It is an action brought by employers of labor to ruin and crush their men. We have spent considerable time in this evidence, discussing the question as to whether Mr. Kidd or someone else brought on this strike, and Brother Houghton will split hairs upon the question as to whether Mr. Kidd spoke before the resolution to strike was passed by the Local Assembly or after the resolution was passed. A fig for all of that. I do not care. Gentlemen, I want to say that Kidd had the right to come from Chicago; had the right to camp in your town; had the right to speak to your people; had the right to raise his voice until the stones and the bricks of your buildings should cry out with him against this unholy oppression in your midst. I am surprised at these counsel. Is it possible that they think that in this day of the world they can brand a man because he happens to be secretary of a labor organization? That they can appeal to a jury of his countrymen to send him to jail because he dares to be secretary of a labor union? All right, gentlemen of the jury, if you can afford to do it, please do not hesitate. If this jury, interested as I am in this land in which we are common citizens, if this jury, interested as I am, and as Kidd is, in every human being that lives, if you can afford to say that because a man is secretary of a labor organization he should be an outlaw and a criminal, say it, and peace be with you.

Gentlemen, Kidd not only had the right to come here and to agitate, and to bring on this strike if he wished, but it was his duty to do it, provided the strike had a show to win; provided he thought it might win; aye, gentlemen, provided he thought that even if it failed, that even if these poor, despondent, hopeless men, who saw before them one glimmer of light, one ray of cheer in the midst of their dark lives, and who struck for that light and that hope, provided he knew that they would go back to their taskmasters despondent and disheartened, with the life crushed out of them, and provided he still thought, as I think, and as you think, that the Paines of this city would hesitate long before inviting another conflict with their men. Kidd was the chief officer of this labor union. He was the shepherd of his flock; and in spite of what these gentlemen may say, I wish all shepherds were as wise, as tender, as loving, as humane, as forgiving as Thomas I. Kidd. Gentlemen, you may or may not believe in a future world; but if there shall be one, I ask you in that future world where you would rather stand, beside George M. Paine or Thomas I. Kidd? In that land and before that court where wealth and power will go for naught, there will be none so weak and poor as to do the bidding of the Paines.

* * *

When George M. Paine said that he did not desire to deal with this union or with Kidd he was a hypocrite, and he knew perfectly well that the only reason was that he thought he could break these men if they came to him individually, as he wished them to come. He desired that these poor slaves should come to him, and petition him singly, beg him as individuals, as Oliver Twist in the almshouse held out his soup bowl and asked for more. The crime with which these men are charged is that they are members of this organization, and Mr. Kidd is its head, and that is why he is charged. George M. Paine is not wise enough to know that if he should send Kidd to jail another man will take his place. He does not know that he is sowing the wind. I tell you, gentlemen, that he may be wealthy and great and strong, but there is no man strong enough to entirely sub-vert the manhood of the workers of the United States; and if the time shall come when there is a man so strong, then American liberty is dead.

Each member of this union says that the union itself agitated the strike and determined on it before Kidd came into Oshkosh. Have that as you will. You may split hairs over a day to prove that Kidd came first, and I care not whether he did or did not come first. But what are the facts? This organization, like every labor organization, is a democratic institution. Every movement must have its inception in the local body, which this autocrat Paine cannot understand, not being a democrat himself, but an autocrat instead. These laborers had been whipped and scourged and outraged for years. Is it any wonder that they themselves originated this movement? They started it; they discussed it for months; they talked about the poor wages; they talked about these women and little children whom they saw coming forward day by day to take their places; these women and little children who were set to work at the machines which they once used themselves. As a man staked out upon the beach, and watching the rising tide as it crept nearer and nearer, until it was ready to engulf and overwhelm him. They watched them coming until a quarter of their members had gone, until a quarter of the men had been driven out and their places filled with little children and with girls, and they discussed it, and discussed it perhaps in blindness—I do not know. No one knows. We are placed in the world; our intelligence is limited at its best; we can see in the darkness but a very little way; sometimes we think we should go this way; again we think we should go that. No one knows. We do the best we can, and these poor fellows, toiling for starvation wages, working day by day, saving nothing, poorly clothed, poorly fed, and seeing day by day that their own wives and children, like a hostile army, were coming to drive them out, that their children must be taken from the schools and placed in the mill in their stead, that their wives and their daughters should be taken from the home to do the work of man, that they should be set adrift—they knew not what was best. I cannot tell. Do you know? Does anybody know? Mr. Paine, your lawyers may split hairs; that's their trade. They may say that one of these men should have said this or that, or that he should have left unsaid this or that. They may say that he should have done this or that, or left undone this or that. But, gentlemen, you and I cannot measure human conduct in any such way. We can look only to the human heart to know whether the man is good or bad. We can look only to the motives of these men, who, seeing ruin before them, struck out in the darkness the best they could.

If I had been here to conduct this strike instead of Kidd, the men would not have been so gentlemanly and orderly, let me tell you that. They did right to be peaceable. Kidd did right. They did right to turn the other cheek to this man who had done nothing but smite them all these years. But I could not have done it. I wonder if you could. I wonder how many men could. I wonder what Houghton would have done when he put his law book under his arm and trotted down to give comfort and consolation to Mr. Kidd.

I am not going over all these preliminaries, for I do not care for them. The organization had several meetings. They agreed to formulate a plan. They agreed to make certain requests, or demands. They should have been demands, for requests do not go with the Paines. They agreed to make certain demands. Were those demands just or not? What do you think, were they just or were they unjust? They formed themselves together, they agreed on the demands they would make; they took a vote upon it. Mr. Kidd came from Chicago, and after they took the vote, as nine tenths of these witnesses say, although a few say it was before. But I do not care whether it was before or after. But either before or after Kidd spoke upon it, he told them that he had not the right to advise them; it was their own battle; they must do the best they could. If they wished to strike, he would get the sanction of the general council; and he did, and that was sent to them about the sixth of May, and then they addressed this letter to their employers. Then commenced the terrible conspiracy. The men wrote a respectable, decent letter. They dared to sign it by the Secretary of the International Woodworkers' Union. They told George M. Paine what they knew was a lie, that they presumed he could not help reducing their wages in the past. They did that much, knowing it was a lie; but they told him this, thinking that possibly it might smooth him the right way, not knowing that there was no right way to smooth George M. Paine. They told him, also, the honest truth, that they could not live from these starvation wages that he had seen fit to dole out to them to make a little more life, and a little more muscle to work up for him. They asked him to increase wages, which is the greatest crime of which a man like Paine can conceive. The idea of any man asking for an increase of wages! They asked him also that he should not employ female labor. And, gentlemen, it is not at all the question of the right or wrong of a woman to work. You know, and I know, that it is only the gaunt wolf of famine that would drive a little girl into these shops to handle those heavy doors at their machines. You know it; and you know, and I know, that if you take the women and the little children out of those factories, it gives more food to the men, and more food to the women and the little children, too. And Paine knew it, and that is the reason he wanted them. He wanted them because it takes less bread to feed a child than it does to feed a man, and a girl will work for less pay than a man.

The first step in the conspiracy was forming this organization; the next step was making this request for wages. The letter containing the request was courteous, it was kind; it was not altogether true because it was too kind; but if any man ever received a courteous letter from a body of his employees, then George M. Paine received such a letter from his men. They respectfully asked him to do four things. First, to raise wages —a terrible crime. Next, to have a weekly pay day. Mr. Houghton had told them that they had a right to do this. Of course, when he said that he did not get a retainer, so perhaps the advice was not good. You cannot trust a lawyer unless you pay him, and you had better watch him even then. The next request was that he should not employ women, and I think that was right. And then they asked that the union be recognized, although they did not make that as a demand; and I think that was right. But it is not what I think. It is not what you think. These men were employees: they had as much at stake in the running of this factory as George M. Paine. They at least had the right to make these respectful requests in a respectful way; and were they not courteous and decent?

* * *

This organization addressed a respectful letter to George M. Paine, and he received it. He received it on Friday morning, and it called for an answer by six o'clock Saturday evening. Only two days to think about it, says the prosecution. Two days is a long enough time for George M. Paine to think about raising wages. If he should think about it any longer he would drop dead. And they gave him two days to answer their respectful letter; and he received the letter and put it in the wastebasket. He is a nice man, is he not?

If I were you, I would send these defendants to jail, just to accommodate him. I asked Paine why he did not answer that letter. "Why," he said, "it was such an unbusinesslike letter—unbusinesslike letter." Here is this man, the monarch of fourteen states in the sash and door business, and he is paying his men the paltry pittance of a dollar a day, and he refuses to reply to their communication because it is unbusinesslike.

These poor men met together at six o'clock to receive the answer from the bosses, and no word came.

Gentlemen, what could these men do? What would you have done? Aye, gentlemen, I do not know what you would have done; but I know that any American citizen that had a spark of manhood and independence left in his body would have sworn that he would give up his life, if need be, unless those just demands were answered. You cannot build a great country out of citizens that would not have done it. You cannot make a free people out of citizens that would not have spurned with contempt an employer like this. They did what you would have done. They did the only thing on earth left for them to do. They did not declare war. War had been declared. When George M. Paine took this letter and threw it into the wastebasket, he threw down the gauntlet to these men, and said,

"Sirs, you might as well understand now as ever that you are to address nothing to me. I am George M. Paine. Who are you? What right have you to invade my sanctuary, even with a letter carried under the seal of the United States?" What else could they do? And several weeks later, when a body of his own employees went to his office to meet him and ask him in the name of humanity to do something for them, to do something for their families, to do something for the starving people of Oshkosh, not making demands, gentlemen, but begging of this lord and master to do something, to make some proposition. When these men were seated in his presence, George M. Paine turned to them and spoke of their letter, and he said: "The reason I did not answer it is because I don't have to. My wastebasket is filled with letters like that." And this prosecuting lawyer on cross-examination says to the witness: "Didn't he say it in a respectful manner?" Shylock said: "The other day you spat on me." The merchant should have replied: "Well, didn't I do it in a respectful manner?" Respectful? Respectful? George M. Paine never learned the meaning of that word. He has no more use for it in his vocabulary than he has for the words justice, or righteousness, or generosity. He never learned it, and it is not there; and we can not blame him, perhaps, for what he does not know. Respectful? To turn to these petitioning workmen, who had been fleeced, and robbed, and starved for years, and say, "My wastebasket is filled with communications like that." And this is the man, Mr. District Attorney, for whom you prostituted the great state of Wisconsin, for whom you prostitute the office that you hold, to whom you have turned over this state to do the work of a bloodhound to track innocent men to jail. I am sorry you have done it. You should not have allowed this wily conspirator to seduce you with his words, for I do not believe it was anything more than that.

What else did Paine tell these employees in that interview when he was so very "courteous" to his men? Mr. Houghton has given us an illustration of courtesy; you remember he shook hands with Paine before he put him on the stand, the only witness in the case who received this distinction. I do not object to it, gentlemen, I am discussing conditions as they are, and I do not care to have you think, for it is not a fact, that I feel bitterness or hatred against George M. Paine. I have a philosophy which consoles me at times like this: When I see a man who is willing to grind his fellow-workmen in the dust that he may have more wealth, or when I see a lawyer who is willing to abandon his convictions for fifteen dollars a day, I have a philosophy which forgives them both, because I think they do the best they can. I wish they knew better. It is not for me to judge them.

*   *   *

Gentlemen, when these poor, half-starved men go to George M. Paine and tell him that they can no longer support life on the pittance that he gives, he replies, "It is true; I don't give you enough to keep my horse." Gentlemen, these Paines know not what they do.

Justice may be stifled for a time. You may hold it down with an iron heel, but you cannot forever violate the laws of the universe under which all must live. And I say to George M. Paine that there are not enough district attorneys, there are not enough Houghtons, there are not enough Pinkerton detectives, there are not enough jails in this broad land of ours to keep down this surging sea of discontent that was born of your robberies and crimes.

These workmen struck, and this was another conspiracy. What is a strike? When a body of men declare that they will not work longer, and quit together, that is a strike. This is what they did; and what else could they do?

*   *   *

Do you mean to tell me that it has come to that point in America, under the guarantee of freedom of speech, and under the Constitution beneath which we live, that a free man cannot go to his neighbor and implore him not to work? If a jury or a court should write a verdict or a judgment like that it would be the death knell to human liberty. I have a right to work or not, as I see fit. I have a right in a decent way to go to my neighbor and implore him to join with me and cease to work. If he refuses to work, well and good. If he says he will work anyhow, then, gentlemen, he has the right under the law to go to work, and if I compel him not to, I violate the law. Now, there never was any other law than that—at least not for fifty years.

What were the pickets to do? Their duties were plain. They were well-understood. They were to keep track of their members to know who was working. They were also to go to the mills and implore others not to work when their brethren were on a strike. This they had the right to do. It may be, gentlemen, that here and there someone did more. I do not know, and I do not care. It may be, gentlemen, that some poor fellow, some man who had been working for ninety cents a day, or for a dollar a day, and who was patrolling those streets and pleading with his fellow-men not to take the bread from his mouth and the roof from his family, but to go with him—it may be that in despair he raised his hand in violence against his fellow-man. It might be Troiber did it. I do not know. I do not care. I do not know whether poor Troiber did or not. Gentlemen, I want to know what you would have done. I want to put it to you as men. In this great conflict for as holy a cause as was ever waged, in this great battle for a right to live, in this great conflict for your homes and your fireside and your civilization: if some poor laborer saw some other man taking the bread out of his mouth, deserting the organization and going back to the mills, would you blame him if in the heat and excitement of the moment he raised his hand in violence against him? It perhaps was wrong. It was a violation of the law. Whoever did it under the law was guilty of assault and battery. Nothing else. He was not guilty under the law of a conspiracy to injure his fellow-man.

But now let us see what took place. We have heard a great deal about riot and bloodshed and violation of the law. Let me talk with you and reason with you for a moment about that. How much disorder was there in the city of Oshkosh? First, let me call your attention to the fact that sixteen hundred men, honest workingmen of your town, were on a strike; that this strike lasted for fourteen weeks. Of course there was excitement; it could not have been otherwise. Men were taking the places of some of the workers; men were idle on the streets; the matter was the chief topic of thought and discussion. The militia was called out, and of course the tension was extreme during those long fourteen weeks. And yet, gentlemen, aside from these riots, which I will speak of later, there was but one single act of violence in the whole fourteen weeks. And yet this act is paraded before this jury, and you are asked to take away the liberty of three of your fellow-citizens, using that as a paltry excuse, but really because George M. Paine makes this request at your hands. There is evidence that somebody struck a boy going over the bridge one night; not seriously, but they struck him with a stick which they call a club, a hardwood club, the boy thought, because it felt hard on his back. What else happened? There were two other instances where men arguing with others against going to work caught them by the arm and walked them up street; this could scarcely approach the dignity of an assault; and one or two instances where somebody had been threatened that certain things would happen if he went to work; and that is all, in fourteen weeks of excitement in the city of Oshkosh. And that is what they magnify, until they try to make a jury believe that they live in the midst of a band of assassins and conspirators, whom your verdict should send to jail. Gentlemen of the jury, I am not here to pass any eulogy upon the Oshkosh woodworkers, but when I remember that through this terrible ordeal, when they saw their bread taken from their mouths, when they saw the clothing dropping from their bodies, when they saw the roof being taken from the little home that it sheltered, when they saw starvation staring them in the face, that nothing but these matters that I have related occurred to disturb the peace and quiet of the city of Oshkosh, it is the greatest tribute that I could pay to the peaceful, orderly conduct of the woodworkers that these gentlemen have denounced as conspirators and villains.

Brother Quartermass says if a conspiracy is formed, and if one man is sleeping peacefully in his bed and someone else commits an act, then the man who is sleeping in his bed is responsible for the act. Is he? Let us see. Now, gentlemen, like everything else in the world, that depends. If an unlawful conspiracy is formed and a man commits an act in pursuance of it, then every person who belonged to that unlawful conspiracy is guilty of the act. If you, gentlemen of the jury, should conspire, which you probably will not, to kill somebody, and all but one of you should go home peacefully at night, and the other should commit the deed, you would all be guilty. But if you conspired to do something which is lawful, something which you have the right to do, and if some member in carrying out that lawful design does an unlawful act, then the rest of you are not guilty of the unlawful act; and it does not require very much sense or law to understand that. It needs a little human, natural justice, that is all. Because, gentlemen, however much these lawyers try to deceive you, the law is not so fearfully unreasonable as it seems to be. If a number of men combine to do something which they have the right to do, and if while carrying out that combination some individual commits an illegal act, then that individual alone is responsible for his act. I see Brother Houghton making a note of that. Now, gentlemen, does not that look reasonable? Suppose you people conspired together to found a hospital. You go home for your dinner, and you make a thorough agreement, and somebody in carrying it out does an illegal act. Do you think the law is foolish enough and brutal enough to say that every person is responsible for that act? No, it never was, even in those dark ages of crime, legal crime, to which these gentlemen like to go back, and over which they linger so fondly, so very, very fondly. But when a dozen men conspire to murder, which is unlawful unless it is done by starvation, then each one is responsible for the act of every other one. Now, gentlemen, I say this in relation to their seeking to fix responsibility on Mr. Kidd, because he is the man they are after, as Paine said at first.

And how have they set about getting him? Let us see. There was just one act of violence committed that was worth considering in fourteen weeks. There was not enough happened in those fourteen weeks, barring the riots, to make up one decent Fourth of July celebration. There was not enough happened to make up a decent Sunday-school excursion of your Sunday-school scholars, Brother Houghton. In fourteen weeks of a strike of criminals sixteen hundred strong, there was one act, and they thought Michael Troiber committed it, and so they picked him out to be one man. And they heard somebody say that George Zentner was captain of the pickets, and they picked him out for another. And then they put in Thomas I. Kidd, who was the real man they were after, and they linked his name with the other two. This poor Austrian, Troiber, who had never done anything but toil, who had grown haggard and old in the employ of this company—they yoked him and Zentner up, to catch Thomas I. Kidd. Now, gentlemen, I do not care whether Michael Troiber struck the blow or not. It does not make the slightest difference in this case either to Kidd or Troiber. Because if Michael Troiber did it, Kidd is not responsible, unless it was a part of the general scheme. Somebody did it, and if it was a part of the general scheme, Kidd is responsible, whether it was Troiber or not. So far as Troiber is concerned, it makes no difference, for if Troiber did not do it, and still it was a general conspiracy, he is guilty; and they can put in the rest of the sixteen hundred, and Brother Houghton and his pastor, too, for they are all guilty, if their theory is right. If Troiber did not conspire to do it, gentlemen of the jury, but if he did it without a conspiracy and a plan he is not guilty under this charge, because that would be simple assault and battery and not conspiracy at all. So I am not going to waste my time and yours arguing as to whether he did this or not. I do not care who did it.

* * *

You might take him and send him to jail, gentlemen, on this evidence, but you cannot take him on this indictment unless his act was done in pursuance of a conspiracy. If it was not, he committed assault and battery. If Brother Quartermass here files an information for assault and battery after we discharge him on this, I will come up and defend him on that just for fun, for I rather like Oshkosh. I have a sort of curiosity to see whether you could find a jury up here who would do a thing because Paine made the request. I think I would move up and see.

Thomas I. Kidd is to be made responsible upon two theories. First, that he knew of and had to do with these unlawful acts, although no human being has yet brought that home to him; not one. Next, because he advised and counseled them. Now, I come to the blackest part of this dark, damnable conspiracy; and I propose to give Brother Houghton some notes and something to talk about. And now we will put Brother Houghton into this conspiracy where he belongs—not the conspiracy with which we are charged, but the conspiracy to take away the liberty of his fellow-men under the sanction of law; and if there is any darker and deeper one, it is hard for me to imagine it.

Thomas I. Kidd made various speeches in this city. There were sixteen hundred idle men, and the leaders wanted to keep them away from the factories and the mills and out of the saloons, and preserve order, and they did it, barring these riots which sprung up here and there; and right here I want to say one word more, and just one, in relation to the riots. I do not know who is responsible. I do not care who is responsible. I know that away back in 1858 or 1860, when they tried to take a poor, fugitive slave from Massachusetts, and when Wendell Phillips and William Lloyd Garrison with their burning eloquence rose in Faneuil Hall and protested in the name of humanity, in the name of God, in the name of all that was sacred, against taking this poor man back to human slavery, and after listening to their eloquent words, a mob took possession of the jail and battered it down, and dragged him out to liberty; and during the riot some one was killed. And yet, for opening their lips in defense of the slave and for giving voice to human liberty, the world has crowned Phillips and Garrison, and has poured out its infamy upon the slave-catchers who sought to take the black man back.

I do not know who was responsible for these riots. I do know that in a town where such a pen as Paine's exists, where there are so many outraged men and hungry women and little toiling children, in times of excitement riots would be the natural result. It can be said in Oshkosh and as a result of Paine, as a great English humanitarian poet once wrote:

Our fathers are praying for pauper pay;
Our mothers with death's kiss are white;
Our sons are the rich man's serfs by day,
And our daughters his slaves by night.

And I want to say to you, gentlemen of the jury, that when this miasma is gathering as it has been for years, and when the lightning strikes, you need not blame the thunderbolt. It is the miasma and the men that made it that are responsible; and I do not propose to stand here and split hairs upon what this man and that man said and did.

But did Kidd advise riot?

*   *   *

Gentlemen, the overwhelming evidence in this case shows that from the beginning to the end Kidd counseled peace and order and quiet, and told the men that only in this way could they gain their ends. He did once make a speech in that dark day when one of his comrades had been slain in this great battle in which he was engaged—this comrade, a poor boy sixteen years of age, who had worked for the Paines at forty cents a day, and who was caught in the great whirlwind of that tumultuous crowd that surged around McMillen's mill, and lost his life—the first victim in the great strike. He was a poor, unknown, almost nameless boy, but still in the mysterious design of Providence he was called upon to give up his life in a holy cause.

I remember that when John Brown took his band of trusted men to old Virginia, and made his gallant but unlawful fight for human liberty, that the first victim of his act was a poor, unknown Negro, a child of that race that he came to serve; but, whoever he was, and whatever he was, in the inscrutable will of Providence it was designed that this man should be the first victim in that great fight which did not end until human slavery was wiped away.

The prosecution have quoted here the speech of Thomas I. Kidd on the day this comrade was laid to rest; the speech of this pacific, humane, upright man, who loves his fellow-men, or he would not be on trial here. And I want to read it, and I want you to tell me whether there is a malignant, unkind drop of blood in that man's heart. I do not know how Kidd felt on that sad, long-to-be-remembered day, but I might paraphrase the words put in the mouth of a great Roman orator; if I had been standing there instead of Kidd and waging this holy fight, and if I had seen beside me the first dead victim of these people's greed; had I been Kidd, and had Kidd been I, there would have been a Kidd that would have put a tongue in every wound of that dead boy, that would have caused the very stones of Oshkosh to rise in mutiny and cry out against the men who took his life.

It is difficult, I suppose, for a jury to understand the emotions of an advocate, especially one who feels his cause as deeply as I feel mine. For I know, gentlemen, that all of you believe me when I say that the cause represented in this case is one that is very, very near my heart. It is difficult, perhaps, for you, sitting there as jurors, seeking only to do your duty under the law between these contending forces, to understand exactly the position of one whose feelings and whose sympathies and whose life is aroused by what he conceives to be one of the darkest plots for the enslavement of man. I have not sought to conceal them. I have given to you my honest sentiments—sometimes possibly severer than they should be—not that I have meant them in malice, but they have come from my heart, and I could speak in no other way. Now, gentlemen, for a little time this morning, I want to direct your attention to some of the efforts that have been made to convict Mr. Kidd. It is because a labor leader has dared to come to the city of Oshkosh and interfere with the holy calling of men who simply wish to get money, and it is to make an example of him, and to all of his kind, that you are called here, gentlemen, and asked to send a man to jail. I referred last night to the one effort, gentlemen, and the only scrap of evidence in these three weeks' search, where every man in Oshkosh who could shed any light, or any darkness, upon this matter has been called before you to state what he heard, what he saw, and what he did not know; and the only statement of consequence proven, every man knows was false.

*　　*　　*

There are two more items, gentlemen, only two more items, where they have sought in any way in all this long struggle, when the hearts of these defendants must have been wrung with emotion, when they were facing a terrible responsibility, and yet bearing it like men—there are only two other occasions when anyone claimed that anything that could possibly approach vituperation, or even angry words or angry acts, ever escaped from the lips of Thomas I. Kidd. And I want to refer to another one now. But I am surprised, gentlemen, at what lawyers will do to win cases; and I am surprised at the depths that men will reach in order to crush out some person they believe is hostile to their interests. I am surprised that any lawyer could stand before this jury, as Brother Quartermass did, and read to you the words of Thomas I. Kidd that were uttered at the bier of his dead comrade, and say to you that they were incendiary and bad. Place yourselves there, gentlemen, not in this courtroom, not under calm deliberation, but place yourselves, as a leader in this great struggle, and in the presence of a comrade who had died in this strife, pronouncing a few plain, simple words above his grave. And yet those plain, simple words of charity, and love, and human kindness have been tortured and distorted by Brother Quartermass until you are asked to believe that words of kindness and love and charity were words of venom and hate.

I shall not read Kidd's speech in full. I should like you to read it. I wish that every man on earth could read it. It is filled with tender sentiments, it is filled with love, it is filled with charity toward all men, it is filled with charity even to the men who were pursuing these unfortunate victims to the brink of the grave. Gentlemen, they have seen fit to read one paragraph and ask you to say that this paragraph is incendiary. One paragraph out of an address made upon an occasion like that; and even this paragraph, gentlemen of the jury, is harmless, and gentle, and kind. What is it? "I hope the heart-gnawing and the worried and worn mind of the father, who has suffered, I am told, more than ordinary men have suffered for the last six months, will touch the hearts of the manufacturers with pity, that they will begin to realize that if this strike is fought to defeat for the strikers that it will be a defeat that may ruin them; it will be a defeat that will be but the beginning of the real work. Because personally I feel that this is as just a fight as was ever waged to better conditions and to better humanity; and if the men should be defeated in this battle, then I will swear that my whole strength will be exerted to prevent a sash, to prevent a door or a piece of mill work made in the city of Oshkosh from being used in any other part of this country." That is where they stopped. Would not you have done as Kidd said he would do? Would not any man have done it? Gentlemen, it would be better for Oshkosh, and it would be better for the world, if not one single sash, or door, or blind, should go out of your town. They are made from the unpaid toil of labor and from the sweat and tears of babes. These gentlemen have seen fit to stop at this point of Kidd's speech.

Let me read the next paragraph and tell me what kind of a man is Mr. Kidd, the despised labor leader, with venom and hatred in his heart: "I suppose that most of you have read Leigh Hunt's remarkable poem, "Abou Ben Adhem," and very touching it is. It speaks about Abou Ben Adhem's having a dream one night, and as he lay in his tent an angel came to him, holding a roll within his hand, and he asked the angel or spirit what it was and the angel answered, 'A list of those whom love of God has blessed.' 'Is mine one?' said Abou. 'Nay, not so,' replied the angel. 'Then go write me down as one who loves his fellow men.' The angel disappeared, but the next night he came again, amid a great awakening light, and held within his hands a list of those whom love of God had blessed, and lo, Ben Adhem's name led all the rest." Brother Houghton, you can take that speech next Sunday and read it to your Bible class and you will teach them more of love and charity and tenderness and human sympathy than from any speech that you can make.

Gentlemen, you are asked to convict a man on that speech. Convict Thomas I. Kidd, who is great enough, and good enough, and wise enough to know that however much these poor workmen have been outraged, still these employers themselves do not know what their actions mean. I think I know this man. I have heard him speak; I have heard him testify, and I believe there is not a particle of hatred or bitterness in the man himself. I believe, gentlemen, that if in the great day when men shall be called upon to answer for the deeds done in the body, if George M. Paine should be arraigned before that Judge, accused by his workmen, accused by the little children, accused by these men whom he is seeking to hound to the jail, I believe that Thomas I. Kidd would say from the depths of his heart, "Father in Heaven, forgive him; he knows not what he does."

I want to read one more paragraph of this speech, gentlemen, and only one; and not because I have fear that any human being who views it as a jury should, and as a jury will, would differ from me in my interpretation of the language of Thomas I. Kidd, but I want to read it to show you what men will do with the foul design of getting rid of some person who they think is in their way. Let me read the last paragraph of this memorable address, for it was the address of a loving chieftain over a dead comrade who had lost his life in as holy a cause as ever men waged for right: "I glory in the fight you have made, only deploring the lamentable occurrence of last Thursday, only deploring these riots, because riots they were; but I believe, however, that we are not altogether responsible for them. I glory in the fight you are making; I believe it is going to benefit labor in Oshkosh; I believe it is going to benefit labor in Wisconsin, and will benefit labor so far as the woodworking industry is concerned throughout the United States and throughout the world.

"All hail to labor; all hail the coming of a new time when men will not travel the highways and byways of this country seeking in vain for opportunity to work and make the world richer by their labor.

"All hail the coming of a new era when children shall work neither on farm, in factory, nor in mines, but shall enjoy the recreation and education essential for their future well being, and the welfare of their country.

"All hail the coming of a new Christianity, a Christianity that will not pander to the wealthy and help perpetuate the present system with all of its horrible inequalities, but a Christianity that will teach what Christ taught, love, brotherhood, humanity and truth.

"All hail the dawning of a new time when right not might shall rule the land, when love not hate shall bind mankind, when worth not wealth shall command the admiration of the people, when paupers shall be scarce as millionaires. Labor is striving to lift the people upward. It is striving to bring about the time of which the poet speaks, 'Upward, onward press the people to the pure celestial heights.'"

Gentlemen, that is Thomas I. Kidd. Those are the spontaneous utterances that were taken down from the lips of a man in the deepest feelings of his life. Not studied, not made, not revised, but welling out from his being, coming from his very soul. Gentlemen, if you and I can do as well, if you and I can feel in our hearts the gentleness, and tenderness, and love that Thomas I. Kidd had in his on that memorable day, then, whatever any human tribunals may say, we may rest assured that in the sight of eternal justice our hearts are pure and clean.

There was another address made once upon a time, and I undertake to say that no man could have made the address of Thomas I. Kidd at the funeral of his dead comrade excepting he had read the address of that other man, of that meek and lowly Jesus who was convicted eighteen hundred years ago. I undertake to say that no person in this country, whatever they might be in some other land, would be filled with the human charity and human love that breathes in every line of the address of Thomas I. Kidd, unless he had studied the words of Jesus, the greatest heretic, and the greatest benefactor, perhaps, of whom we know. There was another address made eighteen hundred years ago; and if these prosecutors had been called on in those days by the powerful and the rich to send that man to the cross, they would have used that address as they have used this of Thomas I. Kidd. They would have pleaded to a jury, as in this case, that while the words that fell from the lips of Christ seemed to bear love and charity and tenderness to all the world, that still these words were "hocus pocus," as Brother Quartermass put it, and they meant something else. It is asked of you, gentlemen of the jury, that you shall convict Thomas I. Kidd on the statements that he made, and then, gentlemen, because his words were kind and humane and loving and tender, you are asked to believe that he did not say what he meant. What should Kidd have said? If in the intensity of his feelings he had spoken as I have spoken, then those words would be there to condemn him. If in the love of his great human heart he should speak words of tenderness and pity, then you are to say that he did not mean these words and that it was all a delusion and a snare. If these gentlemen had been present at that famous trial eighteen hundred years ago, they would have picked up a stenographer to go and hear the Sermon on the Mount, not for the purpose of having him listen to its blessed truths and let its lesson sink deep into his heart, but in hopes that he might find something to send Him to the cross. And then they would have read, "Blessed are the meek, for they shall inherit the earth." And then Quartermass would have said, "Blessed are the meek, for they shall inherit the earth." What does that mean, gentlemen of the jury? How shall the meek inherit the earth unless they go out and take it, gentlemen? There you have it. It is "hocus pocus." Jesus said it, of course, because He was up on a high mountain where everybody could see and hear Him. He said, "Blessed are the meek, for they shall inherit the earth"; but what He meant was that the poor fishermen of Judea should go and take it by force of arms; and there is the "hocus pocus" of it all. Then He would have said, "Blessed are the peacemakers, for they shall be called the children of God." But they would have argued that when He said "Blessed are the peacemakers," He was standing up on a hill, where everybody could hear him; and His reference to peacemakers meant exactly the opposite of what He said, and He meant they should go and stir up riots and destruction; and evil was in His heart instead of good. Don't you remember, don't you remember, when He was gathered together with a few disciples, and said, "I come not to bring peace, but a sword." Ah, and when He got up on the high mountain, surrounded by all the people of the earth and speaking to the multitude that heard His voice, He said, "Blessed are the peacemakers," and He meant, gentlemen, exactly the opposite of what he said; and there is the "hocus pocus" of it all. And, gentlemen, He also said, "Blessed are they that do hunger and thirst after righteousness, for they shall be filled." "They shall be filled." "What does that mean, gentlemen?" would say Quartermass. "It means that they shall have beer, that they shall have plenty to eat, and they shall have plenty to drink. It means, gentlemen, when He said it upon the hill, it meant that they should have plenty to eat and plenty to drink, and they should go out and get it." That's what the Quartermasses of that day and the Houghtons of that day undoubtedly said; "and they convicted him."

Gentlemen of the jury, there never was a man whose words were so pure, there never was a man whose heart was so good, there never was a man whose life was so great, or so holy, but what men of evil thoughts and evil desires would seek to torture their words and contort their utterances and make them bad and vile. There never was a man whom malice and envy had pursued to the door of the jail but what earth and hell would be raked to find something that would furnish an excuse to convict. You may make the most of it, gentlemen; I do not believe a jury ever lived on this earth that would take that speech of love and gentleness and tenderness and construe it into violence and wrong.

* * *

Now, gentlemen, a few words about the nature of this conspiracy. What was it? It is one thing, as I said yesterday, to conspire to do a lawful act; it is another thing to conspire to do an unlawful act. These men were combined for a lawful act, and they can only be held accountable for the unlawful acts committed by themselves, or by the direct procurement of themselves. It is contended here that some of the pickets who were sent out to watch the mills and to look after their fellow-workmen, that some of these pickets did unlawful acts. It is also contended that too many pickets were placed around the mills, and that in this way they made a show of force and resistance. Now, gentlemen, in order to convict Kidd upon any such theory, it must appear to you that Kidd sent men there for the purpose of disorder and riot, or that Kidd sent men there for the purpose of awing other men into submission. That is the law. That is the humanity of it. Now, what is there in this case to justify it? In the first place, the evidence shows that all that Kidd knew of pickets was that pickets were to be placed there for the lawful purpose of watching other men and soliciting others to unite their fortunes with theirs. In the next place, gentlemen, the overwhelming evidence in this case shows that day after day as the strike wore on, men were standing around idle, peaceably sitting down, whittling, not molesting any human being, but leaving everybody to go freely where they wished, but simply appealing to their fellow-men to join with them.

* * *

Now, gentlemen, it may be that in these later days human liberty is not as sacred as it ought to be. We sometimes carelessly fritter it away; and you, gentlemen, sitting in this jury box, and looking at this case, may not be able to judge the feelings and emotions that control the defendants, and the millions of others who feel with them an interest in this historical trial; for although it has happened in the little village of Oshkosh, and in a plain municipal court, and although by chance you men are sitting as a jury in this case, still it is one of the historical trials of the world. It is a precedent to make history. None of you should deceive yourselves with the thought that it is a question of a year in jail for Thomas I. Kidd. That is not worth the talking. It is not a question of whether poor Michael Troiber spends this winter in jail or not, or whether George Zentner shall board here or somewhere else; but it is a question, gentlemen, of whether when a body of men desiring to benefit their condition, and the condition of their fellow-men, shall strike, whether those men can be sent to jail. And I want to say to you, gentlemen of the jury, that if these three men, or any one of them, can go to jail in this case, then there never can be a strike again in this country where men cannot be sent to jail as well. Because it can never happen, it will never happen, it has never happened, that a more peaceable, orderly body of men lay down their tools of trade in a grand and noble fight in humanity's cause. It has never happened, and it can never happen, and you are asked, gentlemen, to say to the millions of toilers all over the United States that whatever the insult and the abuse and the outrage that is heaped upon them they must bear it in silence, or a jury will send them to jail. That is the case you are deciding. I want each one of you gentlemen to feel the occasion, to understand what it is, to know that in the great historical trials of England, the great trials that tested the constitutional liberty of the citizen, in the great battles for freedom of speech, freedom of the press and individual rights, no jury in England, and no jury in America, ever had a more momentous cause submitted to their charge.

We cannot see the events that are close beside us. The great events of the world were scarce noted by those who were a portion of them; but as time wears on, and we leave the scene of action and look back upon the past, and history writes the record, we point to this spot and that as being milestones in the progress of the world. And this is one, and this city of Oshkosh is the scene of the action, and this municipal court has been chosen for it; and in the inscrutable wisdom of Providence it has fallen to the lot of this jury to decide this case. Not, gentlemen, perhaps, because you are wiser or greater or better than your fellowmen. History is not made that way. Men do not make events, but events make men. You are not, and Mr. Kidd is not, writing the labor movement of the world, but this revolution is going on and on and on, and it has fallen to the lot of you, and it has fallen to the lot of him, to be important factors in that great human struggle which is moving and agitating all over the world. You do not know why it happened. I do not know why it happened. I know it is true, and, gentlemen, if I have spoken with feeling, as I know I have, perhaps harshly, perhaps more unkindly than I should, it is because I have felt so deeply the responsibility which is on me and the responsibility which is on each of you. I have said what I thought of George M. Paine. I have told the truth as I saw it of Nathan Paine. I have suggested that I thought Brother Houghton should not have been in this case. But in my heart, gentlemen, I have not the slightest, no, not the slightest feeling of bitterness against one of those men. You may not understand it. Aye, you may not believe it; but I would not wantonly and cruelly hurt the feelings of any man that lives, because I know, down in the depths of my being, that George M. Paine is what he is, and he knows no other way. I know that Nathan Paine was born as he is, and he sees no other way; and I cannot tell, and you cannot tell what causes there were that induced Brother Houghton to take this case. I know they were enough for him. I know I could not do it. I know that the Paines are wrong; and if this trial should teach them something, if it could teach them, gentlemen, not to see themselves as others see them, but to see their acts as they really are, then I shall think that Thomas I. Kidd has not lived in vain, and I shall think that your time and mine have not been wasted in this case.

Gentlemen, there are many things that I meant to say, but I shall leave them untold. There are many points in this case which I have not touched, and which perhaps I would if I were to talk to you for a week, or a month, or a year. I shall leave them unsaid, for I am sensible that I have kept you long—I fear too long, but I want to tell you the reason why. It is not that there are so many points to discuss. It is not that there were so many witnesses in this case, or that the trial consumed so great a length of time. It is not, gentlemen, that from the time I commenced this case until I shall speak my last word that I ever had one single moment of doubt about the verdict of this jury, for I have not, and I say that to you as frankly as I could speak to my God on the judgment day; that it is not, for I do not believe, gentlemen, that anywhere on the face of the earth a jury could be found today that would send men to jail for the crime of loving their fellow-men, and I am willing to rest that with you.

I have spoken at length, and I have spoken freely, because I believe in this cause. I know what will be said in reply. I know some of the things that will be said by Brother Houghton. I can feel them now, and will feel them again, and stand them the best I can, conscious that what I have said has been only as I believed it my duty to say it, and only as the spirit moved me to say it. I know you will be told that I am a labor agitator, a socialist, an anarchist, and I do not know what else, and I do not care what else. They may say what they will and do what they will; names do not count. It may be, gentlemen, that there is not one man on this jury that would agree with me upon the great questions that are moving the world today. It may be that you think I am wild and insane when I look abroad over this fair land of ours and see wealth upon one hand and poverty and misery and want upon the other, and when I raise my voice in season and out against what seems to me to be the crime of the century in which we live. I may be wrong. Kidd may be wrong. So may all of those torch-bearers who in the past have led the world onward and upward to something higher and better and holier than it had known before. But it is not a question of whether I am wrong or right, so far as I am concerned and so far as you gentlemen of the jury see fit to judge me; it is a question of whether I believe it with such intellect and power as the Lord has given me to believe; that is all. It is a question as to the sincerity of my motives, not as to whether the theories are right or wrong. So far as my clients are concerned, and so far as the cause is concerned, what I say and what I think, and what I believe, have nothing on earth to do with this case.

I believe that the world is filled with wrong. I believe that men are imperfect; I believe that institutions are imperfect; I believe that we are gradually, slowly, painfully going onward and upward to something better than the world has known, but I feel there is injustice now. I know, gentlemen, that in the midst of our wealth and our pomp and our power, with all our vain boasting, that there is want and misery and crime and injustice all over the earth. I look at the gorgeous temples reared to the memory of the meek and lowly Jesus, and I know that these are a mockery to the doctrines which He taught. I know that if that humble Man could come back to earth today that George M. Paine would not be bowing his head in a temple reared to His name, but he would be pursuing the meek and lowly one before this jury, with these prosecutors to aid and abet.

* * *

These poor Oshkosh toilers are the images which the god of greed and the god of mammon have made of the Almighty and reared in His name in mockery of the doctrines we profess. These images are in this courtroom now. They have come upon the witness stand and told you their tales of suffering, want, hardship and woe. They will die some day, and those little children will come forward again to be the images in the next generation of that God whom these men in their ignorance and their willfulness have mocked and reviled. These are the images which our greedy men have reared to His memory; and so long as these images are here and over all the face of the earth, so long I wish that I might be spared to speak for these hopeless ones who are too weak to cry aloud.

Gentlemen, I am about to leave this case in your hands. I would like to add one word about Kidd. He has been called a labor agitator, and he is. I will be called one, and I am. Gentlemen, I hope I will continue to be so long as the breath is spared in me to speak. It is common and cheap to abuse labor agitators; common, gentlemen, and cheap. I do not know what effect it will have on you. I think it will have none. I happened to have been born of an Abolition father and mother, back in the Western Reserve of Ohio, one of the stations of the underground railroad in those early days, when it was a crime to take a poor Negro and send him on his way to liberty and light; when the flag of the Union floated over the black slave, and the poor child of bondage was forced to go to a foreign land and live under an alien flag to be free. I was born under these circumstances and conditions, and I well remember when scarce a babe, scarce old enough to go into Paine's factory—when as a little child, I heard my people tell of those brave men and women, Garrison, Kelley, Foster, Pillsbury and others of their kind who took their fortunes, their lives and their reputations in their hands, who traveled up and down the land the best they could, preaching their doctrines to all who would stop and hear. They were criminals, they were outlaws; they could find no church; they gathered a few together as they could; as Jesus of old gathered His disciples about Him where He went; but those outlaws, those disreputables, those men and women spurned, despised and accused, were the forerunners of a brighter and more glorious day; and we in this generation bow down in reverence to the memory of those outlaws who gave their time, their energy and their lives to the suffering black. One of these was John Brown, sometimes perhaps misguided, but the infinite power had planted within him a heart that bled for his fellow-men, and had filled his life so full of the devotion to his cause that he gladly gave it for the slave. John Brown loved the Negro, he loved the poor black workman. He struck a blow in his defense. His body lies moldering in the ground, but his soul is marching on.

Men do not build for today; they do not build for tomorrow. They build for the centuries, for the ages; and when we look back it is the despised criminal and outlaw, the man perhaps without home or country or friend, who has lifted the world upward and onward toward the blessed brotherhood which one day will come. Here is Thomas I. Kidd. He draws a salary of twenty dollars a week. This is more than the Oshkosh woodworkers are paid. It is not a munificent salary, gentlemen. It is not too large for a man who goes up and down the land to help his fellow-men. He has serious responsibilities in his hand. Born in Edinburgh, imbibing in his young years the love of humanity, the hatred of injustice, he came here, like thousands of others, believing in greater opportunity and greater freedom for himself and his fellow-men. He has been in this cause for years; he is devoted to it. He believes it. Gentlemen, it is not a bed of roses in which the agitator sleeps. He may hear himself make speeches, but he often feels that the crowd draws back and shuns him as they would a leper's touch. He may hear himself speak and may receive applause, but it means social ostracism. Aye, gentlemen, it means more. The man who undertakes to serve humanity consecrates his life and he must endure all things, and risk all things, for the cause he serves.

In closing this case I want to say again that I have spoken as a lawyer for his client, the best I could. I have spoken from the depths of my heart. It is possible—aye, probable—that here and there I may have spoken unwisely or rashly. It is possible, yes, probable, that I may have been unduly severe on some person connected with this case. But there is not a thought of bitterness in my heart for one of these men. I wish they were different. I wish they were better. I wish they might feel the sufferings of other men. I wish that George M. Paine might work for a dollar and a quarter a day, and I wish his children might be compelled to labor in his factory for ten hours a day at twelve or thirteen years of age. Not, gentlemen, that I want them to do it, for I do not; but I wish that in some way his heart might be touched and his children be made to know, and that they might feel the kinship which they bear to all the world. I wish they might learn that in the sight of eternal justice George M. Paine is no more than Michael Troiber or George Zentner. I wish they might learn that George M. Paine in the eye of justice has no more right to the blessings of the world than those little children who told you their tales of want.

Gentlemen, I leave this case with you. Here is Thomas I. Kidd. It is a matter of the smallest consequence to him or to me what you do; and I say it as sincerely as I ever spoke a word. No man ever entered this struggle for human liberty without measuring the cost, and the jail is one of the costs that must be measured with the rest; and if you see fit to send him there, he will take his punishment like a man, and ask no odds of any human being on the earth. But, gentlemen, I do not appeal for him. That cause is too narrow for me, much as I love him and long as I have worked by his side. I appeal to you, gentlemen, not for Thomas I. Kidd, but I appeal to you for the long line— the long, long line reaching back through the ages, and forward to the years to come—the long line of despoiled and downtrodden people of the earth. I appeal to you for those men who rise in the morning before daylight comes, and who go home at night when the light has faded from the sky and give their life, their strength, their toil, to make others rich and great. I appeal to you in the name of those women who are offering up their lives, their strength and their womanhood on the altar of this modern god of gold; and I appeal to you, gentlemen, in the name of these little children, the living and the unborn, who will look at your names and bless them for the verdict you will render in their aid.

Gentlemen, the world is dark; but it is not hopeless. Here and there through the past some man has ever risen, some man like Kidd, willing to give the devotion of his great soul to humanity's holy cause. Here and there all through the past these men have come, and through the future they will come again. They will come to move the world onward and upward; they will come beckoning their fellow-men to follow in their lead; they will point to a sunrise far away, so distant that the ordinary mortal cannot see, but which is clear to their prophetic eye.

> 'Tis coming up the steep of Time,
>   And this old world is growing brighter,
> We may not see its dawn sublime,
>   Yet high hopes make the heart throb lighter.

> We may be sleeping in the ground,
>   When it awakes the world in wonder,
> But we have felt it gathering round,
>   And heard its voice of living thunder.

It has fallen to your lot, gentlemen, to be leading actors in one of the great dramas of human life. For some mysterious reason Providence has placed in your charge for today, aye for ages, the helpless toilers, the hopeless men, the despondent women and suffering children of the world; it is a great, a tremendous trust, and I know you will do your duty bravely, wisely, humanely and well; that you will render a verdict in this case which will be a milestone in the history of the world, and an inspiration and hope to the dumb, despairing millions whose fate is in your hands.

DARROW's summation not only presented a history of the workers' grievances against the Paine Lumber Company, but it is also a sociological treatise in simple and direct words; it is both a history of trade unionism and of the struggle of the "downtrodden."

When it is realized that Darrow used no notes in delivering his closing arguments in this case, their clarity and power seem even more remarkable. The classic appeal to personal rights over property rights makes it a pivotal declaration in the history of American social thought.

The trial lasted three weeks. Darrow's summation took two days, the jury was out fifty minutes, took two ballots and voted "Not Guilty."

For his work in the Kidd case, Darrow received $250.

Strike, Arbitration

ANTHRACITE MINERS
Scranton and Philadelphia, Pennsylvania, 1903

DARROW'S CLOSING ADDRESS INCLUDED
A VEHEMENT APPEAL FOR UNION CAUSE
AND A BITTER CONDEMNATION
OF THE OPERATORS FOR
CRUELTY AND BLINDNESS

[Headline, Philadelphia North American, February 15, 1903]

AN ESTIMATED 10,000 anthracite coal miners walked off the job in 1900 under the leadership of John Mitchell, president of the United Mine Workers of America. Within a week, 100,000 miners were on strike.

The average annual wage of the miner was then about $250, according to Mitchell.

Among the union's wage demands was a 20 per cent increase for day laborers who were receiving less than $1.50; a 15 per cent increase for those receiving between $1.50 and $1.75; and a 10 per cent increase for all others. Other improved working conditions were also among the demands.

There was nothing radical or revolutionary about the young John Mitchell. He had none of the fiery class-war philosophy of William Dudley Haywood and the Western Federation of Miners, with which Darrow was to become associated during the Boise, Idaho trial a few years later.

John Mitchell was conservative; he talked of the "common interests of labor and capital"; he frowned upon strikes except when he felt there was a dire necessity. He insisted that the union's cause had a high moral purpose and was based on the American principles of fair play.

The year 1900 was an election year. Republican National Committee chairman Mark Hanna urged the mine owners to compromise with the union. They did. The result was a one-year agreement which included a 10 per cent wage increase.

Though Mitchell admitted that the union did not win all of its demands with this agreement, he was satisfied that it did get a wage increase and some improved working conditions.

According to Perlman and Taft in their History of Labor in the United States, the union had won a decided victory in the strike. "For the first time the entire anthracite region had acted as one group. The strike was very skillfully directed, the men retaining public favor until the end of the struggle."

The contract of 1900 was renewed a year later. However, in 1902, when the union asked for an eight-hour day, a 20 per cent pay increase and recognition of the union, as well as improvements of other conditions, the mine owners balked. In May of that year, an estimated 150,000 miners answered a strike call.

President Theodore Roosevelt was asked to intervene. The union said they would agree to arbitration, with the President of the United States to name the arbitration board. The mine operators, however, declined.

The strike dragged on. A coal famine was in sight, particularly in the hard-stricken eastern part of the country.

So effective was the walkout that at least one department store—Wanamaker's in Philadelphia—advertised in a newspaper that "one good result of the coal strike was to open the eyes of the people to the economy and convenience of cooking by gas."

President Roosevelt finally took a hand in the crisis. After a conference between the President and the internationally known capitalist J. P. Morgan, who met with President Roosevelt as the operators' representative, the mine operators agreed to arbitration and to the appointment of a commission by the President.

A seven-man panel was then named to hear testimony, examine witnesses and look into the working conditions of the mines.

Heading the Commission as chairman was Judge George Gray of Delaware who had been in public life for more than twenty years, and had also served as a member of the Anglo-American Joint Committee on arbitration under The Hague Convention.

Secretary of the Commission was Carroll D. Wright, commissioner of labor who was "known not only in the U.S. but in Europe, as one of the leading students of sociology and kindred subjects," according to the New York Tribune.

Other men on the Commission included:

Thomas H. Watkins whose "appointment was due to his knowledge of the coal mining business," according to the New York Tribune;

Retired Army General John M. Wilson, a man of "distinguished appearance, fine physique and robust health [which] combine to make him one of the notable figures in the life of the national capital";

E. W. Parker, newspaperman and mining engineer, whom the newspaper described as "socially . . . a charming man, a witty storyteller, and sure to keep the Commission in good humor";

Bishop John L. Spalding, "pre-eminently a psychologist. He is especially noted as a clear and logical thinker, possessed of great lucidity of expression, and has frequently been styled 'the modern Emerson' "; and

E. E. Clark who was the labor representative. Clark was the Grand Chief of the Order of Railway Conductors. "He is a representative of the highest type of labor leader—the type which has made the order of railway employees models of conservative and efficient labor organizations," said the Tribune.

President Roosevelt instructed the Commission: "By the action you recommend, which the parties in interest have in advance consented to abide by, you will endeavor to establish the relations between the employers and wage workers in the anthracite fields on a just and permanent basis, and as far as possible to do away with any causes for the recurrence of such difficulties as those which you have been called in to settle."

Preliminary meetings of the Commission were held in Scranton. The hearings then moved to the federal courthouse in Philadelphia.

A battery of twenty-three lawyers presented the case for the operators, including Francis I. Gowen, Philadelphia, representing the Lehigh Valley Coal Company; Simon P. Wolverton, Sandbury, speaking for the Philadelphia and Reading Coal and Iron Company; Samuel Dickson, Philadelphia, for the Independent Operators of the Hazelton region and the Lehigh Coal and Navigation Company; H. C. Reynolds, Ira H. Burns and Alfred Hand, all of Scranton, for the Independent Operators of the Wyoming region; and John B. Kerr, New York, for the New York, Ontario and Western Railroad.

For the miners were Clarence Darrow, James Lanahan and the O'Neil brothers. "These lawyers," said Darrow of Lanahan and the O'Neils, "had once worked in the mines and were familiar with all the terminology as well as the method of work, and were likewise well-equipped lawyers."

The hearings, which received world-wide newspaper coverage, lasted about three months. They concerned themselves with working and living conditions of the miners, their education, cost of food and clothing, rent, education, or as Darrow put it, "Everything that enters into living and toiling."

On February 12, 1903, George F. Baer, president of the Philadelphia and Reading Coal and Iron Company, closed the case for the operators.

p. 408

"With polished sarcasm and powerful rhetoric, [he] plied the lash upon the United Mine Workers of America and their officers," reported the Philadelphia North American.

Mr. Baer ended his speech with the proposal that the miners be paid on a sliding wage scale, but that the scale should not fall below the present basis for the next three years.

On February 13, 1903, Darrow began his summation.

> *"It has come to these poor miners to bear this cross . . . that the human race may be lifted up to a higher and broader plane than it has ever known before."*

GENTLEMEN OF THE COMMISSION: I ought personally to show my appreciation of my brethren of the East who have treated me, from the West, so kindly, feeling as I did that anything from Chicago, and especially myself, might be met with some doubt and uncertainty in this region of the country. I have certainly enjoyed their society, and I trust they have not found me more tractable than they expected.

I scarcely know what to say in opening this case. We have spent a long time in examining this evidence and bringing it before this tribunal. It was the result of a long and bitter strife, a strife in which men on both sides were turned into wild beasts and forgot that common sympathy and common humanity which, after all, are common to all men when they are approached from the human standpoint and the human side. This hearing, coming after this long and bitter siege, looked to me from afar as if it would be bitter, too. I felt as I came here and felt as I was coming here that I would do all in my power to make the feeling less bitter than it was. I felt that I did not wish to go away from this region and feel that I had helped to stir up dissension rather than cure it, helped increase this feeling of bitterness and hatred between two rival parties, instead of bringing them closer together, so that they might live together in that peace and harmony in which it was meant that all men should dwell together on earth.

But I find myself just at the closing in a position where I have to take very good care that all my good resolutions do not go for naught, and I shall take the best care I can. I have listened for nearly three days to the arguments of counsel for the operators, not all arguments, much that is argument, much that is vituperation, much that is abuse, much that is bitterness, much that is hatred, much that should not have been spoken here, much that could not have come from a brain which sees widely and largely and understands fully the acts of men.

I have heard my clients, 147,000 workingmen who toil while other men grow rich, men who go down into the earth and face greater dangers than men who go out upon the sea or out upon the land in battle, men who have little to hope for, little to think of, excepting work—I have heard these men characterized as assassins, as brutes, as criminals, as outlaws, as unworthy of the respect of men and fit only for the condemnation of courts.

I know that it is not true. I have too much respect for the state of Pennsylvania, I have too much respect for any body of my fellow-men wherever they live, to believe that any great mass of them have turned into criminals and cutthroats, excepting for some cause that drives them to it.

These are men, men like any others, men who, in the midst of sorrow, travail and severe and cruel crisis, demeaned themselves as nobly, as bravely, as loyally as any body of men who ever lived and suffered and died for the benefit of the generations that are yet to come. I shall apologize for none of their mistakes, and excuse none of their misdeeds. But I do say it does not come well from their accusers to call them criminals, and I cannot refrain, in speaking of a long series of causes which brought about these dire results, from characterizing some of these acts in such plain English as would be applied to my clients if they were in this court, as they are, and were being charged with some of the many offenses that can be laid to the doors of the operator.

First, how does this case stand? We have had a six months' strike. We have had a three months' arbitration. We have had a condition in Pennsylvania where man was set against man, family against family, class against class. We have had a body of wealthy and respected gentlemen, men who understood the English language and knew how to use it, men who were neither foreigners nor criminals, men who were not even doctrinaires or dreamers, but practical businessmen, sensible men, men who stood against the tide of progress and who boldly said to those in their employ: "We will do nothing; we will pay you no higher wages; we will not submit your disputes to any body of men, either secular or clerical; we will post our notices upon our doors, and that shall be your contract. We give you notice that for one year your wages are so and so, and that is all."

We have seen, as a consequence of this act, 147,000 men lay down their tools of trade, and we have seen 750,000 men, women and children reduced to want and starvation for six long months. We have seen the President of the United States appoint this commission to settle this difficulty, and then, this afternoon, in the last hour of this proceeding, the man [George Baer] more responsible than any other comes before this commission and says: "Ah, we will consent to a portion of the demands you made; we will raise your wages; we will do something; we will recognize your union; we will treat with your agents." In fact, they will do exactly that which these men demanded nine months before, and which they in their blindness, their ignorance and their stupidity refused.

Why did not Mr. Baer go to Mr. John Mitchell nine months ago, as he came to this commission today? Why did not counsel for the operators in this case go to this band of criminals nine months ago and say they would meet their agents and negotiate and talk with them? Why was all of this deferred until 750,000 men, women and children were brought to the verge of starvation and this country was facing the most terrible fuel calamity it has ever known? Yet we are met here today, and in the last two or three days, by these gentlemen, who all these long and weary months have refused to know us, to recognize us, have demanded as a condition that these men must give up their union, dearer to them than their bread (for it is their bread and their life as well), that they must give up their organization and must come to them with their hat in their hand, each one in a position to be discharged the next moment if they dare to raise their voice. This is the condition in which we have met today.

This case has been discussed by lawyer after lawyer. It has been discussed, to my mind, without bringing to this commission any real analysis that could substantially help them in their determination of this case.

We have heard all sorts of theories discussed. Why, I used to be something of a theorist myself, years ago. I could talk to this commission about Socialism, about single tax, even about religion —all sorts of things—if I saw fit to take your time and you saw fit to permit it. We have been regaled with that. My esteemed friend, Major Warren, has told us what he knows about Socialism, or rather what he does not know about Socialism. (*Laughter and applause.*) I would suggest to the chairman that he do me a favor to request that there be no applause.

CHAIRMAN: Oh, well, I think we shall get along.

DARROW: It interrupts me; that is all.

Now, I am not going to discuss Socialism with Major Warren. It is all I can do to point out his errors in this case, to say nothing about his errors in Socialism. I do not propose to discuss New Zealand with Mr. Baer, except to simply suggest that when Mr. Baer tells us of the high price of hauling the traffic in New Zealand it seems to me it can be accounted for only on two theories. One is that New Zealand is a very thinly populated country, and the other is that they take as their basis of freight rates the Reading schedule for hauling anthracite coal in this region. (*Applause and laughter.*)

CHAIRMAN: Gentlemen, the Chair must request that you refrain from applause. The speaker has just told me that it interrupts and annoys him; it is not because I do not want you to applaud what you believe in, but because it interrupts the proceedings.

DARROW: Either one of those reasons that I have stated might account for it. So the commission may dismiss it from their minds.

I have made up my mind to be very dull this afternoon and save my really interesting remarks until tomorrow. For that reason it will be a little more difficult to give attention this afternoon, and a little easier tomorrow. Of course, it follows from that that what I shall say this afternoon is important and what I shall say tomorrow will not be so important.

Seriously, it seems to me that this case has not been discussed by my friends the operators in a way to throw any true light upon the controversies that you have before you. We are all accused of being dreamers on our side, and I will admit for a moment that I have always had a sort of a penchant for associating with dreamers. I have attended all kinds of social and economic and religious meetings in my time, but I do not believe I ever heard a series of papers in my life anywhere that dealt so much with abstract questions—most of them wrong—as that with which they have regaled us for the last three days. We seem to have forgotten this case entirely and what it is about, and why we are here, and what we are to settle. I propose to let Adam Smith and all the rest of the patriarchs rest for this afternoon, at least, and assume that I am here in a court trying a case, where two parties have some substantial matter to be settled by this commission, and nothing else. And I want to settle these questions according to the rules of logic and according to the rules of law so far as the law is applicable to this commission, and, I take it, that is to quite an extent at least.

A large part of the evidence in this case has no bearing upon the issues in the case. So far as the demands of the Mine Workers are concerned, it makes no difference whether crimes have been committed or not. If John Smith earned $600 a year, it is no answer to say that Tom Jones murdered somebody in cold blood. That does not relieve you. It is no answer to say that someone's house was burned. It is no answer to say that some person has been boycotted. The question is what has he earned? Are these men entitled to more money? Are they entitled to shorter hours? As reasonable human beings should we recognize the union or should we run against it like a stone wall and still swear that we do not know it is there? Those are the propositions.

Gentlemen, I can dispose of that very easily. You can do just as you please about recognizing the union. If you do not recognize it, it is because you are blind and you want to bump up against it some more; that is all. It is here. It is here to stay, and the burden is on you and not upon us. There is neither the power nor the disposition in this court, I take it, to destroy the union. It would not accomplish it if it could, and it certainly could not if it would. And if these wise businessmen, with the combined wisdom of business gentlemen and the agents of the Almighty cannot see the union, they had better blunder along still a few more years, and possibly after a while they will know it is there and recognize it themselves. These questions are here to be discussed and they are the practical issues in this case.

When we ask for higher wages, they say: "Oh, no; you are criminals, and therefore we should not raise your wages." When we ask for shorter hours, they say: "Oh, no; you burned a house, and therefore you should work ten hours instead of eight." Suppose we were no more logical than these business gentlemen. We do not claim to be businessmen—we are theorists and lawyers.

When they refuse to raise our wages, suppose I say: "No, Mr. Operators; you are criminals." I say that legislative body after legislative body, court after court, investigating committee after investigating committee have pronounced you criminals and outlaws. What of it? It is true; but what of it? I say that you are carrying on your business in conflict with the spirit and the letter of the Constitution of the great commonwealth in which you live. But what of it? That is no reason why you should pay us any more wages than we are worth. We are not entitled to two dollars for one dollar any more from you than we would be from a body of law-abiding gentlemen. If we work for you, it is not your moral character we are interested in; it is your dollars, that is all.

We are not examining you to see how well you come up to the commandments of the Decalogue or to the civil law. We take you as we find you. If we did not, we could not take you at all, and we only ask of you what our day's work is worth. This commission settled this matter long ago. When we intimated to the commission to show that these gentlemen owned the railroads and they owned the mines, and were taking money out of one pocket and putting it into the other and were charging exorbitant freight rates and making false statements, the commission said: "What has that to do with the question?" And they said wisely. What has it got to do with the question? These men who are engaged in the business of mining coal, if they work for these operators, have no more right to demand anything from them because they are respectable citizens or are not respectable citizens than they would have if the opposite were the case.

Neither have they any right whatever to plead to this organization, or to its people, in answer to our demand for wages anything whatever about the kind of men they are. I do not think it comes with a very good grace from these gentlemen, neither do they say it very squarely, but as such things are generally said in this world by men who do not like to say them openly—I do not think it comes with good grace from these gentlemen, whose breakers, whose mines, whose every dollar is up there surrounded by my clients, whose families are living from the profits that are made from the work of my clients in the ground; these men who have issued their bonds and their stock upon the lives of these despised foreigners and these unruly boys—it does not come with good grace from them to say that the men who have made them rich are criminals and entitled to no consideration from this court. And yet that is their position before this body. I take it that that position cannot appeal to reasonable men; that all that has been said on this line is aside from this case.

It has been said in order that, in some way, they may wring a few more dollars from these men who give their labor and their life that their bonds may be greater and their stocks more valuable on the exchange.

We are here asking for money, independent of any theories of political economy. We are here asking for shorter hours, and it has nothing to do with Socialism or Anarchism, excepting as every demand that the poor makes from the rich is to be construed as socialistic. And in so far as that, why, let it go; we are willing to accept it.

In discussing this question of wages it might be a good idea to find out what we are getting. What we are getting has something to do with whether we ought to have more or not.

We have been told through several long and more or less weary days that the miners did not know what they were getting. Well, they did not—not if these gentlemen are right. These miners, if they were only Christian Scientists, would be all right. If they could believe that they had the fine houses—now, I say this in a popular sense. There may possibly be some Christian Scientists on this commission, I do not know. But I say this in the popular sense. These miners, if they could only believe that they had the fine houses and the money in the bank and the good health and the long life and the good school and church facilities and the grand prospects and the great wages for the composite men, that these gentlemen believe, could be happy, and we could settle this strike. Now, if with all their wondrous other achievements they had instituted some sort of a mind cure to make their unfortunate employees sincerely believe their statement, then we would not have had this trouble.

They say that Mr. Mitchell came here from the soft-coal region, and did not know what the men were getting, and the men themselves did not know. Now, I insist that they do not know. If they do, then they have sought to deceive this commission, to becloud these issues, to cheat and defraud this half-million people who are dependent upon the bounty that these operators see fit to shower upon the anthracite regions. If these miners are receiving such wages as gentlemen have told us of, well and good. Just let us go home and enjoy them, and we will say no more about it.

Now, the operators are smarter men than we are. They say so, and we will admit it and save any proof on that question. They have got all sorts of advantages of us. Their social advantages are better, their religious privileges are better, they speak the English language better. They are not children. They can hire good lawyers and expert accountants, and they have got the advantage of us in almost every particular, and we will admit all that.

CHAIRMAN: Except the lawyers.

DARROW: Oh, they have got the advantage there. We are not worrying so much about the lawyers as we are about the commission.

Now, these fellows keep books. Our men do not keep books. It has hardly been worth while. There is not a miner in the whole region that can hire an expert accountant. It is all they can do, when they combine their 147,000 men, to hire an expert accountant. They have the books in which they put down to every man how much he got or how much he was supposed to have received or how much they say that they think perhaps he got; how much they think somebody else working the same length of time or longer in some other position might possibly have gotten if he had worked so many days more. They have the books there to show it, and those books have been brought before this commission, and every one has given his guess about them before they came and after they came.

I am not here to say that these eminent gentlemen are not as good as other men; are not as kindly as other men; are not as just as other men. I think they have been deceived. They have been deceived by their bookkeepers; they have been deceived by their expert accountants; they have been deceived by their doctors—doctors of figures, doctors who have doctored up figures. They have doctored them up, not only so that they might deceive us, but so that they have deceived them.

And when Mr. Baer informed the Senate of this state, and informed the President of the United States, and informed this commission of how much wages his men were getting, he gave them information at least 30 or 40 or 50 per cent beyond any facts that really existed.

If, at the end of all this time and labor, he is willing to give us 5 or 10 per cent upon the figures that he says correctly represent our earnings, we will be very glad indeed to take it. We will be very glad to take a finding of this commission just as he gave it, and we will ask no more questions and make no more demands. From the beginning of this strike until the end, whatever you may say about whether the miners knew what they were getting or not, these operators have never given out a correct figure or made a statement that would stand the light of day for a single moment when they talked to the public.

Now, in this I do not mean to make any general onslaught upon the figures as they have been finally brought before this commission. I do not mean to make any general charges against the real figures of real, living, flesh-and-blood men that this commission, through the assistance of Dr. Neill, compelled them to give to this commission. It is not the real men I am quarreling with; it is the composite man, the imaginary man, the imaginary figure—all of these matters that have been used by the expert accountants of these gentlemen in order to deceive somebody.

Now, what are these men getting?

I know a little more about mining than I did when I came down here, although I do not know as much about it today as I thought I did when I landed in Scranton. I have learned that many things that the gentlemen say on the other side are true, strange as it may seem. Conditions are various. Your function is not an easy one; I will admit that at once. To bring peace, harmony and justice and equality out of this whole region is not easy. Of course, nothing but my intimate acquaintance with you gentlemen would make me believe for a moment that you would fully accomplish it at one sitting. There are scarcely two men in the whole region who get the same wages, as you all know. There are 147,000 men and boys employed. There are, perhaps, 15,000 or 20,000 different rates of wages. It would be an easy thing to call a commission to settle the difficulty. A settlement of this difficulty is as if they would appoint a commission to go and settle the wages of everybody in Philadelphia, for instance. All right, I am not finding fault with it. I do not see what else we could do, but still it is not an easy task, and when we are all done and through with it, it is utterly impossible that it can be exactly just, and we expect that in advance, although we trust that most of the injustice will be such as the other side will have to complain of.

But let us see, as near as we can, what these gentlemen were getting. Mr. Baer and his first lieutenant, Mr. Veith, do not seem to quite agree. I have a very high opinion of Mr. Veith, and that opinion, taken in connection with Mr. Baer's eulogium upon his chief lieutenant, leads me to think that Mr. Veith is right and Mr. Baer is wrong, so he will pardon me if I take Mr. Veith instead of himself in these matters to ascertain how much

Mr. Baer is paying and how much work he is getting. I am going to be governed by him and by their books and not by the eminent gentlemen whom they put on the stand, and who caused me for the first and, I trust, the only, time to lose my temper in this case; who fixed up the diet of pig iron and raw jute and carbolic acid for the miners to live on, which is a very good diet for his composite man. But it is no good for mining coal. A composite man has got to dig coal or he cannot even stay on the payrolls of an expert accountant.

Who are these gentlemen? I am a little slow in getting to the point, as the commission will observe, because there are so many circumstances that seem to pop in ahead of the real point I am at. Mr. Baer seems to think anybody can mine coal. He seems to think it is as easy a job to be a coal miner as it is to be president of a railroad company, or a lawyer. A man can take the evidence in this case in his office and never come into court until it is too late to put him on the witness stand, and he knows all about it, and anybody can mine coal and these fellows are common laborers.

Now, what does Mr. Veith say? I take it Mr. Baer never mined coal, although the fact that he once worked for $50 a year might seem to indicate he was mining coal.

He did not tell us what he was doing. Mr. Baer informed the country, when he was telling it what a bad set of men the miners were and what an unreasonable demand they had made, that the miner went into the ground and he stayed there from four to six hours, and he got out at eleven o'clock in the morning, and he told this commission the same thing, except that he raised it an hour, he said from five to six. Of course, he was a little more cautious when he came before the commission than he was when he went before the country.

* * *

But Mr. Baer says it does not take skilled labor. Anybody almost can be a miner; it takes nothing except a pick and a reckless disposition. You might get along without the pick. But I do not see how you could get along without the other unless you are horribly hungry. But Mr. Veith says that it takes three or four years' experience to be a good miner. These gentlemen who have performed eminent services in the way of expert figures have laid all the stress upon the contract miner, men who are skilled workmen, men who work longer to be a contract miner than they would to be a carpenter, or a bricklayer, or a lawyer, a might sight harder, or, I guess, even a clergyman, although I am not so well acquainted with that business. Three to four years, and they worked in the ground where six out of a thousand are killed every year, to say nothing of the healthfulness of the occupation, which they can get doctors by the score to swear to just the same as an accountant. But six out of a thousand die. Miners are not very good figurers. They do not think about it. If they were going into war and knew that when they went in that six out of a thousand would be killed in a year, they would hesitate.

They might figure how long a life they would probably have and what sort of a death they would meet; but they go down into the ground—I am speaking of the inside workmen, where six out of a thousand are killed every year—and they learn their trade in three or four years, where 18 to 24 out of a thousand are killed, to say nothing of the hundreds of others who are maimed and crippled by reason of this occupation, which requires neither skill, nor intelligence, nor religion, nor morality, nor wages. You have seen the miners come here day after day, whether called by them or by us, and there was scarcely one of them who had not been seriously injured, bones broken, eyes lost, some blind, some maimed forever, almost all of them more or less disabled, and six out of every thousand every year who do not come at all—and yet anybody can be a miner. It is easy for a railroad president and a lawyer to say that anybody can be a miner. Mr. Baer forgot to tell us what his salary is now. I trust it has been raised since he got $50 a year.

Five hundred dollars a year is a big price for taking your life and your limbs in your hand and going down into the earth to dig up coal to make somebody else rich. These contract miners that they talk of require three to four years' experience. They are working at a trade where six out of a thousand are killed every year, and what do they get? I will show you what they get.

I have had a computation made covering every company that has filed schedules with this commission, and I have taken it from their books, not from our payrolls, but from their books, and in Mr. Baer's company only about a third of them got over $400 in the year 1901. You may lop off a very few who got over $900, and this has been explained; if this commission has not learned it, they have not learned much. There are particular places and soft places even in the mines.

*　　*　　*

Only 2.4 per cent of all of Mr. Baer's skilled workmen get $900 a year. We can safely leave them out, as being of that class who do not mine coal, but who mine men, the same as he, who get their profits not from digging so many tons of coal, but from exploiting so many hours of labor of someone more unfortunate than themselves. Let us take all the men over $800, and in Mr. Baer's system there are but 5 per cent who get $800. These are plainly all contractors. The 5 per cent who get above $800 include the 2½ per cent above $900. We will eliminate those. As Mr. Torrey[1] suggested, the high and the low should be wiped out alike. Let us take the class less than $200. Forty-nine per cent, nearly half of all the men who appear on the payroll as contract miners, get less than $200 a year. Now, I do not want this commission to take those figures. I mean to deal fairly with this commission.

I would be a little afraid, if I were not honest, to ask them to take something that was not reasonable. Our only confidence is that this commission will understand the truth, and I propose to bank upon that. Of those 49 per cent who get less than $200, large numbers worked only a small fraction of the year. That is true. And in the calculations which I make, and which I consider fair for this commission, I entirely eliminate them. I propose to throw out not only that 49 per cent who get less than $200, but 9 per cent more who get less than $300, and then some besides that.

*　　*　　*

[1] A counsel for operator.

Nay, cut every man below $400, and you get rid of much more than half of them. More than half of the men who imperiled their lives, and who carried with them the certificate of the state of Pennsylvania that they were competent men, and who went down into Mr. Baer's mines, received less than $400. Let us assume that they are vagrants and drunkards, and should have no consideration from this court, which is not true, and which our knowledge of human nature and of human life, of the effort of man to live, to perpetuate his race, to make his state, to support life upon the planet, all of these prove that this statement is not true. If it were true, the human race would have died out ages ago.

It is only the few who are weak. Nature lops these off, unrelentingly destroys them. The great mass, the great middle class, survives. But we will give Mr. Baer the benefit of the doubt; he needs it and we will give it to him. We will take off more than half of his men, who get below $400 a year, and we will lop off only 5 per cent who get above $800 a year, and then what have we? We have 95 per cent of all the men who are not lopped off as being too low—the rest is for his benefit, you understand. And how much do you get? In Mr. Baer's company the men from $400 to $800 last year made on the average $528.

Now, what else? That is not all clear money. We have had various testimony as to how much it costs the miner, outside of the powder which the company furnishes. This $528 is independent of the powder and independent of the laborer. Some of our men have said it costs $5 a month. I think that is too high. Some have said it costs $50 a year. Some have said it costs $40. Now, I do not know. I am free to say I do not know. I do know this, that the superintendent of the Lehigh Valley Coal and Navigation Company swore that he made 30 cents a week difference for oil—that is, $15 a year for oil. Now, if my clients were lawyers, or bankers, or judges, or generals, or railroad presidents, I would not be quibbling here over $50. I would say let it go. But $50 is a good deal to the miner, and I do not want the commission to forget it.

It is a good deal to them. In addition to that, they buy their own tools. They buy squibs, cotton, their shoes wear out—they say that they wear only about two months, at the longest, and they are expensive. They buy these supplies, which our miners, some of them, say amount to $40, and some say to $50, and some say to $60 a year, but $15 of it is settled by the operators themselves. I take it that it amounts to $30 or $40 a year—$40 a year would not be extreme. I know there is at least one member of this commission who could figure it more accurately than I can, and I am perfectly willing that his statement shall go entirely upon this matter. Assuming that it is $40 a year, then these gentlemen got $488 last year. That is the amount, the highest average, that could be paid by Mr. Baer for these experienced men.

In this world, you know that the men who get the best pay are always in evidence the most. The lawyers are in front of the miners and the miners in front of the mine workers. Most of the people we have had on the stand were contract miners. The poor devil that loads the coal—we do not want to forget him. What has he been getting? He works in the ground. The falling rock, or a stray car, or a belated blast, will catch him the same as the experienced miner. His business is almost as dangerous as the contract miner's. More than five out of every thousand of his craft are killed every year, to say nothing of the maimed and the crippled and the blind who are turned out under the beneficent laws of the state of Pennsylvania to the almshouses and highways and the byways, because no man can recover in this state, and I say it advisedly, that I believe there is not another state in the Union where it is as difficult to recover as in this commonwealth of Pennsylvania.

When I think of the cripples, of the orphans, of the widows, of the maimed who are dragging their lives out on account of this business, who, if they were mules or horses would be cared for, but who are left and neglected, it seems to me this is the greatest indictment of this business that can possibly be made. There are thousands of them, and many of them have come before this commission to tell their story and to exhibit their misfortunes under our advice.

Of these laborers five out of a thousand are killed every year. There is not any record of how many accidents there were. An accident must be pretty serious to be recorded. As our old friend Gallagher said, you do not account it an accident in the mine unless you get half killed, and you remember he had been half killed twice. They have come in here with broken arms, and disfigured faces, and broken legs, and with one eye and with no eyes, to tell the tale of this business upon which all the industry of this country, especially the East, is resting today. If, forsooth, these poor miners are to have shorter hours or more pay, nothing short of a calamity will overtake the industry of the East!

Well, I do not like calamities, especially when they come to me. But if the civilization of this country rests upon the necessity of leaving these starvation wages to these miners and laborers, or if, as my friend Reynolds[1] indicated to this commission yesterday, it rests upon the labor of these poor little boys from twelve to fourteen years of age who are picking their way through the dirt, clouds and dust of the anthracite coal, then the sooner we are done with this civilization and start over anew, the better for the humanities that after all must survive all forms of civilization, whether good or bad.

I do not believe that the civilization of this country and the industry of the East depends upon whether you leave these men in the mines nine hours, or ten hours, or whether you leave these little children in the breakers. If it is not based on a more substantial foundation than that, then it is time that these captains of industry resigned their commission and turned it over to some theorists to see if they cannot bring ruin and havoc a good deal quicker. These gentlemen will find a way when they have to find it. It is a trick of human nature that they never will find a way until they have to find it.

But I was speaking about the laborers. These laborers got last year $333. Princely wages, and yet we are told that all was peace and joy and happiness in the anthracite region until Mr. Mitchell came. Three hundred and thirty-three dollars a year for these men who shovel coal in the mines nine and ten hours a day, and five out of a thousand killed by accidents every year! What of the

[1] H. C. Reynolds, attorney for independent operators of the Wyoming region.

rest? This was last year. The fact is that they got about $300 on an average until Mr. Mitchell came here with this much abused organization of his to create desolation and havoc among these serfs. It was about $270 a year in those halcyon days. No wonder that they long for the good old days again, the days when everything was so peaceable and so happy before the war.

What about the company men? Here is where we get our composite men. I have not seen one of these composite men yet. All we know is that the composite man gets bigger wages than the real man, and he does not need as much to eat. No wonder their figures love the composite man. He has every element for a good, useful citizen from their standpoint. About 60 per cent of all the employees are composite men, and they are paid by the month. Nobody knows what, but still they are paid by the month. They do not know themselves. They give us a rate of payment and they assume in this rate of payment most of them are idlers and vagrants and drunkards. I think they must buy pretty cheap whiskey, to say the least. On this list the largest number of men are laborers. I will not take the time to go over each company by itself, but assuming they were real men instead of composite men, the laborers got $334 last year. Now they do not get it. Their figurers figured they got it. They would have got it if they had worked every day the breaker worked. But we will take the figures as they are; they are bad enough. If we cannot get a raise on them I do not think we will get a raise on a smaller amount, because if they were down much lower everybody would think they were not worth it.

*　　*　　*

But let us see what else there is on this schedule. The slate pickers are a very large class. Of course, they are children. Mr. Baer told the Commissioner of Labor, and he told the United States Senate, and he told the people of the United States, that the lowest rate that he paid to slate pickers was 85 cents. Of course, Mr. Baer is a busy man. He is a practical man. He is not a dreamer or a theorist. He got the figures transposed. The books that he has filed show that the rate is 58 cents, instead of 85 cents.

But like his other mistakes, he has not found it out yet, at least not until now. He informed the country that the lowest rate to these boys was 85 cents. It is 58 cents. Now, I do not know what you will do, but if I was the commission I would raise these boys' wages to $2.50 a day. So that they would get rid of all of them, every one of them. If the work of this commission does not result in getting rid of this abominably disgraceful evil of child labor in Pennsylvania, then I think the people may well say that it has been a failure. You may not get rid of it at once, but no man ever lived that could make an excuse for it.

I do not think any man ever lived that would not blush because of the money he gets from it. I was surprised that my friend Reynolds in his zeal should defend it—defend the taking of a boy twelve years old, and setting him down to labor in this everlasting cloud for ten hours, or eight hours, or any hours—for what? That you may get gold. That is all. Can any man frame an honest defense for it? Where are your sons and your daughters? Let me say this, that until you, Mr. Railroad President, or you, Mr. Lawyer, will take your child by the hand and lead him up the breaker stairs and sit him down to pick at that trough of moving coal, until you will take your pale girl to the silk mills, let me speak for the children of the poor. Is there anyone who can defend it?

This custom has grown up in the state of Pennsylvania because there is money in it, and the industries of Pennsylvania are dependent upon it. Shame upon the industries of Pennsylvania if this is true! If it is so, of little avail have we protected this great state for half a century, if the result of all of it is that men shall grow rich from the labor of these little children.

Another thing. It is not easy to generalize. I have sought to the best of the ability I have to study some of these important problems. I may have studied them wisely; I may have studied them foolishly; but at least I have sought to find out. The evidence in this case shows that every single one of these industries is run by the labor of these children. It shows more than this. It shows that in the vicinity of Scranton are at least twenty mills—silk mills, knitting mills, thread mills—where little girls from twelve to thirteen or fourteen years of age are working ten hours a day, twelve hours a day and twelve hours at night as well. Do not tell me that

that is due to the inhumanity of the father or mother. It is contrary to natural law. The wolf suckles her young. The wild animal cares for its offspring, and the human being is not less kind than the wolf or the beast. The instinct of life planted deep in all living things provides that the old must care for the young. It provides that the parent, whether man or beast, must care for its offspring. It needs no human law to enforce it. It needs nothing but a chance for those common, eternal instincts which have kept the human race alive.

Is there any man so blind that he does not know why that anthracite region is dotted with silk mills? Why are they not on the prairies of the West? Why are they not somewhere else? Why is it that men who make money that is spun from the lives of these little babes, men who use these children to deck their daughters and their wives—why is it that they went to Scranton and to all those towns? They went there because the miners were there. They went there just as naturally as a wild beast goes to find its prey. They went there as the hunter goes where he can find game. Every mill in that region is a testimony to the fact that the wages that you pay are so low that you sell your boys to be slaves of the breaker and your girls to be slaves in the mills.

These problems are not new. They were threshed out in England fifty years ago—more than fifty years ago—until stringent laws prevented these abuses there. Smaller boys, smaller girls than these worked longer hours in England.

Robert Day Lorn relates in the early days of his campaigning that he went into one of these mines where one of the boys, eight or nine years old, was working, and he asked him if he knew anything about God. The boy replied: "I don't think he works in this chamber. He must work in the next." Why should he? Why could he?

When these railroad presidents were finally called to book before the President of the United States, one of them shed tears because the United Mine Workers allowed these boys to join their organization, because they taught these poor babes doctrines of anarchy and disobedience to law. This railroad president shed tears because the United Mine Workers were spoiling the souls of these poor children, and yet he was willing to take the earnings of these poor children that he and his family might be richer because of their toil.

These babes know their friend. There is not one of these children so ignorant, not one of them so lost to natural instincts, that he does not know who loves him. There is not one who would not run from a railroad president to the open arms of John Mitchell; and they are right. I have no doubt the railroad president loves children. Neither have I any doubt that the wolf loves mutton. These men make a living out of these children and if they can do nothing else in this region, this infamy should end.

408

* * *

I shall have occasion to refer to this again. First I want to dispose of these wages.

These company men, outside of steam men, firemen and engineers, all range from $300 to $350 a year. If that is any reasonable rate of wages, gentlemen, all right. They are not reasonable. They are not just. They are not fair, in any fair meaning of the word. So much for the wages.

This commission has these schedules. The contract miners of this region last year received less than $525. Before that they received in the neighborhood of $460, and that was after the 10 per cent raise of 1900, before which their wages were about $400 a year. Up to 1900 the contract miners of this region were getting something like $400 a year, and the laborers who toiled all day in the mines were getting less than $300 a year.

And these are the halcyon days that the coal operators speak of. These are the days before John Mitchell came to this region, when everything was prosperity and happiness and peace.

Now, I want to say a word about those days, and I want to quote here from a man who is not a theorist. I want to quote from a practical businessman, a man who has employed almost as many men and women and possibly little children as Mr. Baer; and that is Mr. Abram S. Hewitt.[1]

My friend Major Warren[2] shed some tears over Mr. Hewitt's new-made grave; he told the commission how great a man he was.

[1] An industrialist.
[2] A counsel for operators.

Now, I learned to admire him many years ago. I learned some of my first doctrines of political economy from Abram S. Hewitt, and unfortunately, some others from his great father-in-law, Peter Cooper.[1] They do not exactly agree, but they were both good doctrines.

Mr. Hewitt has been quoted here, and I should speak kindly of him even if he was not dead. My Scotch friend, Brother Burns,[2] whose radical speech could only be explained to me upon the theory that for once in his life he had gotten on the wrong side and was talking against everything that he had professed all his life, and so he forgot himself; that is the first time I have heard Mr. Burns speak since he came into our hearing that I have not felt that it was not interesting and instructive, but I will refer to that again. Mr. Burns read from Mr. Gowen, a great criminal lawyer, who was prosecuting the Molly Maguires.[3] Of course, a criminal lawyer or any other kind of a lawyer trying a case is not the very best authority in the world. That is a habit of other lawyers—to look at things from their own standpoint. Pretty nearly all the other lawyers I ever knew did that, so I do not know about Mr. Gowen's arraignment of the Molly Maguires.

I do not know much about the Molly Maguires. I remember that I heard of them when I was a very young child, and I then thought of them about as Mr. Baer thinks of a trade unionist now. I think perhaps if I knew more about them I might find that even they had some redeeming virtues. In fact I have generally found them in everybody when I looked for them. When I do not, of course, I do not find them because I am not looking for them. Human nature seems to be a good deal alike the world over. We are bound to find about what we look for and what we have the eyes to see and the heart to feel.

But, at any rate, this is what Mr. Hewitt said. And as Mr. Hewitt was an extensive coal operator before he died and said some things to President Roosevelt in reference to this strike, he is really brought into it. Perhaps the words are worth quoting in this

[1] Philanthropist, capitalist.
[2] Ira H. Burns, an attorney for the independent operators of the Wyoming region.
[3] One of the first labor organizations in America.

connection, apropos of the halcyon days before John Mitchell came to Pennsylvania.

"In 1876, during the days of the Molly Maguires, I made a tour of inspection through the mining region. I found terrible conditions there. I found the men living like pigs and dogs, under wretchedly brutal conditions. If the same spirit of sacrifice which has sent out our missionaries into every heathen land had been shown in the coal regions, and the same efforts had been made to establish and maintain the schoolhouse, the church, and, above all, the Sunday school, which have borne such fruits elsewhere in this broad land; if the hospital for the sick and the comfortable refuge for the unfortunate had been carefully provided; if reading rooms and night schools and rational places of amusement had from the outset been maintained for a growing and restless population, the coal regions today might have been a paradise on earth instead of a disgrace to civilization."

That is Mr. Hewitt before he became interested in the coal region. Where are the reading rooms? Where are these improvements which Mr. Hewitt says the operators should have brought to have made a paradise of this land that they have converted into a howling wilderness? Where is the little child whose labor they have taken who has ever received as much as a Christmas card or a Christmas present or a remembrance to know that he has a soul, and that there is any human being on earth who has any thought of him except to get money from his toil?

These gentlemen who do not live with their men, who appoint their bosses and their overseers and expect them to produce results—it is well for them to say we are Anarchists and criminals, that we are drunkards, that we are profligates, that we cannot speak the English language, that we are unruly boys. But it would come with far better grace from them if they could show that ever once, ever once in all their administration of these lands and of these natural bounties which Mr. Baer thinks the Lord gave to him to administer—that ever once they have considered anyone but themselves.

Why did they allow this strike? We heard much from Mr. Baer this morning, and we heard the same old story that has been repeated wherever these gentlemen have spoken, and that has been published in the newspapers whenever they are willing to pay advertising rates, which is always—the same old stories, false and misleading and untrue. These gentlemen cannot even learn. Their association here on this commission should have taught them something. Mr. Baer comes here with the old, worn-out story that our men were brigands and highwaymen, because, forsooth, they refused to pump out the mines for a twelve-hour day while their brothers were on strike.

I want to speak of that for a moment. This ancient lie has traveled up and down the land, and it seems that nothing can stop it; and it is recorded again here today, after it has been shown for three months to be false. After these gentlemen have confessed from their own mouths that it was their own ignorant, brutal prejudice that caused all this trouble, they come again to this commission and say we were highwaymen, because, forsooth, we would not work!

How much truth is there in it? This story was repeated to the President of the United States. It was told to the Commissioner of Labor. It was told upon the witness stand. It has been told in the newspapers. It has been told wherever men could be bought or hired to listen to the tale. And what is it?

Why, here it is. Is there any man with a grain of sense who will look at this story in an unbiased way and not understand where all the fault was? When this strike commenced, the firemen, the engineers and the pump men were not at first involved. The evidence is that they attempted to strike a year before, and strike for an eight-hour day; that thereupon the leaders of this organization went to them and told them the time was not ripe, but if they would wait they would help them when the time should come. And when the United Mine Workers determined to enter upon this strike, then the firemen, the engineers and the pump men determined that it was their time to get the eight-hour day.

Now I take it that whatever question there may be before this commission there can be no question about the justice of these demands. Let us think of it a minute.

Here are the firemen, shoveling some days thirty, forty, fifty tons of coal, and even more. Here are the firemen working twelve hours a day, and every day in the year. They have no Sunday.

They do not need to go to church or anywhere else; they are fire-men. No Christmas, no Fourth of July, not even a John Mitchell Day—nothing. They work 365 days in the year, with only one variation, and that is on leap year, when they work 366.

But in order to give this fireman a Sunday off every other week, so that religious privileges should not be entirely denied even to him, they give him the privilege of working twenty-four hours one Sunday and laying off the next; and they do not think that is too long. Twenty-four hours for a day's work! And their only regret, probably, is that they cannot get twenty-five. And some of these men tell about working sometimes two, three, four, even five of these days. Those, of course, are times when there is some diffi-culty; some man is laid off by reason of being sick, or something of that sort.

I wonder, gentlemen, whether any member of this commission could think that these companies should not have given them an eight-hour shift, put on three shifts of men instead of two, and if you believe that the pillars of civilization would have been pulled from out the temple if you should find it in your ruling in this case? And these firemen, by the way, got about $1.75 a day for twelve hours. Why, I would not want to listen to this argument for twelve hours for that kind of wages, to say nothing about shoveling forty tons of coal. One dollar and seventy-five cents a day, and only twenty-four hours every other Sunday!

What of the engineers? They say that is an easy job, they sleep. Do they? Every single employer was forced to admit it was against the rules and that a man would be discharged for sleep-ing. They say that sometimes they sleep at night, because it is not a very hard job to tend an engine. Well, I have no doubt it is sometimes harder than at other times; but there are times when it is a hard job to be an engineer.

In the first place, it takes a skilled, experienced man, a man who must let his fellow-workman down to the bottom of the mines and bring him up again. A moment's forgetfulness, a moment's lack of thought, means the death of perhaps twenty or twenty-five of his comrades. A man whose business it is to raise and lower sixty or seventy cars of coal an hour, more than one a minute, sometimes through ten hours a day, sometimes longer. It surely is not an easy job. At any rate, they too had this twelve-hour day, with the swing shift, twenty-four hours every two weeks.

And the pump men, who must be there, too, the men who man the pumps, who keep the water out of the mines, they must be there all the time, and to save hiring three men, they hire two and make them work twelve hours a day, to keep the water out and keep the air pure.

Now, these men had struck once, they had struck for eight hours. The union thought the time was not propitious and they told them to wait. This strike came on and they said, Let us join, and they sent their delegates. What did the mine workers do? They said, All right, you may strike, but before you strike we will give ten days' notice; we will give notice on the first day of June that if they will not give you eight hours a day by the tenth of June we will strike.

These gentlemen say we held them with a club. We abandoned our post of duty. I supposed that some of the ideas of feudalism had not found root in democratic America. Was this a post of duty? Was he a soldier, a sailor? It was a plain contract to be terminated any day by notice by either party, and these men did not even give notice that they would terminate it, but they said to their employers, Give us an eight-hour day and we will stay at work, and if you do not we will strike. What was the result? They paraded to the country that these poor miners are responsible for flooding the mines.

Gentlemen, this was an industrial war. I do not like to work much better than the chairman, but there are all sorts of wars, and this was no child's play. I am willing to say, although it is entirely aside from this case, you on your side were fighting 147,000 men with their wives and their children, and the weapons you used were hunger and want. You thought to bring them to terms by the most cruel, deadly weapon that any oppressor has ever used to bring men to his terms, hunger and want. You on your side used these weapons. These fighting miners had the legal right and the natural right to use upon their side this weapon, had they seen fit, and say to these men, Unless you surrender to us, accept our terms, your mines will go, we will give them back to nature again, and see what nature will do. But nothing of this sort was done. They could not have complained, one party more than the other, but this was not the case. They went to their employers and they said, Grant us the eight-hour day and we will stay at the pumps, we will stay at the engines, we will fire them, we will attend to the mines while our brethren are on a strike.

Well, if these people had failed to take that opportunity to gain such a righteous thing as an eight-hour day, to my mind, they would not have had the intelligence necessary for American citizens. If they had failed at this time to improve their condition when it was auspicious, it would have shown they had been driven to those depths of desperation that they would not know when to claim their rights.

How did these gentlemen meet them? They met them with contempt. Did they do it because they refused the eight-hour day? Oh, no. Counsel in this case says to this commission now that the firemen ought to have an eight-hour day. They said that much after all these long, weary months. Neither do they seriously object, I take it, to the engineers' having an eight-hour day, or the pump men, too. All of them concede the firemen should have it. These gentlemen did not refuse to give these men the eight-hour day because of the wages, because of the extra shift, because they could not afford it. Oh, no. When I pressed Mr. Rose for an answer, an operator said: "We refused to grant the eight-hour day because we did not wish to recognize the union, and would sooner let our mines fill up." Think of it!

These gentlemen, when met by their employees like honest businessmen and told they would protect their mines during the days of this trouble and strike if they were granted an eight-hour day, said no; rather than do that we will send to the four corners of the earth and bring what Brother Burns characterizes as the scum and the offscourings of creation to run our business, because we are thick-necked and pig-headed—and that was all there was of it.

In one case, in spite of Mr. Baer's declaration, it has been shown in the evidence where this request was granted, and only one. In one or two instances they were willing to grant it to the firemen, but not to the engineers. With their old stubbornness, their old willfulness, they had rather see their property destroyed than to concede that the men in their employ were human beings, with a human mind, with a human soul.

Just one man granted it.

* * *

And now they come to this court like little children, with their contemptible talk that these men who were striking for their liberty, and gave them a notice they did not deserve, and demanded rights that were their due—these men who reasoned with them and sought to save them and protect them—they say these men were to blame, because in their blind and stupid prejudice they destroyed their own property. That lie has traveled up and down the country from the day this strike commenced until now. It is not only false and untrue in its every statement, but it is about as cowardly as anything that can be conceived. If these gentlemen were stupid enough to let their mines fill up with water rather than grant this eight-hour day, all right. But keep still about it. After you have done it, the more you talk of it the more contemptible it makes you look in the eyes of all men who think.

* * *

A good many of our troubles in this world are due to mental condition, and some of the operators' troubles, and possibly some of the miners' troubles, have been due to the same causes.

I have done the best I could, in my humble way, to relieve these operators of some of the delusions they have been laboring under since this strike began, but I find on listening to Mr. Baer's speech that my efforts in most directions seem to have been in vain. He informs this commission, in the same attitude that the operators have used since the beginning of this strike, that we, 147,000 irresponsible miners, irresponsible, as Mr. Baer says, because we have not any property, and therefore cannot be made responsible by the laws of the land; that we, a parcel of Huns and Goths and vandals, men who cannot speak the English language and boys who do not love discipline—that we are responsible for the coal famine through which we have passed and are passing today.

Mr. Baer had a right, and should have been given the privilege, as he was, to state his views and let the country have the benefit of them. But the responsibility of the coal famine rests upon those people who were really responsible for this strike. If the cause of the miners was ill-advised or wrong, or if they struck without any just grievance, they are responsible. If, on the other hand, their grievances were just, their demands were reasonable, their attitude was that of rational men, considering not themselves alone, but their duties to society—and every man must consider that, regardless of what the dead letter of the law may be—if their attitude was broadminded and just and fair, and the operators, through blind and stupid prejudice, refused to deal with them and to accede to their demands, and this strike resulted, the blame is upon them and not upon us.

Our clients have suffered through this strike. We did not have any coal to sell, and we have not been able to double the price on one commodity which these men dispose of to the highest bidder. They have used these winter months to recoup themselves for the losses they have sustained on account of our just demands. We have had no such chance.

I wish this morning to investigate the question as to who was responsible for this strike, and what was the cause of this strike—whether the miners can be charged with causing a coal famine, or whether the operators are the men whom this country rightly holds responsible for the high prices, the great need, the famishing conditions through which we have passed.

I want to say that this strike, from first to last, was due to the blind, autocratic, stupid spirit of these operators, that their men should not organize—nothing else. It was not because they thought they should have no more money, for I am inclined to think that these gentlemen would have raised the wages by this time, strike or no strike. At least they came into this court one after the other and practically conceded that they should have raised them, and should now raise them. They were not willing to do it then; but I cannot understand how Mr. Baer, as president of the Reading Railroad, can raise his wages, and how the president of the Pennsylvania Railroad can raise his when they are dealing with the railroad, and still say that these men, infinitely poorer paid, in an employment generally more dangerous, in an occupation certainly more disagreeable and onerous, should have no share in the increased prosperity which has come to them, and which has come to the common country.

It is not, then, the question of wages. These gentlemen precipitated the greatest conflict between capital and labor which the world has ever seen, the most gigantic strike in history, because in their minds it was a question of mastery—nothing else; because they felt and they believed that upon this contest depended the question of whether they should be the masters or whether the men should be the masters.

Neither should be the result of this contest. They, with their feudal ideas that the men who in some mysterious way have been placed in the ownership and the possession of industry are the masters, that they have the right to make the rules and the regulations and set the wages—set them as I will show they did in this case, by nailing their schedule on a door—they, who believe that for one moment to accede to the demands and requests of these men would mean that they were no longer the masters, thought they had better let the water come into their mines and drown them out and destroy their property rather than submit.

Neither can I believe that this was entirely due to the mine owners, when I consider that they were willing to take these fearful chances, to let the country face this coal famine, to let their mines be destroyed. I see in this stubborn, cruel fight—where the weapon used by the operators was starvation, where they depended not upon starving men alone but expected that the men would listen to the starving cries of wives and children to give up this struggle—I believe the operators were induced and urged by the railroad companies to believe that here in the coal region was the final struggle to determine who were the masters in this country, whether the men were chattels, or whether they were men, endowed with the same right to look the other contracting party squarely in the face, the same right to make their own terms as to the hours of labor, the days of labor, the price of labor when they are selling their lives, as the master does when he is buying the laborer's life.

This was the struggle, and this was the cause, and I wish to prove this matter to this commission, not from our testimony but from that of these gentlemen alone. I prove it from their own mouths, and place the responsibility where it belongs—upon these men, who cannot understand that the human race through its long, sore and bitter travail has been moving onward and upward and forward toward the final democracy of man, to the time when each human being shall be a man, clothed with the right to contract, with the right to live his life, and not to be governed and ruled by such rules as the masters have ever imposed upon him.

Now, to begin with these gentlemen, and to give one illustration of where this matter really begins. I read to this commission the indictment of the operators drawn by an operator—the indictment of the late Abram S. Hewitt—of the conditions in the anthracite regions during those halcyon days of which these operators are so fond of talking—the days when they had loyalty and when they had discipline. How these operators do love that word *discipline!* They love it as the slaveholder loved it when he raised the lash above the bare back of the slave. Those were the days when they had discipline; and in those days, says Mr. Hewitt, these operators had their servants subject to such discipline that the men who went down into the mines and dug up the wealth for them were living like pigs and like dogs. And then Mr. Mitchell came into this region. Now, agitators never make revolutions. They are made by the other people entirely. All the pamphlets of all the dreamers and all the agitators in the days preceding the French Revolution amounted to nothing. It was the tyranny of kings and princes, the blind, lavish expenditures of the rich and great, wrung from the labor of the poor, that gave root to the words of the agitator. So Mr. Mitchell and his "paid agitators," as these gentlemen who work for nothing are so fond of characterizing them—Mr. Mitchell and his paid agitators could never have come into the mining region and rallied these pigs— these men who lived as pigs and dogs, according to Mr. Hewitt, unless through a long series of years they had been compelled to live as pigs and dogs.

Loyalty to these bosses could never come with a whip or with starvation. It could only come through just treatment and the recognition of common, fair, honest rights.

These gentlemen charged with the management of these great interests did not desire to see Mr. Mitchell come. The evidence of this from their own mouths is overwhelming. Away back in 1887, after the strike of 1886, the Congressional committee investigating this region called on Mr. Whiting, then superintendent of the Reading Railroad Company, before the days of Mr. Baer, and they asked him what he thought about labor organizations and the organizing of men in the anthracite region, and this was Mr. Whiting's idea then:

Q: You say these striking men will come back and go to work?
A: Yes, sir.
Q: On your own terms?
A: At the old rate; yes, sir.
Q: What force do you rely on to bring them back?
A: Well, sir, their necessities.

These men have learned nothing in all these twenty years. They are the men who declare that the world stands still and the sun goes around it, and characterize as dreamers and visionaries all who see any new light, or have any new theories, or new aspirations—no, not new, but any aspirations for bettering the condition of their fellow-men.

When this strike began, almost twenty years later, we find these operators would deal with their own employees, but they would not deal, they would not think of dealing, even upon their own terms, with any labor organization, labor union or agent, unless that agent worked for them.

Let us put it concretely. Mr. John Markle,[1] one of the chief figures in this great drama, leases a house to James Gallagher, who worked for him. He has a lease such as I never saw before or read of or heard of in my studies, in some regards. He rents a house for 15½ cents a day. There may have been other leases such as that, but I never heard of one. I think I am on safe ground there. I have made some inquiry as to whether any human being ever leased a house by the day. Why, it is about as much as you want to do to go to a hotel with your trunk or your valise and rent it by the day, where you do not have to anchor a cookstove or take

[1] Mine operator, George B. Markle Company.

in your own folding bed. But Mr. Markle, in order, as his astute counsel says, that he may have room for the men who really work for him in case of necessity—and I have no doubt that is the reason—draws a lease at 15½ cents a day. I am not complaining of the price—a day's notice is pretty short to move a family, but the terms of the lease are even more stringent than that. Lest there be any mistake, lest the subtleties of the lawyer or the subtleties of the judge might help out the tenant, he does not lease it for any term, but he leases it at "the will and pleasure of John Markle." If anybody can tell what that is they can do better than I can. I know something about his will, but I do not know anything at all about his pleasure, unless he got pleasure from evicting these thirteen men. Mr. John Markle has had a great deal to say in this controversy, and I have not any feeling against Mr. Markle as Mr. John Markle. I have no doubt that, as he sees right and wrong, he is as good a man as I am, and intends to do as near right as I do. My quarrel is with Mr. John Markle's ideas and what he makes of them. He probably acts up to his highest light, and that is all that is given to any human being to do. My criticism is not of him, but it is of his position in this case and his position as the overseer of his men.

Mr. John Markle then says to his men: "I will not deal or negotiate with any one of you for wages, unless you are in my employ, which means renting my house at my will and pleasure at 15½ cents a day."

Now, then, I have no doubt that a situation like that would conduce to the independence of the contracting parties. I once in a while put up with some inconvenience at a hotel. I have made up my mind I would strike for ice water, or soft-boiled eggs, or something of that kind, but then when I thought a strike would result in my having to pack up my valise and carry it over to some hotel on twenty-four hours' notice I continued to put up with the discomfort. But here is a man who has his household goods and his household gods all in one palatial residence such as they furnish our clients down there (if you do not believe it, read the statistics of the expert accountants), and they give him his job. There is nobody else within seven or eight miles that he can work for, and no other house within two or three miles that he could move into.

They say to him, "We will negotiate with you because you are in a condition that if you make us any trouble we can get rid of you in just about a minute and we will send our general superintendent to help set your cookstove out in the street, your cookstove and your sauerkraut." That was the condition of these gentlemen in the houses in the days they think so much of and which they pray this commission to restore to them. They had no objection to dealing with their employees, but they could not deal with the men who did not work for them. Their employees could choose an agent, but the agent must work for them. They do not want any divided allegiance, that is, the agent must work for both parties, but especially for the employer. So this was the condition of things when the negotiations for this demand began.

❊　　❊　　❊

Now, this was the condition up to the strike. Every request, every demand, every prayer of these men had been contemptuously refused. Mr. Mitchell had asked to meet and discuss. He had asked, when that failed, that they submit their differences to a body of men, or to an individual man, and let them settle before this civil strife was precipitated upon the people of the United States. No human being could have done more, and no conscientious, intelligent man, true to the high position which he represents, could have done less. These men whose life and liberty and condition in a way were dependent upon him, all the future generations that are dependent upon the just treatment of the generation in which we live, all these caused him to make this demand, which was just and reasonable, and which they have largely conceded in the closing days of this historic hearing. They spurned it with contempt. "We will not meet you, we will not raise wages, we will not shorten hours, we will not submit our differences to unprejudiced, fair-minded men; we will post our notices upon the door and this shall be your contract for twelve months to come."

Gentlemen, you may have all the consolation that you can get. You may take all the notices that you may pay for, but you can never deceive the American republic in understanding where the responsibility for this great strike rested from beginning to end.

You allowed this strike, nay, you forced this strike, that you might demonstrate to your men, that you might demonstrate to the generation in which you live, that you might demonstrate to the generations yet to come, that the owners of capital are the masters and that no divided allegiance could be tolerated for a single moment. This strike from its inception and before was brought about for one purpose and only one, to crush out this union which had brought to these downcast, suffering men, women and children the first ray of light and hope and inspiration that had ever come into the darkness of their lives.

Yet these gentlemen were not only willing, for the sake of destroying the union, to plunge this country into disorder and danger, but they come here in the last days of this hearing and tell this commission that the men who were fighting for their liberty, fighting for their rights to make a fair contract between man and man, fighting for the right to meet their masters and discuss their grievances, and nothing else, that the men were responsible because, forsooth, they were not willing to take the notices that were posted on their employers' doors.

If I thought that there was any sort of danger that any number of American citizens could place the responsibility there I would despair for the intelligence of my countrymen.

Mr. Baer thinks a labor union is a terrible thing. He objects to the United Mine Workers. Every word that he uttered, however well disguised, showed that his real grievance was against this body which had dared to come into this region and dispute his imperial authority. He says it is a cruel thing and a terrible thing that 400,000 mine workers, representing the anthracite and bituminous fields, can form a monopoly of all the coal that is produced in the United States. And he warns the country that if this is possible they may awaken some day and be unprotected from the cold blast of the winter. He says this is still more cruel because these men have no financial responsibility—because they are poor.

Educated in the law and in the ethics of business, he has taught himself to believe that the danger would be less if these mine workers were rich. Does not Mr. Baer understand by this time that the American people fear his monopoly more than ours?

And does he not understand that they fear it because it is so rich and because it has financial responsibility? The poor man is utterly unable, except for a limited time and under limited conditions, to control and regulate the conditions of trade. But take the power of the great railroad companies of this country, which control the trade both of the bituminous and the anthracite fields, and it depends upon the sweet will and the sweet pleasure of one man to paralyze the wheels of industry. Your responsibility, Mr. Baer—and by the word "responsibility" I mean what he means—your financial responsibility is the thing that the American people fear.

Mr. Baer afraid of the mine workers, and the people of this country afraid of these men who dig their coal? Why, let us look at the other side of the picture. I do not believe much in monopoly myself, and I propose to treat both of these monopolies the same way, because an organization of labor to a certain extent is a monopoly, as I shall discuss further on. But Mr. Baer ought to know, and does know, that his people have a monopoly too. The Pennsylvania Railroad and the Reading Railroad and the Baltimore and Ohio Railroad are one thing—in fact, all the great trunk line systems are pretty nearly one thing. And these roads bring not only the anthracite coal but the bituminous coal to market as well. Either one of these under certain conditions might paralyze industry and bring ruin and want, and I am willing to join with Mr. Baer and say that I believe that condition is not right—not right for a single moment. Mr. Baer says: "Ah, the thing to do is to crush the United Mine Workers and leave it with us. We are Christian gentlemen, in whom the Lord in His infinite wisdom has placed the management of these properties, and everybody's interests are safe in our hands."

Mr. Baer might as well understand, and he will learn if he places his ear close to the ground—he has carried his head so high that he has never done that—he might as well understand that the people of America will not always place themselves in a position where they may be dependent for fuel, or any necessity of life, either upon mine owners or mine workers. And I hope they will not.

Mr. Baer and all of his friends ought to understand that the people of the United States do not believe in any such absolute ownership of the earth on which we live as will allow them to hold all the coal that the Lord has placed in it and make the rest of us freeze, unless they give the word; and when the time comes it will be settled not by destroying the mine workers, but by the people taking possession in some way, and under fair terms, of this coal and providing a means for themselves, so that they will not freeze; so that industry will not be paralyzed; so that their necessities and their wants will not be dependent upon one man, or ten men, or 400,000 men; and they never can protect themselves in any other way.

The strike came on, and everybody excepting the operators wanted to settle it.

*　　*　　*

Mr. Olyphant[1] says: "We had twenty-three years of perfect peace—nothing to trouble us in our mines anywhere." Well, this is not the only condition of perfect peace. During those twenty-three years of perfect peace we cannot forget what Mr. Hewitt said about it. It was the perfect peace of the graveyard, except that the men could work.

Mr. Baer says again: "Now, what I have said is that the management of business belongs to the owners." There is the trouble with this case. Gentlemen of this commission, these men can never understand that the management of business does not belong to the owners. The man who builds a mill and equips it and draws his profits from it under the laws of this country has a right, of course, to say how many hours men shall work, what wages they shall get, to say anything not inconsistent with the law. I admit it. But the man who is bound to sell his labor and spend his time inside the doors of that mill has the same right to say how many hours he will work, or how many days he will work, or for how much money he will work; and there can be no gainsaying it.

If they want to place us upon a Chinese level or any other level, under the laws of this country as they exist today they have a perfect right to close their doors and only open them when their

[1] R. M. Olyphant, president, Delaware & Hudson.

demands are acceded to. And we have that right. What does it mean? It means industrial war, and industrial war is all that the laws of America have provided for. So long as they have provided for nothing but industrial war, then we insist upon the part of labor that you have no right to compel the laboring man to lay down his arms upon the field of battle. If it is industrial war, well and good. We can fight as well as you can fight, and until the country provides some other way, we must have our chance as well as you.

That is the law. I take it there is a moral law that is higher. Whatever Mr. Baer may say, and I will be charitable enough to believe that although his words were written he did not think what he said, it is too late in the world for any man, however high and mighty, to say to any intelligent human being that there is no distinction between the laws of the land and the moral law.

Why, a hundred years ago and more, Mr. William Blackstone, the great commentator, and almost the father of English law, wrote it down that the man who squared his conduct by the letter of the law was neither an honest man nor a good citizen. Neither is he. The civil law does not pretend to take into account everything that is good and bad. The civil law does not treat of all the rights and the duties and the obligations of men. If it does, we had better nail up our church doors and close our schoolhouses forever, and burn most of the books which have dealt with the questions of moral conduct.

If a civil strife like this comes on, then those responsible for it must consider the moral questions. The man who owns the factory must consider whether he has any moral duty to the men who are dependent upon him, in a way, for bread, and the danger and evil to society that will result if he closes his doors. The workingmen must consider, too, their responsibility to those dependent upon them and to the community that their labor serves. And I insist that if either one of them recognizes the moral law they will say: "I may be looking at this question from my standpoint. I will submit my differences to someone else." And sometime I have no doubt that the civil law will recognize this much of the moral law.

Mr. Mitchell recognized it. Mr. Mitchell offered to submit this controversy to a board of arbitration, but the operators said, "No." Repeatedly they said: "We have nothing to arbitrate." It is the old, old question: "What is there to arbitrate? Arbitrate wages? Why, we have posted the wages on our breaker doors, and the contract runs until April 1903. There is no question of wages; that is settled." It is settled like every other controversy in the anthracite regions for fifty years; and "there is nothing to arbitrate."

And so the strike came on. For a moment I want to omit the strike and show that this condition continued in the minds of these gentlemen clear to the end. Unfortunately for them, the sentiment of the country was with the miners, and they sent their money and their clothing and their relief to prolong this struggle. We of Chicago have been criticized because we gave them some of our money, and an eminent railroad president said that Boston deserved to freeze this winter because she sympathized with the strikers last summer. The whole country has been criticized by these gentlemen, because in this most gigantic contest that the labor world has ever known their sympathies were with the poor instead of the rich.

We can stand our criticism. I believe the great mass of the citizens of Chicago would have been ready to huddle together during the winter and keep themselves warm by living in one great room rather than to have had these men give up the fight that they were making, not for themselves, but for the common humanity of the world and for the generations that are yet unborn; and I believe that is true of the great mass of men in all the United States.

The strike came on because these men refused to recognize their workmen as human beings, and October came around and they saw the winter in front of them, and they knew then whom the country held responsible for this cruel struggle; and the country has not forgotten today. Then the President of the United States, in obedience to the wishes and the prayers of his countrymen, asked Mr. John Mitchell to come, and he asked the presidents of the railroad companies to come and see if they could not agree on some terms to settle this industrial strife. And they came. And Mr. John Mitchell's words were conservative, calm, wise, ethical, human. The words of these operators breathed the spirit of the serpent, if serpents have spirits; they breathed the feeling of a hyena; they showed that even with the winter in front of them and with the most direful calamity possible that the people were to face, they still had not learned anything. They went there and these are some of the things that were said before the President of the United States as late as October:

Mr. Truesdale said: "It is first and foremost our duty, and we take this occasion to state it and press it upon your consideration, and through you upon that of the authorities of the state of Pennsylvania, to insist upon it that the existing conditions of anarchy and lawlessness, of riot and rapine, a condition which has been raging with more or less violence throughout the anthracite regions during the last five months, be immediately and permanently suppressed. To this end we ask that the entire authority and power of the state of Pennsylvania, civil and military, and, if needs be, that of the United States government as well, be exercised forthwith.

"Second, we ask that the civil branch of the United States government, taking cognizance of and following the decision of its courts rendered in litigation growing out of previous similar conditions, at once institute proceedings against the illegal organization known as the United Mine Workers' Association, its well-known officers, agents and members, to enjoin and restrain permanently it and them from continuing this organization, and requiring them to desist immediately from conspiring, conniving, aiding or abetting the outlawry and intolerable conditions in the anthracite regions for which they, and they alone, are responsible. We are advised by our counsel that such civil action will lie on the part of the United States government, as it is well known that the United States statutes are daily being openly and grossly violated; that previous decisions of the courts justify fully such action being taken at this time, and that ample remedy can be given immediately and effectively for existing conditions.

"Another duty, Mr. President, and we regard it as the most supreme! One sixth of the membership of this illegal organization is composed of young men and boys between the ages of fourteen and twenty, the future citizens and lawmakers of the great state of Pennsylvania. These young men and boys during the past two years have had their young, immature minds poisoned with their most dangerous anarchistic, distorted, wicked views and errors concerning the rights of citizenship and property that anyone can possibly conceive of; all taught the teachings and practice of the officers, organizers and apostles of the United Mine Workers' Association."

If this gentleman were half as tender and careful for the young bodies of these children as he pretends to be for their young minds, then he would close his breakers or place men there to pick his coal. This is the answer the President receives from him.

Mr. Markle said: "I fully endorse these remarks from you, and as an American citizen and a citizen of the commonwealth of Pennsylvania I now ask you to perform the duties vested in you as President of the United States." A modest request from this gentleman, who no doubt believed that the President of the United States held all of his vassals under the form of tenure of a lease at will and pleasure for 15½ cents a day, and that if President Roosevelt said the word he could tell them to move off into the ocean just as Mr. Markle could tell his employees to go! So he says: "Mr. President, you do your duty, and that is all we will need." Then he goes on: "A record of twenty-one murders, a long list of brutal assaults, houses and bridges dynamited, daily acts of violence now taking place and several washeries burned down are actual evidences of this condition of lawlessness existing there. Are you asking us to deal with a set of outlaws? I can hardly conceive of such a thought. The respectable citizens of these United States will insist upon the officers in power giving to the citizens of Pennsylvania law and order and the right to work if they so desire.

"Mr. President, I represent the individual coal operators, and in addition thereto, we represent, far better than Mr. Mitchell does, a majority of the anthracite coal workers, including some 17,000 men who are now working and endeavoring against great odds to relieve the public of the possibilities of a coal famine, in making this appeal to you."

And then Mr. Baer speaks. Sitting there, presumably, whilst all the rest were speaking, he comes last:

" 'The domestic tranquillity' which the Constitution declares is the chief object of government does not exist in the coal regions. There is a terrible reign of lawlessness and crime there. Only the lives and property of the members of the secret, oath-bound order, which declared that the locals should 'have full power to suspend operations at collieries,' until the nonunion men joined their order, are safe. Every effort is made to prevent the mining of coal; and when mined, Mitchell's men dynamite bridges and tracks, mob nonunion men, and by all manner of violence try to prevent its shipment to relieve the public.

"Under these conditions we decline to accept Mr. Mitchell's considerate offer to let us work on terms he names. He has no right to come from Illinois to dictate terms on the acceptance of which anarchy and crime shall cease in Pennsylvania. He must stop his people from killing, maiming and abusing Pennsylvania citizens and from destroying property."

Surely a temperate, judicious, businesslike speech to make to the President of the United States upon this occasion! He showed that he is not only a "businessman," but a constitutional lawyer. "The domestic tranquillity" which the Constitution declares is the chief object of government does not exist in the coal regions! I presume he is more familiar with that provision of the Constitution than the provision of the Constitution which absolutely forbids any man from being an officer in a coal company and an officer in a railroad company at the same time.

These gentlemen were meeting at the request of the President of the United States. They were meeting, not because the President desired to settle the differences between them and their employees, but because the President of the United States, heeding the cry and the prayers of seventy million people, feared the calamity that would come upon us in the winter unless some settlement was reached.

Mr. Mitchell said: "I am willing; I will turn over my case to you. I will do what I have been ready to do from the first. If I am wrong I will submit it to my fellow-citizens to decide. You may appoint a court of arbitrators if you will do it. I will accept every man you appoint, and we will submit to their findings; and in the meantime our men will go back into the earth and bring up coal to prevent the famine that otherwise must come."

These gentlemen said: "No; oh, no, no, Mr. President; this is not what we demand. We demand more soldiers, more guns, more bayonets, more violence. What we want is that you will send the army of the United States to kill these Anarchists, these lawbreakers, these criminals who have been our employees for fifty years."

And then they lied to the President of the United States. Mr. Thomas and Mr. Markle told the President of the United States that this body of mine workers had committed, one said twenty and the other said twenty-one, murders; and that a condition of anarchy and violence and turbulence and disorder existed from one end of this region to the other—as if, instead of this country being settled by peaceable, quiet, Christian men, it was inhabited by wild beasts.

They have had their day in court—and I will refer to this in a few minutes. They have had their months and their weeks in court; and they have brought to the attention of this commission four men who were killed, not one of whom was murdered within the meaning of this language, although one was severely beaten, beaten to death—not, perhaps, by mine workers.

But with all of their research and investigation and their time and their money they have brought four and we have brought four—four of our men that were killed by them, four of theirs that were killed by us. And, regrettable as it is, and unfortunate as it is, the penalty perhaps is not too great a price to pay. Nothing can come in this world without penalties; nothing ever did come or ever can come. It is regrettable that that is the law of life, but it is the law of life, and we must recognize the law of life. There is no evading it, and it had better be recognized than be treated with as these gentlemen propose to treat the union—as if it was not there.

At least, for the sake of inducing the President of the United States to send guns and soldiers and bayonets to shoot down inoffensive men and women and children, if need be, their employees and their wards for fifty years, they deliberately told him that twenty or twenty-one murders had been committed by this set of desperadoes, and they again refused to arbitrate.

They met the request of the President with contempt. "Although the winter is coming, we are still the masters. You, Mr. President, have one duty to perform, and that is to send out the standing army to help us mine coal and shoot down the men who have made our fortunes for us."

But he did not do it.

Now, I will discuss in a few moments the question of violence. But I want to refer briefly to some other reasons, to show that from the beginning to the end this whole strike was precipitated because of the blind and stupid resistance of these gentlemen to the organization. They wanted to destroy it.

* * *

I wish to say that all of the evils and trouble of this great strike grew from the blind determination of these men that there should be no organization of labor. I call your attention, as another example of this, to the Delaware, Lackawanna and Western. Major Warren, with an ingenuity which seemed sincere, and yet I hardly think it was, although he is an estimable gentleman, says to this commission: "Was there any wrong in the Delaware, Lackawanna and Western getting up an organization of their own?" Was there? Now, Major Warren, I take it from his address, is just beginning his study of social economics. I do not want to discourage a young man starting out, because he has done pretty well; but after he has read further, as far as I have, he will need to go but just a little further to find that the very first thing the employers attempt to do when a union is about to be formed among their men is to get up another union, man it with their officers and tie it down with conditions. It is not possible that the Delaware, Lackawanna and Western people did not know that.

If they had read the history of trade unionism in England they would have found out. It has been attempted over and over again in the history of the world from the beginning, and I suppose will be to the end. So they sent their bosses out among their employees and asked them to form a union.

They asked them to leave the other union, too, as one of the witnesses testified. This is the kind of union they wanted to form of their employees. "The object of this union shall be to promote the interest of miners, laborers and all employees of the Delaware, Lackawanna and Western Mines morally, socially and financially, and to spread intelligence among them. It is an organization for the protection of men who believe that by proper action they can secure justice and have their grievances remedied without resorting to strikes. An organization independent from any other organization controlled by soft coal or outside interference."

Everybody, whether miner or boss, was eligible. I know that Major Warren really understood what this meant. I know that anybody who has the first knowledge of these questions understood that when the bosses and foremen went through the mines and urged their men to give up their union and join this, they were doing it to destroy the Mine Workers' Union.

I will not say that it is not possible that they might have got some benefit out of this union. I do not want to misjudge these men. I do not pretend for a moment that every act of their lives has been a selfish act and that sometimes they are not good and kind. But I do say that this old dodge of forming a union by the bosses and the employers and getting the men to leave their own union, is so old and gray and decrepit that I would not have supposed it would have found countenance among the anthracite mine owners of Pennsylvania. I would have supposed that even they would have gone beyond that stage.

That is not all. It is not half.

After this strike was over and the men went back loyally and faithfully, they laid down their clubs and their dynamite and they took up their shovels and their picks and they did their part. But the Coxe company refused to take back 439 men whose names have been given. And the men said no, we will not go back and leave 439 of our men idle, and finally they met Mr. Kudlich and he reduced the number to 135, who they still said should not go back, and up to the time this commission met in Scranton and during its deliberations, Coxe Brothers had not commenced operations because they refused to take back 135 of those men, their employees, who must have been gross agitators, not men who had committed crime, for no attempt has been made from the beginning to reinstate any unfortunate person who has been charged with crime. Not the slightest. The United Mine Workers have not asked it. They simply refused to take back these 135 men because they were gross agitators. These were the men who were responsible for this long and bloody contest and they could not go to work.

Not only would they starve them into submission, but when all the miners in the anthracite region had listened to the voice of the millions calling upon them for coal and had ceased hostilities and gone back to work, they would still starve them and their wives and their children. The war was still on and the 135 must fall victims to it. Mr. Markle came in with his long list that he refused, and there is not a company in this region that did not refuse to reinstate men, not because men had committed crime, gentlemen of the commission, but because these men were agitators—which the smug and comfortable class of the world has always considered the most serious offense that could be committed upon them. Agitators! It was Garrison and Phillips and John Brown and this handful of men who could not be forgiven before the war, but who will be reverenced as long as sentiments of humanity, justice and freedom live in the human breast.

They tell us there has been no discrimination. I can only call your attention briefly to several cases. William Hale was refused work by the D. and H. on account of the union. Balderson was discharged from the same company because he belonged to the union. Miller was discharged from the Erie on account of the strike. Dreisbach, of the Lehigh Valley, was refused work because he struck.

❋   ❋   ❋

They say there is no blacklist. There is nothing in a name. A man may be blacklisted in one colliery, or at all the collieries of a company, or all the companies of the region. If a man has a home, a family, a cookstove, a barrel of sauerkraut in the cellar, even with a one-day lease at the will and pleasure—of a mine owner, it is a pretty serious blacklist if you do not give him work at that colliery or with that company and you send him off adrift to pick his way through the regions, and see if, perchance, some other boss will not hire him, some other boss who has not heard his name and does not know him. A blacklist is something like a boycott. It is not the easiest thing to prove, and it is pretty cruel in its effects. I do not like either of them. I am bound to defend both of them within the limits.

I hardly expected that these gentlemen would come into this court and swear that they had a blacklist. I am free to say I am pretty easy, but I did not look for that. So I was not surprised when man after man came upon the stand and said, Oh, no, we never heard of a blacklist. Although we had proven over and over again where leaders of labor organizations had been discharged, turned from their homes and refused work. In the case of Coxe Brothers, they picked out every man who was a leader, and there was not one officer left. Their sharpshooters were more deadly than the Boers' in the South African War.

They never missed an officer, even though the officer was on a relief committee. That seemed to be worse than any of the rest, because it prevented their favorite weapon of starvation from getting in its deadly work. Over and over again we showed their discrimination.

We brought poor old James Gallagher back here, who had served more than thirty years for Markle, and who was turned from his home on a November night, and who is still without work, although as clever a man as I have met in the anthracite region, not even barring the astute lawyers whom it has been my pleasure to meet.

I suppose the facts are, if the truth were known, that James Gallagher is too clever. If a man is too clever he is not any good as a workingman. He ought to be a lawyer, then the bosses could hire him.

There was one man, however, who could not get out of his blacklist, and that was Warrener. Mr. Warrener is a college graduate, a polished gentleman, the superintendent of a large company. There was a strike at the Maltby colliery. He said the strike developed into a boycott. Thirty or forty men were engaged in this strike. They would not go back to work. I do not know whether the strike was just or unjust, and I do not care. They thought it was just or they would not have struck, and they had a right to strike. Finally these men went away from the jurisdiction of this feudal baron and got a job with Thorne, of the Temple Iron Company, another feudal baron. These thirty or thirty-five men who had laid down their tools in one place got a job in another, and thereupon Warrener, under his own admission, met with the superintendents and said to them they were strikers from the Maltby colliery. I asked him why he said it, whether to get them discharged or not, and he quibbled and he dodged, and he avoided and he evaded and he gave no excuse whatever. He plainly admitted that it was on account of this strike at his colliery, and I take it that anyone with the ordinary amount of intelligence must know that it was true and that Mr. Warrener did not tell the whole truth to this commission upon the witness stand, because the fact remains that these men struck and Warrener went to Thorne and told him of it and Thorne discharged them, every one of them.

Then some trouble was made about it. Thorne took them back, but every single one of them was discharged. The employer of this company was not content to boycott his men in his own collieries because they exercised the right of common American citizens and struck and refused to work, but, forsooth, he followed these men throughout the anthracite region to deny them bread and to reduce their families to want.

This is the condition, and this is the grievous offense of which the United Mine Workers are guilty—that they have taken this mass of men, this 147,000 men, that they have bound them together in one body and said to each man: "Here is a friend; this organization is your friend. You may come to us with your complaints and your grievances and your wrongs, and we will stand by you." And it was for this, for this determination upon the part of these employers to crush out this body so odious to them, that this five months' strike ensued.

Now, what do they tell us about it? "Ah," they say, "but you committed crime." I do not propose, in the discussion of this case, to avoid any question, however much I might think it would be against us. The light of day, so far as possible, must fall upon this region; and men who wish to know and who wish to fairly judge must pass judgment upon these two contending forces, and say which is right and which is wrong, and how far each was right and how far each was wrong.

We have heard the evidence in this case. We came here demanding more pay, shorter hours, recognition of our union, and they have replied: "You are cutthroats and assassins and murderers and outlaws, and therefore you will work for what you get."

Let me examine that. First, it is no answer. It can make no difference in any issue in this case, excepting the recognition of the union, what violence was committed in the anthracite region. That is the first proposition. It can make no more difference in the determination of this commission than the crimes committed by the operators; and they have been many, if you call violation of the law a crime. I refer to those laws about rebates, unjust tariffs, ownership of coal mines by railroad companies. However, I do not care anything about them. They have nothing to do with this case. We are not interested in the moral character or the moral obligations of any of these gentlemen. We are only interested in finding out what wages we can get out of them, and under what terms we can work for them; and I do not ask the commission to go any further.

What about the crimes that they have charged to us? We have heard a good deal about it in the long days and weeks this commission has been in session. The so-called nonunionists have had a lawyer or lawyers in this case. They have been represented at this court; and they say they have been beaten, stoned, abused, called "scabs," and sometimes killed.

I do not admit that anybody hates suffering and injustice any more than I. I hope nobody does; because if they do, they suffer a good deal. I do not like it. I have not any enemy in the world to whom I would like to cause any suffering; and I do not really like to say unkind things about Mr. Baer, although I may seem to like to. And I am sincerely sorry that any workingman or any other man caused any kind of suffering in the anthracite regions. I am sorry I could not help it; if I could have helped it I would. I have no doubt Mr. Mitchell would. I have no doubt that even the men who held the club in their hands would have avoided it if, in their minds and in the way they saw life and the way they were surrounded, they could have helped it. I have not the slightest doubt of it.

❖   ❖   ❖

[Some men] committed some things that are called crimes, just as some are committed every day in Philadelphia—more, but as disconnected and disassociated with anything else; just as others are committed every day in the same region in which this investigation and this terrible strike took place—more, perhaps, but as disconnected, excepting that they grew out of the passions and the feelings and the struggles of this great contest, as any crimes are disconnected from any other acts. In a sense they are disconnected, and in a sense they are connected.

Whenever you raise the price of wheat it means that more men commit crime; whenever you raise the price of coal it means that more men commit crime; because, after all, natural laws control the universe, and ever must control the universe. And the feelings and the despairs and the hopes and the criminal instincts of men grow from this bitter contest, and would grow from it in any country in the world and in any age of the world, and will do so so long as man has aspirations and fears and instincts. And it matters not what is the finding of this commission; they cannot cure this condition, and they cannot change it. It is a natural condition.

I do not expect that many of this commission would agree with my view upon that question, and it is not material to my side of the question whether they do or not. In my philosophy these men, and all of us, are the product of our heredity, of our environment. We cannot help it. I do not believe any man has the right to judge his fellow in any of these relations. I cannot pronounce one of them a criminal. I have no right to pronounce one of them a criminal. There is not any man who can honestly and seriously ask himself the question: "Had I been born as this man was, had I been reared as he was, had I suffered what he did and undergone what he did, would I have done any different from him?" and be sure that he would not.

I cannot say that I would have been in any different position from the poor, unfortunate Pole who, in his clouded intellect, felt it his duty to strike Winsdon[1] over the head with a club, deeply as I regret it. I cannot say that I would be in any different position from Mr. Baer had I been born under his environment and lived under his surroundings. I do not mean to condemn either one of them in this case; and I think it is the only broad and fair and logical way to look at it.

CHAIRMAN: Do you think it right to tell the man who struck down Winsdon that it was his environment that made him do it?

DARROW: I should tell him so, and I do not think he would be a bit more apt to do it again. But that is another question. I would go as fast as I could to tell him not to, to urge the reasons why he should not, as I would to Mr. Baer to tell him he should not have precipitated this crisis upon the country. But I do not think it does any good to scold either one of them after it is over, and I would not do it. I would approach them upon an entirely different basis from that, and I think the whole philosophy of life would teach us to approach them upon an entirely different basis from that.

* * *

Are the men criminals as a class? Does this commission believe that that poor Pole, whatever his name, who struck Winsdon over the back of his head with a club, would have done it under other conditions and other environments? Why, he was a man who took his dinner pail in his hand day after day and went down in the mines to earn money for his wife and his children. I will guarantee he was a man who, if Winsdon had come to him hungry, suffering, to his door, would have taken him in and given him succor and help. He was a man who did this deed which he conceived, in his blind ignorance and his passion, to be a duty to his family and society, although I believe, and all our leaders believe, that in this he was wrong.

We are told by these gentlemen that our clients, the mine work-

[1] Former minor official of the union who went back to work during the strike.

ers, are criminals, anarchists, destroyers; that they deserve no mercy and no justice from any court.

We are not told directly that they deserve no justice, and yet this evidence is arrayed in this court for no purpose except to influence the judgment of this court; nothing else. If this evidence has no bearing upon the wages you will give, upon the hours you will give, upon the questions involved in this case—and they say the recognition of the union is not involved—then it has no bearing in this case.

CHAIRMAN: I can say now that this commission does not believe the United Mine Workers were assassins, cutthroats or criminals.

DARROW: I have had no doubt of it, Judge, from the beginning. I have visited their homes, as this commission has visited their homes. I do not care what language they speak, whether it is English or not; I do not care how strong their passions or their feelings. I know they are men, like us. I have visited their little homes, and on their walls in almost every instance, no matter what language they speak, you find the picture of the Madonna and her child, with its same lesson in every language and in every clime. You cannot tell me that those people—no matter what they do, when moved by strong feelings, strong desires or great provocation—have not the same instincts of love, and pity, and hope, and charity and kindness that are the heritage of every man who lives. I have found that, and upon their walls also I have found the picture of John Mitchell. You need not tell me that the one picture comes from the feeling of love and devotion and reverence, and that the other is born of the brute, of passion, of hatred, and crime. They both come from the same thing, and the organization, no matter what it does, any organization that could take that heterogeneous mass, drawn from every nation on earth, from every land and every clime, and weld it into one common homogeneous mass, with common aims and aspirations and hopes—any such organization must be grand and glorious and doing good on the earth.

*　　*　　*

Gentlemen of the commission, when this commission adjourned I was discussing the question of the violence in the coal regions, and the character of the men, women and children who live in the coal regions and spend their days in the mines and around the mines.

But let us look at this question of the disorder in the coal region from a natural standpoint. You and I may have our theories of crime and of criminal responsibility, but there are some things, I take it, that we can agree upon that have no relation to the question of moral responsibility. Men and women have arranged themselves in a system which we call society, as much a system as the revolving planets, each moving in its orbit, each escaping the others because they keep their place; as much a system as the infinite number of infinitely small molecules that make up a piece of iron or a piece of steel, or a piece of wood, each having a separate orbit, and the harmony of the whole depending upon the observance of the relations between these separate atoms.

That is what society is. That is what it is broadly. Men and women rather automatically fill their places. They live their lives, they tread their paths, they go their way, regarding each other's rights, in their orbits, and living together in harmony and in peace. But if peace and harmony are disturbed, then comes a new adjustment, a new relation. These particles must form again in some other way. It is the same in the physical world, in the moral world, in the spiritual world, the world of beasts as with men. Let some cataclysm occur and destroy all the particles of matter in the physical world, and they must readjust themselves. First in order and tumult, but finally they readjust themselves once more. The same is true of man. In a war, a pestilence, a great strike, all these social relations are changed in a moment. The orbits of the individual atoms are changed. It means force, it means violence, it means a clashing of individuals, a clashing that caused the orbits to change and society is changed. There can be no disturbance of human relations, or of physical relations, that does not bring this conflict. I do not care what it is. You can never have a great strike but that here and there violence arises. You can never construct a great building out of the ordinary but that here and there some violence is done. Nothing can happen to disturb the ordinary, common walks of life except these atoms will clash.

So it was in the coal fields. Here were some 147,000 workingmen, a population perhaps of 700,000 people living very close to the limits of life. We have read of the wealth of these men; it is not worth talking about. The Erie Company brought its land agent to prove how much its employees were worth. What did they say? They went to the tax records and they proved that 28 per cent of them were paying taxes upon property, and they brought, not its assessed value, but its real value, the assessed value multiplied by two and in some instances two and a half, which we will assume is correct, and they figured out that 28 per cent of their employees had property averaging a thousand dollars apiece. Then we sent our people to investigate. They took every tenth man in the regular order upon the list, and it showed that one-half of that property was either mortgaged, or had judgments against it, or was not theirs at all. Wherever a miner has come into this court and has told anything of his possessions, the evidence has shown that he and his children have toiled for years to get a little home above their heads. They were frugal, they were saving, they were self-denying. They worked for years and scarcely an instance has been shown in this case where any man has had one, or two, or at the most three thousand dollars, but what it was the combined savings of all his family covering years. This was the condition. These people were gathered from every portion of the earth, with all degrees of intelligence and all degrees of feeling; and it does not follow that the man or the woman of the deepest feeling is the worst man or woman. The man with cool judgment and little feeling, who is never moved to strong loves and strong hates, may pass along through life in the beaten path. But many of these people are close to nature, people of deep feeling, of other races than ours, no doubt kind, no doubt generous, no doubt of warm sympathies. I have seen them in the coal region: fathers and sons and brothers and neighbors, men kissing each other at parting, which you rarely see with men who can speak good English. I knew they were not operators; I was sure of it.

They were the despised Huns, the Goths and vandals whom the operators employed, but whose natural love and whose natural sympathy would bring men to kiss each other at meeting and at parting. And these are the men who committed crimes—men of strong emotion, men not cool and calculating, and weighing evidence and human actions like a judge upon the bench or a lawyer who is paid to weigh them. They were men who act upon the emotions which God gave them, whose school was the mine and hard work and bitter experience; men who have not learned to control their natural sympathies or their natural passions. And these men were thrown out for five and a half months to fight with famine for themselves and their wives and their children.

It is a shortsighted man who could doubt what would be the result—a shortsighted man. If this commission were sitting here today, and were informed that in a valley a hundred miles in one direction and fifty miles in another and peopled by a miscellaneous people, five hundred thousand souls, they were to be reduced to want for five and a half long months, months of idleness, months of excitement, months of intense social feeling, would you doubt what would happen? Not one man would doubt it. You would know that in spite of every law of man and God, in spite of every instinct of humanity and charity, which, after all, are planted deep in the hearts of men, which after all make for the preservation and the uplifting of the human race—that in spite of these, the feeling of the brute would here and there arise, and these scenes of violence and crime must inevitably come.

Mr. Baer knew it. Mr. Olyphant knew it. Every one of these railroad presidents knew it when they insolently and cruelly refused to meet their men in calm, decent conference and thus let slip the dogs of war.

The responsibility, gentlemen, is not upon these men who were your chattels and your servants, these men who begged and pleaded and prayed for the commonest right that every human being should have from the master for whom he works. The responsibility is for those men who severed their relations with their fellow-man. When Mr. Baer and the other captains of industry severed these relations there could be but one result, and there was one.

When I consider that in this mining region there was a population of 700,000 men and women and children, to say nothing of several hundred thousand more dependent upon them—more than a million of people, more than there are in the city of Philadelphia, always living close to the limits of life—when I consider that these conditions existed there for five and a half long months in the face of the most serious strain, and when the passions of men were awakened, the wonder in my mind is that there was not more violence instead of less. And if it had not been for the loyalty of these men to their union, for the judgment and the coolness and the watchful presence of their leaders, could anything have prevented the destruction of an enormous amount of property? Let us see what it was.

Not a breaker was burned, not a piece of property destroyed that belonged to these coal companies, save that here and there some windows were broken. In all the testimony we have had not one instance has been shown where any leader of this organization ever counseled, advised, committed or tolerated violation of the law—not one. Here and there some poor fellow, driven by desperation at the sight of the man who was going out to take what he called "his job," who was going out for the purpose of destroying the righteous cause for which these men were suffering and fighting, here and there some men, maddened by this sight, committed acts of violence for which we are as sorry as this commission can possibly be. But I cannot overlook the facts, and I do not care to overlook the facts.

They tell us that we were cruel. Were we? I will not charge any of these wrongs upon the poor, stuttering Pole, or the Slav, or the Goths, or the vandals, or any of the rest. I think it comes with a poor grace from these men who have taken their labor for years to charge that they cannot speak English, and are therefore not responsible for their contracts, and are men who commit crime. I will not concede for a moment that the evidence in this case or what I know of my fellow-man shows that this body of men is worse than other men; and I do not want to take the responsibility from the Irish or the Welsh or the English or any other class of men who can speak the language that we speak and place it upon the shoulders of these poor men—unlettered, uneducated, close to nature, but doing the best they can. A warm-hearted, sympathetic, emotional, religious people, living close to the heart of nature and feeling her every pulse beat—these men are the peers in courage, in devotion, in conscience of any man who lived.

The evidence in this case may show that they more often

overstepped the law. It may. But there is the law of the land and there is the moral law.

Let us look at this case of Winsdon, which, I take it, is the clearest and the best-defined of any case that has been brought to the attention of this commission, where it is claimed that mine workers committed some depredation.

Take the case of Winsdon. The evidence in this case shows that three Poles living near Mr. Winsdon's house committed this act. Mr. Winsdon had been a member of the union, and, as I recall it, an officer of the union. He had gone out on the strike. He had stayed out, as his wife tells us, I believe, until he had no money, and being a mine worker, of course that was not very long. Then he went back to work. He and his son-in-law started down the garden walk, out of the back door to go to work, when their brethren were on a strike—a strike in as righteous a cause, I believe, as ever men fought for. In one way I would excuse Mr. Winsdon; in another way I would not. Under the laws of the land he had a perfect right to go to work, and no man had the right to molest him in any way. That is perfectly true.

No man has the right, the moral right—whatever his legal may be—no man has the moral right even to work when that work interferes with the social, the moral, the living relations of his fellow-man, and I do not speak the words of dreamers. I can speak the words of law. We have for years excluded the Chinese from this country because we believe that to bring them here at the wages for which they work will reduce our American workingmen (whom we profess to love so fondly) to the standard of the Chinese, and we say "No, you may not work." We have regulated the hours of children, the hours of women, the pay of men—even the hours at which man may toil in certain callings, and even generally the hours, as was done in Utah, and held to be valid by our Supreme Court, as I understand.

We have by law denied any such absurd principle as that there are no times and occasions when a man has not the right to work. For instance: Supposing a body of men were willing to work eighteen or twenty hours and to live upon rats, or any other cheap diet. Can any man tell me they have the moral right to do it, if by that means, as most inevitably would result, they are lowering the standard of life of the American people, which is the most jealous thing for us to preserve?

Man is an individual animal and he is a social animal. He must even work in such a way as to promote the welfare of his race, and I take it that no mind that feels justice can look in any way except with contempt at the person who will voluntarily, of his own free will, see fit to undermine and underbid his fellow-man and lower his condition in life. Mr. Winsdon was doing this. Mind, I am not charging this up against him. Mr. Winsdon had a wife and children and undoubtedly to him the pressure seemed great, for he himself had been a striker. He had recognized the justice of this holy cause. He had called upon his brethren to lay down their tools with him, and he had gone out to meet this very same condition in which he found himself when he walked down the walk. I presume the necessities were great; and yet, he did not need to starve. Men could live there, even, for ten million men, all the honest toilers of America were turning in their money to support these miners. Every man whose heart beat for humanity was giving his mite to keep them alive in this terrible contest.

These men were out in this struggle. They saw Winsdon and his son-in-law going to work against them, against their wives and their children, against their country, against their instincts of justice and of fair play and of righteousness, and they went out in the morning and hit them over the head with a club. No, I have no idea in the world that they ever intended to kill him. They did intend, of course, to beat him. They did intend to drive him from his work. They did intend to violate the law, and this court may do what this court thinks is right and just as to that matter. But I cannot look at the condition of those men without considering their environment, without considering their long and bitter struggle, without remembering that they did not do this because they were criminals, but they did it from a mistaken, a sorely mistaken sense of what they thought was the right.

We do not excuse it or condone it. We would be glad to welcome any conditions which would make these things impossible; but I want to say to this commission that you cannot preach a sermon loud enough or long enough or use the English language vigorously enough, to abate one jot or one tittle of the same thing if the same conditions should arise again. There is but one way to prevent this, and that one way is to teach our captains of industry that they must respect their fellow-men.

If these gentlemen had met John Mitchell and John Mitchell's organization, Winsdon would have been alive today, and so would the three or four more victims whom they killed, to say nothing of the three more victims whose bodies have been directly or indirectly traced to the doors of the mine workers. You cannot cure it in any other way. It is idle and futile and useless to talk of curing it in any other way. But there was force and violence present in this case for which men are more nearly responsible than this. Let us see about that, for after all it is a pleasanter subject to me, and I think it has more direct bearing upon this case. All these matters were consequences. They were results. Here and there dynamite was used, never once to destroy life, always to frighten. Always deplorable; we deplore it. Counsel for the nonunion men say that the strikers abused women. Where? Where? It must be said for this body of men, 147,000 strong, that in this long warfare there is no one word in this case showing where they have raised their hands against a woman or against a child; not once. They called them scabs at times, that is true; but they were always safe—as safe as if one hundred policemen stood on guard. These men were not criminals. These men were men engaged in a great contest, in which the feelings and passions and emotions of men were stirred, and when the contest is over I will guarantee that you will find that each one of these poor men is as decent, as honest, as humane, as generous, as kind, as loving, as any other man who ever lived. When the feeling and the cause are gone, then the normal man is the man again; whether operator or workman, the rule holds good and must hold good.

But there were some of these operators who were less kind. How about Mr. Markle? There are all sorts of force. I insist that Mr. Baer's definition will never do. I have no doubt but what every gentleman of this commission will at once disagree with Mr. Baer in saying that no man has any duties except his legal duties. He says if we were to consider moral rights where would we come out? Where would we end? One man thinks one thing is a moral right and another man thinks another thing is a moral right. Well, I have known lawyers to disagree as to legal rights quite as much as moralists disagree as to moral rights, and perhaps more. The whole training and education of the youth and the man is to teach them the difference between right and wrong in human relations, to teach them those relations which make for the peace and the good order and well-being of society, and those which are anti-social and tend to the disorder of society. There are moral rights and there are legal rights.

After the strike was over Mr. Markle felt so outraged and so incensed that his men dared to strike that he used force more inexcusable and more to be condemned than any violence of any ignorant man that has been proven in this case. The war, you remember, was over. The President had settled it and the men had gone back to work. Then he evicted thirteen men, not one of whom had committed a crime so far as this record goes. Among the thirteen, he picked out one man who had been more than thirty years in his and his father's employment. He not only said he would not employ these thirteen men again, but he drove them from their homes. All of this took place after this commission was appointed, directly in the face and under the eyes of this commission appointed to settle this controversy, and whilst this man was within the jurisdiction of this commission, corresponding with it at least. Had this commission been a court, with the powers of a court, every bit of this would have been in utter contempt of court and worthy of a sentence in a common jail.

What is the first step in these proceedings? We find Mr. Wright[1] telegraphing to Mr. Markle that this commission had been appointed and asking him whether he wanted to come in. Upon that day we find him sending word to his men to bring in their brass checks, which meant they were to be discharged and hired over again if he wanted to hire them over again. Then we find him answering this communication from Mr. Wright and saying that he did not know whether he would come in or not, that he was having some difficulty with his men. Then we find that his men went there in a body and, hearing the rumors of this discrimination, told Mr. Markle that they would not come back unless they could come all together. Then

[1] Carroll D. Wright, secretary of the commission.

we find Mr. Markle giving notice that he would not hire them all and then sending a communication to Mr. Wright saying that he was having some difficulty with his men, some of them who had committed criminal offenses would not be taken back and he could not tell yet whether he would enter into negotiations with this commission or not. Then he goes to his lawyer and he takes his cutthroat lease, a lease at the will and the pleasure of John Markle at 15½ cents a day, containing a clause allowing a confession of judgment, and he hands it to his lawyer, who signs his name to it, and he confesses judgment to oust James Gallagher from his home. Then when the last one of these men is ousted, he sends word to this commission that he is ready to come into court. That is John Markle. Can anyone imagine a more cruel and heartless eviction than this?

How did he do it? Mind you, there was not one of these men who had ever committed a crime. I will guarantee that if Mr. Gallagher's brain could be taken out and weighed it would be the equal of Mr. Markle's, and if you weighed his conscience in some way you would find there is more of it. I suppose his lungs are blacker, as has been demonstrated in this case happens to all miners, but that is another question.

Mr. Gallagher says that he had served there for 31 years and he defies them to show one black mark against him. If that is so, he has done better than I could have done. Possibly it would trouble any of us to do as well. Nothing but a very faithful and very obedient man could have that record. But, anyhow, he was not discharged because he had committed a crime; neither were any of the rest. What was he discharged for? Why, his son had been a member of the relief committee, that is the nearest he could get to it. He had gone around feeding women and children against Markle's will and pleasure, for under his will and pleasure, which were the terms of his lease, these men, women and children should die, or go back into the mines. The others were officers of the union, everyone of them officers and leading members. He got his attorney to confess judgment, and the men waited, as men always do wait when they are being driven from their homes, not believing that John Markle could do it, or that any human being could do it. They waited and John Markle's lawyer goes over to Wilkes-Barre at twelve o'clock at night and gets the papers and brings the Sheriff, or directs the Sheriff to be there early the next morning. He comes there in the morning at eight o'clock and comes to the door of these men, and he goes to Henry Coll, among the rest, whose wife was lying sick upon her bed and whose blind mother-in-law, a hundred years old, was lying sick upon her bed, and Henry Coll begged of the Sheriff to give him two hours' time, not two days, but two hours, to find a place where he could lay his sick wife and his blind mother-in-law.

The Sheriff said, "I will see what I can do," and he went down to John Markle's office. There he found John Markle and John Markle's lawyer in the office waiting for this eviction and, according to the testimony of his general superintendent of evictions, the Sheriff asked John Markle, and John Markle turned to his lawyer and undoubtedly his lawyer knew what kind of advice John Markle wanted. He had doubtless worked for him before and he said, "No, you had better not do it, they might get out an injunction against you." An injunction! As if any court would ever issue an injunction in a case like that. An injunction to keep a poor devil in a house worth four dollars a month for a few more days. Why, if an injunction had been granted in that case John Markle's mine would have filled with water, and Mr. Baer would have said that the fabric of civilization would tumble down around our heads.

Henry Coll asked for two hours, and, according to one story, he was answered "not ten minutes"; according to another story, "no." Probably the latter is more correct, because it is shorter. John Markle sent his superintendent, while he stayed in the office, his superintendent of evictions Williams, and they got some wagons, because there were some of those fellows who were far away from the highway, the only place where those poor people had to lay their heads, and they had to load the goods into the wagons; and in one place they found a barrel of sauerkraut, which showed they were not quite starved out, and in another place I think thirty bushels of potatoes, and that is all the commissary that was left so far as this record goes.

And they dumped them out into the middle of the street, and

the superintendent was there, and John Markle in his office, closeted with an attorney.

They took out their stoves and their chairs and their beds and their sauerkraut, and they left them in the street. And they got through with this glorious job at six o'clock at night of a November day, when the rain was coming down and it was dark, and they were there upon the street—men, women, children; the well, the sick, the blind, the infirm, the helpless, two miles from any shelter. And then the superintendent turned his back upon them and drove away and went home and got his supper and reported to John Markle!

Gentlemen of the commission, you may roll together all the cruelty and all the violence and all the misery that all of these irresponsible Goths and vandals have committed in the anthracite region; you may pack them in one, and they cannot equal the fiendish cruelty of John Markle when the cause was gone, and he turned these helpless people into the street simply to satisfy his hellish hate.

There are all kinds of violence in this world. It is cruel. I would like to live in a world where there is none of this cruelty and this inhumanity of man to man. I have never found that it was all upon one side or by one class. It flows from the feelings of man; and when judges condemn it they must condemn that feeling wherever it is, and however it manifests itself, or whether it manifests itself at all; because it is the feeling that is bad, and not the man that is bad.

I do not propose to judge John Markle. Very likely he may have some religion or some philosophy that justifies his cruelty. But his acts are bad, inexcusably bad; more inexcusably bad than the casual, uncertain, violent acts of any of the weak and poor people who have been charged here with crime.

There was violence. I regret it. I cannot help regretting it. I know that in this great contest I stand for the weak. I have stood for them, for now these many years. I know that the other side has every means for influencing public opinion. I know that I cannot come even before as fair-minded and as high-minded a body of men as this before me and expect all of our positions to be fairly understood or given fair weight. I know that we speak in a way against things that are. I believe that we dream of things that are yet to come, and hope for things that the future still holds in store for us; and I know that whenever violence and bloodshed ensues, these gentlemen, with all their power and their means of influence, are ever ready to charge it to us. I believe there is no laboring man and no friend of the laboring man but deprecates it and hates it and grieves over it, as I know I deprecate it and hate it and grieve over it. I want to say in fairness to the other side who have said to me: "Oh, but you have not disciplined your men. You have not discharged them from the union," that if my advice were asked, I would not do it.

I would use all my power and endeavor to prevent these things, if I could, but I would withdraw from no human being, no matter who he is, no matter what he had done, or what he might do. I would never think of withdrawing from him one single prop or support that might possibly help him the more to be a man.

But what of the boycott? This is in the same line. I might first, in speaking of boycott, refer to one historical example. You and I may form our notions upon the strict line of ethics as we see that line, but the world does not move upon that line and never did. Hatred and bitterness never produced a result in the hearts of men and in the hands of men. We have one illustrious example, at least, in the United States of the boycott, of violence, of the scab, and that was in the Revolution.

I have just been reading the history of the leaders of the American Revolution, written by one of the professors of the University of Pennsylvania. There is not one specific act that is charged to the mine workers in this case but was charged to these revolutionaries—to those men whom we regard today as patriots, and whom on every fourth day of July we teach our children to love, venerate and respect. Not one.

On the other hand, one hundred thousand men in America, men good and true, men of culture and refinement, clergymen, lawyers, judges, bankers, a hundred thousand loyalists who moved in the highest society, were driven from their homes into exile, their houses burned, men murdered, stoned, hung in effigy, boycotted, refused association, absolutely driven from the United States never to return. Nova Scotia was almost settled by these men. While today you can scarcely find a man in America who would trace his lineage to loyalists, everybody, whether they have a right to it or not, are proud to trace their lineage to the fathers who built up this country through their blood and their suffering and their toil. The forces of the law are sometimes one thing, the forces of society and the forces of nature are quite another.

You and I may sit here and judge men by the dead letter of the law. We may say that this act is right and that act is wrong, but up there sits the living God and He judges the acts of men by another standard from ours. He does not weigh with our scales, nor measure with our short tape lines. He would prepare the continent to raise wheat for men and He sends a glacier from the north to grind it and to pulverize the soil. He would prepare the human race and He chooses a way which may be simply divine to Him, but which we in our weakness and our shortsightedness cannot comprehend and cannot understand. You cannot make me believe that the God who it is said notes the fall of every sparrow was unmindful when James Winsdon was killed, or that He was unmindful when the Coal and Iron Police shot Patrick Sharp, but rather that in His own infinite way and for His own infinite purposes, which we cannot understand, He let this work out for the eternal betterment of all in the end.

Now, what about the boycott? Let me say there is the legal side and the moral side. The boycott is an ancient and a respectable weapon; it is respectable when they use it, but not respectable when we use it. That is like all other weapons—like a gun or a sword or a revolver. It first came into prominent use in this country at the time of the American Revolution, but it was old then. Then our American women, much as they liked pretty clothes, in those days refused to wear them if they were made in England or spun in England. Then they refused to meet anybody who wore clothes made in England or spun in England.

Then they refused to meet anybody that did not refuse to meet anybody that wore clothes made in England or spun in England. (*Laughter*.) This was our ancient boycott. It was in what we now believe to be a righteous cause; and when our historians tell about it they do not say: Oh, how wicked and how cruel and how illegal, and they do not go into a panic and say: Why did you not apply for an injunction to prevent it? They recognize it as one of the means that was used then to gain independence.

We might have got it without. I do not know, nobody knows; but they got it that way. Now, I have been boycotted a great deal myself. I expect to be as long as I live. Sometimes rightfully and sometimes wrongfully, generally wrongfully. It is one of the penalties that we all pay for doing the particular things we do. Sometimes it is a penalty we pay for doing right, sometimes a penalty we pay for doing wrong; it is a penalty for doing differently from what the other people wish us to. It is the very same principle that makes us choose our companions, our society, those we wish to live with and associate with.

We wish to live with and associate with those who are like us, who believe with us, who sympathize with us and are part of us, and we boycott the rest. Now, I take it, that if I wish to trade with John Smith, I can. First, I am talking about the legal part, then I want to say a word about the moral part of it, because I am one of those old-fashioned people who believes there is a difference between the moral law and the civil law. Once in a while they meet, but not often. If I wish to trade with Smith I may; if I do not wish to trade with him, I need not. It may be because I do not like the color of his hair, it may be because I do not believe in the way he worships God, it may be because I think he does not pay enough wages. At any rate, unless I may do this, I am not free; and I may do it.

I may not only refuse to trade with Smith, but if my feeling is strong enough against Smith so that I believe he is an evil force in the community, I may go so far as to say I will not trade with anybody who trades with Smith. It results in this, and it ever must result in this and ever has resulted in this. Wherever the feeling is intense enough and deep enough, men are divided into hostile camps. Take the coal strike, a great contest which interested every man, woman and child.

You were either for it or against it. Take the War of the Rebellion, about which I heard in my old Western Reserve home in Ohio, a place from which John Brown went forth on some of his glorious illegal expeditions to free the slaves. We used to hear of it there, you hear of it everywhere. If the feeling is deep enough, men range themselves into hostile camps. The man who stands for liberty is my friend, the man who stood for John Brown was my friend, the man who stood for slavery was not my friend. I lived with my class. I ate with them, drank with them, worshiped with them. I associated with them and I passed the others on the other side. So we have here in the coal region, in this greatest conflict of modern times. Nothing else was discussed, nothing else could be discussed. From one end of the country to the other men were taking sides, the poor were sending their wages to keep the miners on a strike, the rich were asking for soldiers to shoot them down. I must be on one side or the other. I loved my side and I hated the other side. If a conflict is deep enough these two rival camps live separate and distinct from each other and the boycott is there.

That is the evolution of it, and courts may condemn it to the day of doom and they cannot affect it. Here is the distinction which the criminal law makes. If I, out of malice to John Smith— and the criminal law must look to the human heart, for it is a maxim of the criminal law that there can be no crime unless the heart is criminal—if I, out of malice to him, go abroad and seek to get other men to stay away from him, to destroy him, that is a crime, but if I, for the defense of myself, for the defense of my race, for the defense of what I believe are the rights of men, see fit to avoid John Smith, I have the right to avoid him and he has the right to avoid me.

You may say, and say well, that the law cannot always determine whether the motive is good or bad, but the law must determine whether the motive is good or bad. The boycott is a right. It is a right which they take and have a right to take.

A man wants a lawyer, for instance—I have had it happen to me a good many times—I have been discussed and some say, "Oh,

no, do not get him, he is a disturber, we will get somebody else."
I cannot help it. Of course, I go off and mourn about it, but I cannot help it. I know I have to stand it. It is one of the penalties I pay for my opinion, and if I should run for an office I am dead sure I would be boycotted by any number of people because they would say, "He is dangerous, you cannot trust him." If some other man runs for an office who is a friend of the powers I think are in the wrong, then my friends boycott him and say, "Oh, we can't have him, he is an old fogey."

It always exists, it always has existed. I do not believe in it at all as an ultimate, and if I get along to it, as I think I will, toward five o'clock, I will explain just what I think about it. I am going to finish today and leave the commission to imagine the things I have not said.

The scab stands in exactly the same relation as the boycott. The scab is a man who goes in to take the place of his fellow-man who is working for better conditions. He always has been hated, he always will be hated. Sometimes he is a good man, often he acts from necessity, but he is a man who is a traitor to his class. He is a man who is used by the capitalist to destroy the rights and the aspirations and the hopes of the workingman. We have heard a great deal in this country of late about the scab. I use this word, I want the commission to understand, because it is commonly used, not because I like it or approve of it, because I do not. I speak frankly, because it is the word commonly used and is in all the literature upon this question. We have heard a great deal about him in these modern days.

*　　*　　*

Mr. Baer and his friends imagine, no doubt, that they are fighting for a grand principle when they fight for what they say is the God-given right of every man to work for any wages he sees fit. I do not know about any such God-given right. It is a little uncertain. But that is not a God-given right these gentlemen are interested in. They are interested in the God-given right to hire the cheapest man they can get. They have less use for a scab than we have, and they always have had less use for a scab than we have had.

As a class this body of men, as has been shown in this case, has always been ready to take the benefits that flow from organized labor, and never been willing to fight to obtain them. They have been ready, after the dangers have been encountered and the contest is over, to come in and take the wages, but they never have been ready to face starvation and hunger and abuse in the common cause. As a rule the scab is a man who has no abiding place on the face of the earth. He does not live anywhere or stay anywhere. He does not come because he believes in anything or has any convictions on any subject on earth. He is a wandering tramp, ready to be used by anybody who will pay the price to use him; and they ship him from one city to another and from one country to another, and then ship him from Philadelphia and from New York and from Chicago to the coal regions to take the place of men engaged in a heroic struggle for their liberty. And then, when the strike is over, they let him walk home again or let the union send him home.

That is his history. That is what he has come to be recognized as by men who have studied this question and who have written upon the subject.

* * *

In these great social travails for the elevation of the working classes the union has ever been the most potent power and the greatest influence. The scab is not the man who refuses to join a union. He may have sentimental reasons. He may not care to. He may really believe in it, as some men believe in the church, without absolutely joining it. But he is the man who, in the midst of one of these great conflicts, lends his aid and encouragement and help against his class. He is the man whom they use, as they used him here in this contest with the United Mine Workers, to try to destroy their union and break the strike, and whom they have used in this court under the sanction of an oath up to the last moment of this trial, with the false claim that he is present by attorney in this court.

He has been true to his character from beginning to end. He is the pliant tool of the men who in this great struggle, wisely or unwisely, are against the laboring man. And it cannot be but that he will be despised, mistrusted, hated and reviled by all men who love liberty and who love their fellow-men, and who have the point of view of the organized laboring man.

Now I must say a word about the eight-hour question; and I am sure I am leaving much unsaid, and perhaps I should have left much of the rest unsaid. But I have been talking my honest feelings in this case as they have come to me, regardless of what I think of the judgment or the inclination of any gentlemen of this commission, recognizing simply that they wish me while I speak to speak the truth as I see it and understand it, and leave the responsibility with you.

Let us see about the eight-hour question.

This demand for eight hours is not a demand to shirk work as is often claimed to be the case. It is a demand for the right of the individual to have a better life, a fuller life, a completer life; and this, like everything else, depends upon your point of view. If I were to measure this demand from the standpoint of Mr. Baer, I might be against it. I cannot say. I believe he is wrong, even from his own standpoint; but I do not measure it from his. I measure it from the standpoint of the man, from the standpoint that the interest of government, the interest of society, the interest of law and of all social institutions is to make the best man they can.

That is what you are here for today. That is the purpose of every law-making power. It is the purpose of every church. It is the purpose of every union. It is the purpose of every organization that ever had the right to live since the world began. There is only one standpoint from which you can have a right to approach this question, and that is, what will make the best man, the longest life, the strongest man, the most intelligent man, the best American citizen, to build up a nation that we will be proud of—a nation in which there will be no more strikes and no more violence, either by them or by us.

This commission can view it in no other light, and I would argue it in no other way. Other gentlemen may measure it in dollars and cents. I shall not. Until the American people have gone so far and moved so high that they can view a subject from an ethical standpoint, I do not care to speak to them. If I cannot address them upon that side I will be silent.

Is it in accordance with the evolution of man, with what is best, that we should work eight hours, or more or less? "Ah," these gentlemen say, "but we work longer." No, you do not work longer. I know the lives of men of my class. I come to my office at nine o'clock in the morning, sometimes, and I stay until five, sometimes. Sometimes I may stay longer, sometimes shorter. But the rest of my time I have for those purposes of improvement or of pleasure that seem to me to respond to the necessities of my being and to make as much of myself as I possibly can.

There is nothing high and ennobling and great in digging coal —nothing. This is work. It does not tend to the moral being, to the spiritual being, to the intellectual being. Not that! These gentlemen who toil in the mines or at the breaker must look upon this only as toil—as toil to furnish them the means of life, for bettering their condition or improving their brain, for giving them a wider insight into the great questions of life and the great questions of humanity, which, after all, are the only things worth living for, when everything is said and done.

Is eight hours enough? Is it enough? What one of us—it is right to place ourselves with them—would wish to go down below the earth and work nine or ten hours? It will not do to say, "Ah, but they are a different class from us." They are not. Under other circumstances, with their brains and yours, some of them might have been here and you might have been there. I can point you to men among my clients who are the peers of any of us. Nature sent them to digging in the earth, while it placed you and me in responsible positions where we could develop the highest faculties that God had given us.

That is the difference, and that is all. Now, the manual worker who asks for shorter hours asks for what? He asks for a breath of life; he asks for a chance to develop the best that is in him. It is no answer to say, as some employers have said in this case, "If you give him shorter hours he will not use them wisely."

He will not use them wisely? This is scarcely worth reply.

Our country, our civilization, our race, is formed upon the belief that, after all, God has planted in man something that does make him use his privileges for the best; that, after all, with all his weakness and his imperfection, there is still in him that divine spark which makes him reach upward and upward for something higher and better than he has ever known; and he will use it for the best.

One man may stumble, ten men may stumble, but in the long sweep of time and in the evolution of events it must be that greater opportunities mean a more perfect man, mean a higher being, mean a better individual life, mean a better social life, mean higher and better moral and ethical ideas because of the opportunities that were given. If this were not true, then progress would be impossible. We must assume, in all of these discussions, that the tendency of man is toward perfection: the tendency is upward and upward and onward, toward the heights to which the human race has not even yet aspired in its wildest dreams. And it is given to us, in our humble way, and with our limited power, to help that tendency to build up men, and it is all that we can do.

I do not care to dispute with Mr. Baer as to whether he will be obliged to build a new breaker or not. I could prove from these tables—and I simply suggest it and leave the commission to work it out—that last year it would not have added more than twenty minutes—it would not have shortened the working day more than twenty minutes to have had a full eight-hour day, and I will simply suggest how. The breakers now do not average eight hours. Cut off every day where the breaker runs less than eight hours. Those days would not be affected. Only those days where the breakers have run more than eight hours would be affected, and when you take every day that has run more than eight hours and cut it off you will find it does not decrease the working day twenty minutes, according to the tables that are in possession of this commission and on file here. Nothing is impossible if you want to accomplish it, and anything is impossible if you do not wish to accomplish it.

I have no doubt that Mr. Baer could bring me a string of figures reaching from here to his New York office to prove that the world would come to an end if we did not employ child labor in the breaker; and if he made me believe it I would say: "All right; let us stop working the children. After all, I think perhaps the human race was wrong, and we had better get rid of it and start over again, and see if something cannot be developed."

I presume that the figures of these gentlemen might prove anything, but that has nothing to do with this question. It is not for me to discuss whether Mr. Baer must build a new breaker. That is his business. I do not propose, if I can help it, to have Mr. Baer stand in the way of the progress of the human race for the sake of any breaker in the anthracite region. If they cannot run this industry with what they have got they must build more; and if this commission are as broad and wise as I believe they are they will never consider that question in their deliberations.

Why, the old philosophers 2,000 years ago, who were dreamers then—I do not know who the "practical businessmen" were; their names have been forgotten, and they have not come down to us— the old philosophers of 2,000 years ago used to look forward into this nineteenth and twentieth century and dream of the day when the brain and the intellect and the ingenuity of man would give birth to wonderful machines that would do the work of the human race, and when men could be freed and left to work out their highest development and the best that was in them without the trouble of work. That day has come. We have these wonderful machines. Why, within 125 years, within a hundred years, the productive power of man has been increased in England and America almost twenty-fold; some say more.

We have learned to apply steam and electricity, and have made such cunning machines that they almost seem to think, and yet in spite of this, although the human brain has devised these machines to do the work of man, our men must toil and our boys and girls must continue to be serfs.

If we have the will there is the way, and the way is easy. Let me suggest this: Man, whenever he has turned his attention to improving his condition, has been able to do it. Whenever wages are high he invents machines to supplement his work and aid in the production of things. In America, where wages are the highest, machines are the plentiest. Take these children from the breaker and shorten this day and the clumsy machinery will be improved. You will find ways to increase the production of your breaker and ways to increase the production of your mine, and you will never miss the little boys with their black faces, and you will never be sorry that you allowed these men to live a little while longer on the face of the earth.

You may go back to Egypt and you will find there where you can hire men for ten cents a day and five cents a day, men harnessed to mills and wearily pacing around to draw water up from the earth; because it is cheaper in Egypt to do that than it is to build a windmill or an engine. Here they have a windmill or they have an engine, because they believe in the dignity of man. If man is a machine, set him to work to draw the water, to hew the wood, and consider him principally or solely as to how many dollars and cents you can work him into. If the question is how much you can get out of a man, work him twenty-four hours a day and let him die; or work him fourteen hours a day and kill him in a little longer time; or work him twelve hours a day and destroy him yet more slowly. But if the question is the greater and the broader and the higher question—what is a man worth and what is a man for—then it must address itself to the mind of this commission and to the minds of every man, what hours are best for him? What will develop his highest life, his body, his mind, his soul, his aspirations, his hopes—all that there is in him and of him or may be in him and of him?

Do you doubt that the eight-hour day is coming? Does anybody doubt that it is coming? It is here, in many, many industries. It is here in the soft-coal field. It is here in a large number of industries and vocations pursued by man. Do you suppose ten years from now or fifteen years from now we will be discussing over this eight-hour question? And can this commission, charged with one of the greatest responsibilities that ever devolved on any commission or body of men since history began—and I do not say it lightly, because I can see in it possibilities which perhaps none of us dream of, which perhaps were not even thought of when we were brought together in conference. It seems to me that after this there can never be a great strife or contest like this; that if the commission is wise, as they will be; if they are broad, as they will be; if they build for the future, as they will; if they build for what is the highest for men, the grandest and the best for the human race; this will be one of the milestones in the progress of the world. We will never go back to the past. We will never go back to what has gone. You, my friends, the employers, and you, my friends, the workmen, will learn to be brothers; will learn that there is a better way in this world than calling hard names and throwing stones and shooting guns and invoking starvation to settle your disputes.

* * *

Now, gentlemen of the Commission, I have spoken about as long as I will upon this case. I want to say a few more words about this union and some of the fault that has been found with it.

These labor organizations have never gone to their employers and asked them to fix up a schedule by which they could organize their union. If they had done this they would never have had any union, and if they had had a union it would have been utterly impotent and useless. This is ours, and while it is full of imperfections, like all human work of miners and dreamers, still it is the best we could do. We have tried to patch it somewhat since this commission commenced its sittings, and we are willing to patch it more. There are things in the constitution of which I do not approve. One clause especially, which was placed in there in view of the Homestead riots, which, I believe, has no relation to the miners' case, and that is, that they protest against officers to guard property. I have no doubt that a man who has property may hire anybody he sees fit to go in and guard and protect it, and I have no fault to find with it, neither; I take it. Have they? But they need not expect impossibilities of us. We are willing to accept their friendly aid and counsel, but when they come into court and allege this excuse or that for not dealing with us, or not recognizing that we are on earth, then it comes with a bad grace from them.

We have opened our books; we have shown you all we have; we have given you our by-laws, our rules, and kept no secret from you, and you have not even given us a copy of yours, and we have not asked you for a copy of yours. I assume they are made by your lawyers to serve your ends and not to serve ours. This is our business. Neither do I take kindly to the suggestion of those gentlemen that we should incorporate. As if there is no responsibility excepting the responsibility that comes to incorporated capital. Strange as it may seem, in some respects, I am very old-fashioned. I think a real man is about as important as an incorporated man; that a real flesh-and-blood workman is about as important as a composite workman used to figure wages from. I do not believe in this wild mania of incorporation. It has no sort of place with a trade union. You want to teach the people of the United States this new, strange doctrine, this doctrine of wealth, that, forsooth, a person which man made, which is a corporation, is greater than a person which God made, which is an individual? It is a false doctrine. It has produced infinite evil in America, and its evil has just begun. I am not willing to admit for a single moment that anything can be gained for manhood, for righteousness, for the good of all, by going to some petty state legislature and asking to merge the individual flesh-and-blood man into a corporation created by the State. Why, we were told in the argument that the state of New Jersey—of all places on earth the state of New Jersey— had introduced a law to compel labor organizations to incorporate! I understand they have introduced one at Springfield, Illinois, but it will not pass. They tell us here that the state of New Jersey is going to pass such a law. Nobody can tell what will happen in New Jersey. New Jersey has been busy with the incorporation business, very busy indeed. New Jersey has issued its bogus charters and sent them broadcast over the United States, its charters which have been simply letters of marque and reprisal for every pirate that sails the high seas of commerce to capture what he can get, until New Jersey has become a stench and a byword in the minds of all people who believe in fair dealing and justice between man and man. These gentlemen do not wish to incorporate.

They are good enough as God made them, and they are trying to get better just as fast as their masters will let them. If you want them to be financially responsible, I will tell you how to do it: just raise their wages. An incorporated man has not any more money than an unincorporated man, unless he peddles his watered stock upon somebody more ignorant than himself, and, of course, we cannot do that, we cannot find the people. Of all the nonsense that has been indulged in by the false and chimerical friends of labor unions—and I do not know but sometimes here and there they have got our real friends, I would want further investigation about that, and I think they would want further—this talk about incorporation is about the most useless. It has gone so far that I know in Chicago some of the fellows have commenced incorporating political parties, and they have an idea that if four or five fellows get incorporation for the Democratic party they can go and enjoin anybody else who undertakes to call a convention. They have incorporated the Public Ownership party, the Municipal Ownership League, the People's party and various branches of the Democratic party. They have not yet tried to incorporate the whole Democratic party; perhaps after a few more campaigns they may be able to do it. But that is another question.

We have grown corporation mad, and it all comes from this false and distorted and baneful idea that money is everything. Now we are not interested in money, excepting wages. We want some of it, but we are not in the business of selling watered stock or of issuing bonds or anything, and we do not understand how you can make the coal miners responsible by incorporating them; and if we did, we would not want it and do not propose to have anything whatever to do with it.

Just a few words about the union and what it stands for, and then I am going to leave you to imagine all the rest that I know I would have said if I had had anything like a reasonable time to speak in.

*   *   *

Trade unionism is not all good. I have been its friend in my own way for a good many years. I have fought some of its battles with the best ability and all the sincerity that I could give to its cause, for I believe in it. It is like every other instrument created by man—it is not perfect, and it is an evolutionary stage. I do not claim that this order of the United Mine Workers is perfect. We have brought together in two short years 147,000 men, who speak twenty different languages, of all degrees of intelligence, of all degrees of moral character, and we have molded them as near as possible into one homogeneous mass. God knows they are not perfect. But I ask you, gentlemen of the commission, where else in the history of the world has any general, either in industrial life or on the field of battle, in two short years molded together such a heterogeneous mass into such grand and valiant and brave and noble veterans as these who faced starvation for their fellow-man? Where else has such a body of men done as well? And when you judge us and pronounce upon us, pronounce sentence of good or sentence of evil, I wish you to judge us in the light of all the impossibilities that confronted us; in the light of the severe travail through which we passed; in the light of the material which we were bound to use; in the light of the fearful, appalling odds that we faced. Judge us in that light, and we will stand by this verdict.

I am not here to pronounce any eulogiums upon men, neither am I here to condemn them. But I want to call the attention of the commission to the officers and the leaders of this magnificent body who have fought this glorious fight and who have won this brilliant victory, whose rewards will be reaped so long as men and women live upon the earth. I want to say one word for that cool, calm, considerate, humane leader who, from the beginning to the end, has come out of every contest victorious, has faced every situation and won—not because he is wiser, not because he is greater, not because he is better than the rest, but because his face is turned toward the morning and the future, and he is moving with the progress of the world.

The blunders are theirs, and the victories have been ours. The blunders are theirs because, in this old, old strife, they are fighting for slavery, while we are fighting for freedom. They are fighting for the rule of man over man, for despotism, for darkness, for the past. We are striving to build up man. We are working for democracy, for humanity, for the future, for the day that will come too late for us to see it or know it or receive its benefits, but which still will come, and will remember our struggles, our triumphs, our defeats, and the words which we spake.

These men are not perfect. No men are perfect. No organization is perfect. Trade unionism in some ways is exclusive, is monopolistic. It does think more of the men who are in it and of it and with it. I do not believe in monopolies and exclusion. I, too, am something of a dreamer. I long for a time when there will be no exclusion and no monopoly and no boycott, either by them or by us—for a day of universal brotherhood, when there will be no trade unions and no employers. Trade unions are for today, for the present. They may be characterized as war measures, as agencies in this great problem of lifting the human race to the heights to which it will one day come. They are agencies, mediums for that. They are the greatest agency that the wit of man has ever devised for uplifting the lowly and the weak, for defending the poor and the oppressed, for bringing about genuine democracy amongst men. They cannot fight forever, let us hope, with the boycott or against the scab.

I long for the time when the boycott will die; when no man can look at his brother and say to him, "In my regard you are not my equal"; when each man will associate with his fellow-men on equal terms; when no man will be a unionist or a scab; when no man will be an employer or an employed.

My dreams, in the few moments which I can give to dreams, are of a universal republic, where every man is a man equal before his Maker, governor of himself, ruler of himself and the peer of all who live; where none will be excluded; where all will be included; where the work of the trade union is done and trade unions have melted and dissolved. And I love trade unions, because I believe they are one of the greatest agencies that the world has ever known to bring about this time; one of those agencies for the building up of character and the building up of men, and toward forming that ideal republic which has been the hope and the aspiration and the dream of every great soul that ever lived and wrought and died for his fellow-man.

Gentlemen of the commission, I have talked long in this case. I feel, in leaving it, that there are many things I would have wished to discuss. My regret is only that I could not be of more service than I have. I presume that is the regret of us all. I may have been severe here and there upon some of these operators or all of them. I have meant to say my say kindly, justly, charitably. In my heart I have no feeling against one of these men. No doubt, no doubt they want to do the right. I do believe, as Mr. Olyphant believed of us, that they have been misled; that they are blindly setting their faces against progress; that they are standing in the way of the natural, peaceful, laudable evolution of the human race. I do believe that if they will learn to come to us as brothers, as friends, as kindred, they will find that we will extend the right hand of fellowship. I do believe that if they will recognize the God in our men as we will recognize the God in them, we will join hands with them to make a paradise out of this land which has flowed with blood.

I wish they knew us. I wish they could understand that back of the black hands of these, their servants, back of the black faces of these men that go down into the mines are consciences, intellects, hearts and minds as true as in any man who ever lived. I wish they might know us—that we are here and we are there to do our duty, not only by ourselves and for ourselves, but to do our duty to them; to do our duty to that great mass of people who, while not directly interested in this contest, still have suffered because of it. If they meet us, if they recognize us, if they come to us and let us come to them, we will prove that we are their brothers and their friends.

This contest is one of the important contests that has marked the progress of human liberty since the world began—one force pointing one way, another force the other. Every advantage that the human race has won has been at fearful cost, at great contest, at suffering endured. Every contest has been won by struggle. Some men must die that others may live. It has come to these poor miners to bear this cross, not for themselves—not that, but that the human race may be lifted up to a higher and broader plane than it has ever known before.

I did not come into the state of Pennsylvania to stir up dissension and hatred and bitterness. I should like to feel, as I go away, that I have dealt justly and fairly by every man and every condition which I have met. I should like to feel that my efforts—sincere efforts they have been—have done something to bring peace and harmony and quiet and prosperity to this valley which should be blessed, but which has been cursed.

DARROW SPOKE for eight hours, never once using a note, in contrast to Baer who read his argument most of the time. An even greater crowd was in the courtroom to hear Darrow than was present when Baer delivered his argument. The room was filled to capacity. There wasn't even standing room, and many had to be turned away.

Baer's blows against the union in his summation "were returned with interest by the chief counsel for the mine workers," said the North American. "It seemed at times as though Mr. Darrow must speedily exhaust himself, so completely did he give forth his strength of body and soul."

There were repeated outbursts of applause during Darrow's plea. Darrow asked Commission Chairman Judge Gray to request the audience to refrain from showing their feelings, that it interrupted his line of thinking.

When Darrow concluded, the Commission hearing was temporarily suspended as a result of applause which lasted for more than five minutes. A crowd gathered around Darrow to offer congratulations.

"All the philosophy, all of the hopes and pleas and demands of the anthracite mine workers and, in a measure, of trade unionists everywhere, are summarized in the brilliant final address of Clarence S. Darrow that yesterday brought to a close the history-making sessions of the Anthracite Strike Commission," the Philadelphia North American reported at the end of Darrow's summation.

The Commission went into executive session to study the 10,000 type-written pages of testimony.

A little more than a month later—on March 21, 1903—the Commission published its findings. The miners had gained a 10 per cent pay raise, the sliding scale suggested by Baer was put into effect, an eight-hour day was established for several categories of work, and the miners received several million dollars in back pay.

"It was generally conceded that labor gained greatly by this arbitration," said Darrow.

The settlement, though it did not recognize the union as a responsible partner in labor-management relationship, did however recommend a Board of Conciliation which would handle all disputes between the miners and the operators. It also prohibited discrimination against union and nonunion miners, and criticized the employment of children.

A Governor Is Murdered

STEVE ADAMS
Wallace, Idaho, 1907

HAYWOOD, MOYER AND PETTIBONE
Boise, Idaho, 1907

THRILL AND SHOCK
IN DARROW'S PLEA
DRAWS TEARS AND GASPS

[Headline, Chicago Tribune, July 25, 1907]

A BOMB KILLED Frank Steunenberg, former governor of Idaho, on December 20, 1905. It exploded as he opened the gate to his home in Caldwell, Idaho.

Immediately, Idaho's Governor Gooding offered a $10,000 reward for the apprehension of the guilty party, and the Steunenberg family added another $5,000 to the reward money.

A piece of fish string and some plaster of Paris was found near the gate of Steunenberg's home. The clue led to the room of Harry Orchard in the Saratoga Hotel where authorities found evidence to link him with the murder. Orchard had been living in Caldwell for several months under the name of Tom Hogan.

Though the evidence pointed to Orchard, the immediate reaction of the newspapers and the community was that someone was behind him, and it was openly hinted this could only be the Western Federation of Miners with whom Steunenberg had been at odds.

The former governor had been elected with labor support. He carried a union card; he had been a printer. But during his term as governor, the miners in the Coeur d'Alêne district went out on strike. Violence resulted. Steunenberg declared martial law and implicated every member of the WFM as responsible for the violence. The miners looked upon him as a betrayer.

There were several other reasons why the Western Federation of Miners was presumed to be behind Orchard: Orchard had often acted as a bodyguard for Charles H. Moyer, president of the union; he was a frequent visitor at the union offices; he had been active in some of the union's strikes.

Despite the evidence pointing to him, Harry Orchard nevertheless insisted he was innocent. For more than a week the local authorities attempted to get him to confess, but they were unsuccessful.

Then John McParland, western head of the Pinkerton Detective Agency, came into the case.

Labor charged that the Pinkerton agency came in for the reward money. But William J. Pinkerton denied this, saying: "Our agency . . . was solicited by the governor to send McParland immediately to Boise for consultation with him, and this was done on our regular business terms."

McParland closeted himself with Orchard and in a few days had a confession—a confession which took three days to record and in which Orchard admitted to a series of crimes, among which were 26 murders including that of Steunenberg.

Apparently, more than a confession was necessary from Orchard; the confession had to be wrapped with respectability. So when newspapermen were finally permitted to interview Orchard in prison, they learned he had "got religion."

Orchard said the crimes were instigated by the "inner circle" of the Western Federation. He named William D. "Big Bill" Haywood, secretary-treasurer of the Federation, who later became the spokesman for the Industrial Workers of the World (IWW); George Pettibone who at one time was active in the union; and Moyer. He accused Jack Simpkins, a member of the executive board, as an accomplice to the murder of Steunenberg.[1] Orchard also implicated Steve Adams, a member of the Federation, in various of the crimes. Adams, at the time of Orchard's confession, was living on a homestead in Oregon.

The sheriff when arresting Adams told him he was not wanted in the Steunenberg murder; that he was wanted only to corroborate Orchard's

[1] Jack Simpkins disappeared soon after Haywood, Moyer and Pettibone were arrested, and he was never brought to trial. To this day, his whereabouts remain unknown.

story and if he would do this, he'd "come out all right and would not be prosecuted."

After Adams' arrest and his transfer to the Boise, Idaho, penitentiary, his wife and children were also brought from the Northwest and housed in a cottage on the prison grounds.

Like Orchard, Adams was closeted with Detective McParland. In a few days the detective had an alleged confession which supported Orchard.

Adams was reputed to have confessed that he joined the Federation at Cripple Creek; he knew Haywood, Moyer and Pettibone; it was Pettibone who suggested he see Simpkins because they wanted "to get" Steunenberg; that Haywood gave Pettibone $200 for Adams' expenses, and Simpkins gave Adams another $300 "to get rid of some claim jumpers." Adams reportedly said he took part in the murder of two claim jumpers, Tyler and Boule, in August 1904, in northern Idaho.

Haywood, Moyer and Pettibone were in Colorado at the time of Steunenberg's murder and Orchard's confession—yet the governor of Idaho requested their extradition from Colorado. Since the three union officials were not fugitives from Idaho, legal technicalities developed in obtaining their extradition.

To get the men into Idaho, officials of the state of Colorado co-operated with Idaho officials and on the night of February 17, 1906, Haywood was arrested in his room in a rooming house in Denver, Colorado, near Federation headquarters. Moyer was arrested at the railroad station as he was leaving for a trip to visit the smeltermen's union at Iola, and Pettibone was picked up in his home in Denver.

A waiting train at the depot whisked the union officials into Idaho where carriages were waiting to take them to the penitentiary in Boise.

Haywood in his autobiography relates that as the entourage approached the prison gates, he noted a sign: "Admission 25 cents," but that they were admitted free and were put in murderer's row in the death house.

Labor—which rallied to the defense of Haywood, Moyer and Pettibone—claimed they were kidnaped.

The method of getting the Federation officials into Idaho from Colorado was appealed to the Idaho Supreme Court and finally to the United States Supreme Court, which ruled that though the manner in which the prisoners were extradited was illegal, the case was out of its jurisdiction since the prisoners were already in Idaho. Supreme Court Justice McKenna dissented. Said the Justice: "Kidnaping is a crime, pure and simple. The foundation of extradition between the states is that the accused should be a fugitive from justice from the demanding state, and he may challenge the fact by habeas corpus immediately upon his arrest."

Clarence Darrow came into the case after the U.S. Supreme Court ruling.

When Darrow learned that Adams had repudiated his confession to an uncle, he tried to see Adams but was refused permission by State officials.

The State, on hearing of Adams' repudiation, brought him to Wallace, Idaho, the county seat of Shoshone County in northern Idaho. Here he was indicted for the murder of the claim jumper Tyler.

James H. Hawley represented the State in the case of Idaho versus Steve Adams. Darrow was at the defense table with Edmund Richardson of Denver.

Both the State and Darrow admitted that Adams' corroboration of Orchard's testimony was most important for the conviction in the Haywood, Moyer and Pettibone case.

Reported the Chicago Inter-Ocean on the opening day of the Adams trial on February 10, 1907: "The great legal battle for the life of Steve Adams began here today. On one side are the forces of the State seeking Adams' conviction, the first step toward convicting leaders of the Western Federation of Miners charged with the assassination of former Governor Frank Steunenberg of Idaho; on the other is the powerful Federation, declaring the charges are false and an attempt by the mine owners to break up the union."

Thus was set the prologue to the Haywood, Moyer and Pettibone case.

To prepare the case against Adams after he had repudiated his confession, the government exhumed what it claimed were the remains of Tyler from a grave in northern Idaho. The decayed clothing was taken to Tyler's sole survivor, his mother, who identified some of the clothing as that belonging to her son. The mother was in the courtroom all through the trial dressed in "widow weeds."

When Adams was put on the witness stand, he testified that after he was taken to Boise, he was put in a cell with Orchard. "I was taken to the office of the penitentiary and introduced to Detective McParland. He told me about Kelly the Bum and other men who had turned state's evidence and had been set free. He told me some Bible stories, too, but I cannot remember what they were as I am not familiar with the Bible. He kept me until four or five in the morning trying to make me confess.

"McParland told me," Adams continued, "that he wanted to convict Moyer, Haywood, Pettibone and Simpkins who he called 'cutthroats.' If I would not help convict them, he said, I would be taken back to Colorado and either hanged or mobbed. If I did help I would only be taken back to Colorado as a witness."

Adams also testified that when he was jailed in Wallace he was not allowed to see his attorney but was compelled against his will to talk to McParland.

The trial lasted three weeks. In early March, Darrow presented his summation to the jury.

*"I speak for the poor, for the weak, for the
weary, for that long line of men, who, in
darkness and despair, have borne the labors
of the human race."*

IN opening this case, the district attorney has told this jury
that in many respects it is a remarkable case. It is remarkable.
In some ways, I never heard and never read of a case like this. He
has told you that able counsel have come here from other states
and other cities to defend this common workingman. It is not for
me to say, nor for Mr. Richardson to say, whether counsel from
other states are able counsel or not. But it is true, and I have no
wish to deny it, that I have come 2,000 miles to defend this case,
and Mr. Richardson 1,500 miles for the sake of making a defense
for a man who could not possibly pay either one of us for the services we render, according to the standard that lawyers ordinarily
set for their services. I do not mean to disguise the fact. I do not
believe I could if I would.

I do not propose to be that bird who shoves his head into the
sand and thinks nobody can see his body, because I know you
gentlemen understand it. I am willing to concede the truth of
every word that Mr. Knight[1] has stated upon this proposition.
Much as I love justice, much as I hate to see punishment of any
sort, I have not the time nor the ability, even if I had the inclination, to go up and down this land and defend every poor man
charged with crime throughout the length and breadth of the
United States; and that is not the reason I am here. Gladly would
I do it if I could, and if I had the power and the time and the
means. That is not the reason I am here, and that is not the reason Richardson is here. Mr. Knight speaks truly—I have no desire
to conceal it when he says that back of this man are the funds of a

[1] A state's attorney.

great organization, the small contributions of thousands of workingmen to give him a better defense than the ordinary poor man placed on trial in the courts of this country, with his life in danger from the law, could have.

There are hundreds of men throughout the length and breadth of the land, men who know no trade but work, men who get their small means by the sweat of their brow, who in some unfortunate moment, fall into the clutches of the law, and are tried, condemned and executed almost without defense, because without means. And if it had been that Steve Adams must rely upon himself alone, if he had had no relatives and no friends to speak for him or help him in his cause, he might have been like the rest.

It is true, gentlemen, that a great effort has been made to defend him. It is true that I have been willing to leave my other affairs to come 2,000 miles into this little town in the midst of these mountains amongst unfamiliar people, and a jury that I am not accustomed to, for the sake of looking after this case; and Mr. Richardson has done the same. But that is not all; not only have we come here to give such aid, with such ability as we have in his defense, but the state of Idaho never yet prosecuted a man as they are prosecuting this poor, unimportant, almost nameless laborer, and they have shoved aside Shoshone County and its officers. They have employed as much ability as they could get locally, and they have gone to the capital of the state and employed as great a lawyer as there is in the state of Idaho, to ask for his blood. They have done more than that; the state of Colorado has been called upon, and months of the time of the greatest detective of the West have been given to bring him to the gallows. They have gone to the state of Washington and brought another, and used his time without stint for the same purpose, and they have gone to the state of Colorado and brought here the adjutant general of the state, and one of the head officers of the Mine Owners' Association and brought his influence and his power and his money into this court to help convict this man.

It is a remarkable case; it is unprecedented in the annals of crime prosecutions. I do not need to tell this jury that there is not a man in this courtroom who really cares to take Steve Adams' life. It is not for him, a humble almost unknown workman, that all the machinery of the State has been set in motion, and all the mines and the mine owners of the West have been called to their aid. Not that. It is because back of all this, and beyond and over it all, there is a great issue of which this is but the beginning. Because, beyond this case, and outside of this courtroom, and out in the great world, is a great fight, a fight between capital and labor, of which this is but a manifestation up here in the woods and the hills. You know it; I know it; they know it. There is not a man so blind, there is not a person so prejudiced or so bigoted, as to believe all this effort is being put forth to punish an unknown man for the murder of an unknown man.

That is not all, gentlemen. I want to measure every word I say in this case, and although it may seem harsh, it is true. This prosecution, from beginning to end, is a humbug and a fraud. This prosecution, from beginning to end, is a crime, an outrage, there is not one jot of honesty, not one particle of sincerity, not the least bit of integrity in it, not one single moment from the day this man was taken from his home in Oregon until now. And we say this, gentlemen, without any regard as to whether this man is innocent or guilty of the crime with which you are charging him. He is not being tried today for that. That is not the issue here. That is not the reason that calls these prosecutors from two or three states of the Union, that sets this machinery in motion which would crush out his helpless life. Who is this man? What does it mean? If one of you were arrested, would any such power be brought against you?

If it was, what would happen to you? Would it make any difference whether you were innocent or guilty if the great machinery of the law were turned loose to crush you? Where is the poor man that could stand up against it? Where is the man who could be taken without process of law, sent to the penitentiary, locked up for months without a charge, prosecuted by the greatest in the land, and defend himself if he stood helpless and alone? If there ever was a cause or justification for poor men standing together, this case furnishes that justification.

This man has been characterized by Mr. Knight as a foul murderer, as a man whose breath is putrefaction, as a criminal, as an assassin; bad form, it seems to me for the attorney of the state, to say the least. He has been held up to this jury as one of the worst monsters that the annals of crime have disclosed. Bad form at least, because he is here helpless, his lips are sealed, what they say he must listen to, the charges that they make he cannot answer. He should be tried fairly, calmly, deliberately. I may be forgiven in my zeal for his defense, but the State cannot be forgiven for using malice, for playing upon the passions and upon the feelings of men to take their fellow's blood.

I know but little more about Steve Adams than you. It is not for me to pass eulogiums upon him. I look at him as I do most men, neither good nor bad. I look at him as I look at my friends on the other side in this case, as I look at my associates, as I look upon myself, as I look upon you, gentlemen of the jury—a human being; a human being into whom God breathed the breath of life, neither all good nor all bad. He may have done wrong. I cannot tell. He may have been guilty of many crimes. I do not know. Nobody can tell what will happen to you, or what will happen to me. Nobody can fathom the feelings of hatred, the feelings of despair and of violence that lurk in the breast of every man who lives. But Steve Adams is a man who loves his wife, his children, who is kind to his friends, who has high and holy sentiments and sympathies. It is not for me to judge; I cannot tell. He may be in part what Mr. Knight seems to think he is. I haven't the brain, I haven't the inclination to pass judgment upon my fellow-man. I never had the ability to sort them out and say, this man is bad. Go that way. This man is good. Go that way. It must be left to somebody wiser than I. If Mr. Knight can do it, well and good. If you gentlemen can do it, well and good.

I do not know what Steve Adams might have done in Colorado. I have no information upon that and neither have you. Mr. Knight or Mr. McParland may say what they will upon that subject. I only say this, gentlemen of the jury. If I know anything about the hearts and the feelings and the minds of the Western men, if I have learned anything about your state and your people in my short sojourn here, I don't believe a jury in Shoshone County will hang Steve Adams in Idaho for something he did in Colorado. If he has violated the law in Colorado, gentlemen of the jury, Mr. Wells, the adjutant general of Colorado, is here, and he didn't come here to testify to one sentence, as he pretended to testify on this stand, but to take Steve Adams home. If he has committed any crime in Colorado, the laws of Colorado are there; the prisoner is here. He can be taken there, and we will go there and defend him the best we can; and if he has violated the law of the state of Colorado, I suppose he will have to pay the penalty, but he is not to pay the penalty of it in this proceeding. He is being tried here for the murder of Tyler, a man whose name was scarcely known to the people of this county, but a man whom Providence for some inscrutable reason decreed should agitate these three states, and whose name should be written in the history of one of the most remarkable and one of the strangest criminal trials that history records.

Gentlemen, I have said to you that his prosecution is a fraud from beginning to end. These powerful interests, which are back of this case, are not interested in Steve Adams. They look upon this inoffensive man, so far as his importance is concerned, this ordinary, ignorant, common workingman, as simply a pawn in a game that they are playing; and there's not a man on this jury that does not know it. They are gambling with the life of Steve Adams. They are treating this man as though he were a dice to be thrown, and nothing else. They are willing that his life shall be taken, regardless of who he is, if perchance it may bring them one step nearer to their real prey.

Do you believe that when the governor of the state of Idaho was fondling Steve Adams' babe, that when lawyers of the state of Idaho were meeting him in his prison home, that when he was being fed and visited by the elite of Idaho's capital, that they thought he was the wretch that Mr. Knight has described to you? They were using him then, gentlemen, they were using him then as if he was a pawn on the board to help play their infamous game; and when he turned on them they were willing to take his life. This life they value about as much as they would the life of a fly, if it could bring them one step nearer to their real prey, which is not Steve Adams. They are after bigger game.

Gentlemen, that is not all. Do I overstate this case? Is there one single fact from beginning to end that does not bear out every word that I say? I will say more. You may return a verdict of "guilty" against this man. You may do your part to tie a rope around his neck, if you will, but the state of Idaho does not dare to hang him. Do you suppose that the governor of this state, who fondled his babe; do you suppose that this lawyer, who visited him in his prison home, who got his confidence and trust, who ate with his wife, who watched and stayed and labored day by day with Steve Adams; do you suppose that these men who got the confidence of the weak, humble, common workingman—do you suppose that they dare, by the means of that confidence, to tie a rope around his neck and strangle him to death? No! If Mr. Gooding, governor of this state, if Mr. Hawley, prosecuting this case, if Mr. McParland, infamous as he is, if they should ever dare to take this man they have betrayed, aye, betrayed, and outraged; if they ever dare to tie a rope around his neck, they commit a crime so black and dark that all the waters of the great sea could never wash away the great stain. I am not afraid of that. They are not going to hang him, whatever this jury may do. They would use his conviction to try to get him back into their hands where he was before, and you know it, and they know it.

And that is not all. Let me go a step further. Here is certain paraphernalia laid out upon this table. The State says the over-alls, the undershirt, the jumper, the hat, and the skull are Fred Tyler's. Fred Tyler, a common, unknown woodsman, who started away from Santa, Idaho, without a dollar in his pocket, whom nobody knew outside of his immediate family, and nobody cared for outside of his immediate family, who had made no place in the world, and who was entirely unknown to fame, even in the small town from which he started out. They say it is his, Fred Tyler's remains, that they have brought into this court. And they have brought into this court Fred Tyler's mother, to sit here before you day after day, and I hope, gentlemen of the jury, that I do not need to make an affidavit to prove that I feel as sorry for Fred Tyler's mother as any man can feel. I recognize her as being the saddest actor in this sad and remarkable drama that is being played inside these walls. I recognize it, and I feel it, and if I could say anything or do anything that would make it easier for her, I would say that word, and I would do that act; and I think that is true of every person who has sat in this courtroom day after day. But gentlemen, let us be honest and fair even in the discussion of Mrs. Thomas'[1] relation to this case. Mr. Knight stood before this jury and wept tears when he spoke of Mrs. Thomas. Let me say now, gentlemen of the jury, that every one of those tears were crocodile tears, every one. If one of these men ever cared for Mrs. Thomas, they cared for her because they wished to coin this mother's tears into hatred against three men down at Boise. They have cared for her because they wished to coin this mother's love into munitions of war against this man and the men whom they seek to reach. Have they cared for her in any other way? Gentlemen, has the county of Shoshone cared for her in any other way? Answer me that question, in your verdict, and tell me whether every tear they shed is not a crocodile tear? They used this mother's heart, they used this mother's tears, just as the stage manager uses the contemptible trappings of the stage to produce an effect and nothing else. Let me tell you why.

In 1905, a year and a half ago, a skeleton was found up in the wilds of Idaho. The brother-in-law and the stepfather of Fred Tyler said it was he who had died out there in the woods. What did the county of Shoshone do, gentlemen? What did they do? They took his remains and sewed them into a gunny sack; they dumped in his bones, the skull, his overalls, his jumper, his hat and an old bottle, and sewed them into a gunny sack. Mr. Knight tells you about the sad requiem of the north winds around his unknown grave up in the woods; that was the only requiem that ever was sung about Fred Tyler, if this is he. Did the officers of the state ever even hold an inquest to know whether this was Fred Tyler's body? They knew at least one man had been killed by settlers because he was a jumper. They suspected another man had been killed in exactly the same locality, and for exactly the same reason. They knew, or believed they knew, who that man was. They took the coroner and his deputy, and they sewed these bones in a bag or gunny sack, and they brought them down to Wallace. They didn't even take pains to make an investigation as to whether they had Fred Tyler's remains or not. Did they even

[1] Fred Tyler's mother.

write a letter to his mother? Did anybody sing any requiem above his grave, or did anyone say any masses for his soul? Did they ever make any investigations to find out who took away his life, or to punish anyone for his crime?

Where was the sheriff of the county who is more than interested in these latter days? The coroner of the county who had possession of these remains? They made no effort of any sort. They could have given him Christian burial. They could have had some poor ceremony for an unknown woodsman. They could have shown some respect, instead of shoveling him into a pine box, and not even take care of such evidence as there might be, and then bury him in a pauper's grave in the potter's field.

The first time the state of Idaho ever looked up Mrs. Thomas, the first time it ever shed a tear for her, and the first time they ever cared for that mother's love or that mother's tears, was when they sought to use her love and tears to tie a rope around Steve Adams' neck.

And so, gentlemen, I say again, that from beginning to end there has not been one grain of sincerity in this prosecution.

It is almost a travesty to examine this evidence. It is almost a shame to stand before a jury and discuss whether a jury of this county, knowing that some men were killed up in the north, and killed perhaps by dozens of men, at least four or five, whether you will become conspirators with Gooding, with Hawley, with McParland and the rest, whether you will join with them to put a rope around this man's neck. For what? Not to avenge Tyler, but to furnish evidence to help the Mine Owners' Association crush the life out of the greatest labor organization of the West.

Has this county ever sincerely gone to work to find out who killed Boule? Has it ever gone to work to find out what became of Tyler?

* * *

The law says that before a man can be deprived of his life, or his liberty, the jury must be satisfied beyond all reasonable doubt of his guilt; and that means each one of you, because each one of you is a juror alone. Is there any reasonable ground to believe that this man ever did perpetrate this murder? In the first place, it is perfectly patent that no criminal case could be on trial today in Shoshone County except for the case in Boise. Fred Tyler, if these are Fred Tyler's remains, would have been left to slumber peacefully in his grave instead of being resurrected as he has been, for the purpose of hounding some men to their death, not Steve Adams at that. But did Steve Adams murder Fred Tyler? And does the evidence satisfy you gentlemen of that fact beyond a reasonable doubt? Assuming the case is honest, assuming that it is a fair investigation by the county to punish crime, assuming that nothing was ever heard of excepting a murder upon the headwaters of St. Joe, and a man arrested for it, then how stands this case?

In the first place, gentlemen of the jury, the law says that you must be satisfied that a crime has been committed. This cannot come through a confession—I will discuss the confession a little later—and over and over and over again, in the history of the world, confessions have been shown to be so unreliable that the law says you cannot establish the crime by a confession. You must first show that somebody is dead. You must next show that the death came by foul means. Then you may take confessions or anything else that comes along to prove that the defendant is guilty of the crime.

First, the evidence in this case must show beyond a reasonable doubt that Fred Tyler is dead; that he was killed on or about April tenth, and that it was his remains that were found in the St. Joe district, and buried here in Wallace, and now lie on the table before you.

In 1905, in July or August, a skeleton was found up beyond the head of navigation of the St. Joe River, up in the Marine Cable district, about a mile away from a cabin that was once occupied by Jack Simpkins. That is the starting point of this identification, if there ever has been an identification. There was nothing but some bones, a pair of overalls, a blue jumper, two undershirts, a black hat, perhaps a bottle, and possibly a little piece of an old shoe. This was found lying in the woods, not between two logs, as this confession says, where it would evidently be concealed, but on top of three logs, out in the plain light of day, where passersby could scarcely fail to see and smell it. With these rags and these bones that have lain in the woods, no one knows how long, the State sets to work to prove that Fred Tyler is dead, and that these are Fred Tyler's remains.

Gentlemen, I have discussed the question of identification. How does Steve Adams happen to be here? How do you twelve men happen to be sitting here trying this resident of Colorado and Oregon? He came up here in 1904, and he stayed four or five weeks, and then he went away. Of course, no one knew when he came and nobody knew when he went, and now they are trying him. What is the reason? That proposition is just as plain as any other. You know why it is. He came and left. Two men, perhaps, were killed. One surely was killed while he was here. There was no information, no indictment and practically no prosecution, and he went away. Nearly two years later the ex-governor of this state was assassinated. Now I do not care to talk about that. I trust I feel as most other men feel about any murder. Some time that question will be tried, but not now. A man was arrested. I do not know as I feel quite as my brother Richardson does about that man. I never looked into his brain. I do not know the shape of his skull. I do not know his motive. I do not know his early life. I do not know his feelings and his passions and his desires. I do not know how well he could control himself, or how little he could control himself. I am willing to leave his judgment between himself and the infinite God who made him as he is.

Somebody killed him, and it is true that when a man of importance is killed, ten thousand men seek to find the slayer, where not one will look for the slayer of his humble fellow-man, a common workingman. When Fred Tyler was supposed to have been found again, nobody said anything about it; but when ex-Governor Steunenberg was assassinated, the whole United States had to be turned over to connect everybody possible with the crime.

Now I have nothing to say against the prosecution and the conviction of every person who was implicated in that crime. Every guilty one doubtless will be convicted, but the only fear in a great state trial like this is that somebody will be convicted who ought not to be. But that case will be tried when we get to it. They did capture Harry Orchard. McParland led him to his cell, keen, shrewd, practiced, cunning. This man I suppose was caught red-handed. There was only one chance for him to save his life, and that was to implicate someone else. Amongst the rest he gave McParland the name of Steve Adams, this man whom they brought before this jury and asked you to put to death. Orchard told McParland and others that Steve Adams had committed many crimes. And what did they do? Steve Adams had left these mountains a year before, he had spent a month or six weeks and gone away, he had gone back to Colorado for a short time, and then to Nevada to dig for gold. He had left Nevada, and still having the idea of a homestead, had gone to Oregon and planted his little family upon a homestead, and was living there in quiet and in peace.

Now I do not know what he might have done in Colorado. I know as far as the evidence in this case is concerned, he was arrested and kept ninety-three days in jail without any charge and without any trial, and so far as this evidence is concerned, there is nothing against him in Colorado any more than in Idaho. If there is, I take it the state of Colorado can punish its own criminals and look after its own crime, and will do it after the citizens of this state have got through with him. He was arrested, and spent ninety-three days in jail. An explosion occurred during a great strike in Colorado. As he said, every union man was driven out of Cripple Creek, where he lived. He lived up on top of the mountain, at Altman, away above the world. An explosion occurred and soldiers came, and the people were aroused, whether rightly or wrongly, I am not going to discuss; it will be settled sometime, somewhere. We cannot settle it here. I only speak of it as it affects this case. Steve Adams had been an humble member of the union. He had been digging in the earth and carrying his union card. He was known in the local lodge that he attended, and when the soldiers came, people were after him. He slipped down the hill and ran eight miles, and took a train and got to Denver. The refugees were coming to Denver from everywhere. They gathered at Pettibone's store. They gathered at headquarters. They were being protected and defended the best they could by the union. They were getting relief. They were coming in from the mountains and the hills. Adams changed his name to Dixon; not the first workingman who has changed his name; not the first man who has been obliged to deny the name his mother gave him for the sake of getting a job. He came to the Coeur d'Alène; not the first man who has come to the Coeur d'Alène under some other name. He came to see Vincent St. John,[1] whose name became Vincent when he got to Burke. He went up to see Simpkins. His name was Dixon. He went back to Oregon, took up a homestead, and was living in peace and quietude when Steunenberg was killed. Now we get to this case and his connection with it.

Is there a man on the jury who believes Adams had anything to do with the killing of Steunenberg? You know he had not. There is no evidence in this case that he ever had anything to do with crime in Colorado; yet he was arrested and held ninety-three days in jail without a charge and without a trial.

He was living with his wife and children on his Oregon farm, and some men came here in the night with a fugitive warrant, charging him with being the murderer of Steunenberg. The man who had the warrant, the men who had charge of the case, the governor who was pushing it and every man connected with it, knew the charge was a lie. They knew Steve Adams' hands were clean of the blood of Steunenberg. They never intended to convict him, to try him or hold him for the killing of Steunenberg, and they deliberately made a false and perjured charge so as to get him, with the hope of getting hold of something against the Western Federation of Miners. They sent a warrant for this man, and charged him with the killing of Steunenberg, when they knew he never killed him, when they knew he never had anything to do with it. That warrant came from Canyon County, Idaho, Steunenberg's home county. They took that warrant to Oregon, and they took Steve on a train right through Canyon County, and never stopped until they got to Boise, Ada County, and put him in the penitentiary, a place they had no right to put him. They had no more right, gentlemen of the jury, to do that, than they would have to take one of you when you go to your homes after this trial, and place you in the penitentiary of

[1] An official of the WFM and one of the organizers of the IWW.

Washington or Colorado, without even a paper charge against you. Without trial, without commitment, without any pretense of any charge, they put him in there, and put him in a cell with Orchard. Gentlemen, does anybody need to argue to you, intelligent men, as to why they did it? Is there any one of you who does not know? If so, then I am afraid there will be a disagreement in this case. If there is any man so blind or so ignorant that he does not know why Steve Adams was taken from Oregon and landed in the penitentiary, in the Boise penitentiary, then, gentlemen, such a man should not be passing judgment upon the lives of his fellow-men. Was he taken there for the murder of Steunenberg? Was he taken there for any crime? He was taken there that they might choke out of him some evidence against Moyer, Pettibone and Haywood. He was put in a cell with Harry Orchard, who had already confessed. They had no right under the law to put him in the penitentiary. They had less right to put him in a cell with this confessed criminal. It is not a question of the outrage they perpetrated upon him, but it is a question of the violation of the laws of the state of Idaho, by the officers of the state of Idaho.

Fortune, in some mysterious way, had picked up Whilman[1]; nature meant him for a butcher. Necessity made him a drayman, and a rotten political machine placed him at the head of the state penitentiary. Whilman took this prisoner without any charge or commitment, without any warrant, without any authority of law, and he placed him in this cell with Orchard. Now, gentlemen, there are some rights that a convicted felon has, and an unconvicted citizen, especially with no charge against him, should have more. The keeper of the penitentiary is bound to take care of the persons entrusted to his charge. He is bound to see that nobody is locked up by him excepting by due warrant of law. He is bound to protect them as much as he protects anyone else. But what did he do? The warden of this state of Idaho, under whose tender mercies every convicted felon must live, opened his doors and took in and locked up a citizen of another state, accused of no crime, who had committed no crime, and then he gave the

[1] Warden, Boise penitentiary.

keys to a notorious detective, and left him to place this inmate upon the rack.

Gentlemen, we are confronted with the confession that was extorted from a man in the state penitentiary by a professional detective, aided and assisted by a warden who should have been protecting him in such rights as he had. Whether Steve Adams is guilty of murdering an unknown citizen, is a matter of small consequence, small indeed, because these isolated acts of violence leave no impression on the State. Tomorrow, somebody else will be murdered; next week another; and yet the State will go on, the law will be preserved, its power and its majesty will still protect the humblest citizen. But if the law can be violated, if the officers of the law can take a citizen without charge and without trial, if they can place him in the penitentiary and then turn him over to the tender mercies of every vagabond detective who seeks to entrap him, then you will not maintain the honor of the State which is meant to protect the liberty and life of its citizens from despots and malefactors. It is infinitely more important, gentlemen, to the state of Idaho, to know whether this confession was honestly secured than to know whether any man was murdered, whosoever that man might have been.

They went to Oregon, they got Steve Adams. They brought him back in the early evening and they put him in a cell, and they locked him up with Harry Orchard. Harry Orchard at once commenced to talk to him about Steunenberg, about Colorado and murders. Gentlemen, Steve Adams was charged with the greatest of crimes. The United States was on fire over the killing of Steunenberg. Colorado was ablaze. Idaho was burning. The Mine Owners' Association thought that here at last was a chance to get rid of their hated enemies. The world was talking about it. Every newspaper in the land was talking about it. Unfortunate indeed was any human being whose name was linked with that terrible tragedy. Suppose it was you, suppose it was I, and in some casual way some person had said that we were connected with that offense. Would we have been scared? Would we not have hesitated? Would our faces have blanched? It is not a question of whether you are guilty or innocent, for many a guilty man has escaped, and many an innocent man been convicted. It is a question of the white heat of public opinion, of the mad mobs who devour every person that they attack. The world was against every man who was suspected of this in the remotest degree, and Steve Adams was taken, and he was put in the penitentiary. He stayed there four or five days, and nobody came there but Orchard. The warden came up and asked him how he was getting along and that's all. And then McParland came.

Now, gentlemen, how about that confession? Without it, there is not a breath against Steve Adams in this case. Without it, even if you assume that Tyler is dead, Steve Adams had nothing to do with it. If the confession was made freely, openly, voluntarily, without fear and without hope, then, if the other elements in this case have been proven, and if no other defense is made, the confession should count. If it was not made freely, but was made through hope or through fear, then it is so much blank paper, and should not weigh one single moment with this jury. And, gentlemen, this is not an idle statement, and it is not an unwise law. There may be those who say that a man would not confess unless he is guilty, but all history shows that he will. This law was made for a good purpose. You can count the men by tens of thousands who have gone to their death confessing crimes that they never committed. All Europe was swept by the delusion of witchcraft, and New England was swept by the same. And old women confessed over and over again, that they had ridden to the moon on broomsticks and were witches, and were condemned to death. Spain and France and Italy made their torture chambers, and they took their victims into these torture chambers, and turned the thumbscrew harder and harder until the victim confessed to save his life. In the old times, our good Puritan forefathers in New England, who were so wise, and so holy and so just, made their statutes against the great crime of witchcraft, and brought in old women, and inflicted upon them tortures and all sorts of indignity to get them to confess their crime; and when they could not get them to confess in any other way, they tied their hands together, and their feet together and threw them into the mill pond, and if they floated they killed them as witches, and if they didn't float they didn't need to kill them. And that was in New England. There's not a place in the world where machinery has not been invented to procure confessions. And there is not a sleuth on earth who does not at once set to work to get a confession, by all means, fair or foul, as long as he gets his confession. So the law is wise when it says that a confession cannot be taken unless it is voluntary and free. If the confessor is moved by fear or influenced by hope, then it is fear that is speaking, it is hope that rises above his courage. It is not the man, it is the mind cowed by fear one moment, and raised by hope another, and such a confession cannot count.

Indeed, gentlemen, let me ask you a simple question: Why do you think Steve Adams made this confession? I would like counsel, when they argue this case, to tell the jury why he did it. If he did not do it for hope, if he did not do it for fear, what did he do it for? Did he do it for justice? Did he do it because he wanted to right wrong? Did he do it for love of his family or fellow-man? Did he do it for truth? If so, why didn't he stick to it? If so, why did he come into this court today and repudiate it? If he did it because it was honest and true and plain as day, then will you tell me why it was that the very first chance he got away from under the watchful eye of McParland, the very first human voice he heard that could give him any help, the very first hand that was reached out to him, he said: "For God's sake take me out. This confession is a lie!" If Steve Adams came upon this witness stand and sought to convict someone else, and he stood by this confession, then they might argue that this confession was for some other purpose; but when he is placed in the penitentiary and confronted by detectives and threatened with death, and is in bodily fear of his life, and when they hold up to him hopes of life, and home, and family, and a chance in the world, then that must be the moving cause.

Gentlemen, it is clear upon its face. It will be up to this jury to say why he confessed. There must have been some motive that influenced this humble man when he signed his name to that document. That motive was not the motive expressed in the document, the love of his fellow-workman, the fear of God, or the love of his family. If so, he forgot them, the first chance he had. That motive can be read upon almost every page of criminal prosecutions that the world has ever seen. It was the effort of detectives, of people to create fear and then hold out hope. Was there ever a better chance for that? Here was a man charged with killing the ex-governor of the state. He was placed in a cell with a man whom he knew. This man told him he had killed the ex-governor, and that he had implicated Steve Adams in the crime. Outside, from one end of the United States to the other, was a howling mob of outraged people, who were ready to tear limb from limb any human being, even remotely connected with this crime. Outside was not a friendly voice or friendly hand, and one lawyer whom he saw for a moment, selling himself to the State; his uncle was not near to look to. The governor there, the attorneys for the state there, Orchard there, McParland there; locked for a week in a cell and then brought out before him. What do you think?

He stayed there a week, or nearly that, then one day he was brought down by the warden, and the warden talked to him about what a good man he was, what a good family he had, and how he had better help the state. Steve said nothing. The next day he was brought down again, and McParland was in the room. At nine o'clock in the morning, gentlemen, McParland's mind, matched against Steve Adams' mind. The one astute, trained, cunning, cunning as the spider who weaves his web to catch the fly; cunning, weaving a web to enmesh a life, not the life of Steve Adams, but of someone else whom they wanted to get.

McParland stayed with him. He gave him a good cigar. He told Steve he was a good fellow, that his people were good people, and that he had committed many horrible crimes; that he had been led wrong, that he had been influenced wrong, but it was not too late for him to mend. Does it make any difference whether you take the story of McParland or Steve Adams? Does it make any difference who is speaking when determining what influenced Steve Adams' mind when he made this confession? McParland himself admits it. There is not a line of his testimony where he does not practically admit every charge that we make. He says he went there, he offered him a cigar, he smoked it, he said nothing; and then he commenced to talk to Steve and he first reeled off a lot of Bible stories. You know the devil can quote Scripture, and so can a detective, and McParland knows the Bible. He told him about all the ancient sinners who had been forgiven, and he interspersed his talk with illuminating lessons from the life of St. Paul and of "Kelly the Bum"; of David, and of Jack Horn. He told Steve how David was forgiven, and what a great man he afterward became; a man after God's own heart.

And he told him about the Molly Maguires and "Kelly the Bum." McParland knew the way to get a confession out of him. He related how he saved Kelly the Bum, and gave him a thousand dollars. Although his sins were as scarlet, McParland had washed them white as snow. We asked him why did you do it? And he said, so he would think about it. You remember how he dodged and quibbled and hedged when that question was asked.

Now, gentlemen, why do you think he told about Kelly the Bum? You are twelve men sitting here in the jury box. You are not charged with crime. You are passing upon the criminal conduct of your fellow-man. After you get through, you go home to your families. Nobody has a word against you. It is not easy for you to imagine the condition of Steve Adams as he stood in the Boise penitentiary. Let us imagine it as well as we can. Let us, the best we can, place ourselves in his condition, and then form our judgment of how he acted, or why he acted. Here is a man taken from his home, without a charge, without commitment, without a conviction, lodged in a cell with a confessed criminal; charged with what was then the gravest offense in the civilized world. No other human being perhaps on the face of the earth at that time was so much in the limelight of public hate as the murderers of Steunenberg, whoever they were. Every newspaper was ablaze with condemnation, the press all over the United States was against them, the hand of every man was against them. They were safe nowhere, and here came Steve Adams in a single night, taken out of his state, without due process of law, or practically that, because they had no right to take him. He was not a fugitive from justice. He was taken to the penitentiary charged with this crime, placed in a cell with the man who admitted he did it; told by this man that he had confessed against him, and his only chance was to confess against someone else; left there for five days without friend and without help; then taken by the warden, who violated his oath of office and his duty to his fellow-man by turning his prison over to a detective; then placed in his hand, left for a day, while the detective told him story after story of how men charged with crime had been released and placed in glory in this world and the next by the simple act of swearing against someone else; and how the State was always good to those who were good to the State, offered every opportunity—told that if he failed to confess he would be sent back to Colorado, and be turned over to the law or to the mob; but if he confessed, over here was Oregon, over here was his home, over here were friends and liberty and a new life.

Now, gentlemen, if it had been a stronger man than Steve Adams, he would have signed the confession. Is it strange that a man would lie to save his life? I will venture to say there are men on this jury that have told a lie for smaller things than that. Men will lie to make money; they will lie in business; they will lie in the practice of law; they will lie in any of the callings of life. Is it strange that this man in the penitentiary, without a friendly hand, threatened by death, offered life—that he would lie to save his life?

Why, you have seen people with a cancer, you have seen people with the consumption, who would wander up and down over the face of the whole earth to be cured, and every newspaper that they read that has an account of a patent medicine or a quack remedy, they will spend their last dollar to get it. "All things will a man give to save his life." It is not a literal quotation, but it is the idea. Any man will commit almost any act, not any man perhaps, but most men, make almost any sacrifice, take almost any chance, to save that which is the most precious thing, the most precious boon, the thing without which everything else is useless. Did he do it for justice? Did he do it because he wanted to do something for the State? If so, he has gotten over it; he forgot it the first chance he had. As long as they could keep him locked tight, then he remained true; but when the real

Steve Adams had a chance to speak, then he at once repudiated what he had done.

Gentlemen, the simple statement of that case is enough to show that every line of that confession is a fraud. What else is there in it?

This McParland, what is his trade? Is there any worse trade than the one that man follows? Can you imagine a man being a detective until every other means of livelihood is exhausted? Watching and snaring his fellow-man. Is there any other calling in life can sink to that? But yet we have been told it is an honorable profession. Well, that depends on how you look at it. Maybe they think so. It is honorable compared with some things the State has done in this case. But it is not honorable in any old-fashioned sense of that word. McParland told the jury that this confession was given freely, voluntarily. Did he lie? Is he a liar? Thiele[1] told you the same thing. Did he tell the truth? If he did not tell the truth about that, then how can you believe his whole story? Was it given freely and voluntarily? First, can you believe a detective at all? What is he? A detective is not a liar, he is a living lie. His whole profession is that, openly and notoriously. Let me illustrate. Here is Thiele, a detective, maybe a decent fellow if he would follow a decent calling. What did he say on the witness stand? He went into the detective business, and the first thing he did was to go to Butte and join the union, join the Western Federation of Miners, raised his hand to heaven and took his oath that he was not a detective, and that he was a miner, and that he was true to his brethren, that he was a member of the Western Federation of Miners. And he took another name, and he stayed there under that other name, and attended their meetings night after night as a detective, as a spy. Was it a lie? Was it a living lie? From the moment he entered that lodge until he went away. Can you, gentlemen, understand a man doing that? Can you believe any human being who would be guilty of a lie like that? And he would have you believe that after he had lived this lie, after he had sworn he was not a detective, after he had placed his hand upon his heart as a

[1] Head of the Thiele Detective Agency.

[433]

member of the Western Federation of Miners, while his only purpose was to betray them, and destroy them—that still his word is good against another member of the Western Federation of Miners.

McParland, who is he? I do not care if he confesses ten times a day. According to his own story, he went down into the coal mines of Pennsylvania. He joined the Ancient Order of Hibernians. He took the oath that they gave. He met day after day and week after week with his neighbors and his friends, and his comrades and members of his lodge; he learned their secrets, he ate at their table, he drank at the bar with them. He fondled their children, he was one of them. And every moment, he was working himself into the lives of these men; he was a spy, a traitor, a liar; and he was there to bring them to the gallows! It is all right to punish crime, but there are certain methods that are more dangerous to the State, and are more odious to honest men than crime. It is better a thousand crimes should go unpunished, better a thousand desultory acts of men should go without punishment, than that the State should lend itself to these practices of fraud and treachery and make liars of men.

I want to know, gentlemen, how much confidence you can place in McParland under his own statements about himself. But let us go further than that into this case. Does not every fact corroborate Adams, when he says he was moved by fear and influenced by hope? Did they have him there to punish him for any crime, or did they have him there that they might move upon his poor, weak, simple mind, that they might hold before him the horrid visions of the scaffold upon one hand, and bright visions of liberty and life upon the other, and in that way induce him to bear witness against his fellow-man? You know McParland got this statement patiently, carefully, made him promises, threatened him with punishment, wrote it out, revised it and got his name to it. When you get into the jury room, you will analyze, you will read this statement of McParland's. It is not the statement of Steve Adams.

Then what? He was taken out of Orchard's cell, was he not? This statement was made on the twenty-seventh day of February, and he was taken out the next day and placed in the hospital.

Mind, he had not been charged with anything. He was placed in the hospital, and was told that they would send for his wife. And they did. And his wife was there on the second. And she was placed in charge of the clerk of the penitentiary, and sent to his mother's house, and she came to see him, and then they were so kind and so good to this self-confessed criminal, this criminal whose hands had been bathed in ex-Governor Steunenberg's blood, whose hands were red with the blood of numerous victims in Colorado, who was reeking with crimes in Colorado —they loved him so much that they put him in their private house in the penitentiary, and let his wife and children come there with him. They set up housekeeping in almost as good a manner as on the homestead in Oregon. They took Harry Orchard to board so that his eye could be upon them. And never in their little Oregon home did they have any such guests as they had in their house inside the walls of the penitentiary. There came my friend Hawley, attorney of the state, to visit with them; he sat down and spent an hour with this red-handed murderer who had been slaying his fellow-men. There came Borah, a Senator of the United States, from the state of Idaho. Steve was getting into fine company, and getting in fast. There came McParland, who told him Bible stories about King David, and other stories about Kelly the Bum. And last of all, there came the governor of the state, and took his babe out of its cradle and kissed it on the cheek. But luckily, the baby got well.

All these people came there and visited him; he was treated as the proudest citizen of the state by Boise's first citizens. He was entertaining the elite of Boise, the capital of the state. And he entertained them for six months, six long months. This confession was made on the twenty-seventh day of February, and he was a good fellow until sometime in September, more than six months. I wonder if any of these men had any difficulty in taking his blood-red hand. I wonder if they had any trouble talking with him. Did they promise him anything? Was he charged with anything? Six months in the penitentiary of the state, without a charge, is a good long while. Was he charged with the murder of Steunenberg? Oh, no, four other men were there charged with that crime; he was simply a witness, and was being fed from the guards' table, and furnished with the best of everything that Boise could afford. The warden came to see him, but Steve's brother could not come. No member of the Western Federation of Miners could come, his uncle could not come, until one day in September he got in under the false pretense that he was a delegate to the Irrigation Congress, and he was allowed to take dinner with Steve. For the first time in six long months, a friendly human being had a chance to see him alone. He had committed no crime, he was there voluntarily; they did not want him, oh, no. They were entertaining him purely voluntarily. True, they had a confession, and it had been in their possession six long months at that time. They had this, that is true, but they were not holding him as a prisoner; but the first time in six long months that any human being that could help him came inside his door, he asked him to take him out.

Then what? I wonder if these officers lie; that's too easy a question. Let us see what happened then. This old uncle came to town and got a lawyer, and the lawyer asked for a writ of habeas corpus. They had nothing to hold him on, and he had a right to the writ, and everybody in Boise knew it, but they said they did not try to hold him after he asked for a writ. What did they do? Why, when he asked for the writ, he was living with his family in a house instead of the pen, and entertaining the royalty of the state, but as quick as he asked to get out, they took him and locked him up in a cell that had been vacated a day or two before by a murderer whom the warden had swung off to glory. Why did they do that, gentlemen? Immediately when he raised his hand, immediately when he threatened to be himself and act for himself, they locked him in a cell. They did it purely to heap indignity upon him; they did it because they were mad. They saw somebody getting away. So they locked him in a cell, and he came out next day, and he was released; released! He had been placed there charged with killing Steunenberg. He had been there six months without a hearing, without indictment, without information, without reasonable charge, with nothing. A writ of habeas corpus was asked for, and he was released on that charge. And then what? He was immediately taken on a fugitive warrant from Colorado for some of the numerous crimes that counsel would have you believe he committed there. And he was taken before a magistrate and discharged on those, and then arrested to bring up here to Shoshone County, and as soon as he was placed in the hands of the sheriff of Shoshone County, Angus Sutherland, he was taken out of the county jail, where he belonged, and placed back in the penitentiary, from which the writ of habeas corpus had taken him. Handcuffs were placed upon his arms for the first time. He never needed handcuffs while he was charged with the murder of Steunenberg; he never needed handcuffs while he was charged with the crimes of Colorado; he never needed handcuffs on his arms until he dared, dared to look into the clear light of heaven and say that he wanted to be a free man and proposed to defend his rights. He was handcuffed and taken back to the penitentiary, and again detectives came to coax him back. His lawyers were refused admittance. He was taken out by stealth in the early morning, and brought overland by weary stages to this little town, where we are trying him now.

* * *

Now let's see exactly what is in the confession. Mr. Knight says that this confession has been corroborated by other evidence. Has it?

Mr. Adams says that Orchard told him what to say on these various matters. No doubt Adams knew something about the killing of Boule. He must have known whether he told Orchard or not, he was there at the time. No doubt Adams knew about the quarrel in that country. No doubt he knew the difficulties between the settlers and the jumpers. He might have heard of Tyler's disappearance. Orchard was there a year later. He was there after his body was found. He was there after the newspapers had told all about it. After every neighbor in the whole community could describe every stitch of clothing there was on the skeleton and the place where it was found. Orchard could not have helped hearing about it, except perhaps how it happened, and no human being yet knows whether this statement is true or false. They do not know whether anybody ever took Fred

Tyler out and shot him, and they don't know from the evidence in this case whether Fred Tyler is dead. But I will venture to say this: that if Fred Tyler had taken out a life insurance policy of $5,000 in the New York Life, in favor of his poor old mother, and she had come into a court of justice and asked for the payment of this policy, the company would have said there is no legal evidence on earth to prove that your son is dead. No insurance company would ever dream of paying it upon proof like this. If it were a civil case, they could not recover on this proof, let alone make a case beyond a reasonable doubt.

* * *

I want to examine a little further this confession. What is it for? You will read it when you get in your jury room. McParland got it for the purpose of fastening crime upon the Western Federation of Miners in the Steunenberg matter. It bears upon every page clear evidence that it had no other purpose. He did not get it up for Tyler. He got it up to fasten evidence upon Moyer, Haywood, Pettibone, Simpkins and St. John, if possible. Every word of that confession shows that it was a cunningly devised lie, a lie made by him in which he offered Steve Adams his life, if Steve Adams would corroborate the story. It is hard to be confronted with the gallows on one hand and with liberty upon the other. Let us all hope that no such temptation could ever come to us, but many, and many, and many a man in all the ages of the world, has fallen under temptation like that.

* * *

I have said all I need to about this confession; that a man was taken to the pen, that he was placed in a cell without charge and without crime, that he was guarded and watched and tended, that he was browbeaten and bullied and promised all these things, to save his life, and to get back his home. It is as plain as the sun in the heavens. But this is not the worst. McParland has come here, and in view of these plain facts, and in the face of the written confession itself, has dared to raise his hand to heaven and swear to this jury that this is a free and voluntary confession, made without fear and without hope. Gentlemen, this confession is the record of a band of conspirators who took an American citizen, who outraged his liberty, who violated the laws of the land, who trampled on the Constitution that was made to protect him, and then committed the darkest and deepest perjury in this court of justice to cover up their deeds.

It seems to me that whatever may be said about the facts of this case, whatever may be said about proving that Fred Tyler is dead, whatever may be said about the confession, it would be difficult to imagine a case where clearer evidence has been shown to the jury that whoever did commit the act, still the defendant was not responsible for the crime.

What does the State charge in the first place? The document upon which this case is based was signed more than one year ago; almost six months ago the information was filed in this court. The State has had one whole year in which they might prepare the evidence. Evidence in a criminal case, which involves the life of a human being, must not be guesswork, and surmise and suspicion; it must be facts; it must be so clear and conclusive that it leaves no room for honest doubt. It was for the State to say when this man was killed, where, and how, and by whom. They had a year upon that proposition. After taking all the time it was necessary for them to take, they alleged that he was killed on or about August tenth.

Now, gentlemen, I do not want in the least to attempt to deceive. An allegation that a man was killed on August tenth may be supported by evidence that he was killed about that time; and this allegation says he was killed on or about the tenth of August. And while a man may be convicted if the crime was committed on some other day, still, before there can be a conviction, the jury must be satisfied upon some particular day; they must pick out some time, and you must be able to say that on some particular occasion, it is clear to your own mind that this felony was committed. Then you will take that particular date, and consider that date, and see whether all the evidence in this case sustains that date or not beyond a reasonable doubt. They picked out the tenth day of August; they made it almost as specific and definite as it was possible to make it; they tried their case, they listened to ours, then they come into this court and admit that we proved an alibi from the eighth of August down, and that the date must have been before the tenth. Until they heard our case they believed otherwise, they charged otherwise, they proved otherwise. They put us to the trouble and expense of tracing the footsteps of Steve Adams until we traced them so thoroughly that we satisfied the State itself.

❖ ❖ ❖

The presumption of the prosecution, and the basis of this case, is that we are defending a sort of inhuman machine, who can be detailed, as McParland says, to go here and there, and execute whomsoever somebody wishes to have killed. That up here in Idaho were some people that the old pioneers wished to get rid of, and they sent to Colorado and got this engine of destruction to come up here and put them out of the way. It is all right; that theory is no more fantastic than the other theories out of which they built up this case.

❖ ❖ ❖

Gentlemen, I am going to leave this case with you. It is the case of the state of Idaho against Steve Adams for the killing of Tyler. Both sides, the State upon their side, and we upon ours, have told this jury that it is more than this. Gentlemen, is it a case against an unknown man for the killing of an unknown man? You know it is not. You know what it is. In the greatest struggle and contest of the United States, the fiercest struggle that is known in the whole world that is being waged today, the contest between capital and labor, all sorts of side issues come into light.

Up here in Idaho, in your little mining town, you are engaged in trying one of the side issues of this great, world-wide fight. This man is an insignificant man, his wife is an unknown woman, his children are poor, a man in the humble walks of life, and why is it all this wealth and power is arrayed against him? Simple, gentlemen; because he is part of the great struggle, a struggle in which I do not mean to say the workingman has been always right. I believe in him, I work for him; I have fought for him; I have given him such ability as I had; I have given him all my energy; I have given him every pulse beat of my heart, because I believe in his cause. I know he is sometimes wrong, I know he is sometimes cruel, and sometimes corrupt, I know that he is often unreasonable and unjust. No bitter contest in the world was ever fought by an army which was always right; no bitter contest in the world was ever fought by an army that was always wrong. I know that in this world-wide contest, this contest which has lasted since the human race began, this contest between the rich and the poor, this effort of the weak and the poor and the despised to get more liberty, more prosperity, more life, while they have committed errors and done wrong—I know that in this contest the poor are right, eternally right. I know that the world and the ages are working for them, that time is working for them. The world goes forward, not backward. It looks toward the time when there will be more equality and more justice toward men. Men of the State, are you so blind as to believe that if you hang Steve Adams this war will be over; do you believe that if you hang Moyer, Haywood and Pettibone, this war will end, and that the laborers and mechanics will take up their tools and abandon their dreams and hopes? Aye, you may hang Steve Adams until dead, you may spill the blood of thousands, but you cannot cure hatred by hatred. You cannot blot out a great movement or a great idea, you cannot kill a conscientious liberty-loving movement, as the labor movement is, the whole world over. It will have no effect. You can spill Steve Adams' blood, but what of it? You will live to know that you have done an injustice, that you have committed a crime, because you singled this man out at the behest of someone else. You may kill these other men if you will, but the cause will go marching on.

Sometime the employers will learn, sometime we will learn, that hatred begets hatred, that you cannot cure conditions with policemen and penitentiaries, with jails and scaffolds. Some day they will learn, sometime we will learn, that every man you butcher, whether with a gun or a dagger, or a club, or upon the scaffold, only adds to the hatred and the prejudice of the other side. Sometime these bitter passions will pass away, and if they pass away in the lifetime of the generation which is prose-

[441]

cuting Adams today, and prosecuting Moyer, Haywood and Pettibone today, sane men will look back upon this jury and will thank their God, and thank this jury, that in the bitterness of this strife, you were not swept away, but were willing to listen to the evidence and consider the man, and the circumstances and the time, and the place, and unmoved by passion and prejudice, pronounce a verdict of Not Guilty in this case.

THE JURY was out two days. They couldn't reach a verdict; the count was seven to five for acquittal after several ballots. Adams was held for retrial.

Before Adams' next trial, however, the case of the State of Idaho against Bill Haywood was called.

While Haywood, Moyer and Pettibone were awaiting trial, President Theodore Roosevelt tagged them "undesirable citizens."

At the suggestion of Eugene Victor Debs, union men throughout the country began to wear large buttons with the inscription "I Am an Undesirable Citizen."

Labor, in the meantime, raised a $250,000 defense fund. Darrow's fee in the case was reportedly $35,000.

Haywood was the first to be brought to trial.

Attorneys for the prosecution were James H. Hawley who also prosecuted the Adams case; William E. Borah, who had been elected a United States Senator but did not take his seat until after the trial; Owen M. Van Duyn; and Charles Koelsche.

At the defense table with Darrow were Edmund Richardson of Denver, John Nugent and Edgar Wilson of Boise, and Fred Miller of Seattle.

The judge was Fremont Wood.

Scores of newspapermen from all parts of the country came to Boise to cover the trial, which opened early in May 1907.

The Chicago Tribune on the opening day suggested in a headline that the trial:

MAY BE EPOCH MAKING

Haywood's wife was brought into the courtroom in a wheelchair. She had been an invalid since the birth of their youngest daughter who was now nine years old. She was at her husband's side throughout the trial.

There were 26 men on the panel of veniremen when court opened. Five were excused for personal reasons; eight were challenged for cause; thirteen were accepted by the prosecution. The defense challenged two for cause and three were temporarily accepted.

At court's adjournment at the end of the first day, eleven men were in the box and 100 more veniremen were being called to appear at the next session.

On May 25, sixteen days after the trial began, the newspapers continued to carry headlines: "Boise Jury Hard to Get."

The following day the Chicago Tribune headline read:

DARROW ACCEPTS TALESMAN WHO
SAYS HE WOULD HANG AN
ANARCHIST ON SIGHT

J. E. Tourtellottee, the prospective juror, had said he was opposed to capital punishment "except in case of war and in the case of an organization against society."

Darrow, surprised at this statement, wanted to know what type of organization.

TOURTELLOTTEE: Well, I mean a bunch of anarchists, for instance—

DARROW: But you would vote to hang an anarchist?

TOURTELLOTTEE: Yes, if I understand what an anarchist is, I would hang him on sight. I regard it as a matter of self-defense. It is the right of society to protect itself.

DARROW: Then if you should vote to take this defendant's life, it would be on the theory that he is an enemy of society.

TOURTELLOTTEE: That would be the only ground on which I would do it.

Darrow accepted him. But the following day he was excused by the prosecution on the ground of his opposition to capital punishment.

The jury was finally impaneled on June 3. It was composed of nine farmers, a real estate agent, a building contractor, and a foreman of fence construction on a railroad. Of these, there were seven Republicans, four Democrats, and one Prohibitionist.

At one point when the court was hearing arguments on a technicality, Borah started to read from the record. The crowd in the courtroom began to leave. Confusion followed. Borah stopped reading. Said Darrow: "Never mind. The jury can't get away."

On a hot July 24, 1907, Darrow began his address to the jury.

G ENTLEMEN, I need not tell you how important this case is. How important to the man on trial and to those who still must be placed where he is today. How important to his family and his friends. How important to society. How important to a great movement which represents the hopes and the wishes and the aspirations of all men who labor to sustain their daily life. You know it! You could not have sat here day after day so long as you have without understanding it, and grasping it, and excusing us if, in our haste and zeal, we seemed to say things we should not have said, and forgot things we should have spoken of to you.

And, gentlemen, we are here as aliens to you. Our client and the men who are with him down here in this jail have been brought fifteen hundred miles to be tried by a practically foreign, alien jury—a jury unfamiliar with their method of thought, a jury unfamiliar with their methods of life, a jury who has not viewed life from the standpoints of industry as these men have viewed it. I am here, two thousand miles from home, unacquainted with you, with your life, with your methods of reasoning. All of us are brought here in an alien country, before people, if not unfriendly, whom at least we do not know, and we are here met by the ablest counsel that the state of Idaho ever produced—the peer of any counsel anywhere; and, more than that, we are here in the home of the man who was killed in the most ruthless, cowardly, brutal way that any man could meet his death.

*   *   *

More than that, gentlemen, we are all human. We have come into this courtroom and into this community—a community that has been deliberately poisoned for a year and a half, a community where feeling, and sentiment, and hatred have been deliberately sown against this defendant and his friends; a community where lie after lie has been sent broadcast like poison to infect the minds of men—we have come here after a year and a half of that, and must submit our case to a jury that has been fed upon this poison for all these months. We have no redress. We ask for none. You have sat here for two months, and you know the lies that have been broadcast in almost every paper that is circulated in this community. You have heard it from the witness stand, and you know it, and they could not have failed to have influenced this jury and this court. Men cannot rise above their environments. We are all alike, and if I were to tell this jury that I believed they were great enough and wise enough and strong enough to overcome the environments in which they live, and if I were to say to this Court that he could do what no other judge in Christendom ever did, rise superior to his environments and his life, you would know I was lying to you. You would understand that, if you did not understand anything else. We are all human, we are all influenced alike, moved by the same feelings and the same emotions, a part of the life that is around us, and it is not in the nature of things that this Court or this jury would not to some degree have been influenced by all that has gone before. But, gentlemen, as men go, as we see our neighbors and our friends, I have no doubt that you twelve men before me intend to carefully guard and protect the rights, the hopes, the interests and the life of this defendant. I have no doubt that you mean to give to him the same honest trial, the same benefit of the law, that you would expect twelve men to give you, if by some trick of Chance or by some turn of the wheel of Fate your life was hanging in the balance and twelve of your fellow-men were passing upon it.

Gentlemen, I don't believe that anywhere where the English language is spoken or where the common law prevails, any intelligent lawyer would ever have dreamed of convicting defendants upon evidence like this, except they relied upon the strained, harsh circumstances of this case, and had they not known that these defendants, taken by force fifteen hundred miles away and dropped down before a hostile jury and in a community crying for their blood, would be cruelly handicapped in this, the supreme struggle of their lives. Do you consider how much it means? Suppose one of you twelve men were taken from your farm, charged with murder, not to be tried in a community where you lived, not to be tried by farmers who knew you and knew your way of life, and your method of thought—that you were to be taken to Chicago, to be taken to New York, to be dropped down into a great and unfamiliar city whose men do not think the thoughts that you think, whose people do not lead the lives that you lead, and expected there, over fifteen hundred miles from home and friends, to make your defense; and then suppose that you were charged with a crime which every member of that community regarded as a crime against the sanctity of his own state, against himself—then you could appreciate the condition in which we find ourselves today, and could understand the handicap that has been placed upon us from the beginning of this case.

Gentlemen of the jury, one thing more: William D. Haywood is charged with murder. He is charged with having killed ex-Governor Steunenberg. He was not here. He was fifteen hundred or a thousand miles away, and he had not been here for years. There might be some member of this jury who would hesitate to take away the life of a human being upon the rotten testimony that has been given to this jury to convict a fellow-citizen. There might be some who still hold in their minds a lurking suspicion that this defendant had to do with this horrible murder. You might say, we will compromise; we cannot take his life upon Orchard's word, but we will send him to the penitentiary; we will find him guilty of manslaughter; we will find him guilty of murder in the second degree instead of the first.

Gentlemen, you have the right to do it if you want to. But I want to say to you twelve men that whatever else you are, I trust you are not cowards, and I want to say to you, too, that William Haywood is not a coward. I would not thank this jury if they found this defendant guilty of assault and battery and assessed a five-dollar fine against him. This murder was cold, deliberate, cowardly in the extreme, and if this man, sitting in his office in Denver, fifteen hundred miles away, employed this miserable assassin to come here and do this cowardly work, then, for God's sake, gentlemen, hang him by the neck until dead. Don't compromise in this case, whatever else you do. If he is guilty—if, under your conscience and before your God, you can say that you believe that man's story, and believe it beyond a reasonable doubt, then take him—take him and hang him. He has fought many a fight—many a fight with the persecutors who are hounding him in this court. He has met them in many a battle in the open field, and he is not a coward. If he is to die, he will die as he has lived, with his face to the foe. This man is either innocent or guilty. If he is guilty, I have nothing to say for him.

Gentlemen, I am not going to apologize in any way or seek to belittle the terrible crime that was committed in Canyon County.

My associate said that Governor Steunenberg was a great and a good man. I don't know anything about that, whether he was either one, and I don't care. It is just as much murder to kill a bad man as it is to kill a good man. It is just as much murder to kill the humblest man who tills the fields as it is the king upon his throne. There is no difference. I have taken no pains to study who Governor Steunenberg was, excepting he was the governor of this state. I assume he was like everybody else—like you, like me, like everybody. I assume he had his virtues and he had his failings. If he did not, he would have had no friends. It is a great mistake to think that because a man had been a governor the law should be any swifter to wreak vengeance upon someone by taking his life away than if he had been a plain ordinary man, and yet, gentlemen, it is true. If this man had not at one time been governor of the state, I do not believe there is money enough in the state treasury of Idaho to hire a lawyer with a reputation to ask for another man's blood upon the evidence that has been offered in this case.

Governor Steunenberg was a man. He had a right to live. Whether he was a great man or a small man, a good man or a bad man, wise or foolish, cuts no figure in this case. If any word of mine or any act of this defendant could bring back this life of which we have heard, how quickly we would say that word and do that act! But the past is settled. No result from this jury can call that man back to life. No verdict that you can give can bring back the father, or bring back the husband, or in any degree lessen the pang that must have come to those near and dear for the murder of that man. All you can do, gentlemen, with your power, all you can do toward fixing up the schemes of the Almighty, is to make more widows and more orphans on account of the death of Steunenberg, and if this jury wants to take that responsibility in this case upon this evidence, well and good. May peace be with you.

* * *

You have listened to the argument of Mr. Hawley in this case. He told you how honest he was. Now, I will not tell you anything about that. You will have to find out from my argument whether I am honest or not, and whether I am does not make any difference with this case, and whether Mr. Hawley is does not make any difference in this case. You are the gentlemen who are to determine this—not Mr. Hawley, not I. He said to you, gentlemen of the jury, that he would not prosecute this case unless he believed this defendant guilty. Now, why? Is he prosecuting it because he believes him guilty? Is that it? Or is he prosecuting it because he thinks he may want to put another ell on his house, and wants some more deficiency warrants with which to do it? Which is it? Has any man a right to make a statement like that? I hope there is no one here who cares a fig about what Mr. Hawley thinks about this case. He may be bughouse—and he is, if all of his statements are true—or he is worse. Let me show you what he said, and then judge for yourselves.

He said to these twelve men—men of fair intelligence and fair learning—that you would be warranted in convicting Bill Haywood if you took Harry Orchard's evidence out of this case, and still he says he is honest. Maybe he is, but if he is honest he is crazy, and he can have his choice. There is not an intelligent man who has listened to this case who does not know that it is Orchard from beginning to end; and there is not a word of incriminating evidence in it, let alone enough to take the life of a human being, without Harry Orchard; and Mr. Hawley told you that there was enough evidence in this case to hang Bill Haywood if you left it out. Is he crazy or does he think you twelve men are daffy? One or the other. . . .

* * *

Mr. Hawley talked to you for a day and a half about how guilty this defendant is. What was the burden of his talk? Was there anything in it but Orchard—Orchard—Orchard, from beginning to end? Did he play upon any other string, or can he play upon any other string excepting Orchard—Orchard—Orchard?

But let us cut out the Western Federation men for a moment. I am just going to give you a little object lesson—a little advance sketch of Harry Orchard as I know him. Not the seraph with the wings, supported on one side by Hawley and upon the other by Father McParland—not he. I don't know that Harry—nobody else does, excepting Hawley; even the Senator [Borah] has not become acquainted with him, and I don't think he will stand for it. Even the Senator, if he honestly thought that Harry was going to heaven, would do his level best to go the other way, and would probably succeed. I want to see whether I can get the right focus on this fellow before we get into the serious business. Orchard is all there is from beginning to end of this case, and two lawyers seriously propose to take away the life of a human being upon the testimony of Harry Orchard. Gentlemen, I do not believe it was ever done in any civilized land on the face of the earth, and for the very simple reason that a land could not be civilized where such a thing would be done, and it will not be done here in Idaho.

Well, gentlemen, I am going to discuss this religious question further on, but I am like Brother Hawley, I am long on that subject. I do not know whether the Senator can beat Brother Hawley and me upon that or not. Of course Hawley told you—now you people know better than I do about Mr. Hawley, because I never saw him until he was in this case, and I would not judge him by anything here—but he says when a man gets religion he is all right, and he will not lie, he cannot lie; he has seen this great light, and he is led from above, and the jury must believe he cannot lie because he has got religion. Well, if Hawley has not got it, he ought to have it. The best I could do would be to advise him to go right off and get it, if there is any left after what Orchard has taken.

Gentlemen, I sometimes think I am dreaming in this case. I sometimes wonder whether this is a case, whether here in Idaho or anywhere in the country, broad and free, a man can be placed on trial and lawyers seriously ask to take away the life of a human being upon the testimony of Harry Orchard. Lawyers come here and ask you, upon the word of that sort of a man, to send this man to the gallows; to make his wife a widow, and his children orphans—on his word. For God's sake what sort of a community exists up here in the state of Idaho that sane men should ask it? Need I come here from Chicago to defend the honor of your state? A juror who would take away the life of a human being upon testimony like that would place a stain upon the state of his nativity—a stain that all the waters of the great seas could never wash away; and yet they ask it. You had better let a thousand men go unwhipped of justice, you had better let all the criminals that come to Idaho escape scot-free, than to have it said that twelve men of Idaho would take away the life of a human being upon testimony like that.

Let me illustrate a minute. Here is a man who was depraved enough until he got religion. Hawley will concede that. If I were to get out of here and Orchard were to get out, I would feel uncomfortable. I would feel sort of squeamish if I thought he was anywhere in the same country. I would feel, if I had to go out of my house, I ought to go out through the sewer or up through the chimney, so that if I opened the door I would not run onto a dynamite bomb. It is a pretty fierce game. But that is easy. I will tell you one that is fiercer than that. That is not much of a game. I will tell you the game that Mr. Hawley wishes to stamp with the approval of twelve jurors and play on the American people, and if he can do it, gentlemen, do it, and may God be with you; you will need Him.

If a man may commit every crime known to man; if he may be a perjurer, a thief, a bigamist, a burglar, a murderer; if he may kill man after man, and then, when he is caught with the blood dripping from his fingers, if he can turn to you and say: Here now, you told me to do it; I was down to your house last night, in your parlor, and you told me to plunge the dagger into that man's heart; then if twelve jurors can turn from that assassin, with his hands dripping with blood, and swear it upon you, and take your life, it is the fiercest game that was ever put up in the American republic, and that is what is asked for here.

It is not enough for a plain, simple, honest man to tell his simple story and denounce it as a lie. It is not enough to bring witness after witness to disprove it. This man, taken in his infamy and crime, turns to his neighbor and says, "You are the man," and he says to the jury, "Hang him and save me." Gentlemen, I do not know—I sometimes think it is an insult to argue a case like this to twelve jurors, and I do not believe that twelve men anywhere would do it. If one of you had seen the act, if one of you knew it was true, you would not have a right to convict upon testimony like that. If you can hang Bill Haywood because this criminal says he is guilty, then, gentlemen, no other criminal need suffer in Idaho. There is no doubt about it. Tell me why any man needs to go to the gallows or the prison when he can turn and accuse his neighbor, and twelve men believe him and take his blood? Gentlemen, I am serious about this. I am either right or Hawley has gone crazy over it. And I have wondered and wondered and wondered whether I could be wrong and whether they could find anywhere on the face of the earth twelve men who would do a deed like this. I do not believe it. If twelve jurors could take away the life of a human being because a man like that pointed his finger at him to save his own life, then I would say that human life would be safer in the hands of Harry Orchard than in the hands of a jury who would do it. Would any jury dream of it? What are our teachings, our instincts; what have we learned from the past that we should ever dream of giving credit or countenance to a monster like that?

Let us take a short view of this fellow. Who is he? And is he converted? We will find out whom we have got to deal with before we deal with him. I have sometimes thought I had a fair command of language, but it fails when I get to describing Harry Orchard, so I will just call him Orchard, and let it go at that. Who is this fellow upon whose testimony you gentlemen are asked to shift this crime to Haywood? Let us see: He is unique in history. If he is not the biggest murderer who ever lived, he is the biggest liar, at least, who ever lived, and I undertake to say that the record of the English and American courts cannot show a single man who has been impeached by as many witnesses as Harry Orchard. Why, gentlemen, if Harry Orchard were George Washington, who had come into a court of justice with his great name behind him, and if he was impeached and contradicted by as many as Harry Orchard has been, George Washington would go out of it disgraced and counted the Ananias of the age. No man living could stand up against it excepting a phenomenal murderer like Orchard.

Let me say this, gentlemen: I may be wrong, but I certainly never felt in my life as strongly the impossibility of any American jury giving credit to evidence as I feel it here. I may mistake you twelve men. I have sat with you for nearly three months, and I have been trying to read you day after day. Yet I may mistake all of you; when I look into your eyes I may not see your souls as I think I do; there may be deep down some hideous plan or some method that I cannot understand, or I may have gone daffy myself. But while I have thought of this subject, and lost my sleep thinking of it, I have never felt there could be any danger that any American jury could take the word of a perjured monster like this, and with that word deprive a fellow-being of his life. Gentlemen, if I am wrong, if this jury, upon its oath and its conscience and before its God, can say it demands a sacrifice, well and good. We will furnish you the victim and do it with a glad and cheerful heart.

Who is this fellow [Orchard]? We have not been favored with anything but his own story, and being such a monstrous liar, he has not probably given us the best evidence of himself—the worst evidence. But take his own story. A man who was bred to cheat and to lie; a man who, as a young man, in the first blush of his manhood, gave his soul to Christ—I do not know about these second conversions, whether they are any solider than the first or not. Do you, Senator?

BORAH: I have not had the first.

DARROW: He belonged to the church. He was superintendent of a Sunday school. He was a Christian Endeavorer. He is not endeavoring any more; he has got there. That was when he was a young man. But that did not help him then. Now, maybe he has got religion for keeps this time. If I was the governor and I thought he had, I would kill him quick, before he got a chance to get over it, and thus make sure of his soul. I do not think Harry ought to trust himself. But he had it before, and he commenced to cheat and he commenced to steal and burned down his own cheese factory to get the insurance—and he must have made out a false affidavit in order to get it. It shows that he could lie under oath, too, at that time. And he ran away with his neighbor's wife, and he left his wife and his little child without a penny, and they never heard of him since, until recently, and he went out into the world, not to work—oh, no, not for

Harry, not to work. He knew a better game than that and he commenced a better game still. He came West to grow up with the country. The limited field of Ontario[1] was too small for him. He must have a name and he had to have room to move around in—this man, this wonder who is so great in the eyes of Hawley that the whole world is perjured when placed beside him. Then what? I do not know what he did next. The woman he took away with him left him, which shows that she had some sense, even if she did go away with him.

He went to the Coeur d'Alêne. He says that, although he had been in the union but a month, he touched off one of the fuses that blew up the Bunker Hill mill and killed two men. He wandered around, gambling and doing nothing for several years, and then he says he killed two men in the Vindicator mine, fourteen at the Independence depot, murdered Lyte Gregory[2] in cold blood, tried to kill Peabody,[3] Goddard,[4] Gabbert,[5] and a number of others; tried to kill two hundred men in the Vindicator mine; tried to blow up the Idanha hotel and kill three or four hundred more; intended to blow up Max Malich's boardinghouse and kill five or six hundred more. All of his intentions were away ahead of his achievement. He tried to kill Bradley[6] and did kill Steunenberg. But all this time he was a liar, an unstinted liar, burned a saloon, made a false affidavit to get the insurance, told that he had killed his brother when he had not, told that he had killed John Neville[7] when he had not, got his picture taken as a criminal committing murder—lied and lied and lied—violating, as I have said, every commandment of God and man, and then caught red-handed.

Now you are asked to believe him. For what? Now, let us see about it. Gentlemen, if he had stopped there, do you think you would have taken a chance on Bill Haywood's life? Suppose he had not got religion, then what? Now, if I laid much stress upon

[1] Birthplace of Orchard.
[2] Mine company detective Orchard claimed he murdered.
[3] Gov. J. H. Peabody of Colorado.
[4] Justice L. M. Goddard, Colorado Supreme Court.
[5] Chief Justice W. H. Gabbert, Colorado Supreme Court.
[6] F. W. Bradley, organizer, Mine Owners Protective Association.
[7] John Neville, saloon operator whom Orchard allegedly murdered.

the religious end of this case I think I would want to have it proven. So far we have not anything but Orchard's word for it, and a little corroboration on a vital and material point would not hurt his word. It seems to me we have nothing but that. Father McParland has not come here and told about the laying on of hands. If I was going to take a chance on Bill Haywood's body, on the character of this man's soul, I would want some little bit of a scrap of evidence outside of him. Now, he may be the most religious man who has ever lived. Even then you cannot always trust religious men. I am sorry to say it, but it is true, because religious men have killed now and then, they have lied now and then. It is not a sure thing. If it was, we would have hard work with the evidence in this case, because we have had several religious witnesses ourselves, and it would be a hard job to tell which religious man was truthful. You would have to say Orchard was, of course. But has he got it?

He was captured red-handed at Caldwell. Mark the peculiarities of the fellow. He never did a courageous thing in his life, not one. Can you show me one act of his life that had any courage? If his story is true, he was with a thousand men when he touched off the fuse at the Bunker Hill mill. If his story is true, he sneaked through the dark passages of the mine and fixed a box of powder when he blew up the Vindicator. If his story is true, he sneaked back in the darkness and put the box of powder under the station and ran away in the night when he killed fourteen men. If his story is true, he laid a bomb at Goddard's gate that he might open it and be killed. If his story is true, he met a man coming out of a saloon, drunken, at midnight, and killed him without a chance for a word, for an act. If he has told the truth, he sneaked up the back stairs and poured arsenic or strychnine in milk to poison a man and his wife and little babe.

If it is true, he went up in the night and laid a bomb at Steunenberg's gate, and then he ran back in the darkness and got almost to the hotel before Steunenberg was dead. Will you show me the act that was not the act of a sneaking, craven coward in this man's life? Will you show me where he has ever met bravely a man or beast? Has he ever taken a chance in his miserable life? Has he ever met a foeman where that foeman had a chance to shoot or a chance to strike? Has he ever gone into a court of justice and stood his ground, and is not his action in this case on a par with every act of that monstrous life? And yet you are asked to believe him. And Hawley tells you to say that he is truthful and that our men and our women are perjurers because Harry Orchard, this creature Orchard, has told the truth. All right, gentlemen, Hawley may know you better than I do. He may; I trust he does not. Now, what does Orchard do after he is caught? Did he not do just what he always did?

Why did not Orchard place the bomb under Steunenberg's bed at the Idanha hotel? What does he say? Not that he thought it would blow up a lot of innocent people; oh, no; not that he thought it would kill some women and some little noncombatant children; oh, no; but he was afraid maybe he could not get away. Are you going to believe him? You better leave him to Hawley—he needs a pet in his old age. Afraid he could not get away, and he was caught then at Caldwell, and the first thing he did was to try to get away. Tried to get away—how?

Now, gentlemen, let us have a little common sense about this case, seeing Mr. Hawley has got through with his argument. Suppose I was to go to this jury and try to demonstrate to you that Harry Orchard would kill a man for $50. Would you believe me? You would think he would kill two for $50, wouldn't you? Now, gentlemen, would there be any doubt about it? Could there be one of you twelve men that would hesitate a moment to believe me if I came to you to demonstrate that Harry Orchard would kill a man for $50? Now, suppose I come here and say to you that he would kill a man to save his own neck, then what? Did he ever get as much for any act in his life as he is getting for this? Why, if you rolled together all the money that he ever claims he got from burning cheese factories and killing men and from the gaming table, it would all sink into nothing compared with the bribe that is offered here for Haywood's life. Tell me that you would believe that this man would kill a man for $50 and you would not believe that he would deliver over three men to death to save his neck? Any need to talk about that? But what did Hawley say? Let us see what Hawley said. He says, "We have not promised him anything." Well, now, gentlemen, again is he crazy, or is he just deceiving you? Which? How do you know they have not promised him anything? Has McParland said so? Has Gooding said so? Has Van Duyn said so? The strong man at the back of this prosecution whose orders all the rest obey to the last letter, has he said so? I do not suppose he knows. Hawley has not said so, except in his argument. Lawyers, like everybody else, have to be sworn before you will believe them, and you have to watch a little then, sometimes. Has anybody said so but Harry Orchard? What do you think about a little corroboration on that?

RICHARDSON: He did not say so, either.

DARROW: Well, I do not know as he did, no. He did not say he was not promised anything, but he practically said he thought he might have his life saved. But I do not want to say anything like that. What do you think? Has he been promised anything? I hope the Senator has made a note about this, and maybe he will tell us. Is Orchard to get anything? Or has he got anything, for delivering these three enemies of the Mine Owners' Association into the lion's den? Let us see. I do not know whether he has been promised exactly, but he has been paid. You cannot fool Harry. He got his money in advance.

Let me show you, gentlemen: the Court will instruct you that you have a right to take your common sense into the jury box with you. Instead of Mr. Hawley's argument, you may take that in there. A lawyer is not presumed to have any, but a jury is.

Harry Orchard was captured on the first of January, 1906, about eighteen months ago. He is living, isn't he? No doubt about that. He looks fat and sleek and healthy and not in danger of any sudden death. If, to save his miserable carcass, he had not lied to kill three men, the grass would have been growing above his grave for twelve months past. Is there any doubt about that? You cannot beat him out of the year and a half that he has already had, and if it is worth only a dollar a day to him he would kill these three men for that a good many times over. You cannot beat him out of that. But what else? Why, so long as he is doing this great service for the State, would anybody think of killing Harry Orchard? You might as well kill the avenging angel and get done with the whole scheme. They need him in their business. While Harry Orchard is living, and society is safe, I take it nobody intends to kill him until we get through with Haywood, with Moyer, with Pettibone; until the last trial has been had; until the last appeal to the Supreme Court has been taken; until they shall be hanged and their bodies laid away in the earth or eaten up with quicklime. They will take care of Harry up to that time, won't they? So he has got a fair lease of life, and I think an insurance company might carry a policy on him—at least one of the kind that he used to work for.

But Jack Simpkins is still at large. Jack has been evading the Pinkerton detectives, who, for the time being, have been so busy hunting up this wonderful mass of evidence against Moyer, Haywood and Pettibone that they have not had time to get Jack. Well, I do not know when they will get him. They never ask me about him. I have no idea when this great magician, McParland, will reach out his hands and grasp him. McParland is getting pretty old himself, and if he does not get him before he dies there will never be any other man that will get him, because when he dies all the acuteness of the detective association will die with him. He is the only detective that I ever heard of that could quote Scripture, and it would be too bad to have anything happen to him. Jack is at large, and they surely wouldn't hang Harry Orchard until Jack was caught and prosecuted and the jury had finally passed on him, and the courts had passed on him and his body was laid away. Then, there is a lot more of them. There are 40,000 members of the Western Federation of Miners, all criminals, and Orchard knows them all, and so long as there is a neck to hang, why kill this man? You might just as well do away with the gallows so you couldn't hang any more, as to kill him.

Nonsense! Is there any man on earth who believes that anyone has any purpose of hanging this man? And if so, when? And he would have been dead a year only for this. A year! Thank God, we have had a year of his society on the earth anyhow. We have shown what a wonderful thing the Christian religion is, when it can make over Harry. Now let us see:

I speak under disadvantages with Hawley when I talk about the Christian religion, for at least he talks as if he knew. Now, if I make some slip there is the Senator to come along and pick me up afterward and show me where I am wrong. If he doesn't know himself, Hawley will tell him tonight after I get through, so he will take no chances. But I am going to take a chance to talk a little about that subject, for of all the miserable claptrap that has been thrown into a jury for the sake of getting it to give some excuse for taking the life of a man, this is the worst. I wonder, gentlemen of the jury, if Hawley would ask you to believe him and hang Bill Haywood, without giving him religion? So they had to get religion and throw it into this case, and they have gotten it from nobody but Harry Orchard. McParland hasn't told you anything about it. Nobody who is supposed to be any judge of it has told you anything about it. Nobody has said anything about it excepting Harry Orchard and Hawley. Well, let us see what he has. I want to say a few words for the benefit, not of this jury, but of those sickly slobbering idiots who talk about Harry Orchard's religion. If I could think of any stronger term to apply to them I would apply that term. The English language falls down on Orchard and likewise upon all those idiots who talk about Orchard's regeneration. Now I am going to take a chance and talk about that for a few minutes.

There is one thing that is well for them to remember right at the beginning, and that is that at least a month before Dean Hinks[1] persuaded him to lay his sins on Jesus, Father McParland had persuaded him to lay his crimes on Moyer, Haywood and Pettibone. You might remember that in starting. It is on a par with the character of a characterless man—I am referring to Orchard now, so there will be no mistake. It is a smooth game of shifty Harry. You are asked to give him immunity and to give immunity to everyone of his kind. You are asked to say to the old and to say to the youth, You may kill, you may burn, you may lie, you may steal, you may commit any crime or any act for-

---

[1] Rev. Edwin S. Hinks, Dean, St. Michael's Cathedral, Boise, Idaho, who listened to Orchard's confession and wrote the introduction to his *Autobiography*.

bidden by God or forbidden by man, and then you can turn and throw your crimes on somebody else, and throw your sins on God, and the lawyers will sing your praises. All right, gentlemen. If in your judgment public policy demands it, go ahead and do it. Don't stop for a little matter like Bill Haywood's neck.

Shifty Harry meets McParland. He has lived a life of crime and been taken in his deeds, and what does he do? Why, he saves his soul by throwing the burden on Moyer, Haywood and Pettibone. How can you beat that game, gentlemen? Can you beat it? And you twelve men are asked to set your seal of approval on it and to make that contract good so it may go out to every youth in the land. You may need to do it, but it should be a mighty strong necessity that would lead you to do it, should it not?

Now, gentlemen, like Brother Hawley, and I know like Senator Borah, I, too, have a profound regard for religion. Mine may be broader than Brother Hawley's. I don't want to say to these twelve men that I think the Christian religion is the only religion that the world has ever known. I do not believe it for a moment. I have the greatest respect for any religion or any code of ethics that would do anything to help man, whatever that religion may be. And for the poor black man who looks into the black face of his wooden idol and who prays to that wooden idol to make him a better man and a stronger man, I have the profoundest respect. I know that there is in him, when he addresses his prayers to his wooden idol, the same holy sentiment, and the same feeling that there is in the breast of a Christian when he raises his prayer to the Christian's God. It is all one. It is all a piece of ethics and a higher life, and no man could have more respect for it than I have. In the ways of the world and in the language of the world I am not a professed Christian. I do not pretend to be. I have had my doubts about things which to other men's minds seem plain. I look out on the great universe around me, at the millions and millions of stars that dot the firmament of heaven in the nighttime; I look out on all the mysteries of nature, and the mysteries of life, and I ask myself the solution of the riddle, and I bow my head in the presence of the infinite mystery and say, "I do not know." Neither do I. I cannot tell. But for that man who understands it all and sees in it the work of a Supreme Being, who prays to what he honestly believes to be this higher power, I have the profoundest regard; and any communion with him, any communion of that poor, weak mortal with that higher power, that power which permeates the universe and which makes for good, any communion that lifts a man higher and higher and makes him better, I have regard for that. And, if Orchard has that religion, well and good. I am willing that he should have it. I hope that he has it. I would not deny that consolation and that solace to him, not for a moment. But I ask you whether he has it, and what it means to him? I have no desire to injure Harry Orchard. I am not made that way. I might have once when the blood in me was warmer and my feelings were stronger. But I, like Hawley, have been tempered by years, and I have no desire to hurt even Harry Orchard, despicable as I think he is. I have no desire to take his life. I am not responsible for his being. I cannot understand the purposes of the infinite God who fashioned his head as he saw fit to fashion it. I cannot understand the purpose of that mysterious power who molded Harry Orchard's brain as he pleased. I am willing to leave it to Him to judge, to Him who alone knows.

I never asked for a human being's life and I hope that I may never ask for human life to the end of my days. I do not ask for his. And if the time should ever come that somebody pronounces against him the decree of death and nobody else asks to save his life, my petition will be there to save it, for I do not believe in it. I do not believe in man tinkering with the work of God. I do not believe in man taking away the life of his fellow-man. I do not believe that I understand, I do not believe that you understand, I do not believe that you and I can say in the light of heaven that if we had been born as he was born, if our brain had been molded as his was molded, if we had been surrounded as he has been surrounded, we could say that we might not have been like him.

It is not for me to pass condemnation upon him, but simply to discuss his evidence and to discuss him as he and his evidence affect this case. Then, gentlemen, let us see whether he is changed. I do believe that there is something in the heart of man which, if rightly appealed to, may make him better. But I do not believe in miracles. I do not believe you could change in a minute a man's very nature. I do not believe it was ever done or ever can be done. You can't take Harry Orchard's face or his form and make it over again in a second, and you can't take his crooked brain and his crooked, dwarfed soul, and make it new in a minute; and if you, gentlemen, are going to bank on that in this case, then you are taking a serious responsibility with Bill Haywood's life. I might have a little more confidence in this if he had not confessed to the Pinkertons before confessing to the Savior. You might have a little more confidence in this if he had not sought to save his life before he turned to save his soul. But there are certain things, gentlemen—I will not say they are indications of a Christian spirit: I know that there are Christians on this jury, because we have studied the personnel of this jury as carefully as we can; but I do not propose to make my statement more nor less because of that.

To my mind these religious instincts permeate all systems of life. One may be higher, better, further developed than another; but deep in the heart of the primitive man is that religious instinct which makes him look up to some higher power, as he wonders about the mystery of his being, the mysteries of life and the mysteries of the great universe around him. He forms his prayers, and whether they are to the same God or not, whether the same name or not, and the same substance or not, I have faith to believe that, if they are the honest and sincere expressions of his soul, they reach the same God at last, no matter how men think they disagree. I have tried in my way, and have failed oftener than I have succeeded. I have sworn off on the first day of January, and begun again on the second, sometimes even held out till the third or fourth. I have tried many and many a thing and failed, and sometimes succeeded indifferently, and I know the weakness of the flesh, the strength of human nature, the struggles it takes to make a new man. Gentlemen, Hawley doesn't know half as much about religion as I do. If he knew anything whatever about religion, he never would tell twelve men that something could be sprinkled upon the head of Harry Orchard and his nature would change in the twinkling of an eye. He is as crazy on religion as he is on other things. You can't do it. He might get an insight, and he may struggle on and on and on for something higher and better, and fall while he reaches, and reach while he falls, and in this way men get religion like they get other things that are good.

Let us see what he has got, and then we will see whether it is religion. There are certain qualities which are primal with religion. I undertake to say, gentlemen, that if Harry Orchard has religion now, that I hope I may never get it. I want to say to this jury that before Harry Orchard got religion he was bad enough, but it remained to religion to make him totally depraved. Now, I am measuring my words, and I am going to show it to this jury, and I am going to show it to you so plainly, gentlemen, that I believe nobody can doubt it. I say that there was some spark of honor and integrity and manhood about that depraved man before he got religion, but that after he went into McParland's hands he became totally depraved. We will mention a few things. What does religion mean? It means love, it means charity, it means kindliness, it means forgiveness to a man whose life has been covered with slime and filth. If he had got religion it ought to be kindness and charity and forgiveness to other men whose lives are like his. Would you have any confidence in religion if it didn't mean that? Would you have any confidence in religion if a man was as cruel, as heartless as he was before? Take Orchard. Take his story. He was acquainted with Moyer. He was acquainted with Haywood. He was acquainted with Pettibone. He had worked himself into the confidence of Pettibone at least. He had been invited to his house. He had met his wife. He had eaten at his table. He had slept in his bed. He was his friend. Gentlemen of the jury, I ask you who watched him, who saw this monster on the witness stand, I ask you whether there was the least look of pity, the least sign of regret, the least feeling of sorrow when this man sought to hand over his friends to the executioner? Did he look any different? Was there any different gleam in his eye or different cast in his countenance or a single flutter of his iron nerve that wasn't there when he met a reeling, staggering, drunken man and shot him three times before he could raise his hand? If there is any pity in his soul, if there is any of the heavenly mercy, if there is any of the Christlike forgiveness, it hasn't gone out to Pettibone at whose table he had eaten. But let us take a case that is plainer than that, gentlemen of the jury. You are not emotional men. Here are twelve men who are mainly farmers; you haven't read fairy stories. You work with your hands. Most of you, perhaps, never heard a fairy story until you heard Orchard's. I am not going to appeal to you on any fantastic basis. I am going to put a proposition to twelve hard-handed and hard-headed men of Idaho, and I want you to say, gentlemen of the jury, whether religion has changed the nature of this wretch, and I should expect if any of you were interested in religion you would say that he hadn't got it. You would have to say it to keep from giving up your own.

Let us see how it appeals to twelve men. When you are through with this case and have gone back to your homes and think of it, as you will over and over again (for it is a historical case—it is seldom in the lifetime of any man that he is a juror on a case as historical as this), pictures will come back to you, of this lawyer, that lawyer, this court, of this witness, of this defendant—you will see them while you are waking, you will see them while you are sleeping, you will dream of it and you will think of it, and you will wonder whether your poor weak, human judgment erred, or whether you did right, or whether after all is said and done, you might not have done otherwise. Pictures will come of the figures in this case, and amongst the rest Harry Orchard's. It may not come to all of you alike. It may not come to me as it comes to others.

One of you may picture Harry Orchard as he is meeting this drunken man reeling out of the saloon and shooting him to death in the darkness of the night. Another man may picture him as he places the fagot under Neville's saloon and runs away. Another may picture him as he plants a box of powder under the station and hurries off in the darkness to save his life, while he sends fourteen souls unshriven into the great beyond. Another may picture him placing a bomb at Steunenberg's gate.

Hawley will picture him as a cherubim with wings growing out from his shoulders and with a halo just above his head and singing songs, with a lawyer on one side of him and McParland on the other. I don't know yet how Borah will picture him, but everybody will picture him according to how they see him. My picture is none of these—none of these. I see what to me is the crowning act of infamy in Harry Orchard's life, an act which throws into darkness every other deed that he ever committed as long as he has lived, and he didn't do this until he had got Christianity or McParlandism, whatever that is. Until he had confessed and been forgiven by Father McParland, he had some spark of manhood still in his breast. There have been other criminals in this world, great criminals. Our penitentiaries are full of criminals whose names are unknown. Men have mounted the scaffold, they have fallen through the trap door, they have been strangled to death, their bodies have been eaten up with quicklime inside of the prison walls, and they protected their names. Their name was the only thing sacred that was left to the criminal.

Look at this fellow, you twelve men, and tell me what you think of him, and whether you will take away a life on account of him. Who was he? He left Ontario a young man. His record was bad. It wasn't infamously bad. His name was not Harry Orchard; his name was Albert Horseley when he left. He went to Detroit with another man's wife. When he reached Detroit his name was Harry Orchard. He lied, he stole, he burglarized, he committed arson and became a murderer and his name was Harry Orchard. His best friend never knew any name but that. The name of Horseley was buried deep in this criminal's heart and he protected it as the one spark of goodness that bound him back to his childhood days. He was not totally depraved. He protected his name. He had gone away from Ontario. He had taken the name of Orchard and he had covered it with infamy and slime, but he had left the name of Horseley comparatively pure in the little Ontario town. Now, gentlemen, this is the picture of Harry Orchard that comes to me. You may picture him a saint if you want to or if you can, and, if you can, you may take away the life of a fellow-being on his testimony, and I will say to you as the judge does to the condemned murderer, "May God have mercy on your souls."

You may picture him as you think he should be pictured. But here is this picture: here is a little rural town off in Canada; here is a country graveyard with a white fence around it and a church by its side. Here are two old-fashioned Quaker people who read their Bible and who love their God and who live, in the sight and the fear of their God, a quiet, peaceful, honest life, and who reared their family hoping they would follow in the footsteps of that Quaker couple. They died and are buried in that old graveyard in the country town; the names on the marble headstone are never heard of beyond the limits of the little town where they lived and where they died; but they lived an honest life, an upright, God-fearing life, and they laid down their burden when it was done and sleep the peaceful sleep of the just, and their names were respected and their names were honored. They bore two sons and six daughters. One son went out into the world. He married. He had a child. Temptation overcame him. He left his wife to toil for herself. He left his child, a baby girl, unprotected and unaided, to grow up alone without a dollar or a penny, or a father's love; and he went out into the world and covered himself with mud and dirt and crime until he was revolting in the sight of God and man. The brother stayed at home, a quiet, peaceful, honest man, having children to bear the Horseley name to generations yet unborn. The sisters married. They had children in whose veins flowed the Horseley blood. They are quiet, peaceful, honest citizens. The little girl, growing up neglected, uncared for, has been struggling alone until she is nine years old. The Horseley name is all she has. The honor of the grandfather and the grandmother sleeping in their Quaker graves, that is all she has. She has nothing from the father who deserted her. Suddenly there comes back a story that the monumental criminal of the ages was Albert Horseley; that this man, who went out from this quiet town, covered himself with crime and with infamy, so that every neighbor who goes through that quiet yard can point to the grave of this old Quaker couple and say, "There lie the father and the mother of the greatest criminal of modern times." And the brother and the

[465]

sisters, living and toiling as best they can, with the burden of the world upon them, the world now can point to them, "There is the brother, there are the sisters, these are the nieces and these are the nephews of that monster who has challenged the civilized world with his iniquities and his crimes," and the deserted wife and, above all, the little girl, flesh of his flesh and bone of his bone.

Gentlemen, I want to know what any one of you think of this miserable wretch who blighted the life of this deserted girl to save his miserable neck? Am I still crazy? Are the men of Idaho different from other men? Does not the same sort of blood flow through your veins as flows through the veins of all men who ever lived? Can anybody look upon this act with anything but horror, and yet Hawley says every human being is to be condemned who has dared to run counter to his perjured word. Think of that girl!

Gentlemen, every act of this villain's life pales into insignificance compared to the crime committed against that child. The blowing up of the Independence depot was a sacrament compared with running that poisoned dagger into the heart of a nine-year-old babe, a dagger that could not kill, gentlemen. If it could kill, well and good. But this was a dagger that would fester and corrode and leave its pain and sting and leave the fingers of the world pointed at her and the voice of the world raised against her as long as her offspring remain upon the earth. And why did he do it? You know why he did it. He had protected this one thing through all his crimes; until he spoke his name upon this witness stand nobody knew it excepting that "inner circle" to whom he confided it. He had kept it through all his crime and through all his wandering, and the character of his dead father and the name of his brother and sisters and the helpless babe and the honor of his wife, these at least were unassailed. It was left for McParland to help him commit the crowning infamy of his infamous career. And why did he do it? Not to give any glory or any luster to his family name. Ah, no, he wasn't so proud of his name that he wanted some of the reflection to reach to this child and to these brothers and to these sisters. Not for glory, not for honor.

He did it, gentlemen of the jury, because the miserable, contemptible, Pinkerton detective had persuaded him that his story would gain more credit with the jury if he gave his real name; because McParland had persuaded him if he would give his name it would help to tie the rope around Bill Haywood's neck. That is why he did it. He gave it to wreak vengeance upon an organization which they have been dragging and hounding to the grave.

Gentlemen, am I wrong? Is there any man that can ever think of Harry Orchard—any man but Hawley—is there any sane man, I will say, who can ever think of Harry Orchard except in loathing and disgust? You have seen him here. You have heard his story. You have seen him sleek and fat and well-fed, facing this jury day by day asking for this man's blood. Do you ever want to see him again? Do you ever want to hear his name again? In the future when you are trying to find the most infamous word that the English language has given us, can you think of anything but Orchard? Do you want to read a paper again with his name in it? And yet, gentlemen, upon the testimony of this brute, this man who would assassinate his own nine-year-old girl with a dagger a thousand times more malicious and deadly than one that kills, upon his testimony you are asked to get rid of Bill Haywood. For what? Does anybody else attack his name? Anybody else swear anything against him? Has any other voice been raised to accuse him? Oh, no. You are asked to take his life because down in Colorado and up in the Coeur d'Alène he has been against the Mine Owners' Association, and because he has been organizing the weak, the poor, the toilers; has been welding together in one great brotherhood those men; has been calling them to fight under one banner for a common cause—for that reason he has raised up against him the power of this body of men, and you are asked to kill Bill Haywood.

To kill him, gentlemen! I want to speak to you plainly. Mr. Haywood is not my greatest concern. Other men have died before him. Other men have been martyrs to a holy cause since the world began. Wherever men have looked upward and onward, forgotten their selfishness, struggled for humanity, worked for the poor and the weak, they have been sacrificed. They have been sacrificed in the prison, on the scaffold, in the flame. They have met their death, and he can meet his, if you twelve men say he must. But, gentlemen, you shortsighted men of the prosecution, you men of the Mine Owners' Association, you people who would cure hatred with hate, you who think you can crush out the feelings and the hopes and the aspirations of men by tying a noose around his neck, you who are seeking to kill him, not because he is Haywood, but because he represents a class, don't be so blind, don't be so foolish as to believe you can strangle the Western Federation of Miners when you tie a rope around his neck. Don't be so blind in your madness as to believe that when you make three fresh new graves you will kill the labor movement of the world. I want to say to you, gentlemen, Bill Haywood can't die unless you kill him. You must tie the rope. You twelve men of Idaho, the burden will be on you. If at the behest of this mob you should kill Bill Haywood, he is mortal, he will die, but I want to say that a million men will grab up the banner of labor at the open grave where Haywood lays it down, and in spite of prisons or scaffolds or fire, in spite of prosecution or jury, or courts, these men of willing hands will carry it on to victory in the end.

Gentlemen: I want to apologize for saying too much about Harry Orchard. I have always been just a little careful of my conversation and the topics that I discuss, especially in public, and I feel that I owe you an apology for using his name so often. But I can't help it. Eminent lawyers up here in Idaho have seriously proposed to hang a man, take him out and kill him, on the testimony of Harry Orchard, and that is my excuse for talking about it. I hope after I am done with this case I will never have to use his name again or see it again or hear of it again. I have tried to give you a short sketch of this man upon whose testimony they hope to take away the life of one of your fellow-citizens. If we find who he is, I do not think there is any danger of my overstating it. When I make little references to Bill Haywood or Brother Borah, I might possibly overstate, but I am safe when I am talking about Harry Orchard. I can't overstate that. You would have to make the English language all over again to do justice to that subject, but I have tried to sketch him so that where his evidence appears in this case, and it is all that does appear in condemnation of these men, you would know who he is, and what he is and whether he has been miraculously made into an honest man, and whether a jury would be safe in whipping a dog on his testimony, leave alone hanging a human being on his testimony.

Mr. Hawley tells us that McParland has converted him. He is a wonderful detective, isn't he? But here is a piece of work, gentlemen of the jury, that will last as long as the ages last —McParland's conversion of Orchard! Don't you think this detective is wasting his time down in the Pinkerton office in the city of Denver? From the beginning of the world was ever any miracle like this performed before? Lo, and behold! A man who has spent his life as a Pinkerton—isn't a preacher—he has never been ordained except in the Pinkerton office. But here is a man who has challenged the world—Harry Orchard, who has lived his life up to this time, and he has gotten over what religion he ever had, and he meets this Pinkerton detective who never did anything in his life but lie and cheat and scheme (for the life of a detective is a living lie, that is his business; he lives one from the time he gets up in the morning to the time he goes to bed; he is deceiving people, and trapping people and lying to people and imposing on people; that is his trade), and Harry Orchard is caught, and he meets this famous detective, who speaks to him familiarly about David and St. Paul and Kelly the Bum, and a few more of his acquaintances, and he speaks of them in the most familiar way. And then he holds out the hope of life and all that life could offer to Harry Orchard, and lo, and behold, he soon becomes a Christian. Now, gentlemen, Savonarola, who was a great preacher, and a mighty man in his day, is dead. He went up in flames long ago, and he cannot convert the world. John Wesley is dead. Cranmer is dead. Moody is dead. Pretty much all of them are gone. What is the matter with McParland changing the sign on his office, and going into the business of saving souls instead of snaring bodies? If he could convert a man like Orchard in the twinkling of an eye,

I submit he is too valuable a man to waste his time in a Pinkerton detective office trying to catch men. He had better go out in the vineyard and go to work and bring in souls. A man who could wash Harry Orchard's soul as white as wool need not hesitate at tackling any sort of a job that came his way. He is a wonderful detective, but his fame as a detective would be eclipsed in a moment if he would go into the business of saving souls instead of catching men.

But I might suggest to this good man, who talks of St. Paul and David as if they had been shadows that he had used in his office, I might suggest to Mr. McParland, the wise and the good, who quotes the Bible in one moment and then tries to impose upon some victim in the next, who quotes Scripture in one sentence and then lies in the next, who utters blessings with one word and curses with the next, I might suggest to this good man that William Haywood has a soul, Moyer has a soul, Pettibone has a soul. Why not go to Moyer, Haywood and Pettibone and tell them some of your stories of St. Paul and David, and offer to wash their sins away?

Why not give some attention to the souls of the men whose bodies they are trying to consign to the tomb? Do you suppose McParland is interested in Haywood's soul? Do you suppose he is interested in Moyer's? Do you suppose he is interested in Harry Orchard's? Do you suppose he is interested in his own? Do you suppose he is interested in anything except weaving a web around these men so that he may be able to hang them by the neck until dead? And to do it, like the devil, he quotes Scripture. To do it, there isn't a scheme or a plan or a device of his wily, crooked brain that he won't bring into action, whether it is the Bible or detective yarns—there is none too good for McParland. And then he will have a lawyer to say: "Here, behold McParland's work. Here is Harry Orchard, with a pure soul and a clean heart, and he told you twelve men a story by which you can afford to take away the lives of three men." Well, all right, perhaps you will do it, but I don't think so.

Now I want to take another view of this man Orchard. It seems that I never can get away from him. He has told you a great story. The fairy tales that we used to read are not in it with this story. Baron Munchausen and all the rest of them have to go away back and sit down since Harry Orchard entered literature. He had to tell McParland his real name, and almost the first question that Hawley asked was as to his real name, where he was born and who he was, and he told us it was Horseley. Of course, he had to tell it, because he had already written his autobiography, written this wonderful story of a wonderful life, and he had spread his infamy throughout the land to damn all the people whose blood made them kin to him. He had done that beforehand. Is he a romancer, is he a liar, or is he honest? Now let me call your attention to a few things in the light of what he is. First, he had written a story before he ever got here. Before you men heard him from the witness stand he had woven the story and sold it to a magazine! Well, now I know that you have to look out for a storyteller. I have had a little experience in that line myself, and when the imagination gets active it is a little difficult to tell whether we are telling the truth, or just think it is the truth. He had fixed this up to sell—to sell to *McClure's Magazine*[1]—and in the spare moments waiting every minute for the halter to dangle above his head, he is putting in his time writing this story which is being published now.

Commencing from his earliest youth he has been a liar, that he confesses, and a liar of a singular kind—telling of meaner things than even Harry Orchard ever did, telling of more things than even Harry Orchard ever did. He admits that he said he had killed Neville, hired a man to go and poison him, when Neville was never poisoned and never killed. If he can admit that he told the story that he poisoned Neville when it was a lie, is there any reason that he couldn't tell the story that he put strychnine into Bradley's milk when that, too, was a lie? Time after time he has shown that he is a liar, given to this kind of weird romancing; that tells what an infamous mortal he is. Not man enough to lie in his words and his letters, he goes into a photograph gallery and poses himself with two other men, he standing with a smoking revolver in his hand and one man shot dead before him with the cards in his hand, and another man

[1] *McClure's Magazine* ran Orchard's *Autobiography* in serial form.

standing by his side, Harry Orchard of course being the real hero. He never would take a pose and let the other fellow be holding the revolver and he appear to be dead. Oh, no, never. You can't get a truer picture of the type of this liar than the picture that he posed for and which has been presented to this jury.

Now, gentlemen, while he has perhaps told some things that are true, and many things that are not true, he has told this jury of an infinitely greater number of people that he intended to kill than the number of people that he did kill, which is a circumstance worth considering when you are sizing up a man like that. He told you that he came pretty near blowing up the Idanha hotel, which would kill from two hundred to four hundred people. He told you that he was going to blow up Max Malich's boardinghouse, which would kill from three hundred to six hundred more. He told you that he wanted to touch off a carload of powder in the Vindicator mine, that would kill a third of the men, one whole shift; and that there were about six hundred or eight hundred men employed in the mine and that he would kill a third of them. He told you that he was ready to blow up some institution in the Coeur d'Alêne, that would kill two or three hundred more. The poor fellow has really never had a chance in the world. He has never been where his talents would be recognized. It is unfortunate, from his standpoint, that he has never been able to kill five hundred or six hundred at a time. All of his big schemes seem to have failed, like the big schemes of all the rest of us. But he had them in his head, every one of them. He was going to put a bomb under Governor Steunenberg's seat in the car and blow up the train. He was going to do infinitely more than he ever did do; and in order to make himself a bigger man than he really is, and God knows he is big enough, he boasted of crimes that he never committed, and told you of attempting to commit crimes bigger than he ever did commit. Now I want to know whether there is any chance for a jury to go astray upon a character like his, whether it could be possible that anywhere on the face of the earth you could bring together twelve men who would ever look at the testimony of a monster of this sort? Of a man who, perhaps, is a phenomenal murderer, but who at least is the biggest liar that this generation has known. This is the character of the man upon whose testimony you are to be asked to take away these men's lives.

* * *

Mr. Hawley talks about the wicked unions. He says you have got to destroy the Western Federation of Miners. Wherever they are, there is trouble. Wherever they are, they are calling strikes without reason. You have got to destroy them. They are the greatest enemies to liberty; they are the greatest enemies to the prosperity of the state of Idaho. What does he know about the prosperity of the state of Idaho? If his theory of this case is true, then I can believe rumor—that they have brought him most of the prosperity he has had within the last year and a half, and I don't see why he is finding any fault. They are the enemies to prosperity—we have got to kill them—they strike without cause. Let us see, gentlemen, let us see. There was a strike in Denver and in Colorado City. What were they about? The evidence shows that the Western Federation of Miners was making trouble. What about? There was a strike in Denver, I think, in the year 1902. This was what it was about—this brand of conspirators whom Mr. Hawley calls criminals, who are constantly stirring up trouble, called a strike for this: They had worked long and hard for an eight-hour day in the state of Colorado; they believed that eight hours was as long as a man ought to twist his muscles and twist his bones in a smelter—and I do, and I think you do, gentlemen of the jury. It does not make any difference whether it was long enough or not; I never saw a time yet when the employer did not think the hours of labor were too short, and I never saw a time, to be fair about it, when the workingman did not think they were too long—I think so. In that week when I was a workingman I thought so, and I hope I never will see the time when the workingman won't believe his hours of labor are too long and his wages are too low, because you can never get any prosperity or progress or liberty or what the world has been striving for and reaching for and hoping for until we elevate the poor and weak and give them wages and liberty, and give them life, and release them from their toil so that they may have time to read the newspapers and make themselves wise.

The state of Colorado passed an eight-hour law in 1899—under the evidence in this case, 1899 is right, isn't it? And the Guggenheims[1] fought it, and they took it before the Supreme Court—and the courts are always the last to move, and the higher they are the slower—and they took it before the Supreme Court and of course the Supreme Court declared it unconstitutional. It is unconstitutional to pass a law which won't permit Guggenheim to take ten hours out of the hide of his men instead of eight.

RICHARDSON: It was twelve hours in the smelter.

DARROW: Well, a man that will work in a smelter ought to be worked twelve hours a day.

The courts declared it unconstitutional. Of course they would. What is the Constitution for except to use for the rich to destroy the laws that are made for the poor? That is the main purpose in these latter days. Then what did the workers do? They said, If the Constitution is wrong, let us change it. And they appealed once more to the state—to the people. The people are blind and stupid, but still more generally right upon an issue like this—and they put it to a vote of the people, and the people voted six to one to change the Constitution which was in their way, and the new Constitution provided that the next legislature should enact an eight-hour law. This was the strike which Hawley says was unconstitutional—was unwarranted. They appealed to the people, and by six to one they changed the Constitution of the state and then the legislature came in in 1902 and was asked to pass that law which the Constitution commanded them to pass, and what did they do? Why, the Constitution is only meant to be obeyed by the poor. What is the law for if a rich man has to obey it? Why should they make it if it can reach them? Why should they have the Constitution if it could be used against them? The Constitution said that they must change the law—must pass an eight-hour law, and Mr. Guggenheim and

[1] Capitalists, mine and smelter operators.

Mr. Moffat[1] and the Union Pacific Railroad and the Mine Owners' Association and all the good people in Colorado who lived by the sweat and blood of their fellow-men—all of these invaded the chambers of the House and the Senate and said, "No, you must not pass an eight-hour law; true, the Constitution requires it; but here is our gold which is stronger than the Constitution." The legislature met and discussed the matter, and these miners were there. The evidence in this case has shown you who they were. Haywood was there; the labor organizations were there; and they were there pleading then, as they have always pleaded, for the poor, for the weak, for the oppressed. I don't mean to tell this jury that labor organizations do no wrong. I know them too well for that. They do wrong often, and sometimes brutally; they are sometimes cruel; they are often unjust; they are frequently corrupt; they will be as long as human nature is human nature, and there is no remedy for it. But I am here to say that in a great cause these labor organizations—despised and weak and outlawed as they generally are—have stood for the poor, they have stood for the weak, they have stood for every humane law that was ever placed upon the statute books. They have stood for human life. They have stood for the father who was bound down with his task; they have stood for the wife threatened with being taken from the home to work by his side; and they have stood by the little child, who has also been taken to work in their places, that the rich could grow richer still; and they have fought for the right of the little one to have a little of life, a little of comfort while he is young. I don't care how many wrongs they have committed—I don't care how many crimes—these weak, rough, rugged, unlettered men, who often know no other power but the brute force of their strong right arm, who find themselves bound and confined and impaired whichever way they turn, and who look up and worship the God of might as the only God that they know; I don't care how often they fail—how many brutalities they are guilty of. I know their cause is just. I know that trouble and strife and contention have been invoked, yet through brutality and bloodshed

---

[1] Dave Moffat, mine operator.

ATTORNEY FOR THE DAMNED

and crime has come the progress of the human race. I know they may be wrong in this battle or that, but in the great long struggle they are right, and they are eternally right; and they are working for the poor and the weak, they are working to give more liberty to the man. And I want to say to you, gentlemen of the jury, you Idaho farmers, removed from the trade unions, removed from the men who work in industrial affairs, I want to say, had it not been for the trade unions of the world—for the trade unions of England, for the trade unions of Europe, the trade unions of America—you today would be serfs instead of free men sitting upon a jury to try one of your peers. The cause of these men is right.

If they make a mistake, gentlemen, as they often do, it is not for you and me to judge them—to judge them too narrowly, too critically. It is not for you and me to judge them as we judge the man of leisure and opportunity and learning. They are reaching out in the darkness, they are moving toward the light, they are raising the whole world upon those shoulders which have borne the burdens of the human race. These fellows worked for an eight-hour law. It was submitted to the people and it passed. The mine owners sent their men to the legislature and they blocked the command of the Constitution with their gold, and the legislature adjourned without obeying the Constitution that the people had carried by six to one, and then the miners struck for an eight-hour day. They struck for what the Constitution gave them. They struck for what the legislature had denied them at the behest of the rich, and they struck for what they had a legal right to, and a moral right to, by every law of morals known to man.

Gentlemen, I want to know whether you twelve men condemn that strike. Mr. Hawley says they have made trouble and you ought to get rid of them, and a good way to begin is to hang the secretary-treasurer. That is the way to begin to get rid of the Western Federation of Miners because they have made trouble. Yes, they have made trouble, thank God, and more power to them. Nothing good in this world ever came excepting through trouble and tribulation and toil. Were they to blame because they had trouble in Denver? Were they to blame for calling a strike to provide for a legal day? If you say so, all right, gentlemen, you are more hopeless than I think you are.

That strike was settled and they got their eight-hour day. Do you want them to give it up? Is there a man on this jury who would want to send those men back to the smelters for twelve hours a day? Hawley says you want to kill this union. Do you, gentlemen? Think of it. These men have doubtless done some brutal things; these men have likely done some criminal things, and these men have likely done some cruel things, and some that were not wise, and some that were not just. That is admitted. I know they did. I am not going to tell you any lies upon that subject, for I think too much of them, but, admitting that, would you destroy the Western Federation of Miners and send back these forty thousand workmen, with their wives and children to deal single-handed with the Mine Owners' Association of Colorado? Ah, gentlemen, if you would, I think you would be traitors to that country in which you live. Would you dissolve this union and force every poor man to go to Guggenheim with his hat in his hand and individually beg for a job? Let me tell you, gentlemen, if you destroy the labor unions in this country, you destroy liberty when you strike the blow; you would leave the poor bound and shackled and helpless to do the bidding of the rich. It would not reach you today, for you are far away from the centers of trade and industry, but it would reach you tomorrow. It would take this country back—back to the time when there were masters and slaves. You have not lived in an industrial country; you have not studied trade unionism as some of us have studied it—and I hope I have studied it—but I don't believe, gentlemen, that you can gather up any twelve men—any twelve men even if they have had no more enlightenment than the newspapers—even if they had read nothing but poison—I don't believe you can gather up twelve men anywhere in America, if you take them by chance, who do not know and understand that in some way these labor unions have stood for the rights and the liberties of the human race, and that to destroy them would send the human race back once more toward slavery.

The strike in Denver was for an eight-hour day. Then came the strike at Colorado City, and what was that for? Oh, everything we do is unholy. The best way is to kill us and get rid of us because we are making trouble. Now, gentlemen, I don't want to make any mistake about this—I don't want to mislead you, not for a minute. If you turn Haywood loose, the chances are he will make more trouble. So long as there are Guggenheims, so long as there is a Morgan, so long as there are Rockefellers, and so long as there is anybody who has the spirit of independence and justice in his heart there will be trouble; and if these men can live, and live without trouble, then we are slaves and we will have to begin all over again.

If you, gentlemen, by your verdict, want to do your part in this direction, I cannot help it; you will have to go ahead and do it, but I don't think you do. I don't think anybody does who is in his right mind and who loves his country. They had a strike in Colorado City for a matter just as simple. What was it? Why, the Guggenheims down there were turning off their union men—nothing new about that—they were turning off their disturbers and their agitators to break up the union, and so they struck. They had to, or else give up the union. They had to strike or give up every hope they had for the betterment of themselves and their fellow-men, and they struck. The strike dragged its weary way along for days and weeks and months. I don't know whether you, gentlemen, understand just what it means to strike. Did any of you ever do it? I did not. I don't suppose I would be brave enough. If the lawyers got up and struck for an eight-hour day and wages of three dollars and a half a day, I don't believe I would be brave enough to go out with Senator Borah and Mr. Hawley and the rest. And then it would be unreasonable for us fellows to demand three dollars a day and public sentiment would not support us. When I speak of public sentiment, I mean the newspapers. That is the only way we know what public sentiment is, and the only way we can know about it is to read what they say and then guess the other way. It is a serious thing to call a strike. You never heard of a case where the outsiders did not say that the walking delegate, and the president and the secretaries called the strike. Now, I have known their affairs for a long while and I want to say what all history shows, that they are always the most conservative men in the union, because responsibility brings conservatism. Even if Mr. Hawley was put on this jury I am not sure that he would hang this man without Orchard's testimony. He might get responsibility, and conservatism with responsibility. And they are, gentlemen, conservative, and they hate to call a strike because a strike is a serious thing to the workingman. If some of us who have saved a little, or who have a ranch where we can get chickens and potatoes and one thing and another, and live—we could go on a strike. But for the man who has a family, and is living from day to day and consuming all he earns, as all workingmen are—probably if they were not consuming all they earn they would cut down the wages so they would—if a man is in that position, a strike is a serious thing. To ask a man to lay down the tools of his trade, to lose his job, and face starvation for himself, his wife and children is a serious responsibility, and workingmen hate to take it, and they only take it with the direst necessity.

How many bankers do you suppose you have in Boise who would risk starvation for a cause? Well, I think they are few. How many lawyers would run the chance of starvation for the sake of a cause? How many businessmen would close their stores and face starvation for themselves, their wives and their children, for a cause? Mighty few. That is what the workingmen do. It is what they are bound to do when they bind themselves together in a great organization, each fighting for himself and his fellowmen. They are bound, not to take their lives in their hand, but to place their lives in the hands of their fellow-men.

So these fellows went out on a strike in Colorado City. They failed, and pretty soon they found the smelters were running all right, and were smelting the ore that was mined by their brothers up at Cripple Creek. And the Cripple Creek miners said: We will no longer go down in the mines and dig up the ore to be smelted by the men who are fighting our brothers at Colorado City. So the Cripple Creek miners struck, and their camp, where 60,000 men lived, was at once deprived of all its resources. The men, women and children were almost turned into the streets; they were left to depend on the alms they could get that were distributed from the unions; and they fought it out for months and months; and the strike had scarcely begun before they called in the militia.

They called in the militia because old man Stewart got beaten up. Now, I am sorry old man Stewart was beaten up. I am sorry for him, just the same as I would be for any other man who got injured, but all my sympathy does not go out to old man Stewart, who waked so much sorrow and grief in the heart of my friend Hawley. He forgot all the miseries of the world in looking at old man Stewart; they were all nothing to him in contemplation of the horrible fact that Stewart got beaten up. For what was Stewart beaten? I will tell you. It was a union camp; they had established the eight-hour day; they had fought for it, gentlemen, and they had fought for it as men have always fought for everything that is good since the world began. Do you think any progress ever came without it? Did we ever make progress without struggle and fighting and sometimes bloodshed? And these men had struggled for an eight-hour day. They had built up their unions and the eight-hour day was established, and they found it necessary, in their judgment, to call a strike, to ask all their men to go out until the strike was settled. And old man Stewart who swears he was working eight hours a day—just eight—enjoying the fruits of all the struggles, of all the victory, of all the men who had risked their jobs and their lives to gain an eight-hour day—he was willing to take the short hours which these blunt, rugged, brave men had won; he was willing to take the high wages that had been won by those rugged men; and then he went to work to cut these men's throats. That is what Stewart did.

They had no right to beat him, but when you consider how bad men are, I want you to consider the provocation. Gentlemen, you may take all the deeds of violence and all the unlawful acts of all the men in Colorado connected with the Western Federation of Miners, and they could not reach my contempt for this contemptible man. You might think of this when you think of old man Stewart.

*   *   *

Now, gentlemen, getting back to Orchard— Do you remember the first time Harry Orchard says he saw Moyer and Haywood? He did not have an identification card; he did not have a letter of introduction; he had nothing. He walked into Moyer and Haywood's office—the president and secretary of a great labor organization—"My name is Orchard; I have just blown up the Vindicator mine and have killed McCormick and Beck, the super‧intendent and the boss." And Moyer and Haywood slapped him on the back, and said, "You are a good fellow; and you done noble," or words to that effect. And Moyer reached in his pocket and pulled out twenty dollars and gave it to him, and the next day he went back and Haywood gave him two hundred and eighty dollars more for that job!

Now, gentlemen, do you think that story is true? Of course, if one of you had lived an upright life, had looked after your family, had earned your living by the sweat of your brow, had fought for the poor and the weak and the disheartened, had taken a hand in every good movement that came within your reach—if you had fought the strong and the powerful and the great, and had given your life to this work—and some murdering scoundrel should be caught in his crime and turned and accused you to save his life, you would think it was pretty hard if twelve jurors would not take your word, unsupported, against his, would you not? Of what use is character—of what use is life—of what use are good deeds and a good name—of what use is the hope and the aspiration and the desire to serve your fellow-man, if a scoundrel like this, a scoundrel like this, to save his own neck, can come into a court of justice and take your character and your name and your life to save his own? You would not expect that you had to do much except to give your plain, simple word, and you would expect your words and your deeds and your life would stand as a shield to protect you against all such scoundrels as Harry Orchard. And yet you are asked to hang Bill Haywood on that kind of testimony. He has been more fortunate than you might be. You might be caught by such a scoundrel and no one near to support you; you might be caught with your uncorroborated word, and you might be taken so far away and be so poor that you could not get the witnesses, and you could not hire the lawyers to come and defend you. And even then you would expect the word of an honest man who has lived an upright life to be your shield and your protection and that it would be ample for your cause. But no, not here—not here.

I want to say that these things were always good in any case where labor unions are not involved; any case where it is not the case of labor. But if it is a labor union—if it is a president or secretary or a walking delegate or some man who has devoted his life to the cause of the poor, then such excuses do not go, and they are presumed to be guilty until proven innocent, and the jury is crazy if you can prove his innocence. As Mr. Hawley remarked, this jury would be crazy if it did not believe these defendants guilty in this case.

Well, now, let us look at that story a little further. Does it look reasonable? Let us assume that this man is a cutthroat; let us assume that Bill Haywood is a cutthroat. Nobody ever said he was a fool. His worst enemies have not made that claim. Let us assume that he is like all the rest of us—a Dr. Jekyll and Mr. Hyde, and that the Mr. Hyde preponderates over the Dr. Jekyll; that he would be willing to slay and to kill; and let him be a criminal as bad as Harry Orchard pictures him; he is weaving a net to catch every man who is unfriendly to him; he is making bombs for governors and judges and the strong and the powerful who hate him. He is a plain assassin, and the head of a great labor organization. Is he a fool? Do you suppose a man could carry on those deeds and take no measure to protect himself? Do you think he could leave his doors open to every tramp and every criminal that might enter them, and when this criminal should say to him, I sent two men to eternity, and I blew up a mine, that he could turn to the man, without introduction and without acquaintance, and, slapping him on the back, say, "Well done; here is $300 for your work and we will need more of it in the future." Now do you believe it? Does that look reasonable?

Gentlemen, let me say this: If this jury believes that Haywood and Moyer met Harry Orchard in their room, and without any introduction of any sort, they let Harry Orchard tell them of this murder, and that they then turned and gave him $300—if you believe that story, for God's sake take them out and hang them—they deserve to die. They have not got brains enough to lead any labor movement in the world; they are misfits, and I don't see why they have been alive so long.

Gentlemen, it is not men of that character that could build up a great organization like the Western Federation of Miners; it is not men of that mold that could plant hospitals in all your hills and all your mountains; it is not men of that kind that could dispense a million and a half dollars to widows and orphans in ten years. It is not those men that could take the English and the Irish, the Dutch and the Bohemians and the Italians, and mold this incongruous mass into one great and mighty power so as to make the cause of labor one in the land. It takes brains. It takes courage. It takes devotion. It does not take a man such as Orchard describes. It takes goodness, too, and you cannot make me believe it of Bill Haywood, or of Charley Moyer, or of any other labor leader in the United States.

I don't claim that this man is an angel. The Western Federation of Miners could not afford to put an angel at their head. Do you want to hire an angel to fight the Mine Owners' Association and the Pinkerton detectives, and the power of wealth? Oh, no, gentlemen; you better get a first-class fighting man who has physical courage, who has mental courage, who has strong devotion, who loves the poor, who loves the weak, who hates iniquity and hates it more when it is with the powerful and the great; and you cannot win without it, and I believe that down in your hearts there is not one of you would wish him to be an angel. You know an angel would not be fitted for that place, and I make no claim of that; but he is not a demon. If he were a demon or a bad man he would never be working in this cause, for the prizes of the world are somewhere else. The man who enters the labor movement, either as an organizer, a member, or a lawyer, and who enters it in the hope of reward, is a foolish man indeed. The rewards are on the other side—unless you look for your reward to your conscience and to your consciousness of a duty well done. I presume that this big, strong man is a man, a man that has strength and has power, and has weakness; a man of love and affection, a man of strong nature, of strong purposes—I don't know about that, and I don't care about it; I don't look for anything else in man; I want the man of courage and brains and devotion and strength.

* * *

Now, gentlemen of the jury, there are many things more I would like to say, but I have not the strength to say them. Perhaps it is lucky for you that I have not, and I must leave the case here and hand it over to you. Under the laws of the state of Idaho the State has the last word, and when my voice is silent, and when Moyer and Haywood cannot speak, their accusers can be heard pleading against their lives. I know the ability of the eminent gentleman who will close this case. I know the appeal he will make to this jury. I know that he will talk of law and order and the flag which the mine owners have desecrated time and time again. I know the suspicious circumstances which will be woven into that appeal and handled by a skillful tongue and a skillful brain, and I must sit still and listen to it without any chance to reply. I can only ask you, gentlemen of the jury, to weigh with care and consideration every word that is spoken. I can only ask you to answer when I cannot speak, if there are any facts and any circumstances which will justify an answer. I only ask you to remember that you are to explain every fact and circumstance in this case consistent with this man's innocence, if you can, and I shall ask you to try; and if you try it will not be difficult to accomplish, for there is nothing in this case but Harry Orchard—Harry Orchard, an unspeakable scoundrel; Harry Orchard, a perjured villain; Harry Orchard, bigamist and murderer and coward; Harry Orchard, shifting the burdens of his sins upon these men to save his life. If you men can kill my client on his testimony, then, peace be with you.

Gentlemen, Mr. Hawley has told you that he believes in this case, that he would not ask you to convict unless he believed Haywood was guilty. I tell you I believe in my case. I believe in it as I believe in my very life, and my belief does not amount, nor his belief does not amount to anything, or count. I am not an unprejudiced witness in this case. Nobody knows it better than I. My mind is not unbiased in this great struggle. I am a partisan, and a strong partisan at that. For nearly thirty years I have been working to the best of my ability in the cause in which these men have given their toil and risked their lives. For nearly thirty years I have given this cause the best ability that God has given me. I have given my time, my reputation, my chances—all this in the cause of the poor. I may have been unwise—I may have been extravagant in my statements, but this cause has inspired the strongest devotion of my life, and I want to say to you that never in my life did I feel about a case as I feel about this. Never in my life did I wish anything as I wish the verdict of this jury, and, if I live to be a hundred years old, never again in my life will I feel that I am pleading in a case like this—never will this jury be called upon to act in another case which involves such momentous questions as this. You are jurors in a historical case. You are here, with your verdict to make history, here to make history that shall affect the nation for weal or woe, here to make history that will affect every man that toils, that will influence the liberties of mankind and bring weal or woe to the poor and the weak, who have been striving through the centuries for some measure of that freedom which the world has ever denied to them.

Gentlemen of the jury, this responsibility is on you, and if I have done my part I am glad to shift it upon your shoulders and be relieved of the grievous load.

I have known Haywood—I have known him well and I believe in him. God knows it would be a sore day to me if he should go upon the scaffold. The sun would not shine or the birds would not sing on that day—for me. It would be a sad day, indeed, if any such calamity would come to him. I would think of him, I would think of his wife, of his mother, I would think of his children, I would think of the great cause that he represents. It would be a sore day for me, but, gentlemen, he and his mother, and his wife and his children, are not my chief concern in this great case. If you should decree that he must die, ten thousand men will work in the mines and send a portion of the proceeds of their labor to take care of that widow and these orphan children, and a million people throughout the length and breadth of the civilized world will send their messages of kindness and good cheer to comfort them in their bereavement and to heal their wounds. It is not for them I plead. Other men have died before. Other men have died in the same cause in which Bill Haywood has risked his life. Men strong with devotion, men who loved liberty, men who loved their fellow-men, patriots who have raised their voices in defense of the poor, in defense of right, have made their good fight and have met death on the scaffold, on the rack, in the flame, and they will meet it again and again until the world grows old and gray. William Haywood is no better than the rest. He can die if die he must. He can die if this jury decrees it; but, oh, gentlemen, do not think for a moment that if you hang him you will crucify the labor movement of the world; do not think that you will kill the hopes and the aspirations and the desires of the weak and poor. You men of wealth and power, you people anxious for his blood, are you so blind as to believe that liberty will die when he is dead? Think you there are no other brave hearts, no other strong arms, no other devoted souls who will risk all in that great cause which has demanded martyrs in every land and age?

There are others and these others will come to take his place; they will come to carry the banner when he can hold it up no more.

Gentlemen, it is not for him alone that I speak. I speak for the poor, for the weak, for the weary, for that long line of men, who, in darkness and despair, have borne the labors of the human race. The eyes of the world are upon you—upon you twelve men of Idaho tonight. Wherever the English language is spoken or wherever any tongue makes known the thoughts of men in any portion of the civilized world, men are talking, and wondering and dreaming about the verdict of these twelve men that I see before me now. If you kill him your act will be applauded by many. If you should decree Bill Haywood's death, in the railroad offices of our great cities men will applaud your names. If you decree his death, amongst the spiders of Wall Street will go up paeans of praise for these twelve good men and true. In every bank in the world, where men hate Haywood because he fights for the poor and against that accursed system upon which the favored live and grow rich and fat—from all those you will receive blessings and unstinted praise.

But if your verdict should be "Not Guilty" in this case, there are still those who will reverently bow their heads and thank these twelve men for the life and reputation you have saved. Out on our broad prairies where men toil with their hands, out on the wide ocean where men are tossed and buffeted on the waves, through our mills and factories, and down deep under the earth, thousands of men, and of women and children— men who labor, men who suffer, women and children weary with care and toil—these men and these women and these children will kneel tonight and ask their God to guide your hearts —these men and these women and these little children, the poor, the weak, and the suffering of the world, are stretching out their helpless hands to this jury in mute appeal for Bill Haywood's life.

DARROW *spoke for eleven hours.*

As he talked there were tears in his eyes, Haywood's wife and mother were sobbing, and women in the courtroom wept.

At one point, according to a newspaper report, "a juror asked that Darrow stand further away as it gave some of the jurors a headache to have him stand so close and talk so loud." Darrow said, "Thank you," and stepped back.

On July 29, 1907, the jury brought in a verdict of Not Guilty. Bill Haywood, after spending eighteen months in jail waiting for his case to be called, sitting through eleven weeks of trial and the jury deliberation of twenty-one hours, was a free man.

"He was a master of invective, vituperation, denunciative humor, pathos and all the other acts of the orator except argument. It was ostensibly a plea for the life of Haywood, but, in fact, it was an address not to twelve jurors in front of him but to Socialists throughout the country," said the Chicago Tribune of Clarence Darrow's plea in the Haywood case.

"Big Bill" Haywood, on the other hand, said of the summation: "This was one of Clarence Darrow's greatest."

Commented Borah: "If Orchard had not turned state's evidence he would be on trial, and the eminent counsel from Chicago would be defending him with all the eloquence he possessed instead of denouncing him as the most despicable monster on earth."

William Jennings Bryan who was to meet Darrow in Dayton many years later said, "I am glad to hear of the verdict. I watched the trial and did not see how anyone could be found guilty on Orchard's testimony."

On the day the verdict was announced, President Roosevelt received a telegram: "Undesirable citizens victorious. Rejoice." It was signed by Emma Goldman, Alexander Berkman and Hippolyte Havel, three of the leading anarchists of the era.

Within two weeks after Haywood's acquittal, the State was granted a change of venue in the Adams case. Adams' second trial opened in Rathdrum, Idaho; again the jury disagreed. This time it was ten to two for acquittal.

Adams, however, was still not a free man. He was extradited to Colorado and there was charged and tried for the shooting of the manager of a mine in Telluride during a strike.

He was acquitted and—finally—given his freedom.

Pettibone was the next to be tried.

It was at about this time that Darrow came down with an ear infection. Between Adams' second trial and Pettibone's, Darrow went to Portland and San Francisco to see ear specialists. While in San Francisco visiting such a doctor, Darrow received a telegram from Boise that the trial of Pettibone was scheduled to start. Darrow tried to get a postponement. His doctor felt it might be fatal to him if he went back to Boise at this time. Pettibone wired that it might be fatal to him if Darrow didn't return. Darrow took the next train to Boise.

At the Pettibone trial, Darrow made his opening statement seated in a chair. He could not continue. Even Pettibone urged him to go back to California for treatment. Darrow left. Seven days later he received word that Pettibone had been acquitted.

The case against Moyer was dropped.

As for Orchard, he was sentenced to death by Judge Wood. However, at the judge's recommendation, the Idaho Board of Pardons commuted Orchard's sentence to life imprisonment.

Orchard lived practically a half-century in the penitentiary before he died on April 13, 1954.

PART FOUR

❧

FOR JUSTICE

They Tried to Get Me

DARROW IN HIS OWN DEFENSE

Los Angeles, 1912

JURORS WEEP AS
DARROW PLEADS

CHICAGO ATTORNEY WINS SYMPATHY
OF MEN IN BOX BELIEVED AGAINST HIM

[Headline, Chicago Tribune, August 16, 1912]

THE INDICTMENT and trial of Clarence Darrow charging him with jury bribing, was an outgrowth of the McNamara case of 1911, in Los Angeles.

J. J. McNamara, secretary-treasurer of the International Association of
Bridge and Structural Workers (AFL), and his brother, J. B. McNamara,
were arrested for dynamiting the Times Building in Los Angeles, creating
a blast which killed a score of people.

The violence of feeling which led to the explosion is what Louis Adamic
refers to as "dynamite" in labor history—and what Bill Haywood called the
"class struggle."

At the time of the explosion, the unions were in a concentrated drive to
make Los Angeles a "closed town." The Times, owned by General Harrison
Gray Otis, was notoriously anti-union and was the leading exponent of the
"open shop" policy in that city.

The American Federation of Labor asked Darrow to defend the brothers.
Darrow came to Los Angeles.

Selection of the jury was in progress when Darrow interrupted it to plead his clients guilty.

The change in plea from not guilty to guilty came as a shock to the labor movement which had rallied its forces for the defense of the McNamaras.

But it had become apparent to Darrow as he was preparing the case that the McNamaras were guilty in the sense that they did commit a social crime in the war between labor and management, although he insisted that they had never had any intention of killing anyone with the bombing of the Times Building.

When Lincoln Steffens, newspaperman and muckraker, suggested to Darrow that the defense work out a settlement with the State's Attorney and others involved in the case, Darrow readily agreed. The settlement called for the McNamaras to plead guilty, a conference of labor and management to settle labor disputes, and further prosecution of labor men involved in the case to be dropped.

To Steffens, this meant a practical application of the Golden Rule. To Darrow, it was a means of saving the lives of his clients.

"The experiment was a failure," Steffens wrote in his Autobiography. "There were no local conferences between labor and capital and two other alleged dynamiters were arrested three years later, tried and sent to the penitentiary."

As negotiations for a settlement in the McNamara case were about to be completed, Darrow was charged with attempting to bribe George Lockwood, a prospective juror, through Bert Franklin, one of Darrow's investigators. He was also charged with attempting to bribe Robert F. Bain, the first juror sworn in, as well as trying to influence five other prospective jurors.

Darrow faced a one-to-ten-year prison term on the alleged bribery charge, and not more than five years or a fine of $5,000 on the charge of attempting to influence prospective jurors.

The Darrow trial opened on May 15, 1912, in Judge H. Hutton's courtroom.

Representing the State were John D. Fredericks, Joseph Ford, Arthur Keetch and Asa Keyes.

For the defense besides Darrow were Earl Rogers, Harry Dehme, Horace Appel and Jerry Giesler.

It wasn't until Friday, May 24, that the final juror, the thirteenth, was impaneled. A seldom-used California law permits a thirteenth juror to be selected, but he acts on a verdict only if one of the other jurors becomes incapacitated.

Commented Darrow when the final juror was selected: "Today is Friday; this juror is the thirteenth; it's good. We're not superstitious."

A few days after the trial opened, General Otis, the Times publisher, in a newspaper interview 2,000 miles away while visiting in Chicago, said: "The District Attorney sent word to Mr. Darrow that his confession would not be accepted unless he agreed to tell all. That would implicate labor leaders of prominence, and there is where the delay comes in. They have the goods on Darrow, he knows it and would like to confess and get out as easily as possible."

To such reports Darrow responded: "I never had anything to confess in this case and never had any conversation with anyone regarding a confession nor any intimation or thought of that kind."

The State's case rested on Bert Franklin's testimony.

A number of leading citizens, including a former president of the Illinois State Bar Association, the general counsel of the Chicago, Milwaukee and St. Paul Railroad, a Catholic priest, and several former district attorneys testified as to the good reputation of Darrow.

Lincoln Steffens was also called by the defense.

In his cross-examination of Steffens, Fredericks asked him: "By the way, Mr. Steffens, you are an avowed anarchist, aren't you?"

To which Steffens replied: "Worse than that. I am a believer in Christianity and that is more radical than anarchy."

In his plea in his own defense, Darrow spotlighted the various political and social forces which he claimed were out "to get" him. The Chicago Inter-Ocean headlined its story out of Los Angeles on April 15, 1912:

DARROW FLAYS FOES
AS CUTTHROAT BAND
IN PLEA FOR LIBERTY

CHICAGO LAWYER ON TRIAL FOR AL-
LEGED JURY BRIBERY ASSAILS HIS
ENEMIES AS LIARS AND CONSPIRA-
TORS AGAINST HIS FREEDOM

No Prosecutor Immune from
Denunciation in 3-Hour Talk

The court scene when Darrow began his summation to the jury was dramatic. Men's clothes were torn as they tried to get into the courtroom. Police were called to quiet the mob.

The courtroom was jammed. Jurors were entranced by the indicted lawyer's oratory. Tears streamed down their cheeks. Men in the audience wept. "Women sobbed until the court attachés were forced to quiet them," said one newspaperman.

"I have committed one crime . . . I have stood for the weak and the poor. I have stood for the men who toil."

[493]

ENTLEMEN OF THE JURY, an experience like this never came to me before, and of course I cannot say how I will get along with it. I am quite sure there are very few men who are called upon by an experience of this kind, but I have felt, gentlemen, after the patience you have given this case for all these weeks, that you would be willing to listen to me, even though I might not argue it as well as I would some other case. I felt that at least I ought to say something to you twelve men besides what I have already said upon the witness stand.

In the first place, I am a defendant charged with a serious crime. I have been looking into the penitentiary for six or seven months, and now I am waiting for you twelve men to say whether I shall go there or not. In the next place, I am a stranger in a strange land, 2,000 miles away from home and friends—although I am proud to say that here, so far away, there have gathered around me as good and loyal and faithful friends as any man could have upon the earth. Still I am unknown to you.

I think I can say that no one in my native town would have made to any jury any such statement as was made of me by the district attorney in opening this case. I will venture to say he could not afterward have found a companion except among detectives and crooks and sneaks in the city where I live if he had dared to open his mouth in the infamous way that he did in this case.

But here I am in his hands. Think of it! In a position where he can call me a coward—and in all my life I never saw or heard so cowardly, sneaky and brutal an act as Ford committed in this courtroom before this jury. Was any courage displayed by him? It was only brutal and low, and every man knows it.

I don't object to a lawyer arguing the facts in his case and the evidence in his case, and drawing such conclusions as he will; but every man with a sense of justice in his soul knows that this attack of Ford's was cowardly and malicious in the extreme. It was not worthy of a man and did not come from a man.

I am entitled to some rights until you, gentlemen, shall say differently, and I would be entitled to some even then, and so long as I have any, I shall assert them the best I can as I go through the world wherever I am.

What am I on trial for, gentlemen of the jury? You have been listening here for three months. What is it all about? If you don't know, then you are not as intelligent as I believe. I am not on trial for having sought to bribe a man named Lockwood. There may be and doubtless are many people who think I did seek to bribe him, but I am not on trial for that, and I will prove it to you. I am on trial because I have been a lover of the poor, a friend of the oppressed, because I have stood by labor for all these years, and have brought down upon my head the wrath of the criminal interests in this country. Whether guilty or innocent of the crime charged in the indictment, that is the reason I am here, and that is the reason that I have been pursued by as cruel a gang as ever followed a man.

Now, let's see if I can prove this. If the district attorney of this county thought a crime had been committed, well and good, let him go ahead and prosecute. But has he done this? Has he prosecuted any of the bribe takers and givers?

And who are these people back of him and back of the organization of this county who have been hot on my trail and whose bark I can remember from long ago? Will you tell me, gentlemen of the jury, why the Erectors' Association and the Steel Trust are interested in this case way out here in Los Angeles? Will you tell me why the Erectors' Association of Indianapolis should have put up as vicious and as cruel a plot to catch me as was ever used against any American citizen?

Gentlemen, if you don't know, you are not fit to be jurors. Are these people interested in bribery? Why, almost every dollar of their ill-gotten gains has come from bribery.

When did the Steel Trust—the Steel Trust, which owns the Erectors' Association and is the Erectors' Association—when did it become interested in prosecuting bribery? Was it when they unloaded a billion dollars of watered stock upon the

American people—stock that draws its life and interest from the brawn, the brain and the blood of the American workingman? Are they interested in coming all the way out to this state and to Los Angeles to prosecute a man merely for bribery? There are a good many states between this city and New York City. There are a good many state's attorneys in this broad land of ours. They can begin at home if they would, these men who have made bribery a profession and a fine art.

Gentlemen of the jury, it is not that any of these men care about bribery, but it is that there never was a chance before, since the world began, to claim that bribery had been committed for the poor. Heretofore, bribery, like everything else, had been monopolized by the rich. But now they thought there was a chance to lay this crime to the poor and "to get" me. Is there any doubt about it?

Suppose I am guilty of bribery, is that why I am prosecuted in this court? Is that why, by the most infamous methods known to the law and outside the law, these men, the real enemies of society, are trying to get me inside the penitentiary?

No, that isn't it, and you twelve men know it. Your faces are unfamiliar to me. There may not be a man on this jury who believes as I believe upon these great questions between capital and labor. You may all be on the other side, but I have faced the other side over and over again, and I am going to tell you the truth this afternoon. It may be the last chance that I shall ever get to speak to a jury.

These men are interested in getting me. They have concocted all sorts of schemes for the sake of getting me out of the way. Do you suppose they care what laws I might have broken? I have committed one crime, one crime which is like that against the Holy Ghost, which cannot be forgiven. I have stood for the weak and the poor. I have stood for the men who toil. And therefore I have stood against them, and now this is their chance. All right, gentlemen, I am in your hands, not in theirs, just yet.

In examining you before you were accepted as jurors, Mr. Fredericks asked you whether, if I should address you, you would be likely to be carried away by sympathy? You won't be if you wait for me to ask for sympathy. He has cautioned you against my argument. You will find I am a plain-speaking man who will try to talk to you as one man to another. I never have asked sympathy of anybody, and I am not going to ask it of you twelve. I would rather go to the penitentiary than ask for sympathy.

I have lived my life, and I have fought my battles, not against the weak and the poor—anybody can do that—but against power, against injustice, against oppression, and I have asked no odds from them, and I never shall.

I want you to take the facts of this case as they are, and consider the evidence as it is, and then if you twelve men can find on your conscience and under your oath any reason to take away my liberty, well and good, the responsibility will be on you. I would rather be in my position than in yours in the years to come.

As I have told you, I am tried here because I have given a large part of my life and my services to the cause of the poor and the weak, and because I am in the way of the interests. These interests would stop my voice—and they have hired many vipers to help them do it. They would stop my voice—my voice, which from the time I was a prattling babe, my father and mother taught me to raise for justice and freedom, and in the cause of the weak and the poor. They would stop my voice with the penitentiary. Oh, you wild, insane members of the Steel Trust and Erectors' Association! Oh, you mad hounds of detectives who are willing to do your master's will! Oh, you district attorneys! You know not what you do. Let me say to you, that if you send me to prison, within the gray, dim walls of San Quentin there will brood a silence more ominous and eloquent than any words that my poor lips could ever frame. And do you think that you could destroy the hopes of the poor and the oppressed if you did silence me? Don't you know that upon my persecution and destruction would arise 10,000 men abler than I have been, more devoted than I have been, and ready to give more than I have given in a righteous cause?

I have been, perhaps, interested in more cases for the weak and poor than any other lawyer in America, but I am pretty nearly done, anyhow. If they had taken me twenty years ago, it might have been worth their while, but there are younger men than I, and there are men who will not be awed by prison bars, by district attorneys, by detectives, who will do this work when I am done.

If you help the Erectors' Association put me into the penitentiary, gentlemen, and Mr. Ford stands outside the doors licking his picturesque chops in glee at my destruction, then what? Will the labor cause be dead? Will Ford's masters ride roughshod over the liberties of men? No! Others will come to take my place, and they will do the work better than I have done it in the past.

Gentlemen, I say this is not a case of bribery at all.

Will you tell me if anywhere there could be an American jury, or anywhere in the English-speaking world there could be found a jury that would for a moment lend itself to a conspiracy so obvious and foul as this? If there is, gentlemen, then send me to prison. Anyway, when I reach prison, they can do nothing more to me, and if I stay here, they will probably get me for murder after a while. I do not mean the murder of Ford, he is not worth it; but they will put up a job and get me for something else. If any jury could possibly, in a case like this, find me guilty, the quicker it is done the better. Then I will be out of my trouble.

Gentlemen, if the state of California can afford to stand it, I can. If the state of California, and the fair city of Los Angeles, can lend itself to a crime like this, the victim will be ready when the time comes. But let me tell you that if under such testimony as you have heard here, and under the sort of conspiracy you have seen laid bare here, you should send me to prison, it would leave a stain upon the fair fame of your city and your state that would last while these hills endure, and so long as the Pacific waves should wash your sandy coast. Tell me that any American jury would do it! Gentlemen, I could tell you that I did this bribery, and you would turn me loose. If I did not think so, I would not think you were Americans of spirit or heart, or sense of justice. Gentlemen, if within this courthouse men could be bought and bribed with immunity, could be threatened and coached and browbeaten, and if the gold of the Erectors' Association could be used to destroy human life—if that could succeed, it would be better that these walls should crumble into dust.

*   *   *

Gentlemen, I have tried a good many cases in my time! I have been 35 or 36 years in this profession, and should you send me to prison, why, I have practiced law long enough anyhow; I was going to have a vacation. Of course there are pleasanter places to take vacations than the one where Ford wants to put me —but I have practiced law a good long time, and I tell you I never saw or heard of a case where any American jury convicted anybody, even the humblest, upon such testimony as that of Franklin and Harrington,[1] and I don't expect to live long enough to find that sort of a jury. Let me say this, gentlemen, there are other things in the world besides bribery, there are other crimes that are worse. It is a fouler crime to bear false witness against your fellow-man, whether you do it in a cowardly way in an address to a jury, or from a witness chair—infinitely fouler.

Now, let me put it to you as to men who value your own liberty—because you all value your own liberty, and I trust you value mine, and I have no doubt you do—suppose any infamous scoundrel taken in criminal conduct could know that he could turn on you or on me to save himself, would your liberty be safe? It would not be as safe as mine, for you might not go before as fair-minded a jury as I feel that I am before today. Suppose your hired man could be taken in some act of crime, and the district attorney could say to him, "All right, here is the penitentiary, but I will let you out if you will fasten the crime on your employer." Gentlemen, would you be safe?

*   *   *

Suppose you thought that I was guilty, suppose you thought so—would you dare as honest men, protecting society, would you dare to say by your verdict that scoundrels like this should be saved from their own sins by charging those sins to someone else? If so, gentlemen, when you go back to your homes, you had better kiss your wives a fond goodbye, and take your little

[1] A witness for the prosecution who was formerly an investigator for Darrow.

children more tenderly in your arms than ever before, because, though today it is my turn, tomorrow it may be yours. This consideration, gentlemen, is more important to orderly government, to the preservation of human liberty, than "to get" any one man, no matter how hard they want "to get" him.

Now, gentlemen, I am going to be honest with you in this matter. The McNamara case was a hard fight. I will tell you the truth about it; then, if you want to send me to prison, go ahead, it is up to you. It was a hard fight. Here was the district attorney with his sleuths. Here was Burns[1] with his hounds. Here was the Erectors' Association with its gold. A man could not stir out of his home or out of his office without being attacked by these men ready to commit all sorts of deeds. Besides, they had the grand jury; we didn't. They had the police force, we didn't. They had organized government, we didn't. We had to work fast and hard. We had to work the best we could, and I would like to compare notes with them. I wish, gentlemen of the jury, that some power had been given to us to call before this jury all the telegrams sent by the district attorney's office and sent by Mr. Burns. I wish some grand jury could be impaneled to inquire into their misdeeds. But no, we cannot. They sent out their subpoenas and they got two or three hundred telegrams, public and private, that had been sent from our office. What did they get? Have they shown you anything? Do you think you could run a Sunday school without any more incriminating evidence than they got from those telegrams? I have never tried to run one, but I don't believe you could. What did they get? By the wonderful knowledge of Mr. Ford and by his marvelous genius, they found the key to our code.

They had detectives in our office. They had us surrounded by gumshoe and keyhole men at every step, and what did they secure? Nothing, nothing. I am surprised, gentlemen, that we were so peaceful in fighting the District Attorney and Burns. I scarcely know why we had a code, except that it looked better, and men in business generally use codes, and I knew they had one, for here and there a stray telegraph operator would send

[1] William J. Burns, head of the Burns Detective Agency, hired to investigate the Los Angeles *Times* explosion and to gather evidence against Darrow.

me their dispatches the same as the managers would give my dispatches to Burns. The poor would help me and the rich would help them, but the help of the rich was always of greater avail than the help of the poor, because they were the stronger.

What did they get, with all their grand juries and all their powers, gentlemen? They got conclusive evidence, it seems to me, that everything was regular, that nothing illegal was done, and this with all the witnesses—we interviewed some hundreds —with all the time of twenty or thirty men day and night spent upon that cause, with all the money which we were obliged to spend. Now let us look at the pitiful thing that they have brought to this jury to try to have you think badly of me. No matter if I had killed my grandmother, it would not prove that I had sought to bribe Lockwood; it might cause you to have a bad opinion of me, but you could not convict me of bribery on that opinion.

But what did they get? Why, it is shown here that before I left the city of Chicago in May, a Burns sleuth set a trap to catch me, and he was here and testified—Biddinger.[1] Who is Biddinger? You saw him, you heard him testify. If there is any man on this jury who could see Biddinger and would not take my word against his, then put me away, put me away. If there is any man on earth excepting Ford who would not take my word against Biddinger's, then I wish somebody would shoot me if you cannot get rid of me in any other way.

What did he say? I will analyze his story for a minute—his story which anybody with any brains would know was a fabrication, except what he told on cross-examination, when he very nearly admitted the whole truth. Under the guise of proving to this jury that he was an important witness, Mr. Ford got him to tell of an alleged conversation with J. B. McNamara, which was probably never held; and then, when Ford came to argue his case, he willfully, maliciously, feloniously, criminally, cruelly, distorted the evidence from the purpose for which it was introduced, to show that J. B. McNamara mentioned me before I ever saw him. Therefore I must have been one of the people who inspired his deed! For God's sake, Ford, if you are ever

[1] Guy Biddinger, one of Burns's detectives who arrested J. B. McNamara.

made district attorney of this county, if you are able to climb up the ladder of fame, higher and higher still, I would rather spend my days in the meanest prison pen that the wit and the malice of men can contrive than change places with you, infinitely rather. There are some things worse than prison. Ford introduced that statement, and then he told you it showed that I inspired McNamara's act. What do you twelve men think about a person who could make a statement like that?

Biddinger testified that he had a conversation with McNamara. He said he came to my office and told me about it, and told me about some trinkets that he had, that another detective came with him, one whom I had employed in other matters, and that part was true. He admitted on cross-examination that he did tell me that Burns had traitors in our camp with whom he was consulting, and that he offered to tell me about them. He told me that some of the members of the Executive Board of the organization I was defending were in the pay of Burns, and this, perhaps, was true; they had traitors of ours in their employ. These traitors infest every labor union in this country. The money of the employer is used to hire men to betray their comrades into the commission of crime. I know this. I have fought many of these cases, gentlemen, and I have fought them as squarely as I could possibly fight with such men.

One of the cheapest, meanest, littlest, one of the most contemptible lies that he uttered to this jury was when he discussed the testimony of ex-Senator William E. Mason of Chicago, who testified to my reputation. Ford says, "You mean Mason, the seatmate of Lorimer?" Now, he did not even know better, he did not know anything about Mason, he was willing to perpetrate any lie to take away my liberty. Mason left the Senate ten years before Lorimer ever entered it—and they were always bitter enemies. And yet because Lorimer had been expelled from the Senate, Ford thought if he made that lying, malicious statement, you twelve men would be more apt to send me to the penitentiary.

Why, gentlemen, if I have to do one or the other, if I must choose, I will go down on Main Street and bribe jurors rather than bear false witness like Ford. Is there any comparison?

There is some boldness, some courage, or at least some reckless-
ness to one; there is nothing but cowardice and infamy in the
other.

*   *   *

And here comes another little miserable bit of perjury to
help strengthen their case, a miserable little bit of perjury that
is as plain as sunrise. No man, gentlemen, honestly believes
that I had anything to do with bribing or attempting to bribe
Lockwood down at the corner of Third and Los Angeles streets.
Of course, there may be men who think I would do it. Ford
thinks so, I guess. He would think anything to send a man to
the penitentiary. But could anybody else on earth think that?
I am not talking about my goodness, gentlemen. I have not too
much goodness, but I always had all that I could carry around;
sometimes more than I ought to have carried around; and I
have played according to the rules of the game, and have taken
a little hand in this trial, and you can compare my work, as to
whether it is according to the rules of the game, with any of
the other lawyers in the case; and I have played it that way for
35 years, and I have never done anything of this kind nor had
to do anything of this kind. But that is not what I am discussing.

If you twelve men think that I, with 35 years of experience,
general attorney of a railroad company of the city of Chicago,
attorney for the Elevated Railroad Company, with all kinds of
clients and important cases—if you think that I would pick out
a place half a block from my office and send a man with money
in his hand in broad daylight to go down on the street corner
to pass $4,000, and then skip over to another street corner and
pass $500—two of the most prominent streets in the city of Los
Angeles; if you think I did that, gentlemen, why, find me guilty.
I certainly belong in some state institution. Whether you select
the right one or not is another question, but I certainly belong
in one of them, and I will probably get treated in one the same
as in the other.

I say, nobody in their senses could believe that story, and Ford
knew it, and to bolster it up by a contemptible liar, he has
Biddinger say that I passed $500 in the elevator, and that

Biddinger then told me that it was a careless way to do business. I know who told him to say that. I know who inspired that perjury. Of course, I did not pass $500 in the elevator, but if I had, I had just as much right to give that $500 for that purpose as I would have to buy $500 worth of hogs, just exactly. I was doing exactly what they were doing, what Burns admitted he was doing, what was done in all their cases, what Sam Browne[1] says they did, when he testified that they filled our office with detectives. And here comes this wonderful man, so honest, so pure, so high, so mighty, Ford, who says the State has a right to do that, who says the State has a right to put spies in the camp of the "criminal," but the "criminal" hasn't the right to put spies in their camp. Isn't that wonderful, gentlemen? Here is a contest between two parties in litigation; the prosecution has a right to load us up with spies and detectives and informers, and we cannot put anyone in their office. Now, what do you think of that? Do any of you believe it?

Let me clear up more of this driftwood that has been thrown around the case for the purpose of poisoning the minds of this jury against me, who has spent a lifetime, not all good—I wish it were, I wish it were. I have been human. I have done both good and evil, but I hope when the last reckoning is made the good will overbalance the evil, and if it does, then I have done well. I hope it will so overbalance it that you jurors will believe it is not to the interest of the State to have me spend the rest of my life in prison—though I could find some useful work even there.

Gentlemen, if I am guilty—and I have told you in every way, under oath and not under oath, that I am not, and I have proven, I believe, fortunately by a greater array of honest men and women than are often gathered by a man accused of crime—if I am guilty, is there one man in this jury box, one man, upon your oath, your conscience—is there one man here who loves justice and fair play, who will say that I should be singled out from among this mess, and every crook and thief and spy and informer and traitor in this case get immunity? Who are these wonderful men who hold the destiny of their fellow-men in the hollow of

[1] Captain of Los Angeles detectives.

their hands? Who are they—given the infinite power of forgiving sin—given the power of life and death, and the power of punishment? They say to every thug and crook that comes across their path, "Come to Los Angeles; come to the judgment seat of Fredericks, and 'though your sins be as scarlet, I will wash them white as snow." Gentlemen, under circumstances like this, I could afford to go to prison, but let me tell you that while a verdict of "guilty" would place a blot upon my name, it would place one infinitely darker upon the name of every person connected with an outrage like this.

Now, let's get to the rest of the case. There are a few little things to clear up, just a few little things, sort of specks on the moon. They say that Franklin went to—how many fellows? Smith, Young, Krueger, Yonkin, Underwood? [1] I am not going to spend much time about this, because I want to get where I can discuss this Lockwood case before I go to the penitentiary.

Did I have anything to do with soliciting Yonkin, Smith and Underwood? I sometimes think I did. I'll tell you why—because Franklin says I did not. Franklin says I did not know anything about these solicitations, that he never even told me. Now, that means something; of course he didn't tell me. I never heard of it, any more than any one of you twelve men. Franklin says I didn't. As long as Franklin says I didn't, I suppose even Ford would believe it. But how comes it that this man was going around offering bribes to jurors that I didn't know of? Suppose I had given him omnibus authority, and he had gone to five men who had turned him down, don't you suppose he would have told me? Do you suppose I wouldn't have known it? Think of it, here is a man who goes to five men, without any solicitation from anybody, least of all from me; he never tells me a single word about it. If he went to these five without my knowledge or direction, what about the others? Somebody knew of these attempts, somebody besides me, and I think I can hear Mr. Fredericks saying tomorrow, after my last words have been spoken, "How could all of these things have gone on and the defendant not know of them?" How could it? Of all the people connected with this case, I would have been the last person to know. I was a total stranger in this county.

[1] Five prospective jurors in the McNamara case.

Every other lawyer connected with this case was known through-out the length and breadth of this county. If somebody had been approached at the instigation of counsel, any of the other counsel would have known about it a hundred times more readily than I. Of all the people connected with this case who could possibly have known or heard it in any way, I was the last person and the one most unlikely to have known or heard of it in any way. Ford speaks of me as though I were a cheap jury briber, ready to give a bribe to anybody who happened along. It is a wonder that I didn't try to bribe Ford. You do not know me. Counsel would not let you read my books. If you turn me loose, I hope some time you will have a chance to read my books, so you will see if you have made a mistake.

Now, I am as fitted for jury bribing as a Methodist preacher for tending bar. By all my training, inclination and habit, I am about the last person in all this world who could possibly have undertaken such a thing. I do not intimate for a moment that anybody else would, but in all this situation, mine was the posi-tion which needed to be guarded the most carefully, as these events have shown.

This is the most wonderful case in criminology that I have ever encountered in my profession. You will notice that Franklin had a great penchant for bribing people we couldn't possibly have used as jurors. The more honest the man, the quicker he would offer him something, try to "slip him a little money."

There was George Lockwood, a man of "the strictest integ-rity." Maybe he is—I don't know. I wouldn't think so from his having been a friend of Franklin so long. Guy Yonkin was an honest man, and John Underwood was honest, and Smith was honest; every one of them honest men, every last one, and Franklin goes and visits with their wives and asks them whether they will take a bribe in the McNamara case.

Now, gentlemen, we have got to use a little common sense in this matter. If I am going to the penitentiary, it will be a great solace to me in the long days of my confinement to think you used a little common sense in this case, and were not carried away by Ford. Does it look like a case of jury bribing? Or does it look like something that was framed up? Out of all these men whose names Franklin mentioned he swears that he believes that Yonkin, Smith, Underwood, and the man Lockwood, captain of the chain gang, were honest and incorruptible—and he goes forth to bribe them. But Krueger was not honest—something else was the matter with him. Krueger had been in trouble with the district attorney and Franklin says he knew the district attorney would not take him, and he testified that he told me so. So he tried to force money on to Krueger, when he knew that Krueger could not possibly have been a juror.

Gentlemen, am I dreaming? Is this a real case and have I been practicing law for 35 years and built up some position in the community where I live and where I don't live, and now am I brought to the door of the penitentiary charged with a crime like this?

Gentlemen, don't ever think that your own life or liberty is safe; that your own family is secure; don't ever think that any human being is safe, when under evidence like this and circumstances like these, I, with some influence, and some respect, and some money, am brought here and placed in the shadow of the penitentiary for six long months. Am I dreaming? And will I awaken and find it all a horrible nightmare, and that no such thing has happened?

Now, what about Bain? I think you gentlemen must know that every word said about these other five shows that I had no connection with this Bain matter. Franklin, himself, said that I knew nothing whatever about three. He said that two men were sent after Krueger, and that I was informed he could not possibly qualify. These tales are brought up here against me, and yet if I was not connected with these cases, is it not pretty safe to say that I was not connected with the other two? The same brain and the same hand were back of it all, and the same money was back of it all, or the same job was back of it all, whichever way you put it, and I take it there is not a sane person who could think for a moment that I had any knowledge of, or any connection with these five bribery charges.

I am still under indictment for having offered a bribe to Robert Bain. Of all the silly things in this case, the Bain matter is about the silliest. It was saved by the prosecution as a delectable morsel for the end of this trial, because Mrs. Bain was a woman somewhat advanced in years, and Robert Bain was a veteran of the Civil War. I do not know what that had to do with it, but Mr. Ford evidently thought it had something to do with it, and so it was brought in here at the last, this Bain case. Now, let me just give you a brief recital of some of the evidence in the Bain case, and if I misquote the evidence, any of the jurors or the lawyers are at liberty to correct me. I may sometimes misquote because I cannot carry it in my mind—and I cannot have much of a mind anyway or I would not have sent down to the corner of Third and Main streets to bribe Lockwood and then have gone down to see the job done. Think of it! The Court may sentence me. If he does, I hope he will send me to the right place.

Not content with sending these fellows down to the corner of Main and Third and then over to Third and Los Angeles streets, I would have run down there myself! Lord! And here are twelve jurors to pass on that. This court ought to adjourn until Monday morning and try this case with the insanity cases.

But to come back to Bain. These people connected with the district attorney's office discovered that Franklin made a deposit of $1,000 on October sixth, and, of course, thinking that Franklin could not carry around $1,000 in his pocket very long, they concluded that I had given him a check on October sixth. Fine logic. And on this theory Franklin swore to it, that he came to my office and got a check and hustled off to the bank on October sixth—which was the first day, he said, that I ever spoke to him about Robert Bain, and the day that he saw Bain's wife the first time. He says the first time I ever talked to him about jury bribing was October fifth, the day before he hustled down to see Bain's wife. Remember, the first time I spoke to him about jury bribing was October fifth, and that on the sixth I gave him a check for $1,000—I, a stranger in Los Angeles, a check on a Los Angeles bank to bribe a juror. Another case for the insanity court. Another lie.

What else does Franklin do? He goes to the bank and he draws $500. The bank cashier swears positively that he gave the money to him in fifties and hundreds. The bank cashier swore that he gave him fifty- and hundred-dollar bills, and yet Franklin gave only twenty-dollar bills to the Bains—every dollar he left there was in twenties. Now, gentlemen, this does not rest on the bank cashier's testimony alone. There comes out of their own mouths a bit of corroboration, which shows perfectly that the bank cashier was right. Mr. Franklin puts $500 in his pocket and rushes off to see—not Mrs. Bain—she was out, so he runs over to see one of the neighbor's wives and leaves his card. Here is a detective for your life! Why, he has got Sherlock Holmes faded. He has got Burns beaten forty ways. He is going to bribe a juror, and he goes over and sees this juror's neighbor's wife, and asks her to tell Bain to call him up at his office. No wonder he used Main Street for his field of operation. And you, gentlemen, are expected to stand for it. No, I am to stand for it. All you do is to return the verdict; I stand for it. Ford tells you that you do not have to do anything but return a verdict. Now, what do you suppose he said that for? Did he want to take from the minds of this jury the responsibility involved in their verdict?

Gentlemen, I don't ask for any mercy at your hands. I want a fair deal. I am going to get it. But no man has a right to take from any jurors the responsibility that they bear to the case they are judging, and tell them that they are to hold a man's life in their keeping without thought. If you think I deserve conviction, then convict me, but do it with your own eyes open and your minds clear.

Gentlemen, it is simply insanity to talk about the Bain case. First, the check was given before the bribery was ever spoken of. Second, Franklin got no money from that check to give to Bain. Third, Franklin went to the neighbor's wife, and to Bain's wife, and they called at his office. Fourth, Bain was not bribed at all, and fifth, Bain says himself that he would have found my client guilty after he got in the jury room. And yet, after all this, I am guilty of bribing Bain!

I have told you my story. I have told you of all these matters as simply and as plainly as I could. Ford said that I lied, that I quibbled, that I hesitated. Now, I do not blame anybody for making any argument that is fair and useful to his end. I will just touch on the matter for a moment, and you do the rest. Ford went on the stand. Who quibbled the most, he or I? Do you remember?

*　　*　　*

Why, gentlemen, I don't want to go to the penitentiary, but when Harrington told me, as he admits he did, that all would be forgiven if I told him where Schmidt or Caplan[1] was—do you suppose I would purchase my life at the expense of the life of my fellow-man, no matter if that fellow-man was a criminal? I am not his judge. Only the infinite God can judge the human heart, and I never tried to judge. I never would do it, and hope I never shall, and when Harrington told me that if I would furnish evidence against Sam Gompers in their wild crusade to destroy the trade union, so that men and women might toil longer for less reward, do you suppose I thought or hesitated or waited to draw my breath for a single moment? I had no information to give, but I had as much as Franklin or Harrington had. I could have told them any story that I saw fit. I could have purchased my liberty at the price of my honor, and then Ford would have said that I was a noble man, and that the fellow I was betraying was a Judas Iscariot. Lord! What a mind he has, and what a heart he has, and what a conscience he has! Would a man hesitate? No, and because I did not I am pilloried here before this jury and before the world as a criminal.

Gentlemen, there is one thing I can say in favor of Franklin; by comparison, Harrington has made a gentleman out of him. Anybody is a gentleman compared with Harrington. Perhaps you think I am especially bitter against Harrington, but I don't believe in bitterness—as some of you may have suspicioned this afternoon. I have always tried to curb it, all my life. I don't blame Harrington, and I don't blame Ford. Nobody is responsible

[1] Matt Schmidt and David Caplan who were also wanted for dynamiting. They were later arrested, tried and sentenced to prison. The prosecution of these men was among those which were to be dropped as a result of the McNamara settlement.

for the shape of his brain: it conforms to the skull which is made of bone, and no one can help the shape of his head. You may not believe it, but there is not a man on this jury that cannot go back through the years and see how the smallest circumstances have affected the whole course of his life, circumstances entirely beyond him and outside his control. And a circumstance that might affect you might not affect me. Some have a large brain, some have a small one, some have a symmetrical brain, and some an unsymmetrical brain. We are no more responsible for the shape of our brains than we are for the shape of our faces. I know this as a matter of philosophy. I know Harrington is not to blame for being a coward. I know God made him a coward, and he cannot help it, and I have spoken of him with this view in my mind all the way along. I would not harm him. Talk to this jury about my moral responsibility for crime! I defy any living man to say where, either by speech or word of pen, I have advised anything cruel in my life.

I would have walked from Chicago across the Rocky Mountains and over the long dreary desert to lay my hand upon the shoulder of J. B. McNamara and tell him not to place dynamite in the *Times* building. All my life I have counseled gentleness, kindness and forgiveness to every human being, and, gentlemen, at the same time, even speaking for my own liberty, I do not retreat one inch or one iota from what I really believe as to this. You were told about the horrors of the *Times* explosion by Mr. Ford. Why? So that some of the horrors of that terrible accident might be reflected upon me to get me into the penitentiary.

Now, gentlemen, let me tell you honestly what I think about that. It hasn't anything to do with this case, excepting as they dragged it in here to prejudice the minds of this jury and to argue that this man should not have been defended by me. Do you suppose I am going to judge J. B. McNamara? I know him. Do you know anything about criminals? Did you ever see a man who committed a crime? I take back nothing of what I have ever said or written or known upon that subject. Men who are called criminals are like you and like me, and like all other men. They may do this thing wrong and they may do ten thousand things right. I never saw a case where a wife or a mother or a father or a brother or a sister or a husband or a friend didn't plead for the "criminal" that he or she knew, and point out to the governor and those charged with mercy ten thousand good things in his life and in his character that would commend him to mercy, while his enemies were telling only the wrongs he had done. I know that the same feelings lurk in the brain and heart of every man. I am not responsible for J. B. McNamara's brain; I am not responsible for his devotion to a cause, even though it carries him too far.

Let me tell you something, gentlemen, which I know District Attorney Fredericks will use in his argument against me, and which I have no reason to feel will meet with favor in the minds of you twelve men, but it is what I believe. I will just take a chance.

Did you ever think of the other side of this question? Lincoln Steffens was right in saying that this was a social crime. That does not mean that it should have been committed, but it means this, that it grew out of a condition of society for which McNamara was in no wise responsible. There was a fierce conflict in this city, exciting the minds of thousands of people, some poor, some weak, some irresponsible, some doing wrong on the side of the powerful as well as upon the side of the poor. It inflamed their minds—and this thing happened. Let me tell you, gentlemen, and I will tell you the truth, you may hang these men to the highest tree, you may hang everybody suspected, you may send me to the penitentiary if you will, you may convict the fifty-four men indicted in Indianapolis; but until you go down to fundamental causes, these things will happen over and over again. They will come as the earthquake comes. They will come as the hurricane that uproots the trees. They will come as the lightning comes to destroy the poisonous miasmas that fill the air. We as a people are responsible for these conditions, and we must look results squarely in the face.

And I want to say to you another thing in justice to that young man who was my client, and whom I risked my life, my liberty, and my reputation to save. He had nothing on earth to gain; his act was not inspired by love of money; he couldn't even get fame, for if he had succeeded he could never have told any human being as long as he lived. He had nothing to gain. He believed in a cause, and he risked his life in that cause. Whether rightly or wrongly, it makes no difference with the motives of the man. I would not have done it. You would not have done it. But judged in the light of his motives, which is the only way that man can be judged—and for that reason only the infinite God can judge a human being—judged in the light of his motives, I cannot condemn the man, and I will not.

I want to say more, when you know the man, no matter whom—I have known men charged with crime in all walks of life, burglars, bankers, murderers—when you come to touch them and meet them and know them, you feel the kinship between them and you. You feel that they are human; they love their mothers, their wives, their children; they love their fellow-man. Why they did this thing or that thing remains the dark mystery of a clouded mind, which all the science of all the world has never yet been wise enough to solve.

But this act of McNamara has again been brought before this jury that it may work upon your passions against me—for nothing else. None of the perpetrators of this deed was ever morally guilty of murder. Never. No one knows it better than the people who were prosecuting them. Sixteen sticks of dynamite were placed under a corner of the *Times* building to damage the building, but not to destroy life, to intimidate, to injure property, and for no other reason. It was placed there wrongfully, criminally, if you will, but with no thought of harming human life. The explosion itself scarcely stopped the printing presses. Unfortunately, there was an accumulation of gas and other inflammable substances in the building which ignited, and the fire resulting destroyed these human lives.

Gentlemen, do you think my heart is less kind than Ford's? Do you think he would care more than I for the suffering of his fellow-men? Do you think for a moment that I did not feel sorry at the destruction of those lives, and for the wives and the children and the friends that were left behind? Wouldn't I feel it as much as he? And yet, gentlemen, this *Times* matter is paraded before this jury, in the hope that in some way it may awaken a prejudice in your hearts against me. Gentlemen, I wish in no way to modify anything I have ever said or thought upon this subject. There never was a man charged with crime that I was not sorry for; sorry for him and sorry for his crime; that I could not imagine the motives that moved his poor weak brain; and I tell you today as Mr. Steffens told you from the witness stand, there will come a time when crime will disappear, but that time will never come or be hastened by the building of jails and penitentiaries and scaffolds. It will only come by changing the conditions of life under which men live and suffer and die.

❖ ❖ ❖

Gentlemen of the jury, you cannot have listened here for three months and not have understood this case. No intelligent person could, and I know you do understand it. For the balance of my argument I shall confine my talk almost entirely to the main charge brought against me, and say no more about these outside issues, which mean nothing except an effort on the part of the State, cruel, unjust and unlawful, to prejudice you against me.

The question which you are to decide here is this: Did I give Franklin four thousand dollars on the morning of the twenty-eighth of November to seek to bribe Lockwood? That is all there is to it.

❖ ❖ ❖

I have said about all I care to about Franklin. I have said enough, I have said too much. I have no feeling against him, he is the way God made him. He can't help it any more than you can help being you, or I can help being I. It was a hard choice he had to make; it is a hard choice for a weak man, to offer him honor or comparative honor on the one hand, and security at least from the penitentiary on the other. Some men will take one, some will take the other; it depends on the man; he is not responsible for his brain or his skull. I don't want anybody to think that I would judge him with hardness or bitterness. I have never judged any human being that way in my life, I never shall. I am only asking you, gentlemen of the jury, to consider the reasonableness and the probabilities and the improbabilities and the absurdities of his story—nothing else.

Would I take a chance of that kind surrounded by detectives from the beginning to the end? Leave out the moral question. Leave out the tradition of a profession that I have followed for thirty-five years. Leave out everything except the bare chance; would I take that chance with these gumshoe men everywhere, their eyes on everyone connected with this case—detectives—nine of them testifying in this case—detectives over the town as thick as lice in Egypt, detectives everywhere?

> *Detectives to the right of me,*
> *Detectives to the left of me,*
> *Detectives behind me,*
> *Sleuthing and spying.*
> *Theirs not to question why—*
> *Theirs but to sleuth and lie—*
>   *Noble detectives!*

I hadn't a chance with those fellows. Yet, I did take a chance, I took the chance of being alive where they were, as every man does, unless he could rely on twelve men to judge him honestly and kindly and carefully, as I feel I can rely on you.

Now let me talk a little about Harrington. Do I need to say much about him—a man who came here to work for me, a man who lived in my house, who ate with me and with my wife, who slept under my roof, and who stayed for ten days as our guest—and all the while he was going before Lawler and the Grand Jury and testifying against me? Against me! Great God! Do I need to impeach him? A man sleeping in your house, eating at your table with yourself and your wife, and betraying you! Is there any crime more heinous than that? Would you ever want to look upon Harrington's face again—the man who sat in this courtroom day after day and would not look me in the eye. Did he look at you? Did he look one juror in the eye? Will he ever look a human being in the eye again until he goes down to his unhallowed grave?

And then, gentlemen, think of that man plotting in Chicago with the Erectors' Association—my friend, and asking me for money—meeting these men in a hotel in Chicago, and putting up a scheme to trap me into a hotel room, where a Dictograph hidden behind a bureau could record my words. They knew perfectly well then, as they know today, that they could not pick out twelve human beings on the face of the earth that would throw away the liberty of a man upon the testimony of Harrington and Franklin, and so they thought to trap me where the hidden Dictograph might be made to distort my words. Is there any doubt about that? And Harrington, posing as my friend, came here to lure me into a room where he could secretly record and distort my conversation, in order to land me in the penitentiary!

Gentlemen, where is there a parallel for that in the annals of criminal trials? Let's think of it a moment. Wouldn't it be better that every rogue and rascal in the world should go unpunished than to say that detectives could put a Dictograph into your parlor, in your dining room, in your bedroom, and destroy that privacy which alone makes life worth living? What would you think of it, one of you men, if your hired man should conceal a Dictograph in your home or your office, and seek to destroy you in that way? And do you want to tell me that the Erectors' Association that would be guilty of a shame like this, would not be guilty of plotting my ruin, and charging me with a bribery for which they themselves were responsible?

I want to say this, that if they deliberately put up a job to catch me on the streets of Los Angeles, that job was a sacrament compared with the hidden Dictograph used to trap a man into the penitentiary. They used to have a steer down in the stockyards in Chicago, where Harrington came from, that had been educated; they had educated this steer to the business of climbing an incline to the shambles. There was a little door on the side so that the steer could dart through this door and not get caught in the shambles, and his business was to go out in the pen and lead the other steers up that incline to the shambles, and then just before they reached the place he would dodge down through the door and leave the rest to their destruction. That is Harrington.

If there is a man on earth who would give credit to Harrington in this matter, I would like to look in the face of that man, and I would find he was not a man—that is all. Better, I say again, that all the crimes that men could commit should go unpunished than that credit should be given to a scheme like that which was plotted in the Sherman House by Harrington, Lawler and the Erectors' Association. But what did they get from their infamy?

Nothing. I went to Harrington's room where the Dictograph was hidden behind the bureau and talked with him in a friendly way day after day; but evidently the stenographers in the next room who recorded my language were too honest to distort it. And when I went on the witness stand, Ford asked me if I said this and that while the Dictograph was listening. And all the time they had in their wonderful tin box the full record of my conversation—in that tin box which contains more infamy than any other box in the world—more infamy and less evidence.

More infamy and less evidence—infamy practiced by the district attorney's office. And they did not show this infamy to this jury. They did not dare to show it. Would these Dictograph reports have shown that I told the truth on the stand or that Harrington told the truth? Then they had the effrontery to argue to you that they asked me all they wanted to prove—and my denial of practically every single thing they asked stands unimpeached and you know it. They asked directly if I did not admit to having received ten thousand dollars in bills from San Francisco. I said, "No." Where is the wonderful tin box? Where are the listening Dictograph operators? Would they have testified for me or for Harrington?

Of course they had to have somebody to help Franklin, and so they threatened Harrington. They placed a charge against him, and threatened him with the penitentiary unless he did something for them, and so Harrington comes to the stand, and he lies, and he lies, and he lies, and you twelve men know it. What did he say? There are some links that need filling. Nobody has discovered a single penny that I have spent unlawfully.

And what else about Harrington? He is contradicted by four witnesses. He is contradicted by Fremont Older[1] who came all the way from San Francisco to tell his story, and he told it straight and truthfully. He is my friend. Ford says he is a liar because he is my friend. I would rather go to the penitentiary and stay there the rest of my life with the friendship of a man like that, than to purchase my liberty by betraying my fellow-men.

* * *

Suppose some evening when you are in your jury room, and you, being instructed not to talk about this case, get into an argument among yourselves about matters of philosophy, and the old question of free will and necessity crops up. I wonder if you will all agree, and if you don't, will you say that the man who disagrees with you is a liar, because he has a different philosophy? You won't, not unless your own philosophy is very poor. Suppose you start a little discussion on politics or religion, or who is the best baseball player in America, as you have before now. Will you agree? Not at all, and there may not be one man on this jury who would believe as Lincoln Steffens believes as to what we call crime, and what is punishment, and what are social crimes, and what are not. But he is a big man with a broad vision, a man who sees further than most men.

Gentlemen, because you don't believe a thing today is no sign that it is not true. There are dreams, and the dreams of today become fact tomorrow. Every effort toward humanizing the world, every effort in dealing with crime and punishment, has been toward charity and mercy and better conditions, and has been in the direction of showing that all men are at least partly good, and all men are partly bad, and there isn't so much difference in men as we had been taught to believe. Every effort that will last beyond the day and the year must have a humane idea, must have for its purpose the uplifting of man, must have

[1] Crusading editor, San Francisco *Call*.

its basis in charity and pity and humanity, or else it cannot live.

Lincoln Steffens believes that; you believe it, too. You may not believe this way or that, but it is aspiration that has raised man from the savage drinking the blood of his fellow from his skull, and has led him up through trials and toil and tribulation to the place where he can have mercy and charity and justice, and can look forward to an ideal time when there will be no crime and no punishment, no sin, no sorrow, and when man will visit no cruelty upon his fellow-men.

Almost everything that you believe now was scouted at and hissed scarcely a hundred years ago. Most acts of humanity that we practice today would have been despised and denied two hundred years ago. The world is moving, and as it moves, brutality is further off, and humanity is nearer at hand. I don't care for Steffens' views; it is facts that I am interested in.

Was my practice humane in this case? Among the other heinous charges that Mr. Ford saw fit to bring against me was that I had betrayed my clients—I, who had almost given my life's blood in their service—I, who never had a client in my life that I didn't consider my friend—I, who under the traditions of the profession, and under the feelings of my heart, have put myself in the place of every client that I ever served—I, who worked day and night to save those lives that fate had placed in my hands, and who had bared my breast to the hostility of the world to serve them! I betrayed them!

Gentlemen, I wish you knew, I wish I could make you understand. I didn't need to do it. I was not on trial then. I was living in peace. It was nothing to me except that I made their case my own. And what happened? It was as if I were a boy walking upon the sand by the sea and the sky was clear above me, excepting here and there a fleeting cloud, as there always is in every clear sky; the waves were calm and peaceful, and in a moment the heavens fell and the ocean overwhelmed me. If it shall be written in the book of Fate that I have not made sacrifice enough for them, well and good, let me drink the cup to the dregs.

Did I think the McNamara case was disposed of? Is there any question but what we began the settlement of that case on the twentieth of November? Mr. Ford said I knew these people were guilty from the beginning. Where is the evidence? I did not know. I have practiced law for many a year. I do not go to a client and say, "Are you guilty, are you innocent?" I would not say it to you. Every man on earth is both guilty and innocent. I know it. You may not know it; I know it. I find a man in trouble. In a way his troubles may have come by his own fault. In a way they did not. He did not give himself birth. He did not make his own brain. He is not responsible for his ideas. He is the product of all the generations that have gone before. And he is the product of all the people who touch him directly or indirectly through his life, and he is as he is, and the responsibility rests on the infinite God who made him. I do what I can for him, kindly, carefully, as fairly as I can, and I do not call him a guilty wretch.

I had no knowledge whatever about the McNamaras until it was borne in on me day by day that this man I knew who trusted everything to me could not be saved if he went to trial. Just as the doctor finds that his patient must die, so it came to me that this client was in deadly peril of his life. Do you think that if I had thought there was one chance in a thousand to save him I would not have taken that chance? You may say I should not. That if I believed he was guilty I should not have tried to save him. You may say so; I do not. If this man had suffered death it would have brought more hatred and violence, more wrong and crime than anything else; for, after all, gentlemen, the source of everything is the human heart. You can change man by changing his heart. You can change him by changing his point of view of life. You cannot change him by scaring him, by putting him in the pen, by violence and cruelty. If you look on him as a doctor looks on his patient, and ascertain the cause of his conduct, then you may change him. These acts of violence will occur over and over and over again until the human race is wise enough to bring more justice and more equality to the affairs of life than has ever obtained before.

And let me tell you about these acts that grow from social

conflict. The men who stand for the workers strike out in their blindness. True, they strike out in the night, and often wrongly. These men who built the civilization which we enjoy; these men who have built the railroad bed and laid the tracks, and who man the locomotives when you and I ride peacefully across the country in Pullman cars; these men who go ten, twenty and thirty stories in the air to the top of the high buildings, taking their lives in their hands, and whose mangled remains are so often found on the earth beneath—these are the men who have built our civilization. Let me say to you that every step in the progress of the race, every step the world has taken, has been for the elevation of the poor. There is no civilization without it— there can be no civilization without. The progress of the world means the raising of these through organization, through treating them better, through treating them kindlier, through treating them more justly. Every step in civilization means the elevation of the poor, means helping the weak and the oppressed, and don't ever let yourself think that though these people often do wrong, that though they are blind, rebellious and riotous, that after all they are not doing their part and more in the progress of the world. I knew it, I felt it then. I knew that though terrible were the consequences of this blind act, consequences which nobody foresaw, still it was one of those inevitable acts which are a part of a great industrial war. I believe that the loss of life was an accident. Nobody meant to take human life in the *Times* disaster and the position of the State in the settlement of the matter showed that nobody meant to take human life. I heard these men talk of their brothers, of their mothers, of the dead; I saw their human side. I wanted to save them, and I did what I could to save them, and I did it as honestly and devotedly and unselfishly as I ever did an act in my life, and I have nothing to regret, however hard it has been. Gradually it came to me that a trial could not succeed. Gradually another thing came to me. It was expensive—the money of the Erector's Association, of the state of California, the power of the Burns Agency, everything was against us. It needed money on our side, and a great deal of it. It needed money that must be taken from the wages of men who toil—men whose cause I have always served, and whether they are all faithful to me or not, the cause that I will serve to the end. I could not say to them that my clients would be convicted. I could not say to the thousands who believed in them, and who believed in me, that the case was hopeless. The secrets that I had gained were locked in my breast, and I had to act—act with the men whom I had chosen to act with me. I had to take the responsibility, grave as it was, and I took it.

Was this case disposed of before Franklin was arrested? Why, gentlemen, there is no more question about that than there is that you twelve men are in front of me. Lincoln Steffens testified that on the twentieth day of November after he and I came from San Diego, he made the proposition for a settlement to me. The idea grew out of a conversation we had with Mr. Scripps,[1] and I said I wished it could be done, but I said, "If anything is done it must come from you." On that very day he went to Meyer Lissner[2] and Thomas Gibbon.[3] At first, I had so little confidence in the possibility of a settlement that I scarcely thought about it for a day or two, but soon Mr. Steffens brought back reports which gave me the confidence to wire my friend Mr. Older, and ask his advice.

All the leading men connected with the labor movement on this coast were then at Atlanta. I could not get to them. I had to take the responsibility, and the other lawyers had to take it with me. What else could we do? I could not consider politics. I could not consider my own interests. I had to consider those accused men, nothing else; and there isn't one of you twelve men who would ever hire a lawyer who you didn't believe would consider your interests first of all—and if he did not he wouldn't be true to his profession, or true to his own manhood. Those things alone could I consider. I wired on Wednesday, the twenty-second; I wired to Fremont Older and I wired to Gompers to send me a man at once, and I named certain men; and Mr. Older came down here on Wednesday morning. Now is that all a lie? Did I wire to these men on that day? If so, why?

[1] E. W. Scripps, newspaper publisher.
[2] Politician, reformer in Los Angeles.
[3] Los Angeles businessman.

Ford says I might have got up all this scheme so as to cover up a case of jury bribing. Well, I might—I might. Sometime his bitter heart might be touched by feelings of kindness and charity, it might—if the days of miracles had not passed. And so I might have got up this elaborate scheme because I foresaw that I was going to give Franklin four thousand dollars on the next Tuesday morning and start him off with the money to bribe a juror. Why, gentlemen, I might have done it—and therefore you will argue, says Ford, that I did. And this in a civilized country, at least, presumed to be.

Older and Davis[1] and Steffens and I met together. Was I betraying my clients? Davis spoke up and said to me, "Mr. Darrow, you can't afford to do it." Judge McNutt[2] was there; he was as fine a man as ever lived in the world, as loyal to me as any friend I have ever known, as true to his profession, and as true to the higher ideals of manhood as any man I have ever met.

Davis said, "You will be misunderstood by union labor." I told him I had no right to consider myself. I had no right to consider the men who furnished the money. My duty was over there in the county jail with those two men whose lives depended upon my courage and my fidelity and my judgment. Whatever befell me I must be true to them, and no lawyer lives who is true to his profession and true to himself who ever hesitates in an emergency like that.

McNutt at once agreed with me. Davis went to the District Attorney—and this is uncontradicted. The first proposition that came from Lissner and Steffens was that J. B. McNamara should plead guilty and that all other prosecutions should stop. Davis then went over to the District Attorney, and brought back word that it would require a term of years at least for J. J. McNamara. That was discussed on Wednesday, November 22, between Older and Davis and Steffens and myself. And Judge McNutt is dead, dead, says Mr. Ford. I couldn't help it. If the Angel of Death hovering around the courtroom had come

[1] Le Compte Davis, L. A. attorney who was associated in the McNamara case.
[2] Judge Cyrus F. M. McNutt, former member Indiana Supreme Court and McNamara defense attorney.

and asked my advice, I would probably have told him "Take Ford, and spare McNutt," but he didn't. I cannot help it because the Angel of Death made a mistake.

This matter was considered on Wednesday. Steffens said that he would see that the original proposition went through, and he went back to Chandler, the manager of the *Times*. Chandler[1] was meeting with Steffens, and then word came from the East —from the East—from the seat of money and power and wealth and monopoly; word came that it was not enough to take J. B., but that J. J. must plead guilty to something; and we worked on that. We worked on it the rest of the week, and Steffens swears that he went and interviewed these defendants. Each brother was willing to suffer himself, but J. J. didn't want his brother to be hanged, and J. B. didn't want J. J. to plead guilty to anything. J. B. agreed to plead guilty and take a life sentence, and J. J. said to us that after his brother's case was out of the way he would plead guilty and take a ten years' sentence. Ford said that I should have told J. B. that J. J. was to plead guilty. Why? I was defending J. B., and it was my business to get the best terms I could for him. I was also defending J. J., and it was my business to get the best terms I could for him. I had no right to play either one against the other—no right, let alone what a man would naturally do. Now, that was the condition, going back and forth before Saturday. We had agreed to accept the District Attorney's terms if no better terms could be had. On Saturday, when that jury list was drawn, it was not handed over to Franklin for him to look up the missing names; it was kept until night, until he himself called me for it, and I gave it to him. There was nothing else to do. In the face of the world, and in the face of our employee, we were bound to go on as we had. On Sunday, Steffens, McNutt and I spent most of the day at the jail, where, finally, each of the brothers separately agreed with our plan. On Sunday night McNutt called Davis to his house and told him that the McNamaras had agreed to our plan.

Now, gentlemen, what is there against all that? The testimony as to the settlement of the McNamara case stands here clear as

[1] Harry Chandler, son-in-law of Gen. Otis, publisher L. A. *Times*.

sunlight. On Monday morning, Mr. Davis went to Fredericks and Fredericks agreed that he would accept the pleas of guilty —J. B. to take life and J. J. ten years. Now, what about it, gentlemen? Is all this a lie? Is it another dream? Why even Franklin doesn't testify against this. If they had got Franklin and Harrington to contradict it, then they might argue that I had some motive on the twenty-eighth of November for seeking to bribe a juror. But nobody testifies against it. Fredericks doesn't deny it, Chandler doesn't deny it, nor Lissner nor Gibbon. There is no denial.

In the meantime I had received a telegram from Ed Nockles[1] on Friday, and in reply I wired him to come on immediately. Was that dispatch a fake? Was it sent to cover up a case of jury bribing at the beginning of the next week? On Monday every one of the parties interested had formally agreed to the plan of settlement. We had agreed to it on Sunday. We had agreed to it on Saturday, but we were still trying to do better if we could. Davis had told us that the settlement must be made at once. And with this condition of affairs, when I had no thought whatever that the McNamara case would be tried, is it likely that on Tuesday morning I would take four thousand dollars, not of my own money, but of money that was sorely needed, and not only waste that money, but take a chance of the destruction of my life and a term of years in the penitentiary, by sending Franklin down on the corner of Third and Main streets to bribe a juror?

Gentlemen, if you can believe it, I do not know what your minds are made of. If there is anybody whose prejudice and hatred are so deep that they cannot be removed, who can believe a thing like that, I would like to search him with an X ray, look inside his skull and see how the wheels go round.

The settlement of the McNamara case cost me many friends, friends that have been coming back slowly, very slowly, as more and more this matter is understood. I am not a fool. I can prove that by Ford. I knew I was losing friends. Was I saving myself? Can any man on this jury or any person point to a single place in this whole matter where I ever sought to save myself? Was I

[1] AFL official.

trying to save myself when Steffens came to me after Franklin's arrest and asked if the settlement could still be made, and I said it could, and then he turned to me and said, "Someone may think that some of you lawyers are connected with the Franklin matter." And I said to him promptly, "If anybody has suspicions of anything like that, you tell them for me that this matter is never to be in any way considered in disposing of the McNamara case. Let the law take its course in that." And have I ever haggled or bargained or sought to throw myself into the balance anywhere? I was thinking of my clients, not of myself.

You may pursue me with all the infamy and venom you wish, but I know, I know in my inmost heart, that in all the sacrifices and responsibilities I have taken in my life, I never made one so hard as this, gentlemen. With the eyes of the world upon me, knowing that my actions would call down the doubt and, in many cases, the condemnation of my friends, I never hesitated for the fraction of a second. Perhaps if I had hesitated, my flesh would have been too weak to have taken the responsibility. But I took it, and here I am, gentlemen, and I am not now trying to get rid of the responsibility. Was it wise or unwise? Was it right or wrong? You might have done differently, I don't know.

I have been a busy man. I have never had to look for clients, they have come to me. I have been a general attorney of a big railroad, I have been the attorney several different times, and general counsel, as it were, of the great city of Chicago. I have represented the strong and the weak—but never the strong against the weak. I have been called into a great many cases for labor unions. I have been called into a great many arbitration cases. I believe if you went to my native town, that the rich would tell you that they could trust not only my honor, but my judgment, and my sense of justice and fairness. More than once have they left their disputes with the laboring men with me to settle, and I have settled them as justly as I could, without giving the workingman as much as he ought to have. It will be many and many a long year before he will get all he ought to have. That must be reached step by step. But every step means more in the progress of the world.

This McNamara case came like a thunderclap upon the world. What was it? A building had been destroyed and twenty lives had been lost. It shocked the world. Whether it was destroyed by accident or by violence no one knew, and yet everyone had an opinion. How did they form that opinion? Everybody who sympathized with the corporations believed it was dynamite; everyone who sympathized with the workingman believed it was something else. All had opinions. Society was in open rupture; upon the one hand all the powerful forces thought, Now we have these men by the throat, and we will strangle them to death; now we will reach out the strong arm of money and the strong arm of the law, and we will destroy the labor unions of America. On the other hand were the weak and the poor and the workers whom I had served; these were rallying to the defense of the unions and to the defense of their homes. They called on me. I did not want to go. I urged them to take someone else, but I had to lay aside my own preferences and take the case. There was a direct cleavage in society. Those who hated unions, and those who loved them. The fight was growing fiercer and bitterer day by day. It was a class struggle, gentlemen of the jury, filled with all the venom and bitterness born of a class struggle. These two great contending armies were meeting in almost mortal combat. No one could see the end.

I have loved peace all my life. I have taught it all my life. I believe that love does more than hatred. I believe that both sides have gone about the settlement of these difficulties in the wrong way. The acts of the one have caused the acts of the other, and I blame neither. Men are not perfect; they had an imperfect origin and they are imperfect today, and the long struggle of the human race from darkness to comparative civilization has been filled with clash and discord and murder and war and violence and wrong, and it will be for years and years to come. But ever we are going onward and upward toward the sunshine, where the hatred and war and cruelty and violence of the world will disappear.

Men were arrayed here in two great forces—the rich and the poor. None could see the end. They were trying to cure hate with hate.

I know I could have tried the McNamara case, and that a large class of the working people of America would honestly have believed, if these men had been hanged, that they were not guilty. I could have done this and have saved myself. I could have made money had I done this—if I had wanted to get money in that way. I know if you had hanged these men and other men, you would have changed the opinion of scarcely a man in America, and you would have settled in the hearts of a great mass of men a hatred so deep, so profound, that it would never die away.

And I took the responsibility, gentlemen. Maybe I did wrong, but I took it, and the matter was disposed of and the question set at rest. Here and there I got praise for what was called an heroic act, although I did not deserve the praise, for I followed the law of my being—that was all. I acted out the instincts that were within me. I acted according to the teachings of the parents who reared me, and according to the life I had lived. I did not deserve praise, but where I got one word of praise, I got a thousand words of blame! and I have stood under that for nearly a year.

This trial has helped clear up the McNamara case. It will all finally be cleared up, if not in time for me to profit by it, in time for my descendants to know. Some time we will know the truth. But I have gone on about my way as I always have regardless of this, without explanation, without begging, without asking anything of anybody who lived, and I will go on that way to the end. I know the mob. In one way I love it, in another way I despise it. I know the unreasoning, unthinking mass. I have lived with men and worked with them. I have been their idol and I have been cast down and trampled beneath their feet. I have stood on the pinnacle and I have heard the cheering mob sound my praises; and I have gone down to the depths of the valley, where I have heard them hiss my name—this same mob. But I have summoned such devotion and such courage as God has given me, and I have gone on—gone on my path unmoved by their hisses or their cheers.

I have tried to live my life and to live it as I see it, regarding neither praise nor blame, both of which are unjust. No man is judged rightly by his fellow-men. Some look upon him as an idol and forget that his feet are clay, as are the feet of every man. Others look upon him as a devil and can see no good in him at all. Neither is true. I have known this, and I have tried to follow my conscience and my duty the best I could and to do it faithfully; and here I am today in the hands of you twelve men who will one day say to your children, and they will say it to their children, that you passed on my fate.

Gentlemen, there is not much more to say. You may not agree with all my views of philosophy. I believe we are all in the hands of destiny, and if it is written in the book of destiny that I shall go to the penitentiary, that you twelve men before me shall send me there, I will go. If it is written that I am now down to the depths and that you twelve men shall liberate me, then, so it will be. We go here and there, and we think we control our destinies and our lives, but above us and beyond us and around us are unseen hands and unseen forces that move us at their will.

I am here and I can look back to the forces that brought me here, and I can see that I had nothing whatever to do with it and could not help it, any more than any of you twelve men had to do with or could help passing on my fate. There is not one of you that would have wished to judge me, unless you could do it in a way to help me in my sore distress—I know that. We have little to do with ourselves.

As one poet has expressed it:

Life is a game of whist. From unknown sources
The cards are shuffled and the hands are dealt.
Blind are our efforts to control the forces
That though unseen are no less strongly felt.
I do not like the way the cards are shuffled,
But still I like the game and want to play,
And through the long, long night, I play unruffled
The cards I get until the break of day.

I have taken the cards as they came; I have played the best I could. I have tried to play them honestly, manfully, doing for myself and for my fellow-man the best I could, and I will play the game to the end, whatever that end may be.

Gentlemen, I came to this city a stranger. Misfortune has beset me, but I never saw a place in my life with greater warmth and kindness and love than Los Angeles. Here to a stranger have come hands to help me, hearts to beat with mine, words of sympathy to encourage and cheer, and though a stranger to you twelve men and a stranger to this city, I am willing to leave my case with you. I know my life, I know what I have done. My life has not been perfect; it has been human, too human. I have felt the heartbeats of every man who lived. I have tried to be the friend of every man who lived. I have tried to help in the world. I have not had malice in my heart. I have had love for my fellow-men. I have done the best I could. There are some people who know it. There are some who do not believe it. There are people who regard my name as a byword and a reproach, more for the good I have done than for the evil.

There are people who would destroy me. There are people who would lift up their hands to crush me down. I have enemies powerful and strong. There are honest men who misunderstand me and doubt me; and still I have lived a long time on earth, and I have friends—I have friends in my old home who have gathered around to tell you as best they could of the life I have lived. I have friends who have come to me here to help me in my sore distress. I have friends throughout the length and breadth of the land, and these are the poor and the weak and the helpless, to whose cause I have given voice. If you should convict me, there will be people to applaud the act. But if in your judgment and your wisdom and your humanity, you believe me innocent, and return a verdict of Not Guilty in this case, I know that from thousands and tens of thousands and yea, perhaps millions of the weak and the poor and the helpless throughout the world, will come thanks to this jury for saving my liberty and my name.

THE FOLLOWING DAY, reports of Darrow's summation called it: "One of the most masterly ever heard in an American courtroom."

Darrow himself agreed. "It was a good argument . . . I have listened to great arguments and have made many arguments myself, and consider that my judgment on this subject is sound."

All through the trial, it was the feeling that jurors number seven and number eleven were against Darrow. But when the accused attorney concluded his speech, the two men were openly weeping, as was everybody else in the courtroom including the judge.

The jury was out thirty-four minutes. They had been ready to bring in a "not guilty" verdict from the moment they went into deliberation. They took three ballots however—as one juror explained—so that no one would claim they had acted in "undue haste."

The scene following the reading of the verdict was as dramatic—if not more so—than on the day Darrow started his plea.

The crowd in the courtroom was hysterical; a number of jurymen shouted. Judge Hutton himself was one of the first to congratulate Darrow. He said to him, "Hundreds of thousands of hallelujahs will go up from as many throats when they hear this."

Darrow embraced his wife. Friends and sympathizers gathered around them. Darrow went to the jury box to thank the jurors. Three jurors embraced him. Others patted the shoulder of the man they had just freed.

Three months later, Darrow was brought to trial on the second charge. The jury could reach no verdict and was dismissed. Finally, the second indictment was dropped.

John Brown

1800-1859

Clarence darrow was color-blind when it came to people. "To me," he frequently said, "people are not simply white or black; they are freckled."

This feeling was instilled in Darrow at an early age. The Darrow home in Kinsman, Ohio was a link in the Underground Railroad. His father was an ardent abolitionist. The youngster was told that the Negro had few friends, and the young Clarence was urged never to desert him.

Darrow never did.

He spoke before colored audiences, he defended them in court, he wrote for their press, he was a member of the National Association for the Advancement of Colored People, he fought for their rights, he was always their friend.

Judge Holly in his eulogy at Darrow's funeral stressed, "The colored race will long remember him with grateful hearts for his heroic battles in their behalf."

The following lecture on John Brown was delivered at the Radical Club Forum in San Francisco on December 12, 1912, shortly after Darrow was acquitted in the jury bribery case in California. It was a lecture he was to deliver many times.

J OHN Brown was born in Connecticut in 1800. His parents were farmers, and like all who really work, were poor. His natural instincts were never warped or smothered or numbed by learning. His mind was so strong, his sense of justice so keen, and his sympathies so deep, that he might have been able even to withstand an education. He believed in Destiny and in God. He was narrow, fanatical, and self-willed, like all men who deeply impress the generation in which they live. Had he been broad and profound, he would have asked himself the question, "What is the use?" and the answer would have brought an easier life and a peaceful death. He was a man of one idea, which is all that the brain of any man of action can ever hold. He was not a philosopher, and therefore believed he had a mission in the world, and that he must early get at his Master's work, and never rest by day or night, lest that work should not be done. He was of the type of Cromwell, of Calvin, of Mahomet; not a good type for the peace of the world, but a type that here and there, down through the ages, has been needful to kindle a flame that should burn the decaying institutions and ancient wrongs in the fierce crucible of a world's awakening wrath.

His life was one of toil and hardship and poverty. In his earlier years, he was a farmer, a wool grower, a merchant, a tanner, and with all a fairly successful man. Up to his middle life, the demands of business and the claims of a large family took nearly all his time and strength; but more and more the crime of slavery obsessed his mind, until casting all else aside and forgetting even those of his own household, he answered all carpers "as another dreamer years ago." He turned to the helpless and the poor, and waving aside his kin, he said, "These are my brethren and sisters." Ever the same eternal voice has called to the devoted souls—"Unless you desert father and mother, brethren and kindred, you cannot be my disciple." His own slender means, with all that he could beg and borrow, was from that time devoted to the cause for which he gave his life, and while he lay in the poor Virginia jail waiting for the end, he could not spare the money to bring his family to his side to give their kind ministrations before he mounted the gallows that choked out his life and immortalized his name. His work was so important that he had no time to get money, and no thought of its value. Unlike many other reformers, he went about his Master's work in such great haste that he did not even wait to accumulate enough money before he began his task.

Most of John Brown's biographers tell us when and why he

became the champion of the black, but they do not tell us right. His love of the slave was a part of the fire, that although it seems to slumber, still, now and then, through the long and dreary night, kindles a divine spark in the minds of earth's strong souls which lights the dark and devious pathways of the human race to nobler heights.

Lucky are the sons of men when these prophets are born upon the earth; above their neglected cradles sing the morning stars, and around their humble homes, hushed and expectant, awaits the early breeze that shall drive away the fog and mist before the rising sun.

John Brown found the power of slavery thoroughly intrenched in the United States; no other institution in the land seemed more secure. True, here and there, voices were raised to denounce the curse, but for the most part, these came only from the weak, the poor and the despised. The pulpit, the press, the courts, the wealthy and respectable gave it their sanction, and more powerful still was the fact that slavery was hopelessly interwoven with the commercial and financial institutions of the land, and any attack on these was an attack on the sacred rights of property—the sin of sins!

Even in his business life, he talked and worked against slavery. He was one of the chief conductors of that underground railroad which sent so many helpless captives by devious ways across the continent beneath the Stars and Stripes, until they were landed as free men in Canada, under the protection of the British flag. But to John Brown this was like bailing out the ocean with a dipper. This might free a slave, but it would not abolish slavery. The system must be destroyed. When the slave power, reaching out its arm to perpetuate itself, turned to Kansas to fasten its shackles on a new state, John Brown sent forth four devoted sons and two others of his kinsmen to help fight the battle of freedom in this new land. In the meantime, he was busy in the East raising money and men to help the cause.

Kansas was then in the throes of civil war. It is idle to ask or answer the question as to where the blame should be placed for any special act through these long bloody days and nights.

The war was not between men, but between two systems old as the human race—freedom and slavery. Then, as ever, officials and power and wealth were with slavery, and the dreamer and idealist with liberty. Then as ever, the power of slavery was united, and the forces of freedom divided. Fighting for liberty were the Garrisons, who believed in nonresistance; the Beechers who believed in appealing to the heart—the heart of a system that had no heart; the Sewards and Sumners who believed in the ballot; and John Brown who believed that all of this meant war and could be settled by no other method.

John Brown could not long resist the lure of Kansas. With a slender purse, a few trusted men, a small number of guns, a large family and a devoted soul, he made his way to that historic land. He found the enemy militant, triumphant and insolent. He found the friends of freedom peaceable, discouraged, and submissive. He gathered a small devoted band and prepared to fight. "Where will you get your supplies?" asked one of the peaceful and the meek. "From the enemy," came back the reply.

Guerrilla warfare was the order of the day. Guerrilla warfare is murder because the killed are so very few. In this warfare, the name of Brown was a terror to the other side. He was silent, active, resolute and unyielding; next to his belief in abolition he believed in God. None of his band drank, smoked, told doubtful stories, jested on sacred things or indulged in levity of any kind. They had daily prayers, stern visages, frequent Bible readings, and they knew how to shoot. The commander, like all fanatics, believed he was called of God to do His work, and so he was. Every man is called of God, if he but believes it strong enough. When an army goes to battle singing psalms and muttering prayers with a leader called of God to perform his task, let the world beware; such an army cannot lose, no matter what its size. Even though vanquished and destroyed, from the bones and ashes of the dead will spring a multitude that will prevail against all the powers of hell.

At first, victory seemed with the slaveholder in the guerrilla war; the village of Lawrence, a free-soil town, was sacked and burned without a struggle in its defense. John Brown, chagrined that a town should be given up without a fight, called together his four sons, two kinsmen and two other trusted men, armed them with knives and pistols, bade them mount their horses and follow him. He did not need to tell the party the specific errand for which they rode; whatever the details might chance to be, the cause was freedom, and with them the method did not count. Across the prairies and swamps and through the night they kept their way, until they reached a little settlement where slept the leaders of the Lawrence raid; five of these they dragged from their homes, took to the woods, cut them to pieces, and then rode away. At once Kansas was aflame; the Free Soilers with whom Brown had fought were the ones who most loudly condemned the act. With one accord, they hastened to deny either sympathy or complicity with the deed. A silence profound and deadly fell over all the leaders of the state. A price was put on John Brown's head, but no one seemed overanxious to win the prize. The pendulum swung back, as pendulums always have and always will. Even the nonresistants took up their guns, and the battle for freedom in Kansas was won.

Then John Brown turned East. He did not wait even to run for office, and claim the reward of his labor. There still was work to do and he was growing old. For a time he busied himself gathering bands of slaves and taking them across the United States to the hospitable northern land. Long since he had exhausted his own funds and collected all he could for the great cause; long since he had given up all other business except "his Master's work." At Harpers Ferry, he said, "For twenty years I have never made any business arrangements that would prevent me answering to the call of the Lord."

Perhaps no one knew the exact plan of his last great fight. For years he had given up all hope of a peaceful solution of the cause; he did not believe in moral suasion or political action. To the nonresistant, he answered in the language of the Hebrew prophet, "Without the shedding of blood there can be no remission of sins." As near as can be known, Brown had a plan of forcibly taking possession of various points in the Allegheny and the Blue Ridge Mountains, of fortifying them and collecting forces of men, black and white, to engage in the wholesale business of deporting the blacks from the South. He had long lived in these mountains and looked upon their rising peaks and deep ravines with reverence and awe. He believed that God had raised the Alleghenies as a bulwark for freedom and for the liberation of the slaves. Harpers Ferry was the place to strike the blow. Harpers Ferry was a natural outlet of the great Black Way to the north. This great Black Way lay east of the mountains, running from Harpers Ferry south through the Virginias and Carolinas, reaching three out of four millions of blacks in the United States. Along this way with weary feet had fled most of the poor fugitives in their escape from the land of darkness to the land of light. Harpers Ferry, too, had the government arsenal packed with arms, used by the nation in defense of slavery. These he would capture and place in the hands of the blacks and his comrades to fight for freedom. Immediately surrounding this town was a country where the blacks were more numerous than the whites, and where he might expect to get recruits when the blow was struck.

When Brown had formed his plan, he visited all the abolitionists that he knew and could trust to enlist their help. He received some contributions of money, given for vague, indefinite purposes, but no man of influence would either join the expedition or give sanction to the plan. Frederick Douglass, the leading colored man of his time, counseled him not to undertake the task; he pointed out that it would surely fail, and he believed that failure would seriously harm the cause. But all argument was of no avail; win or lose, he had no choice; whether he had many followers or few, a voice had spoken to his soul, and that voice he must obey. How could he fail? His cause was the greatest cause for which any martyr ever lived and died—the liberty of man. No sordid motive ever moved his life; his Commander was the great Jehovah, and the outcome had been determined since the morning stars sang together and the world was new.

With scarce a score of men he reached Harpers Ferry, rented a farmhouse and began to collect arms and make his plans. It was a strange and motley band that hid for weeks in an old farmhouse awaiting the fatal day. John Brown, tall, gaunt and gray, with serious face and stooping frame, taking upon his devoted head the crime and sorrows of the world. Around him were five sons and kindred whom he loved with a tender devotion, next to the Negro and his God; seven obscure blacks, fresh from the bonds of slavery, and nine more unknown whites, made up the army, that with bowed heads and consecrated souls challenged the strongest institution of the land, made war upon the United States with force and arms. And strange to say this poor and motley band of humble unknown men were triumphant in the cause for which they fought and died.

On the seventeenth of October, 1859, about eight o'clock at night, the little army left the farmhouse for Harpers Ferry, five miles away. They quickly captured the arsenal and took possession of the town. Then their plans began to go awry; the citizens rallied; the regular troops were brought upon the scene; Brown and his followers were penned in the engine house, and made a last desperate stand against overwhelming odds. John Brown was seriously wounded, two of his sons were shot down by his side, six escaped, all the rest were either shot or hanged.

Brown was indicted, immediately placed on trial while still suffering from his wounds, was brought in and out of the courthouse on a cot. Of course, [he was] convicted, and within six weeks after the raid, was hanged. He was convicted and hanged. For though one of the purest and bravest and highest-minded patriots of any age, he was tried by the law; the law which makes no account of the motives of men, but decides upon their deeds alone.

The news of John Brown's raid sent an electric shock around the world; the slave power was aghast at the audacity of the act, and knew not where to turn. The leading abolitionists of the North were stunned and terrified at the manhunt coming on. The great William Lloyd Garrison promptly and fiercely denounced Brown's mad act. Beecher and Seward cried out against the man who had so criminally and recklessly hazarded his friends and the cause. Bold and wrathful were all these old abolitionists when there was no risk to run, but here was a maniac who transformed their words to deeds.

In the first mad days but one man stood fearless and unmoved while the universe was falling around his head, and this man

was John Brown. When faint voices cried out for his rescue,
Brown promptly made reply, "I do not know that I ought to encourage any attempt to save my life; I think I cannot now better
serve the cause I love than to die for it, and in my death, I may
do more than in my life."

But soon the mad frenzy of the mob began to die away. A few
brave souls stood unmoved in the fury of the storm. While Brown
still lived, the calm, sane voice of Emerson called his countrymen to view Brown's deeds in the light of the motives that fired
his soul; he told the world that soon the day would come when
his deeds with their motives would place John Brown among the
martyrs and the heroes of the earth. Theodore Parker did not
lose his head in the mad unseemly haste to save his neck, and
brave old Wendell Phillips fearlessly hurled his maledictions
in the teeth of the maddened and exultant foe. But when the
scaffold bore its fruit, and the dead hero's heart was cold, the
pulse of humanity once more began to beat; the timid, the
coward, the time server, the helpless and the weak looked on the
brave, cold clay, and from a million throats a cry for vengeance
was lifted to the stars. Men cried from the hustings to wake a
sleeping world; newspapers condemned the act; ministers who
still were Christians appealed from the judgment of the court
to the judgment of their God; church bells with sad tones tolled
out the tidings of Brown's passing soul, and men and angels
wept above his bier. And still the tide rolled on, until in less
than two short years the land resounded with the call to arms,
and millions of men were hurrying to the field of strife to complete
the work John Brown began.

Once more at Harpers Ferry was gathered a band pledged to
the same great cause—"the Liberty of Man"—a band that under
the leadership of Grant swept down the great Black Way with
fire and sword, and in a sea of blood washed the crime of slavery
away.

But while the victorious hosts were destroying the infamous
system that had cursed the earth so long, John Brown was sleeping in a felon's grave, and around his decaying neck was the
black mark of the hangman's noose, the reward of a Christian

world for the devoted soul that had made the supreme sacrifice for his loyalty and love. More than any other man, his mad raid broke the bondsman's chain. True, the details of his plan had failed, where the plans of prophets always fail: the men who worked with him, and the poor for whom he fought, left him to die alone. John Brown offered his life and the lives of those he loved for the despised and weak; and while he fought and died, these, idle and nerveless and stupid, looked blindly on as their masters strangled him to death.

But this story, too, is old, old as the human race. Ever and ever hangs the devoted Christ upon the cross, and ever with faint heart and dumb mouths and palsied hands, the poor for whom he toiled, stand helpless and watch their savior die.

The world has long since accepted the results of John Brown's work. Great as was the cost, all men know that it was worth the price. But even now the idle, carping, and foolish still ask, "Did Brown do right, and would it not better have been done some other way?" Of all the foolish questions asked by idle tongues, the most childish is to ask if a great work should not have been done some other way. Nothing in the universe that was ever done, could have been done in any other way. He who accepts results must accept with them every act that leads to the result. And all who think must accept all results. High above the hand of man is the hand of destiny, all potent in the world. To deny destiny is to deny God, and all the forces that move the universe of which man is so small a part. To condemn an act as wrong assumes that the laws of justice laid down by the weak minds of man are the same as the laws of the universe, which stretch over infinite matter, infinite time and space, and regards nothing less than all.

The world may ask the question, "Did John Brown's work fit the everlasting scheme of things?" It cannot ask whether this or that taken apart from all, was good or bad. Nothing in the universe stands or can stand apart from all the rest. Nature works in a great broad way, and makes no account of the laws of justice as man has laid them down. Nature would prepare the earth for the human race; she sends a glacier plowing across a continent carrying death and destruction in its path and leaving powdered rock and fertile valleys in its wake. For some mysterious reason, she would change a portion of the globe, and she sends earthquake to cover the land with sea, to raise islands in the trackless ocean, to shake down cities, lay waste provinces, and destroy the "unjust" and the "just" alike.

John Brown was right; he was an instrument in the hands of a higher power. He acted as that power had given him the brain to see, and the will to do. In answering his inquisitors in Virginia, he said, "True, I went against the laws of man, but whether it be right to obey God or man, judge ye."

Long ago it was said, "By their fruits ye shall know them." The fruits of John Brown's life are plain for all to see; while time shall last, men and women, sons and daughters of bondsmen and slaves, will live by the light of freedom, be inspired by the hope of liberty.

The earth needs and will always need its Browns; these poor, sensitive, prophetic souls, feeling the suffering of the world, and taking its sorrows on their burdened backs. It sorely needs the prophets who look far out into the dark, and through the long and painful vigils of the night, wait for the coming day. They wait and watch, while slow and cold and halting, the morning dawns, the sun rises and waxes to the noon, and wanes to the twilight and another night comes on. The radical of today is the conservative of tomorrow, and other martyrs take up the work through other nights, and the dumb and stupid world plants its weary feet upon the slippery sand, soaked by their blood, and the world moves on.

John Peter Altgeld

1847-1902

"If I pardon the Haymarket anarchists, from that day on I will be a dead man," John Peter Altgeld told Clarence Darrow when his friend indicated impatience at the governor's delay in acting on a pardon.

But six weeks later the governor did act. There was no doubt about his feelings and thinking. The pardon message and the exoneration of the dead men were the results of Altgeld's intensive study of the case. He found the judge prejudiced, the jury hand-picked, and much of the evidence "a pure fabrication."

The pardoning of the anarchists was not the first time Altgeld acted in accordance with his conscience and with what he believed right, and against public opinion.

There were many such instances. One was the exchange of letters with President Grover Cleveland, when the President decided to send Federal troops to Chicago in the Pullman strike of 1894. Governor Altgeld told the President then, "Waiving all questions of courtesy, I will say that the state of Illinois is not only able to take care of itself, but it stands ready to furnish the Federal government any assistance it may need elsewhere."

Lonely days followed the governor after the pardon. But there were at least two men who were ready to be at his side. One, his secretary of labor, George Schilling; the other, Clarence Darrow, who would go to Springfield to see his friend as "often as I could."

The governor was defeated when he ran for re-election.

After the ex-governor returned to Chicago, Darrow took him into his law firm, which then bore the name Altgeld, Darrow and Thompson.

Altgeld died as he was lecturing in Joliet in defense of the Boers. That was March 12, 1902.

The body lay in state in the Chicago Public Library. Thousands of people came to pay homage to their "great and brave champion."

Two clergymen who were asked to officiate at the services refused. Jane

Addams, head resident of Hull House, spoke, and Darrow delivered the address which is given here.

Irving Stone, in his biography of Darrow, said that "many horse-drawn carriages followed the hearse, but Darrow walked alone by the side of his friend."

In 1947, at a centennial celebration of Altgeld's birth, more than 1,000 people attended a dinner in Chicago and heard the Republican Governor Dwight Green, Cardinal Stritch, and Supreme Court Justice William O. Douglas eulogize the governor.

IN THE GREAT FLOOD of human life that is spawned upon the earth, it is not often that a man is born. The friend and comrade that we mourn today was formed of that infinitely rare mixture that now and then at long, long intervals combines to make a man. John P. Altgeld was one of the rarest souls who ever lived and died. His was a humble birth, a fearless life and a dramatic, fitting death. We who knew him, we who loved him, we who rallied to his many hopeless calls, we who dared to praise him while his heart still beat, cannot yet feel that we shall never hear his voice again.

John P. Altgeld was a soldier tried and true; not a soldier clad in uniform, decked with spangles and led by fife and drum in the mad intoxication of the battlefield; such soldiers have not been rare upon the earth in any land or age. John P. Altgeld was a soldier in the everlasting struggle of the human race for liberty and justice on the earth. From the first awakening of his young mind until the last relentless summons came, he was a soldier who had no rest or furlough, who was ever on the field in the forefront of the deadliest and most hopeless fight, whom none but death could muster out. Liberty, the relentless goddess, had turned her fateful smile on John P. Altgeld's face when he was but a child, and to this first, fond love he was faithful unto death.

Liberty is the most jealous and exacting mistress that can beguile the brain and soul of man. She will have nothing from him who will not give her all. She knows that his pretended love serves but to betray. But when once the fierce heat of her quenchless, lustrous eyes has burned into the victim's heart, he will know no other smile but hers. Liberty will have none but the great devoted souls, and by her glorious visions, her lavish promises, her boundless hopes, her infinitely witching charms, she lures her victims over hard and stony ways, by desolate and dangerous paths, through misery, obloquy and want to a martyr's cruel death. Today we pay our last sad homage to the most devoted lover, the most abject slave, the fondest, wildest, dreamiest victim that ever gave his life to liberty's immortal cause.

In the history of the country where he lived and died, the life and works of our devoted dead will one day shine in words of everlasting light. When the bitter feelings of the hour have passed away, when the mad and poisonous fever of commercialism shall have run its course, when conscience and honor and justice and liberty shall once more ascend the throne from which the shameless, brazen goddess of power and wealth has driven them away—then this man we knew and loved will find his rightful place in the minds and hearts of the cruel, unwilling world he served. No purer patriot ever lived than the friend we lay at rest today. His love of country was not paraded in the public marts, or bartered in the stalls for gold; his patriotism was of that pure ideal mold that placed love of man above the love of self.

John P. Altgeld was always and at all times a lover of his fellow-man. Those who reviled him have tried to teach the world that he was bitter and relentless, that he hated more than loved. We who knew the man, we who clasped his hand and heard his voice and looked into his smiling face; we who knew his life of kindness, of charity, of infinite pity to the outcast and the weak; we who knew his human heart, could never be deceived. A truer, greater, gentler, kindlier soul has never lived and died; and the fierce bitterness and hatred that sought to destroy this great, grand soul had but one cause—the fact that he really loved his fellow-man.

As a youth our dead chieftain risked his life for the cause of the black man, whom he always loved. As a lawyer he was wise and learned, impatient with the forms and machinery which courts and legislators and lawyers have woven to strangle justice through expense and ceremony and delay; as a judge he found a legal way to do what seemed right to him, and if he could not find a legal way, he found a way. As a governor of a great state, he ruled wisely and well. Elected by the greatest personal triumph of any governor chosen by the state, he fearlessly and knowingly bared his devoted head to the fiercest, most vindictive criticism ever heaped upon a public man, because he loved justice and dared to do the right.

In the days now past, John P. Altgeld, our loving chief, in scorn and derision was called John Pardon Altgeld by those who would destroy his power. We who stand today around his bier and mourn the brave and loving friend are glad to adopt this name. If, in the infinite economy of nature, there shall be another land where crooked paths shall be made straight, where heaven's justice shall review the judgments of the earth—if there shall be a great, wise, humane judge, before whom the sons of men shall come, we can hope for nothing better for ourselves than to pass into that infinite presence as the comrades and friends of John Pardon Altgeld, who opened the prison doors and set the captive free.

Even admirers have seldom understood the real character of this great human man. These were sometimes wont to feel that the fierce bitterness of the world that assailed him fell on deaf ears and an unresponsive soul. They did not know the man, and they do not feel the subtleties of human life. It was not a callous heart that so often led him to brave the most violent and malicious hate; it was not a callous heart, it was a devoted soul. He so loved justice and truth and liberty and righteousness that all the terrors that the earth could hold were less than the condemnation of his own conscience for an act that was cowardly or mean.

John P. Altgeld, like many of the earth's great souls, was a solitary man. Life to him was serious and earnest—an endless tragedy. The earth was a great hospital of sick, wounded and suffering, and he a devoted surgeon, who had no right to waste one moment's time and whose duty was to cure them all. While he loved his friends, he yet could work without them, he could live without them, he could bid them one by one goodbye, when their courage failed to follow where he led; and he could go alone, out into the silent night, and, looking upward at the changeless stars, could find communion there.

My dear, dead friend, long and well have we known you, devotedly have we followed you, implicitly have we trusted you, fondly have we loved you. Beside your bier we now must say farewell. The heartless call has come, and we must stagger on the best we can alone. In the darkest hours we will look in vain for your loved form, we will listen hopelessly for your devoted, fearless voice. But, though we lay you in the grave and hide you from the sight of man, your brave words will speak for the poor, the oppressed, the captive and the weak; and your devoted life inspire countless souls to do and dare in the holy cause for which you lived and died.

SOURCES

Address to Prisoners in Cook County Jail, Charles H. Kerr and Company, Chicago, Illinois; 1913, 3rd reprint

Plea in defense of Loeb and Leopold, Haldeman-Julius Company, Girard, Kansas

Debate on Capital Punishment, under the auspices of the League for Public Discussion, Haldeman-Julius Company, Girard, Kansas

Massie Case, Honolulu *Star Bulletin*, April 27, 1932, Honolulu *Advertiser*, April 28, 1932

Argument of Clarence Darrow in the case of Henry Sweet, National Association for the Advancement of Colored People, 69 Fifth Avenue, New York City; 1927

Famous examination of Bryan at the Scopes evolution trial, Haldeman-Julius Company, Girard, Kansas

The World's Most Famous Court Trial: Tennessee Evolution Case, National Book Company, Cincinnati, Ohio; 1925

Argument of Clarence Darrow in the case of the Communist Labor party, Charles H. Kerr and Company, Chicago, Illinois; copyright 1920

The Woodworkers' Conspiracy Case, Campbell Printers, Chicago, Illinois; 1898

Anthracite Miner Case, Philadelphia *North American*; February 13, 14, 15, 16, 1903

Argument of Clarence Darrow in the case of the State of Idaho against Steve Adams, February 1907

Haywood Case, *Wayland's Monthly*, Girard, Kansas; October 1907

Darrow in His Own Defense, Golden Press, Los Angeles, California; copyright 1912

John Brown, *Everyman*, March 1913, Golden Press, 512 American Bank Building, Los Angeles, California

John Peter Altgeld, John F. Higgins, printer and binder, 376-80 West Monroe, Chicago, Illinois

SELECTED BIBLIOGRAPHY

Adamic, Louis: *Dynamite*, 1931
Barnard, Harry: *Eagle Forgotten*, 1938
Brownell, Baker: *A Preface to the Universe*
Busch, Francis: *Prisoners at the Bar*, 1952
Chaplin, Ralph: *Wobbly*, 1948
Crandall, Allen: *The Man from Kinsman*, 1933
Debs, Eugene Victor: *Writings and Speeches*, 1948
Ginger, Ray: *Bending Cross* (Biography of Debs), 1949
Haldeman-Julius, Marcet: *Darrow's Two Great Trials*, 1927
Harrison, Charles Yale: *Clarence Darrow*, 1931
Hays, Arthur Garfield: *Let Freedom Ring*, 1928
Haywood, William D.: *Bill Haywood's Book*, 1929
Holbrook, Stewart H.: *Rocky Mountain Revolution*, 1956
Jones, Mother: *Autobiography of Mother Jones*, 1925
Martin, John Bartlow: "Murder on His Conscience," *Saturday Evening Post*, April 2, 9, 16, 23, 1955
Masters, Edgar Lee: *Across Spoon River*, 1936
Orchard, Harry: *Confessions and Autobiography*, 1907
Perlman & Taft: *History of Labor in the U.S.* (1896-1932), 1935
Smith, T. V.: *Live Without Fear*, 1956
Steffens, Lincoln: *Autobiography*, 1931
Stone, Irving: *Clarence Darrow for the Defense*, 1941
Tennessee Evolution Trial, *Complete Report of Scopes Case at Dayton*, 1925
Weinberg, Arthur: "I Remember Father," Chicago *Sunday Tribune* Magazine Section, May 6, 1956
Whitehead, George G.: *The Big Minority Man*
Whitehead, George G.: *Evangelist of Sane Thinking*

Darrow, Clarence:
  A Persian Pearl, 1899
  Resist Not Evil, 1904
  An Eye for an Eye, 1905
  Farmington, 1905
  Crime, Its Causes and Treatment, 1925
  The Prohibition Mania (co-author Victor S. Yarros), 1927
  Infidels and Heretics (co-editor Walter Rice), 1927
  Story of My Life, 1932

INDEX

ABOUT THE EDITOR

ARTHUR WEINBERG *was born, reared and educated in Chicago, the scene of Clarence Darrow's rise to national renown. An early interest in "the attorney for the damned" was kindled by the author's father, a leader in the garment workers' labor movement, who idolized Darrow, the corporation lawyer who became a champion of the working man. While earning his Ph.B. Mr. Weinberg served as editor of the Chicago Campus and the Daily Northwestern; he went straight from college to a career as a professional journalist. His work has appeared in the Chicago Tribune and the Chicago Sun-Times, and he is now a reporter for a group of national business newspapers.*

An unceasing interest in Darrow culminated in the idea for the Clarence Darrow Centennial Celebration held in Chicago in May 1957, for which he served as Executive Chairman. Currently he is teaching a course entitled "Clarence Darrow, His Cases and Causes" at the University College of the University of Chicago.